MENDELSSOHN: A LIFE IN MUSIC

Pencil portrait of Felix by Wilhelm von Schadow, April 1834.

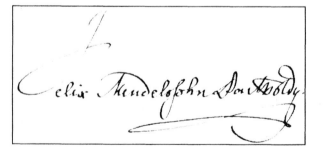

Mendelssohn

A Life in Music

R. Larry Todd

OXFORD
UNIVERSITY PRESS

OXFORD
UNIVERSITY PRESS

Oxford University Press, Inc., publishes works that further
Oxford University's objective of excellence
in research, scholarship, and education.

Oxford   New York
Auckland   Cape Town   Dar es Salaam   Hong Kong   Karachi
Kuala Lumpur   Madrid   Melbourne   Mexico City   Nairobi
New Delhi   Shanghai   Taipei   Toronto

With offices in
Argentina   Austria   Brazil   Chile   Czech Republic   France   Greece
Guatemala   Hungary   Italy   Japan   Poland   Portugal   Singapore
South Korea   Switzerland   Thailand   Turkey   Ukraine   Vietnam

First published by Oxford University Press, Inc., 2003
198 Madison Avenue, New York, New York 10016
www.oup.com

First issued as an Oxford University Press paperback, 2005
ISBN 978-0-19-517988-0

Library of Congress Cataloging-in-Publication Data
is available

9 8 7 6 5 4 3 2

Printed in the United States of America
on acid-free paper

To Karin

Contents

Prologue

Part I: Precocious Deeds

Part II: The Road to Damascus

Illustrations

Illustrations appear following p. 222

Frontispiece. Wilhelm von Schadow, pencil portrait of Felix, April 1834. Staatsbibliothek zu Berlin—Preußischer Kulturbesitz, Musikabteilung mit Mendelssohn-Archiv, *MA BA* 135 (see p. 292); autograph signature, letter of June 27, 1844, Rare Book, Manuscript, and Special Collections Library, Duke University, Durham, North Carolina

1. Moritz Oppenheim, *Lavater and Lessing Visit Moses Mendelssohn*, 1856. The Collection of The Judah L. Magnes Museum, San Francisco, California (see p. 8)

2. Monkey figurine, from the estate of Moses Mendelssohn. Staatsbibliothek zu Berlin—Preußischer Kulturbesitz, Musikabteilung mit Mendelssohn-Archiv, *MA* Depos. MG Fot 5 (see p. 5)

3. Portraits of Felix and his siblings (1816), showing Fanny (age 11), Felix (7), Paul (4), and Rebecka (5). The Bodleian Library, University of Oxford, MS. Eng. c. 2269, fols. 1–4 (see p. 32)

4. Karl Begas, oil sketch of Felix (1821). The Bodleian Library, University of Oxford, M. Deneke Mendelssohn e. 5 (see p. 75)

5. Felix's pen-and-ink drawing of Grindelwald Glacier, August 27, 1822. The Bodleian Library, University of Oxford, M. Deneke Mendelssohn c. 5, fol. 17 (see p. 100)

6. Wilhelm Hensel, pencil drawing of Fanny Mendelssohn Bartholdy as Cecilia, patron saint of music, 1822. Staatsbibliothek zu

16. Felix's final residence on the Königstrasse (now Gold-schmidtstrasse) in Leipzig, where his family moved in 1845. Internationale Mendelssohn-Stiftung e. V., Leipzig (see p. 499)

17. Final autograph page of the full score of *Elijah*, dated in Leipzig on August 11, 1846. Kraków, Biblioteka Jagiellońska (*olim* Berlin, Deutsche Staatsbibliothek), *Mendelssohn Nachlass* 51, fol. 189 (see p. 522)

18. Wilhelm Hensel, portrait of Fanny, 1847. Staatsbibliothek zu Berlin—Preußischer Kulturbesitz, Musikabteilung mit Mendelssohn-Archiv, *MA BA* 44 (see p. 542)

19. Felix's watercolor of Lucerne, July 2, 1847. Staatsbibliothek zu Berlin—Preußischer Kulturbesitz, Musikabteilung mit Mendelssohn-Archiv, *MA BA* 6 (see p. 558)

20. Wilhelm Hensel, sketch of Felix's deathbed, November 6, 1847. The Bodleian Library, University of Oxford, M. Deneke Mendelssohn b. 1 (see p. 567)

Acknowledgments

The present volume owes much to the collective wisdom of many Mendelssohnians and friends to whom I remain greatly indebted. Several scholars, including John Daverio (news of whose tragic passing arrived during the book's production), Stephen Hefling, Wm. A. Little, Nancy Reich, Jeffrey Sposato, and James Yoch, Jr., reviewed the manuscript and offered a host of helpful suggestions and refinements. At the Bodleian Library, Peter Ward Jones not only answered endless queries about the M. Deneke Mendelssohn Collection but generously read the entire manuscript and provided a thorough commentary. The volume is much improved for his counsel and fine eye for detail, and for his impeccable Mendelssohnian sleuthing and valued friendship over the years. My students in a Mendelssohn Seminar at Duke University (2002), including Lily Hirsch, Joyce Kurpiers, Jeff Palenik, and Amy Tabb, were among the first to read and to respond critically to the manuscript.

The expert staff at Oxford University Press, including my editors, Kimberly Robinson and Helen Mules, and copyeditor, Mary Sutherland, greatly facilitated the production of the volume. The determined patience and quiet persistence of Maribeth Anderson Payne, formerly of OUP, convinced me in 1996 to undertake the biography; she offered much appreciated advice along the way. To Mark Faris, of Duke University, I owe a sizable debt for designing and generating the musical examples; and to my friend, J. Samuel Hammond (Special Collections, William R. Perkins Library, Duke University) an earnest thank you for discharging in timely fashion the daunting task of producing the indices, and for detecting numerous, seemingly intractable infelicities in the prose. I am grateful as well to John Druesedow and his able, nimble staff at the Duke Music Library, including Patricia A. Canovai, for bibliographical assistance of various kinds.

The offices of William H. Chafe and Karla F. Holloway (Dean of Trinity College of Arts and Sciences, and Dean of Humanities, Duke University) granted research funds and a sabbatical leave that provided the quietude necessary for completing the volume, and I thank them for their support. To my patient colleagues in the Department of Music at Duke, who have borne with equanimity any number of conversations at our common lunch table that turned inexplicably toward the topic of Mendelssohn, a collective thank you.

Several institutions have generously granted permission to publish illustrations and/or provided microfilms of documents, and it is a pleasure to acknowledge them here: Staatsbibliothek zu Berlin—Preussischer Kulturbesitz mit Mendelssohn Archiv and Cécile Lowenthal-Hensel (Berlin); Duke University, Durham; Biblioteca Jagiellońska, Kraków; Internationale Mendelssohn-Stiftung, Leipzig; Stadtgeschichtliches Museum, Leipzig; British Library, London; The Pierpont Morgan Library, New York; New York Public Library; Bodleian Library, Oxford; The Judah L. Magnes Museum, San Francisco; Stiftelsen Musikkulturens Framjände, Stockholm; and Library of Congress, Washington, D.C. And, over the years, many "Feliciens" and colleagues have generously shared their work, contributed ideas that have shaped positively the writing of this book, and speeded its completion in manifold ways. Though I cannot possibly acknowledge them all here, I would like to thank Clive Brown (Leeds), Anne Elliott (Birmingham), Rudolf Elvers (Berlin), Jürgen Ernst (Leipzig), David Evans (Bangor), John Gough (Birmingham), Christoph Hellmundt (Leipzig), Christopher Hogwood (Cambridge), Hiromi Hoshino (Tokyo), Hans-Günter Klein (Berlin), Friedhelm Krummacher (Kiel), Veronika Leggewie (Coblenz), Roger Nichols (London), Christian Martin Schmidt (Berlin), Thomas Schmidt-Beste (Heidelberg), Françoise Tillard (Paris), Ralf Wehner (Leipzig), and Pietro Zappalà (Pavia), and, in the United States, Leon Botstein, David Brodbeck, Camilla Cai, Elizabeth Cason, Anna Celenza, Michael Cooper, Harry Davidson, Bryan Gilliam, Monika Hennemann, Stephen Jaffe, Stephan Lindeman, Scott Lindroth, Peter Mercer-Taylor, Donald Mintz, Jairo Moreno, Elizabeth Paley, Robert Parkins, Anne Parks, Siegwart Reichwald, Douglass Seaton, J. Rigbie Turner, Sean Wallace, and Marian Wilson Kimber. More specific intellectual debts are recorded in the notes.

To James Bland, a warm thank you for his friendship, on and off the court. And finally, to my family, the greatest debt of all—for several years, they have suffered with good humor the daily vagaries of a biographer, and the music historian's "folly"—chasing the ever receding, chimerical musical past. To my daughter, Anna, may she grow up in a world yet touched by musicians of genius such as Mendelssohn. And to my wife, Karin, whose enduring love and encouragement inform every page that follows, this book is dedicated in heartfelt gratitude.

The Itzig Family

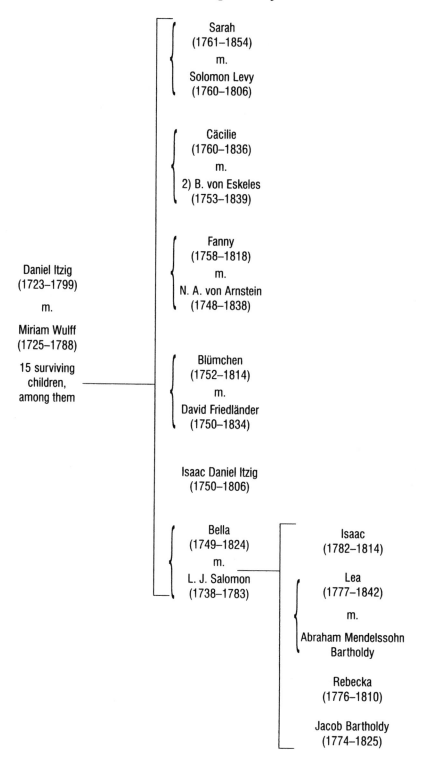

Daniel Itzig
(1723–1799)

m.

Miriam Wulff
(1725–1788)

15 surviving
children,
among them

Sarah
(1761–1854)
m.
Solomon Levy
(1760–1806)

Cäcilie
(1760–1836)
m.
2) B. von Eskeles
(1753–1839)

Fanny
(1758–1818)
m.
N. A. von Arnstein
(1748–1838)

Blümchen
(1752–1814)
m.
David Friedländer
(1750–1834)

Isaac Daniel Itzig
(1750–1806)

Bella
(1749–1824)
m.
L. J. Salomon
(1738–1783)

Isaac
(1782–1814)

Lea
(1777–1842)
m.
Abraham Mendelssohn
Bartholdy

Rebecka
(1776–1810)

Jacob Bartholdy
(1774–1825)

The Mendelssohn Family

Moses
Mendelssohn
(1729–1786)

m.

Fromet
Gugenheim
(1737–1812)

10 children,
of whom 6 survived
to adulthood

Nathan
(1782–1852)

m. ——————————

Henriette Itzig
(1781–1845)

Abraham
Mendelssohn
Bartholdy
(1776–1835) ——————————

m.

Lea Salomon

Henriette (Jette)
(1775–1831)

Joseph
(1770–1848)

m. ——————————

Henriette (Hinni) Meyer
(1776–1862)

Recha
(1767–1831)

m. ——————————

Mendel Meyer
(d. 1841)

Brendel (Dorothea)
(1764–1839)

m. ——————————

1) Simon Veit
(1754–1819)

2) Friedrich Schlegel
(1772–1829)

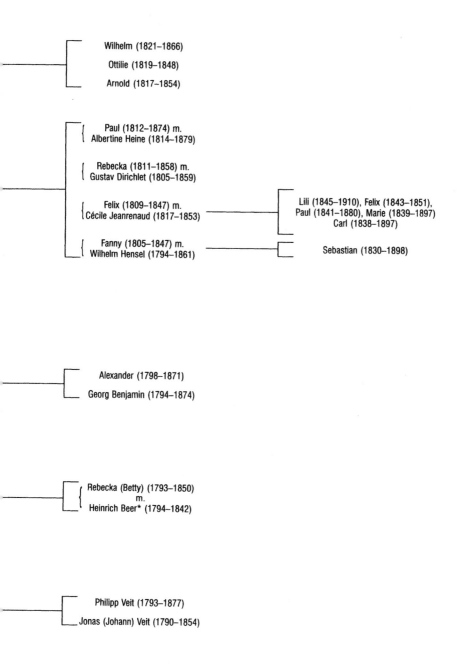

Wilhelm (1821–1866)

Ottilie (1819–1848)

Arnold (1817–1854)

Paul (1812–1874) m.
Albertine Heine (1814–1879)

Rebecka (1811–1858) m.
Gustav Dirichlet (1805–1859)

Felix (1809–1847) m.
Cécile Jeanrenaud (1817–1853)

Fanny (1805–1847) m.
Wilhelm Hensel (1794–1861)

Lili (1845–1910), Felix (1843–1851),
Paul (1841–1880), Marie (1839–1897)
Carl (1838–1897)

Sebastian (1830–1898)

Alexander (1798–1871)

Georg Benjamin (1794–1874)

Rebecka (Betty) (1793–1850)
m.
Heinrich Beer* (1794–1842)

Philipp Veit (1793–1877)

Jonas (Johann) Veit (1790–1854)

*Brother of Giacomo Meyerbeer

Principal Sites of Felix Mendelssohn Bartholdy's Travels

NORWAY (ceded by Denmark to Sweden in 1814, independent after 1850)

SWEDEN

SCOTLAND

Tobermory
STAFFA — •Fort William
IONA •Oban
Mull

•Glasgow
•Edinburgh
•Melrose Abbey
Abbotsford

NORTH SEA

DENMARK

UNITED KINGDOM

ENGLAND

IRELAND

ANGLESEY
•Durham
•York

Bangor• •Conwy •Liverpool
Flint• •Manchester

WALES

•Birmingham

Boundary of the German Confederation

Hamburg• •Bad Doberan
•Schwerin

•Stettin (Szczecin)

EAST PRUSSIA

NETHER-LANDS

HANOVER

GERMAN

London•
Dover•
The Hague•
Rotterdam•
Nijmegen•

Brandenburg• •Berlin
Braunschweig• •Potsdam
(Brunswick)

PRUSSIA

ISLE OF WIGHT
Portsmouth• Calais•
•Düsseldorf
•Cologne

Boulogne•
Oostende•
Antwerp•
Ghent•
•Brussels
Aachen•

PRUSSIA

•Kassel •Dessau •Wittenberg
•Leipzig

STATES

•Weimar •Dresden

SAXONY

•Breslau (Wrocław)

BELGIUM

Liège•

LUXEMBOURG

Koblenz•
Bingen•
•Frankfurt am Main

•Mainz •Offenbach

Paris•

Zweibrücken•
•Heidelberg
Baden-Baden•

Strasbourg•

Freiburg•
•Stuttgart
WÜRTTEMBERG

Danube R.

AUSTRIAN

SWITZERLAND

BADEN• Schaffhausen•

BAVARIA
•Munich

•Vienna
•Bratislava (Pressburg)

Basel• Zürich•
Bern•
Lausanne• Thun•
Geneva• •Montreux
•Interlaken
•Lucerne

Oberammergau•
•Salzburg

•Linz •Baden

FRANCE

Bay of Biscay

Rhône R.

SARDINIA

LOMBARDY-VENETIA

•Graz

EMPIRE

•Milan
•Venice

OTTOMAN EMPIRE

Genoa•

Po R.

PARMA
•Bologna

Florence•

TUSCANY

SPAIN

CORSICA

ITALIAN

PAPAL STATES

STATES

A D R I A T I C   S E A

SARDINIA

•Rome

•Gaeta
•Naples
•Amalfi

CAPRI

KINGDOM OF THE TWO SICILIES

M E D I T E R R A N E A N

SICILY

S E A

MALTA

0   100   200   300 Miles

0   100   200   300 Kilometers

Preface

In the one hundred and fifty-six years since the composer's death in 1847, history has rediscovered Felix Mendelssohn Bartholdy numerous times, with radically different results. Etched into our collective musical consciousness are several vivid images of the man and musician. He was a prodigious polymath/polyglot whose intellectual horizons—embracing music, drawing, painting, poetry, classical studies, and theology—were second to none among the "great" composers, and whose musical precocity, not just in composition but also conducting, piano and organ, violin and viola, was rivaled only by Mozart. Mendelssohn was among the first conductors to adopt the baton and to develop systematic rehearsal techniques that advanced the fledgling art of conducting as an independent discipline. He ranked among the very foremost piano virtuosi of his time and performed feats of extemporization legendary already during his lifetime; in addition, he was probably the most distinguished organist of the century. He was the "prime mover" in the Bach Revival, the stimulating agent behind the posthumous canonization of the Thomaskantor. Mendelssohn was the restorer of the oratorio, who produced two examples judged worthy of Handel: *St. Paul* (1836), which scored early international successes in Germany, England, Denmark, Holland, Poland, Russia, Switzerland, and the United States; and, second only to Handel's *Messiah, Elijah* (1846), premiered in Birmingham, England, and performed at every triennial musical festival there until the demise of the institution at the outbreak of World War I.[1] Mendelssohn was a versatile, craftsmanlike composer whose work effortlessly mediated between the poles of classicism and romanticism, and he convinced Robert Schumann to label him the Mozart of the nineteenth century. Mendelssohn composed several undisputed masterpieces still in the standard repertoire—the Octet and

Midsummer Night's Dream Overture (created when he was sixteen and seventeen), the hauntingly ineffable *Hebrides* Overture and radiant *Italian* Symphony, and the Violin Concerto, the elegiac opening theme of which spawned several imitations.

But balancing these appraisals are commonplaces of a different cast. Mendelssohn was a musician whose delicate "parlor-room" *Lieder ohne Worte* betrayed a proclivity toward the saccharine, whose exploration of a diaphanous musical fairyland in the *Midsummer Night's Dream* Overture, the Scherzo of the Octet and other works revealed a sentimental, effeminate nature. He was a composer of conservative tastes in pre-Revolution Germany who relied excessively on rhythmically predictable melodies with square-cut, symmetrical phrases. His treatment of harmony and tonality offered few innovations. By and large he adhered to classical blueprints and traditional, academic counterpoint, and was by nature a "dry" formalist. His Bach obsession led Mendelssohn, in Berlioz's view, to be too fond of the music of the dead. In the final analysis, Mendelssohn's music evinced a "pretty" elegance and superficiality that could not withstand the weightier "profundity" of Beethoven and Wagner, between whom the winsome Mendelssohn interloped as a "beautiful interlude" (*schöner Zwischenfall*) in nineteenth-century music.[2]

Of the major Western canonical composers, Mendelssohn's posthumous reception traced an especially wayward, volatile course, subject to the pendulum swings of musical fashion. In contrast to Austro-German musicians such as J. S. Bach, Schubert, Robert Schumann, and Bruckner, whose posthumous careers described ascending courses toward recognized "greatness," Felix was canonized by his contemporaries during his lifetime, when, as the preeminent German composer of the 1830s and 1840s, he dominated a German-English musical axis connecting Leipzig and London. After his unexpected death at age thirty-eight, his reputation suffered two seemingly irremediable blows, first from Richard Wagner's anti-Semitic critique at mid-century, then from the reaction against the Victorian age near the turn to the twentieth century. As a composer of Jewish descent and an intimate of Queen Victoria and Prince Albert, Felix proved an irresistible target; his stature diminished rapidly, so that through much of the twentieth century there was little doubt that, his versatile talents notwithstanding, he had not attained the level of Bach, Mozart, Beethoven, or Wagner.

And so, a hundred years after a lionized Mendelssohn had mixed freely among the European cultured elite, the Nazis summarily de-canonized the composer and banned his music. By 1934 German performances of Mendelssohn were nearly fleeting memories. On the night of November 9, 1936, the composer's statue, installed before the Leipzig Gewandhaus in 1892 by Werner Stein, was torn down and replaced by flowerbeds. Sir Thomas Beecham, touring in Leipzig with the London Philharmonic, had visited the site the day before and returned with a delegation of musicians to lay a wreath, only to encounter the eerie absence of the statue.[3] Two years later, at the end of 1938, the Mendelssohn firm, for generations a preeminent German banking house and symbol of the family prestige, was liquidated.[4] The Nazis' attempts to destroy Mendelssohn's legacy, though ruthless and thorough, were not completely successful. Thus, the popular incidental music to *A Midsummer Night's Dream*, commonly used in German productions of the play, proved difficult to extirpate. When, in 1934, Party officials approached several "Aryan" composers to write new music for the play, Richard Strauss,[5] Hans Pfitzner, and Werner Egk refused, and Carl Orff's attempt in 1938 to produce a score that spared his listeners Mendelssohn's "moonlight with sugar water" ultimately failed; in 1944, an Allied bombing raid destroyed the opera house in Frankfurt where it was to have had its premiere. Meanwhile, the emigré Austrian composer Erich Wolfgang Korngold had arrived in Hollywood in 1934 to work on the score for Max Reinhardt's film version of *A Midsummer Night's Dream* (1935), featuring remarkable special effects for the elves and a singular cast with Mickey Rooney as Puck, James Cagney as Bottom, and Olivia de Haviland as Hermia. Korngold drew heavily upon Mendelssohn's own overture and incidental music to *A Midsummer Night's Dream*, and he supplemented these obvious sources with liberal quotations from Mendelssohn's other works to produce a cinematic celebration of his music. Korngold averred that Mendelssohn would outlive Hitler.[6]

Still, even in English-speaking realms, a good bit of twentieth-century discourse about Mendelssohn reflected distinctly negative judgments. Thus, in 1938 Gerald Abraham de-legitimized Mendelssohn's *oeuvre* as a "shady half-brotherhood of romanticism and neoclassicism," and found the *Scottish* Symphony to symbolize "only too well the course of its composer's career: the brief touch of inspired romanticism at the beginning followed by a dreary waste of mere sound-manipulation, relieved only by the oasis of the light-handed scherzo, and ending in a blaze of sham triumph."[7] Philip Radcliffe's 1954 biography, on the whole a sympathetic account of the composer, still labored under the encumbered critical reaction against Mendelssohn—thus we read that a theme from the *Reformation* Symphony is "spoilt by a touch of self-consciousness," there is little in *Ruy Blas* "that can be called tragic at all," the songs are "liable to cloy in too large quantities," Saul's rage aria in *St. Paul* leaves "an impression of rather ineffectual bluster," and *Elijah* is only "worthy at least of respect and sometimes of more."[8] Even Eric Werner's substantial 1963 biography, a major post–World War II effort to rehabilitate the composer's image, occasionally repeated the familiar criticisms. For Werner, *St. Paul* was stylistically so uneven that "probably only parts of it can be rescued for the concert hall or for church music"; the *Ruy Blas* Overture "scarcely sounds the tragic note"; and the Second Piano Concerto is "hardly worthy of [Mendelssohn's] name," but perilously close to the "French salon composers" he despised.[9] It is, as Leon Botstein has noted perceptively, "as if the aesthetic of Wagnerian criticism, shorn of its evident political and racist content, still reigns."[10] Indeed, George R. Marek's biography of 1972, geared toward a popular audience, unwittingly perpetuated stereotypes of the composer as one who evinced mansuetude and effeminateness—notions that ultimately may trace their ancestry to Wagner's notorious 1850 critique—through the title, *Gentle Genius: The Story of Felix Mendelssohn*.

The unusual trajectory of the Mendelssohn reception—a high plateau reached during his lifetime and reinforced by a cult of hero worship after his early death, then a vertiginous descent, and finally, in the latter twentieth century, rebounding efforts at rehabilitation—could form the subject of a separate monograph. A sketch of its outlines would begin with the demonstrably public outpouring of grief in Germany and abroad at his death in 1847 and the elaborate memorial ceremonies on a scale usually reserved for eminent figures of state, the position of honor accorded Mendelssohn's music at the concerts of the Crystal Palace[11] and the establishment in England of a Mendelssohn Scholarship in 1856, offering study abroad (especially at the Leipzig Conservatory), the first recipient of which was Arthur Sullivan. The monograph would continue with the remarkable process of idealization that crystallized in the memoirs of the composer's circle, including the two-volume account compiled from his letters by his nephew Sebastian Hensel, *Die Familie Mendelssohn* (1879)—still an indispensable basis of research—which remembered the Mendelssohns as an upstanding, fully assimilated, upper middle-class German family of the Vormärz, the post-Napoleonic period of political conservatism before the outbreak of revolution in March 1848.

Other accounts, notably the freely embroidered *Erinnerungen* (1868) of Elise Polko (née Vogel), who sang for Mendelssohn in Leipzig during the 1840s, moved the genre of Mendelssohn biography into the realm of fiction, a process furthered by the unusually durable *roman à clef* of Elizabeth Sara Sheppard, *Charles Auchester* (three volumes, 1853), which transformed Mendelssohn into Seraphael, a divinely inspired musician of "unperverted Hebrew ancestry" who dies at an early age and becomes a martyr to the cause of art.[12] English (and American) readers willingly tolerated Sheppard's "frequently mawkish and febrile" prose, so that *Charles Auchester* remained in print well into the twentieth century.[13]

Three years before its appearance, in a Germany seething with revolutionary ferment, a polemical article appeared in the *Neue Zeitschrift für Musik*, the Leipzig journal Robert Schumann had founded in 1834. Attributed to Freigedank ("free thinker"), "Das Judenthum in der Musik" ("Judaism in Music") was written by Richard Wagner, who at mid-century hid behind a veil of anonymity to launch a scurrilous anti-Semitic diatribe against the Jewish element in German music.[14] Because of his political activities in Dresden during 1848, Wagner had fled to Switzerland, where the expatriate developed revolutionary essays about the future course of German music. Franz Brendel, the editor of the *Neue Zeitschrift*, who had replaced Schumann in 1845 and lectured in music history at the Leipzig Conservatory, somehow welcomed "Das Judenthum in der Musik" as consistent with the journal's new agendum—to promote the politically "liberal," *Neudeutsche* "school" of Wagner and Liszt. Mendelssohn's music, now identified with the old political order, came in for heavy criticism. Brendel himself led the attack, though without overt reference to Mendelssohn's Jewishness, in an 1845 serial essay that compared him to Robert Schumann; Brendel found their music incongruent with the expectations of the new age—Mendelssohn's because of its conspicuously retrospective, formalist character.[15]

This critique paled in comparison to Wagner's racist tirade, which opened with an elaboration of why the German people felt an instinctive revulsion to Jews, dismissed by Wagner as a foreign race, lacking its own legitimate language, that could survive only by superficially imitating European art.[16] Midway in the essay "the early departed" Mendelssohn was singled out: as the most visible figure of this process, he had aped the formal complexities of Bach's music, admittedly in the "most interesting and astonishing" way, but had failed to penetrate the "human" spirit of the most important modern composer, Beethoven. Mendelssohn, Wagner wrote, "has shown us that a Jew can possess the richest measure of specific talents, the most refined and varied culture, the loftiest, most tender sense of honor, without even once through all these advantages being able to bring forth in us that profound, heart-and-soul searching effect we expect from music. . . ." Mendelssohn's music lacked originality and passion; it was, for all purposes, impotent.

While Wagner was planting the seeds of a virulent strain of Mendelssohn reception, the British continued to celebrate the life and music of a composer who had visited London ten times between 1829 and 1847, and placed an indelible stamp on Victorian musical culture. In 1858 a state event occurred that legitimized his adoption as a Victorian. On January

25, the Princess Royal, Vicky, married Crown Prince Frederick William of Prussia in the Chapel Royal of St. James's Place, to the strains of the Wedding March from the incidental music to *A Midsummer Night's Dream*. Composed in 1843 to celebrate the nuptials of Shakespeare's Theseus and Hippolyta, Mendelssohn's music now honored an English-German royal alliance and inaugurated a custom that would touch the lives of untold millions. Mendelssohn's delicate projection of musical fairyland in the other movements of his incidental music—his elevation of the "fanciful" as an aesthetic category—may well have helped stimulate the vogue of Victorian fairy paintings and illustrations that began to take hold in the 1840s and endured until the early twentieth century, when Edwardian manners challenged the need for folklore and belief in the supernatural. A significant proportion of Victorian fairy images treated subjects drawn from or related to Shakespeare's play, given new resonance by the English premiere of Mendelssohn's music in 1844.[17]

When, between 1879 and 1889, the first edition of Sir George Grove's landmark *Dictionary of Music and Musicians* appeared, Mendelssohn's place in English music history seemed secure. In addition to writing the entries for Beethoven and Schubert, Grove lavished on Mendelssohn a major article painstakingly researched in Berlin and Leipzig, where Grove interviewed family members and the composer's friends, and examined the autographs meticulously bound in the more than forty green volumes of what became the *Mendelssohn Nachlass* in the Berlin Staatsbibliothek. Grove's work set an unusually high standard for the musical scholarship of the time, and provided a firm foundation for Mendelssohn research. There is little doubt that in Grove's conception of the European canon Mendelssohn occupied an honored position; yet Grove closed his article with this defense of the man, intended, it seems, for detractors who would accuse him of superficiality: "It is well in these agitated modern days to be able to point to one perfectly balanced nature, in whose life, whose letters, and whose music alike, all is at once manly and refined, clever and pure, brilliant and solid. For the enjoyment of such shining heights of goodness we may well forego for once the depths of misery and sorrow."[18]

Nevertheless, by the closing decades of the nineteenth century increasingly disparaging English voices were being heard. Early in 1889, the new music critic of the London *Star*, George Bernard Shaw, later Wagner's apologist in *The Perfect Wagnerite* (1898), likened Mendelssohn to the musical Tennyson of the century and denied the composer greatness of the first magnitude: "We now see plainly enough that Mendelssohn, though he expressed himself in music with touching tenderness and refinement, and sometimes with a nobility and pure fire that makes us forget all his kid glove gentility, his conventional sentimentality, and his despicable oratorio mongering, was not in the foremost rank of great composers. He was more intelligent than Schumann, as Tennyson is more intelligent than Browning: he is, indeed, the great composer of the century for all those to whom Tennyson is the great poet of the century."[19] Shaw revived Wagner's (and Brendel's) earlier line of attack, that Mendelssohn was a pedantic formalist ("The fugue form is as dead as the sonata form; and the sonata form is as dead as Beethoven himself. Their deadliness kills Mendelssohn's *St. Paul* and the 'regular' movements in his symphonies and chamber music"). Shaw reinforced a view of Mendelssohn as effeminate, which gained currency as the century came to a close, perhaps no more vividly than in Aubrey Beardsley's dainty caricature published in *The Savoy* in December 1896, in which the dandified composer appears with feminized curled hair and delicate shoes, and brandishes a plumed pen.[20]

Apart from Wagner's venomous prose, probably nothing harmed Mendelssohn's posthumous reputation more than the early twentieth-century critique of Victorianism. Lytton Strachey's *Eminent Victorians* (1918), which mercilessly discredited four late Victorians (Cardinal Manning, Florence Nightingale, General Gordon of Khartoum, and Thomas Arnold, headmaster of Rugby), is often viewed as firing the opening salvos of this reaction. But, as Michael Mason has suggested, an "increasingly explicit distaste for the 1830s and 1840s was certainly a preparatory step, in the first decade or so of [the twentieth] century, towards full-fledged anti-Victorianism. . . ."[21] Samuel Butler's trenchant indictment of Victorian society, *The Way of All Flesh* (written between 1873 and 1885 but published posthumously in 1903) provoked a reexamination and rejection of earlier Victorian values—Butler targeted Mendelssohn in two chapters, including the final one, where Ernest Pontifex, professing not to like "modern" music, converses with Miss Skinner, whom he imagines says, "as though it were an epitaph: STAY / I MAY PRESENTLY TAKE / A SIMPLE CHORD OF BEETHOVEN / OR A SMALL SEMIQUAVER / FROM ONE OF MENDELSSOHN'S SONGS WITHOUT WORDS." It was an easy step to associate Mendelssohn with those Victorian attributes from which the new century tried to distance itself—shallowness, hypocrisy, prudishness, and all the rest. And so, by 1911, for the eleventh edition of the *Encyclopaedia Britannica*, Donald F. Tovey felt compelled to update the reprinted, eulogizing Mendelssohn article from the tenth edition by W. S. Rockstro, a student of the composer in Leipzig during the 1840s, by noting that "Mendelssohn's reputation, except as the composer of a few inexplicably beautiful and original orchestral pieces, has vanished. . . ."[22]

The dual critiques of Wagner and the anti-Victorian reaction, which generated stereotypes about the composer that have proven difficult to dislodge, account for much of Mendelssohn's precipitous fall from grace. And yet, each critique readily betrays its flaws. In Wagner's case, the anti-Semitic bias is clear enough. If, for the sake of argument, we set aside his vituperative agendum—admittedly impossible, owing to his inextricable weaving of racist arguments into the criticism of Mendelssohn's music— what separated the two composers were two distinctly opposed worldviews. Wagner identified musical "progress" with the "absolute" revolutionary "triumph" of 1848 over the past and its obsolete political order, of course an event Mendelssohn did not live to see. In contrast, during the Vormärz, Mendelssohn developed what Leon Botstein has termed "an aesthetic of creative restoration; a search for historic models; a backward glance tempered by a modern taste for the subjective, emotional, poetic voice of romanticism."[23] For Wagner the future of German music lay in the music drama, closely bound up with German nationalism and aspirations toward unification. He saw Mendelssohn, a member of an elite Jewish family, as belonging to the "antirevolutionary defenders and beneficiaries of the pre-March social order who . . . sought to falsify the past . . . and prettify their surroundings and thereby deny the deeper political and social realities and national possibilities."[24] In reality, despite his family's wealth, Mendelssohn was no blind supporter of Frederick William IV's absolute monarchy but a liberal sympathetic to middle-of-the-road policies. There is little doubt that, like many of his countrymen, Mendelssohn yearned for reforms leading to a constitutional monarchy, even though his political views were doubtless not radical enough for Wagner. To invalidate Mendelssohn's music through a kind of political litmus test, to consign his music summarily to the dust heap of the pre-revolutionary German order, is *prima facie* problematic.

In a similar way, the idea of Mendelssohn as a superficial, effeminate Victorian cannot stand. In recent decades, our construction of the Victorians has been fundamentally challenged by fresh interpretations, including Peter Gay's *The Bourgeois Experience: Victoria to Freud*, and probing readings by Michael Mason (*The Making of Victorian Sexuality*, 1995) and, most recently, Matthew Sweet (*Inventing the Victorians*, 2001), who has thrown down a veritable cultural gauntlet: "Suppose that everything we think we know about the Victorians is wrong. That, in the century which has elapsed since 1901, we have misread their culture, their history, their lives—perhaps deliberately, in order to satisfy our sense of ourselves as liberated Moderns."[25] In a systematic exposé, Sweet debunks the familiar stereotypes about the Victorians that accumulated in the twentieth century. We can profitably extend his corrective to our forming, postmodern views of Mendelssohn. The tenacious idea of Mendelssohn as an overly sentimental composer probably has more to do with layers of interpretations that accrued to his music and biography *after* his death than any intrinsic quality of his music. Thus, the piano miniatures that became celebrated in middle-class parlors as the "Songs without Words," the vast majority of which Mendelssohn published without specific titles, acquired from their publishers in the second half of the nineteenth century all manner of insipid titles—"Consolation," "May Breezes," and the like—titles that Mendelssohn never would have authorized but that ultimately reinforced the view of him as a purveyor of maudlin piano music.

The persistent idea of Mendelssohn as a genteel lightweight, whose refined music buckled beneath the dramatic cogency of Beethoven's or elephantine mass of Wagner's scores, also requires reassessment. We may yet realize that imposing a Beethovenian or Wagnerian yardstick on Mendelssohn does an injustice to his music. The essentially dramatic model of the Fifth Symphony and Wagner's revolutionary theories about music drama do not fit Mendelssohn's music, but not because of its intrinsic inferiority. It is not that Mendelssohn could not write dramatic music—stretches of *St. Paul, Elijah*, and the cantata *Die erste Walpurgisnacht* prove otherwise. Rather, Mendelssohn's aesthetic was broad enough to admit other models as viable avenues of exploration. Several of his scores—the *Hebrides* and *Calm Sea and Prosperous Voyage* Overtures, the *Italian* and *Scottish* Symphonies, for example—seem inspired more by a synaesthetic blending of the visual and musical, and by highlighting the painterly attributes of music than by elucidating a dramatic narrative. Mendelssohn excelled in understatement, chiaroscuro, and nuance, and in subtle, coloristic orchestration that lent his scores an undeniable freshness and vividness. And as for Mendelssohn's "excessive" reliance on history, his music concerns exploring the continuity of the European musical tradition more than celebrating its rupture. As a result, Mendelssohn's music constantly mediates between the past and present: his revival of Bach and Handel—and his attempt to reconcile the classic-romantic dichotomy by overlaying onto richly expressive music the classical attributes of poise, balance, and clarity—has much to do with restoring and preserving, in an age Schumann decried for its philistinism, timeless values drawn from the exemplars of the past.

Of the later twentieth-century efforts to rehabilitate Mendelssohn's image, the first serious attempt came in 1963, with the publication of Eric Werner's *Mendelssohn: A New Image of the Composer and His Age.* Werner was among the first to consult a wealth of unpublished manuscripts and documents unavailable to earlier biographers, including the family correspondence (now in the New York Public Library), some of which had appeared in abridged form in Hensel's *Die Familie Mendelssohn*, and in volumes edited by the composer's brother Paul and son Carl. With memories of the Holocaust still fresh, Werner was in part concerned with exploring Mendelssohn's identity as a Jewish musician and awareness of his Jewish heritage. Now, as Jeffrey Sposato has recently documented, it appears that Werner exaggerated, indeed falsified, some evidence, and that Mendelssohn, who was baptized as a Protestant at age seven, remained throughout his career a devoutly practicing Lutheran—that he willingly paid, as it were, the "price of assimilation."[26] However one may judge Werner's scholarship, he did a great service by raising the question of identity, at the center of a nexus of problems confronting every biographer of the composer. As a member of a Jewish family that had "successfully" entered Prussian society, Mendelssohn would have been reminded of how the search for identity—spiritual, social, political, and aesthetic—was the critical issue affecting his life. Whether in retrospect we regard Mendelssohn as an "assimilated" German Jew who fully embraced Protestantism or who viewed his Christian faith as a "syncretic" "universalization of Judaism," as Leon Botstein has proposed,[27] we must begin to realize the significance of the composer's own project of assimilation, of finding common ground between his adopted faith and the rationalist Judaism of his grandfather, Moses Mendelssohn.

There is another issue in Mendelssohn reception that has come to the fore in recent decades—his relationship with his sister, Fanny Hensel, herself a musical prodigy and composer of several hundred works. While Felix enjoyed an extraordinary international, highly visible career, Fanny's musical sphere was limited primarily to the musical salon she kept at the Mendelssohn residence in Berlin, a gathering place for many musicians of note but one segregated from public view. While Felix produced music for public consumption, Fanny composed in the smaller forms for her intimate circle of friends. Finally, and most controversially, while Felix's authorship was widely celebrated, Fanny's authorship was suppressed until late in her life, when she began cautiously to bring out her songs and piano miniatures in *Lied ohne Worte* style. Felix's early publication of six of her songs under his own name has prompted no small amount of feminist indignation about his motives and "paternalistic" attitudes toward his sister.[28] The evidence suggests, though, as Nancy Reich has observed,[29] that Fanny's "suppression" was as much an issue of class as gender—whereas the middle-class Clara Wieck/Schumann could pursue a professional career as pianist and composer, Berlin society in general did not permit ladies of leisure to do so. Still, the burgeoning, late twentieth-century revival of interest in Fanny Hensel has reclaimed from obscurity a remarkably talented composer whose music demands fresh consideration. Throughout this biography, I have attempted to bring into focus the parallel lives of the siblings and the "public-private" dichotomy that regulated their musical outlets. I have chosen to include Fanny's music, ignored in earlier Mendelssohn biographies, not only because of the light it sheds on the work of her brother but also because of its own merits.

For one buffeted by the inexorable swings of musical fashion, the posthumous Mendelssohn has proven a cooperative subject for a new biography. Now available to the scholar investigating his life and work is a staggering amount of primary source material, encompassing autograph manuscripts, sketches, diaries, letters, paintings, drawings, accounts, concert programs, and countless other documents. One can examine Mendelssohn's honeymoon diary, his school notebooks, his assessments of students in the Leipzig Conservatory, not to mention the sketches and autograph drafts of his major works, and documents revealing the evolution of the libretti of his oratorios. Scarcely a few months elapse without a "new" Mendelssohn letter or manuscript appearing on the auction block. The composer himself preserved his manuscripts and thousands of letters of his incoming correspondence in bound volumes, as if to save the record of his life's work for future scholarly inquiry. Today, sizable deposits of Mendelssohniana survive in Berlin, Leipzig, Oxford, Kraków, New York, and Washington, D.C., with smaller collections scattered among libraries ranging from Stockholm to Aberystwyth to Jerusalem, from Melbourne to Tokyo to St. Petersburg. Scholars are on the trail of several lost works that may yet appear.[30] I have relied heavily upon primary sources and have tried to cling to the facts they divulge about the composer Robert Schumann called the "unforgettable" one.[31] And I have written this biography convinced that the record of Mendelssohn's life, more than anything else, will assist us in peeling away those layers of his reception that have revealed more about how succeeding generations canonize and de-canonize composers than about Mendelssohn himself. In 2003, it is still possible to concur with Friedrich Niecks, who in 1875 concluded his estimation of the composer thus: "Art is wide, there is room for all that are true to her, for all that serve her, not themselves. Such an artist was Mendelssohn. Therefore—honor to him!"[32]

March 2003   Durham, N.C.

MENDELSSOHN: A LIFE IN MUSIC

Prologue

Porcelain Monkeys and
Family Identities

> *Friar:*   Nathan! Nathan! You are a Christian. By God, you are a
> Christian! There never lived a better Christian!
>
> *Nathan:* Alas! For what makes me a Christian in your eyes,
> makes you a Jew in mine!
>
> —G. E. Lessing, *Nathan der Weise,* iv.7

The clarion call of the Enlightenment for religious tolerance found, perhaps, no more illuminating metaphor than the friendship of the philosopher Moses Mendelssohn—the composer's grandfather—and the critic-
playwright G. E. Lessing. Before their meeting in 1754 the young Lessing
broached the issue in the comedy *Die Juden* (1749). A traveler foils two
bandits, disguised as Jews, from assaulting a baron, who, offering his
daughter's hand in reward, discovers his rescuer is a Jew. The mores of the
time thwart the wedding, yet the baron concedes, "How admirable the
Jews would be if they were all like you!" To which the traveler rejoins: "And
how amiable the Christians if they all had your qualities."

Lessing's introduction to Moses Mendelssohn provided an opportunity to test *inter*-faith tolerance. At first sharing a fondness for chess, the
two formed an abiding friendship. Lessing encouraged Mendelssohn to
publish his first major work, the *Philosophische Gespräche* (1755), and the
same year they collaborated on a critique of Alexander Pope's optimistic
Essay on Man. They exchanged ideas about the theory of tragedy that resurfaced in Lessing's *Hamburgische Dramaturgie* (1769), an eloquent attempt to break the grip of French neoclassicism on the nascent German theater.
Mendelssohn brought to Lessing's attention Winckelmann's pithy phrase
about the "noble simplicity and quiet grandeur" of ancient Greek statuary, thereby catalyzing the modern aesthetics of Lessing's seminal *Laokoön*

(1766), in which the critic challenged the classical Horatian formulation, *ut pictura poesis*, that for centuries had linked painting and poetry as sisterly arts.

Two years before his death, Lessing recorded a final act of friendship in *Nathan der Weise* (1779), the title role of which was understood to represent Moses Mendelssohn. Set in twelfth-century Jerusalem, the play revisits the topic of religious freedom. In the pivotal third act, Nathan appears before the sultan to adjudicate whether Judaism, Christianity, or Islam is the true faith and, as Peter Gay has suggested, argues that each creed is the "incomplete incarnation of a larger truth."[1]

I

Moses Mendelssohn's own advocacy of religious tolerance resounded meaningfully for his descendants. Of his ten children, six survived. The eldest, Brendel (1764–1839), divorced her husband, the banker Simon Veit, converted to Protestantism and, assuming the name Dorothea, married Friedrich Schlegel; the couple later embraced the Catholic faith. The second daughter, Recha (Rebecca, 1767–1831), and the eldest son, Joseph (1770–1848), a thriving banker, remained Jewish. Henriette (1775–1831), known as Jette, turned to Catholicism and served as a Parisian governess. The last two children—Abraham (1776–1835), Felix's father and a partner in Joseph's firm, and Nathan (1782–1852), an engineer—became Protestants. Although Moses remained faithful to Judaism, four of his children thus did not, so that one generation confronted issues affecting the three principal European faiths. The children coped also with the ongoing assimilation of German Jewry into the mainstream culture, a process meaningfully accelerated by the work of Moses. The philosopher's struggle to mediate between two German worlds—the dominant Christian society, tied to the monarchy of Frederick the Great, and the disenfranchised Jewish society and subculture—was not lost on Felix Mendelssohn Bartholdy, who, after his boyhood baptism as a Protestant, remained mindful of his Judaic roots. At the zenith of fame in the 1830s and 1840s, the composer pondered his spiritual heritage in *St. Paul* and *Elijah*, oratorios on New and Old Testament subjects addressing issues relevant to his family—the conversion of Saul, and the pre-Messianic prophecies of Elijah.

In 1729 Moses ben Mendel Dessau was born into a modest family in the Jewish quarter of Dessau (eighty miles southwest of Berlin), the center of the small duchy of Anhalt-Dessau. Jews had settled there early in the seventeenth century, but only a few decades after the devastating

Thirty Years War did Jewish communities win official recognition. During the eighteenth century, Dessau became a center of the *Haskalah*, the Judaic revival of scholarship, philosophy, and science often compared to the German Enlightenment. When the local rabbi, David Fränkel, was called to Berlin in 1743 as chief rabbi, Moses, of frail constitution and disabled by a hunchback, followed. According to an anecdote, at the *Rosenthaler Tor* (the only gate Jews could use), a sentry asked the fourteen-year-old Moses why he had come to Berlin. His answer, to study with his rabbi, was probably the only legal way for him to enter the city.

The state rigorously controlled the Jewish community—some 1,200 in a population approaching 100,000—and classified Jews into six categories. At the summit, a few prosperous families enjoyed a "general privilege," a distinction created by Frederick the Great during the Seven Years' War (1756–1763) to reward court Jews who had assisted the war effort. The privilege granted rights to own property, change domicile, and ply business trades, all transferable to children of protected families. At the bottom were private workers, permitted to remain in Berlin only so long as they were employed. Separating the two extremes were four "protected" and "tolerated" categories, with diminishing levels of "concessions." Citizenship was not conferred, except on a few members of the most privileged.

Living frugally in Berlin, young Moses read the Talmud and medieval Jewish philosophy. A turning point came with his decision to study German literature, a bridge to the secular literature of the Enlightenment and to Christian theology. He also learned French (preferred by the court *philosophes*) and English, and parsed a Latin translation of John Locke's *Essay Concerning Human Understanding*. Especially formative for Moses' intellectual development was the philosophy of Leibniz as disseminated by his disciple Christian von Wolff, who expounded a form of Christian rationalism. Leibniz's theory of monads (elemental particles purposefully arranged by divine providence) convinced Moses that German philosophy was compatible with modern Judaism.[2]

In 1750 he found employment as a tutor in the household of Isaac Bernhard, a prosperous silk manufacturer, who established factories in Berlin and Potsdam, and augmented his looms to more than one hundred. Moses became a clerk and a partner in 1761; when Bernhard died in 1768, Moses managed the firm with the merchant's widow. The Prussian court recognized his entrepreneurial acumen, and in 1763 he received the "privileged" status, after the Marquis d'Argens importuned Frederick the Great: "A poor Catholic philosopher begs a poor Protestant philosopher to give the privilege to a poor Jewish philosopher. There is too much philosophy in all this, for reason not to concur with the petitioner."³ (In 1787, the year after Moses' death, Frederick William II extended privileges to his widow and children.) Through Lessing, Moses met J. G. Sulzer, a Swiss aesthetician who nominated him in 1771 to become a member of the Berlin Academy in speculative philosophy. But the king ignored the request and thereby vetoed the nomination of *le juif Moses*.

From Sulzer's musical advisor, J. P. Kirnberger, Moses took lessons in keyboard⁴ and probably music theory as well. A violinist who joined the retinue of Princess Anna Amalia, Kirnberger was a colleague of C. P. E. Bach, the accompanist of the flute-playing Frederick for almost thirty years. Kirnberger was a rigorous instructor; having studied with J. S. Bach in Leipzig, Kirnberger dedicated his career to disseminating the Thomaskantor's pedagogical method and labored for years editing Bach's chorale harmonizations. Kirnberger's imposing treatise, *The Art of Pure Composition* (*Die Kunst des reinen Satzes*, 1771–1779), stood as the last meticulous examination of figured bass. Exactly how far Moses pursued his studies with Kirnberger is unclear, though the theorist's influence remained potent in conservative Berlin into the opening decades of the nineteenth century. When Felix Mendelssohn began composition lessons in 1819, Carl Friedrich Zelter guided him through a course of instruction substantially derived from Kirnberger.

In 1762 Moses married Fromet Gugenheim (1737–1812), daughter of Abraham Gugenheim of Hamburg, descended from the Viennese court banker Samuel Oppenheimer. Fromet's grandchildren later perpetuated her memory as a Xanthippe who challenged her husband's philosophical pursuits, and Felix averred that the children's method of arguing derived from Fromet.⁵ Still, Moses had earnestly wooed her, and, according to family legend, tenderly overcame her resistance with a clever argument when she recoiled from the sight of his deformed back: heaven had preordained their marriage and the disfigurement, which Fromet was predestined to receive until Moses requested it for himself, so that his future wife could be "well made and agreeable."⁶

Another family legend, transmitted by Sebastian Hensel (Felix's nephew) and the novelist Fanny Lewald,⁷ is considerably less endearing. When Fanny visited Felix's sister Rebecka Dirichlet in the 1840s, she made an unusual discovery:

> Soon after I had met Mrs. Dirichlet, I noticed one day that an extensive collection of ugly porcelain monkeys stood in a large cabinet in the dining room of her otherwise very tastefully decorated apartment. Their effect was doubly appalling because of the good quality of the rest of her furnishings. I could not help but ask what had moved her to use these nasty figurines as decorations. "Oh," she replied, "these are not decorations, but heirlooms and his-

torical documents. At the time that my grandfather, Moses Mendelssohn, settled in Berlin, every Jew who had married had to buy a certain number of pieces from the Royal Porcelain Works, which Frederick the Great wished to promote in this manner. It was not enough that this was a real financial hardship at times, but the Jews had no right to select their own figurines and had to take what was given to them by the factory. In this way, my grandparents acquired a whole menagerie of monkeys, which his children later divided as memorabilia and which we in turn inherited from our parents. We keep them as a remembrance of the good old times."[8]

As late as 1929, one of these ungainly creatures was exhibited in Dessau on the bicentenary of the philosopher's birth. But recent research has challenged the story's authenticity, for Frederick the Great purchased the china factory in 1763, more than a year after Moses married, and promulgated the decree affecting Jewish subjects in 1769. As for the figure displayed in 1929 (**plate 2**), it was of Meissen, not Berlin provenance. Thus, two independent events, Moses' wedding and the edict concerning Jewish porcelain, may have coalesced "to form an impressive legend."[9]

Moses Mendelssohn partitioned his Berlin existence into several sectors: he was a faithfully practicing Jew, a successful businessman, and an eminent philosopher. Growing recognition of his formidable intellect facilitated his assimilation into German culture and, as Abraham later explained to Felix, led the philosopher to change his name from Moses ben Mendel Dessau to Moses Mendelssohn, separating himself "irrevocably . . . from an entire class."[10] An initial distinction came in 1763, when Moses entered an essay competition of the Academy of Sciences. His submission, on whether metaphysical truths were susceptible to mathematical proofs, received the first prize (Immanuel Kant settled for an honorary mention). Four years later Moses achieved international fame with *Phaedon*, part translation, part paraphrase, and part reworking of Plato's timeless dialogue. In a modern retelling of Socrates' final conversation with his friends before he drank the hemlock, Moses initially adhered to Plato's text but then departed more and more, refashioning Socrates into a kind of enlightened Leibnizian in classical Athens, who defended natural theology with lucidly reasoned arguments.

Just as Socrates had overcome superstition and sophistry, so Moses Mendelssohn surmounted considerable barriers in emerging from the ghetto to effect a rapprochement with the Enlightenment. Some imagined Mendelssohn could achieve full assimilation only by converting to Christianity, and no one urged this course more ardently than the chiliast J. K. Lavater, who assumed some Jews would willingly commit apostasy. Lavater was convinced the "regeneration" of the most distinguished German Jew could stimulate mass conversions to Christianity, signaling, in turn, the millennium of the rule of Christ. And so, in 1769, Lavater appealed publicly to Moses Mendelssohn. The occasion was a translation of a treatise by the Swiss philosopher Charles Bonnet, who, Lavater believed, had argued convincingly for the superiority of Christianity.[11] Lavater addressed Moses as "an Israelite in whom there is no guile," but then challenged him to rebut Bonnet's arguments, or "do what prudence, love of truth, and honesty bid you do—what Socrates would have done, had he read this treatise and found it irrefutable."[12]

The affair had an effect opposite from what its instigator intended, for it gave Moses an opportunity to reaffirm his Judaic faith. There were further tests: Moses was asked to intervene on behalf of several Jewish communities—in Altona, near Hamburg, against authorities who had falsely accused the rabbinic court of defaming Christian holidays (1769); in Mecklenburg-Schwerin, against the prohibition of Jewish burial practices (1772); in Switzerland, against a proposal to prohibit Jews from procreating (1775); in Königsberg, against the censorship of a Jewish prayer (1777); and in Dresden and Alsace, against the threat of expulsion (1777).[13] With each intercession Moses argued for the oppressed's civil rights, consistent with his agendum of advancing the emancipation of German Jewry. Meanwhile, during the 1770s, he also embarked upon an educational project encouraging the study of the Torah and the Psalms. Initially, his goal was to facilitate his sons' religious education by producing new German translations and commentaries. But as the work progressed, he determined to disseminate his efforts, in order to revive the study of Hebrew and the Bible, and to render the scriptures accessible to German Jews. Published by subscription, the Pentateuch appeared with Masoretic commentary between 1780 and 1782; the Psalms, in 1782. Reaching throughout Europe to Russia, the landmark edition was criticized in some Jewish communities as a sacrilegious blending of the sacred and profane, and banned. But the translations' impact in promoting the moral education of German Jewry was probably incalculable.

While preparing the editions, Moses was also meeting a new challenge to convert to Christianity. In *Jerusalem* (1783), he reexamined the relationship between church and state, and argued that Judaism was compatible with the idea of the liberty of conscience, which had been under attack, owing to imprecise lines drawn between secular and ecclesiastical affairs. The earlier excesses of the Catholic Church, having secured for Montesquieu only a "dreadful calm in a fortress about to be assailed during the night," had been mitigated somewhat by the Reformation, only to yield to new forms of religious fanaticism. For Moses, before mankind had left the state of nature to enter into a social contract, "might and right" had been "heterogeneous ideas" that could not be linked.[14] Even the libertarian politics of John Locke, who had defended religious tolerance, were not completely satisfactory. In the Lockean world, the state concerned itself with its citizens' temporal welfare; the church, their eternal welfare. Moses registered his objection: "To whom are we to entrust the care for the eternal? To the church? Now we are, once again, back at our starting point. ... The state is, therefore, subordinate to religion, and must give way whenever a collision arises."[15]

His solution was to recognize that society represents a complex "matrix of both state and church."[16] While the state depended upon a social contract, the church's domain was the relationship between the individual and God. Confusion about these roles had permitted the church to make illegitimate incursions. In short, the church could have no claim to property, no power of excommunication, and could not require oaths, a "torture of the soul." By entering into a religious society, man had not agreed to a specific kind of social contract; rather, he was solely interested in his moral edification and that of his neighbors. In the second part of *Jerusalem* Mendelssohn demonstrated that "Judaism, *qua* religion, was suited to the secular state."[17] Judaism was not a theocracy based upon strict Mosaic laws but a voluntary association—not a revealed religion, as was Christianity, but a revealed legislation. As such, Judaism was compatible with the interests of the ideal secular state, because it was based upon natural rights and "eternal truths of reason."[18]

Two years before publishing *Jerusalem*, Moses eulogized the deceased Lessing as "more than one generation ahead of his century."[19] Sadly enough, now, in Moses' waning years, a new controversy arose, ostensibly about Lessing's beliefs (was he an adherent of Spinoza, manifesting atheist sympathies?) but manipulated to pose yet another test of Moses' religious convictions. He answered this challenge in a final effort, *Morgenstunden* (*Morning Hours, or Lectures on the Existence of God*, 1785). Designed to guide his son Joseph toward "a rational knowledge of God,"[20] the volume comprised seventeen lectures in dialogue form and laid out justifications of God, among them Moses' own *a posteriori* proof: our very existence, he reasoned, is contingent upon things that exceed the limits of our perception; nevertheless, the concept of our existence must be fully apprehensible by some form of intellect, an "infinite intellect that thinks all things real and possible."[21]

In the preface to the *Morgenstunden* Mendelssohn acknowledged his struggle with the work of Immanuel Kant, whose monumental *Critique of Pure Reason* (1781) had just upended metaphysics. The "all-crushing Kant" was how Moses described his colleague. Undoubtedly, Moses realized at the end of his life that metaphysics was in jeopardy of systematic dismantlement from Kant's vigorous probing. Nevertheless, Moses remained

optimistic that somehow Kant would find a way to restore the traditional branch of philosophy to its earlier prominence. For his part, Kant
respected the *Morgenstunden*, even if he found it "a masterpiece of the
self-deception of our reason."[22] When Moses died in Berlin, on January
4, 1786, he remained a "dogmatic" metaphysician to the end, a pious Jew,
and an unflagging defender of the Enlightenment.

Though hailed during his lifetime as the German Socrates, Moses
Mendelssohn's posthumous reception followed two widely diverging paths.
First, Lessing's idealized image in *Nathan der Weise* was appropriated to af-
firm the philosopher's position as a model Jew who had successfully reconciled Judaism with modern German culture. In the mid-nineteenth century,
Moritz Oppenheim commemorated Mendelssohn's friendship with Lessing
in a painting depicting the two enjoying a game of chess (**plate 1**, 1856).
Ironically, as a result of his "assimilation," Mendelssohn became the symbol of the "regenerated" Jew, a "status" bolstered by Sebastian Hensel's
Die Familie Mendelssohn (1879), which portrayed the Mendelssohns as
fully emancipated, virtuous members of the German bourgeoisie. On
the other hand, the opponents of assimilation "made Mendelssohn the
symbol for everything thought to be amiss with Judaism and the Jews."[23]
At one extreme, in the closing decades of the century, proponents of
Zionism rejected Mendelssohn as a "false prophet of assimilation."[24] Hero
worship and denigration thus solidified into opposing poles of the
philosopher's *Rezeption*, contrasting reactions to his life and work, ironically enough, not unlike those later accorded the philosopher's grandson, Felix Mendelssohn Bartholdy.

II

If Moses Mendelssohn won renown in German letters, a few other Berlin Jews amassed great fortunes. The most successful was Frederick the
Great's court banker, Daniel Itzig (1723–1799), whose father, a horse
merchant, had achieved a "tolerated" status in Berlin. Along with two
partners in 1755, Daniel Itzig won the lease of the Prussian state mints
and began to receive royal commissions for coinage. These were trying
years for the fledgling Prussian state: in 1756, Frederick invaded Austrian
Silesia, touching off the Seven Years' War. Before Frederick emerged victorious as the absolute monarch of a new European power, Prussia suffered severe hardships. To finance his campaigns the king ordered the
devaluation of the Prussian currency. He seized foreign currency, melted
it down, retained its precious metal for his own treasury, and reminted
the coins with impure alloys before recirculating them. Itzig and his part-

ners received handsome compensation for overseeing these currency manipulations.

In 1761 Daniel Itzig became the third Berlin Jew to receive the "general privilege." With his new wealth, he began purchasing fashionable Berlin properties: in 1765, a mansion overlooking the Spree River;[25] in 1769, a house near the Royal Palace, later the residence of his daughter Sarah Levy (a maternal great aunt of Felix Mendelssohn); and during the 1770s, the Bartholdy *Meierei*, a spacious garden near the Schlesisches Tor.[26] Itzig enlarged the mansion by acquiring adjacent buildings to create an impressive edifice with symmetrical wings. It contained a private synagogue and a room with a retractable roof. Among the mansion's treasures was an art gallery with paintings by Rubens, Ter Borch, and Watteau. No less impressive was the garden, landscaped by the royal gardener, with tree-lined walks and orchards, and an open-air theater appointed with sculptures on subjects from Greek mythology.[27] Felix Mendelssohn Bartholdy's mother, Lea, later reminisced about her childhood haunt, its "comfortable little country house, buried in vines, mulberry and peach trees, in which I occupy a neat but very simple little room with my piano, bookcase, and desk as furniture . . . Here my feelings developed, here my youthful mind ripened, . . . here I read my favorite poets with a higher enjoyment, . . . and I even fancy that the weak notes my unskilled fingers produced are here more melodious and pure"—all this on the "meager soil" of Brandenburg, utterly lacking in "anything romantic."[28]

Daniel Itzig's rise to wealth was as exceptional as it was rapid. By 1765 he owned several foundries, and leather and silk factories. He was a cofounder of the Prussian state bank and late in life served as inspector of roads. In dress, speech, and manner he aspired to full assimilation into Prussian high society, a goal underscored by the proximity of his second residence to the royal palace, from which ordinary Jews were excluded. Though a loyal servant of the court, Itzig observed his religion faithfully; in 1775 Frederick designated him "perpetual" chief elder of the Jewish community. Isolated by his enormous wealth, Itzig nevertheless enjoyed strong ties to Moses Mendelssohn's family. Itzig and several of his fifteen children subscribed to the philosopher's biblical translations. Daniel Itzig's son-in-law David Friedländer became a devoted disciple of Moses; Joseph Mendelssohn was a clerk in the banking firm of Itzig's son Isaac Daniel Itzig; and Joseph's brother Abraham married Itzig's granddaughter Lea Salomon.

David Friedländer, an enterprising son-in-law of Daniel Itzig, merits further comment. For the students of the *Freie Schule*, which he and Isaac Daniel Itzig founded in 1779, Friedländer published a Jewish reader to which Moses Mendelssohn contributed. A successful businessman,

Friedländer served for five years on the Berlin City Council. Active in the Jewish community, he came to adopt liberal, indeed radical views, nevertheless tethered to the Enlightenment ideal espoused by Moses Mendelssohn, that all revealed religious faiths were grounded in reason, even if, for Mendelssohn, Judaism conformed most closely to the idea of a rational religion (*Vernunftreligion*).[29] And so, in 1799, the year of Daniel Itzig's death, Friedländer proposed in an anonymous pamphlet that if Prussian Jews could secure emancipation, they would receive baptism into the Protestant Church, provided the conversions could be accomplished "without disturbing their reason, without harming their moral feeling." Animating Friedländer's startling proposal was an optimism that "the two religions would merge sometime in the future."[30]

The Itzig family's female issue also produced noteworthy proponents of assimilation, though their influence was less public than that of their brothers. Three Itzig daughters, Sarah, Fanny, and Cäcilie, presided over elegant salons, which became a neutral meeting ground—accessible to Jews and gentiles, commoners and nobility—for aristocrats, wealthy merchants, intellectuals, writers, and artists. During the heyday of the salons (between 1780 and Napoleon's conquest of Prussia in 1806), some Berliners imagined the salons might achieve the German ideal of *Bildung*, a broad concept that encompassed education and moral development. For well-to-do Jews, the attainment of *Bildung* represented a significant step toward assimilation.[31]

Sarah Itzig Levy (1761–1854), who married the banker Solomon Levy, maintained an active musical salon,[32] where she developed a J. S. Bach cult. Squinting from nearsightedness and physically unattractive, she possessed, according to Fanny Lewald, "a rather unbecoming masculine aspect."[33] Her *habitués* included the Protestant theologian Friedrich Schleiermacher and poetess Bettina Brentano, later the wife of the writer Achim von Arnim. Among Sarah's early visitors were Mozart, who came to Berlin in 1789 in search of royal commissions, and Haydn, whose early biographer G. A. Griesinger gave Sarah the autograph of the *Heiligmesse* (1796), which she later passed on to her most famous great nephew, Felix Mendelssohn.[34] An accomplished musician, she had studied harpsichord with J. S. Bach's eldest son, Wilhelm Friedemann Bach, who had arrived in Berlin in 1774 and won some success as an organ virtuoso before dying impecunious ten years later. As W. F. Bach's main student, Sarah actively promoted the Bachs' music. Thus, she transmitted an autograph of her teacher to Felix, who later made use of it in a Lied[35] (unfortunately, the autograph and Felix's allusive song have eluded detection). Sarah also became a patroness of C. P. E. Bach by commissioning works, subscribing to editions of his music, and acquiring manuscripts, including the autograph of one of his last compositions, the Double Concerto in E♭ major for harpsichord and fortepiano (1788, H. 479).[36] Sarah may have commissioned this peculiar experiment, which sets the refined timbres of the baroque harpsichord against the graduated dynamics of the new fortepiano;[37] she performed it with one of her sisters for connoisseurs assembled at her salon. When Emanuel Bach died the same year, Sarah offered to underwrite a memorial bust and to put his *Nachlass* in order.[38] Sarah Levy's ties to C. P. E. Bach may help explain one singular facet of Felix Mendelssohn Bartholdy's early compositional development: several of his string *sinfonie* from the 1820s recall this Bach's highly mannered style.

Sarah Levy's influence extended to one of Berlin's most venerated institutions, the Singakademie, founded by C. F. C. Fasch in 1791 for the promotion of sacred German choral music. With a rapidly expanding chorus in which Sarah participated (by 1800 it had grown from 27 to 148 members), Fasch specialized in the study of J. S. Bach's motets. When Fasch died in 1800, the directorship passed to Carl Friedrich Zelter (1758–1832), whom Abraham Mendelssohn Bartholdy engaged (probably on Sarah's recommendation) nineteen years later as music tutor for Felix and his sister Fanny. At the Singakademie, Zelter concentrated on Bach's sacred choral works and was ambitious enough to rehearse parts of the B-minor Mass and the Passions. Zelter also resurrected older instrumental music: the Ripienschule, established in 1807 with ten members, met on Fridays to rehearse overtures, concertos, and string *sinfonie* of Handel, J. S. Bach, C. P. E. Bach, Quantz, and Franz Benda. Sarah Levy frequently performed keyboard concerti of the Bachs; thus, in 1807 and 1808, she appeared as soloist in J. S. Bach's Fifth Brandenburg Concerto and Concerto in D minor for harpsichord.[39] Childless, she survived her five siblings, the Revolution of 1848, and the determined effort of Frederick William IV to buy her stately home behind the *Packhof* to make way for a new museum.[40] Likened to Methuselah,[41] she died at the august age of ninety-three in 1854, seven years after Felix's death. Upon her demise, her priceless collection of Bach manuscripts was donated to the Singakademie library.[42]

While Sarah Levy remained in Berlin, her sisters Fanny von Arnstein (1758–1818) and Cäcilie von Eskeles (1760–1836) settled in Vienna. There they married court bankers, among the first Viennese Jews to receive patents of nobility; both Fanny and Cäcilie were ennobled as baronesses. (Felix's sister Fanny Cäcilie, 1805–1847, was named after these two great aunts.) In 1823 Beethoven recorded in Cäcilie's album a short Goethe setting.[43] Her sister, Fanny, who displayed stronger musical interests, arrived in Vienna in 1776. Five years later, the Emperor Joseph II relaxed restrictions upon Jewish subjects by promulgating the Edict of Tolerance, easing Fanny's entrance into high Austrian society. She was a trained pianist who moved comfortably in musical circles. She attended Mozart's concerts and in 1812 helped organize a charity concert that led to the founding of the Gesellschaft der Musikfreunde. During the Congress of Vienna (1814–1815), she held lavish musical soirées that featured foreign musicians such as the young Giacomo Meyerbeer, then an aspiring piano virtuoso. Among the many celebrities visiting her salon were the Schlegels, Madame de Staël, Lord Nelson, Wilhelm von Humboldt, Goethe, and the Berlin song composer J. F. Reichardt. Fanny's daughter, Henriette von Pereira Arnstein (1780–1859), with whom Lea Mendelssohn Bartholdy corresponded, was an accomplished pianist who knew both Haydn and Beethoven.

As one of the few Berlin Jews to receive the "general privilege," Daniel Itzig had enjoyed an exalted status. Still, the protection of the court by no means applied to his entire family or descendants, nor did it confer rights of Prussian citizenship. This situation changed dramatically in May 1791, when Frederick William II took the unprecedented decision to naturalize Daniel Itzig's family and grant them "all the rights of Christian citizens in our sundry states and dominions."[44] The Itzig family thus won exemption from the onerous concessions normally extracted from Jews holding the general privilege. Henceforth the court treated the Itzigs as Christian subjects, even though they freely continued to practice Judaism. But the king tempered his generosity with two qualifications. On the female family side the rights of citizenship extended only to the grandchildren, so that Lea was granted citizenship while her unborn children, including Felix, were not (similarly, they did not enjoy the privileged status extended in 1787 to Moses Mendelssohn's widow and children, although they would be protected by the Prussian emancipation edict of 1812). Second, the king admonished that the rights could be revoked; if any of the Itzigs or their issue "should fall into the Jewish petty dealing that is still common among a great part of the Jewish nation and linked with deceitful frauds, or should even have anything to do with usurious practices, such a person shall be deprived of the benefit of naturalization and the rights bound up therewith in this document, and consequently return into the state of a common Jew."[45] Still, by 1791 the Itzig family had attained a level of emancipation toward which other Berlin Jews could only aspire.

In 1795, four years before his death, Daniel Itzig petitioned Frederick William II to relieve less fortunate Jews from certain discriminatory laws. The answer, delayed until 1798, came in a decree of Frederick William III, who acceded to the throne in 1797. Though his father had recognized the Itzigs as citizens, the new king and his advisors were unwilling to go farther. Remarkably enough, the monarch acknowledged that in the discriminatory laws there existed "a certain harshness and a prejudicial distinction between Jewish subjects of the state and the others; and it is to be desired as much for the honor of humanity as for the good of the citizenship that these laws should be abolished."[46] But Frederick William III refused to repeal them, since their purpose was "to secure the other subjects of the state against the inconveniences which the reception of the Jewish nation among them involves, by virtue of the peculiar character of this nation." The "peculiar character" was the Judaic faith and its customs, viewed officially as "running counter to the purposes of the Christian state."[47]

III

For socially mobile Jews less fortunate than Daniel Itzig's family, converting to Christianity was an alluring means of improving their lot. Through much of the eighteenth century conversions in Berlin were rare, averaging only about three per year. But in the closing decades the number began to rise, so that in 1800 twenty-five Berliners left Judaism, a number that increased to nearly eighty per year by 1830,[48] prompting some to liken the trend of apostasy to an "epidemic of baptism" (*Taufepidemie*).

Several factors explain the growing attraction of conversion. By embracing Christianity, Jewish subjects achieved citizenship, though in reality the converted were still susceptible to discrimination. While some baptisms reflected genuine spiritual convictions, others were encouraged by the proselytizing zeal of Christians. Thus, Schleiermacher likened Judaism in 1799 to a mummified religion, a "mechanical motion from which life and spirit have long vanished," and urged the *salonières* Henriette Herz and Rahel Levin to convert.[49] For well-to-do Jewish women, conversion offered a means of escaping failed marriages and forging new alliances with Prussian noblemen. An early, sensational example followed the death in 1776 of Moses Isaac, a friend of Moses Mendelssohn and brother-in-law of Daniel Itzig, his partner during the Seven Years' War. Like Itzig, Isaac had amassed great wealth, an estate of some 750,000 thalers, and received the general privilege from Frederick the Great. In 1780 two of Isaac's daughters converted and married noblemen; in the process, one daughter, Blümchen, abandoned her husband, Joseph Arnstein (brother-in-law of Fanny Arnstein). What began as a private family scandal erupted into a public imbroglio about the decedent's will. Moses Isaac had stipulated the disinheritance of any of his children who converted, and two of Isaac's sons now petitioned the monarch to enforce the clause. After protracted legal actions, in which Frederick the Great and Frederick William II upheld it, the matter was settled in 1787. Despite favorable rulings, the brothers agreed to pay each sister 75,000 thalers.[50] Remarkably enough, one brother, the physician Joseph Fliess, subsequently converted to Christianity in 1804 and became Carl Friedrich Fliess. In turn, he himself was excluded from the trust along with his descendants, including those who remained Jews.

The rising tide of conversion also affected the Itzig family, but less scandalously than Moses Isaac's issue. Daniel Itzig died in 1799 and left a fortune appraised between 700,000 and one million thalers.[51] According to his will, each offspring received 40,000 thalers, and his grandchildren, smaller amounts. In addition, a family trust was established for Itzig's property, including the mansion, art collection, and the Bartholdy *Meierei*.[52] Like Moses Mendelssohn and Moses Isaac, Daniel Itzig remained true to his religion and, like Isaac, provided that descendants who converted would be disinherited. During Itzig's lifetime none dared challenge his authority, but within a few months of his death, a nineteen-year-old grandson, Isaac Itzig, did so, evidently to advance his career in jurisprudence (professional options for Jewish subjects were then severely limited). Changing his name to Julius Eduard Hitzig, he embraced the Protestant faith in Wittenberg, Luther's stronghold, and became a judicial officer in Warsaw, then part of a Prussian province.[53] Lea Salomon, who would marry Abraham Mendelssohn in 1804, was unimpressed by her cousin's metamorphosis: "he could not resist the desire to be baptized under the image of this great man, and to be in some sort protected by him; and by this step toward the salvation of his soul he has obtained the worldly advantage of soon getting a place in his profession."[54] Hitzig's decision later earned him a withering rebuke in Heinrich Heine's *Hebrew Melodies* (IV, 38–42), where the poet pondered whether the "H" meant "Holy Itzig (for Saint Itzig)?"

The eagerness to convert proved irresistible to Daniel Itzig's grandchildren. Many were baptized during the 1820s, in some cases, including Lea Mendelssohn Bartholdy, *after* their children—Itzig's great-grandchildren—had changed faiths.[55] The case of Jacob Salomon (1774–1825), son of Levin Jacob Salomon and Daniel Itzig's daughter Bella, decisively influenced Abraham and Lea's family. Sometime near the turn to the nineteenth century Jacob added the surname Bartholdy, after his grandfather's dairy farm[56] and then, in 1805, was baptized as a Protestant. Jacob Salomon Bartholdy now became Jacob Bartholdy. In 1809 he fought against Napoleon in the Austrian campaign; his account of the Tyrolese uprising earned Heine's praise as a "clever, well-written book" and provided material for Karl Immermann's tragedy *Andreas Hofer.*[57] After Napoleon's defeat, Jacob served as Prussian consul to Rome, where he resided in the Casa Bartholdy atop the Spanish Steps. An art connoisseur, Jacob commissioned the German Nazarene painters to execute frescoes for his drawing room, on the Genesis account of Joseph.[58]

One of the frescoes, by Peter von Cornelius, treated Joseph's reconciliation with his brothers, seemingly chosen to advance the peace after the devastation of the Napoleonic era. But the painting also bore personal meaning for Jacob Bartholdy. Upon his conversion, his mother, Bella Salomon, had disowned him, a poignant example of how the decision to change faiths could bitterly divide families.[59] Almost certainly this experience helped convince Lea and Abraham Mendelssohn to convert secretly, several years *after* their children had been baptized. A fragmentary letter from Jacob to Abraham reveals that the two discussed conversion; Jacob's views ultimately prevailed:

> You say *you owe it to the memory of your father,* but do you think you have done something bad in giving your children the religion that appears to you to be the best? It is the most just homage you or any of us could pay to the efforts of your father to promote true light and knowledge, and he would have acted like you for his children, and perhaps like me for himself. You may remain faithful to an oppressed, persecuted religion, you may leave it to your children as a prospect of life-long martyrdom, as long as you believe it to be absolute truth. But when you have ceased to believe that, it is barbarism. I advise you to adopt the name of Mendelssohn Bartholdy as a distinction from the other Mendelssohns. At the same time, you would please me very much, because it would be the means of preserving my memory in the family.[60]

Barbarism versus *Bildung*: Jacob placed the issue of conversion in stark terms, brushed aside his brother-in-law's sense of filial duty, and even speculated that as an assimilated Jew Moses Mendelssohn might have pursued the same course. Jacob Bartholdy had no doubt about how Abraham Mendelssohn should raise his children.

IV

Abraham's decision to convert may have had practical consequences for his alliance with Joseph in their Hamburg and Berlin banking firms. As early as 1812, Abraham began to add the surname Bartholdy,[61] probably in response to Jacob's urging. On March 11, 1812, Frederick William III issued an emancipation decree, according to which new Jewish citizens were to choose fixed family names.[62] Abraham and Lea's children became Protestants in 1816, but the parents remained Jews until October 1822, when they secretly embraced Christianity in Frankfurt. At the end

of 1821, Abraham dissolved his ties to the banking firm, which was liquidated and reorganized, with Joseph's son Alexander (1798–1871) replacing Abraham.[63] Although hard evidence is lacking, Abraham's severance
from the firm may have prepared his decision to convert. A few months
after baptism, he received official approval to adopt the name Bartholdy,
and indeed Felix's earliest letters bearing the signature Felix Mendelssohn
Bartholdy date from 1823.[64] In short, Abraham's departure from the bank,
conversion, and change in name thrice underscored his distinction "from
the other Mendelssohns."

How did the fraternal partners come to observe different faiths? Their
age gap and dissimilar professional experiences provide some answers.
The elder by six years, Joseph was fifteen when his father died. Moses
had supervised Joseph's education, introduced him to Hebrew studies
when he was only five years old, and raised him on the philosopher's
translations of the Pentateuch. At nine, Joseph began to study the Talmud under a private tutor; at fourteen, Moses explored with him the
metaphysical complexities of the *Morgenstunden*, specifically created for
Joseph. But the son was willful and by 1783 had interrupted his Hebrew
studies. (Nine years later he would found a Society of Friends, an association of "freethinking" liberal Jews committed to disseminating the
"light of enlightenment" and challenging Orthodox Judaism.[65]) Moses
remained concerned about Joseph's prospects and observed in 1785, "It
is a matter of deep regret to me that I have to withhold him from the
sciences in order to make him a slave of Mammon. For medicine he has
no inclination; and as a Jew he must become a physician, a merchant, or
a beggar."[66]

The "slave of Mammon" found employment in Berlin as a bookkeeper in the court bank, Itzig & Co. After marrying Henriette Meyer,[67]
whom Zelter described as "the most beautiful feminine creature I have
ever seen,"[68] Joseph worked at the bank until 1795. He then mastered his
own destiny by establishing a small banking firm that employed only two
clerks.[69] Two sons were born to him. Alexander, mentioned earlier, followed in Joseph's footsteps, while Benjamin (1794–1874) became a professor of geography at the University of Bonn.[70] In 1799 Joseph allied himself
with Moses Friedländer, the son of David Friedländer, and the firm, now
known as Mendelssohn und Friedländer, remained in business until 1803.[71]
The next year Joseph formed a partnership with Abraham.

We know little about Abraham's early years. Clearly, when Moses
Mendelssohn died, the nine-year-old had not developed as profound a
filial relationship as had his brother, who was more bound to the family
traditions. Nor was Abraham as advanced in Hebrew as Joseph, who had
benefited from his father's tutelage. Not surprisingly, around 1813 Joseph,

not Abraham, contemplated preparing an edition of Moses' writings. When, thirty years later—with the assistance of Felix Mendelssohn Bartholdy—an edition appeared in Leipzig, Joseph's son Benjamin served as the editor, and Joseph contributed a biographical sketch of his father.[72]

Abraham once referred to himself as formerly the son of his father and then the father of his son, as if to limit the paternal role to that of a hyphenlike intermediary linking two great men. Abraham saw himself as a "true Peter Schlemihl" who lacked his own shadow.[73] Like Joseph, Abraham decided to pursue banking; unlike his brother, he began his career not in conservative Berlin but cosmopolitan Paris, where he worked as a bookkeeper for Fould, Oppenheim & Co. from 1799 to 1804 and managed the banking house in 1803.[74] We do not know when Abraham arrived in Paris, but he was en route by 1797[75] so that he witnessed much of Napoleon's Consulate (1799–1804), when the Civil Code was debated, and the reaffirmation of democratic principles of the Revolution, including religious tolerance. In 1803 Zelter recommended Abraham to Goethe as a Parisian correspondent for a new literary paper.[76] According to the music critic A. B. Marx, Abraham was an incorrigible opera patron. Though partial to Gluck, the young clerk attended the premiere of Luigi Cherubini's *Les deux journées* (1800).[77] This sensational "rescue" opera, in which Savoyard peasants conceal an unjustly oppressed aristocrat in a water jug, aroused the egalitarian fervor of the time, and was reportedly based on an actual event.[78] In 1791, French Jews, unlike their Prussian counterparts, had received full rights as citizens and, observing this measure of equality may have influenced Abraham to remain in Paris, where, as he explained to his sister Henriette, he was content to eat dry bread (*manger du pain sec à Paris*).[79]

Nothing could dissuade "Abraham *le citoyen*"[80] from his francophilia until Henriette introduced him to Lea (Lilla) Salomon (1777–1842), a granddaughter of Daniel Itzig "acquainted with every branch of fashionable information." She "played and sang with expression and grace, but seldom, and only for her friends; she drew exquisitely; she spoke and read French, English, Italian, and—secretly—Homer, in the original language."[81] A few early letters reveal that this polyglot was able to converse readily about Wieland, Goethe, Schiller, and the dramatist/diplomat August von Kotzebue. Marx reports that in her "resonances of Kirnberger lived on; she had made the acquaintance of Sebastian Bach's music and perpetuated his tradition by continually playing the *Well-Tempered Clavier*."[82] Among her circle was the music collector Georg Pölchau, who purchased C. P. E. Bach's musical *Nachlass*,[83] and later presided over the library of the Berlin Singakademie, rich in autographs of J. S. Bach.

Henriette Mendelssohn was quick to realize the advantages of Abraham's union with Lea (by marrying an Itzig, he would become a citizen) and encouraged him to return to Berlin: "'Du pain sec' is a very good thing, especially here, where it is so white; but I always fear that if you continue to work for others without the means of getting on, and notwithstanding your great talents are always dependent on caprice and obstinacy, we know it might become 'du pain amer'[bitter bread]...."[84] Abraham conceded and returned in 1804 to cofound the firm J. & A. Mendelssohn[85] and marry Lea on December 26. Apparently Lea's mother forced the issue, for she disapproved of her daughter's union with a modest clerk but was willing to commit her daughter's dowry to support the new bank.[86] In 1805 a second firm, Gebr. Mendelssohn & Co., was launched in Hamburg, where the brothers now settled. We know little about the beginning of this business, though documents reveal that in 1806 the brothers accepted a new partner, presumably to boost capital reserves and expand operations. On September 21 they consummated a contract with the nineteen-year-old Joseph Maximilian Fränckel, son of a wealthy merchant and nephew of Joseph Mendelssohn. Fränckel became a "silent" partner, contributing 30,000 and 75,000 thalers to the Berlin and Hamburg branches respectively. Because he had not yet reached the age of majority, one Philipp Joseph Veit managed the Berlin firm in Joseph's and Abraham's absence.[87] Annual profits and losses were distributed among the three partners according to two formulae. In Berlin, Fränckel's share was 7/12; that of the brothers, 1/8 for each, with the remaining 1/6 divided among all three. From the Hamburg operations, Fränckel received 1/8 of the returns, and Joseph and Abraham divided the remaining 7/8.

While the brothers established one of the preeminent Prussian banks, three of their siblings led more routine lives. Relative obscurity has cloaked Moses Mendelssohn's second daughter, Recha, whose marriage to an agent of the duchy of Mecklenburg-Strelitz, Mendel Meyer (brother of Joseph's wife Henriette), ended in divorce. An "intellectual, clever, but unfortunately very sickly woman,"[88] Recha founded a boarding school for young girls in Altona, near Hamburg, and remained close to Abraham. Her daughter, Rebecka (Betty), converted to Christianity but returned to Judaism in 1818, in order to elope with Heinrich Beer, brother of Giacomo Meyerbeer.[89]

The life of the youngest sibling, Nathan, whom Moses dubbed "Nathan the Wise," is more fully documented. Inclined toward the natural sciences and engineering,[90] he traveled as a young man to Paris and London, where he invented mathematical instruments and improved the pneumatic pump. In 1806 Alexander von Humboldt helped fund his

Berlin workshop for astronomical, geodetic, and physical instruments. Baptized as a Protestant three years later, he became Carl Theodor Nathaniel Mendelssohn. During the War of Liberation, he served as a second lieutenant in the infantry; after the war, he married Henriette Itzig, a granddaughter of Daniel Itzig, and became an inspector of an armaments factory in Neisse. In 1821 he resettled in the resort town of Bad Reinerz in lower Silesia, where, with Joseph's backing, he established a foundry (see p. 121), severely damaged by flooding in 1827 and 1829, so that Nathan abandoned the enterprise. Tragedy and misfortune plagued him: no fewer than seven of his children died, and in 1846 his eldest son, Arnold (1817–1854), a doctor with socialist sympathies, became entangled in a bungled minor theft. A futile flight to Paris to enlist Heinrich Heine's aid led to Arnold's incarceration for five years.[91]

Moses Mendelssohn's youngest daughter was Henriette. Small in stature and deformed, she resembled her father.[92] Henriette followed Abraham to Paris, where she directed a boarding school for young girls. Highly cultured, she counted among her acquaintances Helmina von Chézy (a librettist for Schubert and Weber, and with whom Felix later considered collaborating); Gaspare Spontini, smugly triumphant from his opera La Vestale (1807); Madame de Staël, expelled from France in 1810 for her book about German manners, De l'Allemagne; and the statesman/novelist Benjamin Constant, who also managed to arouse Napoleon's displeasure.[93]

Initially offended by her sister Brendel's conversion to Catholicism, Henriette herself became a devout Catholic in 1812, and assumed the name Maria Henriette, without, Sebastian Hensel reassures us, adapting "any of the disagreeable qualities often seen in converts."[94] Around this time she met one of Napoleon's generals, Horace-François Sebastiani,[95] and became the governess of his daughter Fanny. Hensel describes her service in this household until 1824 as a "brilliant misery."[96] A rich heiress, Fanny Sebastiani was by nature indolent and untalented—and unresponsive to Henriette's fastidious grooming. The spinsterish governess now lived in opulence and occupied a suite of rooms staffed by servants in an hôtel in the Faubourg St. Honoré, with a view of the Champs Elysées. Here she remained during Napoleon's regime, penned discreet letters to her Berlin relatives during the early years of the Empire, and reported in July 1815, as the allies advanced for the second time on Paris, "Europe is once more in France."[97] After Louis XVIII made an inglorious return to Paris "in the baggage of the allies," Sebastiani arranged an opportunistic match between his daughter and the young Duke de Praslin, "neither rich, agreeable, nor clever," Henriette noticed, "but . . . a duke of ancient

descent."[98] After performing her final service, arranging Fanny's trous-
seau, in 1825 Henriette returned, escorted by Abraham and Felix, to Berlin.[99] Her misgivings about Fanny's fiancé proved clairvoyant, for in 1847
the duke became hopelessly smitten by an English governess and murdered his wife. Then, during his trial before the Peers, he committed
suicide by taking arsenic and inadvertently helped precipitate the crisis
that undermined the reign of Louis-Philippe, the "citizen king."

V

The respectable lives of the Mendelssohn siblings considered thus far
contrasted utterly with Brendel's notorious relationship with Friedrich
Schlegel. The eldest child of Moses, she received, like Joseph, an excellent education, and was well versed in literature, drawing, and music.
According to one contemporary, she was "trained to a masculine independence of thought and character"; [100] in Sebastian Hensel's more genteel estimation, her mind "developed to a higher degree than usually
falls to the lot of her sex."[101] But the father's care in raising her proved a
"dangerous gift." Observing the Jewish custom of the time—for Hensel,
an "oriental view of woman as merely a chattel"[102]—Moses selected her
husband. At age eighteen, she entered into a loveless marriage with Simon
Veit (1754–1819), an irreproachable but dull banker. Brendel fulfilled her
needs in the salons of Henriette Herz and Rahel Levin,[103] and organized
a weekly Jewish Lecture Society at the Veit home. For sixteen years Brendel
endured the marriage and bore two children, the painters Jonas (1790–
1854) and Philipp Veit (1793–1877), who later joined the Christian brotherhood of the German Nazarenes in Rome (Philipp was one of four artists
commissioned by Jacob Bartholdy to execute the frescoes for the Casa
Bartholdy).

In July 1797 Brendel's life changed irreversibly when a brilliant, nearly
destitute young literary critic arrived in Berlin. Friedrich Schlegel (1772–
1829) had half-heartedly studied law before becoming a freelance writer.
In his first efforts he committed himself to classicism and decried modern poetry as a chaotic mixture of conflicting impulses. But, Schlegel believed, a new literary age was about to dawn, and he stood ready to develop
a radically different theory of poetics. What emerged near the turn to the
new century as a dramatic *volte-face*—Schlegel's vision of romantic poetry as a "progressive, universal poetry"—was largely elaborated in Berlin, where Schlegel shared a room with Schleiermacher and associated with
Ludwig Tieck and Wilhelm Wackenroder, authors of *Herzensergiessungen
eines kunstliebenden Klosterbruders* (*Outpourings of an Art-Loving Friar*,

1796), which stimulated a romantic revival of Dürer. At the Berlin salons, the twenty-five-year-old fell madly in love with Brendel Veit, seven
years his senior.

By November 1798 Schlegel was confiding his situation to his school-
mate Friedrich von Hardenberg (Novalis), about to write the early romantic novel, *Heinrich von Ofterdingen* (1801). Brendel had "gradually"
become Schlegel's wife, though in a "civil sense" she was still married to
another man[104] (nearly all marriages, Schlegel opined in his thirty-fourth
Athenäum Fragment, were but provisional approximations of a true marriage). Within weeks Brendel left Veit and her two sons and moved to the
outskirts of Berlin, where she enjoyed assignations with Schlegel. Her family
and most acquaintances ostracized her; the novelist Jean Paul Richter dismissed her as a concubine. For support, she relied on Schlegel and a few
steadfast friends, including Schleiermacher and Henriette Herz, who de-
fied her husband's express command to shun Brendel. Remarkably, early
in 1799 this social outcast won a divorce and custody of her younger son,
Philipp, on the conditions she neither remarry nor change her faith. But
an even more extraordinary event transpired that year, when Schlegel
published his novel *Lucinde*, soon recognized as an allegorical account
of his illicit relationship with Brendel. Here, veiled as Julius and Lucinde,
they preside like a priest and priestess over a religion of idealized spiritual, physical, and emotional love. No continuous narrative thread runs
through this (for the time) salacious work, perhaps prompting Wilhelm
Dilthey to dismiss it in 1870 as, "aesthetically considered, a little monster."[105] Among its thirteen parts is a central narrative, flanked by free,
arabesque-like passages. Schlegel blends letters, straight narrative, allegory, and literary criticism to create an autobiographical novel that also
encompasses the "theory of the allegorical novel."[106]

In 1799 Friedrich and Brendel moved to Jena, a small university town
not far from Weimar, that briefly became the epicenter of early German
romanticism. Here they joined Friedrich's brother, A. W. Schlegel, then
completing his German translations of Shakespeare (one later inspired
Felix's *Midsummer Night's Dream* Overture). Other members of the circle
included Tieck, Novalis, the philosopher F. W. J. Schelling, and A. W.
Schlegel's wife Karoline, who left him to marry Schelling. To support the
insolvent Friedrich, Brendel took up writing and published her own
novel, *Florentin* (1801). Suppressing her authorship, Friedrich identified
himself on the title page as the editor (Brendel made the compunctious
comment that in her prose "the devil too often governed where the da-
tive or accusative should have done").[107] Like *Lucinde*, *Florentin* mixes
various genres to create Schlegelian "romantic confusion." Unlike the
unpredictable turns of *Lucinde*, however, *Florentin* adheres to a plot that

rarely strays from the development of its principal characters, the young, wandering artist Florentin, the fifteen-year-old Juliane, and her mysterious aunt Clementina, a thoroughly musical figure likened to Cecilia, patron saint of music. Before *Florentin* appeared in print, Brendel began its autobiographical sequel, *Camilla*, of which a few fragments survive.[108] In contrast to the anti-Catholic sentiments of *Florentin*, the sequel portrays Camilla as a devout Catholic and reflects Brendel's deepening attraction to the faith. She abandoned work on it by 1808, when three significant events—her baptism, marriage to Friedrich, and conversion to Catholicism—altered her life yet again.

Discouraged by his bleak prospects in Jena, Friedrich had moved with Brendel and Philipp in 1802 to Paris. There he studied Persian and Sanskrit, and launched a new periodical, to which she contributed unsigned articles. The couple solicited support from Brendel's siblings by circulating the rumor that she intended to separate from Friedrich. The ruse failed and further damaged the tenuous relationship with her family. Her brothers, it seems, were intent upon resisting claims Brendel had on an inheritance from Moses Mendelssohn's estate.[109] To Schleiermacher she confided: "My brother Abraham is a barbarian without feeling, and is not one hair better than any young Berlin Jew; he only wears finer linen, and possesses a coarser arrogance."[110] As for Joseph, "my oldest brother is the richest but also the most mean."[111] Estranged from her family, she decided to convert and on April 6, 1804, became a Protestant. Taking the name Dorothea, she married Friedrich and—as Dorothea Schlegel—finally legitimized her infamous relationship.

The Schlegels now left France to pursue a peripatetic existence that led them to Cologne. Increasingly drawn to Catholicism, they secretly converted on April 16, 1808. For Friedrich, Protestantism had come to represent the rationalist Enlightenment; by embracing Catholicism, he sought to rediscover the emotional roots of Christianity and reaffirm his intellectual separation from the Enlightenment. For Dorothea, conversion symbolized a further emancipation from her eighteenth-century upbringing and her father's values.

Pursued by scandal, Schlegel—revolutionary critic, author of *Lucinde*, companion of a Jewish *divorcée*, husband of the Protestant and Catholic Dorothea, and a religious convert—now committed another *volte-face*: he took up the role of a conservative diplomat. In 1808 the couple moved to Vienna, where Friedrich joined the civil service. Later, and in declining health, he succumbed to visions of grandeur. Assuming a pretense of nobility, he presented himself as Friedrich von Schlegel and with Dorothea pursued the modish quackery of mesmerism (animal magnetism); he even fancied himself a faith healer. Schlegel's creativity finally exhausted itself in the revision of his collected works, ten volumes of which appeared before he died, insolvent, in 1829.

Through all these intellectual and spiritual sea changes Dorothea remained faithful to Friedrich. She devoted herself equally to the spiritual well-being of her sons, whom she encouraged to convert to Catholicism in 1810 and thereby delivered another blow to their father, Simon Veit.[112] In 1818 and 1819 Dorothea sojourned in Rome, where she reaffirmed her faith and visited her sons and their artistic brethren, the Nazarenes.[113] After Friedrich's death, she moved to Frankfurt and lived with Philipp, who became the director of the art institute there. In 1830, after a separation of twenty-six years, she was finally reunited with her sister Henriette and reconciled with her brothers Abraham and Joseph, who supported Dorothea in her later years.[114] Her nephew Felix Mendelssohn Bartholdy could not tolerate the Nazarenes' fanaticism, but he did correspond regularly with Philipp Veit[115] and was especially fond of Dorothea. In a curious twist, when the Lutheran Felix arrived in Frankfurt in 1837 to marry the daughter of a French Huguenot minister, the Catholic Dorothea Schlegel was the only Mendelssohn to attend.

Part I

Precocious Deeds

Chapter 1
1809–1819

In Nebel und Nacht: Hamburg to Berlin

Maxima debetur puero reverentia.

The greatest reverence is owed the child.

—Juvenal, *Satires* xiv, 47

When bankers Joseph and Abraham Mendelssohn established Gebrüder Mendelssohn & Co. in 1805, Hamburg was a thriving center of commerce and shipbuilding with a population of some one hundred thousand. It had belonged to the old Hanseatic League and, as a "free city," was relatively immune to the affairs of neighboring regions. A few decades before the brothers opened their firm, Salomon Heine was pursuing the same profession in Hamburg. At his death in 1844 he left a vast fortune of some forty-one million francs; his silver holdings prompted Heinrich Heine to cavil about "that magically powerful metal of which the uncle often has too much and the nephew too little."[1]

Though Joseph and Abraham moved in the same social circle as Salomon, who described Abraham as his "best friend,"[2] their business operated for only about six years before the French annexation of the city forced them to return to Berlin. The bank was located on Grosse Michaelisstrasse (No. 71a); their winter residence (No. 14), just behind the Michaeliskirche, was Felix Mendelssohn Bartholdy's birthplace, a three-story edifice where Abraham and Lea Mendelssohn lived with Joseph, his wife Henriette, and their sons Benjamin and Alexander.[3] Neither building is still extant, though in the nineteenth century the residence inspired the preservation-minded "Swedish nightingale," Jenny Lind. Distraught when the composer died in 1847, the soprano ceased performing her friend's music for several years; in 1869 she and her husband, Otto Goldschmidt, placed a commemorative marble tablet above the entrance to No. 14,[4] where it remained until the Nazis removed it in 1936.

An undated letter from Lea described the newlyweds' cramped domicile—presumably the two families shared the second and third floors—as lacking in "comfort in the Berlin style" and announced their interest in a country cottage "with a balcony!!! situated on the Elbe close to . . . Neumühlen."[5] Known as Martens' Mill after its former occupant, Daniel Martens, the cottage became the couple's summer residence in 1805. At the time, Neumühlen was part of Altona, an adjacent Danish community where merchants sold duty-free wares, and where French Huguenots, Dutch Mennonites, and Spanish, Portuguese, and German Jews found tolerance for their faiths. Jews could worship publicly in Altona, in contrast to Hamburg, where owing to a lack of synagogues they observed their faith privately.[6] Abraham's mother, Fromet, spent her last years in Altona and may have encouraged her sons to move to Hamburg in 1805.[7]

For the next several years, Abraham and Lea divided their domicile between Hamburg and Altona, imitating, albeit modestly, the luxuriant lifestyle of Salomon Heine, who possessed a stately summer house in Altona.[8] Three of their four children were born in Hamburg: Fanny on November 14, 1805, Felix on February 3, 1809, and Rebecka on April 11, 1811. No. 14 Grosse Michaelisstrasse was also the birthplace on June 19, 1810, of Ferdinand David, later Felix Mendelssohn's concertmaster at the Gewandhaus Orchestra in Leipzig. The earliest surviving document about any of the children is Abraham's letter to his mother-in-law of November 15, 1805, announcing Fanny's arrival and recording Lea's observation that the matriclinous daughter had "Bach fugal fingers."[9]

On the day of Fanny's birth Napoleon entered Vienna, after decisively defeating the Austrians at Ulm. Prussia observed neutrality in the conflict, and Hamburg maintained her independence, so that the port's merchants were more or less able to pursue unrestricted trading opportunities. But the delicate political equation changed dramatically in July 1806, when Napoleon created the Confederation of the Rhine, sixteen forcibly allied German kingdoms, principalities, and grand duchies. German soil now accommodated a French garrison, provoking the usually lethargic Frederick William III to order a mobilization and demand the dissolution of the Confederation. Instead, on October 14, Napoleon outflanked and routed the ill-prepared Prussian army at Jena, while Marshal Louis Davout decimated a second, numerically superior Prussian force near Auerstädt. Within weeks the emperor established the Continental System, a bid to interdict English trade with the Continent. Henceforth, English subjects and property in French realms were declared prisoners of war and contraband. Though the French lacked the naval supremacy to enforce a blockade, these measures had an immediate impact upon German territories; for Hamburg, the result was devastating. There fortunes had been made from free trade; there fortunes were suddenly lost.

The sovereignty of Hamburg now yielded to a succession of French regimes, culminating with the arrival in 1811 of Marshal Davout, the dreaded Duke of Auerstädt, who offered to dispatch his own brother on the emperor's command. In 1810 Napoleon imposed the French Civil Code upon Hamburg and began conscripting citizens into the French navy. Finally, on January 1, 1811, he formally annexed the city as a French territory. Henceforth, Davout proclaimed, the well-being of Hamburg was linked to Napoleon's fortunes.

The annexation effectively transformed the city into a smugglers' den. Blockade-runners practiced a brisk trade, under the corruptible eyes of French officials. How Gebrüder Mendelssohn & Co. fared during the early years of the French occupation remains unclear. Among the firm's Parisian clients was Alexander von Humboldt, who, monitored by the French secret police, was nearly bankrupt after his epic five-year expedition to South and Central America; in 1809, the celebrated geographer received lines of credit from the Mendelssohns to prop up his finances. Abraham and Joseph also participated in the precarious business of insuring goods. Meanwhile, the Berlin branch continued to expand: its international clients of 1806 represented Amsterdam, London, Lyon, Paris, Riga, Warsaw, and Vienna.[10] The brothers' Parisian banking connections and Berlin family ties strengthened their business (as a member of the Itzig family, Lea Mendelssohn maintained an account producing the considerable yearly income of nearly 7000 thalers).[11]

When Felix was born, the direst effects of the French occupation— including the expulsion of 25,000 Hamburgers before the Russian siege of the city in 1813—were yet to be felt. Nevertheless, according to Jules Benedict, the infant Felix "indicated his strong dislike to the sound of brass instruments and military music, while he listened with fixed attention to anything of a softer and more refined character."[12] The earliest reference to Felix occurs in a letter of May 2, 1809 from Lea to her cousin Henriette von Pereira Arnstein in Vienna: "Tomorrow my little son will be three-months old; he is a nice little lad and promises to be more pretty than Fanny" —an allusion to a slight orthopedic deformity of Fanny, a trait inherited from her grandfather.[13] As for Fanny, Lea reported that at age three-and-a-half, she was reading her letters plainly and constructing phrases correctly, with purpose and clarity.[14]

Curiously, no entry for Felix appears in a birth register of the Jewish community of Hamburg and Altona from 1781 to 1811. A revealing though prejudiced remark by Carl Friedrich Zelter may explain the omission. In October 1821, Zelter described his "best student" to Goethe as "the son of a Jew, to be sure, but no Jew. His father made the significant sacrifice of not having his sons circumcised and has raised them as is proper; it would be truly something rare [Yiddish: *epes Rohres*] if the son of a Jew became an artist."[15] A literal reading suggests that Abraham intended to raise Felix outside Judaism.[16] Indeed, as Jeffrey Sposato has argued, there is no hard evidence that Felix ever "set foot inside a synagogue" or "received any kind of Jewish religious instruction, either formal or informal."[17] Some evidence to support Sposato's conclusion appears in a little-known Viennese review of a Berlin concert in which the thirteen-year-old Felix appeared on December 5, 1822. Here an anonymous correspondent asserts that the "boy was born and raised in our Lutheran religion."[18] Perhaps Abraham, who himself had converted to Christianity only months before, in October 1822, disseminated this bit of misinformation—Felix was, in fact, baptized in 1816.

I

At the beginning of February 1811 Marshal Davout arrived in Hamburg as the new *gouverneur*. Two months later, Lea's and Abraham's second daughter, Rebecka, was born. Apparently, around this time Abraham and Joseph ran afoul of the French authorities, so that, according to Sebastian Hensel, "they were obliged to flee the town, and in mist and darkness (*in Nebel und Nacht*) they escaped one night in disguise, turning their steps towards Berlin."[19] Unfortunately, Hensel does not explain their plight, nor does he disclose when they reached Berlin. Presumably they were involved in some anti-French activity and were in jeopardy of Davout's repressive measures. Ironically enough, after Napoleon's fall, their sister Henriette, governess of the Parisian family of General Sebastiani, became Davout's neighbor. The ruthless tyrant had now mellowed into a hen-pecked husband: "I must tell you as a curiosity that this dreadful Davoust [*sic*], the terror of the north, the author of such unutterable misery, is at home the meekest of men. He has not the courage to give any orders to the lowest servant without the consul of his lady, who governs the household as sternly as he used to govern the conquered countries." And further, "When he first heard my name, he asked General S[ebastiani], who happened to be with us, whether I had any relations at Hamburg, as he had known very worthy people of the same name in that place."[20]

Two documents suggest the worthy Mendelssohns' surreptitious flight occurred near the end of June 1811. Six years before, the music lover Abraham had acquired a collection of J. S. Bach manuscripts auctioned in Hamburg. In June 1811, Abraham sent forty-three of them to the Berlin Singakademie (including the Suite in D major, BWV 1068, and ten cantatas). Zelter acknowledged the gift on June 29 and urged Abraham to "save" other Bach choral masterpieces, for, excepting connoisseurs, "who [else] during our times would understand these things?"[21]

If Abraham and Joseph were still in Hamburg in late June 1811, on July 1 they were in Berlin, where they concluded with their "silent" partner, Joseph Fränckel, a contract dissolving the Hamburg and Berlin firms on December 31, 1811.[22] Subsequently, a new agreement, dated January 8, 1812, reorganized the firm of J. & A. Mendelssohn, owing to "changed circumstances," and provided that each partner would receive one third of the profits and be liable for one third of the losses.[23] Exactly where the Mendelssohns first lived in Berlin remains unclear, but they appear to have resided principally at Markgrafenstrasse No. 48 (between the Jägerstrasse and Französische Strasse), which belonged to the Pastor Stegemann, before they moved to Neue Promenade No. 7 (between the Spree and Haacksche Markt), since 1812 the property of Lea's mother, Bella Salomon Bartholdy.[24]

The first few Berlin years challenged the brothers' business and personal lives, though the access of Lea's family to the French ambassador advanced their interests.[25] In March 1812 the Prussian administration had to raise funds to support Napoleon's Russian campaign, and J. & A. Mendelssohn was assessed 15,000 thalers (upon additional levies, the Mendelssohns refused to cooperate and paid the maximum penalty of 25,000 thalers[26]). The same month the Prussian monarch decreed the Edict of Emancipation, rescinding many restrictions on Jewish subjects and guaranteeing them rights as citizens. On October 30, Abraham and Lea's second son, Paul, was born;[27] by this time, Napoleon, having failed to conclude a truce with Tsar Alexander, had begun the retreat from Moscow. Within weeks the orderly withdrawal disintegrated into a desperate flight from the Russian winter and marauding attacks of the enemy. The emperor reached Paris in December 1812; only about one sixth, or 100,000 men, of the *grande armée*, the largest military force ever assembled, followed him.

The Russian disaster emboldened Prussian patriots to liberate German territories. In February 1813 the minister Hardenberg issued a call for volunteers, and the irresolute king, pressured by increasingly belligerent advisors, formed an alliance with the tsar and declared war against France on March 17. J. & A. Mendelssohn helped supply the Prussian army; in a secret communiqué of April 26 the firm offered to arrange for the delivery of 40,000 Austrian flintlocks.[28] Berlin was at once apprehensive about engaging the enemy and aroused by patriotic fervor: "For fourteen days fear and hope have alternated here in a dreadful way."[29] So wrote Joseph Mendelssohn on May 22, 1813 to his son Benjamin, who at nineteen was experiencing combat as a lieutenant at Bautzen, where Napoleon managed to extract a costly victory from the allies. Joseph outfitted Benjamin and also Dorothea Schlegel's son Philipp Veit, who served with the poet Joseph von Eichendorff at the Battle of Leipzig, where in October the allies dealt Napoleon a crushing defeat. In this culminating Battle of the Nations, a French army of 450,000 clashed with Austrians, Prussians, Silesians, Bohemians, and Swedes. Among the fatalities within the city of Leipzig was the police chief Friedrich Wagner, father of the six-month-old Richard.[30] Among the surviving combatants was the nineteen-year-old artist Wilhelm Hensel, Fanny Mendelssohn's future husband, who was wounded several times and nominated for the Iron Cross,[31] a commendation newly created to honor the military valor of ordinary Prussians. Meanwhile, to support the war effort, Abraham provided funds for a military hospital and equipped several volunteers; for his contributions, he was later elected a city councilor of Berlin.[32]

One of Benjamin Mendelssohn's comrades was the Mecklenburg artist August Grahl, who made the earliest known drawings of Felix and his siblings. According to Rudolf Elvers, Grahl executed four miniature, oval-shaped portraits subsequently reproduced during the family's Parisian sojourn of 1816.[33] The seven-year-old Felix reveals a boyish face with ringlet locks of hair, an alert expression in his large, rotund eyes, and perhaps the beginning of a puckish grin. His eleven-year-old sister Fanny appears in a more serious, self-possessed pose; she wears earrings, and has gathered her hair in a chignon behind her head (**plate 3**).

On March 31, 1814, the victorious Allies entered Paris and imposed a peace treaty upon France (upon learning of Napoleon's abdication, Hegel wrote of the "tremendous spectacle" of seeing an "enormous genius destroy himself"[34]). The Bourbon monarchy returned with the accession of Louis XVIII, and Napoleon's once vast empire shriveled to the eighty-six square miles of Elba, over which the Corsican now ruled as sovereign. At the resplendent Congress of Vienna, convened in September to re-map European political terrain, the allies regaled themselves in ballrooms with a new, socially daring dance, the waltz, prompting Prince de Ligne's *bon mot*, *Le Congrès danse et ne marche pas* ("The Congress dances and does not march"). But that "object of unanimous hatred and fear"[35]—Napoleon—unexpectedly returned to Paris in March 1815 and shattered the allies' triumph; phoenixlike, his vanquished army now rematerialized. When, in April, the Prussian minister issued a second call for volunteers, Benjamin Mendelssohn again reported for active duty. This time he served under Marshal Blücher, whose late arrival at Waterloo on June 18 secured Napoleon's final defeat and led to his second abdication and exile to St. Helena in the South Atlantic.

The emergence of Prussia as a post-Napoleonic power facilitated the rapid rise of the Mendelssohns' bank. At the beginning of 1815 the brothers moved their business to the financial center of Berlin, the Jägerstrasse, where the firm remained until its liquidation by the Nazis in 1938. According to the second peace treaty of Paris, France garrisoned allied troops for five years and paid reparations of seven hundred million francs. J. & A. Mendelssohn joined a consortium of banks led by the Rothschilds of Frankfurt to oversee the payments, which began on December 1, 1815.[36] At the end of October, Joseph took up residence with his family in Paris[37] and established a *bureau* to manage the fund transfers.

On March 21, 1816, Abraham and Lea witnessed the baptism of their four children by Johann Jakob Stegemann, the Reformed Protestant minister of the Jerusalemskirche near the Gendarmenmarkt. The baptismal record reveals that the children added the surname Bartholdy, and Felix the names Jacob Ludwig, so that he now became Jacob Ludwig Felix Mendelssohn Bartholdy (Fanny became Fanny Cäcilia; Rebecka, Rebecka Henriette; and Paul, Paul Hermann).[38] The ceremony was a clandestine affair in the family residence, and the parents withheld news of the conversion from Lea's mother Bella, who had disowned Jacob Bartholdy in 1805 upon his apostasy. As late as December 1823, Bella was unaware that her grandchildren were Christian, and that Lea and Abraham too had converted in 1822.[39]

No doubt by 1816 Lea was instructing Fanny and Felix in piano; according to Jules [Julius] Benedict, Lea offered five-minute lessons and "gradually increased the time until he and his sister Fanny went through a regular course of instruction."[40] Felix's formal education began at the Lehr-, Pensions- und Erziehungsanstalt, a private elementary school on the Kronenstrasse directed by a Dr. Messow. School reports document Felix's progress from 1816 to 1818. At age seven, he earned praise for his memory, and on April 1, 1816, was promoted from the fourth to third class for his "laudable efforts and good manners." Exactly two years later, Dr. Messow declared him fit to enter the first class.[41] By July 1818, Abraham altered course: "Felix has now finished all the classes of elementary school, and his father has finally decided to engage a tutor for him, an instructor from his school, of whom Felix was very fond. I am convinced he will learn much more through private instruction and still have the leisure time to cultivate his talents. Outside his musical interests, he is also inclined toward drawing, which he could only practice from lack of time in a limited way during his attendance at school."[42]

Abraham's choice as a tutor was G. A. Stenzel, a history docent at the University of Berlin employed at Dr. Messow's school. For more than a year, from Midsummer Day through Michaelmas (June 24, 1818–September 29, 1819), Stenzel instructed Felix and his younger brother Paul. Felix, it seems, developed a childlike attachment to the young man, which elicited Lea's disapproval: "The father was a reasonable man and not displeased by the influence Stenzel had on Felix. But the mother could not at all grasp why her son followed every word, indeed every glance of his teacher. She was visibly dissatisfied that Felix clung to him with such affection. For this reason Stenzel probably gave up his position half a year before he left Berlin."[43] His replacement was C. W. L. Heyse, a young classical philologist who fathered the writer Paul Heyse, the first German to win the Nobel Prize in literature. For seven years, from October 1819 until April 1827, Heyse instructed the Mendelssohn children and prepared Felix for the university entrance examination.[44]

Writing from the Bartholdy *Meierei* in 1818, Lea disclosed that Felix was athletically inclined: "here in the country he also has the opportunity to practice gymnastics, for which we have found a little equipment; he visits too the very good swimming school in the immediate vicinity, and so physical exercise should prepare him and make him fit for intellectual endeavors."[45] The Mendelssohns owed their athletic interests to the *Turnvater* Friedrich Ludwig Jahn, "father" of the modern gymnastics movement. During the French occupation Jahn had established near the Kreuzberg a gymnastic society that "blended paramilitary drills and spurious Teutonic symbols with classical ideals of bodily strength."[46] A German nationalist intent upon purging French cognates from the mother tongue, Jahn sought to liberate the *Volkstum*, or cultural essence, of his countrymen. In 1818, the nine-year-old Felix must have been among the youngest athletes to visit Jahn's society.[47] But by 1819 Jahn's populist elocutions prompted the regime to curb the gymnast's activities.

II

Though receiving scant discussion, a few sources establish that the Mendelssohns visited Paris in 1816 and in 1817. En route in 1816 they stopped on April 10 at Goethe's residence in Weimar, where Abraham appeared bearing a letter from Zelter. "He has lovely, worthy children," Zelter noted, "and his eldest daughter can let you hear something by Sebastian Bach. ... He, the husband, is very well disposed toward me, and I have an open till with him, for during the times of general need he became rich, without blemishing his soul."[48] The poet received only Abraham, who stayed one afternoon.[49] By May 1816 the Mendelssohns reached Paris, where Abraham relieved his brother Joseph,[50] and by mid-November returned to Berlin.[51] In Paris, Abraham and Lea renewed their relationship with Henriette Mendelssohn and procured lessons for Fanny and Felix from two celebrated musicians, Marie Bigot and Pierre Baillot.[52]

The Alsatian Madame Bigot de Morogues (née Kiené) settled in Paris in 1809. During Napoleon's Russian campaign, while her husband, librarian of Count Razumovsky, was incarcerated as a prisoner of war, she gave piano lessons to support her family; she died of consumption eight years later at age thirty-four. Her performance of one of Haydn's works nearly convinced the composer she had created the composition. With Beethoven she developed a more complex relationship. On one occasion, while sight-reading the *Appassionata* Sonata from the autograph, she negotiated its illegible scrawls so successfully that the startled composer gave her the manuscript. According to J. F. Reichardt, Marie specialized in the more difficult piano works of Beethoven, whom she idolized as a saint.[53] But when he innocently asked her to accompany him on a walk, she misunderstood the invitation, and the mortified composer had to repair the strained relationship.[54]

In Paris Marie performed chamber music with Pierre Baillot, a Viotti disciple and perhaps the last serious exponent of the French classical school of violin playing, distinguished by its full tone, seamless legato, and varied bowings and articulations. (Baillot reportedly grimaced when he witnessed Paganini's pyrotechnical feats.) Among the first to join the faculty of the Paris Conservatoire in 1796, Baillot won fame as a virtuoso and chamber musician; in 1814 he established a public concert series that endured through the post-Napoleonic Restoration and featured quartets by Boccherini, Haydn, Mozart, and Beethoven.[55] Henriette Mendelssohn was among the subscribers to the 1816 season and reported that Baillot was especially fond of Fanny and Felix, whom he coached in chamber music. "You know Baillot's sensitive face," she wrote to Lea in November 1816; "this expression remained as long as he spoke of Fanny and Felix, and we spoke of no one else."[56]

The Mendelssohns' itinerary between Berlin and Paris led them through Frankfurt, where they stopped midroute during their 1816 journey. Fanny and Felix met their aunt Dorothea Schlegel, who marveled at the "energy, skill, precision and expression" with which her niece and nephew performed her favorite composers, Bach and Handel—Fanny with a virtuosity and Felix an ingenuity that boggled the mind.[57] Exactly when the prodigies departed Paris has eluded scholarly investigation, although the children resumed their studies some time in 1817 with Bigot and Baillot.[58] Eight-year-old Felix was apparently transposing at sight the etudes of J. B. Cramer into different keys, a pastime probably encouraged by Bigot, who later recommended Cramer's exercises to Fanny.[59]

On April 27, 1817, Friedrich Schlegel inscribed some paternalistic verses for Fanny that likened her to fragrant flowers blossoming in the fields;[60] presumably the Mendelssohns were then visiting Frankfurt en route to Paris or Berlin. By July Abraham was in Berlin, where he signed a letter of credit for Wilhelm von Humboldt.[61] In August, Felix may have been in Weimar, when he wrote a French letter to Carl von Stein, grandson of Charlotte von Stein, Goethe's intimate friend. Rediscovered in 1987 as Felix's earliest surviving letter, the text concerns an invitation from Carl delivered by messenger, from which we may infer Felix's reply originated around Weimar.[62] Abraham's business often separated him from his family; from Hamburg in October he chided Felix for careless orthography,[63] though Lea no doubt assumed a strong matriarchal role during Abraham's absences.

<h1 style="text-align:center">III</h1>

By 1818 the siblings' prodigious talents were a frequent topic of conversation among the Mendelssohns' circle. Rebecka Meyer declared the "angelic" Felix a veritable musical genius, and the twelve-year-old Fanny strikingly precocious.[64] An astounding demonstration of Fanny's acumen came later that year, when she performed from memory for Abraham twenty-four Preludes from J. S. Bach's *Well-Tempered Clavier*. Aunt Henriette reacted from Paris with appropriate awe but fretted, "I think the thing decidedly blamable: the exertion is too great, and might easily have hurt her. The extraordinary talent of your children wants direction, not forcing."[65]

From all reports, Felix's progress was no less exceptional. If we are to believe a 1906 auction catalog, on November 14, 1817, he presented to the twelve-year-old Fanny a Breitkopf & Härtel published arrangement of Mozart's opera *Marriage of Figaro*.[66] The arrangement has not come to light, and the catalog entry strains credibility, unless we imagine an eight-year-old negotiating a complex Mozart operatic score at the keyboard. But in 1818 Felix did make his public piano debut, accompanying on October 28 the horn virtuoso Heinrich Gugel and eleven-year-old son Rudolf in a Trio for two horns and piano by Joseph Wölfl.[67] During his ninth year Felix also appeared as soloist in the *Concert militaire* by J. L. Dussek, a now forgotten showpiece bristling with fanfares, arpeggiations, and scales in thirds and sixths; like his sister, the young pianist astonished his audiences by his phenomenal musical memory.[68]

In the review greeting his debut, Felix was identified as a pupil of Herr Berger. Both Felix and Fanny had already taken piano lessons with the Moravian Franz Lauska,[69] whose other pupils included Meyerbeer and members of the Prussian court. Around April 1817, the siblings began studying with the leading Berlin pedagogue, Ludwig Berger (1777–1839), and continued until a strain between Berger and their parents terminated instruction in 1822.[70] He has remained a shadowy figure in Mendelssohn biographies, owing to paucity of information about his early tutelage of Felix. Berger had been a colleague of the painter Philipp Otto Runge, who had conceived his masterpiece, *Die Tageszeiten* (*The Times of Day*), for exhibit in a Gothic chapel accompanied by Berger's music and Ludwig Tieck's poetry. In 1804 Berger met the Italian piano virtuoso Muzio Clementi and the next year followed him to St. Petersburg. There Berger endeavored to establish a Russian market for Clementi's pianos[71] and became a colleague of the Irish pianist John Field. When Berger's wife died in childbirth, he began to suffer from hypochondria. Napoleon's approach forced him to flee in 1812. After concertizing in England, where he was a founding member of the Philharmonic Society, he recommenced his career in Berlin and gave his last public concert in 1814. E. T. A. Hoffmann honored him in a madcap tale, "A New Year's Eve Adventure" (*Die Abendteuer einer Sylvesternacht*), where he improvises "hurricanes and roaring surf" at the keyboard. Forced to retire by an arm injury, Berger established himself as a piano instructor; along with Felix and Fanny, his students included musicians with whom Felix later associated, such as Wilhelm Taubert and Adolf Henselt.

Berger composed not only piano sonatas and nondescript etudes reminiscent of Clementi but also nearly two hundred Lieder and male partsongs. Berger's most celebrated songs were ten settings for the musical play *Die schöne Müllerin*, published in 1819,[72] four years before Schubert created his masterful cycle about the miller maid. *Die schöne Müllerin* brought Berger into contact with its poet, Wilhelm Müller, and also Müller's friend Wilhelm Hensel, his sister (and amateur poetess) Luise Hensel, and the poet Clemens Brentano. These were the principals of a circle that met regularly in 1816 and 1817 at the Berlin salon of Elisabeth von Stägemann and her husband, privy councilor F. A. von Stägemann,[73] to perform a new form of domestic entertainment, the Liederspiel.

Around 1800 Reichardt had created this popular Berlin genre as a hybrid of the Singspiel and Liederkreis, that is, a narrative play with interspersed lyrical songs. In an example of art imitating life, the play about the miller maid and her suitors mirrored a real drama that unfolded within the Stägemann circle, as the bachelors Müller, Brentano, and Ludwig Berger wooed the eighteen-year-old Luise Hensel in vain. The daughter of a Lutheran minister who had died when she was eleven, Luise found the "strength of her sensual impulses" something "to be fought with considerable desperation."[74] In December 1818 she converted to Catholicism and pursued an ascetic life devoted to charities. Berger was crushed by the rejection. Felix was too young to appreciate fully this *contretemps* in his teacher's life, though the potential of the Liederspiel was not lost upon him; in 1829 he would compose for his parents the Liederspiel with orchestral accompaniment, *Heimkehr aus der Fremde* (see p. 221).

IV

If Berger's instruction of Felix and Fanny remains mysterious, their relationship with Carl Friedrich Zelter (1758–1832), who emerged in 1819 as Berger's rival in composition instruction, is amply documented. A gruff man, Zelter was described by the socially refined Lea as not especially sensitive (*kein empfindsamer Mensch*),[75] and by the actress Karoline Bauer as "bristly like a shoe-brush."[76] The son of a Berlin mason, Zelter took up his father's trade in 1774 and became a master mason in 1783. His early musical instruction was not rigorous, and when he submitted a cantata to Kirnberger, the highly respected music theorist was blunt in his judgment: "There is nothing more pitiable than an ordinary artist, of whom there are many; on the other hand a common craftsman, even one of modest talent, always remains a worthy person, . . . Do you wish to build houses and then compose, or do you wish to compose and then build houses?"[77] Undeterred, Zelter turned to C. F. C. Fasch (1736–1800),[78] who, after C. P. E. Bach departed for Hamburg in 1767, had served as Frederick the Great's accompanist. Between 1784 and 1786 Zelter took 168 lessons from Fasch in theory and composition, all the while maintaining a double identity as a musician and stonemason. When during the summer Fasch followed the king to Potsdam, Zelter routinely rose early in the morning, trudged the dusty road to Potsdam for his lesson, and returned the same day to Berlin to resume work as a mason. Among his building projects were renovations to the Bartholdy *Meierei*, which brought him into contact with the Itzig family. He also frequented the family of Benjamin Veitel Ephraim,[79] through whom he met Moses Mendelssohn and his son Abraham.

Zelter's autobiography describes Fasch's method of instruction, of interest because Zelter later followed a similar model in tutoring Felix and Fanny:

> For a long while I wrote four-part chorales before turning to five-part ones. Next we progressed to counterpoint and canon, which gave me intense joy, for during my lonely, sandy walks to Potsdam I would create little canonic hatchlings and became entirely proficient in the genre. Finally we got down to three-part composition. . . From here I turned to the so-called character piece and the French dances, and with that the method *per se* was finished and the fugue begun. . . .[80]

The progression from chorale to counterpoint and canon, and the treatment of four-part chorale writing as the norm are all features of Kirnberger's *Kunst des reinen Satzes* and reflect his own study with J. S. Bach.

Consigned today to the obscure annals of music history, Fasch was in his time a well-established composer. Our chief source about him remains a biographical essay by Zelter.[81] Here Fasch emerges as an eccentric bachelor contrapuntist with obsessive-compulsive routines. To test his readiness for creative work, he habitually multiplied complex series of figures. Any miscalculation would banish his musical inspiration for the day. He kept registers of sea-faring ships and constructed miniature houses out of playing cards.[82] One musical obsession shared with Kirnberger—and which Zelter in turn instilled in Felix—was the writing of learned canons. When Kirnberger enlisted Fasch's aid in solving some intractable canons, Fasch hit upon a few solutions but noticed that some canons were irreparably flawed and did not admit realizations with strict imitation between the parts. Kirnberger was so flustered that he wrote fugues in penance.[83]

The abstract, mathematical beauty of high counterpoint fascinated Fasch. A central aspect of his musical legacy, handed down through Zelter to Felix, was an effort to revivify the splendor of baroque counterpoint and its most demanding forms—canon and fugue. Not surprisingly, Fasch's primary creative thrust was in sacred choral music, traditionally associated with complex counterpoint. Among his choral works are cantata-like chorale and psalm settings, including one (for six-part chorus and organ continuo) of Psalm 30 (1794), using the translation of Moses Mendelssohn. But dwarfing these efforts was Fasch's ornate Mass for sixteen-part chorus (in four four-part choirs) and organ continuo.

The stimulus for this *magnum opus* was a polychoral Mass *a* 16 by the seventeenth-century Italian composer Orazio Benevoli,[84] which Fasch had examined in 1783 but found deficient in part-writing and hackneyed in its modulations. Fasch approached the task of composition as if undertaking a series of mathematical calculations, dividing the ensemble now into four choirs, now into two eight-part ensembles, and occasionally resorting to the most intimidating texture, that of a sixteen-part fugue. As he lay on his deathbed, Fasch instructed Zelter to destroy all his compositions except the Mass. Instead, Zelter preserved the manuscripts and laid plans to publish a collected edition (delayed until 1839, seven years after Zelter's death[85]). There is striking evidence that Fasch's revival of the monumental polychoral style piqued Felix's curiosity: a copy of the Kyrie in Felix's boyish hand survives,[86] and in 1828 he composed a sacred motet for sixteen-part chorus and organ continuo, *Hora est* (see p. 181).[87]

In 1789 Fasch began assembling his students to rehearse sacred choral music, including J. S. Bach's motets.[88] From its modest beginnings the ensemble, known as the Singakademie, expanded rapidly from 55 members in 1793 to 148 in 1797.[89] A Berlin correspondent reported in 1799 that the chorus was made up primarily of dilettantes, though it could execute "the most difficult polyphonic vocal works with a purity and precision beyond all belief."[90] As Fasch's health declined, Zelter became increasingly involved with the ensemble and assumed its directorship upon Fasch's death in 1800.

Four years earlier, in 1796, Zelter published his first song collection;[91] among its settings appeared some of the celebrated Harper and Mignon texts from Goethe's novel *Wilhelm Meisters Lehrjahren*. Zelter dispatched the songs to Weimar but not until 1799 did he muster the courage to address the laureate of German letters. The reply was heartening: ". . . for if my Lieder," Goethe wrote, "inspired you to write melodies, I can well say that your melodies have aroused in me many Lieder, and, if we lived closer to one another, I would surely feel transported to a lyrical mood more often than now."[92] As a token of his esteem, Goethe enclosed the ballad *Die erste Walpurgisnacht* and invited Zelter to set it. But, unable to conjure up music to capture Goethe's Druids and their pagan rites,[93] Zelter left the task to his former student Felix, who in 1831 set the ballad as a large-scale cantata (see p. 247).

For more than thirty years—Goethe and Zelter died within weeks of each other in 1832—the two corresponded about music, literature, and aesthetics, and exchanged nearly nine hundred letters but met only fourteen times. Their correspondence reveals the similarity of their views and depth of their friendship. When Zelter's eldest stepson committed suicide in 1812, Goethe began addressing his friend with the familiar *du*, and Zelter observed that in place of a son he had gained a brother.[94] If Goethe remained the arbiter of all matters literary, Zelter became Goethe's musical confidant. Both found Beethoven's music difficult to approach, and both remained wary of the "excesses" of romanticism, which, in an often-cited remark, Goethe compared to a disease. Above all, Goethe found in Zelter the ideal writer of songs: "your compositions are identical to my poems; like a stream of gas, the music propels the balloon into the heavens."[95]

Of Zelter's approximately two hundred Lieder, fully more than one third are devoted to Goethe's verses. Emulating the artful simplicity of folksong, Zelter favors strophic arrangements with undemanding piano accompaniments and syllabic vocal parts. Rarely does his music challenge the text; rather, the music typically recedes into the background: as in Goethe's metaphor, the music elevates the poem into our consciousness. As one example, we may consider Zelter's setting of the Harper song, "Wer sich der Einsamkeit ergibt" (**ex. 1.1a**), conspicuous for its severe economy of means to convey the Harper's sense of alienation and of guilt about his incestuous relationship with Mignon:

Wer sich der Einsamkeit ergibt,	Whoever yields to solitude,
Ach, der ist bald allein!	Ah, he is soon alone!
Ein jeder lebt, ein jeder liebt	This one lives, that one loves,
Und lässt ihn seiner Pein.	And leaves him to his pain.
Ja, lasst mich meiner Qual	Yes, leave me to my torment,
Und kann ich nur einmal,	And can I only once
recht einsam sein,	Find true solitude,
dann bin ich nicht allein.	Then I am still not alone.

Forgoing a piano introduction, Zelter has the singer begin alone; not until later in the setting does the music achieve four-part harmony, where we encounter increasingly chromatic, dissonant passages to depict the Harper's pain.

Elsewhere, Zelter limits himself to two- and three-part writing, and even bare octave doublings (mm. 5–6) to express the abject journey

Ex. 1.1a: Zelter, "Wer sich der Einsamkeit ergibt" (1796)

Ex. 1.1b: *Wer nur den lieben Gott lässt walten* (J. S. Bach's harmonization)

toward self-negation. The haunting vocal line commences with an apparent allusion to the familiar chorale *Wer nur den lieben Gott lässt walten*, as if the Harper invokes divine providence; indeed J. S. Bach's harmonization of the chorale, which Zelter would have known, anticipates the opening of the song (see **ex. 1.1b**). This striking reference enriches an otherwise stark, sparse setting. In decided contrast, Franz Schubert's famous through-composed setting of the same text (D478b, 1816) celebrates the expressive power of the piano, with rolled chords and arpeggiations to simulate the Harper's instrument, and a piano prelude and postlude that frame the poem. But Schubert's vision of the German Lied as a union of music and text found no place in Goethe's aesthetics, which championed instead the North German style of Zelter and his contemporaries Reichardt, Berger, and Bernhard Klein. When in 1816 Schubert posted to Weimar a volume of Goethe settings, including the treasures *Erlkönig* and *Gretchen am Spinnrade*, the poet simply returned them.

Three editions with thirty-six Zelter Lieder appeared between 1796 and 1802; the fourth, announced as the inaugural volume of his collected songs, was delayed by the war until 1810. On entering Berlin in 1806, Napoleon's first act had been to dismiss the municipal council and order the city's burghers to elect seven *chargés d'affaires*. Among the chosen few, Zelter was selected to serve as the committee's representative to the emperor, an honor Zelter was able to decline by pleading inability to converse in French.[96] Instead, during these years of privation, he contributed to Berlin musical life. The Singakademie resumed its rehearsals in 1807, and the same year Zelter established the Ripienschule, which met on Fridays to rehearse instrumental works. Originally comprising ten musicians, this ensemble quickly expanded to an orchestra of about fifty;[97] its exclusively eighteenth-century repertoire offered what Lea Mendelssohn later described as "the most serious things."[98] The founding of the Ripienschule broadened the resources of the Singakademie and facilitated, for example, the Berlin premiere of Handel's *Alexander's Feast* in 1807. Meanwhile, the Singakademie continued to rehearse J. S. Bach's motets and even took up parts of the B-minor Mass and St. John Passion. Yet another creative outlet emerged in 1809, when Zelter established a *Liedertafel* for the performance of male part-songs, to which he contributed about one hundred settings, many overtly patriotic in nature (the Prussian court was then exiled in Königsberg). In recognition of these activities, the Prussian monarch appointed Zelter a professor of music at the Berlin Academy of Fine Arts.

V

Though Zelter was respected in his day as a composer, his lasting contribution was as a teacher and music educator. In 1804 he submitted to Frederick William III a plan for transforming "music from a courtly decoration to an essential part of the cultivated person's education."[99] Zelter established choral schools in Königsberg, Dresden, and Berlin to promote clear diction and the natural, supple qualities of the German language, all with a view toward advancing the national *Bildung*. His students included several Berlin musicians of distinction: the opera composers Giacomo Meyerbeer and Otto Nicolai; song composers Bernhard Klein and Carl Loewe; choral composer Eduard Grell (later director of the Singakademie); music theorist Adolf Bernhard Marx; and, of course, Felix and Fanny Mendelssohn.[100]

Not every student profited from Zelter's instruction. After two years of study, Meyerbeer turned to the unconventional Abbé Vogler, whom Mozart had dismissed as a "trickster pure and simple." For A. B. Marx, who completed only a few figured-bass exercises, Zelter was a pedant of the old school offering uninspired technical training.[101] But Zelter's instruction of Felix stands in marked contrast. For some seven years, beginning in 1819, Zelter remained the dominant musical influence on the boy and young man, and groomed him in the hallowed traditions of the eighteenth century.

According to Eduard Devrient, a member of the Singakademie and Zelter pupil, when Felix's lessons concluded in 1826, the prickly musician claimed Felix had "learned everything from him and not yet outgrown his guidance."[102] Ludwig Berger and A. B. Marx held decidedly different views: in 1822, Berger claimed credit for influencing Felix's compositional development,[103] while Marx likened Zelter's role to that of observing a fish swim and then imagining he had somehow instructed the fish to swim.[104] Still, both Abraham and Felix acknowledged Zelter's authority. Abraham wrote near the end of his life that Felix's "musical existence and direction would have been entirely different without Zelter."[105] And in 1829, during his first English sojourn, Felix paid this tribute to his teacher:

> I often have to laugh, when the musicians here ask me, whether I learned according to Marpurg or Kirnberger, or perhaps might prefer Fux, . . . to which I answered, *how* I have learned, I wouldn't even know. I would only know that you taught me, and unfortunately would have read nothing at all, since you placed little value on that. . . Cramer still maintained that I definitely must have learned from a book, for without one, wasn't it impossible? Then I laughed, as I said, and thought of you, and thank you, that you raised me not according to rigid, constricting theorems, but in true freedom, *i.e.*, in the knowledge of proper boundaries.[106]

Felix's statement flies in the face of Marx; rather than dismissed as a theorem-bound pedant, Zelter emerges as a practical musician who allowed his pupil latitude to discover the "proper boundaries." But despite Felix's assertion of freedom from treatises, Zelter circumscribed those boundaries around certain model texts, in particular Kirnberger's *Kunst des reinen Satzes* (1779) for figured bass and chorale and Marpurg's *Abhandlung von der Fuge* (1754) for counterpoint. Essentially, Zelter served as a musical hyphen to connect Felix to eighteenth-century German musical culture, epitomized by J. S. Bach and expounded in the music theory of the Berliners Kirnberger and Marpurg. Figured bass, chorale, and counterpoint formed the triangular foundation of that tradition and thus of Zelter's instructional method.

Exactly when Felix and Fanny began lessons with Zelter remains unclear. Presumably formal instruction was underway by May 1819, for Felix and Fanny were then attending Zelter's Ripienschule.[107] On June 12, Zelter referred to himself in Fanny's album as her teacher,[108] and by July 19 Lea was able to assess Zelter's pedagogical style:

> ... he weaves so much spirit, taste, meaning, humor, even genius into his discourses everywhere, that I often regret not having jotted down the best of it. In his case the belief of the ancients, that man has two souls, seems to be true, for I cannot deny that the same man who charms us with inspiration of an artist, touching seriousness of thought, and jokes *à la* Jean Paul, can also be downright insipid and prosaic.[109]

At this time, her children's studies had reached a hiatus— in June Zelter had departed for Vienna. In the imperial city he took walks with the aging court composer Antonio Salieri (still spinning out compositions, Zelter found, like a silkworm[110]) but evidently did not meet Salieri's former pupil, Schubert.

Instead, traveling to Mödling, Zelter encountered on September 12 a musician he had met in 1796 in Berlin. That occasion had been a visit to the Singakademie by Beethoven, who had improvised on a fugal subject from Fasch's setting of Psalm 119.[111] Now, in 1819, Zelter embraced a composer imprisoned by deafness yet on the brink of exploring the transcendent late style, an abstract realm well beyond the limits of Zelter's musical sensibility. When, in 1823, Beethoven offered to sell subscription copies of his colossal *Missa solemnis*, Zelter agreed to purchase it for the Singakademie, but only if Beethoven could supply an a cappella arrangement practical for performance.[112] Zelter admired Beethoven's earlier, middle-period works—the *Egmont* Overture and *Pastoral* Symphony— in which he had "depicted the most strange [ideas]."[113] And Beethoven's programatic symphony celebrating Wellington's victory at Trafalgar transported Zelter to some uncharted, "brave, fearful-fearless and spiritual" realm. But ultimately Zelter remained a child of the eighteenth century, and, like many contemporaries, unwilling or unable to fathom Beethoven's genius, against which Zelter's own efforts as a composer indeed seem insipid and prosaic.

While Zelter was in Vienna, Felix was sedulously churning out figured-bass exercises (the more advanced Fanny was writing baroque gavottes, twelve of which she finished by August 18, just before the family departed on a trip to Dresden[114]). A few survive in a bound manuscript volume transmitting his composition studies from late 1819 through January 1821 and documenting his astonishing progress.[115] Several stages of instruction are evident in Felix's workbook: figured bass (through October 6, 1819), chorale (through January 1820), invertible counterpoint and canon in two and three parts (through May 1820), and fugue in two and three parts (through January 1821). In addition, scattered throughout the volume are some of Felix's earliest surviving free compositions, chiefly variations and movements in binary-sonata form for piano solo or piano and violin.

The pieces for piano and violin (and similarly scored three-part fugues) raise an intriguing issue: who played which part during Felix's lessons? We might assume Felix took the keyboard part while Zelter, a trained string player, read the violin part. But according to Lea, by May 1819 (around the time lessons with Zelter began) Felix took up violin as a surprise for Abraham.[116] His teacher was C. W. Henning, a court conductor and composer who eventually rose to become a royal Kapellmeister.[117] Succeeding the "accurate Henning"[118] was Eduard Rietz (1802–1832), with whom Felix was performing string quartets as early as 1820, and for whom he would compose several works. Felix's early pieces for violin and piano thus may have served two purposes, as composition studies and to promote his development as a violinist.

The figured-bass exercises betray a conspicuous debt to Kirnberger. For each one, Felix added figures to a bass line, and on the staves above, made two realizations in four- and three-part harmony. Finally, on a stave beneath the figured bass, he abstracted a separate, imaginary bass line according to the precepts of the *Grundbass*, or fundamental bass, an analytic tool Kirnberger had adapted from the *basse fondamentale* of J.-P. Rameau to reveal the essential harmonic root movement of tonal music. Kirnberger had devised a system of rules governing the Grundbass and had even published a meticulous analysis of a Bach fugue to which he subjoined a fundamental bass.[119] That Felix was trained in 1819 to analyze chord progressions according to Kirnberger's Grundbass reveals Zelter's conservatism, especially when one considers that around this time the theorist Gottfried Weber was developing a new analytical technique, the series of Roman numerals still familiar to students of harmony today.[120]

After completing figured bass, Felix notated some thirty chorales in four-part harmony, the first of which dates from October 1819. Zelter provided melodies in the soprano voice, for which Felix devised a figured bass line, tested it at the keyboard, and filled in the tenor and alto parts. Several melodies were Zelter's own invention, though they appear alongside such Protestant staples as *Allein Gott in der Höh' sei Ehr, Nun danket alle Gott,* and *Allein zu dir, Herr Jesu Christ.* The last, a melody several centuries old, evinces archaic features recalling the medieval church modes; indeed, Kirnberger recommended harmonizing the tune by modal rather than modern tonal progressions,[121] a bit of advice Zelter imparted to his student. One of Zelter's newly minted melodies merits special comment: the opening of the sixth chorale recalls *Wer nur den lieben Gott lässt walten,* to which, as we have seen, Zelter alluded in his setting of Goethe's Harper Song (cf. **exs. 1.1** and **1.2**). Probably not by accident, Zelter emended the second and third measures of Felix's bass line, as if to make them conform to the Bach harmonization of the chorale recalled by the Lied. Completed on October 23, 1819, Felix's exercise required considerable effort, for he committed several errors and gauche doublings that earned Zelter's reproving comment, "produced totally without thought" (*war ganz ohne Gedanke verfertigt*).

Though a demanding taskmaster, Zelter was quite aware of Felix's extraordinary musical aptitude. He later informed Goethe of a compelling demonstration of the boy's analytic abilities, which may have occurred in late 1819 or early 1820, as Felix pondered in his own exercises the centuries-old prohibition against parallel fifths (two parts progressing in parallel motion from one perfect fifth to another):

> In the score of a magnificent concerto by Sebastian Bach the hawk eyes of my Felix, when he was ten years old, became aware of a succession of six pure fifths, which I perhaps never would have found, since I did not pay attention to them in larger works, and the passage is in six parts. But the handwriting is [Bach's] autograph, beautifully and clearly written, and the passage occurs twice. Now is that an oversight or a license?[122]

In 1911 Albert Schweitzer uncovered the passage in the 1721 holograph of the Fifth Brandenburg Concerto Bach gave to the Margrave of Brandenburg. Early in the first movement, Bach attempted to ameliorate hidden octaves between the viola and solo violin, only unwittingly to fall "out of the frying-pan into the fire."[123] Altering the viola part, he inadvertently produced a new series of parallel fifths between the viola and harpsichord. We know that Zelter's Ripienschule rehearsed the Fifth Brandenburg; indeed, Felix's great aunt Sarah Levy had performed the keyboard part in 1808. Clearly the fifths were an oversight, not a musical license. It is difficult to imagine Zelter's musicians executing the passage

Ex. 1.2: Mendelssohn, Chorale Exercise (1819)*

*Zelter's corrections shown in solid notes (●).

with unmediated parallel fifths; rather, the ensemble parts probably transmitted the hidden octaves of the earlier version, the lesser of two evils. In any event, Felix's discovery of Bach's error must have chastened the redoubtable Zelter.

VI

By 1819 Zelter's pupil was not only correcting Bach but also composing. Surprisingly, his first efforts have attracted scant scrutiny. We know that for his father's birthday on December 11, 1819, Felix wrote a short Lied[124] and some weeks before, by the end of October, had produced a double piano sonata, in the midst of Latin, French, and arithmetic lessons with Carl Heyse.[125] We can confidently identify the song as the *Lied zum Geburtstage meines guten Vaters*, which eventually came to rest in an album of Felix's *fiancée*, Cécile Jeanrenaud, in 1836.[126] Though the manuscript's date, "den 11ten December," lacks the year, the text of the Lied is identical to that of Fanny's salutation dated December 11, 1819, *Lied zum Geburtstag[e] des Vaters*.[127] As for the double sonata, no dated autograph survives, although a manuscript of a Sonata in D major for two pianos, written in a juvenile handwriting suspiciously similar to that of the Lied, has come down to us. The English scholar Peter Ward Jones has proposed that this work is the double sonata of 1819.[128] If so, the sonata and the Lied represent the earliest surviving compositions of a ten-year-old musician.

In all likelihood Felix designed the double sonata for performance with Fanny. By 1819 the two were appearing together in private musical gatherings, including a dinner party Zelter hosted in May 1819, during which they entertained Hegel and other dignitaries. According to Goethe's daughter-in-law Ottilie, the siblings exhibited "unbelievable skill, precision, and knowledge of art."[129] The double sonata, which we may tentatively place ca. October 1819, has three movements (Allegro, Minuet and Trio, and Prestissimo). Occasionally it simulates the transparent textures of Mozart's two-piano sonata in the same key (K. 448, 1781), but Felix's limited tonal compass and insecure treatment of form betray the neophyte's hand. All three movements (excepting the B-major Trio) are centered on D major. In the sonata-form first movement, the contrasting theme of the exposition fails to reappear in the recapitulation, while the finale begins with what resembles a rondo refrain, only to unfold as a monothematic sonata-form exposition. The maladroit handling of form stamps this composition as an early effort, consistent with a dating from 1819. So, too, do several awkward harmonic doublings, revealing that the boy had not yet progressed far with his chorale exercises. Even so, the sonata is a remarkable effort for one so young, not fully versed in harmony and counterpoint.

Far less ambitious is the twenty-six-measure Lied for Abraham's birthday, set syllabically to a congratulatory quatrain:

Ihr Töne, schwingt euch freundlich durch die Saiten,	Ye tones, vibrate gleefully through the strings,
erklingt heller heut,	Resound more brightly today,
Ihr sollt ein frohes Jubellied bedeuten,	You should signify a happy song of jubilation,
das fromme Kindesliebe beut.	That gathers a child's devout love.

Felix's chordal style recalls Zelter's Lieder, in which the upper voice of the piano occasionally doubles the vocal line and distributes the text evenly between four-measure phrases. Felix does indulge in one liberty: extending the last phrase into a ten-measure piano postlude, he playfully disrupts the predictable symmetry of the song.

Inevitably, Felix's youthful efforts prompt comparison with those of another prodigy to whom he would often be compared—Mozart. At age five, Wolfgang had begun to compose simple keyboard pieces, and within a year or two violin sonatas and orchestral music, culminating in his first symphony, at age nine. Both Wolfgang and Felix had older sisters who exhibited precocious musical gifts; both were proficient at the keyboard and violin; and both composed fluently at early ages in a variety of genres. And yet, their educational and social backgrounds were strikingly dissimilar. Felix's musical authority during his formative years remained Zelter. In Wolfgang's case, musical and paternal authority was vested in Leopold. As a servant of the Salzburg court, Leopold had a specific motivation for supervising his children's education: their precocity was marketable. Thus the siblings experienced public scrutiny early and during a "Grand Tour" appeared before the courts of Europe. For Abraham, since his family had already attained the highest levels of Berlin society, Felix's and Fanny's musical training was part of their general education, not a means of economic betterment.

Wolfgang's early travels exposed him to a variety of musical influences—Italian opera, Parisian sonatas of Johann Schobert, London concerti of J. C. Bach—so that the young composer developed a cosmopolitan style. In comparison, Felix's genius blossomed in the conservative atmosphere of Berlin, where Zelter nourished him on German models of Bach, Mozart, and Haydn, but also sheltered his charge from newer, implicitly more questionable, avenues of musical expression. Thus, contemporary musical styles—the "heroic" style of Beethoven, the onslaught of romanticism (Carl Maria von Weber's "romantic opera" *Der Freischütz* would premiere in Berlin in 1821)—were not a significant factor in the very earliest stage of Felix's training.

Paralleling this musical conservatism was the reactionary temper of the time, which reached a critical phase in 1819, as Felix and Fanny were beginning their study with Zelter. On March 23 of that year, the theology student K. L. Sand murdered the playwright August von Kotzebue in Mannheim, sending shock waves throughout German realms. An isolated example of political fanaticism, the incident nevertheless provoked repressive countermeasures from the authorities, who viewed with alarm the growth of popular student associations. In 1815 the *Burschenschaft* (student union) movement had sprung up at the University of Jena. Initially inspired by a "vague patriotic sentiment," the students extolled an "abstract Germanism," in which "all distinction between Prussia, Bavaria, and Saxony was to disappear...."[130] The movement spread to other universities, but Berlin remained relatively unaffected. Then, on October 18, 1817, at a festival in Eisenach, nearly five hundred students, dressed in medieval garb and carrying black, red, and gold banners, marched on the Wartburg castle. Three hundred years before, signaling the beginning of the Reformation, Luther had posted in Wittenberg his ninety-five theses to protest the sale by the Catholic Church of indulgences, and at the Wartburg, in 1521 had begun to translate the New Testament into vernacular German. As it happened, October 18, 1817 marked the fourth anniversary of the Battle of Leipzig, so that the festival coupled observance of the Reformation and Napoleon's defeat, and symbolized the liberation of Germany from religious and political tyranny.

At the Wartburg, books by reactionary authors were burned, a ceremony witnessed by Sand. One book consumed was a history of the Reich by Kotzebue, a German who had become a Russian nobleman. A prolific playwright read by Lea Mendelssohn and acquainted with Henriette Mendelssohn,[131] Kotzebue was suspected by student organizers of being a Russian agent. His murder prompted Metternich to convene the Germanic Confederation in Carlsbad and issue decrees prohibiting student associations and tightening control of the press. In Berlin, Jahn was arrested and his gymnastic society banned.

Among the extreme expressions of the student movement was an increasingly virulent strain of anti-Semitism. The students now "regarded themselves as a neo-Christian knighthood, displaying their hatred of the Jews with a crude intolerance which strongly recalled the days of the crusades."[132] Animating them in part was an inflammatory pamphlet of the Berlin historian Friedrich Rühs that argued against Jewish citizenship unless accompanied by conversion to Christianity.[133] For Rühs and other nationalists, Christianity was "one of the elements of German national culture, and a Jew who acquired German culture also acquired Christianity as one of its parts."[134]

The pamphleteers incited the so-called "Hep-Hep" Riots, which began in August 1819 in the Bavarian town of Würzburg and spread for two months through Germany.[135] Taunted by the slogan "Hep, Hep" (from the Crusaders' Latin rallying cry, *Hierosolyma est perdita*, or "Jerusalem is lost"), Jews were harassed and attacked and their property vandalized. From Carlsbad, Metternich saw the riots as confirmation of a Jacobinist uprising and convinced his colleagues to suppress them. The Carlsbad Decrees, originally in response to Kotzebue's murder, now attempted to quell what the authorities regarded as a counterreactionary movement threatening the very stability of the post-Napoleonic political order.

Was the young Felix victimized by these social tremors? The only evidence we have is a sketchy account from the belletrist and minor Prussian diplomat Karl August Varnhagen von Ense:

> In one middle-sized town, I can't remember which, there suddenly started up, for no good reason, a wild anti-Jewish clamor. With the wild yell of "Hep, Hep!" individuals were assaulted and followed in the streets, their homes attacked and partly plundered, and abuse and violence of all kinds used on them. But no blood was shed—that was where the courage or the ill-nature of the malefactors ended. . . . The violence was accompanied by a heedless mockery and pleasure in making mischief; one royal prince jovially shouted 'Hep, Hep!' after the boy Felix Mendelssohn in the street. Not all of this was done with malicious intent, and some of those who shouted like that would, if necessary, have come to the Jews' assistance if things had gone any further.[136]

We might accept the account and view the *Neuchrist* Felix as a target of anti-Semitic sentiments. Some have gone farther; in a 1963 biography of the composer, Eric Werner maintained that the unidentified prince spat at and taunted the young composer, a detail not found in Varnhagen's text. What is more, Werner believed the incident prompted Abraham and Lea to have their children baptized—a clearly untenable conclusion, since they had already converted in 1816.[137] Was the Mendelssohn family exposed in 1819 to the new wave of anti-Semitism? Probably they were; in August Abraham described Berlin as "wretched" (*erbärmlich*) and apparently considered moving his family to Paris.[138] Still, we can no longer corroborate the veracity of Varnhagen's report. It is as if, in order to record something worthy of recollection (*denkwürdig*), he linked the pogrom to an event in the young composer's life and then deflated the incident by asserting the prince's comment was all in jest. Part journalistic anecdote, and possibly part confabulation, the passage revives Treitschke's judgment that Varnhagen's writing was a "medley of profound thoughts...intermingled with sparkling nonsense," a "storehouse of aphoristic half-thoughts for the *feuilleton* writers."[139]

Whatever the reality of Felix's life in 1819, there can be little doubt that the Mendelssohns' high standing in Berlin society partially insulated them from the political tremors. When news of the banning of Jahn's athletes reached Abraham, he reacted, "I hope the prohibition of gymnastics will not extend to our innocent place."[140] For the moment, Felix could pursue his education largely sheltered from a changing world; for the moment, Felix's surroundings, including the conservative musical arena of figured bass and Bach chorales, were secure. In this environment the fledgling wunderkind would take flight.

Chapter 2
1820–1821

Apprenticed Prodigy

... a genius can curl the bristles of a pig.

—Zelter[1]

Between the ages of eleven and fourteen, in an explosion of precocity, Felix produced well over a hundred compositions, a quantity no less astonishing than its variety—keyboard and chamber works, symphonies, concerti, Lieder, sacred choruses, and operas. When the first collected edition of Felix's music appeared during the 1870s, most of these efforts, judged stylistically jejune, were excluded.[2] But the launching of a second edition a century later refocused interest on Felix's apprenticeship, and several early works, including concerti, the twelve string symphonies, and the Singspiel *Die beiden Pädagogen*, appeared during the 1960s and 1970s, opening new windows into Felix's formative years.[3] Still, much of this music awaits publication. To the biographer, it reveals a musical diary of a prodigy comparable to precious few European composers.

Zelter scrupulously oversaw Felix's apprenticeship of bursting creativity. Scarcely less industrious was Fanny, who completed her thirty-second fugue by December 1824; the siblings, Zelter reported to Goethe, were like diligent bees gathering nectar.[4] But Fanny's parents never imagined she would entertain serious musical aspirations, and it fell to Abraham to temper her enthusiasm. From Paris he wrote in July 1820, as Felix was crafting fugues and beginning his third piano sonata:

Music will perhaps become his profession, while for *you* it can and must only be an ornament [*Zierde*], never the root [*Grundbass*] of your being and doing. We may therefore pardon him some ambition and desire to be acknowledged in a pursuit which appears very important to him, ... while it does you credit that you have always shown yourself good and sensible in these mat-

ters; ... Remain true to these sentiments and to this line of conduct; they are
feminine, and only what is truly feminine is an ornament to your sex.[5]

Fanny was thus to hang musical ornaments, not build a foundation (*Grundbass*, a pun on Kirnberger's fundamental bass). While her brother essayed
increasingly ambitious compositions, she chose piano pieces and songs—
the smaller, intimate genres of domestic music making associated with
the feminine. In particular, her songs (seventy-four date from 1820 to
1823) earned parental approval. Pampering Abraham's Francophilia, Fanny
preferred the verses of Jean-Pierre Claris de Florian (1755–1794), who
had specialized in pastorals and fables derived from Cervantes and Aesop.
Typically strophic, Fanny's settings evince a lyrical melodic gift and a certain "lightness and naturalness,"[6] thereby approaching Abraham's ideal of
the feminine musical decoration. In contrast, Felix wrote few songs during this period, and set only one of Fanny's Florian texts, about Jeanette,
who would choose a shepherd over a king. A rapprochement with Fanny's
musical world, *Pauvre Jeanette* (ca. March 1820[7]) momentarily bridged
the gender gap between the siblings' musical ambitions, as Felix adopted
Fanny's tuneful, chordal style to produce a simple folksonglike setting
that utterly obscured his devotion to Bach's fugues.

I

By December 1819 Felix was preoccupied with chorale harmonizations.
The exercise book contains several melodies in Zelter's unrefined hand
for which Felix devised a figured-bass line and filled in the alto and tenor
parts (Fanny received similar instruction around this time[8]). The next
step was to decorate the note-against-note exercises with flowing eighth-
note embellishments. Zelter included three examples of a more specialized technique, derived from Kirnberger, in which the chorale melody
migrated to the alto, tenor, or bass. Finally, Zelter allowed Felix himself
to compose and harmonize several melodies to verses of the Leipzig poet
C. F. Gellert (1715–1769).

Largely neglected today, Gellert was a widely read figure of the German Enlightenment who produced fables, sentimental comedies, and
the devotional *Geistliche Oden und Lieder* (*Sacred Odes and Songs*, 1757),
designed, while sung to popular chorales, to elevate awareness of the religious sublime.[9] Moses Mendelssohn held Gellert in high regard, and Haydn
reportedly favored him above all other authors. Several composers—J. F.
Doles and Quantz in the eighteenth century, and J. F. W. Kühnau and M.
G. Fischer in the nineteenth—created new tunes for these poems, while
others set them as a cappella canons (Haydn) or solo Lieder (C. P. E.

Bach and Beethoven). Felix's assignment proved challenging: more often than not, his chorale phrases are melodically stale (some he recycled
from earlier exercises), and his cadences are not always harmonically
compelling. But the childhood efforts later bore fruit: several of Felix's
mature works contain free chorales, which thus evolved from the modest Gellert chorales to become a compositional device.[10]

Late in March 1820 Zelter began to initiate Felix, barely eleven years
old, into strict counterpoint, for centuries the domain of learned musicians. The first topic was double counterpoint at the octave, which Kirnberger had explicated in the conclusion of *Die Kunst des reinen Satzes.*
Felix mastered the technique by writing two-part inventions *à la* Bach, in
which the parts are periodically exchanged. Next Felix took up two-part
canon, including the esoteric diminution and augmentation canons, in
which one voice replicates the other at twice or half the speed. These musical conundrums reflected Zelter's own training under Fasch. Probably
by the end of May 1820, Felix was analyzing fugal subjects and negotiating the thicket of rules governing "real" (literally transposed) and "tonal"
(adjusted) answers in fugal expositions. Since Kirnberger's massive tome
omitted canon and fugue, Zelter now drew upon Marpurg's *Die Abhandlung von der Fuge* (*Essay on the Fugue*), which in 1754 had unraveled Bach's
most cerebral contrapuntal techniques. By the latter part of 1820, Felix
was progressing from two- to three-part fugue and canon, over which
he labored through the early months of 1821. All told, he recorded about
thirty fugues in his exercise book,[11] the last of which, a three-part fugue
in C minor, dates from late January 1821. Here the eleven-year-old emerges
as a Bach *devoté* by writing a fugal gigue, recalling the Thomaskantor's
fondness for combining that stylized baroque dance with artful contrapuntal displays (as in the finale of the Fifth Brandenburg Concerto). Thus
did Felix, as Marpurg quipped of Bach, shake "paper intricacies out of his
sleeve."[12]

Felix attacked four-part fugue by March 24, 1821, when he notated
the first of twelve fugues for string quartet, the last of which probably
dates from May.[13] Here again, Bach was the model, inspiring Felix to
explore fugal artifices such as stretto, diminution, and augmentation. The
fifth quartet fugue (April 11) marked yet another stage—Felix's first double
fugue, using two subjects, presented in separate expositions and then
combined. Several of his double fugues cite chorales and form a sub-
group of specialized (for 1821, old-fashioned) chorale fugues. The eighth
quartet fugue (April 27, 1821), based on the Good Friday chorale *O Haupt
voll Blut und Wunden*, offers an example. It begins with two expositions
on subjects derived from the chorale (ex. 2.1), one moving largely in

Ex. 2.1: Mendelssohn, Chorale Fugue on *O Haupt voll Blut und Wunden* (1821), subjects

eighth notes, the other, in sixteenths. Later, Felix inserts phrases from the chorale in slower half and quarter notes, before recalling the two fugal subjects. We might dismiss all this display as reflecting Zelter's pedantry, but once again, Felix's study of chorale fugue positively influenced his mature music. Thus, this arcane form would reappear in the Overture to *St. Paul* (1836), Felix's most popular composition during his lifetime, and then in the Third Organ Sonata of Op. 65 (1845).[14]

In 1821 the chorale fugue led Felix to sacred vocal music, the climax of his studies during the summer of 1821. The exercise on *O Haupt voll Blut und Wunden* may reflect his familiarity with C. H. Graun's Passion cantata, *Der Tod Jesu* (1755), which employed the chorale and was often performed on Good Friday (in 1821, the Singakademie gave it on April 15, not quite two weeks before Felix finished his chorale fugue[15]). In October 1820 Felix and Fanny had joined the institution, and on October 10 Felix sang for the first time as an alto; in the choir register Zelter dryly labeled his voice *brauchbar* (usable).[16] At the Singakademie Felix was exposed to a distinctly eighteenth-century repertoire—in addition to Graun's cantata, the polychoral motets of Fasch, oratorios of Handel, and motets of J. S. Bach—all supporting Zelter's musical diet of austere counterpoint.

Felix's engagement with sacred music produced motet-like exercises, mostly fugal settings of psalm verses on wooden, academic subjects, but also an ambitious, cantata-like rendition of Psalm 19. All these pieces follow the string-quartet fugues in the second volume of Felix's Berlin *Nachlass*; in addition, surviving in Oxford are two choral fugues on verses from Psalm 119.[17] The chronology of these manuscripts has proven refractory: only one exercise, the double fugue *Die Himmel erzählen*, bears a date—curiously enough, June 16, 1820. Almost certainly, "1820" was a

slip for 1821, a misattribution occasionally found in Felix's early manuscripts.[18] Other evidence (the autographs of two movements for Psalm
19 appear before a piano sonata finished in August) permits us to place
the choral fugues around June–August 1821.

For this stage of instruction Zelter again drew upon Marpurg, who
had treated the motet (*Singfuge*) in detail. By 1820 this genre, for centuries associated with sacred, polyphonic music, was well beyond its prime;
still, Zelter performed motets and used them as didactic tools. Motets
were sectional, a cappella compositions organized according to textual
breaks, with each line of text assigned its own portion of imitative counterpoint. Essentially the composer generated a series of *kleine Fugen*,[19]
and then combined the various subjects in a culminating display. This is
how Zelter instructed Felix, by assigning first double fugues *à 4*, and then
challenging him with triple fugues *à 5*.

All but one of Felix's choral fugues were conceived separately. But
the five-part double fugue *Die Himmel erzählen die Ehre Gottes* ("The
heavens declare the glory of God") introduced a larger scale setting of
Psalm 19, bringing the exercises into the realm of free composition.[20]
Three other movements have survived, including a duet for soprano,
alto, and continuo ("Ein Tag sagt es dem andern," "Day unto day uttereth
speech"), with a keyboard part alternating between florid solo writing
and an unrealized figured-bass line, for 1821 a distinctly outmoded approach rooted in the eighteenth century. Whether Felix set the entire
psalm is unclear, but we do know that on September 18, 1821, Zelter read
part, if not all, of the work at the Singakademie and found Felix talented
but somewhat voluble and lacking in composure.[21]

The surviving torso (verses 1, 2, 4, and 7) reveals Felix planned a work
in several movements, blending homophonic and polyphonic choruses
with smaller ensembles and solo settings along the lines of C. F. C. Fasch's
psalms from the 1790s. These youthful studies foreshadowed Felix's later
efforts in setting psalms, for during the 1830s and 1840s he would compose
several cantata-like sacred works with prominent imitative counterpoint.
Zelter's instruction thus again cast a long shadow upon the mature composer. For yet another reason the early psalm exercises merit reconsidera-
tion: some use Moses Mendelssohn's German translation of the psalms
(Berlin, 1782). Was Felix merely following Fasch's precedent in relying on
the philosopher's work?[22] Two of Felix's double fugues, "Deine Rede präge
ich meinem Herzen ein" ("Thy word have I hid in mine heart") and "Ich
weiche nicht von deinen Rechten" ("I have not departed from thy judgments"), draw on Moses' rendition of Psalm 119. Whatever Felix's motivation, these neglected exercises from 1821 provided an audible reminder of
his distinguished paternal ancestry.

II

By the sheer quantity of music he produced, 1820 and 1821 rank as *anni mirabili* in Felix's accelerated development. In particular, the first two bound autograph volumes of the Berlin *Nachlass* chronicle his remarkable ability to work simultaneously on unrelated compositions. Freely intermingled are piano, organ, and chamber works, solo Lieder and part-songs, sacred choral works, small dramatic scenes, and, of course, fugues. The distribution of compositions is revealing. Thus, the first movement of the Piano Sonata in F minor (December 1820) fills the closing pages of *Mendelssohn Nachlass* (*MN*) 1, though its second and third movements appear only some twenty pages into *MN* 2. Filling the gap are fugues, a minuet for violin and piano, organ prelude, piano etude, male part-song, and arrangement of the overture to Felix's first opera, *Die Soldatenliebschaft*—a compelling display of a prodigy's multiple compositional urges.

During these two years Felix composed no fewer than eight sonatas, including six for solo piano, and one each for two pianos, and violin and piano.[23] Of these, only three are published,[24] and one, a sonatina for Fanny, was until recently virtually unknown in the literature.[25] Stylistically the sonatas are largely beholden to the eighteenth century. Thus, we find in the Sonata in A minor the old-fashioned *Trommel* (drum) bass, and, in the Largo of the Sonata in C minor dotted rhythms and sweeping scales, like a superannuated French overture, in which Felix momentarily dons a baroque wig. Generally thematic contrast yields to monothematic treatments of sonata form, another conservative feature. The passagework does not yet exceed the limits of eighteenth-century piano technique; Felix seems oblivious to the music of virtuosi such as Hummel, Kalkbrenner, or Weber, all of whom were appearing in Berlin during the 1820s.

Instead, Felix took to heart Zelter's injunction to model his compositions after Mozart and Haydn.[26] Thus, the Duo Sonata in G minor, of which only one movement survives, introduces a sighing treble melody over a pulsating accompaniment designed to revive the mood of Mozart's Symphony in G minor, K. 550, while the scampering finale of the Violin Sonata in F major recalls the *Allegro vivace* of Haydn's Symphony No. 102. Felix's sonatas are never far removed from his counterpoint exercises; for example, within a few bars the minuet of the Sonata in A minor lapses into a strict canon.

Two sonatas exhibit more modern stylistic traits. The Sonata in E minor commences with a slow *Introduzione*, replete with dissonances and dotted rhythms signifying the heightened pathos of Beethoven's *Pathétique* Sonata (1799) and Ludwig Berger's own *Sonata-Pathétique* in

Ex. 2.2: Mendelssohn, Piano Sonata in G minor, Op. 105 (1821), Second Movement

C minor, Op. 7 (ca. 1804). In the Piano Sonata in G minor, Op. 105, two conventional, monothematic outer movements frame a romantic Adagio that breathes a different atmosphere. The movement begins with an expressive leap exceeding two octaves, a breach filled with dissonant chords that delay the full tonic chord for several measures. Felix then introduces mottled, fluid arpeggiations, and through the liberal use of the damper pedal generates adventurous dissonant blurs (ex. 2.2). By 1821 he was cognizant of the "open-pedal" technique—raising the dampers to permit discordant sonorities to well together. Haydn, Dussek, and others had tested this license during the 1780s and 1790s, before Beethoven revolutionized the technique in his piano works, including the last movement of the "Waldstein" Sonata (1805).

The piano etude also allowed Felix to distance himself from classical models. *MN* 1 and 2 contain about a dozen etudes, many provided with metronome marks to underscore their practical function. Felix's interest in the etude reflects the instruction of Ludwig Berger, who contributed several didactic works for the piano, and of Berger's teacher Clementi, whose piano compendium, *Gradus ad Parnassum*, began to appear in 1817 and 1819. Felix numbered six etudes, as if he contemplated a cycle treating various technical difficulties, e.g., arpeggiations, hand crossings, wide leaps, and parallel sixths and thirds. But at least one etude had a special purpose, as Abraham revealed to Fanny: "Mother wrote to me the other day that you had complained of a want of pieces for the exercise of the third and fourth finger,[27] and that Felix had thereupon directly composed one for you."[28] Fanny's etude has repetitive patterns to strengthen both hands, and a design possibly inspired by J. B. Cramer's *Studio per il pianoforte* (1810, **ex. 2.3**).

Ex. 2.3a: Mendelssohn, Etude in E minor (1820)

Ex. 2.3b: J. B. Cramer, *Studio per il pianoforte* (1810)

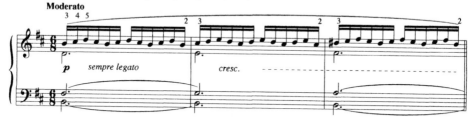

In the closing months of 1820, Felix began to study the organ, an instrument he perhaps first played in the Rochuskapelle just west of Bingen, during a family visit to the Rhine in August.[29] Ironically enough, his Berlin instructor was August Wilhelm Bach (1796–1869), a pedagogue sometimes mistakenly assumed a relation of the Thomaskantor.[30] A member of the Singakademie and pupil of Berger, A. W. Bach had ample occasions to witness Felix's precocity. In 1819 and 1820 Bach had worked with the organist M. G. Fischer, a disciple of J. C. Kittel (a former J. S. Bach pupil). A. W. Bach edited his namesake's organ works and mounted the first complete performance of the B-minor Mass in 1834. Described as a "very thorough and scientific musician" and a "capable maker of fugues,"[31] he was also envious of his young pupil and susceptible to anti-Semitic sentiments. When Felix desired to examine a prelude of J. S. Bach from A. W. Bach's library, he observed to another student, "Why does the young Jew need to have everything? He has enough anyway; don't give him the fugue."[32] Somehow, Bach marshaled sufficient "tolerance" to instruct Felix from late 1820 to 1822. Fanny was permitted to observe her brother's lessons at the Marienkirche,[33] where Bach held the organist's post; but, unlike her brother, she did not compose fluently for the instrument. From Felix's hand in 1820 and 1821 we have an austere *Praeludium* in D minor, some academic three-part fugues (adapted from fugues for violin and piano in the Oxford exercise book), and the beginning of a florid, toccata-like piece in baroque style.[34]

In 1820 he also tested his mettle in chamber music. That year the young protégé of Pierre Rode, Eduard Rietz, who had met the Mendelssohns in

1816,[35] replaced Henning as Felix's violin instructor. Apart from small pieces for violin and piano[36] and the Violin Sonata in F major, Felix essayed three more substantial chamber works: a *Recitativo* in D minor for piano and strings, Trio in C minor for violin, viola, and piano, and Piano Quartet in D minor.[37] Begun on March 7, 1820, the sixty-three-bar *Recitativo* has three sections: a fantasia-like accompanied recitative marked Largo, a compact Allegro, and an abridged return of the Largo. The instrumental recitative and harmonic freedom of the opening recall the eighteenth-century fantasies of C. P. E. Bach, whose telltale jagged melodic lines left their mark on this youthful effort. But the score contains several *Tutti* and *Solo* cues, and the hint of a piano cadenza, as if Felix had in mind a miniature piano concerto, and the string parts are identified in the plural as *Violini*, *Viole*, and *Bassi*, as if the accompaniment was a string orchestra rather than quartet.

In contrast, the Trio and Quartet are unambiguous about their generic identity. The substitution of the viola for a cello in the Trio is unusual but not unprecedented: Mozart had used a viola in his "Kegelstadt" Trio K. 498 (1786). The opening theme of Felix's Trio revives a stock baroque fugal subject, even though subsequently he does not employ fugal procedures. But Felix does invoke an antiquated baroque style in the slow movement, which begins with repetitions of a *basso ostinato* figure. Quite anomalous is the third movement in G minor, *sempre staccato e pianissimo*, and filled with light string work adumbrating the elfin world of Felix's mature scherzi. Still, unable to conceal his training, Felix introduces here a scalelike figure pursued by all three instruments in imitation.

More substantial is the undated three-movement Piano Quartet in D minor, almost certainly from 1821. When the young Jules Benedict visited Berlin in June 1821, he found Felix putting the finishing touches on a "new Quartet for piano and stringed instruments."[38] Of its three movements, the first is among Felix's earliest sonata-form trials with a contrasting second theme. The ternary-form Andante juxtaposes a lyrical opening in B♭ major with a turbulent G-minor middle section. The finale offers a homespun, rustic rondo. Models for the Quartet are easy to discern, for the genre was among the more specialized examples of chamber music. Surely Felix was well acquainted with Mozart's piano quartets (K. 478 and 493), although another source may have been two quartets Prince Louis Ferdinand composed in 1806.[39] A friend of Beethoven, pupil of Dussek, and pianist fêted for his improvisations, the gallant prince died at the Battle of Saalfeld in 1806. His best-known work was his last, the Piano Quartet in F minor Op. 6; Felix may have had its somber hues in mind when, in 1823, he composed the Piano Quartet Op. 2, also in F minor.

Among Felix's most impressive accomplishments of the early 1820s are the twelve string *sinfonie*, of which he finished six by October 19, 1821. On that date Lea described them as "in the old manner, without wind instruments."[40] According to the theorists A. B. Marx and Heinrich Dorn, members of the elite royal orchestra performed these works during Sunday musicales at the Mendelssohn residence.[41] Felix led the ensemble from a piano, where he provided a continuo part by playing the bass line and improvising a harmonic accompaniment above, to substitute for the missing winds. The archaic genre of the string symphony, use of the obsolescent continuo, reliance on monothematic sonata form and baroque "spinning out" of the thematic material all reflect Zelter's conservative guidance. And the eighteenth-century antecedents of the *sinfonie*—admixtures of C. P. E. and J. S. Bach, Mozart, and Haydn— also betray the teacher's tastes.

Most striking in the *sinfonie* are their stylistic discontinuities recalling C. P. E. Bach's mannered style known as *empfindsam* (roughly, "ultraemotional"), characterized by strong unison openings, wide leaps, sudden interruptions, and abrupt shifts in dynamics—all common to six *sinfonie* of Bach (1773, W. 182) performed by Zelter at the Ripienschule.[42] Thus, the energetic opening of No. 5 brings to mind the second of Bach's set, which shares the key of B♭ major and plummeting descending scale (ex. 2.4a, b). A proponent of Emanuel Bach's music, Zelter took exception when the historian J. N. Forkel suggested Emanuel lacked his father's originality.[43] For Zelter a "great genius" who bore "not the slightest

Ex. 2.4a: Mendelssohn, *Sinfonia* No. 5 (1821)

Ex. 2.4b: C. P. E. Bach, *Sinfonia* in B♭ (W. 182, 1773)

resemblance" to his father, the Hamburg Bach had revitalized instrumental music and prepared the Viennese classicism of Mozart and Haydn.[44]

Hardly less pronounced in Felix's *sinfonie* is J. S. Bach's influence, evident in any number of contrapuntal exhibits. The finales of Nos. 5 and 6 bristle with fugatos, but a more erudite display occurs in the slow movement of No. 2. Conceived as a baroque trio sonata, the Andante weaves together two melodic strands in canon that later reappear in mirror inversion against each other. Occasionally the *sinfonie* explore more contemporary styles, as in the Andante of No. 4, where an expressively arching melody in the violins unfolds against lush arpeggiations. The romantic Andante contrasts starkly with the first movement, which begins as a baroque French overture with ceremonial dotted notes. In the second movement of No. 6, in E♭ major, an eclectic stylistic juxtaposition produces an innovative result. Here Felix uses a compact, Haydnesque motive to construct a classical minuet. The Trio, in the unusual key of B major, recalls too Haydn's occasional experiments with submediant (lower-third) relationships. But Felix springs a surprise by adding a second trio in B♭ major, with a prominent chorale-like melody, articulated by interludes between its phrases, that seemingly reenacts *O Haupt voll Blut und Wunden*, though it soon diverges into another example of a freely composed chorale. The interludes imitate a performance practice documented in A. W. Bach's treatises: the custom of organists improvising interludes between the phrases of congregational chorales. In Felix's Minuet the chorale and organ music thus penetrate Viennese classicism, yielding a distinctive hybrid experiment.

Conspicuously neglected by Felix in 1820 and 1821 was Fanny's preferred medium of the Lied. The early manuscripts reveal only four solo songs and two part-songs for male choir, compared to Fanny's nearly thirty songs from the same period.[45] Two of Felix's Lieder have familiar texts: Adam Storck's translations of songs from Sir Walter Scott's *Lady of the Lake*, "Raste, Krieger, Krieg ist aus!" ("Soldier, rest! Thy warfare o'er") and the well-known *Ave Maria*. Published in 1810, Scott's Highland poem inspired a European craze for Scottish history and culture, and transformed into a tourist attraction the rugged terrain of the Trossachs, which Felix would visit in 1829. Scott illustrations were in great demand, as were operas, among them Rossini's *La Donna del lago* (Naples, 1819). In 1820, both Felix and Fanny set *Ave Maria*, and afforded another comparison between the siblings.

Conjuring up the romantic wilds of Scotland—a challenge Felix admirably met later in the *Hebrides* Overture—the eleven-year-old was no match for his sister. Felix imagined a sacred aria, taking as his models J. S. Bach and Handel.[46] Supporting the vocal part is a "walking" bass

Ex. 2.5a: Mendelssohn, *Ave Maria* (1820)

Ex. 2.5b: Fanny Mendelssohn, *Ave Maria* (1820)

line and chords, like a figured-bass realization (**ex. 2.5a**). But this baroque affect fails to transport us to Loch Katrine, where Ellen and her father, outcasts from the court of James V of Scotland, seek refuge on an island:

> *Ave Maria!* Maiden mild!
> Listen to a maiden's prayer!
> Thou canst hear though from the wild,
> Thou canst save amid despair.[47]

In Scott's poem the enchanting "harp of Allan-bane" accompanies Ellen's "melting voice." Fanny begins with harplike preluding in the piano (**ex. 2.5b**), an image missed by her brother (though not by Schubert in his masterful setting from 1825, D839). And she concludes with a murmuring piano postlude, as if capturing the next line in Scott's epic, "Died on the harp the closing hymn." At fifteen, Fanny showed greater sensitivity to the text than Felix; indeed, the Scottish musician John Thomson later issued her song in 1832—the first publication with her authorship identified.[48]

III

An inveterate opera lover, Abraham longed to see his son compose for the stage, and at eleven and twelve—the age when Mozart turned to opera—Felix obliged by writing small-scale dramatic pieces and two substantial Singspiele. Sometime between March 7 and April 1, 1820, he finished a short French scene for soprano, tenor, winds, and strings, "Quel bonheur pour mon coeur de toujours aimer" ("What happiness, my heart always to love").[49] The occasion for this idealized musical *amour* is unknown, though it may have been Lea's birthday, which fell on March 26. His next attempt, confidently titled *Lustspiel in 3 Szenen*, drolly explores the relationship between Abraham and his older brother Joseph.[50] The undated *Lustspiel* falls in the autograph volume from 1820 and was probably written for one of the brothers' birthdays; a reasonable choice would be Joseph's fiftieth, on August 8, 1820 (for Abraham's birthday, December 11, Felix surprised his father with the Singspiel *Die Soldatenliebschaft*).

Felix planned at least two scenes for the *Lustspiel*, although he finished only the first. Joseph (tenor) and Abraham (bass) pledge their eternal fraternal affection, only to fall into a heated debate about Gasparo Spontini's opera *Olympia*. In May 1820 Spontini arrived in Berlin as the Prussian monarch's *Generalmusikdirector*. *Olympia* reached the stage in May 1821 but was overshadowed a few weeks later by Weber's "romantic" opera *Der Freischütz*. The two operas galvanized critical opinion, humorously anticipated in Felix's *Lustspiel*, when Abraham dismisses *Olympia* as totally wretched, while Joseph defends it as very beautiful. Their altercation disturbs an accountant, unable to finish his work in the family's banking firm. Next, an opera singer seeking the Mendelssohns' patronage arrives; rejected, he turns his obsequious coloratura passagework into a rage aria, all cleverly designed to caricature the Berlin stage. The second scene, set within the bank, was to have begun with a chorus of clerks. Felix drafted only a few pages before breaking off work. The reason is not difficult to discern: his inspiration flagged, compelling him to borrow heavily from Mozart's *Don Giovanni*.[51]

The cantata "In rührend feierlichen Tönen" ("In sweet ceremonial tones"), finished on June 13, 1821, almost certainly was for the wedding the following day of Lea's niece Marianne Seeligman and Alexander Mendelssohn, second son of Joseph.[52] Unpublished, the cantata includes two a cappella choruses, of which the first returns at the end to round out the work; there are also two recitatives and a somewhat saccharine soprano duet with a piano part. Felix rendered the textual image of the felicitous union of two souls by having the soloists sing separately and then together. Just as two vines become entwined, two brooks flow together, and two dewdrops form one, so do two souls fuse into one tender flame.

Felix's one-act Singspiel, *Die Soldatenliebschaft* (*Soldiers' Love Affairs*), had an unusual gestation. The librettist was the forensic pathologist Johann Ludwig Casper (1796–1864), who spent the summer of 1820 with Abraham in Paris. There he visited Henriette Mendelssohn and attended vaudeville comedies, from which he probably cobbled the text for Felix's Singspiel. By August Felix was envisioning music for the libretto; composition began at the end of September but, according to Abraham's stipulation "not to show parts of the work to anyone before all was completed," other than Fanny "no one saw a single note until the work was rehearsed."[53] Casper himself played the two bass parts, "in order to keep everything strictly *incognito*." Felix thus created the work in artistic isolation, producing an overture and eleven numbers in orchestral score with little advice from family or friends—and, evidently, without Zelter's direct supervision. Felix accomplished this extraordinary feat in about ten weeks, and the work was performed with piano accompaniment on Abraham's birthday, December 11.[54]

So that Felix could hear the opera with an orchestra, the parents underwrote a production in their residence for his twelfth birthday, February 3, 1821. A little-known account of the proud mother reports the event:

> In the spacious hall . . . a most charming, ample theater was constructed. The orchestra, selected from the best members of the royal *Kapelle*, occupied the middle area; Felix sat in their midst at the piano; and the area behind was raised and filled with the audience. Before [the Singspiel] a French farce was given, . . . called *L'homme automate* [*The Human Automaton*] and . . . truly delightful. Fränkel played an innkeeper and Dr. Casper the automaton most splendidly. Felix wrote an overture for it, into which he wove popular folksongs according to French taste. . . . The character of [*Die Soldatenliebschaft*] is alternately cheerful and full of feeling, as the text requires. The ensembles reveal a knowledge of contrapuntal writing, but above all the orchestration an insight that for a first attempt borders on the incredible. The instrumental rehearsals were on this account very interesting; it seemed to me impossible that a child could be so confident writing for each section of the orchestra—not even twenty errors occurred—and that many found his score not unplayable, when one considers that no expert had seen even one line of it,

let alone retouched it. The old musicians were most surprised to find every-thing fluent, correct and appropriate to the character of each instrument. . . . After the conclusion he was called, and when he refused to appear, Stümer and Casper overcame his resistance and carried him out. . . . It was a uniquely lovely moment for the parents' hearts, to see their beautiful child with Raphael-like locks sitting among all the artists, his eyes always enlivened by the music, radiant and flashing with uncommon energy, and above the child's features streamed an expression of bliss and coyness, . . . And so his calling appears to have been determined, dear Jette! May heaven grant that he remains happy. These days the career of an artist is really full of thorns![55]

The soprano soloists were Fanny and Friederike Robert, wife of the poet Ludwig Robert; the tenors, J. D. H. Stümer from the Berlin royal opera and Heinrich Beer, brother of Meyerbeer. Although *L'homme automate* is lost, *Die Soldatenliebschaft* has survived, along with its spoken dialogue, rediscovered in Oxford in 1960. But despite some attention[56] and a 1962 revival in the German Democratic Republic, which touted the work as an indictment of bourgeois society, the Singspiel remains unpublished.

Set in Spain during the Napoleonic occupation, the plot concerns two pairs of lovers separated by class. Felix, colonel of the French hussars, courts the Spanish Countess Elvire. Her maid, Zerbine, is in love with the ser-geant Victor but is pursued by Tonio, overseer of the countess's castle.

To the young Felix, the parallels between Casper's libretto and Mozart's *Marriage of Figaro* and *Don Giovanni*, also set in Spain and treating com-moners' relationships with nobility, were obvious enough. The stage for *Die Soldatenliebschaft* is set with a brisk overture on a scurrying theme foreshadowing the intrigues to come. Felix delineates his characters with music alternating in mood between *heiter* and *gefühlvoll*, thus bearing out Lea's observation. Tonio, Victor, and Zerbine sing strophic songs in folksonglike idioms, vivified with deft touches of instrumental color— for instance, horn calls for Victor's celebration of the soldier's rustic life (No. 5), and a cello solo for Zerbine's tender *Ariette* (No. 7). Especially effective is the Rondo (No. 4), in which Tonio conceals alarm bells to foil a mysterious suitor, to a distinctive accompaniment of pizzicato strings, horns, bassoon, and piccolo (**ex. 2.6a**). In stark contrast is the Countess's music. Her cavatina (No. 11), "Still und freundlich ist die Nacht," strikes a more serious, noble tone reminiscent of Barbarina's cavatina in Act 4 of *Figaro* (**ex. 2.6b**). Enriching the neutral shades of the string background are echoes in the oboe and bassoon, which also perform a duet in the postlude. Here Felix produced poignant music well beyond his years. To be sure, *Die Soldatenliebschaft* relies upon stock roles from comic opera: the countess and Victor are serious lovers, and Tonio a comic bass re-calling Osmin in Mozart's *Entführung aus dem Serail*, while Zerbine plays a *soubrette*. The score contains too some stereotypical musical gestures,

Ex. 2.6a: Mendelssohn, *Die Soldatenliebschaft* (1821), No. 4

though it projects a remarkable buoyancy and vitality. *Die Soldatenliebschaft* remained a favorite of Felix's parents, and in 1829 the nostalgic composer considered reviving it for their silver wedding anniversary.[57]

Even as preparations for his first Singspiel were underway, Felix began receiving from Casper late in January 1821 installments of a new libretto, *Die beiden Pädagogen* (*The Two Pedagogues*). Abraham challenged his son to have the score finished for a reading *am Klavier* on Lea's birthday. Once again she reviewed her son's achievement, how in six weeks he

wrote an opera, which, finished a few days before March 15, was quickly rehearsed and performed at the piano. You know Zelter is not a particularly sensitive, easily moved man; so imagine how I felt, when I relate that he sat next to Felix, turning the pages of the score, and could not keep his eyes dry. ... Zelter, Pölchau and several other solemn gentlemen were not ashamed to sing in the chorus. The text is again by our house poet Dr. Casper, derived from the French and quite cheerful, light, and musical. As is appropriate for the text, there is less feeling and tenderness in this operetta than in the first, but more comic caprice and mature execution.[58]

Ex. 2.6b: Mendelssohn, *Die Soldatenliebschaft* (1821), No. 11

Although Lea did not identify the cast, we know that the tenor Stümer and baritones Casper and Henning (Felix's violin teacher) took three of the six roles.[59] Toward the end of April 1821, Felix entertained the traveling piano virtuoso J. N. Hummel with a performance of the Singspiel with strings.[60] The next year plans were laid for a fully staged production with full orchestra. The young actor-singer Eduard Devrient (1801–1877) replaced Henning; and on Zelter's recommendation, Devrient's future wife, Therese Schlesinger (1803–1882), sang one of the soprano roles.[61]

Therese has left an engaging account of the frenetic preparations for the performance. The solicitous parents dispatched servants to deliver parts to the soloists, and rehearsals took place at the family residence in a room "not at all luxuriously appointed," though projecting an "aristocratic tone" and offering "piquant and spirited conversation." Therese received coaching from Zelter, who already had subjected her to a tedious course in figured bass; also attending were gentrified members of Berlin society and *literati* such as Varnhagen von Ense. Felix presided confidently from the piano and amazed his listeners by playing with such skill that one could "hear individual instruments of the orchestra."[62] But the much-anticipated production of *Die beiden Pädagogen*, planned with a reprise of *Die Soldatenliebschaft*, never materialized, owing to Lea's ill health.

The source of *Die beiden Pädagogen* was an early *comédie-vaudeville* of Eugène Scribe, *Les deux précepteurs, ou Asinus asinum fricat*, which premiered in 1817 in Paris where Casper and Abraham perhaps encountered it in 1820. Its bilingual title, *The Two Preceptors, or the Ass Rubs the Ass*, betrays the subject, a satire about children's education. In transforming the vaudeville into a Singspiel, Casper accommodated German taste. Thus, *Die beiden Pädagogen* concludes with a choral finale that replaces the rhyming couplets of *Les deux précepteurs*. Still, interspersed throughout Casper's libretto are songlike couplets that recall the light-hearted *airs* of Scribe's comedy. Casper converted the French roles into German characters: the two preceptors (Cinglant and Ledru) become Kinderschreck (scare child) and Luftig (airy). In No. 8, for Zelter a quartet worthy of the comic-opera composer Cimarosa,[63] Kinderschreck and Luftig debate not about Rousseau and Voltaire (as in the original) but two reformers celebrated in German realms, Pestalozzi and Basedow. The Swiss J. H. Pestalozzi (1746–1827), a passionate advocate for educating the poor, argued for nurturing the child's innate faculties. From exile in Königsberg during the French occupation of 1809, the Prussian Queen Luise imagined that Pestalozzi's method was the only means of securing the domestic tranquility of her citizens.[64] His predecessor J. B. Basedow (1723–1790) won Goethe's admiration in 1774 by publishing a massive tract for educational reform and establishing a school in Dessau. There Basedow's colleagues approximated a state of nature by assigning their students *Robinson the Younger*, an entertaining revision of Defoe's *Robinson Crusoe*.[65] In Felix's quartet the pedagogues' argument is nothing more than absurd patter, with the adversaries rapidly exchanging the reformers' names, while the landowner Herr von Robert and his son Carl, the object of the disputation, interject comments from the sideline.

In characterizing Kinderschreck, a mediocrity who rules by the whip while pretending to be versed in Pestalozzi, Felix revealed a genuine gift for comic opera. Kinderschreck's entrance aria (No. 4) pompously asserts his authority by invoking the Latin refrain, *Probatum est* ("it is approved"). Accompanying his pronouncements is stilted music—repeated pitches and phrases mechanically transposed through sequential repetition (ex. 2.7). To conjure up Kinderschreck's instrument of torture, the orchestra periodically executes snaplike figures. No doubt Felix, a product of more humane tutors, enjoyed this bit of parody.

Though Eduard Devrient detected the influence of Carl von Dittersdorf,[66] an 18th-century Viennese composer of comic opera, *Die beiden*

Ex. 2.7: Mendelssohn, *Die beiden Pädagogen* (1821), No. 4

Ex. 2.8a: Mendelssohn, *Die beiden Pädagogen* (1821), No. 10

Ex. 2.8b: Mozart, Violin Sonata in G (K. 301, 1778)

Pädagogen again draws upon the wellspring of Mozart's genius. The D-major overture, "spinning a rapid and witty series of musical events out of virtually nothing,"[67] reminds us of the overture to *The Marriage of Figaro*, also in D major. Both begin with compact *piano* motives; both employ unison writing and a surprise *forte* explosion. In the penultimate No. 10, an ensemble with a chorus of peasants, Luftig is obliged to provide dance music, and he performs a solo violin melody borrowed from the second movement of Mozart's Violin Sonata K. 301 (**ex. 2.8**). Eventually the $\frac{6}{8}$ dance melody is combined with choral music in $\frac{2}{4}$, a polymetrical experiment reminiscent of the Act I finale of *Don Giovanni*, in which Mozart's celebrated minuet appears with other dances in $\frac{2}{4}$ and $\frac{3}{8}$. Elsewhere Felix seems intent upon recapturing the sound of Mozart's late orchestral style, as in the end of the C-major finale, resplendent with allusions to the *Jupiter* Symphony.

IV

Herr von Robert's effort to mold Carl into a *Gelehrter* would have resonated with Felix, then pursuing a rigorous classical education with his tutor, Carl Heyse. Eduard Devrient relates that when Lea noticed her son idle, she would admonish, *Felix, thust du nichts?*[68] A letter from March 1821 to his former tutor, G. A. Stenzel, reveals the extraordinary development of an exceptionally gifted child.[69] After casually mentioning the two Singspiele, Felix summarized his academic regimen, beginning with six hours of Latin a week (four for Caesar and Ovid, one for grammar, and one for exercises). If the prose of the *Gallic War* presented few obstacles, the poetry of the *Metamorphoses* required prepared translations, at the rate of fourteen verses an hour, in order to reach Daphne's transformation into a laurel in Book 1. In mathematics he was reading the fifth book of Euclid's *Elements* and with Fanny had lessons in history, arithmetic, geography, and German conversation.[70] On Mondays and Tuesdays he attended the Singakademie, while twice a week Zelter came to the residence for lessons (around this time, as we have seen, Felix was beginning fugue in four parts). Finally, there were two hours of violin lessons each week; Felix was now practicing etudes of Rodolphe Kreutzer, prized for their innovative extensions of left-hand technique.

The letter presents a budding polymath. Music was at the center of the child's existence, but his studies also led him to delve into poetry. Thus, we have in his hand part of a mock epic (*ein Spott-Heldengedicht*), probably from 1820 or the early months of 1821, about the exploits of Felix's younger brother Paul, assigned the Greek sobriquet Paphlos. Titled *Paphlëis*, this little-known poem comprises three cantos, of which the last two and part of the first survive.[71] *Paphlëis* is indebted to classical antiquity, for Felix crafted its approximately 450 verses in dactylic hexameter, a meter he encountered in Ovid.

Goethe's *Achillëis* (1799, a sequel to Homer's *Iliad*) was a major source for Felix's *Paphlëis*, though a second stimulus was Goethe's idyll *Hermann und Dorothea* (1798), also in dactylic hexameter and fraught with classical allusions (its nine cantos bear the names of the Greek muses). Goethe sought to appropriate a classical genre to tell a modern story, about refugees fleeing the horrors of the French Revolution. Imitating Goethe, Felix devised titles for his cantos and placed the Roman gods Mercury and Bellona at the beginning of the second and third. Unlike *Achillëis* and *Hermann und Dorothea*, though, *Paphlëis* treats no cataclysmic event; it sings, instead, of quotidian activities in the Mendelssohn household and sets the epic aspirations of the poetry against the mundane reality of a child's life in Berlin.

The first canto introduces the eight-year-old Paul with a Homeric epithet. The "fleet-footed Paphlos" (*leichtfüssiger Paphlos*) is a Greek field commander who has marshaled his comrades against Fesca's band. But Paphlos turns heel in a skirmish and flees, only to faint into a pile of mud. His companions rally, defeat their opponents, and incarcerate Fesca in a cellar, and then, with water from a pump, clean off their besmirched leader, who promptly claims credit for the victory.

In the second canto, presided over by Mercury, god of cunning and commerce, Paphlos's companions assemble for a game of marbles. Here Felix bends his hexameters to fit the German titles of Shakespeare's plays *Twelfth Night* (*Was Ihr Wollt*) and *As You Like It* (*Wie's Euch Gefällt*), revealing that by 1821 he was reading A.W. Schlegel's translations.[72] The main portion of the canto is Paphlos's account of his great deeds, prefaced by an invocation to the muses for inspiration. But the story of his life, little more than a chronicle of academic studies with Heyse, impresses as a parody of Felix's letter to Stenzel of March 1821.

Thus, our hero is a polyglot who reads Latin fables of Phaedrus and *A Thousand and One Nights* in Arabic, peruses a Greek primer, and has mastered Syrian, Chaldean, and Sanskrit—all mere child's play. Paphlos studies arithmetic with his father and geometry, history, geography, French, politics, and Greek mythology. He plays the cello, accompanied by Fanny (*Mamsell Benicke*) on the piano and Felix on the violin, and is learning etudes by "Quikrack," no more demanding than hair cream (*Pomade*). He draws and paints, is skilled in sepia, and has even composed a *Morgenlied* with a key signature of fifteen flats. He rises at five in the morning before his brother, and sometimes awakens Felix by splashing water in his face. "And so," he sums up, "I am at once an artist and a scholar, and now you know with what sort of man you have to deal."[73] Nevertheless, Paphlos is mortal: when a flower box suddenly collapses and he feigns injury, his companions turn on him as "the most cowardly inhabitant of the earth." In the final canto, titled after the Roman goddess of war, Fesca wins release and plots a surprise attack on Paphlos, who once again faints in the thick of the fray. Police break up the melée, and he returns home, only to be boxed on the ears and sent to bed by Abraham. Maintaining the epic conceit to the end, our young bard closes with a final Homeric allusion: "And so they laid to rest in bed the hero's corpse."

Although centered on Paul, *Paphlëis* reveals of course as much about Felix, who projects his own worldview onto his brother. There is a wistful, if playful, sense that Paul's path has already been trodden by Felix, that Paul's misadventures comically reflect and replicate Felix's own, more serious experiences as a child. Ultimately the authority of the classical epic and its crisp hexameters provide only a comical foil to a certain truth Felix must have known, that despite his precocity and sensitivity, in the real world his status as a baptized Jew was questionable. Paphlos is a younger version of Felix, who indeed became a great artist, while the pragmatic Paul entered the family's banking business.

The closing lines of *Paphlëis* refer to Paul's residence and identify its address as Neue Promenade No. 7. This stately abode, owned by Lea's mother, Bella Salomon, was in the Spandauer Vorstadt near the eastern end of Unter den Linden. Though the chronology of the Mendelssohns' Berlin residences remains unclear, a letter of Lea dated February 18, 1819, already mentions the new residence.[74] Unaware of this letter, and drawing on evidence from contemporary address books, Manfried Kliem suggested that the family moved to Neue Promenade no later than October 1820. Writing to Fanny from Paris on October 15, 1820, Henriette Mendelssohn observed that Abraham now had a greater distance to traverse from his new quarters to his firm on the Jägerstrasse. This statement does not quite square with Lea's letter of 1819 but might well if she mistakenly misdated the year as 1819 instead of 1820, a type of oversight to which Felix too was susceptible in his correspondence. From Henriette's letter Kliem deduced that the family had moved from Markgrafenstrasse 48 (their other documented residence of the early Berlin years), near the Gendarmenmarkt, a short distance from the Jägerstrasse. The owner of Markgrafenstrasse 48 was Pastor Stegemann, who had baptized the Mendelssohn children in 1816 and died in March 1820.[75] If Kliem is correct, Neue Promenade No. 7, where Bella occupied the ground floor and Abraham's family the second, while the third was rented out, was the site of the lavish productions of Felix's early Singspiele. And if Lea's letter was indeed written in 1820, February 1820 might serve as a *terminus post quem* for *Paphlëis*.

At Neue Promenade No. 7 the Mendelssohns enjoyed a rich musical life. Here Felix and Fanny entertained traveling dignitaries, including, in 1821, Hummel and Weber. Another visitor was the part violin virtuoso, part charlatan A.-J. Boucher, who likened Felix to a phoenix. Boucher impressed audiences with a Napoleonic physiognomy with which he struck various poses from popular engravings—for example, the emperor upon the smoldering ruins of Moscow.[76] (Jacob Bartholdy found the resemblance ludicrous; in his view, a conquering emperor was so far removed from a musician's life that the one should not imitate the other.[77])

At a musical gathering during the winter of 1820, the French flutist Louis Drouet witnessed Felix's compelling abilities. The piano being out of tune with the flute, Drouet strained to transpose his part down a step, only to abandon the attempt, while Felix effortlessly raised the piano part a semitone. "I listened with the greatest apprehension," Lea reported, "though the young devil succeeded with only a few mistakes."[78] Drouet was equally impressed with Fanny, but he found her *rares talen[t]s* more difficult to describe than writing counterpoint and opted to inscribe a fugue in her album.[79] On another occasion, in October 1820, a colleague of Pushkin, Wilhelm Karlowitsch Küchelbecker, later exiled to Siberia for his participation in the Decembrist uprising of 1825, attended a performance at the Mendelssohn residence of a Requiem (almost certainly Mozart's), and documented an early example of a Sunday musical soirée. Much impressed by Felix, who sang in the chorus, Küchelbecker penned an intimate, sensual portrait: "Never have I seen such a perfectly beautiful youth. His dark locks fell in natural freedom halfway down his back, his snow-white neck and chest were open; his dark southern eyes glowed and betrayed future conquests over souls! His small, roseate mouth seemed to have been shaped for kisses; in his voice resonated a spirit that knew and felt more than one thought usual for one of his age to know and feel."[80]

An especially close relationship now developed between Felix and Fanny. According to Lea, he routinely submitted compositions to Fanny's judgment and took her criticisms to heart, "mercilessly" striking passages she questioned.[81] Fanny became his Minerva, the Roman goddess of wisdom and decorative arts, who in classical mythology sprang fully mature from Jupiter's head. Felix's respect for Fanny's musical acumen, playfully expressed through mythological fantasizing, was high praise, indeed. Though Fanny at age sixteen offered penetrating critiques of Felix's music, she could only stand by as his musical horizons continued to expand. And so, more spectator-like than divine, she expressed curiosity about Henriette von Pereira Arnstein's plan in 1821 to send Felix a "naive-sentimental" opera libretto on a Swiss subject. There would be choruses with *obbligato* bellowing of cattle, sunlit glaciers, and a nostalgic, languishing shepherdess[82] (the libretto evidently never materialized). As for her own creative efforts, Fanny continued to write Lieder and submitted her idyllic settings of Florian to the visiting French violinist Pierre Rode, who praised some but found others "too French." According to Lea, Fanny was "musical through and through," a pianist whose accomplished technique elicited words of praise from the usually taciturn youngest son of Mozart, Franz Xaver Wolfgang Mozart (1791–1844), who concertized in Berlin and played duets with her.[83]

A special opportunity for the siblings to collaborate arose in June 1821, when Karl Begas (1794–1854) visited the family. The young painter had apprenticed in the Parisian atelier of Antoine-Jean Gros, a leading exponent of Empire art.[84] Though Gros provided Begas a solid grounding in technique, he found the Frenchman's panegyrizing canvases on Napoleonic subjects politically difficult in the post-Waterloo Restoration, and potentially compromising to his career. By 1817 Begas had turned to religious subjects, and attracted the patronage of Frederick William III, who funded further study in Paris. Four years later, Begas returned

Ex. 2.9a: "Begas" represented by pitches

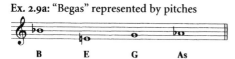

B   E   G   As

Ex. 2.9b: Fanny Mendelssohn, Piano Piece in A♭ major (1821)

to the Prussian capital with a new canvas for the altar of the Berlin cathedral, *Die Ausgießung des Hl. Geistes* (*The Outpouring of the Holy Spirit*),
and on this occasion met the Mendelssohns. According to Lea, Begas
was passionately devoted to music and drawn to her children, and they
responded with musical mementos of his visit, including a piece by Fanny
based upon the musical letters of his name.[85] Her customized offering,
unrecognized since 1821, can now be identified as a fifty-five bar piano
work in A♭ major, recorded on June 27, 1821, on some staves beneath a
chorale exercise for Zelter.[86] Along with J. S. Bach and the Dane Niels
Gade, Begas possessed an exceptionally musical surname; Fanny recognized that musical pitches could represent all its letters (in German nomenclature, B=B♭; and As=A♭). Ex. 2.9 gives the opening of her solution,
a serpentine melody that touches on F minor, before turning to A♭ major.

Felix's piece for Begas remains unidentified. As for Begas, he recorded
his impression of Felix by painting the youth's portrait. Lea found the
result a "splendid souvenir" of Begas's "masterful brush."[87] Even though
the original oil was destroyed in a fire early in the twentieth century, two
nineteenth-century pastel copies by the Englishman Charles Horsfall
(grandson of Alexander Mendelssohn) survived,[88] as did a preliminary
oil sketch by Begas (**plate 4**). After his 1821 visit Begas retained this sketch
for reuse in a historical canvas (whether in fact Felix's boyish face was
again pressed into service remains unknown).[89] The copies and oil sketch
impress as the very realization of Küchelbecker's literary portrait of 1820:
Felix appears with shoulder-length locks flowing down his back, roseate
lips, an exposed white neck and chest, and penetrating, dark eyes turned
askance, as if contemplating some visual or musical object.

Earlier in 1821 another young painter entered the Mendelssohns' lives.
Wilhelm Hensel (1794–1861) was the son of a poor Protestant minister
from Brandenburg, who opposed his son's artistic aspirations (Wilhelm

could draw before he could speak), and in 1811 sent him to Berlin to study engineering.[90] Shortly thereafter the pastor died, leaving Wilhelm free to pursue painting; by 1812 he was exhibiting work at the Academy of Art. But when the War of Liberation erupted, he enlisted. Thrice wounded, he served with distinction and in 1815, as an officer of the victorious allies, entered Paris, where he perused the masterpieces of the Louvre. After the war Hensel earned his living by producing illustrations for calendars and almanacs. A turning point came early in 1821, during a state visit from Grand Duke Nicholas of Russia and his Prussian wife, the Grand Duchess Alexandra Feodorovna (formerly Princess Charlotte). The royals needed entertainment, and Wilhelm was among several artists engaged to provide it. This occasion brought Wilhelm and Fanny together, though no one would have predicted their future union, because, as their son Sebastian later observed, they were from dissimilar backgrounds, one of a "Christian-Teutonic" type, the other "of pure Jewish descent."[91]

The entertainment chosen was a series of tableaux vivants ("living pictures": staged scenes in which actors assumed fixed poses) on Thomas Moore's *Lalla Rookh*. Today largely forgotten, the Irish poet Moore was a biographer of Byron and a political satirist of the Regency who never forgot the suppression of the United Irishmen in 1799. Among his poems were ten volumes of *Irish Melodies* (1808–1834), which elicited from Hector Berlioz several elegiac *chansons*. Moore also composed the popular song "The Last Rose of Summer," the inspiration for a wistful piano fantasy by Felix (Op. 15, 1830). In 1817 the Irishman created a sensation with the escapist "Eastern romance" *Lalla Rookh*, about a sixteenth-century Indian princess who journeys from Delhi to Kashmir to marry Akiris, the young king of Bucharia. Moore's publisher payed £3000 for the manuscript sight unseen. Structuring the romance as four allegorical verse tales, Moore stitched together the whole with a prose introduction and interludes. The second tale, "Paradise and the Peri," later inspired Robert Schumann's secular oratorio *Das Paradies und die Peri* (1843), about a fallen Persian fairy seeking to reenter Paradise by discovering the gift "most dear to Heav'n" (after two attempts, she succeeds with a repentant sinner's tear). The fourth, "The Light of the Harem," about a lovers' quarrel between the Emperor Selim and his concubine Nourmahal, prompted Spontini to compose an operatic rendition for the Prussian court.

In designing tableaux vivants, Hensel drew upon a tradition several centuries old.[92] Opinions vary about the aesthetic merits of this unusual diversion, but with some imagination one might recognize in the genre the precursor of several later art forms. As a posed, framed space, the tableau vivant anticipated photography; when presented as a sequence of tableaux, it was a forerunner of cinematography; and when "performed" with music, it foreshadowed the multimedia synthesis of the Wagnerian *Gesamtkunstwerk*.

The Prussian exchequer spared little expense for the event, held at court on January 27, 1821, and repeated on February 11 before an audience of three thousand. According to Hensel's friend the novelist Theodor Fontane,[93] a Spontini march escorted a bejeweled procession of nobility and guests (symbolizing the wedding party of the Indian princess) into the palace. The assembly viewed successively twelve tableaux depicting scenes from the four fables, to the accompaniment of *romances* by Spontini. For the occasion the architect K. F. Schinkel provided decorations, and the English historian Mountstuart Elphinstone designed oriental costumes. Nobility, including the family of Prince Radziwill, Beethoven's patron, struck the poses. Entering the hall on a gold stretcher, the Grand Duchess Alexandra played Lalla Rookh.

Fontane's account places Fanny among the audience but fails to divulge how she met Hensel. Presumably she attended the second performance, to which the Intendant Count Brühl had invited several artists and literati.[94] But in *The Mendelssohn Family* Sebastian Hensel offers a different scenario. After the second performance the Grand Duchess Alexandra imagined that future generations should have a remembrance of the event, whereupon the king instructed Hensel to prepare a "drawing-room book" with paintings of the tableaux. Once again, the royals assumed their poses, while Hensel executed his drawings *nach der Natur*. Before sending them to Russia, Hensel exhibited them in his studio and there "made the acquaintance of Fanny Mendelssohn Bartholdy, who had come with her parents to admire his beautiful drawings."[95] In 1823 the volume was published in Berlin, one of several royal attempts—ranging from commissions for Persian vases to Spontini's exotic opera *Nurmahal* (1822)[96]—to preserve the festival for posterity.

During this period Abraham continued to tend to the religious education of his children. On May 21, 1820, Fanny was confirmed as a Protestant.[97] In July Abraham broached from Paris a difficult, sensitive subject—the religious divide separating the parents from their children. His letter opens optimistically with a vision of natural religion, an ideal not far removed from Moses Mendelssohn's enlightened views or Lessing's vision in *Nathan der Weise*. Seeking a common spirituality binding all faiths, Abraham wrote, "I know that there exists in me and in you and in all human beings an everlasting inclination towards all that is good, true, and right, and a conscience which warns and guides us when we go astray. I know it, I believe it, I live in this faith, and this is my religion."[98] Although Abraham and Lea had been able to "follow the divine instinct" without forsaking Judaism, they had chosen Christianity for their children, because "it is the creed of most civilized people, and contains nothing that can lead you away from what is good, and much that guides you to love, obedience, tolerance, and resignation, even if it offered nothing but the example of its Founder, understood by so few, and followed by still fewer." Having obtained "the *name* of a Christian" by confessing her Protestant faith, Fanny could now realize her full potential by following the inner voice of her conscience. In August 1821 that voice moved her to accomplish a remarkable deed, the reconciliation of her uncle Jacob Bartholdy with his estranged mother, Bella Salomon.[99] Fanny's talent so impressed Bella that she offered as a reward "anything Fanny liked." Bella honored the unexpected request—forgiveness for Jacob—thereby healing the sixteen-year-old wound caused by his baptism in 1805. For his part, Jacob praised Fanny's "skillful and felicitous negotiations," and observed that her heart had somehow accomplished what the mind could not.[100] But offsetting this joyful event was a tragedy, for around this time Lea gave birth to a stillborn infant.[101] During her recuperation, J. G. S. Rösel, later Felix's drawing instructor, gave her an inscribed stone from a Roman temple[102]:

> In Aesculapius' temple was I found
> By a cheerful, lucky customer,
> In a most blessed hour.
> Therefore luck to me is bound,
> Whoever wears me soon will be sound.

Lea had the stone set, and wore the ring faithfully as a talisman of good luck.

Chapter 3
1821–1822

The Second Mozart

[Mendelssohn,] the greatest, specifically musical genius to appear
in the world since Mozart.

—Richard Wagner[1]

At precisely 7:00 P.M. on June 18, 1821, a slightly lame, bespectacled man
entered the hall of Schinkel's Schauspielhaus on the Gendarmenmarkt
and limped to the rostrum. This was the Dresden Kapellmeister Carl Maria
von Weber, in Berlin to premiere his "romantic opera," *Der Freischütz*. As
a folksonglike melody wafted from four *Waldhörner*, the overture exuded
a German flavor. The natural horn had been revived in the Arnim-
Brentano folk anthology, *Des Knaben Wunderhorn* (*The Youth's Magic
Horn*, 1805), and Weber himself would receive the dedication of Wilhelm
Müller's *Gedichte* "from the Posthumous Papers of a Traveling *Waldhorn*
Player" (1824). Müller's poems inspired Schubert's song cycles *Die schöne
Müllerin* and *Winterreise*—replete with horn calls worked into the piano parts. The male-dominated world of German romanticism centered
on sylvan settings in which hunters wandered toward self-actualization;
the *Waldhorn* was their instrument of choice. Among Weber's audience
were Felix and his parents, Dr. Casper, Heinrich Heine, E. T. A. Hoffmann,
and scores of veterans of the War of Liberation, their chests emblazoned
with Iron Crosses.

The portentous premiere fell on the anniversary of the Battle of Waterloo. A polemic erupted in the press, with Weber's adherents and detractors exchanging verbal volleys. The champion of a new, nationalist
German opera, Weber was opposed to the court Kapellmeister, Spontini,
creator of un-German, Empire-style operas. Spontini's neoclassical *Olympia*, commissioned by the Prussian monarch, was based on an earlier French

tragédie lyrique. The new German version offered stately processions (Statira, Alexander the Great's widow, entered on an elephant, accompanied by a clamorous band crammed onto the stage), a bacchanal, and an apotheosis with the macabre specter of Alexander. Straining with hyperbolic effects, *Olympia* was a stentorian affair: a German physician reportedly cured a deaf patient by taking him to the opera, even though the therapy cost the physician his own hearing.[2] Spontini's music appealed to royal taste, and the court responded by patronizing three performances.

Weber's score addressed a distinctly different, middle-class audience. The music teemed with popular tunes that were all the rage; Heine reported that Berlin barbers, washerwomen, and schoolboys hummed the catchy bridesmaids' song from Act III, and Zelter endured a cobbler's apprentice singing the same number off pitch.[3] The core of the opera was the Wolf's Glen scene concluding Act 2, a continuous, twenty-minute complex in the unfamiliar key of F♯ minor, representing the hour between midnight and 1:00 A.M. Worlds removed from Spontini's pomp, this diabolical scene took place in the depths of a German forest, where the young huntsman Max, to win the hand of Agathe, sold himself for seven magic bullets to the satanic Samiel. As each was cast over a seething cauldron, a fresh apparition appeared, nearly exhausting the theater's special-effects resources. There was a mechanical owl with eerily lit eyes and flappable wings,[4] a wild boar, a carriage with fireworks to depict flaming wheels, an unseen chorus of wild huntsmen, and other "chilling" effects that touched the German soul.

The morning of the premiere Weber completed another major work, the *Konzertstück* in F minor, Op. 79. A telescoped piano concerto, with four connected movements, it belonged almost as much in the opera house as the concert hall, for it was pure musical theater. Felix's friend Julius Benedict sketched its mawkish medieval program[5] of a damsel pining for her knight, a variation on the theme of separation and reunion, explored a few years earlier by Beethoven in his piano sonata *Les Adieux* (Op. 81a). Weber premiered the *Konzertstück* on his farewell Berlin concert (June 25), an event Felix almost certainly attended.[6] The audience witnessed an extraordinary scene. The violinist Boucher, accompanying Weber in a chamber work, inserted a cadenza, into which he managed to blend a *"pot-pourri* of motives" from *Der Freischütz*. But when he conjured up the "Wolf's Glen" scene on his E-string, he floundered and had to save himself by feigning exhaustion and exclaiming to the dumbstruck Weber *"Ah! grand maître! que je t'aime! que je t'admire!"*[7]

Weber's triumphant reception in Berlin overwhelmed young Felix, then grinding out fugues for Zelter. What Spontini contemptuously dismissed as the "little deviltries" (*Teufelein*) of *Der Freischütz*[8] offered Felix a glimpse of a musical world remote from the sacred motets of Bach that Zelter prized so highly. Even before the premiere Felix begged his friend Julius Benedict to play the opera at the piano, and after Weber's departure Fanny and Felix eagerly awaited the appearance of the piano score.[9] The *Konzertstück* later became a staple of Felix's piano repertoire and provided a model for several of his virtuoso concert works. But in 1821 the young apprentice was still under Zelter's sway, and Zelter was unimpressed by the opera, though he conceded to Goethe the music "is so good, that the public doesn't find all the nonsense and gunpowder unbearable."[10]

I

In the same letter, Zelter mentioned a promising young student hard at work on his third comic opera. Now Zelter decided to exhibit Felix to the German poet laureate and, late in October 1821, announced an imminent departure for Weimar with his daughter Doris and prize student, whom he described as "cheerful and obedient," and, as an afterthought, the uncircumcised son of a Jew.[11] En route to Weimar, they stopped in the Lutheran bulwark of Wittenberg, where three hundred years earlier the Reformer had preached and nailed his theses to the door of the Schlosskirche. For the 304th anniversary of the Reformation (October 31), a new statue of Luther by J. G. Schadow, director of the Berlin Academy of Art, was to be unveiled. Into this cradle of the Reformation Zelter, Felix, and Doris arrived on the morning of October 27. Felix busied himself with a new opera, *Die wandernden Komödianten*, which had already progressed to the finale, and played the organs in the local churches. But the highpoint of the visit was his meeting with E. F. F. Chladni (1756–1827), an amateur musician/acoustician.

In the 1780s Chladni had observed that "if a plate of glass or metal were sprinkled over with a fine powder, the vibrations of the plate, as they varied in direction or strength, would throw the grains of powder into different shapes on the surface of the plate."[12] To demonstrate the phenomenon, he stroked plates with a violin bow and generated nodal patterns, including stars with varying numbers of rays.[13] Even Napoleon took notice; in 1809 he instructed the Académie des sciences to offer a prize to whoever could explain the elastic qualities of solids. Finding plates constraining, Chladni invented two new musical instruments. Related to Benjamin Franklin's glass harmonica of the 1760s, the euphon comprised several thin glass rods, about the thickness of goose quills, which, when moistened and rubbed, produced pitches. Most listeners found the sound more pleasant than that of the glass harmonica and less grating on the nerves.[14] The clavicylinder was considerably more elaborate. Resembling a small piano, its depressed keys activated an interior mechanism that contacted a revolving glass cylinder. A skilled performer could elicit dynamic shades and perform rapid passages, although the instrument was ideally suited to music "of a slow, sustained, and even melancholy cast."[15] Felix compared its sound to that of a "very soft oboe."[16]

Zelter chose to celebrate the Reformation in Leipzig, where the travelers arrived on October 30. For centuries the bustling *locus* of the German book trade, Leipzig was also a center of Bach's legacy, a distinction only partially rivaled by Berlin. But by 1821 Leipzig had lapsed into musical dormancy. On his death in 1750, the Thomaskantor had been succeeded by a series of modest musicians: Gottlob Harrer, J. F. Doles, J. A. Hiller, A. E. Müller, and J. G. Schicht. Of these, only Hiller had made a lasting contribution by establishing in 1781 the Gewandhaus concerts, which eventually expanded to comprise an annual subscription series that began after Michaelmas (end of September) and ran to Easter.

At age twelve Felix could scarcely have imagined that fourteen years later he would lead the Gewandhaus Orchestra to unprecedented heights, or that by mid-century, *Leipzigerisch* would connote in musical circles Mendelssohnism. Rather, in October 1821, he dwelled upon past glories. His first priority was to visit Schicht, for whom he played a fugue, etude, and the Sonata in G minor, Op. 105. At Schicht's request, one of Felix's motets, most likely Psalm 19, was copied; Schicht later performed the work at the Thomaskirche, as Lea proudly reported to her Viennese cousin.[17] Awestruck by shades of Bach in the Thomasschule, Felix rambled in a report to Berlin that the elderly Schicht "sleeps in the same chamber in which *Sebastian Bach* lived, I have seen it, I have seen the little spot, where his Clavier stood, where he composed his immortal motets, where he (in Professor Zelter's expression) 'punished' [*kuranzte*] his young charges, and hopefully I will bring along a drawing of this honorable house, in which Rosenmüller, Bach, Doles, Hiller, and Schicht worked and still work."[18]

On the last day of the month Felix heard the Thomanerchor perform Mozart's *Hymnus* in the Paulinerkirche but found the trombones inept, the orchestra out of tune. On Reformation Day a festive gathering of magistrates processed from the Nikolai to the Paulinerkirche; the director of the orchestra conducted the ensemble with a telescope.[19] At the Gewandhaus the next day Felix heard Mozart's resplendent *Jupiter* Symphony, a composition with which Felix formed a special relationship.[20] The famous stretto of the finale in five-part invertible counterpoint stimulated his curiosity, and he sent Eduard Rietz his own contrapuntal sketch of the principal motive.[21]

In Weimar, Zelter and his companions tarried for two weeks in November. The short distance (seventy-five miles) concealed two dissimilar socioeconomic realms. Leipzig, with its burgeoning middle class, was a vibrant center of commerce. Weimar—for Madame de Staël in 1803 a large château; for George Eliot in 1854 a "huge village rather than a town"[22]—had fewer than ten thousand inhabitants, most of whom supported Duke Carl August, ruler of the small Grand Duchy of Saxe-Weimar-Eisenach. When, in 1775, the eighteen-year-old duke invited Goethe to Weimar, what began as an interview became a residency of nearly sixty years.

Initially attracted to Goethe for his literary distinction—the twenty-six-year-old had already produced the sensational, epistolary novel *The Sorrows of Young Werther*—the duke soon involved the young celebrity in the affairs of the duchy, such as the administration of its mines, roads, and even its Lilliputian army. Ennobled in 1782, Goethe became a hardened administrator; it was "as if Byron, after publishing *Childe Harold*, had joined the Civil Service."[23] For about ten years Goethe served the court faithfully. There were some compensations—his friendship with the critic J. G. Herder, who had stirred the young poet's enthusiasm for Ossian; an intimate, probably unconsummated relationship with the attractive wife of the chief equerry, Charlotte von Stein; and a deepening interest in the natural sciences (in 1784 Goethe was examining human skulls for vestiges of the intermaxillary bone). But the drudgery of administration took its toll, and one night in September 1786 Goethe fled to Italy to seek renewal in classical art, in completing his tragedies *Iphigenie auf Tauris* and *Egmont*, and in the arms of his mistress Faustina, idealized in the mildly lubricious *Roman Elegies*.

Goethe returned to Weimar in 1788 and produced several lifetimes of work, the tragedy *Torquato Tasso*, idyll *Hermann und Dorothea*, novels *Wilhelm Meister's Years of Apprenticeship* and *Elective Affinities*, the *Theory of Colors*, and, of course, *Faust*, Part 1 (1808). Weimar was made even more illustrious by the arrival in 1799 of Friedrich Schiller, with whom Goethe raised the Weimar Theater to new eminence. After Schiller's death in 1805, Goethe managed the theater until an absurd scandal defaced his grand vision in 1817. When the duke ordered a performance of a melodrama with the main role assigned to a poodle, Goethe viewed the canine intrusion an affront to art and resigned his theater post. By the time Zelter and Felix reached Weimar, in November 1821, Goethe had rekindled his inspiration. Bridging occidental and oriental worlds, and drawing on the fourteenth-century Persian poet Hafiz, was the *West-Eastern Divan*

(1819), an anthology of sensual lyrics that silently assimilated into its central Suleika section contributions by Goethe's friend Marianne von Willemer. The sequel *Wilhelm Meister's Years of Travel* (1821), a novel with interpolated short stories and aphorisms, resumed the story of the young actor's education and development.

For two weeks Felix lived in the gabled Goethehaus on the Frauenplan. Here Goethe had settled with his wife, Christiana, and son, August, whose principal occupation was to organize the poet's vast collections of scientific specimens (minerals, fossils, and plants) and art objects (medallions, coins, sculptures, prints, porcelain, paintings, and thousands of drawings, including erotica). After Christiana's death in 1816, Ottilie von Pogwisch married August and assumed the matronly role. In this house Goethe entertained a galaxy of literary celebrities—the Schlegels, Novalis, and Heine, Achim and Bettina von Arnim, the Austrian playwright Franz Grillparzer, the Polish poet Adam Mickiewicz, and the English novelist Thackeray. Musical parties were held in the Junozimmer, dominated by an imposing bust of the Roman goddess and containing a six-octave grand piano from the Viennese firm of Nanette Streicher, newly installed in July 1821.[24] Felix numbered among several virtuosi, including Hummel and Clara Wieck, who performed on this instrument. At least one famous musician, however, was denied the pleasure. In 1825 Carl Maria von Weber was kept waiting in an anteroom and then given only a short audience with Goethe before being summarily dismissed, infuriating the sickly musician.[25]

When Zelter, Felix, and Doris arrived on November 2, Goethe was in Jena, so they were received by August, Ottilie, and their two young children. Awaiting the laureate, Felix sketched the houses of Schiller and the Reformation painter Lucas Cranach the Elder. Then, on November 4, the "Sun of Weimar" returned:

> He was in the garden, and was just coming around a hedge; isn't that odd, dear Father, just the way it happened when you met him? He is very friendly, but I don't think any of his portraits look at all like him. He then inspected his interesting collection of fossils, which his son organized, and kept saying: Hm, Hm, I am quite pleased; afterward I walked around the garden with him and Prof. Zelter for another half hour. Then we sat down to eat. One would think he was fifty years old, not seventy-three. After dinner Fräulein Ulrike, [August] Goethe's wife's sister,[26] requested a kiss, and I did likewise. Every morning I receive a kiss from the author of *Faust* and of *Werther*, and every afternoon two kisses from Goethe, friend and father.[27]

After dinner Felix entertained the household with Bach fugues and improvisations, an art the young pianist only recently had begun to develop in Berlin.[28]

Ex. 3.1: Fanny Mendelssohn, *Erster Verlust* (1820)

Felix had brought with him some of Fanny's songs, including her first Goethe setting, *Erster Verlust* (*First Loss*, 1820), composed when she was fifteen.[29] A few years before, the eighteen-year-old Franz Schubert had sent his setting to Weimar with other Goethe treasures, including *Gretchen am Spinnrade* and *Erlkönig*, only to have the parcel returned unopened. Goethe responded more favorably to Fanny's Lied, which subtly conveys the poem's nostalgic sense of loss through a piano figure that oscillates between F major and D minor (ex. 3.1). The yearning for lost love, which frames the poem ("Ah, who brings back those sweet days, Those days of first love?") is associated with F major, while the central lament ("Lonely I nurture my wound, And with a lament always renewing, I mourn that lost happiness") turns to D minor. As it happened, Felix would employ a similar musical conceit in his own setting of 1841 (Op. 99 No. 1), which juxtaposes the same keys.

To thank Fanny, Goethe later, in 1827, composed a poem for her:

Wenn ich mir in stiller Seele
Singe leise Lieder vor,
Wie ich fühle dass sie fehle,
Die ich einzig mir erkor.

Möcht' ich hoffen, dass sie sänge
Was ich ihr so gern vertraut,
Ach! aus dieser Brust und Enge
Drängen frohe Lieder laut.

When to quiet musings given,
With my songs and strains alone
All my thoughts to her are driven,
Whom I fain would call my own.

Might I hope to hear her singing,
What to her I would impart,
All my bosom would be ringing,
With the transports of my heart.[30]

According to Max Friedlaender, Fanny set these verses, but evidently never sent her music to Goethe. It expressed in a "charming" way the yearning quality of the poem, and recalled Beethoven's song cycle *An die ferne Geliebte.*

Among the Weimar guests who heard Felix perform were the grand duke and duchess and other nobility; the writer and painter Johanna Schopenhauer and her daughter Adele Schopenhauer (sister of the philosopher); and the Greek lexicographer F. W. Riemer, of whom Felix later reported, "Dictionary writing suits him well. He is wide, fat, and radiant, like a prelate or a full moon."[31] There were also several musicians, including Carl Eberwein, J. N. Hummel, and two who left accounts, Ludwig Rellstab and J. C. Lobe. The violinist-composer Eberwein had spent two years in Berlin, where, after the requisite examination in counterpoint, Zelter accepted him as a pupil.[32] In Weimar, Eberwein was recognized for his Lieder and early attempt to set *Faust* to music.

In 1821 the reigning Weimar musician was Kapellmeister Hummel (1778–1837), whom Felix had met in Berlin earlier that year. A child prodigy, Hummel had read music at age four and played the violin at five and piano at six. Between the ages of seven and nine he lived in Vienna with Mozart, who taught him *gratis* and prepared him for a grand tour of Europe, orchestrated by the boy's father to imitate Mozart's own childhood peregrinations. Before settling in Weimar, Hummel served Prince Nikolaus Esterházy for seven years and in Vienna was a well-known pianist second only to Beethoven. Hummel's Weimar contract granted him annual leaves, time he devoted to lucrative tours and preparing a highly successful piano method (1828).

Hummel's piano music displays a purling elegance reminiscent of Mozart. But Hummel was not immune to Beethoven's influence, and the larger piano works show signs of stylistic dissatisfaction, as if Hummel too were engaged in an epic struggle to transcend Viennese classicism. Thus the Fantasy in E♭ major, Op. 18 (ca. 1805), which Felix performed during his almost daily meetings with Hummel, contains some striking harmonic progressions lifted from the first movement of Beethoven's *Eroica* Symphony. To Felix's delight, Hummel judged that the youth's playing had advanced considerably since their last meeting; still, he recommended Felix pay greater attention to his posture,[33] a criticism Felix evidently took to heart. When the grand duchess invited the two to play, the temperamental youth declined to appear after Hummel.[34]

Various entertainments and the Weimar ladies diverted Felix. He visited the theater,[35] and played an end-rhyme game (*bouts-rimés*) with Zelter, Ottilie, and her sister Ulrike. Devising verses for lists of rhyming words, the contestants often appealed to Goethe to adjudicate their trials.[36] Meanwhile, Adele Schopenhauer fabricated a delicate silhouette on the subject of Jacob's Ladder for Jacob Ludwig Felix; the ladder comprised two musical staves above Jacob resting on a cloud, with angels representing notes borne heavenward (a second silhouette, "Psyche's Hobby-Horse," followed in January 1822).[37] There were drawings to finish, the new opera, and the fourth book of Caesar's *Gallic War*.

The highlights of the visit were two parties at Goethe's house on November 8 and 11. At the first were the grand duke and Princesses Luise and Maria Pavlovna (sister of the Russian tsar), Zelter, Riemer, Eberwein, and Ludwig Rellstab, who left a detailed report.[38] In 1816 Rellstab had studied with Ludwig Berger, through whom he may have met Felix. Rellstab later established a reputation as an acerbic music critic with a bias for German opera, and his unflattering views of Spontini twice led to an incarceration. As a poet, Rellstab considered writing a libretto for Beethoven, but his principal fame came in 1828, when the terminally ill Schubert set several Rellstab poems, seven of which appeared in the pseudocycle *Schwanengesang*. Rellstab is also credited with comparing Beethoven's Piano Sonata, Op. 27 No. 2, to a moonlit scene on Lake Lucerne, thereby securing immortality for what the composer had dismissed as a prosaic composition.

When Rellstab arrived at Goethe's house on November 8, he found Felix flirting with ladies. Zelter appeared first in ceremonial, outmoded dress—black silk breeches, silk stockings, and shoes with silver buckles, like a scene from E. T. A. Hoffmann's *Ritter Gluck*, in which the eighteenth-century opera composer rematerializes in nineteenth-century Berlin. Only after the entire audience had assembled did Goethe enter, conversing briefly with his *Duzbruder* Zelter before explaining the purpose of the gathering. There was to be a test of the prodigy's abilities to stimulate comparisons with Mozart, whom Goethe had witnessed in 1763 playing a harpsichord with his hands covered by a baize cloth and identifying the pitches of clocks and glasses.

The first trial measured Felix's prowess at improvisation. Zelter chose a short song, "Ich träumte einst von Hannchen," and with arthritic fingers played the tune to an accompaniment of triplets. Displaying perfect pitch, Felix repeated the melody, and dabbled briefly with the triplets before launching into the "wildest Allegro." From the gentle melody flared up a contrapuntal fantasy, a "turbulent, lustrous parliament of tones" reminiscent not so much of dreams of Hannchen as of Hummel's better improvisations. Concluding with an energetic chord, Felix resumed a tranquil state, leaving the astonished audience silent. First to speak was Zelter, chary of praise: "What hobgoblins and dragons have you been dreaming about, to drive you along in that helter-skelter fashion!"[39]

Ex. 3.2: J. S. Bach, Fugue in F♯ major, *Well-Tempered Clavier* I, 1722

Next, Zelter selected a Bach fugue, which Felix confidently dispatched, but the subject of the fugue contained a trill that disappeared in subsequent entries. Once again Zelter carped, bidding Felix not to omit the trill. But due to the complexity of the passagework, he could not physically add all the trills. Assuming the fugue was drawn from the *Well-Tempered Clavier*, we can narrow it to a handful of fugues with trills in their subjects. In particular, the Fugue in F♯ major from the first volume is an attractive candidate, for Bach indeed omitted the trill in several entries of the subject, owing to the limitation of the hand (ex. 3.2).

When Goethe asked Felix to play a minuet, Felix offered the "most beautiful in the world," from *Don Giovanni*. But when, testing the child's ability to render a complex orchestral score from memory, Goethe requested the overture, Felix balked, arguing that the piano could not adequately accommodate Mozart's music; instead, he performed the Overture to *The Marriage of Figaro*. Again, Rellstab's judgment: Felix "began with a lightness of the hand, an assurance, roundness and clarity in the passagework as I have never again heard. At the same time he reproduced the orchestral effects so splendidly, made evident so many of the nuances of the orchestration by adding or clearly bringing out voices, that the effect was thrilling, and I might almost maintain that I experienced greater pleasure with his version for piano than with any orchestral performance."[40]

Withdrawing into his study, Goethe returned a few minutes later with two manuscripts. The first was a fragment of a Mozart sonata for violin and piano the poet had acquired in 1812.[41] Mozart's hand was reasonably clear, and the movement was an Adagio, even though it contained thirty-second-note passages. Felix sight-read it as though he had "known it from memory for a year." But the second manuscript, "bespattered with ink and smudged all over,"[42] gave him pause. Zelter immediately recognized the handwriting of Beethoven, who "wrote as if he used a broomstick, and then wiped his sleeve over the wet ink."[43] The autograph, now in the Goethe und Schiller Archiv in Weimar, was the first draft of the Lied Op. 83 No. 1, a setting of Goethe's poem "Wonne der Wehmuth" ("Rapture of Melancholy"). Felix's task was to find his way through the tortuous labyrinth of a Beethoven sketch. Understandably, Felix stumbled in this effort but eventually deciphered the shorthandlike scrawls to perform the song flawlessly. During a later visit to Weimar, he prepared a clean copy of the song for Goethe.

On November 11 another musical gathering convened, this time to verify Felix's compositional talents. Among the participants were three Weimar court musicians; one was the violist J. C. Lobe, who had produced an opera two years before. Some twenty years later, Lobe would move to Leipzig, where he enjoyed close contacts with Felix and became the editor of the *Allgemeine musikalische Zeitung*.[44] In the Junozimmer in 1821, Lobe found among Felix's manuscripts a piano quartet, which he and his companions now read. Like a sergeant-at-arms, Zelter comported himself with military bearing and bid the musicians to temper their praise, preferably in a "moderate tempo, scored not too noisily, and in C major, the most neutral tonality."[45] After the performance, Felix was excused while his elders deliberated. Lobe did not identify the work, but almost certainly it was the Piano Quartet in D minor, Felix's most substantial chamber work.[46] Comparisons with Mozart now flowed freely. "Musical prodigies," Goethe began,

> "as far as mere technical execution goes, are probably no longer so rare: but what this little man can do in extemporizing and playing at sight, borders on the miraculous, and I could not have believed it possible at so early an age." "And yet you heard Mozart in his seventh year at Frankfurt?" said Zelter. "Yes," answered Goethe; "at that time I myself had only just reached my twelfth year, and was certainly, like all the rest of the world, immensely astonished at his extraordinary execution; but what your pupil already accomplishes, bears the same relation to the Mozart of that time, that the cultivated talk of a grown-up person does to the prattle of a child."[47]

The three musicians agreed, and detected in Felix's quartet "many more independent thoughts" than in Mozart's music from the same age. For his part, Zelter confirmed Felix had composed the quartet without any assistance. The company thus came to a stunning conclusion: Felix was an improved version of the young Mozart.

II

Buoyed by the "pole star" of German poets, Felix departed Weimar on November 19 and returned to Berlin. Scarcely had his father thanked Goethe for "ennobling" Felix's youth[48] before he finished *Die wandernden Komödianten*. By December 9 the Overture was ready, one day after Abraham severed ties to his banking firm.[49] Exactly what prompted this decision is unclear, though its cause may have been a fraternal dispute; perhaps the two disagreed about the management of their business, or perhaps

Joseph disapproved of Abraham's temptation to convert to Protestant-ism. Without shedding much light on the matter, Joseph's wife Henriette wrote in January 1822, "the separation of the brothers grieves me very much; however, they are both men, and, therefore, must have it their different ways. I hope that neither of them will regret that he's stuck to his own will so obstinately."[50]

The new, one-act Singspiel was promptly scheduled for production at the Mendelssohn residence in March. But after a dress rehearsal, misfortune struck. On the evening of March 8, Felix appeared in a children's play. His role required him to brandish a rapier, and when he drew the rusty weapon, he lacerated his thumb. Concealing his bleeding hand in a pocket, he persevered, but after the performance found a half-inch wound that required stitches.[51] The premiere was postponed until April, when the opera was given with *Die beiden Pädagogen*;[52] among the cast were Eduard Devrient, Stümer, and Henning, and probably the librettist, Dr. Casper.[53]

The libretto for *Die wandernden Komödianten* (*The Wandering Players*) survives in Oxford, while Felix's unpublished score of nearly two hundred pages in meticulous calligraphy is in Berlin.[54] The plot turns again on mistaken identities.[55] Three itinerant actors, Fröhlich (Cheerful), Hasenfuss (Chicken-Hearted), and Fixfinger (Nimble Finger), have played in Krähwinkel, a fictitious cultural backwater, where their director, Flink (Nimble), has run afoul of the magistrate, Schwarzauge (Blackeye), engaged to Mme. Germain. Flink is her former lover, and she warns him that Schwarzauge has allied himself with Holzbein (Pegleg), magistrate of Schilda. After Mme. Germain rebuffs Schwarzauge's advances, Flink pretends to be Holzbein; then, when Holzbein arrives, he masquerades as Schwarzauge. A trumpet fanfare announces the troupe's performance before the prince, but the play within the play is amended when the bumbling magistrate attempts to arrest Flink, initially impersonated by Hasenfuss, and then by Fröhlich. Just as Schwarzauge is about to apprehend Flink, Fixfinger announces that the prince has appointed the actors *Hofkomödianten*, and the opera draws to a happy conclusion.

For dramatic pacing *Die wandernden Komödianten* relies upon a brisk succession of ensembles; only two of its twelve numbers are solo arias. As a result, the characters are not as sharply drawn as in Felix's earlier Singspiele but materialize through contrasting groups. The deftly scored Overture in A major, an energetic if circumspect application of classical sonata form, again employs a moderately sized orchestra of strings and double winds. The bustling opening figure, accompanied by string tremolos, is reused in No. 3. The most impressive stretch of the work is the finale (No. 12), prefaced by a rustic, on-stage orchestral overture (No. 11), de-

Ex. 3.3: Mendelssohn, *Die wandernden Komödianten* (1822), No. 11

signed to caricature "the fairly threadbare musical manner that must have characterized most Wandertruppen."[56] After the strings tune in a descending succession of fifths, the overture commences with a simple motive accompanied by plain harmonies (ex. 3.3), including later on some questionable fifths. Farther on in the mock overture, the second oboe staggers one eighth-note behind the first, recalling a similar conceit in the "Merry Gathering of the Peasants" of Beethoven's *Pastoral* Symphony, where a bassoon enters "late." Unlike the formal overture, the mock overture offers a rudimentary version of sonata form; the development, for example, reduces to little more than an ascending unison scale on the dominant. Felix seems intent upon parodying lowbrow musical culture, a compositional challenge he would revisit some twenty years later in the incidental music to Shakespeare's *Midsummer Night's Dream*. There, too, a play within a play inspired well-worn, tattered music—the Mechanicals' Funeral March in C minor.

"Well-behaved and diligent" (*brav und fleissig*) was how Zelter described Felix in March 1822.[57] Since returning from Weimar, Felix had finished the opera and a Gloria, and had begun a concerto for Fanny and *Magnificat*. Though still little known—the Gloria and *Magnificat* were published near the end of the twentieth century—these compositions rank among his most impressive achievements of 1822. Felix's first large-scale choral work with orchestra, the Gloria in E♭ major was probably written during January and February 1822, and in any event finished by March 17.[58] It dwarfs another work not mentioned by Zelter, a modest setting of verses from Psalm 66 for female chorus and continuo, finished on March 8.[59] The autograph of the Gloria betrays signs of haste— numerous corrections, unemended errors in part writing, and some awkward text underlay.[60] Felix set the text of the Ordinary as a cantata in six movements, with a mixture of choral and solo movements, arranged in a tonal plan orbiting around E♭ major (E♭–B♭–c–A♭–E♭–E♭). The variety of textures is impressive, including homophonic and imitative writing *a 4*, a cappella writing *a 5* (*Gratias agimus tibi*), and an ensemble scored for alto and tenor, chorus, bassoons, and strings without violins (*Domine*

Deus). There are, too, traditional displays of counterpoint associated with *Laudamus te* and *Cum sancto spiritu*, for which Felix generated double fugues brimming with learned devices.

He may have set the Gloria aside to take up the more ambitious *Magnificat* in D major, begun in March and finished at the end of May.[61] In 1930 Rudolf Werner found its treatment of the Marian text scarcely less masterful than that yardstick of the composer's genius, the *Midsummer Night's Dream* Overture of 1826.[62] Werner believed Felix emulated the "most splendid of all *Magnificat* creations," by J. S. Bach (BWV 243a), composed in 1731 in E♭ major but reworked in a D-major version (BWV 243). Georg Pölchau, who published the original version in 1811, could have placed it at Felix's disposal in 1822 (Felix acquired a copy for his own library in 1824[63]). Werner pointed to similar figurations in the opening movements, and to Bach's expressively drooping *Quia respexit humilitatem ancillae suae* ("For he hath regarded the low estate of his handmaiden"), which Felix indeed appears to have imitated.

But several features distinguish Felix's score from Bach's masterpiece and render the issue of stylistic indebtedness more complex. Bach writes for five-part chorus; Felix, four-part. Bach specifies among the winds three trumpets and timpani; Felix, two trumpets, two horns, and timpani. Bach apportions the canticle into twelve compact movements, teeming with word paintings; the chorus *Omnes generationes* ("all generations shall call me blessed"), to cite one, contains florid melismas to depict the coming together of "all generations." Felix's setting, in contrast, requires only six movements, and *omnes generationes* does not inspire specific musical imagery.

As Ralf Wehner has demonstrated,[64] Felix would have known another *Magnificat*, composed for Berlin in 1749 by C. P. E. Bach and available through the Singakademie library. This work is also in D major, employs four-part chorus, supplements the three trumpets with two horns, and fits the text into nine movements, a compromise between the grandiloquence of J. S. Bach's twelve and the compression of Felix's six. Emanuel Bach's *Magnificat* recalls, yet is stylistically removed from, his father's high-baroque splendor. Thus, in *Quia respexit*, again in B minor, Emanuel avoids a choral outburst for *omnes generationes*.

A compelling resemblance between Emanuel's and Felix's compositions lies in the concluding *Gloria patri*. After a pause on the dominant, Emanuel unfurls a stunning double fugue on *Sicut erat*. Not to be outdone, Felix too reaches a caesura and introduces a fugue, with a subject patently derived from Emanuel's (**ex. 3.4a–b**). Within two bars Felix superimposes a fresh subject for *Et nunc, et semper* (**ex. 3.4c**), so that his finale begins with two subjects (in contrast, Emanuel's second subject enters some sixty bars into his fugue). Then, for *et in saecula saeculorum*

Ex. 3.4a: C. P. E. Bach, *Magnificat* (1749), "Sicut erat"

Si - cut   e - rat   in prin - ci - pi - o et nunc et sem-per et in   sae - - - cu - la

Ex. 3.4b–e: Mendelssohn, *Magnificat* (1822), "Sicut erat"

b)

Si - cut e - rat in prin - cip - i - o et nunc, et sem - - - per,

c)

Et nunc, et sem - - - - - - - - - per,

d)

et   in   sae - - - - - cu - la sae - cu - lo - rum

e)

A - - - - - men,

and the *Amen,* a third and fourth subject enrich the polyphonic tapestry
(**exs. 3.4d–e**). Felix's quadruple fugue at once surpasses Emanuel Bach's
double fugue and attains a complexity of part-writing rarely seen since
J. S. Bach.

Whether Zelter performed the Gloria or *Magnificat* at the Singakademie is unknown. They were heard in 1822 on a Sunday concert at the
Mendelssohn residence, but with unsatisfactory results; Felix lamented
that anxiety caused him to imagine heavenly angels replacing the "piping"
sopranos, and that a *Miserere* would have been more appropriate.[65] Nevertheless, the concerts, which had begun in the latter part of 1821, now
became a regular institution, with frequent readings of Felix's choral
and orchestral works before patrician guests. One of the earliest documented musicales occurred on March 24, 1822,[66] before a brother-in-law
of the king, Prince Antoni Henryk Radziwill, to whom Beethoven later
dedicated his *Namensfeier* Overture, Op. 115. For the musicale the Frankfurt pianist Aloys Schmitt performed, and Fanny played a piano concerto
by Hummel. Then, the prince asked Felix to improvise on the subject of
Mozart's Fugue in C minor for two pianos (K. 426). An amateur cellist

and composer, Radziwill was the governor of the Polish grand duchy of Poznań, where he maintained an opulent musical establishment and participated in readings of Beethoven's string quartets. The Mozart fugal subject bore special meaning, since the prince had used it in his music for Goethe's *Faust*, on which he labored for some twenty years.

Which Hummel piano concerto Fanny presented is unknown, but it may have been the second, in A minor (Op. 85), performed by Hummel in Berlin in 1821. At the end of March Felix made his second "public" appearance, in a concert of Aloys Schmitt[67] that featured Dussek's *Grande symphonie concertante*, Op. 63, a double piano concerto with an unusual history. The musical confidant of Prince Louis Ferdinand, Dussek had composed this work in 1806; the prince performed it on October 9, the night before he fell at the Battle of Saalfeld.[68] If in 1822 Dussek's concerto still resonated in the Prussian musical consciousness, Hummel's Piano Concerto in A minor thoroughly captivated Felix, then composing his first piano concerto in the same key and scored with string orchestra for Fanny. The resemblances between the two concerti are numerous and have inspired an elucidating study by Wolfgang Dinglinger.[69] Thus, we find similar three-movement plans: a sonata-form first movement with a double exposition for orchestra and soloist, and a slow movement that proceeds without pause into a rondo finale, culminating with a stretto-like coda.

The opening theme of Felix's concerto unabashedly reveals its parentage (ex. 3.5a, b), as do any number of piano figurations, including extended double trills and interleaved percussive chords, a technique in Hummel's concerto that one English reviewer described as a "weaving passage."[70] Like Hummel, Felix allows the pianist to begin the first solo as if in search of a theme; the effect is like a miniature improvisation, a device Hummel had inherited from his teacher Mozart. Stretches of Felix's first movement refract the poignant subtleties of Mozart's concerti through the prism of Hummel's effulgent passagework. But Felix is no slavish follower; his early concerto reveals signs of independence, including a *martellato* passage later pressed again into service in the First Piano Concerto in G minor, Op. 25, of 1831 (ex. 3.6a, b).

The sensitively scored slow movement in E major evinces startling evidence of stylistic maturation. Against a noble, hymnlike theme in the muted strings, the pianist responds with a recitative-like commentary. Was Felix pondering the *Andante con moto* of Beethoven's Fourth Piano Concerto, Op. 58, also for piano and strings? The comparison is inviting enough, even with its obvious differences: there a plaintive piano melody in chordal style interrupts an orchestral recitative. All in all, the 1822 Concerto in A minor marks an impressive achievement of an apprentice, who anticipated elements of his own mature style while he assimi-

Ex. 3.5a: Hummel, Piano Concerto in A minor (ca. 1816)

Ex. 3.5b: Mendelssohn, Piano Concerto in A minor (1822)

Ex. 3.6a: Mendelssohn, Piano Concerto in A minor (1822), First Movement

Ex. 3.6b: Mendelssohn, Piano Concerto in G minor, Op. 25 (1831), Finale

lated the legacy of Mozart's concerti and tested Hummel's innovations in piano technique.

Fanny was not the only musician honored by Felix in 1822 with a concerto. That same year he composed for Eduard Rietz the Violin Concerto in D minor,[71] also in three movements (with the second movement again linked to the finale) and scored for string orchestra. Two autograph versions survive, of which the first transmits the first two movements, while the second (a revised version reflecting Rietz's suggestions) includes all three. Some prominent musicians have been associated with these manuscripts. In 1853 Felix's widow Cécile presented the first version to the violinist Ferdinand David, and in the twentieth century Yehudi Menuhin, who published the first edition of the composition in 1952, owned the autograph. In the 1890s the second version belonged to Clara Schumann before its incorporation into the *Mendelssohn Nachlass* in Berlin.[72]

Ex. 3.7: Mendelssohn, Violin Concerto in D minor (1822)

Two influences converging on this work again tap eighteenth-century stylistic roots. The first is the French violin concerto, represented by G. B.Viotti and his Parisian followers, including Rode, Baillot (Felix's instructor in 1816 and 1817), and Kreutzer (whose etudes Felix was practicing in 1821). The second is the North German keyboard concerto, exemplified by musicians active at the court of Frederick the Great and J. S. Bach pupils such as C. P. E. Bach, Christoph Nichelmann, and J. G. Müthel. Rode had popularized in Berlin several features of Viotti's technique, including a cantabile style with seamless legato, bold treatment of the resonant G string (especially in its upper positions), and varieties of bowings, often in quick succession, a distinctive feature that impressed itself upon Felix's concerto (ex. 3.7).

Three features of the work invoke the eighteenth-century North German keyboard concerto. First, the accompaniment is limited to a string orchestra in four parts, an obsolete scoring for 1822. Second, the first movement does not strictly observe the template of the Mozartean concerto, with its synthesis of sonata form and the baroque ritornello principle. Thus, Felix's contrasting second theme, presented by the violin during its first solo, fails to figure in the opening orchestral *tutti*; and when the theme returns toward the end of the movement, it enters not in the expected tonic D minor but minor subdominant G minor. This oddity, along with the restatement of the opening *tutti* in different keys throughout the movement, suggests Felix was indebted here less to sonata form (as in the first movement of his Piano Concerto in A minor) than to the older ritornello principle, with its frequent alternation of orchestral and solo passages. Third, the turbulent opening thematic material (ex. 3.8), marked by angular contours, interruptions, dynamic contrasts, and energetic tremolos, impresses as a revival of the quirky style of Emanuel Bach and his colleagues. Felix's choice of D minor may have triggered this association, for a number of North German composers—including the Bachs and Müthel, composers favored by Zelter and Felix's great-aunt Sarah Levy—had used that tonality in their keyboard concerti to explore the stronger emotional affects.[73]

Ex. 3.8: Mendelssohn, Violin Concerto in D minor (1822)

III

On July 6, 1822 a caravan of carriages departed Berlin for Potsdam, the beginning of a leisurely three-month journey to Switzerland. The passengers were Abraham and Lea, their children, the tutor Dr. Heyse, a Dr. Neuburg, and servants. Later, near Frankfurt, the charming Marianne and Julie Saaling joined them. Cousins of Lea through their father, the court jeweler Salomon Jacob Salomon, the sisters had taken the surname Saaling years before upon their conversion to Christianity. Marianne had already attained social recognition and, at the Congress of Vienna, earned the confidences of the aristocracy. Having imitated Dorothea Schlegel's spiritual course by embracing Catholicism, she returned to Berlin to become active in charities. Many years before, the comparable beauty of Julie Saaling had been marred by a tragic mishap. During a smallpox epidemic, a superstitious grandmother had prevented her inoculation, and Julie became the only one of six siblings to contract the disease. A botched operation caused her to lose her right eye. Despite her disability, Julie's endearing qualities impressed Heyse, and the two became secretly engaged during the Swiss holiday.[74]

Another member of the party, Fanny, also had reason to contemplate a clandestine romance, for Wilhelm Hensel had recently inscribed these verses for her:

Ein Liedlein hör ich rauschen,	I hear a little song murmuring,
Das folgt mir überall,	That follows me everywhere,
Die Englein selber lauschen,	Even the angels eavesdrop,
Es horcht die Nachtigall.	As does the nightingale.
Und wie der Mond die feuchten,	And as the moon disperses
Tiefbraunen Schatten bricht,	The damp, dark brown shadows,
Ergeht ein stilles Leuchten	There escapes a soft glow
Vom lieben Angesicht.	From a lovely face.[75]

Sixteen years old, Fanny longed to reach Italy, to experience Goethe's blooming, fragrant Arcadian realm. Meanwhile, Felix recorded his travel impressions in drawings executed in situ. For some time, Felix had been studying drawing with J. G. S. Rösel (1768–1843), an instructor at the Berlin Bauschule and acquaintance of Goethe.[76] From this journey Felix would bring back to Rösel more than forty landscapes, generally drawn in pencil and then worked over in ink—the earliest, compelling documentation of Felix's talent at draftsmanship.[77]

When Felix was inadvertently left behind at Potsdam, Heyse rode back to retrieve him, only to find the errant pupil trudging along the dusty road with a peasant girl. The first two days of the journey brought the tourists no farther than Brandenburg and Magdeburg, ninety miles west of Berlin. In the Harz, they elected not to ascend the Brocken but climbed less formidable mountains and spent an hour in the Baumann's cave:

> One wanders among the strangest figures formed by the stalactites, here there is a monk, there a crucifix, here a baptismal font, there a Virgin Mary, here a flag—which is *transparent*—there an organ, a waterfall, a cow, and only God and the guide could know the huge multitude of forms which the unfathomable cave has created for itself.[78]

Traveling "like princes—poets, artists, and princes all in one,"[79] the party proceeded to Göttingen and Cassel, capital of the Electorate of Hesse. Bearing a letter from Zelter, they paused to visit the newly appointed Kapellmeister, the violinist-composer Louis Spohr (1784–1859), who had concertized in Berlin in 1819 when the Mendelssohns may have heard him.

Early in 1822, Spohr arrived in Cassel, where he remained for the rest of his career. He strengthened the orchestra (among the first conductors to wield a baton, Spohr presided over fifty-five musicians), founded a Cäcilienverein for choral music, and directed opera at the court theater. In many ways Spohr's comfortable existence in Cassel mirrored the stability of Felix's later career in Leipzig: each musician developed a municipal musical culture supported by a literate, art-loving middle class, even though Spohr had the disadvantage of settling in a small, repressive police state, in which, during the Restoration, the Elector Wilhelm II had imposed a rigorous censorship.

At the time of the Mendelssohns' visit Spohr was engrossed with his exotic opera *Jessonda* (1823), set in Malabar and offering choruses of Brahmins and Portuguese soldiers, and a ballet of *bayaderes* (female votaries). Spohr's conversations with the Mendelssohns may well have turned to opera, for in May Felix had taken up his fourth libretto from Dr. Casper, *Die beiden Neffen*. Spohr regaled his guests with a chamber-music party, performing two of his own quartets and participating in one by Felix, presumably the Piano Quartet in D minor.[80]

On July 18 the travelers arrived at the elegant Frankfurt hotel White Swan. The pianist Aloys Schmitt procured a Viennese piano for Felix and Fanny,[81] and they met Schmitt's prize pupil, ten-year-old Ferdinand Hiller (1811–1885), later one of Felix's closest friends. At Darmstadt, Felix called on the noted organist J. C. H. Rinck (1770–1846), a former pupil of J. C. Kittel and thus second-generation disciple of J. S. Bach. Continuing through Heidelberg and Stuttgart, the party reached Switzerland on the 28th and spent a day contemplating the swirling cataracts near Schaffhausen during a raging thunderstorm, before they continued to Constance. After examining the subtropical flora of the Island of Mainau, the male members of the party sailed across Lake Constance to visit Meersburg; Felix was impressed by the "half tints" and blends of colors in the lake that "no painter would venture."[82] The reunited travelers then proceeded through St. Gallen, celebrated for its Carolingian monastery. At the southeastern extremity of Lake Constance Lea was surprised to see the Rhine metamorphose into a "chalky, colorless river."[83] By August 4 her family was resting in Zurich.

Their next excursion led them to Glarus and Linthal, a *wildromantisch* area heavily populated but not really suitable for human habitation,[84] where they observed snow-covered mountains from close proximity. Returning to Zurich, Felix met the musician Anton Liste (1772–1832), who agreed to guide the party up the Rigi. While Liste and Heyse ventured by foot "across fields, over hedges and fences, and over cemeteries,"[85] the main procession crossed the Albis and reached Zug. Across its picturesque lake they visited Immisee and Tellskapelle, where the Swiss national hero allegedly had dispatched the tyrant Gessler. The scene, for Felix an "attractive and yet somehow ghastly ravine,"[86] later inspired Franz Liszt to compose the opening piece of the *Années de Pèlerinage*; Felix decided to capture the beech-tree-lined gorge in a drawing.

From Goldau, a village buried in 1806 by a horrific landslide, the travelers plotted their ascent of the Rigi, which began on August 12 with a party of thirty-four, including porters to convey the luggage. Halfway up, the Mendelssohns had to wait out a storm, and when they finally reached the *Rigikulm* they were fogbound an entire day. On the second evening, Lea reported,

> the fog dispersed, and we enjoyed the most beautiful sunset in this heavenly region; only the southern mountains continued to be veiled. To wake up on the Rigikulm on a lovely morning is striking and highly moving. An hour before sunrise, when the heaven is clear, the Alphorn sounds, rousing all the residents of the house with its sharp, piercing tone. Now amid the darkness stirs the liveliest bustle in the narrow quarters, . . . and figures worthy of Hogarth's brush emerge.[87]

At the inn erected on the summit in 1816 Felix took in the magisterial view, the sunrise turning the snow-clad peaks reddish hues, day breaking over the Rigi and, across the serenely aquamarine lake below, the Pilatus. "Dawn can easily be this beautiful on the Rigi," an old guide opined, "but more beautiful it cannot be."[88]

After their descent, the Mendelssohns boarded a boat to Lucerne, and next day cruised across the breathtaking span of the Lake of the Four Cantons. On the Urnersee they were beset by a hailstorm but disembarked, pushed on to Altdorf, and continued south along the Reuss River, following a road "worked into the rocks with the aid of gunpowder," a "grand illustration," according to Fanny, "of the power of human perseverance, which can even bend the will of Nature."[89] On the way to the St. Gotthard Pass Fanny felt an intense longing to see Italy and completed a setting of Goethe's "Kennst du das Land."[90] Near Andermatt, she wrote, "you feel, however, no less powerfully affected by what you do *not* see than by the visible surroundings." But Fanny would have to wait until 1839 to satisfy her romantic *Reiselust*; lacking supplies, the family turned back to Lucerne.

Sometimes traversing only six German miles a day,[91] the tourists proceeded to Thun and on August 22 crossed the Thunersee to Interlaken. En route to Lauterbrunnen, they counted forty waterfalls, and looked with wonder at the Staubbach, with its plummeting cascade turning to spray some 900 feet below.[92] Ascending the Wengern Alp, they viewed the Jungfrau from a "poetic chalet," a modest cowherd's hut, before continuing on to Grindelwald. Sketching along the way, Felix recorded striking views in his drawings, supplemented by a meticulous travelogue that would have satisfied Karl Baedecker. Thus, on August 27, the artist executed a drawing of the Grindelwald Glacier (**plate 5**) and described some salient features: the towering Eiger, whose summit resembled the dome of a cathedral; the distant, craggy peaks of the Fiescherhörner; the debris-covered lower glacier, inexorably advancing to the valley below; and the Lütschine River, gushing from caves beneath the glacier's moraine.[93]

After visiting Bern, the Mendelssohns reached Vevay on Lake Geneva. While Fanny dreamed of the Borromean Islands on the *Lago Maggiore*,[94] Felix sketched Lake Geneva and the French Alps, and completed the first act of *Die beiden Neffen* in Lausanne on September 11. Two days later they registered at Secheron, an inn near Geneva, and Felix's reawakened muse inspired two Lieder and the beginning of the Piano Quartet in C minor, Op. 1.[95] The tourists saw Voltaire's château at Ferney and visited Chamonix to view Mont Blanc before beginning their journey back to Germany, via Neuchâtel and Basel. At the end of September they again lingered in Frankfurt, while Felix completed the first movement of his Piano Quartet.

Throughout the Swiss sojourn Felix remained an astute observer of local musical culture. He recorded folksongs for use in two of his string symphonies and reported his impressions of yodeling to Zelter. If the ululating intervals nearby sounded "harsh and unpleasant," their effect was quite beautiful when experienced from afar with "mingling or answering echoes." But in the Bernese *Oberland* the folk songs of Swiss girls did not impress Felix: ". . . everything is spoiled by one voice which they use like a *flauto piccolo*. For this girl never sings a melody; she produces certain high notes—I believe just at her discretion—and thus, at times, horrible fifths turn up."[96] And finally, he sent back mixed reports about Swiss organs, including a "grand instrument with fifty-three stops" in the Bern cathedral and a modest instrument in the Canton of Fribourg with a pedal board too short to accommodate Bach's music.

Felix visited Switzerland three more times, in 1831, 1842, and a few months before his death in 1847, when, crushed by Fanny's death, he found solace in re-creating in watercolors their fondest childhood memories. But now, in 1822, his artistic horizons were still expanding—Felix, Fanny observed, could not remain idle for one hour.[97] And so, there was much music making in Frankfurt. Felix performed his piano quartet (either in D minor or the recently completed first movement of Op. 1) and, accompanied by Ferdinand Hiller, sight-read his way, presumably, through a violin sonata by Aloys Schmitt.[98] Eduard Devrient, then completing his musical studies in Frankfurt, witnessed Felix's precocity before the musicians J. A. André and J. N. Schelble.[99] In 1799 André had inherited his father's music publishing firm, which he expanded by acquiring rights to the new technology of music lithography. He also purchased Mozart's *Nachlass* from the composer's widow Constanze, and thus laid the groundwork for Köchel's pioneering catalogue. A stout, garrulous man, André contributed Lieder to the Frankfurt musicale and asked Felix to improvise, whereupon Felix "had a quiet bit of fun," working into his fantasy a song by André that had just been sung and then, drawing upon "his all-retaining memory," another song by Devrient.

There was more serious music making at the Cäcilienverein, a choral society founded in 1818 by the actor, singer, and pedagogue J. N. Schelble (1789–1837) and specializing in Catholic sacred music and Handel's oratorios.[100] According to Devrient, Felix's improvisations on Bach motets won Schelble's lifelong friendship.[101] Their meeting inspired Felix to compose a short a cappella setting, finished in October not long after his return to Berlin and then dispatched to Schelble in November. *Jube Domine*, for two four-part choirs, was Felix's first work for the Catholic liturgy.[102] The Compline text entreats the Lord to grant a quiet, perfect ending to the day and includes a reading from 1 Peter (5:8): "Be sober, be vigilant; because your adversary the devil, as a roaring lion, walketh about, seeking whom he may devour." Despite his Bachian predilections, Felix avoided imitative counterpoint and relied instead on descriptive word paintings and antiphonal exchanges between the two choirs in block harmonies. Thus, the devil lurks in dissonant chords, with the interval of the tritone—the traditional *diabolus in musica*—prominently displayed in the outer voices (A♭–D, **ex. 3.9**) on the exact word *diabolus*.

Ex. 3.9: Mendelssohn, *Jube Domine* (1822)

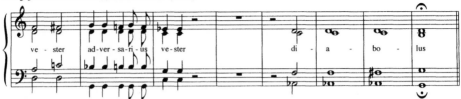

While in Frankfurt, Abraham and Lea converted to the Protestant creed, filling a family breach opened by their children's baptisms in 1816 but dissolving their family's ties to Moses Mendelssohn's philosophy of enlightened rationalism. In a strikingly symbolic gesture, Abraham Moses Mendelssohn now became Abraham Ernst Mendelssohn Bartholdy,[103] and Lea, adopting her sons' names, Lea Felicia Pauline Mendelssohn Bartholdy.[104] The clandestine ceremony occurred on October 4, 1822, and the family soon left the city to resume their journey. Further details are not known, but in 1925 C. H. Müller, archivist of the Cäcilienverein, claimed that the celebrant for the baptism was Pastor Jeanrenaud of the French Reformed Church,[105] father of Cécile Jeanrenaud, whom Felix would marry in 1837. But Auguste Jeanrenaud, a "vigorous pioneer of the Protestant faith," had died of consumption in 1819, two years after Cécile's birth. Almost certainly the Mendelssohns had no contact with the surviving members of the Jeanrenaud family in 1822, for Felix later dated his introduction to Cécile precisely to May 4, 1836.[106]

For the moment, Abraham and Lea kept their new faith a well-guarded secret and probably chose not to discuss it with Goethe, whom the family again visited in Weimar on October 7.[107] Instead, the poet spoke for hours with Abraham about Felix and enjoyed the sophisticated pianism of Fanny, who performed Bach and her Goethe Lieder. Felix again obligingly entertained the poet, who likened the young man to the Old Testament psalmist: "You are my David, and if I am ever ill and sad, you must banish my bad dreams by your playing; I shall never throw my spear at you, as Saul did."[108]

IV

By the middle of the month, Felix had returned to Berlin. His appearance was considerably changed: "the pretty brown curls were cut short to the neck, the child's dress had given place to the boy's suit,—an open jacket over a waistcoat."[109] According to Fanny, prone to idealizing him,

Felix "had grown much taller and stronger, . . . His lovely *child's face* had disappeared, and his figure already showed a manliness very becoming to him."[110] The youth shared his drawings with Rösel, who gave two of his own sketches to his pupil.[111] Meanwhile, on October 18 Felix completed the Piano Quartet in C minor and by November had advanced well into the second act of *Die beiden Neffen*. The same month he began work on his eighth string symphony. Fanny and Felix now resumed their activities as pianists: at Zelter's on October 22 she performed the Piano Concerto in A minor,[112] which Felix played on December 5 at a public concert of Anna Milder-Hauptmann, *prima donna assoluta* of the Berlin opera,[113] for whom Beethoven had created the role of Fidelio.

When Fanny celebrated her birthday on November 14, Wilhelm Hensel, now an active suitor, presented a drawing of Fanny as the patron saint of music and thus linked the object of his affection, Fanny Caecilia, with Cecilia, whose feast day fell eight days later. Seated, the robed, barefooted Fanny holds a scroll of music, her hair adorned with a floral wreath, as three haloed angels peer over her shoulders (**plate 6**). Wilhelm also drew portraits of other family members, including Felix,[114] and their close friends, and thus assumed "mentally his place in the circle to which he wished to belong."[115] Only one month later, Wilhelm pressed his case more directly. On Christmas Eve he gave Fanny a volume of poetry by his friend Wilhelm Müller, the recently published *77 Poems from the Posthumous Papers of a Traveling Waldhorn Player*, which, of course, contained *Die schöne Müllerin*, the Liederspiel Müller and his friends had performed in Berlin in 1816 (Hensel had played the role of the hunter). If Müller had filled his lyrics with thinly disguised fantasies about Hensel's sister, Luise, Wilhelm now appropriated the poems to symbolize his longing for Fanny. To this end, he prepared a new title page for the volume, with Müller's portrait and a dedicatory poem to Fanny, "signed" below with Wilhelm's own portrait.

But the vigilant Lea intercepted the volume, and took exception to Wilhelm's amorous quatrains, addressed to her daughter with the intimate *du*:

Dies Buch voll Lust und Wehmuth	This book full of joy and melancholy
Im bunten Liedertraum	In a motley dream of Lieder
An Deinen Weihnachtsbaum	I hang in quiet humility
Hang' ich in stiller Demuth.	On your Christmas tree.
Und hätt ich es gedichtet	And had I created it,
Du Holde, glaube mir,	Thou dear one, believe me,
So spräche viel von Dir,	It would speak much of thee,
Wär viel an Dich gerichtet.	Much of it would be for thee.

Sey Dir denn zugeeignet,	May its contents, then,
Was es enthält in sich,	Be dedicated to thee,
Und zum Beweis hab' ich	And as proof
Mich selber unterzeichnet.	I myself am signatory.[116]

On Christmas Day, Lea returned the present to the "sensitive, reverent ladies' knight," because she found Hensel's portrait, regardless of the form it took, inappropriate for a maiden; but were he to remove the offending title page, there would be no violation of social propriety, and Fanny could accept the volume.[117]

While Wilhelm was wooing Fanny, she was making her first foray into chamber music. On November 23 she dated the finale of a Piano Quartet in A♭ major, a work begun in May with Zelter's assistance[118] and then set aside during the Swiss sojourn. It was her first essay in a large form. Was Fanny attempting to rival Felix, who had already performed a piano quartet for Goethe? Did Fanny's effort in turn spur her brother to write his Piano Quartet in C minor, begun in Geneva in September and then finished less than a month later in Berlin? Whatever the case, the publication history of these two quartets delineates the gulf separating the siblings' musical worlds. Felix's second piano quartet, published as Op. 1 with a dedication to Prince Radziwill in 1823, marked Felix's debut as a professional composer, while Fanny's quartet lay dormant until its premiere and first edition late in the twentieth century.[119] Fanny never intended to publish her composition; it belonged to her private musical realm, in contrast to the increasingly public arena in which her brother appeared. Indeed, as Rainer Cadenbach suggests, Fanny's work evinces a tentative quality. Dominating the composition is its piano passagework, which overshadows the modest demands of the string parts. The application of sonata form in the first movement is unsure, the trio of the minuet is a piano solo with a bass line in the cello, and the concluding Presto, joined to the minuet, leaves the listener "somewhat helpless, since it is too weighty for a coda, but too compact for a finale and of too little importance."[120]

In contrast, during the closing months of 1822 Felix seems to have acted upon Goethe's pronouncement heralding him as a second Mozart. Comparisons between the two prodigies gained currency. Thus, Heinrich Heine admitted that "according to the judgment of all musicians," Felix "is a musical miracle, and can become a second Mozart. . . ."[121] Expectations in Berlin society ran high, and for Felix, testing his musical mettle meant producing compositions that would invite comparisons with his illustrious predecessor. In the case of the piano quartet, a genre with relatively few examples, Felix was familiar with Mozart's two (K. 478 and 493) and had absorbed the wealth of instrumental combinations ex-

Ex. 3.10a: Mozart, Piano Sonata in C minor (K. 457, 1784), First Movement

Ex. 3.10b: Mendelssohn, Piano Quartet in C minor, Op. 1 (1822), First Movement

ploited therein—the piano as a virtuoso soloist set against the strings, the marshaling of all four instruments in unison, the use of the strings alone, and the like. But for the C-minor Piano Quartet Felix found inspiration in another work of Mozart, the Piano Sonata in C minor K. 457 (1784). Thus, the quartet begins with a rising triadic gesture in the cello and viola that replicates the opening of the sonata (ex. 3.10a, b). Felix arranges his theme into symmetrical antecedent and consequent phrases, a Mozartean feature that attracted critical attention in 1824.[122] The ties between the two works are even more explicit in the finale, which begins with a theme adapted from the opening of Mozart's finale (ex. 3.11a, b). Felix's slow movement, an Adagio in A♭ major, offers a graceful theme that could be by Mozart, but with the Scherzo in C minor we find a more original contribution: a fleet-footed Presto in duple meter that contains the seeds of Felix's mature scherzo idiom. Elsewhere, too, we glimpse a more modern style, as in the lush second theme of the first movement, set in the dark registers of the cello and viola and reminiscent of Carl Maria von Weber. Felix's *opus primum* impresses as a composition that acknowledges its Mozartean parentage while searching for its own identity.

Ex. 3.11a: Mozart, Piano Sonata in C minor (K. 457, 1784), Finale

Ex. 3.11b: Mendelssohn, Piano Quartet in C minor, Op. 1 (1822), Finale

No work of Mozart stimulated Felix as profoundly as the finale of the *Jupiter* Symphony, with its ne plus ultra synthesis of fugal counterpoint and sonata form. Felix's full engagement with the work occurred in November and December 1822, when, attracted by the intricate combinations of the finale, he composed the eighth String *Sinfonia* in D major. Dispatching it in three weeks, he immediately rescored it for a classical orchestra with double winds and gave the composition a sonorous luster that further enhanced its relationship to the model. The revised version, of which he dated the first movement on December 21, 1822, was Felix's first symphony for full orchestra.[123] Preceding it was an undated pendant work, the seventh String *Sinfonia* in D minor, Felix's first symphony to adopt the four-movement classical paradigm with minuet. In the seventh *Sinfonia* Felix made his approach to Viennese classicism. The work begins in the mannered world of Emanuel Bach with yet another dramatic unison opening. The second movement, in contrast, is built upon a theme, marked *amorevole*, that brings us considerably closer to Mozart and Haydn. For the Minuet, Felix devised a theme susceptible to imitative counterpoint, and indeed the movement teeters on becoming a canon in the style of the canonic minuet from Haydn's String Quartet, Op. 76 No. 2 (1799). In the finale Felix introduced an academic fugue that alternates with classical homophony, to produce a rondo-like hybrid.

These contrapuntal stirrings paled in comparison to the eighth string symphony, in which Felix vied with the radiant complexities of the *Jupiter*. The very outset of Felix's work announces a stately tone in a slow introduction with dotted rhythms that comes to a pregnant pause, like so many preambles to Mozart's and Haydn's symphonies. The ensuing Allegro unfolds a monothematic exposition along classical lines, but in its bridge section Felix begins to indulge in canonic imitation (a technique Mozart employed in the first movement of the *Jupiter*)—anticipating even more contrapuntal gambits in the finale. The darkly hued Adagio, much of it scored for low, divided strings, begins with an ambiguous series of harmonies perhaps meant to allude to Mozart's "Dissonance" String Quartet (K. 465). Felix devoted considerable effort to the brightly

Ex. 3.12: Mozart, *Jupiter* Symphony (K. 551, 1788), Finale

Ex. 3.13: Mendelssohn, *Sinfonia* No. 8 (1822), Finale, subjects

scored Minuet and rewrote its trio when he revised the work for full orchestra. But the pièce de résistance is the finale, a fusion of sonata form and contrapuntal gamesmanship that returns us to the *Jupiter* Symphony.[124] Like Mozart, Felix constructed a complex sonata-form edifice upon four subjects, ultimately combined in a stunning display of invertible counterpoint. In Mozart's symphony the first and fourth subjects substitute for the first and second themes of a sonata-form exposition, while the second and third function as transitional and bridge material (**ex. 3.12**). Felix adapted this strategy somewhat (**ex. 3.13**). His monothematic exposition, which reuses the first theme on the dominant, vitiates the need for a contrasting second theme; thus, his fourth subject does not emerge

Ex. 3.14: Mendelssohn, *Sinfonia* No. 8 (1822), Finale, *stretto*

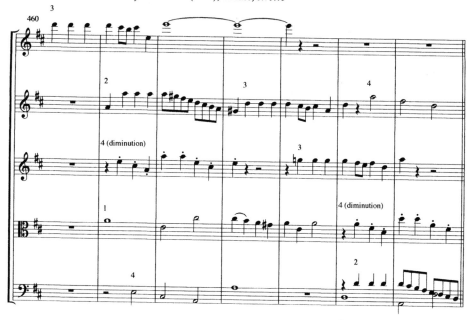

until the development, where it launches a fugato in five parts. The summarizing coda of the work reconstructs the concluding *stretto* of the *Jupiter*. Introducing a "fifth" subject, Felix here spins an intricate web of invertible counterpoint in which all five appear simultaneously in various combinations, his response to the breathtaking mastery of Mozart's stretto (**ex. 3.14**).

In no other early work did Felix assimilate so thoroughly Mozart's peerless craft, or attain a greater level of complexity. Only the culminating quadruple fugue of Felix's *Magnificat* approaches the intricate patterns of his symphony. Judged by Mozart's accomplishments of his thirteenth year (1769), Felix had indeed become a second Mozart; but whether the prodigy's extraordinary talents would support a musical genius of the first magnitude still remained to be seen.

Chapter 4
1823–1824

From Apprentice to Journeyman

Now work on until you become a master.
—Zelter to Felix, February 3, 1824[1]

"He is growing beneath my eyes"[2]—so Zelter described Felix's unbridled development as a composer in 1823, when he created a spate of string symphonies, two concerti, another piano quartet, string quartet, violin sonata, Kyrie, Lieder, piano and organ works, and completed his fourth opera, *Die beiden Neffen*. Capping this startling productivity was the publication late that year of the C-minor Piano Quartet, Felix's professional debut. Released by A. M. Schlesinger, the work was actually engraved in Paris by Schlesinger's son Maurice,[3] himself a music publisher, who also brought out in 1823 a more weighty composition in C minor—Beethoven's transcendent final piano sonata, Op. 111. Felix's Op. 1 was thus an international event. The Parisian virtuoso J. P. Pixis, "thrilled by the splendid genius which expresses itself in this music,"[4] read the quartet, and a Leipzig reviewer lauded the work of a young genius following the footsteps of Mozart.[5] But a Berlin critic was more tempered—the quartet lacked Mozart's "invigorating freshness."[6] The scherzo was original, the finale worthy of praise, but Felix still needed to produce something to advance the art significantly. The mantle worn by the second Mozart was heavy indeed.

I

In spite of this public scrutiny, Felix continued to explore privately the string symphony and dispatched the last four works in the series (Nos. 9–12) along with an unnumbered, one-movement *Sinfoniesatz* in C minor.[7]

Pendulum-like, these compositions swing between cerebral Bachian counterpoint and graceful Viennese classicism. Excepting No. 10, all contain fugal movements or passages. In No. 9, Felix's fugal musings bring together stylistically strange bedfellows: thus, the classically symmetrical first theme of the Allegro later transforms itself into a chromatic fugue. The *Sinfoniesatz* and first movement of No. 12 have double fugues with slow introductions in the archaic style of the French overture, again suggestive of a neo-baroque revival. In particular, the first subject of No. 12, constructed upon the old chromatic tetrachord, bespeaks Felix's preoccupation with Bach's music, as do the origins of this *sinfonia* in an unfinished organ fantasy and fugue Felix sketched on the same subject.[8] And yet, the elegant slow movements of Nos. 11 and 12 display just how fully he had assimilated Mozart's limpid style.

For all their reliance on Bach and Mozart, these *sinfonie* show signs of experimentation. By dividing the violas, Felix now works with an enriched, five-part texture (first and second violins, first and second violas, and a bass line performed by celli and contrabass), in contrast to the traditional four-part writing of the first six string *sinfonie*. Again, by dividing the violas and separating the contrabass from the cello line, he occasionally expands the ensemble to six parts; and by segregating the violins into four parts in the slow movement of No. 9, he even achieves an eight-part texture hinting at the opulent string writing of the Octet, composed only two years later.

Elsewhere the final *sinfonie* reveal an increased independence from familiar models. Thus, the double fugue of the *Sinfoniesatz* in C minor contains some stylistically incongruous passages. In the closing measures, Felix unleashes a unison passage that anticipates a remarkably similar effect in the coda of the *Hebrides* Overture of 1830 (**ex. 4.1a** and **b**). Other innovative signs include the airy scherzo of No. 9, the engaging, Weber-like second theme of No. 10, and the yodel call in No. 9 (Trio) and *Volkslied* of No.11 (second movement), materials recorded during the 1822 Swiss sojourn. The *Schweizerlied* of No. 11, based on a wedding

Ex. 4.1a: Mendelssohn, *Sinfoniesatz* in C minor (1823)

Ex. 4.1b: Mendelssohn, *Hebrides* Overture, Coda (1830)

dance from the Emmental region,[9] offers ingratiating staccati, deft writing for the violas, and a surprise rescoring in the final section. Here a percussion complement of timpani, triangle, and cymbals joins the strings, as if recreating the boisterous Janissary ensemble in the *Allegretto* of Haydn's *Military* Symphony.

The juxtaposition of folk elements and high art in No. 11 is a sure sign Felix was enlarging his compositional canvas. In contrast to the three- and four-movement schemes of his earlier string symphonies, No. 11 has five movements: (1) sonata-form with slow introduction; (2) *Schweizerlied;* (3) Mozartean Adagio; (4) Minuet (oddly enough in $\frac{6}{8}$ instead of $\frac{3}{4}$); and (5) an amalgam of sonata form and fugue. The presence of Swiss folk materials in an expanded symphonic format suggests also the influence of Beethoven, whose *Pastoral* Symphony has five movements and employs in its finale a Swiss herdsmen's tune from the Rigi, which Felix's family ascended in 1822.

The *sinfonie* of 1823 forcefully document Felix's first serious engagement with Beethoven's music, in their off-beat accents and interruptions, prominent diminished-seventh sonorities, and animated stretti. The finales of Nos. 9 and 11 contain passages of massive dominant preparations, a hallmark of Beethoven's insistent, middle-period style. Thus in No. 11, dissonant harmonies accumulate in a manner reminiscent of Beethoven's *Appassionata* Sonata (**ex. 4.2a and b**).

Among Felix's other orchestral works of 1823 are two double concerti— in D minor for violin, piano, and string orchestra; and E major for two

Ex. 4.2a: Mendelssohn, *Sinfonia* No. 11 (1823), Finale

Ex. 4.2b: Beethoven, *Appassionata* Sonata, Op. 57 (1804–5)

pianos and full orchestra. Felix designed the former for Eduard Rietz; the two presented it privately at a Sunday musicale on May 25 before some sixty invited guests and publicly on July 3 at the Schauspielhaus, where Felix appeared on a concert of the Neapolitan contralto Nina Cornega.[10] In laying out his score Felix ruled staves for only the two soloists and string orchestra; but a separate score for winds and timpani[11] establishes he re-orchestrated the work, perhaps for the public performance. This worthy concerto then fell into oblivion until its twentieth-century revival in Berlin on June 8, 1957. Three years later an abridged version appeared, and a reliable critical edition waited until the end of the century.[12]

The three movements include a dramatic Allegro with a classical double exposition, an intimate Adagio with muted string accompaniment, and a Rondo that begins off the beat with an energetic piano solo. The Allegro is built upon a compact figure that in another context could have served as a fugal subject, though here Felix resisted that temptation. Rietz's French-school style of violin playing is evident in varied bowings for the soloist, and in the first movement the lyrical second theme placed in the high register. The piano figuration includes widely spaced chords and sparkling arpeggiations now further removed from the Mozartean style of the A-minor Piano Concerto of 1822. The two soloists frequently appear alone: the center of the Adagio forms an unaccompanied duet, and the soloists' initial entrance in the Allegro, a series of improvisation-like flourishes, is marked *più lento*, a tempo change that separates them even more from the orchestra. Much of the development of the first movement yields to an impassioned, romantic duet between the soloists in the distant key of D♭ major, possibly inspired by a similar passage in Weber's *Grand Duo Concertante*, for clarinet and piano (1817). The recapitulation features an impressive cadenza that culminates, in a brisk *Presto*, on the traditional six-four harmony, signaling the close of the cadenza.

Felix finished the E-major double piano concerto on October 17, 1823, and probably presented it to Fanny on her birthday. The siblings premiered it at a Sunday musicale on December 7, 1823, attended by the pianist Kalkbrenner,[13] and read the concerto the next year for Ignaz Moscheles. Six years later, Felix brought the score to London, where he retouched and performed it with Moscheles.[14] Then, the work "disappeared" until Moscheles arranged an informal reading at the Leipzig Conservatory in 1860, nearly thirteen years after the death of his former student, colleague, and friend. Moscheles perplexed his associates by announcing the composer as F. Knospe, the German word for bud, as if to underscore Felix's Mozartean precocity.[15] Like the Double Concerto for violin and piano, the E-major Double Concerto entered the Berlin *Nachlass* in 1878, before its rediscovery in the twentieth century, when the manuscript (and that of the Double Concerto in A♭ major of 1824) became a pawn of the Cold War. In exchange for Western books smuggled into East Berlin, a microfilm copy made its furtive way from the partitioned city to New York,[16] and the work was heard again and recorded in the early 1950s.

The unusual key of the concerto may unmask a debt to Fanny, who in 1822 had composed a sonata-form piano movement in E major that begins with suspiciously similar material.[17] But Felix's elaborate first movement (450 measures) dwarfs Fanny's modest effort (140), which lacks a second thematic group in the exposition and again discloses inexperience in sonata form. The breadth of Felix's concerto betrays Beethovenian preoccupations. Thus, the two pianists enter with forceful cadenzas on the tonic and dominant harmonies exploiting nearly the instruments' entire range, not unlike the adamantine opening of Beethoven's *Emperor* Concerto, with its three sculpted cadenzas. There are other reminiscences of the *Emperor*—the second theme that appears initially in parallel major and minor keys, for example, and third-related mediant relationships, tonal pairings increasingly conspicuous in Felix's early concerti.[18] The key schemes of the two concerti— Mendelssohn, E–C–E; Beethoven, E♭–B–E♭—are similar, too, although Beethoven mixes flat and sharp keys, yielding some sophisticated enharmonic relationships. All in all, Felix's concerto remains stylistically conflicted. The warm lyricism of the first movement does not support its Beethovenian pretensions, and the slow movement occasionally brings Mozart to mind. The weakest movement is the Rondo, where considerable stretches are filled with repetitive passagework—widely spaced chords, *bravura* runs, and prevalent diminished-seventh sonorities—all familiar to Felix in the piano music of Weber and other virtuosi, technically effective but overused and musically unsatisfying.

Curiously, in the outer movements Felix notated reductions of the orchestral *tutti* passages for the piano part,[19] as if to facilitate an optional performance for piano duet, with Felix and Fanny providing the requisite orchestral passages at the keyboard. But some reductions consist of only a figured-bass line, possibly indicating Felix's awareness of the *col basso* tradition, in which during orchestral passages soloists assumed the role of a continuo instrument, and played the bass line and improvised chords above it. Indeed, there is compelling evidence that as late as the *Emperor* Concerto (1809) Beethoven was still observing this practice,[20] and, of course, Mozart in his piano concerti had devised figured-bass lines for the soloist to realize.

In size and scope, the orchestral works dominated Felix's musical landscape of 1823. Unlike Fanny, he devoted little attention to the art song; while she produced more than thirty Lieder that year, Felix wrote only a handful, all unpublished.[21] One, a charming rendition of Friedrich Matthisson's *Andenken* ("Ich denke dein," "I think of you," 1792) is of particular interest: this poem inspired verse imitations by Frederike Brun and Goethe, and, between 1795 and 1821, Lieder by Zelter, Reichardt, Beethoven, and Schubert (D99 and 162).[22] Felix's autograph bears the incomplete date October 1, but we may infer the year 1823, since the song follows another (*Am Seegestad*) dated September 26, 1823. In *Andenken*, the poet, obsessed about a distant lover, associates her with nightingales, the encroaching twilight, and anxious longing. The concluding stanza breaks the pattern: he interrupts his sensuous reveries to ask when, where, and how she thinks of him. Felix captured the verses in a strophic setting for the first three stanzas, and a variation for the fourth. As in the poem, the music poses three questions, by exploiting a simple musical conceit—three unresolved dissonant chords in the piano, held by fermatas to underscore the syntactical break and extended to allow a free cadenza for the piano, as if the music conveys the question to the distant lover (ex. 4.3). For the final line, the piano resolves the "dissonant" question by reaffirming the tonic key. Now the poet thinks only of her, as the piano subtly revives through metrical shifts the fanciful figuration of the cadenza and the question-answer dialectic of the poem.

In 1823 Felix produced piano and organ pieces with contrasting stylistic tendencies. A discursive Fantasia for piano impresses as a notated extemporization and perhaps gives an idea of Felix's formidable improvisational skills.[23] Unpublished, it alternates between several Adagio and Allegro sections before culminating in a toccata-like fugato. Tonal latitude unusual for Felix complements the work's structural freedom: it begins in C minor and digresses through different keys before concluding in D major. In considerable contrast is the Sonata in B♭ minor, a taut, sonata-form movement based upon a motive related to the opening of the Piano Quartet in F minor, Op. 2, also from 1823.[24] The Sonata begins with a slow introduction, later recalled in the recapitulation, a technique Felix may have borrowed from his teacher Ludwig Berger. In marked relief to the thematic diversity of the Fantasia, the severe monothematicism of the Sonata also suggests not only Berger's influence but Clementi's.

The three organ compositions of 1823[25] mark the zenith of Felix's studies with A. W. Bach. In a lyrical Andante in D major, Felix approaches his teacher's melodious, accessible style. Considerably more ambitious are the chorale variations on *Wie gross ist des Allmächt'gen Güte*, possibly inspired by Felix's meeting in 1822 the Darmstadt organist J. C. H. Rinck, who had included a similar set in his *Praktische Orgel-Schule* (1821). Inevitably, the genre led Felix to ruminate about J. S. Bach's organ music.

Ex. 4.3: Mendelssohn, "Ich denke dein" (1823)

In the first variation, the chorale phrases intermittently appear cantus-firmus-like in the pedal, and in the second variation Felix subjects the melody to a variety of Bachian canons. A more specific debt is evident in Felix's most substantial early organ work, an untitled Passacaglia in C minor, which presents twenty-two variations on a repeated eight-bar ground bass, a neo-baroque edifice unabashedly inspired by Bach's monumental passacaglia in the same key (BWV 582). Like Bach, Felix arranges the variations into three groups, with the ground entrenched in the bass, then inverted to the upper voices for several "free" variations before it returns to the bass in the closing section. Nowhere does Felix seriously challenge the model, though his passacaglia is among the earliest nineteenth-century revivals of the genre, and as such it stands alone for several decades before the historicist experiments of Brahms in the *Haydn* Variations (1874) and Fourth Symphony (1886), and of Joseph Rheinberger in the Eighth Organ Sonata (1882).

A historicist impulse lies too behind Felix's a cappella Kyrie in C minor, composed in five days in November 1823 for Schelble's Cäcilienverein, which performed it in 1825.[26] Like the earlier *Jube Domine*, the Kyrie requires two four-part choirs, from which Felix extracts soloists to explore various textures: the entire eight-part ensemble, the two choirs in alternation, the soloists alone (as in the midpoint, "Christe eleison"), and the soloists supported by one of the choirs. And, like *Jube Domine*, the Kyrie reflects the seventeenth-century polychoral tradition, which Zelter and Schelble had endeavored to sustain at their institutions. However, in much of the Kyrie the earlier ideal of *Doppelchörigkeit*—the alternation of discrete, four-part choirs—yields to eight-part writing and succumbs to Felix's tendency toward dense part-writing.[27] Only in the final section, the return of the text "Kyrie eleison," does Felix temporarily reduce the texture to four parts, to accommodate a double fugue, a new layer of contrapuntal complexity in this richly hued, expressive composition.

Notwithstanding Beethoven's increasing influence, Felix firmly grounded the three chamber works of 1823 in the classical tradition. The String Quartet in E♭ major, his first full-length quartet, required only eleven days to compose.[28] Its four movements include a Mozartean *Allegro moderato* with two contrasting thematic groups; a brooding Adagio in C minor that occasionally anticipates the slow movement of the Octet; a Haydnesque minuet and trio; and a learned double fugue that draws upon the finales of Haydn's String Quartets Op. 20 and Mozart's String Quartet K. 387. The Violin Sonata in F minor, Op. 4, conceived between May 21 and June 3 and dedicated to Eduard Rietz,[29] opens with a free recitative for solo violin that pauses on a descending sighing gesture, subsumed by the piano into the principal theme. As a reviewer noticed, Haydn could have composed the beginning of the slow movement, though later Felix conjures up a romantic "mist of feelings" (*Empfindungsnebel*).[30] Toward the end of the finale, the violin again breaks into recitative, before an explosive Beethovenian coda. The work ends *pianissimo* with two descending sighs that link the outer movements.

Similar in mood is Felix's most substantial chamber work of 1823, the second Piano Quartet Op. 2, published in 1824 and dedicated to Zelter. If Op. 1 invokes Mozart, Op. 2 embraces Beethoven. The first movement alone contains several clear signs: a sonata form with pronounced and expanded bridge, closing sections, and coda, a second theme indebted to the *Waldstein* Sonata, and a tumultuous conclusion for which Felix specifies the extreme dynamic level of *fff*. The expressive slow move-

Ex. 4.4: Mendelssohn, Piano Quartet No. 2 in F minor, Op. 2 (1823), Finale

ment, in D♭ major, explores an enharmonic palette that includes several sharp keys. The lightly scored *Allegro moderato*, the first movement Felix labeled Intermezzo, provides a diversion from the more weighty Adagio and explosive finale, which erupts with a rocketlike theme, propelled by a rising chromatic bass line (ex. 4.4). Its parallel statements on F minor and G♭ major betray Felix's fascination with Beethoven's *Appassionata* Sonata Op. 57, which also stimulated Fanny's imagination at this time.[31]

In 1823 Felix's principal musical outlet remained the private musicales of high society, including the fortnightly gatherings at his residence, a proving ground where he developed into a virtuoso of the first rank. The proud Lea, enjoying her role as a *Musenmama*, reported that Felix and Fanny were transcribing at sight full opera scores into piano duets. (Lea solicited from her cousin Amalia Beer scores by her son, Giacomo Meyerbeer, with which the siblings regaled their guests.[32]) In December Felix and Fanny met the French virtuoso Frédéric Kalkbrenner, then concertizing in Berlin. According to Fanny, after hearing Felix's compositions, Kalkbrenner "praised with taste, and blamed candidly and amiably."[33] There is little evidence that the gaudy virtuosity of the Frenchman, who placed his lucrative relationship with the Parisian piano firm of Pleyel ahead of purely musical concerns, impressed Felix. Still, Fanny found "precision, clearness, expression, the greatest facility, and most untiring power and energy" in Kalkbrenner's playing, and composed piano pieces "*alla K*," including an etude featuring left-hand octaves, the pianist's trademark.[34]

Inevitably, Felix's growing fame brought public scrutiny. While Fanny was shielded from this exposure, Felix now participated more frequently in public concerts, at least three of which are documented for 1823. On March 3 he appeared with the tenor J. D. H. Stümer to perform an amorous *romance* of Felice Blangini, a voice professor at the Paris Conservatoire.[35] More notably, Felix's string symphonies now piqued Spontini's curiosity, and on his incentive,[36] Karl Möser, concertmaster of the court orchestra, performed one in April. From Lea's disclosure that it was in four movements and for full orchestra, we can identify it as No. 8 in D major. Lea feared its length (and fugal seriousness) would not impress the "frivolous" Berlin audience, but the performance scored a success.[37] Finally, on July 3 Felix and Eduard Rietz performed the Double Concerto in D minor at the Schauspielhaus, but other opportunities were declined—Lea remained mindful of the advice of the French flutist Louis Drouet not to exhaust one's audience (*il ne faut pas fatiguer le public*).

II

Felix's emergence into the Berlin limelight contrasted starkly with Fanny's musical reality. In 1822 she had courageously attempted her first large work, the Piano Quartet in A♭ major, but there had been no recognition of her precocity before Goethe, no publication of an *opus primum*. Instead, she mused wistfully, "I have watched the progress of [Felix's] talent step by step, and may say I have contributed to his development. I have always been his only musical adviser, and he never writes down a thought before submitting it to my judgment."[38] But this vicarious coping strategy was now complicated by her relationship with Hensel.

On Christmas Eve 1822 Hensel had given Fanny a volume of Müller's poetry. In 1823 Fanny responded by setting no fewer than eight poems. Almost certainly, she shared them with the poet, who socialized in July at the Mendelssohn residence, where he found everything musical.[39] Fanny's first three Lieder, from *Die schöne Müllerin*, date from January 1823. They include *Die liebe Farbe* (*The Lovely Color*), in which the despondent miller lad requests a burial in green, the maid's preferred color. Fanny chose the bright key of E major for her song, introduced by horn calls in the piano introduction, but had second thoughts and judged Ludwig Berger's rendition superior.[40] She also selected two more optimistic poems from the cycle. In *Der Neugierige* (*The Curious One*), the lad asks the brook if the maid loves him, and in *Des Müllers Blumen* (*The Miller's Flowers*), he associates the blue hue of his beloved's eyes with flowers beneath her window.

Fanny's remaining Müller settings were inspired by two other sections of the poet's anthology. From the *Reiselieder* (*Songs of Traveling*) she excerpted poems about separation, *Seefahrers Abschied* (*Sailor's Departure*), *Einsamkeit* (*Solitude*), and *Abendreih'n* (*Evening Rounds*), in which a wanderer asks the moon for a message from his lover. These Lieder provided an outlet for her feelings about Wilhelm's imminent departure to Italy, where the Berlin Academy of Art sent him in 1823 to further his studies. Fanny also set two poems from *Johannes und Esther*, a minicycle about a relationship between a young Christian and a Jewess. In *Vereinigung* (*Union*, November 1823), she pondered these verses:

Wenn ich nur darf in deine Augen schauen,	If I may only look into your eyes,
In deine klaren, treuen, frommen Sterne,	Into your clear, true, devout orbs,
So fühl' ich weichen das geheime Grauen,	So I feel the secret horror abating,
Das Lieb' und Liebe hält in stummer Ferne.	That in muted distance restrains
	my beloved and our love.

Here, Johannes addresses Esther. The "secret horror" is the separation forced upon the lovers by their differing faiths. Of course, several years before meeting Wilhelm, Fanny had been baptized, thereby removing, or so it seemed, a potential objection to their relationship. But in 1823 another "*geheimes Grauen*" threatened their happiness, as Wilhelm explained in a heartfelt letter from Rome to his sister.[41] For some time, Wilhelm had been drawn increasingly to Catholicism and intended to follow the example of his sister Luise, who, swayed by Clemens Brentano, had converted in 1818.

The prospect of the Protestant Fanny marrying a Catholic provoked a family crisis in 1823. But the drama took an unusual course when Wilhelm, with Fanny's approval, spoke to her parents about their engagement; they did not broach the matter of religion, and Wilhelm interpreted their silence as acquiescence. Lea and Abraham made only one stipulation, that the engagement remain secret, because they did not wish to disturb Lea's mother, the elderly Bella Salomon, an Orthodox Jew still unaware that Lea, Abraham, and their children were Protestants. Wilhelm willingly agreed and enjoyed a period of happiness, until one evening,

> when her mother unexpectedly asked me what my views about religion were and whether it was true, as she had heard, that I desired to convert to the Catholic faith. I replied that she would have known that for a long time, since I had declared it to her daughter before professing my love. And now it was revealed that Fanny, in order not to turn her parents against me and to preserve the domestic peace, had not dared to tell them. Now the mother's wrath turned against the daughter, and she declared that, had she known this, she never would have given her permission, since it did not at all accord with her views to have a Catholic son-in-law, for Catholicism always led to fanaticism and hypocrisy. . . . The father, though he agreed with his wife, intervened, and the upshot was this: she did not wish to be tyrannical, and if her daughter did not change her feelings, the mother would not separate us by force, though she admitted to me freely, that if I converted she would do all in her power to convince her daughter to break off the engagement. Further, if I did not bind myself to remain true to the Protestant church, she must for the time being forbid any lengthy private meetings with Fanny and any correspondence. I stood firm, and said I could not restrict my conscience; I only promised not to take the step without deliberate reflection, and if it happened, to tell them in good conscience.[42]

The tempestuous scene ended in stalemate, with Wilhelm unyielding and Lea, suffering severe nosebleeds from the stress, forbidding the lovers to meet. Still, Fanny reaffirmed her loyalty to Wilhelm. In July 1823 he left for Rome. Accompanied by the actors P. A. Wolff[43] and Eduard Devrient, Wilhelm stopped in Marienbad, where he sketched Goethe's portrait; but the poet found the artist "stuck in the shallow dilettantism of the time," and obsessed with a false piety (*Frömmelei*) and the art of antiquity.[44] Safely in Rome, Hensel took up a time-honored pursuit—replicating the treasures of the Italian Renaissance—and began copying Raphael's monumental *Transfiguration* for the Prussian king. The project took nearly four years and began with a cleaning of the original, exposing "a quantity of details hidden under the crust of the dirt of centuries."[45] Hensel's copy later hung in Sans souci in Potsdam.

Barred from corresponding with Fanny, Wilhelm sent ingratiating portraits of the Mendelssohns and their friends to Berlin. Many of his subjects were idealized beyond recognition; thus, Lili Klein (née Parthey), who had sung in Zelter's Singakademie and knew the Mendelssohns well, reported Wilhelm often had to reveal the identities of his portraits.[46] Surprisingly, Lea and Abraham kept a regular correspondence with Wilhelm. Though Lea found that his renderings represented her children "as they were," she was quite taken by his drawing of four angels watched over by Cecilia; indeed, Wilhelm Schadow was astute enough to recognize Lea as the "original" of the saintly organist.[47] Meanwhile, Abraham arranged for honoraria to be sent to Rome. After the death of Fanny's uncle Jacob Bartholdy in July 1825, Wilhelm reciprocated by settling the deceased's affairs in Rome and offered to ship the frescoes of the Casa Bartholdy to Berlin. Abraham and Lea maintained an almost parental interest in Wilhelm's progress: in January 1826 they urged him to exhibit work in Berlin and chided him that in two years he had not completed anything substantial.[48]

Why did Lea so strenuously object to Fanny's engagement? The parents' own recent baptism in 1822 had symbolically completed the family's assimilation into upper-class Berlin society and the dominant culture of Protestant Prussia. Wilhelm's plan to embrace Catholicism—especially problematic because he was the son of a Protestant minister—threatened the stability of Fanny's social position. Lea surely had in mind the scandalous precedent of Abraham's sister Brendel, now the Catholic Dorothea Schlegel after her earlier flirtation with Protestantism. Finally, Lea was unimpressed by Wilhelm's modest career prospects. His opportunity to secure a court position in Berlin, and thereby provide a respectable livelihood for Fanny, was in jeopardy should he convert. As Wilhelm reported to his sister Luise, Lea was especially concerned about social standing,[49] and indeed, she made herself clear on this point:

You are at the commencement of your career, and under beautiful auspices; . . ., rest assured that we will not be against you, when, at the end of your studies, you can satisfy us about your position. Above all, do not call me selfish or avaricious, my gentle tyrant! Otherwise I must remind you that I married my husband before he had a penny of his own. But he was earning a certain although very moderate income at Fould's in Paris, and I knew he would be able to turn my dowry to good account.[50]

For five years, Wilhelm sent drawings to Berlin instead of love letters. Somehow, throughout the Roman sojourn he remained a Protestant, and when he returned to Berlin in 1828 Fanny was still eligible. They married in 1829.

Shortly after Wilhelm departed for Italy, Felix left Berlin with his father, brother, and Heyse for Bad Reinerz in Lower Silesia, where they visited Abraham's younger brother, Nathan. Felix's letters home, his first to include Greek quotations, reveal that studies with Heyse had advanced well into Homer (according to Eduard Devrient, Felix shared Greek lessons with his sister Rebecka, "in order to make the study more attractive to him"[51]). En route they saw Felix's great-uncle B. D. Itzig (1756–1833) in Frankfurt an der Oder, before proceeding to Breslau (Wrocław), where on August 9, 1823, Felix met Zelter's colleague F. W. Berner (1780–1827), organist of the St. Elisabeth Church. In 1806 Berner's intervention had probably saved the life of Carl Maria von Weber, who had fallen unconscious after imbibing engraver's ink carelessly left in a wine bottle. Berner's celebrated improvisations resonated with Bach. At the church, Berner launched an elaborate organ fantasy on a theme chosen by Felix, first in the manual, and then—to Felix's surprise, because the theme contained sixteenth notes—in the pedals, before harnessing it to augmentation and adding a countersubject. Fortifying himself with wine, Berner next produced droll variations on "God save the King" in the obsolete phrygian and aeolian church modes. But the pièce de résistance was his treatment of the chorale *Vom Himmel hoch*, into which he contrived to introduce the melody in diminution as a fugal subject, though the exertion "tired him very much, so that he had to take two or three glasses of wine."[52]

Berner's erudition contrasted sharply with Felix's musical experiences in the spa town of Bad Reinerz, where he arrived in the middle of August. A "favorite watering-place, with alkaline springs, . . . efficacious in nervous disorders, poverty of blood, and the like,"[53] the region also contained sizable deposits of iron ore. Here, supported by his brother Joseph, Nathan Mendelssohn constructed in 1822 a smelting furnace and, on the slope of a hill, a house with a quaint turret that "resembled a modest little castle."[54] In 1823 he established an iron foundry, and on August 18 Nathan and Abraham laid the cornerstone of a new furnace.

Fifty thalers were distributed to the poor, and six days later the brothers hosted a banquet for the workers, whom Felix entertained.

Two accounts of this event have survived. According to Sebastian Hensel, Felix chose a Mozart piano concerto, but since the bedraggled orchestra could not keep time, Felix instead improvised on themes of Mozart and Weber.[55] A more engaging story comes from Paul Dengler, Bürgermeister of the resort from 1867.[56] The orchestra mustered only the seven musicians of the spa's wind band (*Harmoniemusik*) and some amateurs. When the ensemble could not maintain the tempo, the first movement of the concerto lapsed into a snail's pace. But Felix

> knew how to help. While the orchestra continued to play in a *Comodo* [comfortable tempo], he filled out his piano part, in effect composing in a double tempo [*Doppeltakt*]; thus, for each measure the worthy musicians played, he doubled the number of notes in the piano part, thereby transforming it into a cheerful Allegro. . . Only a genius could have accomplished that.[57]

Felix gave some piano lessons to Nathan's son Arnold and promised to compose a violin piece for Johannes Latzel, rector of the local school.[58] As for Nathan, he persevered in his enterprise for a few years but suffered substantial losses from flooding in 1827 and 1829. As we shall see, the industrious Felix found a way to help then, as well.

III

On Christmas Day 1823 Felix supposedly showed Eduard Devrient a score of J. S. Bach's St. Matthew Passion, the document that would prompt "an actor and a Jew-boy" to "bring back to the people the greatest Christian music."[59] According to Devrient, the score, prepared by Eduard Rietz, was a Christmas present from Bella Salomon.[60] In 1815, Zelter had begun to rehearse portions with a select group of singers; in 1818, Devrient joined the effort to disentangle the "bristly pieces" (*borstige Stücke*) of Bach, then generally viewed as "an unintelligible musical arithmetician."[61] Zelter zealously guarded his Bachiana and concealed the cache from a world "which he supposed no longer capable of prizing it." Among his treasures were a copy of the Passion and the autograph Bach cantatas Abraham had sent from Hamburg in 1811. Occasionally Zelter led Felix to the closet where the manuscripts were stored, only to deny him access, causing a deep hurt the sensitive musician revealed years later to Ferdinand Hiller.[62] Devrient reports that Bella overcame considerable difficulty to procure a copy of the Passion from Zelter and thereby fulfill her grandson's fervent wish.

As an actor, Devrient would have appreciated the dramatic events leading to Felix's 1829 revival of the Passion, precipitating, in turn, the modern Bach revival; indeed, Devrient seems to have enhanced his account on one critical point. How are we to understand Bella—an orthodox Jew who had cursed the Protestant Jacob Bartholdy in 1805 and was unaware in 1823 that her children and grandchildren had converted—presenting Bach's Passion as a Christmas present? Bella was musically sophisticated and numbered with her sister Sarah Levy among Berlin cognoscenti dedicated to preserving the music of the Bach family. No doubt her musical interests supported the decision to have the Passion copied, in order, according to A. B. Marx, to present her grandson an essentially unknown composition.[63] Although Bella was among the first to recognize possibly the greatest musical composition of the Lutheran faith,[64] she did not give the score as a Christmas present. *Pace* Devrient, an inventory Fanny prepared of the family music library establishes that Bella made the gift in 1824, after other Bach acquisitions for 1823; furthermore, the copyist was Eduard Rietz's father, Johann Friedrich Rietz.[65] Peter Ward Jones has surmised that Bella probably gave her grandson the present on his birthday in 1824 (she died in March 1824).

Though Felix's score survives, Zelter's score along with much of the Berlin Singakademie library disappeared at the end of World War II.[66] What were the origins of Zelter's copy? Marx averred that Zelter purchased it from a cheese merchant, who had treated it as mere waste paper, a probably fictitious, if amusing anecdote. In 1928 Friedrich Smend and Georg Schünemann studied the Passion manuscripts, including Zelter's score; Martin Geck was later able to trace the primary source of Zelter's manuscript to a copy prepared by J. C. Altnikol, a son-in-law of J. S. Bach.[67] After Altnikol's death, the copy passed to Kirnberger in Berlin and entered the music library of Princess Anna Amalie, which Zelter helped catalogue in 1799. He thus could have prepared his copy from the Altnikol manuscript. (Like Zelter's score, Altnikol's copy omits the chorale fantasy "O Mensch, bewein' dein Sünde gross," with which the first part of the Passion concludes.)

At some point in 1824 J. S. Bach's autograph score of the Passion[68] arrived in Berlin. Like Zelter a devoted antiquarian, Georg Pölchau acquired this treasure from the estate of C. F. G. Schwencke (1767–1822), C. P. E. Bach's successor in Hamburg. Lea Salomon knew Pölchau as early as 1799, several years before she married Abraham; when Pölchau returned to Berlin in 1813, he remained on friendly terms with Bella Salomon's family. Moreover, Geck's 1967 research found that Felix's copy agreed fundamentally with the version of the Passion transmitted by the Pölchau autograph, and thus argued, contrary to Devrient, that Felix's copy, at least initially, was made from this source. But in 1974 Alfred Dürr proposed instead that the basis of Felix's copy was a score in the Singakademie library prepared from Bach's autograph parts.[69] By December 1823 the only portions of the work Felix likely knew were the six movements Zelter had been rehearsing since 1815[70]—four solo numbers and two short choruses, a few, tantalizing glimpses at the choral monument.

Bella's gift was revelatory: Felix was now free to fathom the manifold beauties of Bach's most profound work. The double orchestras and choruses, enriched eight-part writing and antiphonal effects, reflective arias and chromatically imbued recitatives, halolike enveloping of Jesus' part with string accompaniment,[71] and strategic placement of chorales—all of this deeply impressed Felix, for whom the St. Matthew Passion became a cornerstone of his musical faith. For Zelter, the fundamental impediment to reviving Bach's masterwork had been how to make the music accessible to modern audiences. Zelter's solution was to simplify the recitatives and choral parts in order to produce versions imitating the popular style of C. H. Graun.[72] But Zelter's tinkering only scratched the surface of Bach's colossus and never resounded beyond the secretive Friday rehearsals. Instead, the task of revival fell to Felix.

On Felix's fifteenth birthday, February 3, 1824, Zelter proclaimed him a journeyman. Among the celebrants was Samuel Rösel, who gave Felix an album of sepia Swiss landscapes, several scenes of which Felix had duplicated during his 1822 Swiss sojourn (Rösel's motto—"To live by reminiscence is a doubled life"—thus alluded to his own experiences and those of his student).[73] But the main event was the first full rehearsal of Felix's fourth opera, *Die beiden Neffen*, or *Der Onkel aus Boston* (*The Two Nephews*, or *The Uncle from Boston*).[74] Based, like its predecessors, on a Casper libretto, the opera had originated in May 1822. Felix dated the first act on September 11 in Lausanne; the second and third acts, in March and October 1823 in Berlin. Following a time-honored tradition, he composed the overture last and put the final touches on the score early in November. Once again, Abraham underwrote a production at the family residence, with two performances before one hundred and fifty guests on February 7 and 9, 1824.[75] Therese Devrient reports that among them was Savary, the Duke of Rovigo, a former aide-de-camp of Napoleon who had perpetrated atrocities during the war but was an enthusiastic music lover.[76] According to the young Heinrich Dorn,[77] who sang in the chorus, the cast included Eduard and Therese (they were married on February 11 of that year),[78] Johanna Zimmermann, and the Doctors Andrissen and Dittmar.[79] Presumably Casper participated as well. The orchestra again consisted of the king's elite musicians, and before this august company at the first orchestral rehearsal on Felix's birthday, Zelter delivered his speech, ratified by toasts and merry part-songs.

"Now work on until you become a master," Zelter exhorted Felix, tapping him on the cheek as if knighting him.[80] In elevating Felix, Zelter invoked Mozart, Haydn, and "old father Bach," though the opera had little to do with them and more with Weber, now a significant influence on Felix (just weeks before, he had performed with Spontini Weber's *Konzertstück*).[81] Like *Der Freischütz*, *Die beiden Neffen* consisted of an overture and three acts, with spoken dialogue conveying the dramatic action. The expanded compass contrasts with Felix's other Singspiele, all of which fitted comfortably into one act. Still unpublished, *Die beiden Neffen* has attracted scant attention, partly because the dialogue for the third act is lost, and because the libretto is among Casper's poorer efforts.[82] The plot concerns Theodor and his servant Carl (tenors), eventually revealed to be nephews of Colonel Felsig (bass). The nephews have returned to Germany from America, where their father reportedly died during the Revolution (in the third act, he miraculously appears and is reunited with his family).

Despite the libretto's weaknesses—most of the action occurs in the first act—the score contains some impressive music. Of the adroitly orchestrated overture Zelter reported: "Imagine a painter flinging a dab of color on his canvas and then working it about with fingers and brushes till at last a group appears, and you look at it with fresh wonder, and only see that it must be true because there it is."[83] The "dab of color" is the series of *piano* horn calls with which the overture begins (**ex. 4.5a**), presumably a symbol of separation, as in Beethoven's *Les Adieux* Piano

Ex. 4.5a: Mendelssohn, *Die beiden Neffen* (1823), Overture

Ex. 4.5b: Mendelssohn, *Die beiden Neffen* (1823), Overture

Ex. 4.5c: Mendelssohn, *Die beiden Neffen* (1823), Ballet

Sonata. From this material Felix shapes an expressive Andante for winds, linked to the *Allegro vivace* for full orchestra, a bright Weberian movement probably meant to depict the nephews' return from abroad (**ex. 4.5b**). There is also orchestral music for two ballets (finale of Act I and middle of Act II), brimming with infectious folksonglike melodies reminiscent of Weber (**ex. 4.5c**). According to Eduard Devrient, the most successful number was a chorus some friends compared to the bridesmaids' chorus in *Der Freischütz*.[84] A brother-in-law of Varnhagen von Ense, the poet Ludwig Robert, actually offered to prepare a new libretto based on Felix's chorus.[85] But his parents vetoed the proposal and by the time of the premiere, Felix was already contemplating a new opera on an episode from Cervantes's *Don Quixote*.

By 1824 Felix's circle of friends was expanding considerably. From the middle of the year dates the first reference in his letters to Karl Klingemann (1798–1862),[86] who had entered the diplomatic service of the Kingdom of Hanover, newly created after the dismantling of Westphalia, the puppet monarchy over which Napoleon's brother Jérôme had briefly ruled. Dispatched to Paris to assist with the collection of reparations, Klingemann moved in 1818 to the Hanover embassy in Berlin and gained access to the Mendelssohns' circle. Heinrich Dorn found him "unaffectedly aristocratic."[87] According to Klingemann's son, who published his correspondence with Felix,[88] the diplomat's musical abilities exceeded those of the average dilettante. A volume of his Lieder appeared in Berlin in 1826 and a second volume in Leipzig in 1859.[89] He also produced an abundance of lyrical verses that Felix set.[90]

Among Felix's other friends was the Hamburg violinist Leopold Lindenau, who figured increasingly in Felix's musical life after Eduard Rietz injured his left hand while performing Spontini's *Olympia*;[91] the law clerk Wilhelm von Boguslawski, who submitted compositions to Felix's review;[92] and Louis Heydemann, a law student at the university. Then there was the young critic/reformer Hermann Franck (1802–1855), whom Felix probably met in Breslau in 1823. Franck moved in the circles of Alexander von Humboldt, Goethe, and Jean-August-Dominique Ingres, the painter and amateur violinist whom Franck accompanied in Rome. His politics tilted toward the republican Ludwig Börne and Heinrich Heine, whose "admission to European culture"[93] (baptism into the Protestant Church) Franck witnessed in 1825. Among his musical acquaintances were Meyerbeer, Liszt, Chopin, the Schumanns, and Wagner, whose *Tannhäuser*, Franck believed, captured the spirit of the times.[94] Franck appreciated the momentous significance of Felix's 1829 revival of the St. Matthew Passion, and during the 1820s Franck contributed articles to a music journal inaugurated under the polemical editorship of A. B. Marx (1795–1866), destined to have an especially complex relationship with Felix.

This estimable music theorist—Marx later developed a textbook definition of sonata form—had come to Berlin to study law. His first love, though, was music, and he found inspiration in the multifaceted E. T. A. Hoffmann, a judge of the Prussian Supreme Court, notorious for rendering legal opinions while scribbling caricatures of his colleagues. Hoffmann's madcap tales were all the rage in Berlin, and, what counted more for Marx, Hoffmann had won fame as a composer. In an example of homage or narcissism, he had added the name Amadeus ("loved by God") after his celestial model, Mozart, and in 1816 launched the opera *Undine*, based on a romantic fairy tale by de la Motte Fouqué. No less telling for Marx was Hoffmann's music criticism, including his review that plumbed the ineffable content of Beethoven's Fifth Symphony and the innately romantic qualities of instrumental music.[95]

A Hoffmannesque turning point for Marx's career came during a performance of Gluck's opera *Armide*. In the slumber scene of Act 2, when the vengeful Armida plots the sleeping Rinaldo's murder only to fall in love with him, Marx detected parallel fifths.[96] His theater companion refused to concede the faux pas, so the two visited the music shop of A. M. Schlesinger to consult the score. When Marx located the fifths, the publisher offered him the editorship of the new *Berliner allgemeine musikalische Zeitung*. The first issue appeared on January 7, 1824; Marx led the weekly periodical for seven years, until it ceased publication late in 1830. Schlesinger's goal was to establish a house organ to rival the *Allgemeine musikalische Zeitung*, founded in 1798 by the leading Leipzig firm of Breitkopf & Härtel. The young Marx seized the opportunity to promote a new type of music criticism for what he perceived as a new musical age.

In the early issues Marx brought out a serial manifesto, "Concerning the Demands of Our Age on Music Criticism," which described his own time as a third musical era following those of J. S. Bach (characterized by counterpoint) and Mozart (associated with melodic lyricism). Influenced by Hoffmann's vision of musical romanticism and Hegel's idealism, Marx explicated a fundamental "art principle" (*Kunstprinzip*) that undergirded seminal musical compositions.[97] The new age, still in a nascent state, required a radically new type of music, and Marx seized upon Beethoven as a pioneering musical aesthete. Marx was particularly struck by Beethoven's depiction of extramusical ideas through "tone painting" and read the Fifth Symphony as a "sequence of soulful states with deep psychological truth."[98] In contrast, musicians supporting the status quo came in for heavy criticism. Thus, Marx rebuked Zelter for performing irrelevant eighteenth-century repertoire, failing to add "modern" wind instruments to Handel's orchestral scores, choosing improper tempos, and altering composers' scores (e.g., smoothing out expressive leaps in Graun's recitatives).[99] Perturbed, Zelter later vented some anti-Semitic spleen to Goethe.[100]

How Marx met the Mendelssohns is unclear, but he soon became a *habitué* of the Sunday musicales. Fourteen years Felix's senior, Marx "gained an ascendancy over Felix such as no one ever exercised over him"[101]—for some, a particularly baneful effect. Varnhagen von Ense was especially blunt: ". . . he immediately impressed me as unpleasant through his common appearance and coarse manner. He crawled like a cockroach before Felix, uttered obsequious admiration for him. . . [Marx] was so fat and short, so overly plump, so unpleasantly pungent and suffocating. . . . 'Man as bug,' one said of him."[102] According to Devrient, Marx's "intellectual and flowing speech dominated every conversation, his many new and striking ideas, his adroit flattery, so discreetly veiled, made him, for a time, very popular with the family, notwithstanding his awkward manners, his ungainly appearance, short trousers, and clumsy shoes."[103] Initially, Abraham was attracted to the *Abbé*, as Marx was dubbed after his initials, for the "elder Mendelssohn was very fond of contradicting, and of being contradicted."[104] But at some point the repartee lost its charm; because "people of that kind, who talk so cleverly and can do nothing, act perniciously on productive minds,"[105] Abraham was concerned enough to entreat Devrient to break Marx's hold on his son.

In 1869, Marx's widow, Therese, published a spirited rejoinder to Devrient's account.[106] As for Marx, he believed his relationship with Felix was based on unaffected openness, which matured quickly and developed a "strength that may be rare even between brothers."[107] The friendship "grew so close and fast that scarcely a day passed when we did not exchange visits and notes," filled with "certain expressions and references that only we understood, musical passages, and a crazy quilt of fantastic pictures, for Felix drew assiduously."[108] Felix candidly criticized Marx's inept fugal setting of Psalm 137, while Marx found Felix's string symphonies technically proficient but lacking in depth. Marx thus joined Fanny as a musical intimate of Felix, and indeed helped shape some of Felix's instrumental works. Above all, Marx encouraged Felix's engagement with Beethoven, which reached a new level of intensity in 1824.

During the first half of the year the journeyman Felix composed prolifically. Two sacred works bear the stylistic stamp of the eighteenth century. In *Salve regina*, for soprano solo and strings (April 1824),[109] Felix set the Marian antiphon in three parts (ABA), with pellucid, balanced phrases and supple melodic lines reminiscent of Mozart's arias; the inclusion of coloratura cadenzas suggests he conceived the work for a particular soloist, perhaps Anna Milder-Hauptmann. The chorale motet *Jesus, meine Zuversicht*, presumably for the Singakademie, was dispatched quickly in June 1824.[110] Its five movements employ the Crüger chorale in the first three, all *a cappella*, where the cantus firmus appears in the soprano, then the second soprano and tenor. The fourth movement, a bass aria with organ accompaniment, proceeds directly to the finale, a stiff double fugue on "Halleluja" and "Amen." Felix's first extended sacred work to employ a chorale, *Jesus, meine Zuversicht* may reflect his study of the St. Matthew Passion. However, the migrating cantus firmus and bookish double fugue recall his exercises with Zelter.

In contrast are instrumental works exhibiting the influences of Weber and Beethoven. Weber's bubbly virtuoso style surfaces in the Piano Sextet in D major, composed between April 28 and May 10, 1824,[111] and published in 1868 as Op. 110. Stretches of its outer movements contain sprightly runs in the high treble against bass chords (the work's scoring, for piano, violin, two violas, cello, and double bass, may owe a debt as well to Hummel's Piano Septet in D minor, Op. 74, for piano, flute, oboe, horn, viola, cello, and double bass). Several compositions Weber wrote for the clarinetist Heinrich Baermann may have encouraged Felix to compose the Clarinet Sonata in E♭ major, probably completed in April 1824 for the Baron Karl von Kaskel, a Dresden art patron.[112] While the outer movements offer conventional treatments of sonata form, the middle movement invokes folksong in a melody unfolding in three expanding strophes articulated by piano cadenzas. Its G-minor strains recall Osmin's rustic Lied "Wer ein Liebchen hat gefunden" from Mozart's *Entführung aus dem Serail*, but the lilting rhythms also conjure up a siciliano, a dance favored by Weber. Finally, the unpublished, two-piano Fantasia in D minor, a composite work in four connected movements completed during the early hours of March 15,[113] utilizes an explosive subject reminiscent of the Overture to Weber's *Euryanthe* (1823; ex. 4.6a, b).

Beethoven's dramatic style erupts with special force in the music of 1824. Thus, the Capriccio in E♭ minor for piano, written for Felix's friend Louis Heydemann, borrows from the "Moonlight" and "Tempest" Sonatas.[114] The last two movements of the Piano Sextet betray Felix's immersion in Beethoven's Fifth Symphony and its technique of thematic recall. Though labeled *Menuetto*, Felix's third movement (*Agitato*, in $\frac{6}{8}$

Ex. 4.6a: Weber, *Euryanthe* (1823), Overture

Ex. 4.6b: Mendelssohn, Fantasia in D minor for two pianos (1824)

meter) suggests a demonic scherzo. In the finale, the glittery, D-major recapitulation culminates in a massive *fff* passage on the dominant that spills over into a surprise return of the scherzo (in the Fifth Symphony, Beethoven reincarnates his macabre third movement just *before* the recapitulation of the finale). Then, in the stretto-like coda, the original theme of Felix's finale appears, transposed into the minor mode of the *Menuetto* before a brusque ending in the major. About a year later, Felix would revisit this stratagem of interrupting and linking disparate movements in the Octet.

The Viola Sonata in C minor, composed between November 1823 and February 1824 but unpublished until 1966,[115] also evinces a Beethovenian persuasion. The work begins with a pensive first movement ending *pianissimo*, and a *Menuetto* Felix reused in the Symphony No. 1 in C minor, Op. 11. Dwarfing these two movements is the finale, a weighty theme-and-variations set that decidedly shifts the structural balance to the third movement. Felix begins with a classical binary theme articulated in four phrases. Most of the ensuing variations respect the theme's integrity, but in the second half of the sixth and seventh, he deviates from the original melodic course. The extended eighth, in C major, begins as a piano solo, taking us farther afield from the theme with melodic arabesques recalling the free variations in the finale of Beethoven's Piano Sonata, Op. 111. Reduced to a few laconic comments, the viola now outlines only vestigial traces of the theme. A free recitative then ushers in a dramatic coda in C minor.

The most impressive work of 1824 is Symphony No. 1 in C minor, the only composition of the year Felix later published. The autograph bears the title *Sinfonia XIII*,[116] as if he were continuing his string *sinfonie*. But Op. 11 marks a definitive break from the student symphonies: he conceived it for full orchestra and limited the academic display of coun-

terpoint to a brief fugato in the finale. Moreover, the principal influences are no longer J. S. and C. P. E. Bach, Haydn, and Mozart, but the
Beethoven of the Fifth Symphony and Weber of *Der Freischütz*. The C-
minor tonality is one of several links to these two compositions. Others
include the heightened dissonance level of the first movement, the
Weberian élan of the closing theme in the first movement, the transition
from the Trio of the third movement to the *Da capo* of the minuet (scored
to allude to the third movement of the Fifth),[117] and the triumphant,
stretto-like conclusion of the C-major finale that revisits the brightly lit
conclusions of the Fifth and *Der Freischütz*, where a C-major chorus
vanquishes the diabolical C-minor power of Samiel.

IV

For most of 1824 the Mendelssohns remained in Berlin; in July Felix accompanied his father to Bad Doberan, near Rostock and the Baltic,
where Felix swam in the ocean for the first time. Resisting the resort's
leisure, he sketched the thirteenth-century cathedral,[118] read Cicero and
Homer, played the piano at the summer court of the grand duke of
Mecklenburg, worked on *Die Hochzeit des Camacho*, and solved a musical riddle from Zelter. Likening himself to the wise centaur Chiron and
his pupil to Achilles, the gruff Bachian had chosen two countersubjects
from a fugue of the *Well-Tempered Clavier*, hidden them through transpositions into different keys, and then asked Felix to discover the missing subject.[119] The resort's wind band intrigued Felix. Its personnel
included a flute, paired clarinets, oboes, bassoons, French horns, a trumpet, and a bass-horn. The last named, a novelty of English provenance,
prompted Felix to send a description to Berlin. Related to the ancient
serpent, it possessed a "lovely, deep tone" and resembled "a watering can
or a syringe."[120] For this ensemble Felix composed the insouciant *Notturno*
in C major,[121] later revised for a larger wind ensemble as the *Ouvertüre
für Harmoniemusik*, Op. 24 (1839). Bipartite, it joins a softly illuminated
Andante linked to a vivacious sonata-form movement. The principal
theme seemingly recalls Weber's *Preciosa* Overture (premiered in Berlin
in 1821), in which a wind band presents a C-major gypsy march. The
closing bars of Felix's work contain a phrase reused nearly *verbatim* in
the *Midsummer Night's Dream* Overture of 1826.

    According to Eric Werner, an ugly anti-Semitic incident disturbed
the idyllic visit to Bad Doberan:

> . . . both Felix and his beloved sister Fanny were insulted by street urchins,
> who shouted "Jew-boy" and similar epithets and finally threw stones at them.

Felix defended his sister vigorously and staunchly, but seems to have collapsed afterwards. His tutor J. [*recte* C.] L. Heyse writes tersely about the
incident: "Felix behaved like a man, but after he had returned home could
not conceal his fury about the humiliation, which in the evening broke out in
a flood of tears and wild accusations."[122]

Werner gave as his source the unpublished diary of Dr. Heyse, owned by
a great-grandson of Felix, Joachim Wach (1898–1955). The elusive source,
however, is not in the Wach papers, now at the University of Chicago,
leading Jeffrey Sposato to doubt Werner's reliability.[123] Additionally, Heyse
and Fanny were not even present in Doberan but in Berlin, as Felix's letters from the resort make clear. Indeed, Fanny expressed her anxiety over
her brother's departures in two compositions of July 1824. *Das Heimweh*
(*Homesickness*), finished on July 19,[124] projects onto the traveling Felix
an intense longing for home; Felix later revised and published the song
as his Op. 8 No. 2. Fanny also wrote a poignant Piano Sonata in C minor,
inscribed "For Felix, in his absence."[125] This work shows a considerable
advance in her treatment of sonata form and of motivic and thematic
development. The expressive slow movement plays on the theme of separation by alluding to Weber's *Konzertstück*, well known to Fanny and
Felix, which of course portrays a damsel pining for her crusading knight
(**ex. 4.7a, b**).

Returning to Berlin, Felix nurtured his relationship with Fanny by
embarking on his second double piano concerto, composed between
September 5 and November 12. Like its sibling, the A♭ major Concerto
contains reductions of the orchestral tutti for the solo parts, further evidence of the strength of the *col basso* tradition in Berlin during the 1820s.
The autograph reveals another striking link to the eighteenth century.
Here Felix began to alter his clefs (see **plate 7**)—reversing the bass clef
to a "C" clef, and refashioning the treble to produce a "G" clef with a
loop around the fourth space and fifth line, characteristic of J. S. Bach's
autographs—and from 1824 an identifying feature of Felix's autographs.
These notational changes may reflect his Bachian pursuits. Indeed, the
manuscript of a contemporaneous Fugue in G minor (September 11, 1824)

Ex. 4.7a: Weber, *Konzertstück* in F minor (1821), First Movement

Ex. 4.7b: Fanny Mendelssohn, Piano Sonata in C minor (1824), Second Movement

also exhibits the new clefs; in this double fugue, Felix altered the clefs midway, as if to strengthen the Bachian reverberations by emulating the Thomaskantor's calligraphy.[126]

The Double Piano Concerto in A♭ contains little to suggest the cerebral counterpoint of Bach, with the exception of a fugato in the finale, revived in mirror inversion toward the end of the work. For the most part, the concerto celebrates the piano virtuosity of the day. The work's massive proportions (the first movement alone runs to 600 measures) suggest again Beethoven's influence; indeed, the key scheme of the movements—A♭–E–A♭—replicates through transposition the plan of the *Emperor* Concerto (E♭–B–E♭). There are other allusions to Beethoven: in the first movement, the characteristic motive of the Fifth Symphony insistently appears,[127] and in the finale, Felix resorts to a distinctive harmonic relationship (A♭–G♭, or tonic to lowered leading-tone) pioneered by Beethoven in several instrumental works.[128]

Still, Felix's concerto raises suspicions about other models, if for no other reason than its unusual key. The search leads to the Second Piano Concerto in A♭ major of John Field, who, like Ludwig Berger, had followed Muzio Clementi to Russia. Published in 1816, Field's concerto was performed in Berlin by Carol Lithander on February 26, 1823.[129] Stylistic contacts between the two concerti are especially striking in the orchestral openings. Both begin *piano* with two statements of similar first themes, built upon symmetrical eight-bar periods (**ex. 4.8a, b**) and follow a similar course of events in their orchestral *tutti*. Felix expanded Field's *tutti* of 84 bars to 109 by enlarging the transitions, where he introduced the motive from Beethoven's Fifth Symphony, as if to inject a symphonic dimension into the serene, Field-like character of the concerto. But elsewhere, the Irishman's gentle lyricism prevails, as in the nocturne-like slow movement, characterized by infrequent harmonic changes and liquescent arpeggiations.

While Felix was completing his concerto, the arrival on October 31 of Ignaz Moscheles (1794–1870) stimulated Berlin musical life. Raised in

Ex. 4.8a: Field, Piano Concerto No. 2 in A♭ major (1816), First Movement

Ex. 4.8b: Mendelssohn, Double Piano Concerto in A♭ major (1824), First Movement

Prague, the pianist had participated in the Viennese salon of the Baroness Eskeles, Felix's great aunt. Moscheles's principal composition teacher had been Salieri, who, on his deathbed in 1823, implored his former pupil to refute the "malicious" charge of having poisoned Mozart in 1791.[130] Moscheles's idol was Beethoven, under whose supervision he arranged the piano-vocal score of *Fidelio* in 1814. When Moscheles recorded at the end "Finished with God's help," Beethoven, self-reliant but nearly completely deaf, commented, "O man, help yourself."[131] Beethoven also supported Moscheles in 1823, when the Bohemian gave a highly publicized concert, alternating between a Viennese Graf piano and Beethoven's English Broadwood. The Broadwood, seriously damaged from the aging composer's "pitiless thumping," failed to impress the audience, and the Graf won the day with the partisan audience.

As a composer, Moscheles attracted attention during the Congress of Vienna, with some bravura variations for piano and orchestra on a military theme of Tsar Alexander (*La marche d'Alexandre*, Op. 32). But Moscheles expended much of his subsequent compositional energy on technically less demanding rondos, fantasias, and variations, typically fitted with fanciful titles (e.g., *Les charmes de Paris*) and described by his great-great-grandson as "ephemeral music intended for salons or for the newly expanding amateur market."[132] Catapulted into the front ranks of pianists, Moscheles became an itinerant virtuoso, appearing in Paris, London, and throughout Germany, before marrying Charlotte Embden in 1825 and settling in England. In 1824, one of his tours finally led him to Berlin and to the Mendelssohns.

During a six-week stay Moscheles made several appearances, including three concerts (November 11 and 18, and December 6) featuring as many of his concerti and a variety of solo piano works. A reviewer praised the "almost wondrous elasticity" of his playing and his incomparable execution of rapid thirds, octaves, and trills.[133] Zelter ranked his compositions just below those of Hummel but compared the experience of hearing Moscheles to imbibing the intoxicating waters of Lethe, so that one simply forgot the pianist's predecessors.[134] Between performances, Moscheles attended the Mendelssohns' Sunday musicales, dined with the family, and visited the households of Zelter and Joseph Mendelssohn.

According to Elise Polko, who in 1869 penned a sentimental, half-literary account of Felix,[135] Abraham and Lea hosted a dinner party for Moscheles, Hummel, Zelter, Ludwig Berger, Bernhard Klein, and the poet Ludwig Robert, after which the sensitive Felix declined to play before the virtuosi. There is no firm documentation for this scene, which we may safely relegate to Polko's fictive embroidery, although her other claim, that Felix's rendition of Moscheles's Piano Concerto in E♭ from the manuscript brought tears to his eyes, is probably not far from the truth. Moscheles witnessed the Sunday musicale for Fanny's birthday on November 14, at which Felix performed one of his symphonies, Mozart's Piano Concerto in C minor, K. 491, and (presumably with Fanny) the Double Concerto in E major.[136] The following day Moscheles may have attended a public concert of the pianist Carl Arnold, the crown of which, according to A. B. Marx, was a performance of Felix's Symphony No. 1 in C minor (whether he conducted the work is not clear).[137] A few days later, Lea was writing the *prince des pianistes* to request lessons for Felix and Fanny.[138] Initially Moscheles demurred, but filled his diary with notes about their precocity:

> This is a family the like of which I have never known. Felix, a boy of fifteen, is a phenomenon. What are all prodigies as compared with him? Gifted children, but nothing else. This Felix Mendelssohn is already a mature artist, and yet but fifteen years old! ... His elder sister Fanny, also extraordinarily gifted, played by heart, and with admirable precision, Fugues and Passacailles by Bach. I think one may well call her a thorough "Mus. Doc."[139]

On November 22 Lea repeated her request, and that day lessons began, continuing every other day, without Moscheles losing sight he "was sitting next to a master, not a pupil."[140] Moscheles's role was to provide finishing lessons for Felix and reassure the pragmatic parents that Felix's gifts would "lead to a noble and truly great career." Felix showed his newest compositions and probably shared the first movement of the Piano Quartet in B minor, Op. 3, begun only a few weeks before Moscheles's arrival,[141] and the Double Piano Concerto in A♭. On Sunday, November 28 he heard the Piano Quartet Op. 1, *Sinfonia* No. 8 in D major, a Bach concerto, and a piano duet composed by the visiting pianist Carl Arnold. The attending violinist Wilhelm Speyer wrote Spohr that Felix was a "phenomenon such as nature produced only rarely."[142] At the Singakademie Fanny and Felix played music of J. S. Bach, and at Zelter's residence on December 3 an astonished Moscheles heard Fanny read through a Bach concerto from a manuscript. Only two days later, for Privy Councilor Crelle, Felix was leading a performance of Mozart's Requiem, on the anniversary of the composer's death, and supplying the orchestral accompaniment from a piano. At the next Sunday musicale (December 12), Felix and Moscheles performed the latter's duet, *Hommage à Handel*, a sprightly Allegro prefaced by a slow introduction in the style of a French overture. After his own farewell concert in the middle of the month, Moscheles departed. He would return to Berlin in 1826 and again sit next to a "master."

Chapter 5
1825–1826

The Prodigy's Voice

For unto whomsoever much is given,
Of him shall much be required.
—Luke 12:48

On March 9, 1824, the matriarch of the Itzig family, Bella Salomon, died. Examining the will, the bereaved Lea and Abraham made a discovery: Bella's fortune—the residence at Neue Promenade No. 7, the old *Meierei*, and other assets, valued at more than 150,000 thalers—was bequeathed equally to her son Jacob Bartholdy, the children of her granddaughters Josephine Benedicks and Marianne Mendelssohn (wife of Joseph Mendelssohn's son Alexander),[1] and Lea's unborn grandchildren. Unlike Jacob, cursed by Bella upon his baptism in 1805 but reconciled by Fanny's intervention years later, the daughter and son-in-law were thus "completely disinherited" (*völlig enterbt*).[2]

Had Bella discovered Lea's and Abraham's clandestine conversion to Protestantism, or that of their children? We can only speculate about Bella's motivation,[3] but the action was decisive, for the Mendelssohns now could remain in Neue Promenade No. 7 only by purchasing or renting it. Neither option was desirable, and Abraham began the search for a new residence. By the end of 1824, he found it in a dilapidated mansion at Leipzigerstrasse No. 3, just off the Leipzigerplatz.[4]

Part of the Friedrichstadt, Leipzigerstrasse had been developed during the 1730s by the "soldier-king," Frederick William I, who, when not preoccupied with military campaigns, indulged in *Baulust*. In 1735 the monarch had authorized a Lieutenant von der Groeben to build a house at No. 3, described as a "slender towel" (*schmales Handtuch*)—that is, a lot 59 by 380 meters. During the next few decades the property was the

site of a silk mill; James Boswell described one of its owners, J. E. Gotskowsky, as "a gallant German, stupid, comely, cordial," and his wife, a
"stout, good looking Frow."⁵ Through mutual business interests Gotskowsky had dealings with Moses Mendelssohn. When Gotskowsky died
impoverished in 1775, Leipzigerstrasse No. 3 was sold for 14,000 thalers.
The new owner, Baron K. F. L. von der Reck, was a minor nobleman whose
titles included *"maitre des plaisirs"* and *"directeur des spectacles"*—that
is, he directed royal entertainments and the opera houses. During the
French occupation, he relinquished his silverware to help satiate
Napoleon's demands following the Peace of Tilsit, and after the decisive
Battle of Leipzig his gardens were the scene of a joyous festivity celebrating the victory of Blücher's Prussian army (around this time the octago-
nal baroque square near the house was renamed Leipzigerplatz). By then
the estate had begun to fall, according to Lea, into "that state of decay
and neglect that will always arise from there being many owners,"⁶ and
on February 18, 1825, Reck's son-in-law, Major von Podewils, deeded it
to Abraham for 56,000 thalers.

By the time of the Restoration, the stretch of Leipzigerstrasse between
Leipzigerplatz and Wilhelmstrasse was still a relatively quiet, if fashionable residential area. As a young man Felix wagered he could stroll down
the street with a rosary on his head and did so without encountering
anyone.⁷ On the north side were sixteen houses but on the south, only
six, more spacious properties, including No. 3. No. 2 was owned by the
Prussian emissary to Constantinople; and No. 4 was the site of the royal
porcelain factory, established by Gotskowsky during the reign of Frederick
the Great. The two-story residence of No. 3, the breadth of which accommodated nineteen windows (**plate 8**), faced the street. One interior
room on the ground level opened "by means of three arches into an
adjoining apartment," and became Lea's spacious sitting room, the site
of family entertainments. Behind the principal structure, on either side,
were symmetrical wings (Felix's room was in the left wing, on a mezza-
nine level⁸), with a carriage house and stables. At the back of the mansion an elegant Gartenhaus adjoined the wings, so that the entire
rectangular configuration enclosed an interior courtyard of half an acre.
The south side of the Gartenhaus looked out onto a park of about seven
acres that bordered the lush gardens of Prince Albrecht.

The Mendelssohns moved to Leipzigerstrasse around the middle of
1825; on July 11, Felix was still able to record a view from his old room in
Neue Promenade No. 7.⁹ Because renovations were necessary, they initially lived in the Gartenhaus and delayed occupying the main residence
until mid-December. Encompassing sixteen rooms and three kitchens,
the Gartenhaus was arranged around a commodious Gartensaal, 14 by

7.5 meters, with a height of about eight meters and thus "too large to be called a drawing-room." Sebastian Hensel informs us that the ceiling, "covered with fantastic fresco-paintings," had a shallow cupola, and that the room could accommodate several hundred during Sunday musicales. Here he may have exaggerated, unless we consider an unusual architectural feature: the south side, terraced to command a view of the gardens, had movable glass panels, separated by Doric columns, "so that the hall could be transformed into an open portico."[10] The Gartenhaus afforded Felix a private, romantic space where his genius fully blossomed and where, some one hundred yards from Leipzigerstrasse, he discovered the "deepest loneliness of a forest."[11]

To realize a return on their investment, Abraham and Lea considered adding to the mansion a third floor to rent out; to that end, the young architect C. T. Ottmer drew up plans to convert the baroque facade into a classical design.[12] Because of prohibitive costs they abandoned the plan, though they did rent eleven rooms on the second floor (*Beletage*) to the Hanoverian emissary, Baron von Reden, annually for 2000 thalers. In 1826 Abraham and Lea welcomed as a new tenant Karl Klingemann, then an "extraordinary clerk" of the legation. Other residents later included Eduard and Therese Devrient (from 1829 to 1830); the mathematician Peter Gustav Lejeune Dirichlet (from 1832 to 1845), who married Felix's sister Rebecka in 1832; and the classicist August Böckh (from 1840 to 1846). When Wilhelm Hensel married Fanny in 1829, the newlyweds moved into rooms adjacent to the Gartensaal; in 1830, Abraham added northern windows to refine the lighting of the artist's *atelier*.

Leipzigerstrasse No. 3 came to symbolize the comfortable existence of the Mendelssohns, a point stressed by Sebastian Hensel, who spared little effort to depict his relatives as successfully assimilated, upstanding Prussian citizens of the Vormärz. Somewhat smugly, Lea reported to Henriette von Pereira Arnstein that the residence was only one of three private Berlin estates with a park not already purchased by the king.[13] Here Abraham, Lea, and Fanny lived until their deaths, and Felix's widow, Cécile, and their children resided there from 1848 until June 1851, when the only other family member on the estate was the widower Wilhelm Hensel. That year Paul Mendelssohn Bartholdy sold the property for 100,000 thalers to the state, which converted it into the Upper House (*Herrenhaus*) of the new Prussian Parliament, formed after the revolutionary tremors of March 1848. The main residence became assembly rooms; the Gartenhaus was demolished for additional space. For decades, Leipzigerstrasse No. 3 retained its political function before its razing in 1898, when its memories of the Mendelssohns, of music, painting, culture, and of politics, were lost.

I

For Felix, 1825 began auspiciously enough. On January 18, he put the finishing touches on the Piano Quartet in B minor, published later that year as Op. 3, and on February 12 began the Overture to *Die Hochzeit des Camacho*, having finished the first act of the opera in December 1824. But a family obligation interrupted progress on the second act begun in March; Felix accompanied his father to Paris to escort back to Berlin the recently pensioned Henriette Mendelssohn. En route the two spent a weekend in Weimar,[14] where they found Goethe laboring over the second part of *Faust*. One member of Goethe's circle now judged Felix's improvisations more soulful than the virtuoso displays of his earlier visits.[15] For his efforts, Felix received a medallion of the poet by the Frenchman Antoine Bovy.

Proceeding through Frankfurt, father and son reached Paris on March 22, after Felix had raised a sensitive issue, as Abraham later recalled in 1829:

> On our journey to Paris after that neck-breaking night, you asked me the reasons why our name was changed. . . . A Christian Mendelssohn is an impossibility. A Christian Mendelssohn the world would never recognize. Nor should there be a Christian Mendelssohn; for my father himself did not want to be a Christian. "Mendelssohn" does and always will stand for a Judaism in transition, when Judaism, just because it is seeking to transmute itself spiritually, clings to its ancient form all the more stubbornly and tenaciously, by way of protest against the novel form that so arrogantly and tyrannically declared itself to be the one and only path to the good.[16]

Because a Christian Mendelssohn was no more plausible than a Jewish Confucius, Abraham, upon arriving in Paris, had calling cards engraved "Felix M. Bartholdy," for his son "was about to step into the world and make a name for [himself]." But curiously enough, the Piano Quartet Op. 1 had already appeared in 1823 as the work of Felix Mendelssohn Bartholdy, setting a precedent the composer observed for the rest of his career.[17] Did Abraham allow the use of both surnames for his son's compositional debut, or did Schlesinger attempt to increase sales by linking Felix to his illustrious grandfather?

Felix's choice of profession weighed no less heavily than his religious identity on Abraham. Jacob Bartholdy, for one, was not convinced that Felix should pursue music. "In the beginning you are just as far as at the end," Jacob opined, and he recommended a career in law or banking, with music remaining his "friend and companion."[18] Happily, Abraham did not follow his brother-in-law's advice, and instead made use of the Parisian sojourn to seek counsel about Felix's prospects.

Through a new residential section, the faubourg St. Lazare, Abraham and Felix entered a metropolis of nearly 800,000 at the height of the Restoration. They found the *haute bourgeoisie* enjoying *la grande cuisine* and strolling in arcades lined with opulent shops. Portions of the city, including the Opéra and arcades, "as loud and bright" as "a great celebration in Berlin,"[19] were illuminated by coal gas, by which one could read comfortably at night. After Napoleon's fall, Louis XVIII had pursued a middle-of-the-road policy, keeping in check the liberals and ultra-royalists. In 1820 a fanatic assassinated the king's nephew on the steps of the Opéra, and when Louis XVIII died in December 1824, his brother acceded to the throne as Charles X and began pursuing regressive policies. He resuscitated the ancient right of divine rule, strengthened ties to the Catholic Church, and sought to compensate the nobility for losses during the Revolution. During the Mendelssohns' visit (March 22 to May 13), preparations were underway for Charles' coronation, which took place at Rheims on May 29. At the cathedral the new king was solemnly anointed with holy oil—miraculously preserved from the ravages of war—that for centuries had ordained dozens of previous monarchs.

For the event, the Italian Luigi Cherubini (1760–1842) crafted a resplendent Mass. Twenty-five years before, Abraham had admired him as a composer of dramatic rescue operas such as *Lodoïska* (1791), which captured the revolutionary fervor of the time by ending with the destruction of a palace. Cherubini himself had survived harrowing adventures during the Revolution; his music never fully found favor with Napoleon, who preferred the tuneful fare of Paisiello. But Cherubini was highly regarded in musical circles: Haydn had given him the autograph of his *Drum-Roll* Symphony, and Beethoven admired a musical clock that performed two favorite operatic excerpts, a trio from *Fidelio* and the Overture to Cherubini's *Médée*. Around 1807 Cherubini withdrew from composition to take up painting and botany. When his inspiration returned in 1808, he abandoned opera for Catholic polyphony. His most ambitious work, the Mass in D minor (1811), may still stand as the longest Mass ever composed: its sesquipedalian girth extends to 2,563 measures, surpassing Beethoven's *Missa solemnis* by more than 600. The abrupt stylistic shift in Cherubini's music served him well: he became musical arbiter of the Restoration and embraced conservative Bourbon values. As *surintendant de la musique du roi*, he composed motets, a Requiem to commemorate the execution of Louis XVI, and coronation Masses for Louis XVIII and Charles X. At the height of his fame, Cherubini was installed as director of the Conservatoire, where he produced students who scored successes at the Opéra, including Auber, Halévy, and Boieldieu.

In the view of Edward Bellasis, Cherubini was a musical genius who "restrained mediocrity" at the Conservatoire.[20] For some, however, his eccentric habits bordered on pedantry. Probably with some apprehension, Abraham submitted Felix to the Italian's judgment. The two met at the firm of the piano manufacturer Sébastien Erard, and later at a musical soirée on March 31, when Felix joined the orchestra as a violinist to perform Mozart's Requiem.[21] Against all expectations, Cherubini was on his best behavior; his prickly demeanor, attributed by Felix to his status as a henpecked husband, softened, and Felix was allowed to hear one of Cherubini's Masses in the *Chapelle royale*. Then, on April 4, Felix presented his Piano Quartet in B minor, Op. 3. The performance was marred by an auditor who comforted herself with a noisy, tinsel-adorned fan; still, the usually taciturn Cherubini dumbfounded his colleagues with the prolix assessment, *Ce garçon est riche, il fera bien; il fait même déjà bien; mais il dépense trop de son argent, il met trop d'étoffe dans son habit. ... Je lui parlerai alors il fera bien!* ("This lad is rich; he will do well. He already has done well, but he spends too much of his money, and he puts too much fabric into his clothes ... I shall speak to him—he will do well").[22] The "extinct volcano," as Felix likened him, could still spew some cinders.

At Abraham's request, Cherubini devised a special challenge for Felix: to compose a Kyrie for five-part chorus and orchestra. Undaunted, he dispatched the task in a few days and dated the score on May 6. According to Zelter, Felix cast the work in Cherubini's style, either to emulate or surpass the elder musician.[23] Cherubini was so impressed that he offered to accept Felix as a student and advised Abraham to leave his son in Paris to complete his musical education.[24] Abraham declined and departed for Berlin with Felix and Henriette around the middle of May. Henriette found a "refined, cultivated young man" in place of the "wild lad" she had known ten years before.[25]

The composition that won Cherubini's praise, the Kyrie in D minor, remains among Felix's least known choral works.[26] The thickened, five-part choral textures and orchestra augmented by three trombones imbue the score with solemn, dark hues. Several stylistic idiosyncrasies reveal that Felix was familiar with Cherubini's magisterial Mass in the same key (1811). Among them is the final cadence with raised third, supported by somber invocations of the subdominant G minor, and especially telling is a fugato modeled on the artful fugue from Cherubini's Kyrie (ex. 5.1a, b). Like Cherubini, Felix treats the subject in mirror inversion and combines the two forms in an impressive contrapuntal exhibition.

As if to link Cherubini's Mass to an older, eighteenth-century tradition, Felix's Kyrie invokes a second sacred work, Mozart's Requiem. The inversion of Cherubini's fugal subject simulates the bassoon solo that

Ex. 5.1a: Cherubini, Mass in D minor (1811), Kyrie

Ky - - - rie e - le - - - i - son, e - le - i - son,

Ex. 5.1b: Mendelssohn, Kyrie in D minor (1825)

opens Mozart's Requiem (ex. 5.2a, b); not surprisingly, Felix begins his Kyrie by incorporating in the second bassoon the first few notes of Mozart's bassoon part. There are other Mozartean features, including exchanges between major and minor harmonies, and intensely chromatic part writing. All in all, the Kyrie is a richly expressive work that affords a rewarding glimpse at how Felix might have approached setting the Ordinary of the Catholic Mass.

Felix gave no public performances in Paris but participated in the private salons of high society, where he introduced his piano quartets,[27] including the newly completed Piano Quartet in B minor, Op. 3. Supporting him were Pierre Baillot's colleagues, of whom the most peculiar was the violist Chrétien Urhan, a spiritual ascetic who demurred from ogling ballet dancers from his chair in the orchestra of the Opéra, observed a regimen of radishes and bread to banish evil thoughts, and experimented with scordatura retunings of his instrument.[28] At the time few Parisians were producing worthy chamber music, although an exception was Georges Onslow (1784–1853), who wrote dozens of string quartets and quintets in the tradition of Viennese classicism. From an aristocratic English family tainted by scandal,[29] Onslow resided in a

Ex. 5.2a: Mozart, Requiem, K. 626 (1791), *Introit*

Ex. 5.2b: Mendelssohn, Kyrie in D minor (1825)

château in Auvergne and wintered in Paris, where he introduced his new works. Felix found Onslow's String Quartet in E minor reasonably attractive—*on a galoppé un quatuor*, Onslow mused after a performance—but was shocked at the musician's ignorance of Beethoven's *Fidelio*, modeled on the genre of the French rescue opera.

When not attending soirées and public concerts or translating Tacitus with Halévy's brother, Felix sent penetrating reports about French musical taste to Berlin. Like a magnet, Paris attracted illustrious musicians, native and foreign. Of pianists, Felix numbered among Moscheles, Kalkbrenner, Pixis, the Herz brothers, fourteen-year-old Franz Liszt, and Hummel, who concertized at the piano firm of the *frères Erard*. Among the French musicians were the violinists Baillot, Lafont, Rodolphe Kreutzer, Boucher, and Pierre Rode, who had grown old but still "spat fire." At the Conservatoire Cherubini was joined by the composer-theorist Anton Reicha, author of an early definition of sonata form and creator of unorthodox fugues, and at the musical salons one encountered the pianists and piano manufacturers Ignaz and Camille Pleyel, the composer Lesueur, conductor Habeneck, and the widely traveled composer Sigismund Neukomm, who had returned from Brazil to enjoy the patronage of the Duke of Orléans, the future King Louis-Philippe. In 1825, opera remained the dominant musical form in the French capitol, despite thriving public concert series, including the *Concert spirituel* and *Concert de la Loge Olympique*, founded in the eighteenth century, effaced by the Revolution, and then reinvented in time for the Restoration. At the Théâtre-Italien, Parisians were gripped by a Rossini *manie*, while at the Opéra, the French operas of Cherubini and his pupils ruled the stage.

Felix's letters teem with unflattering vignettes of Parisian musical life. He found a *Stabat mater* hackneyed and proposed to rename its composer, Neukomm ("newcomer"), Altkomm ("old-timer"). The eccentric Anton Reicha, professor of counterpoint at the Conservatoire, was feared "as the wild huntsman (he hunts parallel fifths)." Felix directed his most scathing criticism at Camille Pleyel, who took unconscionable liberties with Mozart: "He made two cadenzas longer than the entire concerto, and decorated the entire piece with coquettish affectations, at best appropriate for Rossini; now he played above, now below, here a trill, there a run, here a double appoggiatura, there a suspended ninth, in short, a concerto by Mozart revised and corrected by C. Pleyel."[30]

Even Gioachino Rossini, the new director of the Théâtre-Italien, fared no better. If Stendhal found in Rossini a "smile of pleasure at every bar" that banished all "those grave, half conscious musings" of Mozart,[31] Felix dubbed Rossini the "Great Maestro Windbag," a "mixture of roguishness, superficiality, and ennui, with long sideburns, wide as a church

door, elegantly dressed, surrounded by all the ladies." At a soirée of the
Countess of Rumford, Rossini introduced into the piano accompaniment of Mozart's *Ave verum* all manner of dissonant suspensions, "for
the benefit and enlightenment of all his listeners, or rather non-listen-
ers," so that his audience was obliged to call out *charmant* and *délicieux*—
thus one savored "the joys of music" in Paris.[32] And finally, the young
Liszt's glittery improvisations were "wretched," inflated with vapid scales;
Franzi possessed many fingers but meager mental faculties (*er hat viel
Finger, aber wenig Kopf*).[33]

Felix found the private salons and public concerts *ennuyant*. The
endless *potpourris* and *romances* were superficial; the esteemed soprano
Giuditta Pasta, far from conjuring up Stendhal's "visions of celestial
beauty,"[34] sang Rossini out of tune; the orchestra of the Théâtre-Italien
had mediocre winds, and that of the Opéra was only good. Conspicuously absent in Paris was Beethoven's music. Since the late eighteenth
century, French *mélomanes* had embraced Haydn's symphonies as de
rigueur in orchestral concerts; only owing to François-Antoine Habeneck,
conductor of the Opéra, did audiences gradually become familiar with
Beethoven's symphonies. In 1825 Felix attended a performance of a
"nouvelle Sinfonie de Beethoven," but the novelty was only the Second
Symphony (premiered in Vienna in 1803); not until the closing years of
the decade did Habeneck venture beyond the *Eroica*, and not until 1831
did he attempt the Ninth Symphony. Felix was unconvinced by the
conducting of Habeneck, who led the ensemble with a violin bow, clutch-
ing his instrument in the other hand and reading the music from a violin part instead of the full score.[35]

For Felix this state of affairs paled in comparison to French opera.
At the Théâtre Feydeau, specializing in *opéras-comiques*, the orchestra
and spacious hall did impress him. Nevertheless, Auber's *Léocadie*, based
upon Cervantes' novella *La fuerta del sangre*, inspired a withering rebuke. The opera alternated between feeble reminiscences of Cherubini
and Rossini, all presented with a monochromatic orchestration:

> Fancy that among the numerous music-pieces of the opera there are perhaps
> three in which the piccolo does not play the principal part! The overture
> begins with a tremulando on the stringed instruments, and then the piccolo
> instantly begins on the roof and the bassoon in the cellar, and blow away at a
> melody; in the theme of the allegro the stringed instruments play the Span-
> ish accompaniment, and the flute again drawls out a melody. Léocadie's first
> melancholy air, "Pauvre Léocadie, il vaudrait mieux mourir," is again appro-
> priately accompanied by the piccolo. This little instrument serves to illus-
> trate the fury of the brother, the pain of the lover, the joy of the peasant girl;
> in short, the whole opera might be transcribed for two flutes and a Jew's harp
> *ad libitum*.[36]

Léocadie probably caught Felix's attention because just then he was engrossed with his own Cervantes opera, *Die Hochzeit des Camacho,* based on an episode from *Don Quixote.*

Felix endured as well a performance at the Théâtre de l'Odéon of *Robin des bois,* an unauthorized version of Weber's *Der Freischütz* perpetrated by that "species of theatrical tomb-robber,"[37] F. H. J. Blaze. Known as Castil-Blaze, this impresario-composer-arranger concocted garbled French versions of Mozart, Weber, and Rossini, a lucrative enough venture, though the results scarcely resembled their models. Thus, the locale of *Der Freischütz* shifted to Yorkshire during the time of Robin Hood; the Wolf Glen to the ruins of St. Dunstan's, somehow losing in the process four of Samiel's seven magic bullets. Among other *castilblazades,* as these mutilations were dubbed, were the insertion of a duet from Weber's *Euryanthe* and the doubling of flutes an octave above Agathe's devout aria, "Leise, leise, fromme Weise," an offense scarcely less serious than Auber's perennial piccolos: "What a miserable, vile, infamous, lousy, boring quodlibet, in all my life I have never dreamed of such a scandal."[38]

Felix's Parisian experiences exacerbated his sense of the divide between German and French musical life, and reinforced his identity as a German musician. His unrelenting criticism—Fanny faulted his silence about nonmusical experiences—anticipated the views of Robert Schumann, who about a decade later seized upon Meyerbeer's grand opera *Les Huguenots* and Felix's oratorio *St. Paul* as representing a widening schism in European music, the one leading to the base and crass, the other to the sublime and noble. Try as Felix might (and admittedly he spent little effort), in 1825 he could not reconcile French tastes with his German upbringing: to the French, J. S. Bach was a wig stuffed with learning;[39] the Parisians were largely ignorant of Beethoven's music; and Weber's nobly Teutonic operas were corrupted by all manner of vulgar licenses. And so, as Felix left France, he concurred with Pierre Rode's terse estimation of Paris as the *locus* of musical decadence (*"C'est ici une dégringolade musicale"*).[40]

II

During the return trip, the Mendelssohns paused in Frankfurt, where Schelble was rehearsing Handel's *Judas Maccabaeus.* Felix extracted themes from the oratorio and dexterously wove them into an improvisation, "thoroughly Handelian" yet with "no pretension to display."[41] When Felix visited the publisher André in neighboring Offenbach, Ferdinand Hiller was struck by the "precocious positiveness" of Felix's speech and manners. A confirmed Mozartean, André dared criticize Beethoven's Seventh Symphony. Felix's response was to render the symphony at the keyboard so powerfully that André ceased his carping—not the last occasion when Felix found music more precise than the ambiguities of words.

In Weimar Felix astonished everyone on May 20 with the Piano Quartet in B minor. Lea had already requested permission to dedicate the work to Goethe[42] and sent an exemplar of the newly published composition from Berlin. Ironically enough, the same day the copy arrived (June 16), Goethe also received from Vienna three of his settings by Schubert. The poet promptly sent what Zelter termed a "love letter" to Felix, praising the quartet as the "graceful embodiment of that beautiful, rich, energetic soul which so astonished me when you first made me acquainted with it."[43] But he posted no acknowledgment to Vienna.

The B-minor Piano Quartet heralds Felix's mature style; indeed, the leap from the Quartet to the high plateau of the Octet, finished in October, is not great. The Quartet impresses with its Beethovenian length, compelling themes, and formal novelties. In the first movement, Felix eschews the classical repeat of the exposition (observed in Opp. 1 and 2) and instead dramatically expands its closing section. The development exploits an unusual conceit: the tempo abruptly shifts to *Più Allegro*, and a fresh thematic gesture, nervously rising in the piano, appears like a digression within the sonata form. After the reprise, the new subject returns in an elongated coda, with tonal meanderings reminiscent of the development. Felix thus reconfigures ternary sonata form into a four-part Beethovenian scheme, with the exposition balanced by the recapitulation; the development, by the coda.

The other endpoint of the Quartet is a massive finale of nearly five hundred measures, an amalgam of sonata and rondo forms animated by string tremolos and brilliant piano writing. Here again, Felix rejuvenates the development to form a culminating coda. In marked contrast are the lyrical, monothematic Andante in E major and gossamer-like third movement in F♯ minor, originally labeled Intermezzo, a prototype of the mature Mendelssohnian scherzo. The diminutive piano arabesques impress as a dizzying *Spinnerlied*, though examination reveals their origins figure in the turning motive with which the first movement commences (**ex. 5.3a, b**). Not by accident Felix recalls this *Ur-motif* in the closing bars of the finale four times in the strings, reinforcing the thematic unity of the entire composition.

Safely returned to Berlin, Felix resumed work on *Die Hochzeit des Camacho* and in August put the final touches on the opera. With the scherzo of Op. 3 still in his ears, he finished on July 23 a virtuoso piano

Ex. 5.3a: Mendelssohn, Piano Quartet No. 3 in B minor, Op. 3 (1825), Scherzo

Ex. 5.3b: Mendelssohn, Piano Quartet No. 3 in B minor, Op. 3 (1825), First Movement

piece, the Capriccio Op. 5 in F♯ minor. Here he again explored those light, filigree textures for which he became celebrated, with whimsical leaps (the composition reminded Rossini of Domenico Scarlatti's zesty sonatas[44]) and a measure of counterpoint in the middle section, where Felix treated a fresh subject in mirror inversion. During this period he found companionship in two new friends. At Easter the young theologian Julius Schubring (1806–1889) arrived to study with Schleiermacher at the university and through Wilhelm Müller gained entrance to the Mendelssohn household, where he received far more than he could offer "so brilliant an intellectual circle."[45] In June Felix met *ein recht guter Baßsänger*[46] ("a pretty good bass singer") from Cassel, Franz Hauser (1794–1870). A kindred Bach enthusiast, Hauser sang an aria from the B-minor Mass for Zelter[47] and copied Lieder by Fanny and Felix, including Felix's still unpublished setting of sentimental verses by Friederike Robert, "Mitleidsworte, Trostesgründe" (June 7, 1825).[48] Hauser was conceivably the beneficiary of another unpublished composition, an aria for baritone and piano completed on September 5.[49] Felix's first setting of an Italian text, *Ch'io t'abbandono* draws its heroic if maudlin verses from Metastasio's *Achille in Sciro*, a popular eighteenth-century libretto but already outmoded by 1825. (In a fanciful reworking of Greek mythology, Achilles' mother secretes her son on the island of Scyros, where he dons female attire to avoid military service. But Ulysses craftily uncovers the disguise, and the two depart for Troy.) Felix cobbled together verses of the young hero from two different parts of the libretto and set them as a continuous scene falling into an introductory recitative, a slow aria (see **ex. 5.4**), and concluding Allegro, a formula familiar in nineteenth-century Italian opera, which often paired an arialike cavatina with a concluding, energetic cabaletta. Felix's score contains imaginative harmonic twists and calls out for orchestration. But there is no evidence he pursued the project further; it fell onto the refuse pile of his lifelong quest for a suitable opera libretto.

Ex. 5.4: Mendelssohn, *Chi'io t'abbandono* (1825)

In October the Mendelssohns entertained Sir George Smart (1776–1867), who recorded some impressions of Felix and Fanny. Smart was a founding member of the Philharmonic Society and served as organist of the Chapel Royal. He directed the English premiere of Beethoven's Ninth Symphony in March 1825 and later that year consulted the composer about the proper tempi. Returning from Vienna, Smart visited Weber in Dresden to discuss the forthcoming London premiere of *Oberon*[50] and then proceeded to Berlin, where he arrived on October 11.

A punctilious man, Smart habitually measured the pitch and tempi of musical ensembles he encountered in his travels. During two weeks in Berlin, he attended a Singakademie concert, conversed in English with Lea at her new residence, and toured the adjacent royal porcelain factory, where he examined a dinner service for the Duke of Wellington. He played Mozart duets with Felix and Fanny and heard several of Felix's compositions, including the Kyrie for Cherubini, a "quite modern and good" piano quartet, and "clever" piano works "rather in the old school,"[51] performed on an English Broadwood grand Abraham had purchased in Paris. Finally, Felix played organ works of J. S. Bach, apparently on a small chamber instrument, while Fanny executed the pedal part on the piano.

Curiously, Smart failed to mention one "clever" composition completed on October 15, 1825—the Octet, Op. 20, which catapulted Felix into the Western canon of "great" composers. The prodigy's sixteen-year-old creative voice now reached full maturity in an irrepressibly masterful, ebullient composition. No work of Mozart from a comparable age matches the consummate skill of the Octet; indeed, the search for models is largely a frustrating one. Still, some have occasionally assumed the Octet was inspired by Louis Spohr's Double Quartet in D minor, Op. 65 (1823), the first of four chamber works exploring question-and-answer effects between two string quartets. (The bipartite division of an ensemble also motivated Spohr to score his Seventh Symphony for two orchestras representing the earthly and divine attributes of human life.) Drawing upon his experience with polychoral music, Spohr observed that the two quartets were like two choirs, now singing in alternation, now together.[52] But Spohr carefully distinguished his experiments from Felix's Octet, in which "the two quartets do not concert and alternate in double choral style, but in which all eight instruments collaborate."[53] Actually, the Octet does contain examples of antiphonal effects, as in bars 21ff. of the first movement and the opening of the slow movement, where the ensemble divides according to register, with the four lower strings answered by the four violins. But Spohr's ideal of *Doppelchörigkeit* was not the primary motivation for Felix's composition, which exploits the rich textural resources of the ensemble, ranging from minimalist unison passages (first movement, bars 211ff., and conclusion of the scherzo) to resplendent eight-part counterpoint (the fugal opening of the finale) and encompassing a multitude of instrumental divisions and subdivisions as well.

The Octet exhibits a tensile, symphonic strength; when it appeared in 1832, Felix appended a note insisting it "be played by all the instruments in the style of a symphony." If we judge by the finale, with its dramatic infusion of fugal elements into a sonata-rondo design, Felix must have had in mind the crowning conclusion of Mozart's *Jupiter* Symphony, the inspiration for the intricate fugal finale of the eighth string *sinfonia* in 1822. Yet another symphonic influence was Beethoven, manifest in the Octet's striving for monumentality, the broad proportions of its outer movements, and also the recall of the scherzo in the finale, again revealing Felix's debt to Beethoven's Fifth Symphony.

Despite the Octet's magnitude, there is vexingly scant documentation about its conception. But Fanny provided a vital clue; in the scherzo, her brother

set to music the stanza from the Walpurgis-night Dream in "Faust" [Part 1]:—
"The flight of the clouds and the veil of mist / Are lighted from above. / A breeze in the leaves, a wind in the reeds, / And all has vanished." ... To me alone he told this idea: the whole piece is to be played staccato and pianissimo, the

tremulandos coming in now and then, the trills passing away with the quickness of lightning; everything new and strange, and at the same time most insinuating and pleasing, one feels so near the world of spirits, carried away in the air, half inclined to snatch up a broomstick and follow the aerial procession. At the end the first violin takes a flight with a feather-like lightness, and—all has vanished.[54]

The "Walpurgis Night's Dream, or the Golden Wedding of Oberon and Titania," is an intermezzo-like dream sequence in which an amateur cast performs on the Brocken in the Harz Mountains a masquerade in doggerel. Here Goethe offers a satire about the cultural values of his time and caricatures dilettantes and snobs, critics, philosophers, and the religious orthodox. The phantasmagoric train of players includes mythical figures, an idealist, dogmatist, realist, supernaturalist, and members of the witches' Sabbath, all supervised by Puck and Ariel, who have come to celebrate the reconciliation of Oberon and Titania, king and queen of the elves. Providing the music for the entertainment is a Kapellmeister and miniscule orchestra of flies, mosquitoes, frogs, and crickets, and a bagpipe blowing soap bubbles. At dawn, the parade is over, and all vanish, captured by the feathery flight of the first violin at the end of Felix's scherzo (**ex. 5.5a**).

Though Fanny specified the closing quatrain of the scene, little imagination is needed to read Felix's scherzo as a fanciful representation of the orchestral backdrop to the dream sequence, through which Goethe interspersed references to the Kapellmeister, his musicians, and the magi-

Ex. 5.5a: Mendelssohn, Octet, Op. 20 (1825), Scherzo

Ex. 5.5b: Mendelssohn, Octet, Op. 20 (1825), Scherzo

Ex. 5.5c: Mendelssohn, Octet, Op. 20 (1825), Scherzo

cal bagpipe, powerful enough to mesmerize animals, like Orpheus's lyre. Felix's finely nuanced, delicate string writing thus suggests the orchestral personnel, with leaping figures at the opening for the crickets and frogs, buzzing trills for the flies (**ex. 5.5b**), and brisk *spiccati* for the stinging mosquitoes. Even the drone of the Dudelsack is present, with open fifths and octaves against a scurrying figure in the violas (**ex. 5.5c**). The whole fits into a miniature sonata form as the ensemble evolves through a kaleidoscope of textures, beginning with a string quartet and attaining imitative writing in seven parts in the development (a charming foretaste of the eight-part fugato in the finale), before dissolving into the ethereal unison conclusion.

The extramusical stimulus for the scherzo raises the intriguing possibility that the other movements of the Octet are related to *Faust* as well. How are we to understand, for example, the propulsive opening theme of the first movement, which emerges in the first violin from quivering tremulos and ascends nearly three octaves (**ex. 5.6a**)? As we know, Felix composed the Octet for Eduard Rietz, whose birthday fell on October 17. Clearly the florid first violin part was intended for Rietz, but did Felix also have in mind a certain Faustian quality, evidenced by the soaring, grandiose lines and exploitation of the instrument's full register? (According to Heinrich Dorn, "when the two friends were together, the idea was always suggested to me of Faust and Mephistopheles, though there was certainly little enough of the diabolic in either of them.")[55] There is, too, the protracted length of the first movement, originally notated with rhythmic values twice as long as those of the printed version, yielding initially a movement exceeding six hundred measures.[56]

The exuberant Allegro contrasts with the subdued Andante, which establishes at the outset a severe tonal dichotomy between the somber C minor of the lower strings and serene D♭ major of the violins. This half-step relation imbues the music with an archaic quality, as if Felix intended to invoke the ancient Phrygian church mode. There are other

Ex. 5.6a: Mendelssohn, Octet, Op. 20 (1825), First Movement

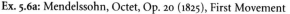

Ex. 5.6b: Mendelssohn, Octet, Op. 20 (1825), Scherzo

clues as well, such as the prominent descending chromatic tetrachords, a traditional symbol of a lament (ex. 5.6b), and the surprise ending in C major, with the raised third (*tierce de Picardie*). The movement is stylistically at odds with the tonal grandiosity and modernity of the first movement. The order of movements suggests the Andante refers to the cathedral scene before the Walpurgisnight (before Faust's capricious ride up the Brocken, Gretchen attends a service where, wracked by guilt and persecuted by the chanting of the *Dies irae*, she faints).

The brilliant finale completes the Faustian analogy by introducing the fugue as a topic of struggle, by reviving the music of the scherzo in a dramatic, now (contrary to Dorn's opinion) diabolical vein, and by ultimately resolving the contrapuntal and tonal dissonance. In 1825 Felix would have known only the first part of *Faust*, so the fugal struggle would be for Gretchen's soul, in the concluding scene, where, visited in the dungeon by Faust and Mephistopheles, she rebuffs their attempts to free her, commits her soul to the Lord while she awaits execution, and receives heavenly redemption. Over four-hundred measures in length, the movement employs three thematic elements, from which Felix constructs an imposing sonata-rondo edifice (ABACABA, **diagram 5.1**). The first is the energetic fugal subject of the opening (*a*). The second, initially presented in a fortissimo unison passage (mm. 33ff), serves as the second theme in the dominant (*b*). The third, anticipated as early as mm. 25ff (*c*), emerges fully in the development-like C section, where it appears as a nearly literal quotation of "And He shall reign for ever and ever" from the "Hallelujah" Chorus of Handel's *Messiah*. All three undergo contrapuntal manipulations, reaching a critical stage in C, where the music of the scherzo briefly intrudes as a fourth subject (*d*), before being symbolically vanquished by the Handelian figure, triumphantly reintroduced over a massive pedal point.

To interpret the Octet as a youthful reaction to *Faust* is admittedly speculative, but such a reading helps to explain several distinctive thematic and formal elements of the work: the monumental striving of the first movement, the remote "churchly" style of the Andante, the Walpurisnight music of the scherzo, and its struggle with the Handelian theme in the finale. Ultimately, though, the Octet resists exhaustive interpretations; its myriad instrumental combinations revolve in their own miraculous sphere, exuding the ineffable magic of a sixteen-year-old genius.

Diagram 5.1: Mendelssohn, Octet, Op. 20 (1825), Finale, Structural Plan

Sonata-Rondo

III

Around the time of the Octet, Felix took up another, hardly less challenging task: a German translation of the *Andria*, Terence's first comedy. The translation was a surprise gift for Heyse's birthday, October 15, 1825, the very day Felix completed the Octet.[57] Dutifully impressed, the tutor published the work the next year,[58] identified his student as "F****," and supplemented the play with a scholarly preface about classical poetry and his own translation of a Horace satire. Heyse observed there were two basic approaches to translating: reclothing the original in modern garb, preserving only the essential content, and adhering to the original meter and versification to produce a faithful imitation. Felix chose the latter; indeed, for him, translating Terence was rather like writing a fugue in the style of Bach. But for Heyse, in contrast to Greek and later Latin poetry, the language of the second-century Carthaginian slave somehow anticipated the accents and quantifications of German folk poetry. The goal of Felix's translation, therefore, was not to follow Terence slavishly but to imitate the prevailing meters and use shifting accents and caesuras to capture the feeling of the original—and thereby discover a link to the artful stresses of German folk poetry.

As Heyse noted, the translator was gifted "in the other Muses" and so worked on the project during leisure hours. As a respite from the intricacies of the Octet, we must imagine Felix, then, finding recreation in parsing Terence; eight-part counterpoint briefly yielded to *octonaria*, the eight-footed lines in iambic tetrameter prevalent in the play. With an acute ear, Felix fabricated deft German counterparts for Terence's lithe verses, as in this passage, when the slave Davus reacts to an impending prearranged marriage between the Athenian Pamphlius and a daughter of the gentleman Chremes. Here Felix mirrors Terence's internal pairing of *segnitiae* and *socordiae* with *Trägheit* and *Lässigkeit*, all the while maintaining a preponderance of iambs:

> *Enim vero, Dave, nil locist segnitiae neque socordiae,*
> *Jetzt also Davus ist keine Zeit, zu Trägheit oder zu Lässigkeit,*
>
> *Quantum intellexi modo senis sententiam de nuptiis.*
> *Wenn anders ich des Alten Meinung über die Hochzeit recht verstand.*
>
> (Upon my word, Davus, it's no time for slackness or stupidity, if I took in just now the old boy's view about the match.[59])

At the end of September 1826, Felix sent a copy of this "poor attempt by a poor schoolboy"[60] to Goethe, who entertained his Weimar circle with readings. On October 15 Felix honored Heyse with another translation, this time of Horace's treatise *Ars poetica*,[61] celebrated down through the centuries for its simile "poetry is like a painting" (*ut pictura poesis*) and its condemnation of "purple" prose. Felix's manuscript, nearly five hundred acatalectic German lines in meticulous calligraphy, remains unpublished.

The year 1825 had closed for Felix with considerable intellectual and artistic ferment, capped by his classical pursuits and the Octet. There had been other stimulations as well. On November 2 Felix appeared on a concert of the violinist Ludwig Maurer as the soloist in the Beethoven Choral Fantasia, Op. 80; Felix also conducted "with fire" his own Symphony in C minor, Op. 11, though whether he used a baton or led from a piano is not clear.[62] Then, for Fanny's twentieth birthday, Klingemann gave her a copy of Beethoven's *Hammerklavier* Sonata, with a mock letter from the "master," who directed Fanny to play the sprawling composition only when time allowed, for he "had much to say" in the sonata.[63] In December 1825 Carl Maria von Weber returned to Berlin to produce his "grand, heroic, romantic" opera *Euryanthe*; Felix attended the rehearsals and was astonished at "what the man did with a strange orchestra."[64] And finally, he was confirmed as a Protestant. In response to his avowal of faith, his pastor, F. P. Wilmsen, cited Luke—much was expected of him to whom much was given[65]—and prayed that art, uplifted and sanctified by religion, would make Felix's soul strong and free, noble and great.

Late in 1825, the Mendelssohns moved from the Gartensaal to celebrate their first Christmas in the mansion of Leipzigerstrasse No. 3. At first Lea complained the "palace-like residence" was too splendid, and not bourgeois enough.[66] She declined Hensel's offer to ship Bartholdy's frescoes to Berlin, because "a plain citizen's house" was not the place for costly adornments.[67] But she spared little expense on the gardens, where new lawns and a hundred rose stocks were planted. The family entertained themselves with musicales, charades, and word games; one object of delectation was the word *Philister* (Philistine), variously rendered as *viel isst er* ("he eats much"), *viel liest er* ("he reads much"), and *viel ist er* ("he is much").[68] For Lea's birthday in March 1826 the children designed a masquerade with *commedia dell'arte* figures and depictions of the months of the year. Two children represented Titania and Oberon, whose magic horn was intoned (an image Felix rediscovered later that year). Felix himself appeared as a Tyrolese peasant reciting newly written verses, including a poem about critics.[69] If a composer were too serious or happy, Felix mused, he put his listener to sleep or was commonplace; if he were longwinded or brief, his listener was exhausted or could not warm up to the music; if he wrote clearly or profoundly, he was a poor rogue or rattled his listener's head. However he wrote suited no one, so he should create as he wished and could.

Leipzigerstrasse No. 3 drew a steady stream of visitors. During the spring of 1826 a young Swedish musician stayed at the Mendelssohn residence. Adolf Fredrik Lindblad (1801–1878) had arrived in Berlin to study with Zelter and Berger and became a close friend of Felix.[70] Motivated to revive Scandinavian folksong, Lindblad arranged twelve ballades, dedicated to Felix and published as *Der Norden-Saal* (1826), the first collection of Swedish folk music to reach an international audience. In July 1826 Felix met the young ballade composer and Stettin music director, Carl Loewe (1796–1869), whose Op. 1, including a dramatic setting of Goethe's *Erlkönig*, had appeared in 1824. A talented pianist, Loewe accompanied his own performances of his Lieder. Felix shared his newer piano pieces[71] and, early in 1827, visited Pomerania to attend Loewe's premiere of the *Midsummer Night's Dream* Overture. Late in 1826 the Mendelssohns again welcomed Moscheles, who arrived on November 11. Moscheles celebrated Fanny's birthday, gave two public concerts, and heard Felix's Sonata in E major, Op. 6 and other piano works, the *Trumpet* Overture Op. 101, and the *Midsummer Night's Dream* Overture, presented as a piano duet by the siblings and then with a full orchestra, "which for the first time brought to light its richness of coloring."[72] Felix composed for him the *Perpetuum mobile* in C major (Op. 119, published posthumously in 1873), a thinly disguised reworking of the finale of Weber's Piano Sonata in C major, Op. 24.[73] At the time, Karl Möser was preparing the Berlin premiere of Beethoven's Ninth Symphony, and Moscheles attended the rehearsals. At one (November 12) Felix reduced the complex score at the piano, while at the performance (November 27), he joined the orchestra, probably as a violinist.[74]

In 1826 Felix's productivity continued unabated; as in 1825, the annual harvest culminated in a seminal masterpiece, the *Midsummer Night's Dream* Overture. Impressed by Felix's "gigantic strides," Moscheles nevertheless observed that few, other than Zelter and Berger, truly recognized the youth's genius. One musical authority who steadfastly opposed Felix's progress was Spontini. On June 14, 1826, Hermann Franck published in Marx's journal a damning review of Spontini's opera *Fernand Kortez*; Felix was implicated by his association with Franck and Marx.[75] For Franck, the Italian's gaudy spectacles—the mutiny of Cortez's army, a cavalry charge with live horses, the burning of the Spanish fleet, and an Aztec temple with sacrificial victims—magnified rather than relieved the monotony of the vapid music. Franck's comments completed the rupture between Marx and Spontini, who now "led the whole opposition against Mendelssohn." Thus, when Felix visited Spontini on July 6 to discuss the premiere of *Die Hochzeit des Camacho*,[76] the royal Kapellmeister refused to commit to a date, and the opera did not reach the stage until April 1827.

Ex. 5.7a: Mendelssohn, Fugue in E♭ major (1826)

Ex. 5.7b: J. S. Bach, St. Matthew Passion (1729), No. 15

The compositions of 1826 alternately project old and new stylistic *personae*, as if Felix, having broken through to the mature, modern idiom of the Octet, gauged its originality by reverting in other works to older styles. Thus, we encounter an etude-like Vivace in C minor that studiously treats its principal theme in mirror inversion, and two Bachian piano fugues, one, in a severe C♯ minor, a virtuoso double fugue,[77] the other, in E♭ major, seemingly modeled on the recitative from the St. Matthew Passion in which Jesus prophesies his betrayal (**ex. 5.7a, b**).[78] Looming over these historicist curiosities is the impressive *Te Deum*, for eight-part choir and continuo, conceived for the Singakademie, where, in a late extension of baroque continuo practice, Zelter habitually supported his ensemble from the piano. Finished on December 5, the *Te Deum* was rehearsed in February 1827 and performed two years later, with Felix presiding at the piano.[79]

Its twelve movements contain an eclectic mixture of eighteenth- and even seventeenth-century styles. Its inspiration was Handel's *Dettingen Te Deum* (1743), which Felix arranged in 1828; Felix's *Te Deum* begins by paraphrasing Handel's final chorus (**ex. 5.8a, b**), with the traditional D-major melody intoned over a "walking" bass line. Handelian textures abound too in the brisk double fugue of *Tu rex gloriae* (No. 7),[80] and in *Per singulos dies* (No. 10), for double four-part choirs, with sprightly, high-pitched figures in the sopranos that imitate the *clarino* register of Handel's trumpets. On the other hand, the graceful *Te ergo quaesumus* (No. 8), for four soloists, is redolent of Mozart. The most exotic section of the work is the *Sanctus* in the *Tibi cherubim* (No. 4), in which Felix imitates seventeenth-century Italian polychoral music, as if transplanting us from Berlin to Venice to ponder the antiphonal mysteries of Gabrieli and Willaert in St. Mark's (**ex. 5.9**). No less moving is the *Miserere* of the

Ex. 5.8a: Handel, *Dettingen Te Deum* (1743), Final Chorus

Ex. 5.8b: Mendelssohn, *Te Deum* (1826), Opening Chorus

penultimate *Dignare Domine* (No. 11); here Felix weaves a dense web of sixteen-part counterpoint, scored for two double choirs (each with four soloists) and based on an expressive figure spanning a ninth. The most original section of the composition, it yields to a Handelian finale, which revives the baroque textures of the opening.

The juxtaposition of old and new styles rises to a compositional dialectic in the *Sieben Charakterstücke*, Op. 7, dedicated to Ludwig Berger and published by February 1827.[81] Between 1824 and 1826 Felix wrote seven piano miniatures and shaped them into a cycle fitted with expressive German headings. Wolfgang Dinglinger has demonstrated how they alternate between disparate historical styles,[82] including, in one group, a Bachian invention and sarabande (Nos. 1 and 6) and Handelian fugue

Ex. 5.9: Mendelssohn, *Te Deum* (1826), No. 4

(No. 3), and, in the other, three "modern" sonata-form movements (Nos. 2, 4, and 7). No. 5 bridges the two groups. It is an erudite fugue crammed with augmentation, diminution, and mirror inversion, as "though the composer officially wished to demonstrate how diligently he had studied and mastered his subject through counterpoint."[83] Not surprisingly, some scholars have detected here Bachian echoes, though another inspiration was Beethoven, for Felix designed his composition as an acceleration fugue, a device he would have examined in the finale of Beethoven's Piano Sonata in A♭ major, Op. 110 (1822).

The "older" pieces of Op. 7 convey serious affects—thus, Nos. 1 and 6, both in E minor, are marked *sanft, mit Empfindung* (gently, with expression) and *sehnsüchtig* (yearningly)—while the "newer" pieces are in distinctly lighter moods. The cycle concludes with a nimble Presto in E major, which impressed Robert Schumann as adumbrating the *Midsummer Night's Dream* Overture.[84] Felix transports us to fairyland with scurrying, *pianissimo* staccato figures; at the end, all vanishes in a turn to the minor, with arpeggiations rising over low lying bass chords—as Hermann Franck noted, reenacting the conclusion of the scherzo from the Octet: "All flies past hastily, without rest, gathering together in colorful throngs, and then scattering in a puff."[85]

Felix reemployed the same key to celebrate the "modern" in the only piano sonata he saw through the press, Op. 6, completed in March 1826 and released later that year by the Berlin firm of Friedrich Laue. According to Schumann, here Felix touched "Beethoven with his right hand, while looking up to him as to a saint, and being guided at the other by Carl Maria von Weber (with whom it would be more possible to be on a human footing)."[86] If Weber's influence is evident in the vivacious virtuosity of the finale, elsewhere Felix's music is steeped in the late piano sonatas of Beethoven. Points of contact include the singing lyricism of the first movement, pairings of keys separated by a step, special pedal effects, expanded registers and broadly spaced chords, the cyclic use of thematic material (thus, the conclusion of the first movement returns at the end of the finale), and the incorporation of a free, unmeasured recitative into the slow movement.

The influence of Beethoven's Piano Sonata, Op. 101 (1817), is especially evident. Both sonatas open with *Allegretti* in $\frac{6}{8}$ meter; though Beethoven's movement is in A major, it begins "out-of-key" in E major, the tonic of Felix's composition. The second movements of the sonatas offer a march and minuet, and continue with expressive Adagios linked, via thematic recalls from the first movements, to Allegro finales. Like Beethoven, Felix inaugurates his Adagio with an E-major chord (in first inversion) and turning motive. While Beethoven treats his motive in two-part imitative

Ex. 5.10: Mendelssohn, String Quintet in A major, Op. 18 (1826), First Movement

counterpoint, Felix builds up a denser counterpoint of four descending imitative entries. Marked *senza tempo*, his Adagio begins with an unmetered recitative alternating with a hymnlike Andante, as if searching for a theme, a quest ultimately answered by the extroverted finale (and seemingly related to a similar process in the concluding movements of Beethoven's Piano Sonata in A♭, Op. 110).

In the spring of 1826 the Octet cast its lengthening shadow over a remarkable chamber work, the String Quintet in A major, Op. 18. Finished at the end of May, the original version comprised an Allegro, Scherzo, Minuet and Trio, and *Allegro vivace*.[87] As in the Octet, Felix here painted with a broad brush. In the exposition of the first movement, the opening graceful, Mozartean theme yields to accommodate a second thematic group in the dominant, and a third, closing group in the submediant F♯ minor, an unexpected intrusion of a distinctive, now familiar style (**ex. 5.10**)—*pianissimo*, with staccato and pizzicato articulations, and playful cross rhythms disrupting the $\frac{3}{4}$ meter—as if an otherwise conventional sonata form momentarily fell under the spell of an elfin world.

Much of the Scherzo, launched by a mischievous five-voice fugato, is in a staccato, *pianissimo* style, and the movement concludes with a delicately rising arpeggiation in the first violin, reaffirming its kinship with the scherzo of the Octet. For the Trio of the Minuet,[88] Felix crafted an austere double canon, in which the first viola mediates between the two canonic strands, by participating now in one, now the other. The purpose of this erudition becomes clear in the finale, a sonata-rondo complex in the middle of which the second canonic subject returns in a fugato. As in the Octet, a contrapuntal struggle thus energizes the development of the finale, and the soaring second theme of the finale, assigned to the first violin and supported by lush tremolos, completes the allusion by reviving the opening texture of the Octet. As we shall see, when Felix published the Quintet in 1833, he recast the work and jettisoned the Minuet in favor of a pensive Intermezzo in memory of the deceased Rietz. But in 1826 Felix still basked in the glow of the Octet and delighted in its Faustian apparitions and riddles.

Also wrapped in the same airy gauze of the Octet's third movement is Felix's masterpiece of 1826, the Overture to *A Midsummer Night's Dream*. Here the scherzo encouraged creative association: Goethe's golden anniversary of Oberon and Titania in the *Walpurgisnachtstraum* stimulated the short leap to Shakespeare's "dream." But before undertaking this veritably Mendelssohnian work, Felix created another orchestral work, the *Trumpet* Overture in C major, Op. 101, completed on March 4, 1826.[89] With its use of a recurring motto, third-related harmonies, and colorful approach to orchestration, Op. 101 impresses as an unjustly neglected *Vorstudie* for its more famous sibling. Thus the robust trumpet fanfares (according to Devrient, later redeployed in the *Hebrides* Overture) introduce the overture, figure near the end of the development and beginning of the reprise, and reappear in the final cadence. Continually reharmonized, they function as a unifying motto. Spanning the interval of a third, they promote mediant relationships (e.g., C major versus E major or A major, a third above and below), further explored in the development, where Felix juxtaposes shifting wind colors against a neutral harmonic wash in the strings. Many of these techniques resurface in more sophisticated ways in the *Midsummer Night's Dream* Overture, though, Devrient assures us, the "Trumpet" Overture remained Abraham's favorite composition of his son.

On July 7, 1826 Felix wrote to Fanny of his desire to undertake an "immense boldness"—to dream the "midsummernightsdream."[90] That summer his creative center shifted to the garden, where he played games with his friends; there, it appears, he conceived the immortal music. The work cost him immense effort: when he shared a draft with Marx, his friend approved the four introductory chords and elfin dance but could perceive "no *Midsummer Night's Dream*" in the rest. At Marx's prodding, Felix recast the work, filled it with a spectrum of characteristic motives, added material for Bottom and the Mechanicals,[91] and dated the completed score August 6. In one month, Felix thus produced a seminal work of German musical romanticism and transferred the spirit of Shakespeare's comedy into the realm of pure instrumental music. But there is striking evidence another composition had a role in shaping the overture. On July 17, Felix participated as a violinist in a performance of the Overture to Weber's final opera, *Oberon*; writing to his father and Fanny, Felix outlined several of its motives, including those associated with the magical horn, the elves, and the Turkish march,[92] all prominent in the opera's libretto, based on C. M. Wieland's epic poem *Oberon* (1780). In composing the Shakespearean overture, then, Felix conceived a kind of operatic overture with recurring motives that "weave like delicate threads throughout the whole."[93] Of course, the early audiences that heard the work at the Mendelssohn residence depended utterly upon their knowledge of the comedy to understand the overture. Still, Felix's music was entrancing enough to provoke one "highly unmusical Frenchman," unversed in

Shakespeare, to react, after hearing Felix and Fanny play it as a duet, *c'est comme un songe* ("it's like a dream").[94]

Between 1797 and 1810 A. W. Schlegel had translated seventeen Shakespeare plays, all reissued in 1825, when Felix presumably became intimately acquainted with *Ein Sommernachtstraum*. For Schlegel, Shakespeare occupied a central place in the Western canon, prompting the critic during the 1790s to review each play in a Viennese lecture series. Praising Shakespeare's "organic" unity, Schlegel defended the bard's liberties with the Aristotelian unities, declaring him "more systematic than any other author," through "those antitheses which contrast individuals, masses, and even worlds in picturesque groups. . . ."[95] Here Schlegel may have had in mind the fanciful interactions in *A Midsummer Night's Dream* between distinct groups—the elves, lovers, Athenian court, and bumptious tradesmen. Like Shakespeare, Felix delineated these characters through sharp contrasts, generating a network of "characteristic" motives nevertheless interrelated and susceptible to subtle manipulations.

Thus, after the wind chords (**ex. 5.11a**), Felix conjured up the elves with *pianissimo* staccati in the violins, divided *a 4* (**ex. 5.11b**). The first *forte* passage for full orchestra, with its majestic descending scale, connotes the court of Athens (**ex. 5.11c**), while the yearning second theme, again given to the violins but performed legato, in deliberate rhythmic values, suggests the pairs of lovers (**ex. 5.11d**). The closing section of the exposition introduces the tradesmen with rustic drones and a braying figure for Bottom (**ex. 5.11e**).[96] And the horn fanfares that close the exposition symbolize the royal hunting party of Theseus and Hippolyta (**ex. 5.11f**).

All these motives impress us vividly in different ways, yet they all spring from the magical wind chords that, like a motto, frame the overture and mark the recapitulation. Thus, embedded in the chords is a descending tetrachord (E–D♯–C♮–B), which transforms itself into the natural minor version of the elves (E–D♮–C♮–B) and major version of Theseus' court (E–D♯–C♯–B). In a further metamorphosis, the lovers' motive, now in the dominant B major, compresses the fourth of the tetrachord to the interval of a third (B–A♯–A♮–G♯). But these subtle shifts account only partly for the chords' special properties. Bearing fermatas, they are suspended outside the brisk *Allegro di molto* tempo of the composition. They evoke a timeless quality and assist the audience in suspending belief and accepting the ensuing illusions. Along with the threefold statement of the chords, Felix masterfully inserts individual, prolonged wind chords at several points into the composition, temporal dislocations that disperse their potent charm throughout the motivic network.

Ex. 5.11: Mendelssohn, *A Midsummer Night's Dream* Overture, Op. 21 (1826), motives

The motto chords are harmonically unconventional, ambiguous, and dreamlike. Felix begins with the ambivalent third E–G♯, which could mean either E major (the actual tonic of the work) or C♯ minor. We are on more secure ground with the second chord, the dominant B major, but are then seduced by an unusual turn to the subdominant A in its minor form—the first of many modal shifts between major and minor—before the fourth chord defines the tonic. And finally, there is the distinctive scoring of the chords, with their blended colors: flutes alone, and then flutes coupled with clarinets, bassoons, and horns. The exposed, evanescent flutes, which almost inevitably begin slightly out of tune, lend the music an almost unreal affect (and recall Cherubini's *bon mot* that two flutes were "worse" than one[97]). Containing the seeds of change, the chords thus represent the nectar of the "love-in-idleness" flower, through which Puck transforms the mortals. It is as if Puck leaps from the stage to befuddle our senses as the overture begins. The agent that transports us to fairyland, the chords are ultimately "no more yielding than a dream."

The idea of metamorphosis also inspired Felix to adapt the conventions of sonata form. At the most obvious level, the wind chords interrupt the mechanical unfolding of the sonata principle, which now becomes a dynamic, flexible process bending to the caprice of the play. Thus the exposition, expanded to introduce the colorful *dramatis personae*, presents the essential "argument." The dampened development, emerging seamlessly in an undertone from the bright *forte* chords of the exposition, transfers us to the play's central acts in the forest, where the lovers' affections are crossed, and where Titania falls in love with Bottom, whose head is transformed into that of an ass. The lovers' and Mechanicals' wanderings and echoing horn calls of the hunt are magically captured in a series of tonal deviations, all suffused by a softly lit orchestration, with pointillistic dabs of wind colors set against the *pianissimo* revelries of the elves. Only at the end of the development does the elves' energy momentarily abate, as the lovers fall asleep through a protracted *ritardando*, gently dovetailed with the motto chords to mark the recapitulation. In the final section, we return to the Athenian court, but when the overture appears to draw to a regal conclusion, Felix springs one more surprise and reintroduces the elves' music as a coda, for Puck's charming epilogue. As the elves bless Theseus's house, Felix transforms his motive into a serene, descending gesture, an apparent quotation of the Mermaid's Song from Act 2 of Weber's *Oberon* (**ex. 5.12a, b**), and perhaps alluding to Act 2, Scene 1 of Shakespeare's play, where Oberon recalls having "heard a mermaid, on a dolphin's back, / Uttering such dulcet and harmonious breath, / That the rude sea grew civil at her song, / and certain stars shot madly from their spheres, / To hear the sea maid's music." Then the overture concludes with the timeless wind chords, and we are released from Puck's spell.

During the summer of 1826, Felix thus led a "fantastic, dreamlike life."[98] In the family gardens he did gymnastics exercises, and established a swim club, for which he set Klingemann's verses to humorous songs.[99] An accomplished equestrian, Felix made excursions with Schubring to the Schönhauser Gardens near the village of Pankow. Resting on a shady lawn after one energetic ride, Felix listened attentively to a passing fly and later applied musical onomatopoeia to incorporate its buzzing into the overture.[100]

Ex. 5.12a: Weber, *Oberon* (1826), Act II, Mermaid's Song

and _____ the last faint light of the sun _____ hath fled! _____

Ex. 5.12b: Mendelssohn, *A Midsummer Night's Dream* Overture, Op. 21 (1826), Coda

In many ways, Felix's life thus imitated art. If Shakespeare remained his passion, with Klingemann's encouragement he now became a *devoté* of Jean Paul Richter, whose quirky novels, teeming with digressions and intrusions of the narrator, offered meteor-like visions of humanity that captivated a generation of German youth coming of age. And Felix's own poetic musings found an outlet in the *Gartenzeitung* (*Garden-Times*), a mock literary journal "founded" in August 1826, just weeks after the completion of the *Midsummer Night's Dream* Overture. Launched on August 21 under the putative editorship of the first-century Roman biographer Cornelius Nepos (i.e., Klingemann), the paper comprised fanciful contributions from Felix's circle, including his father's friends such as Zelter and the Humboldts,[101] in the form of aphorisms, short essays, poems, and drawings.[102] Felix himself contributed a "puzzle" canon, two sketches of the garden house and gardens, and dithyrambic and Sapphic poems.[103] In one game the friends crafted poems based on the "theme," "If loving nature, / If the spirit gave you wings, / follow my light traces, / Up, to the rosy hills!"[104] One of Felix's intimates wove these lines into forty verses titled *Der alte Ariel* (*The Old Ariel*), revealing that *The Tempest* also inspired Shakespearean reveries that summer. Felix recorded his own effort in a "Dithyrambic Non-Gloss." We might read its opening quatrain—"If loving nature / gave you strength's pleasure, / Create freely and merrily! / Only youth may dare it."[105]—as Felix's motto for the summer of 1826, when his voice gave full expression, as Devrient noted, to "the Mendelssohn we possess and cherish."[106]

Chapter 6
1827–1829

In the Public Eye

The old, antiquated phoenix is only waiting for his funeral pile,
and will not be long finding it, for the time is at hand, and we
shall live to see great things.[1]

        —Fanny to Klingemann, April 14, 1828

Early on June 30, 1825, Zelter and the young builder C. T. Ottmer, escorted by bricklayers, carpenters, and the Singakademie management, assembled off Unter den Linden to lay the cornerstone of a new musical temple. Wielding a hammer, Zelter consecrated the first stone in the name of old Fasch.[2] Designed by K. F. Schinkel, architect of Berlin neoclassicism, the new Singakademie became a living musical museum, its construction linked to Zelter, master mason and guardian of the Prussian musical heritage: on July 11 he secreted official documents inside the cornerstone and on December 11, his birthday, observed the capping-off ceremony.[3] Work continued for about a year before Zelter held his first rehearsal in the new building; the public dedication followed on April 8, 1827, with a performance, appropriately, of Fasch's monumental sixteen-voice Mass. Felix's response was to compose his festive *Te Deum* for the new hall, which could accommodate 250 singers and an orchestra of 50, arranged in an amphitheatric arch within an oblong hall 84 by 42 feet.[4] Zelter no doubt approved of the historicist composition, with its baroque, polychoral formations and ornate counterpoint, all furthering his agendum of glorifying past musical monuments. But by 1827, as Abraham realized, Felix had matured to the point that "his genius was now self-existent, and that further teaching would only fetter him."[5]

    The Octet and *Midsummer Night's Dream* Overture had indeed unlocked for Felix musical romanticism, worlds removed from the eighteenth-

century finery of the Singakademie. The overture impressed Zelter variously as a meteor, airy phenomenon, and colliding mosquitoes descending to the earth.[6] But Felix's testing of the power of instrumental music
to express ideas external to music—an experiment encouraged by Zelter's
nemesis, A. B. Marx—may have strained the limits of the elder musician's
aesthetics. By early 1827 Felix's formal lessons with Zelter were discon-
tinued, to the irritation of the aging musician, who, as Devrient relates,
maintained the adolescent had "not yet outgrown his leadership."[7]

Furthering Felix's new artistic independence were the growing performances of his music outside Berlin. Early in February, the Symphony
in C minor, Op. 11, received praise in Leipzig for its youthful energy.[8] The
same month, Felix departed for Stettin (Szczecin) in the Prussian province of Pomerania, where, on February 20, he performed the double Piano
Concerto in A♭ major with Loewe, who premiered the *Midsummer Night's
Dream* Overture and directed Beethoven's Ninth Symphony and Weber's
Konzertstück (Felix took up a violin part in the symphony and was the soloist in the *Konzertstück*, performed—unusual for the time—from memory).
The overture did not fail to impress, despite its juxtaposition with
Beethoven's colossal score. A reviewer likened the ribald intrusions of the
bassoon and English bass horn to a pair of ass's ears in genteel company,
and an artistic lady compared the fluttering, divided strings to swarms
of mosquitoes.[9] During his visit, Felix also appeared in private soirées,
where he dispatched from memory sonatas of Weber and Hummel, and
Beethoven's *Hammerklavier*, the culminating, "almost unplayable" fugue
of which Felix "conquered" with a "roaring tempo."

I

Having returned to Berlin, Felix corrected proofs for the piano-vocal
score of Weber's *Oberon*, brought out by Schlesinger in March.[10] Overshadowing this editorial work were preparations for the premiere of *Die
Hochzeit des Camacho*, finally scheduled for April at the Schauspielhaus.
On finishing his opera in August 1825, Felix had submitted it to Count
C. F. von Brühl, Intendant of the royal theater, who passed it on to Kapellmeister Spontini, holder of a near veto power. Playing the uncoopera-
tive bureaucrat, Spontini procrastinated before summoning Felix in July
1826. Ironically enough, Spontini resided in the same building on
Markgrafenstrasse where Felix's family had lived years before. But Spontini had transformed his quarters into a narcissistic gallery, with busts,
medals, and sonnets in his praise, and a dais from which he received
visitors.[11] Here Spontini deprecated Felix's score and commented, while

pointing through a window to the dome of the French Church, "*Mon ami, il vous faut des idées grandes, grandes comme cette coupole*" ("My friend, you must have grand ideas, grand like that dome").[12] Spontini demanded enough revisions to provoke Abraham into an angry exchange, forcing Brühl to intervene early in 1827. And there were other impediments. No sooner had stage rehearsals begun, early in April,[13] before Heinrich Blume (Don Quixote) contracted jaundice, so that the premiere was delayed until April 29.

Despite late twentieth-century attempts to revive the opera,[14] *Camacho* has always occupied an uncomfortable position in Felix's oeuvre. The librettist, variously identified as the *Regisseur* Baron Karl von Lichtenstein, Karl Klingemann, or the elder August Klingemann, remains unknown, although Rudolf Elvers has demonstrated that the Hanover writer Friedrich Voigts actively participated in at least the first act and probably the second as well.[15] The subject of the opera derives from Cervantes' *Don Quixote*, the source for over one hundred operas. But few composers selected the episode of Camacho's wedding from the second part of the novel (ch. 20–21), and of these only J. B. Schenk's *Der Dorfbarbier* (*The Village Barber*, 1796) enjoyed some success.

Felix's attraction to *Don Quixote* reflected a German fascination with Cervantes. In 1799 Ludwig Tieck had translated the novel, and Felix would have also been familiar with the criticism of his uncle, Friedrich Schlegel, who viewed *Don Quixote* as "the model of the novel, fantastic, poetic, humorous."[16] No less enthusiastic was Friedrich's brother August Wilhelm, among the first to defend Cervantes's technique of inserting digressing stories (such as Camacho's wedding) within the novel and to recognize the significance of its second part, in which the knight achieves an increasing independence from the chivalrous persona of the first part.

In transforming Cervantes's tale (in which Carrasco attempts to marry off his daughter Quiteria, in love with the poor Basilio, to the wealthy landowner Camacho) into a romantic Singspiel, Felix had to contend with certain issues. For Devrient the story was suitable only for "a comic *dénouement*," and the librettist's inability to develop dramatic contexts—Felix himself complained of the overused strophic settings that interrupted the dramatic flow[17]—was ultimately "paralyzing."[18] Unlike the *Midsummer Night's Dream* Overture, in which he could draw upon an entire play for a twelve-minute overture, he now had to produce several hours of music for a single episode from Cervantes's epic. There is some evidence that, as in the concert overture, Felix considered deploying a network of motives throughout the opera; thus, as the Scotsman John Thomson observed, "each character has a language of its own, so that one can never mistake the strains of Sancho for those of his mas-

Ex. 6.1: Mendelssohn, *Die Hochzeit des Camacho* (1827), Overture

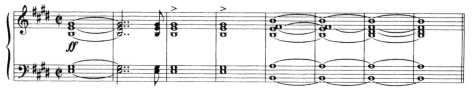

ter...."[19] The Overture commences with a brass fanfare indelibly associated with the Don (**ex. 6.1**), whose first entrance occurs with the fanfare near the end of Act I, when, imagining Quiteria to be his idealized Dulcinea del Toboso, he springs to her defense. Progressing from tonic to dominant, the motive is ultimately extended to form a complete cadence in the closing bars of the opera, so that the fanfare functions like a motto, framing the opera and renewing itself in the middle. The technique is thus not unlike the motto in the *Midsummer Night's Dream* Overture, though now applied across a much larger temporal span. But the knight's motto proved a miscalculation. Felix covered the Don with too much musical armor; if the nebulous wind chords of the concert overture effortlessly conjure up Oberon's elves, the ponderous fanfares of *Don Quixote* fail to convey an "ironical sense of knight-errantry."[20]

Curiously, in the Overture Felix avoided delineating the other principals with their own motives. Instead, for the second theme of the exposition, he utilized material from the ballet of Act 2, where the opposing forces of Cupid and Wealth clash; a tender phrase from the theme reappears just before the ballet, sung by a chorus to the text, "Love is all conquering, love triumphs in every contest" (**ex. 6.2**). The ballet itself adheres closely to the novel. Cervantes describes a masquelike entertainment in which rows of nymphs, led by Cupid and Interest, endeavor to free a maiden imprisoned in a wooden castle. Accompanying Cupid's forces are a flute and tambourine, employed by Felix in an exotic bolero (**ex. 6.3a**). On the other hand, Interest dances a fandango, in which Felix replaces the seductive tambourine with a shimmering triangle to suggest Camacho's wealth (**ex. 6.3b**). The Spanish dances inject local color into Felix's score and recall the precedent of Mozart and Weber, who incorporated a fandango and bolero in two operas set in Spain, *The Marriage of Figaro* and *Preciosa* (the latter based on a Cervantes *novella*).

Ex. 6.2: Mendelssohn, *Die Hochzeit des Camacho* (1827), Act II

Lie - be, Lie - be ist all - mäch - tig, Lie - be siegt in je - dem Streit

Ex. 6.3a: Mendelssohn, *Die Hochzeit des Camacho* (1827), Act II, Bolero

Ex. 6.3b: Mendelssohn, *Die Hochzeit des Camacho* (1827), Act II, Fandango

Elsewhere, the Germanic quality of Felix's music protrudes, especially in two numbers strongly reminiscent of Weber. In the finale of Act 1 (No. 11) Vivaldo sings off-stage to the jaunty strains of a *Waldhorn*, and in Act 2 (No. 16), a bridesmaids' chorus replicates the key and style of the popular chorus from *Der Freischütz*. These concessions to Berlin taste could not conceal the libretto's threadbare quality, and for Devrient, who played Carrasco, the score still represented the "musical thought" of Felix's earlier Singspiele.

An audience filled with family friends greeted the premiere. But the chorus was unsteady, and an exasperated Felix fled before the conclusion of the opera, leaving Devrient to apologize for his friend's absence. The second performance, scheduled for May 1, was abruptly canceled.[21] At once critics seized on the libretto's weaknesses. Ludwig Rellstab reported the encouraging, if not deafening, applause,[22] and also the excessive length of the libretto. According to a Leipzig correspondent, the performance precipitated "stormy applause" but opposition to the partisan calls for the composer to appear.[23] Felix was guilty of "overstriving" for effect. The noisy overture was too bloated for the "romantic, idyllic" material; and the composer, known for serious instrumental compositions, was out of his element, so that Cervantes's tale did not spring fully to life. Meanwhile, a French correspondent hinted that the production was owing to Abraham's wealth and dismissed the libretto as perhaps the most "maladroit" opera book yet derived from Cervantes.[24] Most damning, the score was "completely Germanic"; ignoring the ballet, the reviewer found no evidence of *couleur locale*.

These critiques paled against invidious comments in a minor gossip column, the *Berliner Schnellpost*, edited by M. G. Saphir: "At the Wedding of Camacho a Sunday public [April 29 fell on a Sunday] danced a contra-dance with a Sabbath public. After both sides had been stood up in vain, they fainted."[25] Felix was hurt when he learned the author of these anti-Semitic sentiments was a "highly gifted musical student, . . . who had witnessed and shared the excitement of the family during the preparation of the opera, and who knew the score well."[26] Though Felix later referred to *Camacho* as "my old sin"[27]—even Zelter had acknowledged its libretto contained no gold[28]—Felix drew from the episode a lifelong distrust of journalism: the most lavish praise from demanding critics could not offset the most contemptible abuse of the tawdriest literary rags. He also developed a phobia of committing to another libretto and henceforth examined numerous subjects only scrupulously to reject them, one by one. (Thus, during the summer of 1828, he declined Eduard Devrient's libretto on the legend of Hans Heiling, owing to its similarities to *Der Freischütz*,[29] and even before *Camacho* was staged, Felix was unable in 1826 to come to terms with Helmina von Chézy, who had proffered a libretto on a romantic Persian subject.[30]) The brilliant composer of boyish Singspiele for his parent's residence failed at age eighteen in the public opera house. Curiously enough, in 1828 the Berlin firm of Friedrich Laue issued a piano-vocal score of the opera in heavily revised form, even though Felix did little to encourage the work's revival.[31] Almost certainly Abraham underwrote this publication, since it was clearly unviable commercially; indeed, a reviewer commented that its price was *sehr hoch.*[32]

II

While readying *Camacho*, Felix passed the entrance examination to the University of Berlin. At Easter (April 15) Heyse ended his tutorship of Felix in order to pursue the *Habilitation* at the university; as a replacement, Abraham hired the student J. G. Droysen (1808–1884), who had arrived in 1826 to study with the philologist August Böckh.[33] The son of a Pomeranian minister, Droysen possessed "knowledge far above his age"[34] and became a lifelong friend of the Mendelssohns. Felix and Rebecka studied Greek with him "as far as Aeschylus,"[35] Droysen's specialty. On May 8, 1827, Felix matriculated at the university, to obtain the *Bildung* "so often lacking in musicians."[36] Founded in 1807, the institution attracted within twenty years a distinguished faculty that boasted Wilhelm von Humboldt as the first rector, and his brother, the natural scientist Alexander von Humboldt, the geographer Ritter, theologian Schleiermacher, philosophers Fichte and Hegel, astronomer J. F. Encke, Indo-Europeanist Franz Bopp, historian Ranke, jurists Savigny and Eduard Gans, and Böckh. Among its students were the future "Young Hegelian" Ludwig Feuerbach (1824), and Heinrich Heine (1821–1822), who, like Felix, spent four semesters at the institution. Felix's lecture notes in history and geography,[37] and matriculation records confirm he was a most diligent student, though evidently between classes he preferred to improvise on the *Midsummer Night's Dream* Overture on the piano of a "beautiful lady."[38]

Felix attended the lectures of the historian Leopold Ranke and zoologist M. H. K. Lichtenstein but was especially drawn to the offerings of the geographer Carl Ritter,[39] who in 1822 had begun to publish his *magnum opus*, the twenty-one-volume *Erdkunde*, destined to fill by 1859 some twenty thousand pages. Its full title (*Geography in Relation to Nature and Human History, or General Comparative Geography as a Firm Foundation for the Study of and Instruction in Physical and Historical Disciplines*) reveals its daunting scope. For Ritter, the globe had "a life of its own—the winds, waters, and landmasses acting upon one another like animated organs, every region having its own function to perform, thus promoting the well-being of all the rest."[40] It was probably this aspect of Ritter's scholarship, stressing the "organic" connectedness of the natural world, which particularly impressed Felix, as he pondered "organic" thematic relations in his own instrumental compositions.

During the spring of 1827 the death of a friend, August Hanstein, shook Felix. He sought refuge in counterpoint, and by the invalid's bedside conceived an unusual piano fugue in E minor, completed on June 16 along with a second fugue. [41] Later Felix coupled the two with preludes and published them as the Prelude and Fugue, Op. 35 No. 1 (1837) and a contribution to the album *Notre temps* (1842). These dissonant compositions, featuring subjects rent by angular sevenths and tritones (**ex. 6.4a, b**), were meant to depict his friend's illness; in the "accelerando" fugue of Op. 35 No. 1, the increasingly agitated counterpoint symbolized for Schubring the "progress of the disease as it gradually destroyed the sufferer." Climaxing with stentorian octaves, the fugue culminates with a "chorale of release,"[42] a freely composed hymn in E major in which

Ex. 6.4a: Mendelssohn, Fugue in E minor, Op. 35 No. 1 (1827)

Ex. 6.4b: Mendelssohn, Fugue in E minor (1827)

soothing conjunct motion smoothes out the jarring fugal contours. A quiet epilogue, rather like a devotional organ postlude, brings the composition to a hushed close. Schubring took this "specifically church coloring" as evidence of Felix's fundamental spirituality and noted that his friend habitually began his autographs by inscribing an abbreviated prayer (Lea identified two recurring throughout Felix's manuscripts: *H.D.m.*, for *Hilf Du mir*, "Help me, [O Lord]," possibly from Jeremiah 17:14, and *L.e.g.G*, for *Lass es gelingen, Gott*, "Let it succeed, O Lord"[43]). But this religiosity later exposed Felix to charges of excessive sentimentality; for Charles Rosen, who has regarded Op. 35 No. 1 as "unequivocally a masterpiece," Felix was essentially the "inventor of religious kitsch in music," substituting the "emotional shell of religion" for religion itself,[44] and spawning a strain of musical piety that ran through the nineteenth century.

Contemporaneous with the E-minor fugues is the Piano Sonata in B♭ major, finished in May 1827, perhaps in response to Beethoven's death on March 26. When the sonata appeared posthumously in 1868, it received the opus number 106, linking it to Beethoven's magisterial Op. 106, the *Hammerklavier* Sonata, with which Felix's sonata shares its key and several features. The two begin with similar ascending figures and explore the submediant G major in their first movements. Felix's second movement is a scherzo in B♭ minor, not unlike the middle of Beethoven's scherzo, though here again the young composer invokes the elfin imagery of the Octet and eventually disperses his scherzo in another evaporating puff. Considerably less Beethovenian is the Andante in E major, which impresses as an improvisation on the concluding pages of the *Midsummer Night's Dream* Overture. But this nocturne-like trance concludes with a dramatic gesture: transitional horn calls that introduce the sprightly, widely spaced Weberesque subject of the finale. Near its midpoint the scherzo suddenly returns, injecting minor-hued shades into an otherwise carefree finale. Unlike the recall of the scherzo in the Octet, though, the technique here flags, and when at the end Felix sums up with a cadential figure, it too sounds somewhat lame, a weak reminiscence of a familiar idea from the *Midsummer Night's Dream* Overture.

Around the beginning of May 1827 Schlesinger brought out the twelve *Gesänge*, Op. 8 (the first six had already appeared at the end of 1826). Scholarship has not viewed them as among Felix's strongest efforts. Admittedly, Op. 8 exudes a certain comfortable domesticity; indeed, several of the texts are by intimates of Felix's circle, including the poets Karl von Holtei and Friederike Robert, and Droysen, who masqueraded behind the pseudonym of J. N. Voss. Friederike commissioned at least one, No. 6 (the *Frühlingslied* in Swabian dialect) and specified for its accompaniment a chamber ensemble instead of piano. The song was performed with one flute, one clarinet, two horns, and cello at a Sunday musicale in 1824; later Felix reworked the colorful birdcalls of the flute and clarinet into a piano accompaniment.[45]

In a review greeting Op. 8, Marx distributed the songs into groups of courtly love (*Minne*), desire (*Verlangen*), deep thought (*Sinniges*), and contemplation (*Anschauung*).[46] Many employ simple strophic settings with repeated music and unobtrusive piano parts. In some, Felix opts for modified-strophic arrangements, with alterations in the vocal line and accompaniment. One example is the operatic *Romanze* (No. 10), ambiguously labeled *aus dem Spanischen*, a clue that it was a rejected number from *Camacho*.[47] Another is the *Hexenlied* (No. 8), in which Holtei's image of the Brocken inspired another version of Felix's supernatural G minor. The most ambitious of the twelve, *Hexenlied* falls into three sections, of which the first two are identical, while the third takes on its own life and transforms the mischievous staccato work and horn calls of the witches' dance into blurry piano tremolos and a turn to the major (**ex. 6.5**).

Other *Gesänge* aspire toward the artful simplicity of folksong, perhaps none more than the *Erntelied* (*Harvest Song*, No. 4), described as an "old church song" and set with austere modal harmonies to convey the grim image of Death the Reaper. *Pilgerspruch* (*Pilgrim's Saying*, No. 5) seeks comfort in the devotional poetry of the seventeenth-century lyricist Paul Fleming. The same verses had inspired Fanny to write a part-song in 1823,[48] and Felix later reused the opening phrase of his

Ex. 6.5a: Mendelssohn, *Hexenlied*, Op. 8 No. 8 (1827)

1.Die   Schwal-be fliegt, der Früh-ling siegt und spen-det uns Blu-men zum Kran - ze!

Ex. 6.5b: Mendelssohn, *Hexenlied*, Op. 8 No. 8 (1827)

Die Schwal-be fliegt, der Früh - ling siegt, die Blü-men er-blü-hen zum Kran - ze!

Ex. **6.6a:** Mendelssohn, *Pilgerspruch*, Op. 8 No. 5 (1827)

1.Lass dich   nur nichts nicht   dau - ern, mit   Trau - ern sei   stil - le!

Ex. **6.6b:** Mendelssohn, *Lied ohne Worte* in A major, Op. 38 No. 4 (1837)

Pilgerspruch in the *Lied ohne Worte*, Op. 38 No. 4 (**ex. 6.6a, b**). Fanny chided her brother for faulty voice leading in *Pilgerspruch*, where she uncovered an awkward set of parallel octaves.[49] No innocent bystander, Fanny played a special role in the opus, to which Marx teasingly alluded. No. 12, a setting of Suleika and Hatem's duet from Goethe's *Westöstlicher Divan*, portrayed a "sweet, inward, most pure" form of love, so that one was inclined to label the Lied *weiblich* ("feminine"), "if there were female composers, and if ladies could absorb such profound music." Similarly No. 2 (*Das Heimweh*, "Homesickness") expressed a certain feminine, languishing quality. As Marx knew, Fanny had composed both, as well as No. 3, *Italien*, in which she again gave voice to her yearning for southern climes.

Italien became one of "Felix's" most popular songs and enjoyed an unusual afterlife. During the 1840s, it inspired A. H. Hoffmann von Fallersleben's poem *Sehnsucht*, which appeared in 1848 with Fanny's music. The sensuous quatrains of *Italien* were drawn from a poem of the Austrian Franz Grillparzer that had appeared in 1820.[50] Here the poet transports us from the onerous world of prose into a magical Italy of poetry, fragrant olives, cypresses, and murmuring seas, all captured by Fanny's lilting melody and light chordal accompaniment. When, in 1842, Felix visited Buckingham Palace (see p. 439), Queen Victoria chose to sing *Italien* and executed its climactic high G as skillfully as any dilettante.[51] After admitting Fanny's authorship of the song, Felix persuaded Prince Albert to render the *Erntelied*, whereupon the composer wove motives from both into an improvisation and thus united the feminine and masculine.

Why did Felix subsume three of Fanny's songs into his own opus? Postmodern standards might vilify his action as artistic theft. But Fanny's anonymity reflected her time, when many women writers and artists (e.g., the Brontës, George Sand, and George Eliot) adopted masculine pseudonyms to circumvent societal restrictions; indeed, Felix's aunt Dorothea had published several articles under Friedrich Schlegel's name. No less meaningful for Fanny than the gender divide was the class divide, which restricted ladies of leisure from pursuing "public" professions. Perhaps for that reason, when Fanny's first publication, the Lied *Die Schwalbe*, appeared in an album in 1825, her name was suppressed.[52] In Fanny's case, her creative voice occasionally merged with that of Felix, a credible stratagem since her compositional style had developed in tandem with his. A balanced view might see Felix's decision as a compromise, allowing her a public outlet without violating the family's privacy. Felix's mantle and Marx's veiled comments thus offered a limited means of "legitimizing" Fanny's authorship without exposing her to public scrutiny in the press, all the while preserving lines between the private and public so scrupulously observed in Restoration Berlin. But even this subterfuge was soon enough exposed; John Thomson, after visiting Berlin in 1829, reported about Op. 8 to English music lovers: "three of the best songs," he wrote, "are by his sister. . . . I cannot refrain from mentioning Miss Mendelssohn's name in connection with these songs, more particularly, when I see so many ladies without one atom of genius coming forward to the public with their musical crudities, and, because these are printed, holding up their heads as if they were finished musicians."[53]

During Pentecost in early June 1827, Felix spent idyllic days in Sakrow near Potsdam with a fellow student, Albert Magnus, and composed there the "impromptu" song *Frage* (*Question*). According to Sebastian Hensel, Felix himself crafted the amorous verses, though in 1902 Droysen's son claimed his father as its author (the song appeared in 1830 as Op. 9 No. 1, with an attribution to J. N. Voss, Gustav Droysen's pseudonym).[54] Is it true, poet and composer wonder, pausing longingly on a dissonant harmony (**ex. 6.7**), that a secret admirer asks the moon and stars about him? Only she who shares his feelings and remains faithful can grasp his emotions. Now if Felix actually wrote the poem, who was the object of his affection? A likely candidate is Betty Pistor (1808–1887), who sang in the select Singakademie group Zelter directed on Fridays, when Felix accompanied at the piano. Betty became an intimate of the Mendelssohn children and stirred the younger Felix's adolescent passion. *Frage*, in turn, inspired his String Quartet in A minor, Op. 13, the first movement of which he completed, again at Sakrow, on July 28.[55] Did the quartet, which quotes the Lied, symbolize their relationship? The idea does not seem far-fetched, for in 1830 Felix would add a secret dedication to Betty on the manuscript of his next string quartet, Op. 12 in E♭ major.[56]

Ex. 6.7: Mendelssohn, *Frage*, Op. 9 No. 1 (1827)

Late in August, at the end of the summer term, Felix joined one of the Magnus brothers,[57] the law student Louis Heydemann, and Eduard Rietz for a holiday. Playfully simulating Ritter's lectures, they analyzed the geography of the Harz Mountains but lost their way climbing the Brocken. In Wernigerode, Felix made good on a promise to visit the vacationing Betty Pistor. Living a carefree, students' existence, the friends continued through Franconia and Bavaria, and on September 8 they reached Stuttgart, where Felix met a musician he later hailed as the finest conductor in Germany, P. J. von Lindpaintner.[58] Pausing in Baden-Baden, Felix encountered Ludwig and Friederike Robert, the diplomat Benjamin Constant, and an enthusiastic Frenchman who offered a half-finished opera libretto on the subject of Alfred the Great. Now well advanced into Op. 13, Felix wrote Fanny to ask whether he should incorporate *Frage* into the work's conclusion.[59]

By September 19 he reached Heidelberg, where he spent several hours with the jurist A. F. J. Thibaut (1772–1840), who in 1814 had argued for codifying German law. When the "Hep-Hep" Riots erupted in 1819, he led his students in defending Jews from attacks.[60] In 1802 Thibaut had begun to collect sacred music and by 1811 was directing an amateur chorus. For Thibaut, ignorance of the musical past, neglect of figured bass, and blending of sacred and secular styles of expression had corrupted music. In *Über Reinheit der Tonkunst* (*On Purity in Music*, 1825), he advocated a return to the "pure" style of Palestrina but was less certain about the complex music of J. S. Bach, who had not considered the "needs of ordinary people."[61] Thibaut's monograph impressed Felix, but the principal reason for the visit was to consult Thibaut's library, rich in Italian sacred polyphony of the sixteenth through the eighteenth centuries. Just then Felix was beginning to compose the motet *Tu es Petrus*; without asking his name Thibaut graciously lent him a setting by the Venetian Antonio Lotti. While Thibaut revealed "the merits of old Italian music," Felix argued for J. S. Bach's position as the "fountainhead" in music, and when they parted company Thibaut proposed they build their friendship on Bach and Palestrina, "like two lovers who promise each other to look at the moon, and then fancy they are near each other."[62]

From Heidelberg Felix and friends continued to Darmstadt, where he found the "minister of war for musical affairs," the theorist Gottfried Weber, who committed a faux pas by labeling Beethoven "half again as crazy as he ever was divine," so that Felix demoted Weber to a "horse-doctor-like scoundrel."[63] In Frankfurt Felix stayed with Schelble and saw Hiller, who accompanied the students on an excursion on the Rhine to Cologne. At Horchheim, near Coblenz, Felix, Magnus, and Heydemann disembarked to visit Felix's uncle Joseph, who owned a substantial estate and vineyards overlooking the river. Felix stayed behind to celebrate the annual vintage and then, with Joseph and his wife, Hinni, traveled to Frankfurt to hear Schelble direct a Handel oratorio. By mid-October, Felix had returned to Berlin, where he spent his first evening in Betty Pistor's company.[64]

On October 27 Felix inscribed the title page to his new string quartet, Op. 13, and a few days later finished a Fugue in E♭ major for the same scoring,[65] on a subject elaborated from the "Jupiter" motive. If the latter, posthumously published as Op. 81 No. 4, impresses as a student exercise, Op. 13 effects a worthy *rapprochement* with Beethoven's late quartets, which preoccupied Felix during 1827.[66] Thus, the outer movements—centered largely on A minor—recall textures from those of Beethoven's String Quartet in A minor, Op. 132. Beethoven's late style especially impresses itself on the second movement, a heartfelt Adagio with at least three allusions. The opening is similar to the *Cavatina* of Beethoven's Op. 130, which Felix nearly quotes in one passage. The center of the Adagio, a chromatic fugue, invokes the second movement of Beethoven's *Serioso* Quartet, Op. 95, and the end of the Adagio revives the high-pitched, ethereal sonority concluding the *Heiliger Dankgesang* of Beethoven's Op. 132.

To Lindblad Felix revealed his immersion in Beethoven's late quartets, which offered a guiding principle for Felix's own work, "the relation of all 4 or 3 or 2 or 1 movements of a sonata to each other and their respective parts, so that . . . one already knows the mystery that must be in music."[67] Linking the movements of Op. 13 are references to *Frage*, the "theme" of the entire quartet: "You will hear its notes resound in the first and last movements, and sense its feeling in all four."[68] Thus, Felix incorporated explicit quotations from the song in the outer movements but left more subtle traces in the inner movements. The Quartet begins by reviving the plagal cadences from the end of the Lied before citing its characteristic dotted-rhythmic motive. Reworked at the beginning of the second movement, this figure is present as well in the ingratiating Intermezzo, where the meter shifts from the $\frac{3}{4}$ of the Lied to $\frac{2}{4}$ (**ex. 6.8a**). The scherzo-like center of the Intermezzo delicately outlines the second phrase of the Lied (**ex. 6.8b**). The impassioned finale, which erupts with a free recitative, assimilates a dotted figure into its primary theme but subsequently recalls material from the first two movements. Eventually, Felix returns to the A-major Adagio with which the composition began and now cites the final thirteen bars of the Lied, completing the thematic circle. The dramatic, questioning recitatives (the first movement ends with a recitative-like gesture, the second movement employs a recitative after the fugue, and the finale has several recitatives) challenge the thematic con-

Ex. 6.8a: Mendelssohn, String Quartet in A major, Op. 13 (1827), Intermezzo

Ex. 6.8b: Mendelssohn, String Quartet in A major, Op. 13 (1827), Intermezzo

tents of the composition and lead us inexorably back to the Lied, a technique of recall and denial seemingly related to the finale of Beethoven's Ninth Symphony.

The lyricism of the Quartet broaches a second issue—the extent to which absolute instrumental music can express extramusical ideas. In 1828 Felix began to compose what he later termed *Lieder ohne Worte* (*Songs without Words*), textless piano miniatures that imitate features of art song. Op. 13 anticipated these "piano songs" by transplanting "Ist es wahr?" into the realm of absolute chamber music. Felix's experiment is not unlike Schubert's String Quartet in D minor, D810 (1824), in which his Lied *Death and the Maiden* appears in the slow, theme-and-variations movement and imbues the surrounding movements as well. Though Felix could not have known this masterpiece (published in 1831), the two quartets dismantle in similar ways the boundaries between art song and string quartet. Felix's frequent recitatives, as if beckoning for a text, remind us again that a vocal model was the direct inspiration for his composition.

During the closing months of 1827, Klingemann's transfer to the Hanoverian legation in London diminished Felix's circle. The friend's absence was the subject of a new, mock literary paper launched by the poet Holtei. The *Thee- und Schneezeitung* (*Tea and Snow Journal*), of which eight issues coalesced between September and November, replaced the *Gartenzeitung*.[69] Lea reports, however, that Felix declined to contribute to the new undertaking.[70] Meanwhile, he enjoyed making new musical acquaintances. In December the clarinetists Heinrich Baermann and his son Carl appeared in Berlin,[71] and Felix himself participated in two public concerts on November 13 and December 25, when he performed Schubert's ballade *Erlkönig* (likely his first exposure to that composer's music) and Lieder of Mozart and Beethoven.[72] For Rebecka, Felix composed a toy symphony (lost; according to Sebastian Hensel, Felix modeled it on Haydn's

"Toy" Symphony, now known to be by Leopold Mozart) and during the winter months organized a small chorus that began to rehearse on Saturdays "rarely heard works," including parts of the St. Matthew Passion.[73] Returning in earnest to sacred music, Felix completed rapidly the motet *Tu es Petrus*, Op. 111, and cantatas *Christe, Du Lamm Gottes*, presented to Fanny on Christmas Eve, and *Jesu, meine Freude*, finished on January 22, 1828.[74]

The cantatas were the first in a series linked to Felix's Bachian pursuits, including his study of the Passion and also his examination of W. F. Bach's musical estate, acquired by Betty Pistor's father, the astronomer K. P. H. Pistor, after a bidding war with Zelter. To Felix devolved the task of sorting through and organizing the manuscripts, among them thirteen cantatas of J. S. Bach; in exchange, Felix received a priceless gift, the autograph of Cantata No. 133 (*Ich freue mich in Dir*)[75] and frequent contacts with Betty. But an incident early in 1828 damaged their budding relationship: upon arriving at the Pistor residence to study the collection, Felix was greeted with laughter from Betty's friends. The hypersensitive composer took offense and refused to attend her birthday celebration on January 14. When, a few weeks later, Betty's father forbade her to attend his birthday festivities, the Mendelssohns suspected the reason was anti-Semitism, for some of Betty's relatives had mocked her as "the music- and Jew-loving cousin."[76] Eventually the families reconciled, but Felix never again visited the Pistor residence.

Christe, Du Lamm Gottes and *Jesu, meine Freude* follow closely Bachian prototypes, as if bearing out Berlioz's observation that Felix studied the music of the dead too closely.[77] Both are in one movement and suspend the chorale melodies in the soprano above a web of imitative counterpoint. Orchestral passages frame the movements and separate the chorale strains. In *Christe, Du Lamm Gottes*, the Lutheran Agnus Dei appears three times in F major, with the second statement skillfully worked into a jagged, chromatic fugato in F minor. Similarly, *Jesu, meine Freude* relies upon a minor-major exchange: two-thirds through the composition, the initial E minor shifts to a serene E major for "Gottes Lamm, mein Bräutigam" ("Lamb of God, my bridegroom"), where Johannes Crüger's chorale melody unfolds against a fresh harmonic coloration.

Initially Felix viewed *Tu es Petrus*, composed for Fanny's birthday (November 14, 1827) but not published until 1868 as Op.111, as among his most successful works.[78] In setting this fundamental Catholic text ("Thou art Peter, and upon this rock I will build my church," Matthew 16:18), Felix invoked not the Lutheran cantatas of Bach but the Italian *stile antico*, which ultimately traced its roots to Palestrina, the sixteenth-century foundation of Roman sacred polyphony.[79] According to Fanny, the score alarmed Felix's friends, who "began to fear that he might have turned

Roman Catholic."[80] Whether he was able to consult in Thibaut's library Palestrina's two settings is unknown, but clearly Felix sought to emulate the Palestrinian ideal—lucid, imitative points of polyphony with carefully regulated dissonances—prized by Thibaut as the "pure" sacred style. Even the appearance of the score, ruled in the archaic meter of $\frac{2}{1}$ and filled with obsolete breves (double whole notes, ⊨), bespeaks Felix's fascination with a remote historical period. There is also in the motet a striving for monumentality. Felix specified a chorus in five parts, accompanied by an orchestra expanded to include trombones. Both Felix and Fanny referred to the work as *19 stimmig* (in nineteen parts), and indeed Felix treated the orchestral parts as full participants in the contrapuntal tapestry. After a chordal exordium, the chorus introduces a falling figure in five-part imitation, subsequently magnified by entries in the strings, winds, brass, and even timpani—in all, fourteen entries that suffuse the music with the subject in texted and textless counterpoint, and thus erect a cathedral of sound upon motivic bedrock.

III

On January 9, 1828 an anonymous poem, *Der neuen Zeit* (*To the New Time*), appeared in Marx's journal,[81] with an unusual vision of the classical underworld: Ixion is no longer chained to his wheel, Sisyphus successfully rolls his boulder to the top of a mountain, and Tantalus slakes his thirst and tastes the fruit suspended above his head. The three judges of Hades ignore the "empty shades" clamoring to cross the river Styx and enter Elysium, but grant an audience to a youth (likened to Theseus and Hercules), who, reminded that the living have forgotten the great deeds of the departed, returns to the upper world, his soul inspired by the music he has heard in the underworld.

As we know, Droysen was the poet of this dreamlike allegory[82] that celebrated Felix's efforts to revive the music of the "eternally living dead." In the *Te Deum* and *Tu es Petrus* he had already revived historical periods remote from Bach's cantatas and the familiar corpus of Protestant chorales. In 1828, Felix continued these historical excavations in another "monumental" motet, *Hora est*, scored for four four-part choirs and organ continuo. Written for Fanny's birthday,[83] it was heard at the Singakademie, probably at an early 1829 rehearsal of the St. Matthew Passion and then performed there privately in March 1829 and publicly in November 1829 and January 1830.[84] The inspiration for the motet was a work tied to the Singakademie—Fasch's identically scored Mass (1786), based in turn upon a sixteen-part Mass by the seventeenth-century composer Orazio Benevoli.

Its antiphonal effects, sculpted harmonic blocks, and contrapuntal density offered Fasch a model for his own ideal of sacred music, although he endeavored to improve upon the prototype by rejecting certain licenses of Benevoli, enriching his monochromatic selection of harmonies, and adhering scrupulously to the rule that each four-voice choir should be harmonically independent. Now, in 1828, Felix aspired toward the grandeur of Fasch's Mass by renewing the techniques of the seventeenth-century polychoral style.

The texts, from the Catholic Office for Advent, comprise the antiphon *Hora est* and responsory *Ecce apparebit*.[85] The antiphon summons the faithful from their slumber to behold Christ resplendent in the heavens; the responsory proclaims the Lord will appear upon a white cloud with hosts of saints. For A. B. Marx, who reviewed *Hora est*,[86] the music explored the mysteries of the monastic rites of early Christendom. The composition projects an unusual tonal pairing, with the dark G minor of *Hora est* followed by the luminous A major of *Ecce apparebit*, a juxtaposition calculated to deemphasize the traditional tonic-dominant relationships of tonality in favor of the modal and prototonal colorings of Benevoli's period. The minor-major contrast and ascending modulation by step underscore the idea of spiritual awakening and renewal. In the first part, priestlike male voices summon the faithful in austere textures that range from monody to four-part harmony. Then, in *Ecce apparebit*, the four choirs enter as separate harmonic masses. Gradually, they accumulate and spill over into a *Più vivace* in which all sixteen parts descend in a radiant spiral of imitative counterpoint (**ex. 6.9**), a level of complexity Felix's choral music never again attained.

In 1828 Felix enrolled for his second year at the university. During the summer semester he attended lectures by the physicist Paul Erman on light and heat; Ritter on the geography of Asia, Greece, and Italy; and Gans on legal history since the French Revolution. The winter semester, which ran into the early months of 1829, offered the continuation of Gans's legal history and "natural law or the philosophy of law," and Hegel's lectures on aesthetics.[87] One might suppose that Hegel's views of music

Ex. 6.9: Mendelssohn, *Hora est* (1828)

piqued Felix's curiosity, but the search for Hegelian influence on the composer is, in the main, a frustrating enterprise. Though Hegel enjoyed social exchanges with the Mendelssohns, he seems to have used his visits not so much to discuss music as to enjoy whist.[88]

In Hegel's lectures on aesthetics, assembled after his death in 1831 and edited from student notes probably similar to those of Felix,[89] the philosopher elaborated a dialectical approach to the history of art with three principal eras, the archaic or symbolic, classic and romantic.[90] For Hegel art had achieved its most "adequate" representation in the classic period, in which the aesthetic Idea and its form were perfectly united in the idealized human body. But in the romantic (i.e., "Christian") era, the noncorporeal art of music had distanced itself from classic art and receded into an "unending subjectivity." Hegel's sweeping view of art history appears to have elicited skepticism from both Zelter and Felix. Writing to Goethe in March 1829, Zelter observed: "This Hegel now says there is no real music; we have now progressed, but are still quite away from the goal. But that we know as well or not as he, if he could only explain to us in musical jargon whether or not he is on the right path."[91] Felix too bridled at the Hegelian notion that art had somehow declined, or indeed ceased, "as if it could cease at all!"[92]

The life and career of Eduard Gans (1797–1839), with whom Felix studied legal history and natural law, intersected meaningfully with the Mendelssohns, for the jurist's career was bound up with the question of Jewish assimilation into the modern Prussian state. The son of a prosperous banker who had died insolvent in 1813, Gans studied with Thibaut and finished a dissertation in 1819 on Roman contract law. By 1820 Gans had returned to Berlin and, in the reactionary environment of the Carlsbad Decrees, established a Union for the Culture and Science of Jews. He also joined the Society of Friends (*Gesellschaft der Freunde*), organized in 1792 to counter the "terrible state" (*Unwesen*) of Orthodox Judaism, and there met two of its founding members, Joseph and Abraham Mendelssohn.

For a while Gans pondered establishing a Jewish colony in America, but instead he came to support the assimilation of Jews into the dominant Prussian culture and likened the process to a river flowing into a sea ("neither the Jews will perish nor Judaism dissolve; in the larger movement of the whole they will seem to have disappeared, and yet they will live on as the river lives on in the ocean"[93]). But when Gans sought a professorship at the university, the king summarily declared Jews ineligible. Gans's conversion to Christianity in 1825 enabled him to join the faculty, and he became Hegel's friend and eventually prepared his *Philosophy of Law* for publication in 1833. In politics Gans adopted increasingly liberal views, and when he commented favorably about the July 1830 Revolution in Paris, his lectures, which drew audiences of over a thousand, came under suspicion from the authorities. Felix's 1828 lecture notes clarify that Gans viewed the French Revolution as the defining moment of the modern period, when "all other histories paused," and when the Hegelian dialectical process indelibly affected the *ancien regime*; thus, Prussia was no longer an absolute state, but a "guardianship" state.[94] Gans's fervent desire, well ahead of his time, was to advance a pan-European synthesis. While playing out the unpredictable role of the assimilated Jew in Berlin society, Gans enjoyed social intercourse with the Mendelssohns and became the "commander and protector of the younger ones."[95] A "mixture of man, child, and savage,"[96] he actively pressed for the hand of Rebecka, with whom he read Plato, but in 1831, as we shall see, lost the prize to a worthy competitor.

IV

Between lectures Felix pursued several new compositions. In January 1828, he drafted a sprightly Etude in E minor, later reused in the *Rondo capriccioso*, Op. 14.[97] By February a considerably larger work was forming in his mind, an orchestral overture on Goethe's two short poems *Calm Sea* and *Prosperous Voyage* (*Meeresstille und glückliche Fahrt*).[98] Felix's musical inspiration was once again Beethoven, for whom a memorial concert, in which Felix performed a piano trio, was given on March 26.[99] Beethoven's cantata, Op. 112 on the same poems had appeared in 1822, and in 1824 Marx had actually criticized his favorite composer for representing the solitude of a becalmed vessel by a chorus and orchestra.[100] Quite likely Marx encouraged Felix to "set" the poems without text, as part of the theorist's agendum to test music's capacity to express substantive ideas. Indeed, in a spirited defense of programmatic music published in May 1828, *Über Malerei in der Tonkunst* (*On Painting in Music*), Marx identified Felix as a "student" of Beethoven who had brought "this idea to perfection, expressing *Calm Sea and Prosperous Voyage* without using Goethe's words,"[101] as if Marx were already familiar with Felix's score (the first version was not performed until September).

Among Felix's lesser works of the year is a setting of the Marian antiphon *Ave maris stella*, commissioned in June by the prima donna Anna Milder-Hauptmann, whom Lea described as a "cold princess."[102] Composed on one day in July, it received its premiere at the Berlin Marienkirche on May 27, 1829.[103] Felix divided the celebrated Vespers hymn into two sections. Mary's invocations (*Ave maris stella, . . . funda nos in pace*, "Hail, star of the sea," . . . "disperse us in peace") are set in a quasi-operatic, Mozartean vein, with florid embellishments tailored for Milder's voice. A dissonant Allegro in the minor mode forms the center of the work, with energetic supplications for *solve vincla reis* ("Loosen the chains of evil"), which yield to an abridged return of the opening, lending the work a rounded ternary, ABA´ shape.

"You see [Felix] is the fashion," Fanny wrote to Klingemann;[104] indeed, 1828 brought two commissions—the tercentenary of Albrecht Dürer's death in April, and an assembly of physicians and scientists in September. Felix hurriedly composed two festive cantatas, which have fallen into obscurity, largely owing to their mediocre texts. Sebastian Hensel described the occasions as "universal festivals," by which "the Germans tried to forget their want of political union";[105] the nationalistic subtexts of the cantatas are certainly not difficult to discern.

On the first occasion (April 18, 1828) the philologist E. H. Tölken extolled Dürer as the founder of German art, and the archaeologist Konrad Levezow celebrated Dürer's art as a testimonial to Christian piety.[106] Held in the Singakademie before a royal audience, the festival was a lavish affair, with decorations by Johann Gottfried Schadow and Schinkel. Behind the orchestra appeared a wall in the patriotic colors of red and gold, and in the center stood a six-foot statue of Dürer, framed by smaller statues symbolizing four facets of his work—painting, geometry, perspective, and military engineering. Above the statue loomed a painting based upon a Dürer woodcut (*The Peace of the World Redeemer in the Lap of the Everlasting Father*).[107] For the overture Felix pressed into service the *Trumpet* Overture. After Tölken's address came the cantata, a score of 143 pages lasting one hour and fifteen minutes. At a dinner feast Schadow feted Felix and proclaimed him an honorary member of the Academy of Art.

From all indications, Felix struggled to find inspiration in Levezow's insipid verses. Composed in February and March in about six weeks, the cantata included choruses, solo arias, and recitatives ("dry," i.e., performed at a piano, and "accompanied," with orchestral support)—in all fifteen numbers divided into two parts, each culminating in a fugue. The choruses and arias are thoroughly Handelian and reflect Zelter's deepening attraction to that composer, evidenced by Zelter's performances of *Joshua* (1827), *Judas Maccabaeus*, *Alexander's Feast*, and *Samson* (1828), and *Messiah* (1829; a planned performance of *Acis and Galatea* in an arrangement by Felix did not materialize).[108] The distinctly Bachian recitatives seem to anticipate Felix's efforts to commemorate the Thomaskantor the following year by reviving the St. Matthew Passion.

Ex. 6.10: Mendelssohn, *Dürer* Cantata (1828), No. 1

The cantata opens with an expansive plagal cadence later reworked in the unusual conclusion of the *Calm Sea and Prosperous Voyage* Overture (ex. 6.10). The ensuing orchestral *Festmusik* presents three strains of a marchlike theme that recurs throughout the cantata as a unifying device; in the first number, this theme leads to a chorus imploring the temple of art to open its gate to an unnamed artist, not identified until the third number, where Felix was unable to elevate musically Levezow's mundane revelation, "Albrecht Dürer ward er genannt" ("He was called Albrecht Dürer"). There follows a review of the virtuous Dürer, who rises to the heavens, aided by flowery metaphors—he is a rock uplifted to the clouds, an eagle soaring beneath the sun.

The second part associates Dürer's divine gifts with Christ the Redeemer. "Gaze upon Dürer's sacred works," the amateur poet urges, and the devout will "see the countenance of the Redeemer," the "radiant light of hope." Here Felix conceived the most imaginative portion of the score (No. 10), a tenor aria with violin solo (written for Eduard Rietz) and chorus. In the text the burning tears of a penitent find solace in Dürer's sacred art. The music begins with a questioning recitative for the violin, which then introduces a falling, sighing figure accompanied by string chords (ex. 6.11a). A simple chorale-like melody (ex. 6.11b) expresses the restorative power of Dürer's art. These two thematic elements alternate before the movement concludes with more recitative-like flourishes in the solo violin. The sobering, G-minor tints and brooding tremolos of the aria left their mark on the slow movement of the *Reformation* Symphony (ex. 6.11c), which Felix may have associated with the forceful spirituality of Dürer's art.

For one of the soloists, Eduard Devrient, the cantata did not reflect Felix's genius.[109] Nor was Devrient convinced by Felix's cantata for Alexander von Humboldt, who in 1827 had returned to Berlin as the Prussian monarch's scientific and cultural advisor. Initially, the world-traveled scientist faced an uncertain repatriation, since some nobility regarded him as a Francophile, but he allayed this concern in November, by lecturing on geography at the university. These lectures, which ran through

Ex. 6.11a: Mendelssohn, *Dürer* Cantata (1828), No. 10

Man - che Thrä - nen sah ich fal - len von des Men - schen An - ge - sicht

Ex. 6.11b: Mendelssohn, *Dürer* Cantata (1828), No. 10

Blick auf Dü - rers heil - ge Wer - ke Schau des Hei - lands An - ge - sicht

Ex. 6.11c: Mendelssohn, *Reformation* Symphony, Op. 107 (1830), Andante

April 1828, later formed the basis of his masterpiece, *Cosmos*, a two-thousand-page "sketch of a physical description of the universe." Their success encouraged Humboldt to offer at the Singakademie additional lectures, open to the public; here, in a forum most unusual for the time, royalty, aristocrats, commoners, and women attended, among them, Fanny ("Gentlemen may laugh as much as they like," she wrote, "but it is delightful that we too have the opportunity given us of listening to clever men"[110]).

Humboldt endeavored to counteract the influence of the "nature philosophers," including Hegel, who wished to "comprehend nature *a priori* by means of intuitive processes . . . without using scientific methodology."[111] A new opportunity to promote Humboldt's agendum came in September, when the state allowed him to convene an international convention of naturalists and physicians. Six hundred scientists converged upon Berlin, including the Englishman Charles Babbage, who in 1833 would design a prototypical calculator, and the mathematical genius Carl Friedrich Gauss, who piqued Humboldt's interest in terrestrial magnetism. From Warsaw came Professor Jarocki, traveling with an introverted, eighteen-year-old musician, Frédéric Chopin, who saw Felix but was too insecure to approach him.[112] At the opening session in the Singakademie (September 18, 1828), Felix directed his cantata, and Humboldt gave an address on the social utility of science.

The text of the cantata, by Ludwig Rellstab, charts the progress of the natural world from chaos to unity. Midway in the work a voice of reason interrupts the earth's struggle against the raging elements, and the light of truth countervails the strife. Now the competing forces collaborate to create the "glorious world," and the Lord is asked to "bless

Ex. 6.12: Mendelssohn, *Humboldt* Cantata (1828)

Ja, seg-ne Herr, was wir be - rei-ten, was die ver - ein - te Kraft er - strebt

the strivings of the united force" (**ex. 6.12**). Writing to Klingemann, Fanny commented on Felix's unusual scoring—male choir, clarinets, horns, trumpets, timpani, cellos, and double basses: "As the naturalists follow the rule of Mahomet and exclude women from their paradise, the choir consists only of the best male voices of the capital."[113] Felix chose a male choir to invoke the sound and traditions of male singing societies in Berlin, including Zelter's *Liedertafel*, founded in 1809 during the French occupation. Thus, Felix's music, apportioned into seven choruses, solo numbers, and recitatives, relies less on the Handelian and Bachian models of the Dürer Cantata than on the male choruses of Weber's *Der Freischütz*, which evoke a brand of German patriotism associated not so much with the court as with the educated middle class.

As an occasional piece the Humboldt Cantata was quickly forgotten, though it later had a strange political afterlife: in 1959, the centenary of the scientist's death, Felix's score was revived by the German Democratic Republic. An article appeared in the East German journal *Musik und Gesellschaft*, where quotations from Rellstab's text were retouched to conform to the needs of a secular state. Thus, in the final chorus, "Ja, segne Herr was wir bereiten" ("Yes, bless, O Lord, what we prepare") became "Ja, schützet nun, was wir bereiten" ("Yes, now protect what we prepare").[114] Alexander von Humboldt's reaction to the 1828 premiere is not known, although the conference did bring him closer to the Mendelssohns. At Gauss's urging he renewed his interest in magnetic observations and constructed a copper hut in the garden of Leipzigerstrasse No. 3. Here, while Felix rehearsed the St. Matthew Passion in the *Gartensaal*, Humboldt and his colleagues recorded changes in the magnetic declination, measurements also taken concurrently in Paris and at the bottom of a mine in Freiberg. Within a few years, what had begun in the Mendelssohns' garden as a modest laboratory became part of a "chain of geomagnetic observation stations" that stretched around the world, an early instance of international scientific exchange.[115]

Felix's most significant accomplishment of 1828 was the orchestral overture on Goethe's *Meeresstille und glückliche Fahrt*. In 1787, returning from Sicily to Italy on a French merchantman, the poet had been becalmed within sight of Capri. A resurgent wind averted disaster when the ship began to drift toward the Faraglioni Rocks, and in 1795 Goethe compressed his experiences—including the "deathly stillness" and "monstrous" breadth of the ocean—into the two poems. Now, in 1828, Felix, having seen the ocean only once (at Bad Doberan in 1824) and never having sailed, endeavored to translate Goethe's metaphors of stasis and kinesis into orchestral images, as an example of Marxian programmatic music.

Marx's treatise *Über Malerei in der Tonkunst* had allied "modern" music with the visual arts to reorient the Horatian simile linking poetry and painting, to explore ties between painting and music. Felix's musical inspiration was Beethoven's cantata—among other similarities, the two works share their key, D major, display broadly spaced sonorities, and are bipartite, with linking transitions[116]—yet there is compelling evidence Felix approached his score as a tone painting. Thus, he "wanted to avoid an overture with [a slow] introduction"; rather, the work comprised "two separate tableaux."[117] What is more, Lea reported that around this time Felix began to paint,[118] an activity that found its counterpart in Felix's manipulation of instrumental colors and timbres. To expand the orchestral palette and extremes of its registers, he added a piccolo, contrabassoon, and serpent (a now obsolete bass instrument related to the cornet family), and, in the coda, a third trumpet. And he experimented with subtle instrumental mixtures, as in the opening harmony, a symmetrical string sonority, the middle of which is inflected by clarinets and bassoons (**ex. 6.13a**). *Calm Sea* projects static pedal points in the neutral strings, with occasional touches of woodwinds, and, at the end,

Ex. 6.13a: Mendelssohn, *Calm Sea* (1828)

Ex. 6.13b: Mendelssohn, *Prosperous Voyage* (1828)

Ex. 6.13c: Mendelssohn, *Prosperous Voyage* (1828)

a fluttering figure in the flute, the first suggestion of a breeze. In contrast, *Prosperous Voyage* begins with a transition energized by woodwind and brass chords, as, in Goethe's classical allusion, Aeolus releases his winds.

The thematic material of the overture derives from a murky motive, initially submerged in the contrabass, that outlines the tonic D-major triad in its unstable first-inversion, descending from the root D through A to F♯. This motive washes over much of *Calm Sea*, as in bars 36–40, where five statements appear in the first and second violins, clarinet, cellos, and double bass, and underscore the impenetrable, static quality of Goethe's verse. But in *Prosperous Voyage*, the motive undergoes metamorphosis. Its characteristic dotted rhythm reemerges in the windswept first theme, while the lyrical second theme, which later served as a musical greeting between Felix and Droysen, outlines the motive in *ascending* form (**ex. 6.13b, c**). The tonal stasis of *Calm Sea*, primarily associated with a D major destabilized by non-root-position chords, gives way in *Prosperous Voyage* to a tonal voyage in sonata form that eventually finds haven in the port. The coda depicts the triumphant ending of the journey, a scene conceived by Felix (Goethe's poem ends with just the sighting of land): the dropping of anchor, cannonades from the shore greeting the vessel, and joyous fanfares performed by three trumpets, which secure the tonic triad in root position. But the surprise ending, with its *pianissimo* plagal cadence (D major–G-major–D-major), brings us full circle to the beginning, where the inaugural harmonic progression moves to the subdominant G major. As in the *Midsummer Night's Dream* Overture, the end thus refers to the beginning, and Felix emerges as a romantic tone poet, whose vivid score not only depicts images in Goethe's poetry but also extrapolates from its verses new interpretations.

After *Calm Sea and Prosperous Voyage* was premiered privately on September 7, 1828,[119] the concertmaster of the king's orchestra, Leopold Ganz, offered to present it publicly. But Felix declined for two reasons.[120] In effect, he himself had become becalmed in his compositions; the public was tired of his work, and he had "gently slipped into forgetfulness," where he wished to remain until his own return from travels abroad. Felix was still recovering from the failure of *Camacho* and the intense scrutiny of the public eye. There was, however, another cause for concern: "It was a great grief to me to hear that the King's band has refused to be led by me in public; but I cannot feel hurt, for I am too young and too little thought of." The exact nature of this contretemps—perhaps it was an anti-Semitic incident—remains a mystery, but the hurt was sufficient to convince Felix to withdraw. Not until 1832 was the overture heard publicly in Berlin; meanwhile, he repeated it at his residence, including at least one performance with Fanny as a piano duet, with lights dimmed to create the appropriate mood.[121]

V

For much of 1828 Felix's studies kept him in Berlin. The holidays, though, permitted some travel. Around Pentecost in May he escorted his brother, Paul, and school friends on a walking tour of Eberswalde, a summer resort northeast of Berlin. There they visited modern factories and drank *Bierkaltschale* with Droysen and Ferdinand David. And in October, between the semesters, Felix traveled to Brandenburg, where he met Justizrat Steinbeck, director of the local Singverein. At the piano Felix rendered Beethoven's Ninth Symphony and at the local churches performed fugues from the *Well-Tempered Clavier* and as many Bach organ works as Felix knew from memory. At a pastor's behest, Felix even endeavored to explain to some military officers the mysteries of fugues. The pièce de résistance was his improvisation on *Christe, Du Lamm Gottes*, which, Felix explained to Lea, Fanny could play for her since Fanny already knew it by heart and understood thoroughly his "manner."[122]

Upon returning to Berlin, Felix celebrated Fanny's and Zelter's birthdays. For Fanny, he completed *Hora est* and some piano pieces, including examples of the new *Lied ohne Worte*. To Klingemann, Fanny divulged that Felix had "lately written several beautiful ones," though only one from 1828, a Lied in E♭ major recorded on her birthday, has survived.[123] Its lyrical melody and chordal accompaniment provided a prototype for several piano Lieder that followed; indeed, one passage, marked *Grave*, impresses as a sketch for the *Lied ohne Worte* Op. 19b No. 4 (**ex. 6.14a, b**, 1829). Felix's textless songs of 1828 may have been related to a musical game he had played as a child with his sister, in which they devised verses to fit to instrumental pieces.[124] If so, Fanny may have played a role in developing the new genre; the Lieder may have been a "means of communication for Felix and Fanny,"[125] though Charles Gounod's assertion, that Felix published several of Fanny's *Lieder ohne Worte* under his name, has never been proven.[126]

On Zelter's seventieth birthday (December 11, 1828) the Singakademie held a grand celebration. Goethe contributed verses symbolically uniting

Ex. **6.14a:** Mendelssohn, *Grave* (1828)

Ex. **6.14b:** Mendelssohn, *Lied ohne Worte* in A major, Op. 19b No. 4 (1829)

the arts of architecture, poetry, and singing, but this time the task of composing a festive cantata fell to Zelter's assistant, C. F. Rungenhagen.[127] Was Felix asked to set the verses but declined? We do not know, though he did contribute a modest part-song for male voices, the *Tischlied* "Lasset heut am edlen Ort," hastily set to verses Goethe dispatched to Berlin on December 6.[128]

Hardly less festive were the Christmas celebrations in the Mendelssohn residence. Felix composed another toy symphony (lost), and the circle of friends expanded to greet new arrivals, including the mathematician Peter Gustav Lejeune Dirichlet (1805–1859), whom Alexander von Humboldt introduced to the family. In Cologne, Dirichlet had studied with G. S. Ohm, formulator of the law of electric resistance (1827). When Dirichlet became enamored of Rebecka, Gans quarreled and fought with him "like a schoolboy"[129] and endeavored to win the prize by reading Plato in Greek with her (their relationship, Fanny noted wryly, remained Platonic). Dirichlet joined the faculty of the university in 1831, the year of his engagement to Rebecka. They married the next year and lived in Berlin until 1855, when he filled a vacancy at the University of Göttingen caused by the death of the century's leading mathematician, Gauss.[130]

In October another suitor, Wilhelm Hensel, arrived after five years in Italy. Since he had not been allowed to correspond with Fanny, they had grown apart. The old circle of friends had changed (according to Sebastian Hensel; the new circle practiced a "coterie-slang not intelligible to the uninitiated");[131] Fanny had developed an intimate psychological dependence on Felix, through whom she sublimated her musical needs, arousing Wilhelm's jealousy; and the family was pulled toward politically liberal views through their friendship with Gans. Meanwhile, Wilhelm had become more conservative and expressed royalist leanings. Nevertheless, Fanny and Wilhelm rekindled their relationship; on Christmas Eve, he gave her a miniature Florentine pocket album in the shape of a heart, with delicately scalloped, gilded pages, in which he inscribed, "This little book is very like the heart, / You write in it joy or sorrow."[132] Here, through August 1833, Fanny recorded musical sketches, while her fiancé and, later, husband entered poems and drawings around events in the couple's lives, including Fanny's pregnancy and the birth of their son Sebastian in 1830, and the tragic delivery of a stillborn daughter in 1832.

From Italy Hensel had brought his imposing canvas *Christ and the Samaritan Woman by the Well* and the copy of Raphael's *Transfiguration*. Viewing the paintings at the Academy of Art, the king noted that the artist had "not used his time in Rome unproductively."[133] In January 1829 the academy nominated Hensel for membership, clearing the way for his appointment as court painter. His improving prospects overcame Lea's lingering reservations, and on January 22 Fanny and Wilhelm were engaged. In a poem for the occasion, Hensel contrasted the cold Berlin winter with the rejuvenating springtime within his breast.[134] On February 2 the lovers resumed corresponding, and the next day they were alone together for the first time.[135] Through Wilhelm's servant, they exchanged daily letters. Twenty-one have survived (February–October 1829), including thirteen by Fanny available to Sebastian but suppressed in *Die Familie Mendelssohn*, where he alluded only to their "truly pathetic, heart-moving beauty."[136] With filial devotion Sebastian strove to preserve the harmonious image of his parents' relationship; still, reading between the lines of his account suggests the engagement was anything but smooth. Thus, Fanny's "constant task" was "to shape two natures into one harmonious integrity."[137] Indeed, the letters, published only in 1995,[138] reveal a troubled engagement, as do several elliptical entries in Fanny's diary. In January, Fanny took exception to one of Wilhelm's drawings of her; on February 4 there was controversy about one of his letters; on February 17 he had a fit of jealousy; and on March 1 there was a dramatic scene with Lea about the wedding. Only on March 19 did Fanny feel "truly engaged"; yet, at the end of September, just days before the wedding, she noted another *Streit*. Through all this, Wilhelm impresses as an emotionally distraught, insecure man of thirty-five; Fanny, at twenty-three, as a woman bent on mollifying her fiancé, while becoming increasingly anxious herself about Felix's impending departure for England.

VI

The early weeks of the engagement coincided with the intensifying rehearsals of the St. Matthew Passion, in which Fanny was intimately involved, even though her role was subordinate: while Felix conducted Bach's masterpiece before the social elite of Berlin, Fanny sang as an alto in the chorus, reinforcing the gender divide between public and private. Eyewitness accounts of Eduard and Therese Devrient, Marx, Fanny, Schubring, and Zelter, among others, document the preparations for the event, Felix's two performances in March, and their enthusiastic reception.[139] But the primary sources contain inconsistencies, and the significance of the revival—the prime mover in the nineteenth-century rediscovery of Bach—has provoked no little controversy.

The revival began as a private initiative at the Mendelssohn residence, where Felix assembled a small chorus of friends to rehearse portions of the Passion. Schubring informs us that the devotees numbered only about sixteen, including the Devrients, Schubring, his theology class-mate E. F. A. Bauer, and the painter and art historian Franz Bugler. At this stage Felix merely intended to explore the Passion to disprove Schubring's skeptical assertion that Bach's music offered only a "dry arithmetical sum."[140] But another incentive may have been Marx's announcement in April 1828 of Schlesinger's decision to publish the work. Appearing in 1830, Marx's piano-vocal score of the Passion was an important by-product of Felix's performances; indeed, Marx used his journal to wage a "press cam-paign" for the work and issued a stream of reports before and after the performances in March and April 1829.[141]

Exactly when the rehearsals at Leipzigerstrasse No. 3 began remains unclear. Eduard Devrient claims they were underway by the winter of 1827, while his wife Therese dates the first meetings from October 1828.[142] Initially, like Zelter, Felix had no thought of a public revival; rather, the rehearsals were intended for the private edification of his circle. To ven-ture before the public was to raise formidable obstacles: largely ignorant of Bach's music, Berlin audiences would not tolerate the complexities of the Passion, and its unusual scoring—requiring two orchestras and two choruses—offered another hindrance. But as the rehearsals advanced, a new musical world opened to Felix. In particular, the "impersonation of the several characters of the Gospel by different voices" impressed Eduard Devrient as the "pith of the work," a practice "long forgotten" in old church music.[143] Devrient yearned to sing the role of Christ and to realize through performance the dramatic continuity of the Passion.

The rest of Devrient's entertaining account is well known: how, one day in January 1829, he roused Felix from his slumber to convince him to perform the work, how the two set off to Zelter, how Zelter demurred, comparing the venture to the brazen child's play of two "snot-nosed brats" (*Rotznasen*), how Devrient held firm and overcame Zelter's resistance, and how the two—dressed in a *Passionsuniform* of blue coats, white waist-coats, black neckties and trousers, and yellow leather gloves—enlisted the vocal soloists from the Royal opera and secured the approval of the Singakademie management. Finally, Felix captured the significance of the undertaking with the observation, "And to think that it has to be an actor and a young Jew who return to the people the greatest Christian music!"[144]

Other documents encourage us to refine Devrient's account. First, the issue of the performance was raised not in January but a few weeks earlier: on December 13 Felix and Eduard petitioned the Singakademie to use the hall for the performance, which was granted in exchange for a fee of fifty thalers.[145] Around this time, the two friends must have come to terms with Zelter, for on December 27 Fanny was able to report to Klingemann about another "special" condition not mentioned by Devrient: "[Felix] has many different projects before him, and is arranging for the Academy Handel's cantata *Acis and Galatea*, in return for which the Academy will sing for him and Devrient the Passion, to be performed during the winter for a charitable cause. . . ."[146] Felix sent his arrangement to Zelter on January 8 and promised to begin work on another one, of a Handel *Te Deum*.[147]

We can identify three other concurrent "projects." From Fanny's diary, we know Felix was absorbed in a "heavenly symphony"; indeed, on January 3, Fanny recorded in her heart-shaped diary a few bars from the finale of the *Reformation* Symphony, proving her brother was already pondering that composition early in 1829.[148] Then, at the end of the month, he dated the autograph of the *Andante con variazioni* for cello and piano,[149] published in 1830 as the *Variations concertantes* Op. 17. Built upon a graceful D-major theme, the work comprises eight variations, of which the first six adhere closely to the theme. But in the turbulent seventh variation in D minor, the piano part erupts in a *martellato* octave passage that disrupts the symmetry of the theme. In the final variation, the theme returns, only to undergo expansion in a free, stretto-like coda before the composition comes to a tranquil close. Dedicated to the composer's brother, the variations reveal Paul to have been an amateur cellist of considerable ability.

Felix's third project from this period proved more burdensome: on February 23 he completed a recitative and aria for soprano and orchestra, "respectfully dedicated" to Anna Milder-Hauptmann—one might speculate, in exchange for her agreement to sing one of the soprano roles in the Passion. Only a few pages of the score survive, revealing a fairly conventional recitative with agitated string tremolos (*Tutto è silenzio*), in which we learn that the unidentified character has been accused of murdering her husband, and the beginning of a soothing Handelian aria (*Dei clementi*, "Merciful gods").[150] In April, after Felix departed for England, Fanny rehearsed this piece with the prima donna, who insisted Fanny phrase the vocal part, a request she considered ridiculous but agreed to oblige, as she realized how "thoroughly sick" Felix had become of the composition.[151]

On February 2 choral rehearsals of the Passion began in the Singakademie, one day before Felix's twentieth birthday, when wind musicians serenaded him with arrangements of the Doberan *Harmoniemusik* and Overture to *Camacho*. Joining the celebration, Ludwig Robert contributed a poem inspired by the piano fugue for Hanstein (see p. 172), and Wilhelm gave Felix Jean Paul's serendipitous novel of adolescent awakening, *Flegeljahre* (*Fledgling Years*;[152] two years later the novel's twins, Walt and Vult, would inspire Robert Schumann to compose the piano cycle *Papillons*). As the rehearsals continued, additional members of the Singakademie augmented the chorus. Felix rehearsed from the piano until the orchestra joined the chorus on March 6. The dress rehearsal was held on March 10, and the following evening he presented Bach's masterpiece publicly for the first time in one hundred years.

The soloists were the sopranos Anna Milder-Hauptmann and seventeen-year-old Pauline von Schätzel, alto Auguste Türrschmidt, tenors Heinrich Stümer (Evangelist) and Carl Adam Bader (Peter), baritone Eduard Devrient (Christ), and basses J. E. Busolt (High Priest and Governor) and Weppler (Judas). The chorus was 158 strong (47 sopranos, 36 altos, 34 tenors, and 41 basses), nowhere near the 300 to 400 mentioned in Devrient's account.[153] Most of the orchestral personnel were amateurs from the Philharmonische Gesellschaft founded by Eduard Rietz in 1826 (the first chairs of the strings and the winds were members of the royal Kapelle). Using a baton, Felix conducted from a piano placed diagonally on the stage, with the first chorus behind and second chorus and orchestra before him. According to Devrient, instead of continually beating time, Felix occasionally lowered his baton, so as to "influence without obtruding himself."[154] Therese Devrient reported that the familiar Protestant chorales were sung *a cappella*, though Marx, contradicting her claim, maintained the orchestra accompanied all the chorales except *Wenn ich einmal soll scheiden*.[155]

By the day of the concert the tickets were oversubscribed, necessitating the turning away of a thousand Berliners. Attending were the king and his retinue, Schleiermacher, Hegel, Heinrich Heine, Rahel von Varnhagen, Spontini, and Zelter, who, after participating in the early rehearsals, took his place with "exemplary resignation" in the audience.[156] There a visiting Italian violinist may have joined him. Nicolò Paganini had arrived early in March and played in Berlin eleven times to rave reviews. After hearing his first concert, Fanny confided "he had the look of an insane murderer and the gesticulations of a monkey."[157] Only months before, Paganini had undergone a painful operation to remove his teeth, after which his countenance assumed a macabre, sunken quality. The Mendelssohns received the edentulous musician on March 12, when Wilhelm drew his portrait.[158] His acrobatic virtuosity—playing the violin on one string or upside down, and executing unfathomable trills and multiple stops—must have been seen as a complete contrast to the spiritual solemnity of the St. Matthew Passion, a stark juxtaposition of the new and old, the secular and religious sublime.

To render Bach's colossal work accessible to Berlin audiences—there was no question of performing it in toto—Felix made cuts and revisions, all entered into his score. The excisions included ten arias, four recitatives, and six chorales.[159] The question of how Felix deleted material has recently sparked controversy. In 1993 Michael Marissen proposed that the cuts partly reflected Felix's desire to de-emphasize anti-Semitic passages in the text,[160] but in 2000 Jeffrey Sposato drew another conclusion. Felix acted "as he perceived any other Lutheran conductor would," for he "must have been aware that the idea of a Mendelssohn bringing forth this 'greatest Christian musical work' would be viewed with skepticism and subjected to microscopic scrutiny."[161] Sposato argued that many cuts were intended to remove passages deemed textually or musically redundant; in addition, Felix's abridged version won wide acceptance in subsequent performances of the Passion throughout Germany.

His treatment of the chorale *O Haupt voll Blut und Wunden*, occurring no fewer than six times in the Passion, seems to support Sposato's conclusions. In Part 1 Bach juxtaposed two statements of the melody (No. 21, "Erkenne mich, mein Hüter" in E major and No. 23, "Ich will hier bei dir stehen" in E♭), separating them only by a brief recitative. In Part 2 the chorale recurred in No. 53, "Befiehl du deine Wege," D major; in No. 63, where two verses, "O Haupt voll Blut und Wunden" and "O Haupt zu Spott gebunden" are sung in F major; and finally in No. 72, "Wenn ich einmal soll scheiden" in A minor, sung after Jesus expires on the Cross. Of the six Felix retained only the first, fourth, and sixth, thereby removing three repetitions, though also disturbing Bach's use of the chorale as a unifying device, with its chromatic tonal descent (E major, E♭ major, and D major) giving way to an ascending trajectory (F major and A minor). Of course, this particular chorale was well known to Berliners; Graun had featured it in his Passion cantata *Der Tod Jesu*, frequently performed by Zelter on Good Friday. Felix was cognizant of the chorale's popularity, for he took the trouble to alter the text of "O Haupt voll Blut und Wunden" to make it conform to the Berlin version.[162] Thus, in the third phrase, the reference to Christ's "adorned" (*gezieret*) head was modified to "crowned" (*gekrönet*), and in the fourth "mocked" (*verhöhnet*) was exchanged for "insulted" (*schimpfieret*).

The purpose of these subtle changes seems clear enough: Berliners were encouraged to discover in Bach's cerebral masterpiece roots of their own spiritual experiences as German Protestants. The Singakademie now became a kind of musical sanctuary, as Bach's score swept over the audience like a divine revelation. As conductor, Felix symbolically presided over the "congregation" and reaffirmed his ties to the leading Prussian theologian present at the performance—Schleiermacher. In 1830 Felix would disclose he had become a follower (*Anhänger*) of Schleiermacher,[163] author of the *Der Christliche Glaube* (*The Christian Faith*, 1821–1822). Here Schleiermacher expounded his concept of *Gemeindetheologie*, which emphasized the collective fellowship of the congregation over the spirituality of the individual. Felix would have attended the theologian's sermons in Trinity Church, and at the university would have had personal contact with him as well.

The reception accorded the Passion was nothing short of extraordinary. The Bachian mysteries of Zelter's inner circle were now publicly revealed, in Ludwig Rellstab's words, as the "most perfect creation of German art."[164] Despite Spontini's machinations, the crown prince authorized a second performance on Bach's birthday, March 21, and after Felix had left for England, Zelter led a third performance on Good Friday, April 17, instead of *Der Tod Jesu*. The Bach Revival erupted in full force throughout Germany, where the St. Matthew Passion became the emblem of the ideal Protestant artwork. But in time Felix's triumph was tarnished by voices seeking to minimize his contribution. In 1883 Eduard Grell, a Zelter pupil who had become the Singakademie director in 1853, claimed in a private letter that if someone had "excavated" the Passion, that individual was Zelter. Then, in 1929, on the bicentenary of the composition, Georg Schünemann put forward a similar view and designated Zelter, not the "genial" twenty-year-old, as the "leading head" of the revival, a position Schünemann disputed in print with the musicologist Friedrich Smend.[165] And, of course, the Nazi regime would summarily deny the signal contribution of the *Neuchrist* Felix, who had restored Bach's music only eventually to fall victim himself to anti-Semitism.

The revival of the St. Matthew Passion was the culminating event of Felix's youth. Through the public success he symbolically achieved full assimilation into Prussian culture and thus confirmed his Christian faith through Bach's ineluctable Passion, a work that had frustrated Zelter's timid efforts at rediscovery. This epoch-making composition had indeed risen phoenixlike from the ashes, and Fanny and Felix had lived to see great things. Once again Felix had come before the public eye—for the moment, in triumph. Now, at age twenty, the mature composer prepared to visit England in order to escape the stultifying atmosphere of Berlin, to experience a different musical culture, and to establish an international career.

Part II

The Road to Damascus

Amateur Gentleman

This prophet, too, is not honored in his own
country; he must go elsewhere.[1]

—Ignaz Moscheles

The idea of sending Felix abroad on an extended journey—the "grand
tour" of European gentlemen—was Abraham's. Never fully comfortable
with his family's position as integrated Berliners, he harbored a desire
that Felix would escape to launch a career elsewhere. Though Abraham
preferred cosmopolitan Paris, Felix had already formed in 1825 a decidedly contrary view. Abraham's solution was to subsidize three years of
travel to allow Felix to examine firsthand several European musical cen-
ters. And so, between 1829 and 1832 Felix visited England, Bavaria, Austria, Switzerland, Italy, and France; his experiences, richly documented
in letters, diaries, and drawings, and transformed into several major compositions, ultimately reinforced his identity as a German musician.

His declared purpose was "not to appear in public, but . . . to consolidate my own taste."[2] For advice Abraham turned to Moscheles, who recommended that the young "genius" be introduced "to the great London
world"[3] around Easter, in the midst of the concert season. Largely on this
counsel, Felix planned to travel to London in April, return to Berlin for
Fanny's wedding, and proceed to Munich, Vienna, and Rome. Zelter supported the leave-taking of the parental nest;[4] still, the old musician tried
unsuccessfully to delay the journey until after the third performance of
the St. Matthew Passion, scheduled for Good Friday, April 17.[5]

Late March and early April were fraught with preparations for the
departure. But Felix found time to play the organs at the Dreifaltigskeit

(Trinity), Garnison (Garrison), and parish churches—to her diary Fanny confided that nothing was more fearful than Felix's rendering of the opening chorus of the St. Matthew Passion.[6] There were conversations with Heinrich Heine, whom she found affected (still, "though for ten times you may be inclined to despise him, the eleventh time you cannot help confessing that he is a poet, a true poet!"[7]) and Paganini, for whom Fanny played for hours. The family admired a new, three-quarter portrait by Wilhelm Hensel of Felix seated on a garden bench before lilac bushes, with his fingers expressively arched, his face turned, lost in thought.[8] Droysen captured the imminent departure in the short poem *Wartend* (*Expecting*), set by Felix as a strophic *Romanze* and later incorporated into his second volume of songs as Op. 9 No. 3. The first verse reads: "She bore a falcon on her hand, and sent him across the ocean. Come soon, come soon!" In the second, the falcon returns with a traveler who expresses his pleasures and woes on a *Waldhorn*; in the third, the young maiden awakens from her morning dream. Cast in a stark B minor, Felix's setting approaches folksong, underscoring his intention, announced to Klingemann, to "rake together" Scottish folksongs during his journey.[9] Thus, there are hollow, open-fifth sonorities, a surprise *pianissimo* ending in B major, and high-pitched fanfares, like those in the *Hebrides* Overture, which Felix would conceive in August 1829.

Early on April 10, Felix departed with Abraham and Rebecka for Hamburg, where Salomon Heine regaled the trio with a formal dinner. Felix visited the violinist Leopold Lindenau and, at the local Singverein, heard some choral works of Spohr that did not please. ("They hang Jews for poisoning fountains," he commented mordantly, "but music is just as valuable as a fountain, I hope, and therefore Spohr will have to die."[10]) At the Michaeliskirche, not far from his birthplace, he improvised on the organ. Then, after receiving from Berlin his copy of Jean Paul Richter's *Flegeljahre*, he embarked on the steam packet *Attwood* on April 18.

Ironically enough, the vessel was named after a musician Felix would soon meet, Thomas Attwood,[11] Mozart's celebrated English pupil. But this coincidence failed to secure a prosperous voyage; adversely affecting the three-day crossing were contrary winds, impenetrable fog, and a breakdown of the engine. On Easter morning a seasick Felix was experiencing fainting spells, and when, on the evening of April 20, the *Attwood* anchored at the mouth of the Thames in order to avoid collisions, he cursed his own *Meeresstille*.[12] Through the moonlight he could make out hundreds of "becalmed" vessels. The following day the *Attwood* steamed up the Thames, and for the first time he beheld "the awful mass of London,"[13] a sprawling metropolis of over one million.

I

When Felix reached the Customs House at noon, Klingemann took him to a coffee house where the two perused the *Times*. Rossini's *Otello* with the celebrated Spanish mezzo-soprano Maria Malibran was announced for the evening, and the exhausted Felix borrowed Klingemann's stockings and donned a black cravat so that he could appear in genteel society. In 1829 Italian opera in London was the monopoly of the King's Theatre (near the bottom of the Haymarket), which depended upon a retinue of highly compensated opera stars and leasing boxes to an exclusive audience. Felix secured a seat in the pit, apart from the "six tiers of boxes with crimson curtains, out of which peep the ladies, bedecked with great white feathers, chains, jewels of all kinds." Four years before, he had heard the Italian soprano Giuditta Pasta play Desdemona in Paris, and now he found the talented Malibran's singing, if full of "clever embellishments of her own invention," occasionally hyperbolic and bordering on the "ridiculous and disagreeable." Between the acts was a vacuous *divertissement*, with "gymnastics and absurdities just as with us," so that only after midnight was Malibran-Desdemona dispatched, "panting and screaming disagreeably."[14] When the opera then yielded to a ballet (appropriately enough, *La Sonnambule*), the weary Felix retired to his lodgings.

Moscheles had secured rooms for his young friend at 103 Great Portland Street, the residence of Friedrich Heinke, a German ironmonger in the fashionable West End. Here, in sitting rooms on the second floor, Felix had the use of two grand pianos (one from the firm of Muzio Clementi) and could practice as well on a "dumb" keyboard.[15] His only complaint was the expense; for half the cost, rooms were available on the third floor, but Moscheles and Klingemann insisted he remain on the second, to accommodate the social calls he would doubtless receive. Other adjustments had to be made: Felix's visiting cards lacked the English "Mr.," and Moscheles recommended new cards be engraved, lest Felix appear *unmodisch* whenever he offered his card to a duke or minister.[16]

Felix's London circle included several transplanted Germans. In addition to Klingemann, Moscheles and his wife, Charlotte, with whom Felix went riding in Hyde Park, there was Neukomm, in whose music Moscheles had found a "pitiful lack of Attic salt."[17] Felix also renewed his friendship with Wilhelm Horn, son of a German physician, and Adolphe d'Eichthal, son of a wealthy Parisian banker, whose Jewish family had converted to Catholicism in 1817 (Sebastian Hensel deleted references to the d'Eichthals in *Die Familie Mendelssohn*, owing to the "excesses" of Adolphe's brother Gustave, a disciple of the positivist Auguste Comte, who later joined the radical Saint-Simonians in Paris). And finally, there were two Germans who held appointments at the new University of London: a new acquaintance, Ludwig von Mühlenfels (1798–1861), professor of German and Nordic literature, who had fled Prussia owing to his activities in the student movement;[18] and a Berlin friend, the brilliant Sanskrit scholar Friedrich Rosen (1805–1837), who at twenty-two had become a professor of Oriental literature.

Assisted by Moscheles, Felix easily mingled with English musicians: the music publisher Vincent Novello and his daughter, the soprano Clara; the glee composer William Horsley; the critic and Beethoven devotee T. M. Alsager;[19] the impresario William Ayrton, former manager of the King's Theatre and editor of the musical periodical *The Harmonicon*, founded in 1823; and Sir George Smart. The two leading English pianists, Charles Neate and Cipriani Potter, had met Beethoven in Vienna in 1815 and 1818. In London they often concertized with the Cramer brothers, the violinist Franz, concertmaster of the Philharmonic, and the pianist-composer Johann Baptist, who, Felix reported, usually appeared inebriated. When, during a visit to 103 Great Portland Street, Johann Baptist began to improvise on the piano, Felix recorded his own perfect pitch by charting Cramer's perambulating modulations in a letter to Berlin.[20] Eager to meet Muzio Clementi, Felix had come to London with a letter from Clementi's former pupil Ludwig Berger. But by 1829 the septuagenarian had retired and moved to central England, and Felix contented himself with playing instruments from the virtuoso's firm.

An especially warm friendship developed between Felix and Thomas Attwood (1765–1838). Sent in 1785 by the Prince of Wales to Vienna, Attwood had studied for a year and a half with Mozart; Attwood's exercises, blending species counterpoint and "free" composition, form an invaluable record of Mozart's didactic method. In 1796 Attwood was appointed organist of St. Paul's Cathedral, and through him Felix gained access to its organ and impressed the Englishman with improvisations and performances of Bach. On June 2 Felix witnessed an imposing spectacle in the cathedral: on an immense scaffold erected beneath the dome, several thousand orphans sang Psalm 100 under Attwood's direction. But St. Paul's was also the site of musical controversy. On May 14, anniversary of the charitable institution for the Sons of the Clergy, anthems by Boyce, Handel, and Attwood, and Henry Purcell's *Te Deum* and *Jubilate* in D were performed. Felix attended with the Belgian critic F.-J. Fétis, editor of the *Revue musicale*, who had offered to arrange a Parisian performance of the Symphony Op. 11. In a letter dispatched to Paris on June 5 and translated in the *Atlas* on July 12, Fétis reproved Purcell's composition for its "long succession of insignificant phrases, ill-connected modulations, and incorrect, albeit pretending, harmonies,"[21] and mischievously added that "a young and highly distinguished German composer ... received precisely the same impressions" and was so nonplused by the Purcell that he left before the *Jubilate*. A minor controversy now erupted in the press, with one irate English music lover dubbing Felix the "*unhappy [infelix] Mendelssohn*" and treating him with "that kind of disdain which liberal critics seldom feel, and discreet people never express." Appalled that his private comments were bruited about, Felix drafted a reply, published in German in Marx's journal,[22] and in English (presumably with Klingemann's assistance) in the *Britannia* and *Harmonicon*.[23] The *Britannia* issued an apology, but the rift with Fétis was never healed.

Moscheles did all he could to facilitate Felix's entrance into English musical society. Thus, the choice of Felix's lodgings on Great Portland Street was not arbitrary; Sir George Smart lived on the same street, and nearby were the Hanover Square and Argyll Rooms, the preferred venues for concerts. During the 1820s the character of English concert life changed, as the tastes of the upper middle class impinged more and more on the musical domain of the aristocracy. Two institutions which Felix observed firsthand show this development compellingly. The Ancient Concerts, founded by peers in the eighteenth century, were held at Hanover Square Rooms, where Haydn's London Symphonies had been premiered during the 1790s. Directed by aristocratic amateurs, the Ancient Concerts programmed music at least twenty years old and favored works of Handel. In contrast, the Argyll Rooms, on Regent Street near Oxford Circus, became the venue of the Philharmonic Society, founded in 1813 and emerging a few years later as a professional orchestra devoted to modern music, including Beethoven's symphonies. Here Spohr led the orchestra in 1820 with a baton, challenging the English custom of dual directorship, a "conductor" at the piano and the first violinist as a "leader." Here Smart gave the English premiere of Beethoven's Ninth Symphony in 1825, albeit with mixed results (William Ayrton, for one, observed that Beethoven had "drawn out the thread of his verbosity finer than the staple of his argument").[24] Here, finally, Carl Maria von Weber conducted the ensemble only ten days before his death in 1826.

Each year the Philharmonic performed eight concerts between February and June, timed to coincide with the annual calendar of "high society." Around Christmas, before Parliament convened, the nobility and gentry began to arrive in sumptuous West End residences from their country estates. After the Easter recess, the season commenced in earnest, "a three-month whirlwind of parties, balls, and sporting events,"[25] the chief purpose of which was to marry off eligible young ladies. The height of the

concert season fell in May, June, and July, with the continuation of subscription concerts, a rash of "benefit" concerts for individual performers,
Italian opera at the King's Theatre, and "English opera" (usually severely
truncated reworkings of continental operas) at Covent Garden and Drury
Lane. Then, in August, Parliament adjourned, and the elite returned to
the country to pursue their favorite avocations—grouse, partridge, pheas-
ant, and fox hunting—before the cycle renewed itself.

True to his declared aim, Felix became thoroughly acquainted with
English musical institutions and was most partial to the Philharmonic
Concerts, which offered a mixture of new and recent orchestral, chamber, and solo works. Programs always fell into two "acts," often in a nearly
symmetrical pattern: a symphony, aria, chamber work, vocal ensemble,
and overture for the first, and a symphony, vocal work, concerto, aria,
and overture for the second.[26] Though Felix was not uncritical of the
organization—Smart, Felix noted, simply sat at the piano and turned
pages—he discovered a positive artistic environment in the Argyll Rooms.
The audience, drawn largely from a newly affluent upper middle class
distinct from the nobility, easily related to Felix, who performed without compensation and thus observed the code of the amateur, was from
a prosperous but not noble German family and, of course, was a musical
talent of the first magnitude.

Not surprisingly, Felix abstained from public appearances until the
Philharmonic performed one of his compositions. Instead, he participated in private gatherings and, on May 8, joined the orchestra at King's
Theatre as a violinist or violist for Moscheles's "morning concert," which
featured appearances by Malibran and the German soprano Henriette
Sontag. Near the end of April, the secretary of the Philharmonic, William Watts, asked to examine Felix's compositions, and he submitted his
three concert overtures (Opp. 21, 27, and 101) and First Symphony. But
confusion about Felix's status delayed the decision, for Smart had told
the directors that Felix was a "gentleman," not a "professor."[27] And the
selection of his debut composition proved somewhat problematic: *Calm
Sea* was ruled out because the three-stringed instrument of the principal contrabassist, Dragonetti, could not accommodate the low F♯ of the
opening motive.[28] The final choice was the First Symphony. On May 25,
at the seventh concert, the "conductor" J. B. Cramer escorted Felix "like
a young lady" to the piano in the Argyll Rooms. From there he directed
with a new baton, still such a novelty that its English maker had mistaken Felix for an alderman and insisted on "decorating it with a crown."[29]
The occasion marked one of Felix's first public appearances with a baton; Schubring later reminisced that Felix "had hitherto modestly stated
his opinion, from the piano or the desk of the tenor [i.e., viola]."[30]

According to Sir George Smart, "not much notice" was taken of the symphony,[31] though Felix proudly reported that the middle movements were encored. But the performance was significant for another reason. Felix had determined that the minuet was a dispensable "pleonasm," and in its place he substituted an arrangement of the scherzo from the Octet, thereby injecting some whimsy into the dramatic C-minor composition[32] (curiously, when in 1834 Felix published the parts of the symphony in Germany, he reverted to the minuet). At the concert the movement, announced as an "intermezzo," was performed "by only a limited number of violins, tenors, and basses, . . . and all the wind instruments,"[33] reinforcing its elfinlike character. In addition, Felix compressed the second half of the scherzo and retouched the scoring by adding delicate intrusions of winds and soft trumpet fanfares, and giving the final evanescent arpeggiation to the flute, to produce a "silly" but novel effect. The next day Felix presented the autograph of the symphony with a dedicatory letter in French to the Society,[34] and on June 10, at a concert of the flutist Charles Nicholson, the work received its second English performance.

Felix participated in four other public concerts. On May 30, he offered Weber's *Konzertstück*, performed from "recollection" (i.e., memory),[35] and on June 15, his own Variations Op. 17 with the cellist Robert Lindley. Felix's final appearances were considerably more elaborate affairs. For the benefit concert of the flutist Louis Drouet, which fell on Midsummer Day (June 24), Felix gave the English premieres of Beethoven's *Emperor* Concerto and the *Midsummer Night's Dream* Overture. To the audience's astonishment, he played the concerto from memory on an instrument from the London factory of Sébastien Erard, whom Felix compared to a sorrowful parody of Goethe's Werther.[36] The overture posed new challenges: there were difficulties in securing a bass-horn player; and in the first measure the two flutes were not together, causing the audience to chuckle. At the "false" *fortissimo* ending in E major, the audience began to applaud, only to be surprised by the puckish epilogue of the work. At the end, though, there was sufficient clamor for the encore of the overture, through which the appreciative audience maintained a mouselike silence.[37]

Felix's final appearance occurred on July 13, at a benefit concert of Henriette Sontag for victims of flooding in Silesia. Abraham had received news from Nathan Mendelssohn about the widespread suffering, and Felix now resolved to promote a musical relief effort. Despite the lateness of the season, he was able to secure the Argyll Rooms *gratis* and organize a *concert monstre*[38] lasting over four hours, featuring Sontag, who sang six times, Malibran, Drouet, Moscheles, and himself, and raising some three hundred guineas. Felix and Moscheles performed the

Concerto for two pianos in E, fitted with a new cadenza,[39] and once again Felix directed the *Midsummer Night's Dream* Overture. A reviewer in the *Harmonicon* found the overture "sparkling with genius and rich in effect; some parts playful and sylph-like, others lofty and solid; the whole indicating that the musician has studied the poet, has entered into his thoughts, and even caught some of his imagination."[40]

Felix's success generated new commissions, though most remained unfulfilled. Covent Garden suggested at least two opera libretti, while Drury Lane offered him three hundred guineas to set a book by James Robinson Planché (1796–1880),[41] librettist of Weber's last opera, *Oberon*, which had premiered at Covent Garden in April 1826. Nothing came of the proposals or of a plan to invite Felix to conduct his choral music at the Birmingham Musical Festival of 1829. But most unusual of all was a commission in June to compose an anthem jointly commemorating the abolition of slavery in Ceylon and birthday of George IV. Sir Alexander Johnston, the former governor of the island, gave Felix some verses by the Scotsman Allan Cunningham, among which we read: "A two-fold joy is ours—this morn, / Our king, our freedom, both were born; / Great George, our isle's and ocean's lord, / A conqueror more with mind than sword."[42] Felix viewed the task as something of a joke and signed himself "Composer to the Island of Ceylon." No copy of the music has survived, although it was published in 1836 by the London firm of Paine & Hopkins and clearly pleased Johnston, who went so far as to claim, "This air will have more effect in India in the cause of humanity than all the philanthropic measures which have been adopted in different parts of Europe in favor of slaves."[43]

From Berlin Abraham grew concerned that his son appeared in the English newspapers not as Mendelssohn Bartholdy, but Mendelssohn. On July 8 the father chided Felix that a "Christian Mendelssohn is as impossible as a Jewish Confucius."[44] The same day Fanny wrote to Felix about their father's distress, even though she approved of his "intention to lay aside some day this name that we all dislike."[45] In 1955 and 1963, Eric Werner interpreted Felix's behavior as an "open contradiction to his father's wishes," and possibly an "act of hostility against his uncle Bartholdy."[46] But Jeffrey Sposato's reexamination of the evidence casts doubt on Werner's conclusions. Felix received Abraham's letter on July 14, *after* the final concert appearance at the Sontag benefit of July 13. In a reply of July 16 he explained that he had remonstrated with the English editors, but that they wished to underscore his relation to his grandfather.[47] Felix never dropped the surname Bartholdy, and, heeding his father's wishes, he continued to sign himself formally Felix Mendelssohn Bartholdy.

II

When not appearing at concerts, Felix mixed in high society and attended fashionable balls (at one he encountered the prime minister, Wellington, and secretary of home affairs, Peel). With Lord Sandon, former Lord of the Admiralty, he visited the House of Commons, where he heard the Irish orator Daniel O'Connell, whose election to Parliament had precipitated a crisis that led to the Catholic Emancipation Act.[48] There were other adventures as well. At the Royal Music Library (then still housed in one of the royal residences) Felix pored over Handel's autographs, and through some musicological sleuthing discovered the composer's habit of reusing material, detailed in a report to Zelter.[49] Felix played the art connoisseur, admiring paintings of van Eyck, Titian, and Correggio owned by the Duke of Devonshire, and the sculpture gallery of the Marquis of Lansdowne. But at the Royal Academy of Art exhibition at Somerset House, he reacted viscerally to canvases of Thomas Lawrence, David Wilkie, and William Turner, and dismissed Turner's blurry art as "the most hideous smearing" (*greulichste Schmierereien*).[50] Felix himself was the subject of a portrait taken during his sojourn and completed in 1830 by the English miniaturist James Warren Childe, which shows the twenty-year-old elegantly attired, with top hat in hand and wearing a cravat and gold watch chain, a somewhat dandified English gentleman.[51] Felix's love of Shakespeare inevitably drew him to the theater, but he found performances corrupted by the "insertion of ridiculously bad arias and songs";[52] one could make a tragedy of all the omissions from the plays, and the celebrated Kemble, who played Hamlet at Covent Garden with one yellow and one black leg "to indicate madness," behaved more like a "John Bull Oxford student" than a tragic Danish prince.[53]

As a sightseer Felix was awestruck by the Docks, which dwarfed the "mere pond"[54] of the Hamburg harbor. No less impressive was the subaqueous excavation undertaken in 1824 by Marc Isambard Brunel, the Rotherhithe-to-Wapping Tunnel under the Thames. In 1828 the project was halted about midway when the shaft flooded, drowning several workers (construction resumed in 1835, and the tunnel eventually opened in 1843). Probably through a letter from Alexander von Humboldt, who had visited Brunel in 1827, Felix met the French engineer and on June 13 toured the tunnel with his son, Isambard Kingdom Brunel, who later built the Great Western Railway.[55]

Felix's colorful letters describe one other unusual London introduction. In May he called at the office of J. C. Spurzheim (1776–1832), founder of phrenology and author of *Observations on the Deranged Manifestations of the Mind, or Insanity* (1817). When the *Edinburgh Review* pronounced his research "thorough quackery," Spurzheim moved to Edinburgh to counter his critics. There, in 1828, Moscheles encountered him and, without revealing his identity, asked for a reading of his skull. Spurzheim noted a "disposition for fine art," and after Moscheles disclosed his name, continued with a disquisition about cranial bumps.[56] Presumably Moscheles encouraged Felix to visit the doctor's London office, where, on May 8, a cast of Felix's skull was made. But he was unconvinced by the scientific rigor of the discipline and doubted whether the genius of a composer such as Gluck could be precisely located, even though the "difference between Gluck's brow and that of a parricide" was "probably beyond all doubt." Palpation of Felix's cranium revealed he was "rather greedy, loved order and small children, and liked to flirt—but music was supposedly the predominant characteristic."[57]

<h1 style="text-align:center">III</h1>

Implausibly enough, given his full social calendar, Felix found time for creative work. First, he acquainted Moscheles and Klingemann with recent compositions, among them a new cantata in A minor, *Wer nur den lieben Gott lässt walten* (based on the seventeenth-century chorale by Georg Neumark), which Klingemann found pale and almost sentimental.[58] No dated autograph survives, but the cantata presumably stems from the early months of 1829; in July, Felix gave a manuscript copy to Charles Neate.[59] Its four movements include a homophonic setting of the chorale; a polyphonic chorus with the melody placed as a cantus-firmus in the bass; a freely composed Andante for soprano solo (which Fanny found "overly simple," even "childish");[60] and a final statement of the chorale by the chorus in unison, accompanied by dissonant figuration in the strings. The cantata is unabashedly Bachian, though when it was composed, Felix did not yet know Bach's cantata on the same chorale (BWV 93), to which Felix's work nevertheless bore some affinities.[61]

In London Felix dispatched several musical curiosities, including a miniature Scherzo in B minor for piano, characterized by delicate staccati and shifts from major to minor, all revisiting the *Midsummer Night's Dream* Overture.[62] On May 24 he penned for the contralto Marian Cramer (daughter of Franz) a setting of Thomas Moore's amorous poem *The Garland*, with a gently pulsating figure in the piano accompaniment for "my love shall twine thee round her brow." But Felix had not yet forgotten Betty Pistor and planned to dedicate his major new work of the summer, the String Quartet in E♭, Op. 12, to her. By the beginning of July, he had progressed as far as the slow movement.

Markedly in contrast to Felix's public London life was Fanny's domestic Berlin routine. There were continuing strains in her engagement
to Wilhelm and delays in setting their wedding date. Fanny pined for
Felix, noting even before he departed that his absence cast a "deep shadow
on this sunny time of my life."[63] Clearly the siblings' separation undermined the fraternal support essential for Fanny's creative world. And so
she compared the brilliance of Felix's revival of the St. Matthew Passion
to Zelter's inept performance on Good Friday: at a rehearsal "Zelter himself played, and you can well imagine what he created with his two fingers and his *complete lack of knowledge* of the score."[64] During the
performance of the recitative "Ach, Golgatha," Milder remained a half
bar behind; seldom had "such misery . . . been heard."

To remember her brother, Fanny admired Hensel's new portrait (see
p. 202). And she was drawn to Felix's music, in particular to the "Scottish"
Sonata (*Sonate écossaise*). Released in 1834 as the *Phantasie* in F♯ minor,
Op. 28, this was one of the few large-scale piano works Felix published. In
May 1829 Fanny acknowledged borrowing a melodic phrase Felix had used
in the work the previous year. From this evidence we may date the sonata
to 1828, though on July 7, 1829, Klingemann playfully asserted to Fanny
that it still remained to be finished in England.[65] Like so many of Felix's
larger works, it continued to gestate long after its first draft.

The piece opens with a dreamy, Andante fantasia in the minor, followed by a lighter, major-keyed Allegro. The impetuous finale, again in
the minor, erupts as a substantial sonata-form Presto that dramatically
shifts the weight of the composition. Externally Felix modeled the composition upon Beethoven's own three-movement hybrid of fantasy and
sonata, the "Moonlight" Sonata, but Fanny was attracted to Felix's music because of its evocation of Scotland in the first movement. As Roger
Fiske observed, it "begins with some preluding meant to sound like a
harp, presumably the Celtic sort, and this leads into a slow movement
which might well have suggested an Ossianic melancholy in Berlin."[66]
Several stylistic features betray Felix's attempt to capture a Scottish mood—
there are widely spaced chords and open-fifth sonorities, turbulent cre-
scendos, and misty applications of open pedal, as at the end of the first
movement, where the brooding first theme echoes among vestigial wisps
of arpeggiations, anticipating the magical close of the *Hebrides* Overture (**ex. 7.1**).

Fanny herself coped with the separation through composition. The
day Felix departed, April 10, Droysen brought her some verses, which by
early June had expanded into a *Liederkreis* of six songs dedicated to Felix
"during his first absence in England, 1829," with illustrations drawn on
the manuscript by Wilhelm Hensel.[67] The cycle shows a taut tonal plan

Ex. 7.1: Mendelssohn, *Phantasie* in F♯ minor, Op. 28 (1834)

favoring sharp minor keys and gives compelling evidence of Fanny's lyrical gifts and her attempt to extend individual Lieder into a larger, cyclical work. Droysen's poems continue in the same vein as *Wartend*, set by Felix one week before, but now the "dreaming maiden" is fully awake and acts out her fantasies about separation and reunion. In the first song, *Lebewohl*, she would steal into her brother's dreams; in the second, spring tulips and clematis appear dreary to her; and in the third and fourth, she begins to think of his homecoming. No. 5, *Hochland* (*Highlands*) stands by itself. Here Fanny imagines her brother roaming the Scottish highlands; she transplants herself from Berlin to join him on a secret island in the middle of a loch, probably an allusion to the second canto of Sir Walter Scott's *Lady of the Lake*, in which Helen and her father Douglas seek refuge on an island in Loch Katrine. Cast in a *volkstümlich* style, Fanny's Lied clearly imitates the inflections of *Wartend*, linking her style to her brother's with jaunty dotted rhythms and the key of B minor, common to *Wartend* and the *Hebrides* Overture. The sixth, concluding song closes the cycle by treating the homecoming (*Wiedersehen*), though in a surprise setting: the piano falls silent, and an a cappella trio sings of the joyful life the future holds. Here Fanny borrowed a phrase from Felix's "Scottish" Sonata, again symbolically stressing the siblings' bonds.[68] But the scoring, for two sopranos and a tenor, is enigmatic. Who is reunited? Certainly Felix and Fanny, but who is the third, feminine *persona*? Is it Rebecka, or Lea, or did Fanny symbolize her divided loyalties as sister and fiancée?

Significantly, the trio excludes Wilhelm (Fanny could have added a bass to achieve a quartet). Instead, Wilhelm participated by embellishing the first page of the manuscript with illustrations, including one of Felix and Fanny sailing in a vessel toward some auspicious future. On Midsummer Day, a few weeks after Fanny sent the cycle to England, Wilhelm designed a circular drawing to accompany the "circle of songs." In *Das Rad* (*The Wheel*) he symbolized the hierarchy of the Mendelssohn siblings and friends. Felix appears in the hub, playing a wind instrument and attired in "an English tailcoat with Scottish accessories," while a dolphin nibbles at some music in his pocket. Revolving around the composer, like so many spokes of the wheel, are his siblings and several friends, including Albert Heydemann, Droysen, and Albertine Heine, who later married Paul. But Wilhelm, tethered by a chain to Fanny and Rebecka, appears as a brake shoe on the wheel. The droll symbolism is clear enough: by August 1829, when Felix received the drawing in Scotland,[69] he was still Fanny's "alpha and omega and everything in between."[70]

IV

With the end of the "season" Felix and Klingemann planned a walking tour of Scotland. They intended to travel by coach to Edinburgh and then by various means across the Highlands to Oban and the Isle of Mull. From Sir Alexander Johnston, Felix received a walking stick and introduction to Sir Walter Campbell, the "tyrant" of the Isle of Islay; there was also discussion of crossing the Irish Sea to Dublin, but these two destinations fell from the itinerary. Dining with Sir George Smart on July 21, Felix made an uneven musical exchange—a copy of the *Midsummer Night's Dream* Overture for a canonic drinking song; Oberon's sprightly elves encountered vapid images of "pretty warblers" and "gay larks," reconfirming Felix's earlier impression of the English glee as a "horribly infamous thing" (*höchst infames Ding*).[71] The next morning Felix and Klingemann departed by coach from Charing Cross and reached Durham on the 24th. Felix had brought an album for sketching, and while he drew memorable points along the way, Klingemann added verses on interleaved tissues, blending the visual and poetic. One of the first and most striking scenes was of Durham Cathedral, which Felix viewed from the far bank of the Wear River, and framed with a border of trees and lush vegetation (**plate 9**). Klingemann's verses contrasted the serenity of the sanctuary with the politics of the day:

In Durham wäre gut wohnen,	In Durham one might live well,
Am Flusse ist's kühl und leis,	The stream is cool and gentle,
Die Priester hoch oben thronen,	High above the priests are enthroned
Im Dom ist's still und weiss.	The cathedral within is still and white.
Doch sammeln sich schwere Gewitter	But heavy storms are gathering,
Verderben die gute Station,	Spoiling the rest stop,
Und oben sprechen sie bitter	And above they speak bitterly
Von Irland und Emancipation.	Of Ireland and emancipation.[72]

Two days later, they were in Edinburgh. Their first act was to climb the volcanic outcropping of Arthur's Seat and, at eight hundred feet, take in the stunning view of the castle, the sea, and Firth of Forth, studded with white sails and smokestacks, and the distant outlines of Stirling Castle and obscure "shadow" of Ben Lomond ("When God in heaven takes up panorama painting, you can expect something terrific," Felix wrote[73]). The next day Felix heard Scottish folk music; escorted by George Hogarth, a Lothian barrister and music critic who became Charles Dickens' father-in-law in 1836, Felix attended a bagpipe competition at the Highland games. Intrigued, he sent his card to a piper staying in the same hotel and was able to study the instrument at close range, putting to rest Leigh Hunt's "idea of martyrdom," to be "tied to a post within a few yards of a stout-lunged piper."[74] But the deepest impression was made during the twilight of July 30, when Felix visited Holyrood Palace, where Mary Queen of Scots had reigned and, in 1566, witnessed the murder of her secretary, Rizzio. At the roofless ruins of the adjacent abbey, Felix found everything "broken and moldering" and overgrown with grass and ivy. There too he discovered the haunting beginning of his *Scottish* Symphony.[75]

Among his Scottish acquaintances was the composer John Thomson (1805–1841), later, on Felix's advice, the first Reid Professor of Music at the University of Edinburgh. Thomson gave Felix a song, prompting an acknowledgment in English. In a creatively confused phrase, Felix thanked his friend for "renovating the recollections of the most happy hours" in Edinburgh.[76] But an introduction the following day to Thomson's countryman, Sir Walter Scott, ended in disappointment. To meet the international celebrity (among Lea's favorite authors), Felix and Klingemann traveled south to the Borders region along the Tweed River, where, between 1812 and 1818, Scott had committed the royalties of his immensely successful poetry to building Abbotsford, an eclectic, baronial mansion-*cum*-museum, rather like a review of his literary works, with artifacts from the fourteenth to early nineteenth centuries. Felix and Klingemann found the author about to depart and enjoyed at most a half hour of "superficial conversation." There was no opportunity for Felix to perform for Scott, who knew Moscheles well and enjoyed flirting with his wife (in 1828 Moscheles had dedicated his *Anklänge aus Schottland*, a medley of Scottish folk tunes, to the "great wizard of the North"). Though still at the height of fame—Scott's authorship of the anonymous *Waverly* novels had been revealed only in 1827—by 1829 he had suffered economic reverses owing to his publisher's collapse and spent his remaining years repaying debts, "spinning gold from his entrails," as Thomas Moore observed. Before returning to Edinburgh, Felix and Klingemann stopped at the nearby thirteenth-century Cistercian abbey at Melrose, where Felix sketched the fanciful red sandstone gargoyles.

They started for the Highlands on August 1 by steaming up the Firth of Forth and traveling by carriage to Perth. Near Dunkeld, Felix sketched the Shakespearean "wood that wanders," Birnam Wood. From Ossian's Hall, a folly built by the Duke of Athol, he rendered the Falls of Braan,[77] nearby where, according to legend, the Celtic bard had died in a cave. This was Felix's first Scottish encounter with Ossianic lore, reinforced, just days later, on the Isle of Staffa. Along Loch Tummel the travelers experienced inclement weather, which Felix captured in his drawings by rubbing in impressionistic clouds and "painting" gray mountains[78] with his pencil, a visual indistinctness that would find its musical counterpart in the *Hebrides* Overture. By August 6 they had "stumbled upon a bit of culture" on the Western coast, Fort William, though Klingemann recorded that the town had only one street.

The next morning the two boarded the *Maid of Morven* and, after cruising down Loch Linnhe, disembarked at Oban. In 1826 the architect Schinkel had found there a community of about one hundred houses, from which one could "see almost all the Ossianic islands and cliffs, picturesque, eerie and awesome in the confused way they are thrown together."[79] A mile up the coast Felix sketched the remnants of Dunollie Castle, the thirteenth-century stronghold of the MacDougalls, keepers of the Brooch of Lorne. The ruins appear on a promontory in the middle-ground, encircled by the gnarled foliation of a half-completed tree in the foreground, while in the background loom the distant outlines of two of the Hebrides, Mull and Morven (**plate 10**). Later that day the travelers boarded the steamer *Ben Lomond*; navigating between the islands Felix had just drawn, it reached the quaint fishing port of Tobermory, where that evening Felix wrote to Berlin, "In order to make you understand how extraordinarily the Hebrides affected me, the following came into my mind there."[80] The "following" was a draft in piano score of the opening of the *Hebrides* Overture, complete with orchestral cues and dynamics and in nearly final form. Here we find the rising, three-tiered statement of the evocative bass motive, with layered chords above in the violins and winds ("passable," was Fanny's reaction; not "in vain" did the violins cling to their sustained $F\sharp$[81]). Indulging in romantic tone painting at its purest, he recorded synaesthetic experiences: the images of the Oban drawing became sonorous; the orchestra, a palette of softly mottled hues and shades, to capture the unforgettable Scottish sea- and landscapes.

The inspiration for the overture thus predated August 8, when the *Ben Lomond* conveyed Felix and Klingemann to Fingal's Cave on Staffa, six miles off the western coast of Mull. The seas were calm enough for them to land, though Felix again succumbed to queasiness, and deferred to Klingemann's prose:

> Staffa, with its strange basalt pillars and caverns, is in all the picture books. We were put out in boats and lifted by the hissing sea up the pillar stumps to the famous Fingal's Cave. A greener roar of waves never rushed into a stranger cavern—its many pillars making it look like the inside of an immense organ, black and resounding, absolutely without purpose, and quite alone, the wide gray sea within and without.[82]

In 1772, the botanist Joseph Banks had published a notice of the singular geological formation, with its plicated, polygonal columns that enticed a train of notable tourists, among them Samuel Johnson, Schinkel, Sir Walter Scott, Keats, Turner, Wordsworth, Queen Victoria, Jules Verne, Tennyson, and Robert Louis Stevenson.

From Staffa Felix and Klingemann proceeded to the nearly desolate island of Iona, six miles to the south, where in 563 the Irish monk Columba had founded the stronghold of the early Celtic Christian Church, and where Scottish kings were interred. Once again Felix recorded no verbal impressions, though after visiting the ruins of the abbey, his companion commented: "Iona, one of the Hebrides-sisters—there is truly a very Ossianic and sweetly sad sound about that name—when in some future time . . . the wish arises to retire into the loneliest loneliness, I shall think of Iona, with its ruins of a once magnificent cathedral, the remains of a convent, the graves of ancient Scotch kings and still more ancient northern pirate-princes—with their ships rudely carved on many a monumental stone."[83]

From Oban the travelers used several conveyances to reach Glasgow— horse-drawn open carts, a steam ferry at Inveraray to cross Loch Fyne, and a Clyde paddle-steamer; they even considered trying a new technological curiosity, a steam-coach, but the apparatus "stood idly by the roadside, . . . looking very ridiculous with a high funnel and a rudder."[84] In Glasgow there was more stark evidence of the Industrial Revolution, a cotton mill with hundreds of sallow girls who toiled "there from their earliest days." The Trossachs, which Klingemann thought "ought to be published and packed up as supplements to Sir Walter Scott's complete works," provided an escape from civilization, though a storm nearly capsized their boat on Loch Lomond. Having returned to Glasgow, Felix authorized Fanny to choose the contents of his second volume of Lieder, Op. 9,[85] and then departed south with Klingemann on a mail coach.

In Liverpool they separated on August 19, but not before boarding an American steamer from New York, the *Napoleon*, where Felix found a mahogany Broadwood piano. According to Klingemann, he played parts of Fanny's Easter Sonata, a mysterious composition that has eluded scholarly inquiry. Roger Fiske believed it was synonymous with Felix's Scottish Sonata, Op. 28, but both Fanny and Klingemann referred to it as her composition.[86] Compounding the confusion, in 1973 a recording of an "Easter" Sonata attributed to Felix appeared, but the authenticity of the manuscript, sequestered in private possession, remains unverified.[87] After Klingemann's departure, Felix had one more Liverpudlian adventure: exploring a new railroad tunnel, he rode a car down a one-mile incline to the docks; when the wind extinguished its lights midway, for the first time in his life he saw nothing.[88]

While Klingemann returned to London, Felix continued to northern Wales, where he visited the Taylor family on their rented country residence, Coed Du (Black Wood), near Rhydymwyn in Flintshire. Through a letter from Benjamin Mendelssohn in Bonn, Felix had met Sarah Austin, whose brother, John Taylor, owned mines in Wales and England and a fashionable residence on Bedford Row in London.[89] With Taylor's nephew Felix traveled to Bangor and Anglesey but, wary of inclement weather, thought the better of crossing from Holyhead to Dublin and returned to Coed Du. Playing the gentleman, he read Scott's *Guy Mannering*, hunted with Mr. Taylor's son, and visited his host's lead mines (in one, at a depth of five hundred feet, Felix contemplated the ending of his *Reformation* Symphony). He also sketched the opening of a festive recessional for Fanny's wedding, scheduled for October 3 (events conspired against the timely completion of the piece, and Felix later incorporated it into the opening of the Organ Sonata Op. 65 No. 3 in A major[90]). Much of his time he spent drawing and flirting with Mr. Taylor's three daughters, for whom Felix composed the three *Fantaisies*, Op. 16, in which he transformed Welsh impressions into piano character pieces. No. 1, in a pensive A minor that yields to a lithesome Vivace in the major, depicted a bouquet of Anne's carnations and roses, with rising arpeggiations to suggest the wafting scent. No. 2, for Honora, represented a creeping vine with trumpetlike flowers in her garden. Here Felix's imagination unleashed a capricious scherzo in E minor, with fanfares and light, detached chords (ex. 7.2; in 1939, this fantasy would serve another purpose, to accompany Toto's escape from the Witch of the West in the American cultural icon, *The Wizard of Oz*). No. 3 in E major, for the "prettiest" daughter, Susan, was titled *The Rivulet*, and lazily traced a meandering stream by which Felix and his hostesses had sketched.

Ex. 7.2: Mendelssohn, Fantasy in E minor, Op. 16 No. 2 (1829)

V

On September 6 Felix was once again in London. During the Scottish holiday he had begun to envision with Klingemann an "idyll" for his parents' silver wedding anniversary, and now the idea materialized into a libretto for the Liederspiel *Heimkehr aus der Fremde*. The return to London also brought renewed composition. On September 14 Felix drafted for Sophia Louisa Dance (daughter of William Dance, treasurer of the Philharmonic Society) the piano "Song" in A major, released in 1832 as Op. 19b No. 4.[91] And the same day he completed the major work of the summer, the String Quartet in E♭, Op. 12. Like Op. 13, Op. 12 suggests engagement with Beethoven's quartets; indeed, the Adagio introduction to the first movement recalls the opening of Beethoven's "Harp" Quartet, Op. 74, in the same key. But much of Felix's composition impresses as fresh and original—the infectious *Canzonetta* in G minor, the middle of which becomes a fleet-footed scherzo; the expressive slow movement in B♭ major that introduces the finale; and the formal elasticity of the whole. Thus, in the first movement the development commences with a feigned repeat of the exposition but then takes up a fresh theme. Much of the agitated finale, in the compound meter of $\frac{12}{8}$, is centered on C minor; only in the coda, which recycles material from the first movement, does the music swerve to the true tonic, E♭. Finally, there is the secret dedication to Betty Pistor, whose initials, "B.P.," appear at the head of the autograph.[92] Felix may have impressed Betty's name into the Allegro of the first movement: its first theme begins with the prominent rising fourth, B♭–E♭, in German nomenclature B–Es, the three musical letters extractable from Betty's name (**ex 7.3**). Echolike, the first and fourth movements end with the same interval. But Felix's feelings for Betty remained unreciprocated. In 1830 he learned of her engagement to the jurist Adolf Rudorff. By then the score had passed to Ferdinand David, who, on Felix's instruction, altered the dedication to "B.R.," by a deft stroke of the pen.[93] Felix never shared the dedication with Betty, fondly remembered as a "musical soul," and she learned of it only some thirty years later.[94]

Three days after dating his quartet, Felix was seriously injured when he fell from a cabriolet that overturned and pinned his leg. He had intended to join Abraham in Holland and return to Berlin in time for Fanny's

Ex. 7.3: Mendelssohn, String Quartet in E♭ major, Op. 12 (1829), First Movement

Allegro non tardante

wedding, but the recuperation took more than two months. Klingemann and other solicitous friends tended to him, and his physician, Dr. L. W. Kind, prescribed a jalapic purgative to promote digestion.[95] Meanwhile, Fanny's wedding banns were read in Berlin, and she composed an organ processional in F major for the ceremony,[96] her first work for the instrument. On October 1 the betrothed couple signed a wedding contract with Abraham and Lea. Fanny's fortune, calculated at nearly 19,000 thalers, earned interest of five percent as long as the principal remained under Abraham's control; in addition, he agreed to supplement the sum with an annual income of 1500 thalers.[97] There was merriment on the eve of the wedding (*Polterabend*), though at nine o'clock Fanny was still hastily composing an organ recessional in G major,[98] since Felix's contribution had not arrived. On the morning of October 3 Fanny Mendelssohn Bartholdy penned a last, emotional letter to her brother and gazed adoringly at his portrait, without "doing Hensel an injustice."[99] The ceremony was in the afternoon; Wilmsen, officiant for Felix's confirmation, presided, and Zelter's assistant A. E. Grell played the organ. The couple moved into a wing of the Gartensaal at Leipzigerstrasse No. 3, where Hensel established his atelier.

For several weeks, Felix rested impatiently in his lodging (now at 35 Bury Street, St. James's, near Haydn's residence in 1794), like a prisoner from Beethoven's *Fidelio*.[100] Through the custodian of the King's Music Library, G. F. Anderson, Felix was able to copy Handel's *Dixit Dominus* for Zelter.[101] On October 27 Dr. Kind allowed him to change the position of his leg, and on November 6 his incarceration finally ended when he took his first drive through the city. Thinking a change of venue might hasten the recovery, he visited Attwood on Beulah Hill, Norwood (November 13–18),[102] and there began to take regular exercise. In the elderly musician's library, Felix perused Weber's *Euryanthe* and gratefully gave Attwood a copy of *Tu es Petrus*.[103] Felix also composed for Attwood and his daughter a curiosity for harp and piano, *The Evening Bell*, filled with imitations of a gate-bell at the Englishman's residence.[104] Preparations for the homeward journey now preoccupied Felix, but there was still time to visit Horsley at Kensington and to see Kemble in *Romeo and Juliet*. And two days before Felix departed for Dover, he dispatched Cramer's commission for a piano-duet arrangement of the Symphony in C minor, finished on November 26.[105]

At the end of the month Felix endured a three-hour crossing to Calais, as the Philharmonic Society prepared to elect him an honorary member. Traveling by diligence, he hastened to Lille, Brussels, and Maastricht (December 2), composing in as many days the first three numbers of his *Heimkehr*. But in Arnsberg, between Cologne and Cassel, he suffered a frostbitten foot and again had to consult a physician.[106] Finally, around midnight on December 7, he embraced his family in Berlin. Within a day he immersed himself in preparations for the silver anniversary, and assembled his co-conspirators in Hensel's atelier to read through the Liederspiel. The tone-deaf painter, for whom Felix fashioned a small part on a single, repeated pitch, played an elderly mayor, and Fanny took the part of his wife. Rebecka sang the role of their virtuous ward, Lisbeth, while Devrient took the *buffo* part of the traveling vagabond Kauz. Felix was to play the mayor's son, Hermann, who, returning incognito from soldiering abroad, outwits the scheming Kauz to win Lisbeth's hand. But Felix's injured foot forced him to recruit the young tenor Eduard Mantius, so that, as Rebecka punned, Herr Mantius impersonated Hermann.[107]

On December 19 Felix finished the score,[108] and rehearsals began the following day. With Devrient's assistance he oversaw the construction of a theater in the main residence, but his efforts nearly came to naught when the king ordered a performance of *Faust* for December 27, preempting Devrient's services. Undeterred, Felix advanced the performance one day, though other difficulties remained. Fanny had not yet written her contribution, a Festspiel on a text by Hensel, so Felix motivated the newlyweds to draft the text in a day and compose the music in a week. Scored for orchestra and six soloists, it celebrated the virtues of matrimony: three heralds introduced Therese Devrient, Rebecka, and Fanny in allegories of the first, silver, and future golden wedding anniversaries.[109] When Therese balked at singing her solo, which ascended to an exposed high B♭, Felix again intervened; his upraised baton, she later reminisced, became her balancing pole. The Festspiel was Fanny's first orchestral essay, and Felix relieved her trepidations by assisting with its orchestration.[110] In 1848 the work enjoyed something of an afterlife when Hensel presented the three solos to Frederick William IV and Queen Elisabeth, in honor of their silver anniversary.[111]

The festivities at Leipzigerstrasse No. 3 actually began on the evening of Christmas Day, when relatives and friends surprised Abraham and Lea *zu Hause*. The preparatory celebration included poems, a chorus from Cherubini's *Les deux journées*, and a play by Gans, with a movement from Felix's second toy symphony for its overture.[112] Among the spectators were the young Henrik Munktell, son of a wealthy Swedish businessman, and his compatriot, the composer Franz Berwald (1796–1868), struggling in Berlin since June to compose an opera. Munktell was frustrated in engaging Felix in conversation, for he found the "most genial musician of our time" smothered by his mother's skirts.[113] But on request Felix improvised and then, with consummate musicianship that dumbfounded Munktell, offered two Beethoven sonatas and the Op. 12 string quartet. Felix, for his part, found Berwald arrogant (the Swede dared to criticize *Fidelio*), his harmonies overly "stuffed," and his melodies reminiscent of Lindblad's folksong anthology.[114] Berwald does not seem to have developed much of a relationship with Felix, though the Swede remained in Berlin for several years and eventually founded a successful orthopedic institute.

On December 26 the children presented gifts to their parents, including a porcelain vase from the royal factory, ornamented by Hensel, and a silver goblet from Felix. In the evening, before one hundred guests, Felix directed Fanny's Festspiel and the Liederspiel. To underscore the "private" nature of the celebration, he restricted the size of the orchestra by limiting the first violins and cellos to two each (Eduard Rietz, Adolf and Moritz Ganz, and Paul), and lending the entertainment the intimate quality of chamber music. The subject of the returning prodigal son personalized the domestic music making, as did Kauz's tantalizingly brief references to Scottish bagpipes in No. 4.

The majority of the fourteen numbers are strophic Lieder (one, No. 12, was composed by Klingemann and scored by Felix[115]), but their simplicity does not conceal the composer's sureness in dramatic technique. Most ingratiating is No. 8, where Hermann serenades Lisbeth, only to be interrupted by Kauz masquerading as the night-watchman (in 1849 the Lied inspired a paraphrase-like homage by the French pianist Stephen Heller[116]). The text conjures up midnight as the domain of mischievous spirits, and Felix obliges with delicate textures of pizzicato strings and flutes (ex. 7.4). Three times Kauz cuts short Hermann's puckish G-minor strophes (retouched with delicate nuances in scoring) with the watchman's call in B♭. When, in No. 9, Hermann turns the tables by impersonating the real watchman, Kauz's B♭ yields to Hermann's cross-cutting B♮, a delightful dissonance that curiously anticipates Wagner's similar treatment in the night-watchman scene of *Die Meistersinger* (Act 2).

By incorporating musical self-references into his score Felix further reinforced the autobiographical elements of *Heimkehr aus der Fremde*. The A-major overture captures the buoyancy of *Calm Sea and Prosperous Voyage*; its principal theme seems derived from a transitional subject in *Prosperous Voyage*,[117] and the concluding plagal cadence of the Liederspiel alludes also to the earlier overture—the security of the harbor is replaced, as it were, by that of the Mendelssohn home; Hermann's

Ex. 7.4: Mendelssohn, *Heimkehr aus der Fremde*, Op. 89 (1829), No. 8

Ex. 7.5a: Mendelssohn, *Heimkehr aus der Fremde*, Op. 89 (1829), No. 5

doch der Sol - dat drauss'   im wei - ten   Feld

Ex. 7.5b: Mendelssohn, *Hebrides* Overture, Op. 26 (1830)

(Felix's) journey has been prosperous. In No. 5 ("Wenn die Abendglocken läuten"), Hermann contrasts the peaceful evening bells of his village with the soldier's life abroad, and again, the imagery is clear: pizzicato strings, horn pedal points, and drones to create a pastoral village, and militant B-minor fanfares for the soldier on his forlorn sentry post—the very fanfares Felix would employ in the *Hebrides* Overture, the sketch of which he now shared with his family (**ex. 7.5a, b**).

After the performance Felix sent a copy of the score to Klingemann, gave the piano-vocal score to Therese Devrient, and made copies of No. 5 for Mantius and Betty Pistor. But despite the care lavished on the work—and despite Lea's urging—Felix cherished no thought of a public production. The score was unpublished until 1851, when, four years after the composer's death, it finally appeared as Op. 89 and reached the Leipzig stage, to be withdrawn after only two performances. At midcentury, the innocence of Felix's youthful musical play had been lost; what the theorist Moritz Hauptmann described as *harmlose Musik* and Eduard Devrient a "delicate little work"[118] had no chance against Wagner's weighty music dramas and politicized musical agendum after the Revolution of 1848.[119] But in the relatively halcyon 1829, *Heimkehr aus der Fremde* stood as an emblem of domestic happiness and security at Leipzigerstrasse No. 3.

Lavater and Lessing Visit Moses Mendelssohn, by Moritz Oppenheim, 1856.

Monkey figurine from the estate of Moses Mendelssohn.

Portraits of Felix and his siblings (1816), showing Fanny (age 11),
Felix (7), Paul (4), and Rebecka (5).

Oil sketch of Felix by Karl Begas, 1821.

Felix's pen-and-ink drawing of Grindelwald Glacier, August 27, 1822.

Pencil drawing of Fanny Mendelssohn Bartholdy as Cecilia,
patron saint of music, by Wilhelm Hensel, 1822.

Autograph of the Double Piano Concerto in A♭ major, 1824.

Leipzigerstrasse No. 3, Berlin, as it appeared ca. 1890.

Felix's drawing of Durham Cathedral, July 24, 1829.

Felix's drawing *Ein Blick auf die Hebriden*, showing
Dunollie Castle, Oban, and a view of Mull, August 7, 1829.

Felix's watercolor of Amalfi, November 1836 (from a sketch of May 1831).

Felix's honorary doctorate, University of Leipzig, March 1836.

Pencil drawing of Cécile Jeanrenaud, undated, by Philipp Veit.

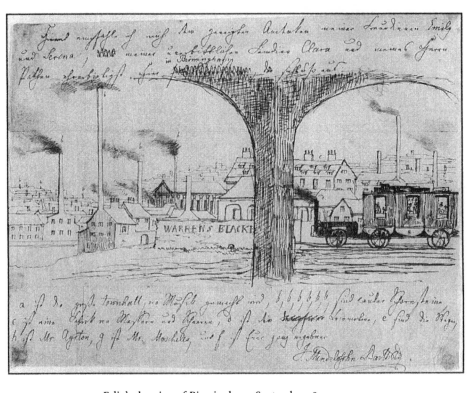

Felix's drawing of Birmingham, September 1840.

Felix's drawing of a domestic scene, September 23, 1844.

Felix's final residence on the Königstrasse (now Goldschmidtstrasse) in Leipzig, where his family moved in 1845.

Final autograph page of the full score of *Elijah*,
dated in Leipzig on August 11, 1846.

Portrait of Fanny by Wilhelm Hensel, 1847.

Felix's watercolor of Lucerne, July 2, 1847.

Sketch of Felix's deathbed, by Wilhelm Hensel, November 6, 1847.

Chapter 8
1830–1832

Wanderlust

I can hardly await the time when the boy will . . .
get to Italy, ... There the very stones have ears,
while here they eat lentils and pig's ears.

—Zelter[1]

Succumbing to Wanderlust, Felix yearned to depart for Italy, though he first celebrated his twenty-first birthday with panache: a military band serenaded him, and Heinrich Beer presented a Mozart autograph sketchbook.[2] But some professional concerns intruded. At the beginning of 1830, the University of Berlin created a new professorship in music for Felix.[3] Declining the honor, he advocated for Marx, who won the position later that year; Felix also refused an invitation to conduct again the St. Matthew Passion.

Meanwhile the *Zwölf Lieder*, Op. 9, and *Reformation* Symphony occupied his creative energies. Fanny had begun assembling Felix's second song collection while he was in Scotland, and by February he was composing the last few Lieder. Like Op. 8, Op. 9 appeared in two *Hefte* of six songs each, now bearing titles, *Der Jüngling* (*The Youth*) and *Das Mädchen* (*The Maiden*), which superimposed on the opus a topical organization, though the texts sprang from several poets, including Heine and Uhland, and the composer's friends Devrient, Droysen, and Klingemann. Felix expended some effort on the musical coherence of the opus. Thus, *Geständniss* (*Confession*, No. 2) begins by glossing the opening bars of *Frage* (No. 1) in the same key, A major (**ex. 8.1** and p. 176, ex. 6.7). Nos. 3 and 4 (*Wartend* and *Im Frühling*) move to B minor and D major, but retain the motivic kernel of Nos. 1 and 2, now rearranged and rhythmically modified. The six Lieder of *Der Jüngling*, all in sharp keys, reflect a male

Ex. 8.1: Mendelssohn, *Gestandniss*, Op. 9 No. 2 (1830)

perspective: in Nos. 1 and 2, the protagonist addresses his lover; in Nos. 4 and 5, springtime and autumn arouse and subdue his passions; and in the barcarolle-like No. 6, he departs from the land of youth and its painful memories. Here the composer's *persona* asserts itself, as Felix, about to set out on life's journey, begins his song by alluding in the bass to the submerged opening of *Meeresstille* (ex. 8.2 and p. 189).

If Felix is the youth, then the romanticized maiden of the second *Heft* is Fanny. Not coincidentally, three of her Lieder appear here, again without attribution: *Sehnsucht* (No. 7), the female counterpart to the male longing in the first half; *Verlust* (No. 10), in which the maiden's lover breaks her heart (Fanny depicts the loss by ending with an inconclusive half cadence); and *Die Nonne* (No. 12), in which a maiden, mourning her paramour's death, expires in a convent garden before an image of Mary. For the remaining Lieder Felix assumes the feminine perspective: No. 8, a spring song, is a counterpart to No. 4, while No. 11, *Entsagung* (Renunciation), set to pious verses of Droysen, was inspired by his sister's confirmation. No. 9 (*Ferne, Distance*), also on a poem of Droysen, refers to a separation and reunion; indeed, near the end, the song pauses on the

Ex. 8.2: Mendelssohn, *Scheidend*, Op. 9 No. 6 (1830)

phrase, *wenn du heimkehrst* ("when you return home"), again linking the cycle to recent events in the siblings' lives.

In contrast, Felix composed the *Reformation* Symphony for a public event, the tercentenary of the Augsburg Confession (June 25, 1530), at which Melanchthon had presented Charles V a summary of the new Lutheran faith. Three hundred years later Frederick William III appropriated the Confession to advance the union of Prussian Lutherans and Calvinists into an Evangelical Church.[4] Quite likely Felix conceived his symphony in 1829 for the anniversary, but for reasons unclear its premiere did not occur until 1832, and in 1838 he renounced it as "youthful *juvenilia.*"[5] Thirty years later, in 1868, it appeared as Op. 107, and like Schubert's "Unfinished" Symphony, published the year before, entered the canon in the closing decades of the nineteenth century.

Felix described the work as his *Kirchensinfonie*; indeed, its programmatic narrative, culminating in the triumph of the Reformation, is not difficult to decipher. Thus, the introduction to the first movement simulates Catholic polyphony through imitative counterpoint based upon the "Jupiter" motive, in its pre-Mozartean incarnation as a psalm intonation (**ex. 8.3a**). The rising entries form a point of imitation in Palestrinian *stile antico*. Chordal wind fanfares, the first suggestion of conflict, answer the counterpoint, but then Felix inserts a second telltale motive—the "Dresden Amen," a response used in Catholic regions of Germany and associated with the Holy Spirit (**ex. 8.3b**). The simple, scalelike ascent in high, ethereal strings later figured in Wagner's *Parsifal* and precipitated a controversy in 1888 when the American musician Percy Goetschius asserted Wagner derived the idea from Mendelssohn. How Felix happened upon the response in 1830 remains a mystery, though he knew at least two composers who had employed it, Carl Loewe and Louis Spohr.[6]

The first movement proceeds with a fiery Allegro in D minor rent by militant fanfares to suggest the spiritual strife. The extramusical significance of the second movement, a light Scherzo in B♭ major, remains unclear,[7] though the introversion of the Andante in G minor would seem

Ex. 8.3a: Mendelssohn, Symphony No. 5 (*Reformation*, Op. 107, 1830), First Movement

Ex. 8.3b: Mendelssohn, Symphony No. 5 (*Reformation*, Op. 107, 1830), First Movement

to owe its inspiration to Felix's *Dürer* Cantata of 1828 (see p. 186) and probably does not suggest, as Paul Jourdan has hypothesized, a "rare reflection by Mendelssohn on his Jewish ancestry."[8] The finale is a symphonic fantasy on the Lutheran chorale *Ein' feste Burg ist unser Gott* ("A mighty fortress is our God"). Introduced by a solo flute, the melody is soon buttressed by winds and brass, symbolizing collective, congregational worship. A transition leads to an Allegro that revisits the idea of spiritual division through a dissonant fugato. Ultimately the symphony concludes with triumphant chorale strains for the entire orchestra.

In 1830 Felix was still under the sway of A. B. Marx: essentially, the symphony was an attempt to render the Reformation as a Marxian *Grundidee* by resorting to Beethovenian models. The sharply differentiated music for the two faiths—Catholic polyphony versus the Protestant chorale—betrays the influence of one of Marx's favorite scores, Beethoven's *Wellington's Victory*, with its musical opposition of French and English forces. There is compelling evidence Felix was also responding to the Ninth Symphony, which, like the *Reformation*, has outer movements in D minor and D major. Felix's autograph reveals that his finale originally began with a flute recitative leading to the "discovery" of the chorale.[9] Felix deleted the recitative as perhaps too obvious an allusion, but the emergence of the chorale as the goal of a spiritual quest surely owes much to Beethoven's final symphonic odyssey.

According to Devrient, Felix attempted an unusual experiment in the first movement: notating the score vertically one measure at a time, instead of sketching melodic and bass lines and then filling in the missing parts. Devrient watched the serried movement progress "like an immense mosaic."[10] By late March 1830 Felix had reached the third movement but was distracted when Rebecka contracted the measles. Even though she was quarantined, Felix too fell ill and postponed his journey. By April 9 he was well enough to begin the finale; then, on May 1, he paused to compose a small cycle of four Lieder.[11] Their poet remains unknown, but their subject—the journey from childhood to manhood—recalls Op. 9 No. 6, as if Droysen had a hand in crafting the verses. The overarching theme of lovers separated and reunited revives somewhat the sentimental program of Carl Maria von Weber's *Konzertstück* (see p. 80), but now from a masculine point of view. In *Der Tag*, the innocent child becomes a youth and falls in love; after an arduous ride on his steed (*Reiterlied*), he arrives at a castle and searches for his lover in the woods. Summoned to serve his country, he bids her farewell in *Abschied*, and then, after returning from the ravages of war a common beggar (*Der Bettler*), seeks reunion with her. "Recognize me," he entreats her, and Felix's music responds with the ending of *Der Tag*, unifying the Lieder and hinting at what he might have achieved in a more ambitious song cycle.

I

On May 13, having dated the autograph of the *Reformation* Symphony the previous day, Felix departed with his father. In Dessau he saw Wilhelm Müller's widow and visited the Kapellmeister J. F. Schneider. *Meeresstille und glückliche Fahrt* was "wildly" rehearsed, and at a party Felix played trios with Schubring and W. K. Rust and improvised on the opening of Beethoven's Ninth Symphony.[12] In Leipzig Felix established ties with the leading music houses, Breitkopf & Härtel and F. Hofmeister, while Abraham returned to Berlin. Through Heinrich Marschner, immersed in an opera on Sir Walter Scott's *Ivanhoe*, Felix sold the String Quartet, Op. 13, to Breitkopf & Härtel; its sibling, Op. 12, to Hofmeister, who informed the astonished composer that a pirated edition of the First Symphony, Op. 11, was already circulating in Leipzig.[13] But in a precopyright age, Felix was powerless to stop the theft and instead laid plans with Heinrich Dorn, director of the Leipzig opera, to premiere the *Reformation* Symphony on June 1. Felix also examined Bach manuscripts before traveling to Weimar on May 21.

Sensing he would not see the Nestor of poets again, Felix extended his stay to two weeks and asked Goethe to use the familiar *du*. There were discussions about Schiller, Scott, Hugo, Stendhal, and Hegel, and Goethe gave his friend a bifolio from the second part of *Faust*[14] and commissioned a crayon sketch of the composer, which Felix found "very like, but also rather sulky."[15] Felix played almost daily on Goethe's Viennese Streicher piano. During these structured sessions Felix presented compositions by "canonical" composers in chronological order. The octogenarian listened intently from a dark corner, his eyes occasionally "flashing fire" like a *Jupiter tonans* ("thundering Jupiter"). But when Felix approached modern times by playing Beethoven's Fifth Symphony, Goethe reacted, "That causes no emotion; it is only astonishing and grandiose."[16]

In Weimar Felix revised the *Reformation* Symphony and dispatched a copy to Leipzig—too late, for Dorn had already cancelled the performance. Felix also flirted with the ladies, composed for Ottilie von Goethe a tender Andante in A major,[17] and contributed to a new journal titled *Chaos*. Launched under Ottilie's editorship in September 1829, *Chaos* was a weekly publication comprising madcap poems, letters, and riddles, appearing anonymously or with pseudonyms, solicited from Goethe's circle.[18] Felix now took his place among Chamisso, Holtei, de la Motte Fouqué, Thomas Carlyle, and Thackeray. To the first series (1830) Felix contributed two letters.[19] One, signed "Felix," purports to be by a visitor of the Rheinfall near Schaffhausen. The other, signed "Sophie Stbrn.," caused much merriment in Weimar, where readers were unable to identify the author. Here a zealous aunt admonishes her niece against visiting the town, for it has been overrun by the *Engländer* John Knox, Rob Roy, and Jonathan Swift, all contemplating harmful deeds. Felix also exchanged humorous verses with his lady friends and composed *Chaoslieder*, including the folksonglike *Lieblingsplätzchen* (Op. 99 No.3), for which he disseminated the misinformation that the text was from the folk anthology *Des Knaben Wunderhorn*.[20]

On June 6 Felix arrived in Munich. The capitol of Bavaria, created upon the dissolution of the Holy Roman Empire in 1806, was developing into a southern German arts center under its Wittelsbach king, Ludwig I. An ardent philhellene, Ludwig embarked upon a massive construction program: the Renaissance-styled Pinakothek to display Flemish and German art; Ludwigskirche, after Byzantine and Romanesque models; and Glyptothek, a marble temple finished in 1830, to exhibit Greek and Roman statuary. The king positioned triumphal arches around the city and recruited celebrated artists to support its rejuvenation. Among them were Peter Cornelius, who adorned the walls of the Glyptothek with murals of Greek mythology, and J. K. Stieler, who specialized in portraits of attractive models. Ludwig had tried unsuccessfully to bring Goethe to Munich; now Felix, armed with letters from the poet, mixed with members of the court, including J. N. Poissl, Intendant of the royal theater and opera. Felix tried the organs of the local churches, appeared with the clarinetist Carl Baermann, and introduced Beethoven's *Moonlight* Sonata at soirées that prized Kalkbrenner and Field as "classic or learned music."[21] Through Stieler, who escorted Felix to Munich art galleries, he met the talented fifteen-year-old Josephine Lang (1815–1880), the artist's goddaughter, who sang Lieder. The encounter encouraged her to pursue composition; she later produced about one hundred and fifty, several of which won acclaim. When Felix departed from Munich, he inscribed a volume of Goethe's poems with the gentle monition, "Do not read, always sing, and the entire volume will be yours."[22]

In Munich, Felix conceptualized the *Scottish* Symphony[23] and read Op. 11 with the royal orchestra. Instead of celebrating the Augsburg Confession with the *Reformation* Symphony, he observed colorful Corpus Christi processions in Catholic Munich. There was another distraction—the pianist prodigy Delphine von Schauroth (1814–1887). The two had met in Paris in 1825, where she had studied with Kalkbrenner. By 1830 she had blossomed into an attractive young woman of seventeen, of a noble but impecunious family. Felix's pocket diary records frequent meetings.[24] To Rebecka he confided that Delphine was "slim, blond, blue-eyed, with white hands, and somewhat aristocratic"; she possessed a good English

Ex. 8.4a: Mendelssohn, *Rondo Capriccioso*, Op. 14 (1830)

Ex. 8.4b: Mendelssohn, *Rondo Capriccioso*, Op. 14 (1830)

piano, which, along with her charms, seduced him into visiting her (Felix's sisters considered her a potential sister-in-law, and Lea was concerned enough to make inquiries about the Schauroths).[25] They performed a Hummel duet and made a musical exchange.

First, Felix revived for her the Etude in E minor (1828) and added a nocturne-like introduction in E major to produce the *Rondo capriccioso*, Op. 14.[26] A slow movement linked to a *bravura* finale, this ebullient showpiece later served as a paradigm for Felix's *Capriccio brillant*, Op. 22, and *Serenade und Allegro giojoso*, Op. 43, both for piano and orchestra. Felix diligently covered all traces of the recomposition, adding, as he put it, "sauce and mushrooms." Thus, he assimilated the characteristic descending fourth of the elfin rondo (E–B) into the lyrical descending phrase of the Andante (ex. 8.4a, b), so that the rondo seemingly sprang from the slow movement. Delphine reciprocated by doting one night upon a *Lied ohne Worte* for Felix.[27] Not coincidentally, it is in E major, as if she intended to replicate the nocturne-like textures of Op. 14 (ex. 8.5). Dated July 21, Delphine's Lied was preserved by Felix in his autograph album.[28] Finally, early in August he read with her a new piano-duet arrangement of the String Quartet Op. 13.

Ex. 8.5: Delphine von Schauroth, *Lied ohne Worte* in E major

As we shall see, from Italy Felix often thought of Delphine, and their relationship deepened upon his return to Munich in 1831.

From Berlin, Felix received worrisome reports about Fanny's health. Pregnant with Sebastian, she experienced an *Unfall* on May 24, 1830;[29] her concerned brother sent letters, including one to Lea, to be shared with Fanny if the baby survived. Resorting to music, he concluded a letter on June 14 with an Andante in A major, expressing what he prayed God would grant her.[30] Its dotted rhythms and key recall the style of *Frage*, Op. 9 No. 1, and a cadence near the end reproduces the close of *Geständniss*, Op. 9 No. 2; Felix endeavored from afar to comfort the bedridden Fanny with the familiar music of *Der Jüngling*. Sebastian was born prematurely on June 16, sickly and frail, and not expected to survive. He received the names Sebastian Ludwig Felix, after the three principal composers in Fanny's pantheon, and at his christening the sculptor C. D. Rauch and Zelter, who stood in for Felix, served as godparents.[31] From Munich Felix sent a congratulatory *Lied ohne Worte*, an early version of his Op. 30 No. 2.[32] Its agitated opening in B♭ minor, reflecting his sister's tribulations, gives way to a joyous conclusion in the major. The infant gained weight and thrived, and even became a symbol of political sensibilities. Euphoric with republican sympathies following the July Revolution in Paris, Fanny sewed the French tricolors into Sebastian's swaddling clothes, much to the dismay of her husband.

During the last week of July, Marx joined Felix on an excursion to the Bavarian Alps. In Oberammergau they attended the Passion Play, performed every decade since the seventeenth century, and in Garmisch Felix sketched the Zugspitze. While Marx returned to Berlin, Felix proceeded to Austria and arrived on August 7 in Salzburg, where Metternich's police seized a parcel of his music. In Linz four days later, Felix's carriage passed one conveying Lea's Viennese cousin, the Baroness Henriette von Pereira Arnstein; then, he changed mode of transportation. Forwarding his personal belongings to Vienna, he engaged a skiff with a gondolier's deck, and "flew away . . . like an arrow at noon" down the Danube.[33] He detailed his impressions of the whirling eddies, the soft cacophony of church bells echoing from either bank, the nocturnal heavens illuminated by bursts of shooting stars, and the enveloping serenity, as if he "were eavesdropping on the music of the spheres."[34] Near the middle of the month, he was in the Austrian capitol.

For some six weeks Felix resided in the Imperial City, unimpressed by its secret police and bureaucracy (most Viennese musicians, poets, and artists had government posts, confirming Metternich's observation the city was administered, not ruled). In the few years since Beethoven's death, Vienna had begun to stagnate in the arts; its chief musical prod-

ucts were light opera and uninspired piano music for middle-class households. At the court-controlled Kärtnerthortheater, where Beethoven's
Fidelio had been premiered, Felix found his friend Franz Hauser, the
principal baritone, singing entrenched Italian opera ("until some fire
falls from heaven, things will not mend," Felix reported to Devrient[35]).
Matters did not improve when the theater's director, Franz Lachner, asked
Felix if the St. Matthew Passion was by Bach. Vestiges of Beethoven's genius were difficult to discern (not a single pianist, Felix noted, played the
master's music), though Felix met several of the composer's acquaintances who had served at his funeral: the poet Grillparzer, aging Bohemian
composer Adalbert Gyrowetz, violinist Mayseder, piano manufacturer
Streicher, music publishers Haslinger and Mechetti, Beethoven's faithful
acolyte Carl Czerny, and cellist Merk, with whom Felix played billiards.[36]
Felix sent to Berlin distinctly uncomplimentary reports: Merk, smoking
a cigar without exhaling, performed an Adagio, and the industrious Czerny
was "like a tradesman on his day off," churning out piano variations, arrangements, and salon pieces (among his hackwork was a revamping for
sixteen pianos of the overture to Rossini's *Semiramide*). In short, the glories of Viennese classicism had passed: "Beethoven is no longer here, nor
Mozart or Haydn either," Felix wrote, and he took little solace when the
octogenarian Abbé Stadler, musical confidante of Constanze Mozart,
showed him the piano on which Haydn had composed *The Seasons*.

With Simon Sechter, who had instructed Schubert in fugue just weeks
before the composer's death in 1828, Felix exchanged "sweet canonical
phrases." And, he found stimulation in the company of the music historian R. G. Kiesewetter, who had assembled an imposing library of early
choral music and regularly performed Palestrina, Victoria, Carissimi,
and J. S. Bach.[37] An especially warm friendship developed between Felix
and Aloys Fuchs (1799–1853), a passionate collector of musical autographs.[38] Felix later acquired for Fuchs manuscripts of composers ranging from Durante and Paisiello in the eighteenth century to Clementi,
Attwood, and Moscheles in the nineteenth. On September 16 Fuchs offered his new friend a priceless gift, the "Wittgenstein" sketchbook of
Beethoven, filled with hieroglyphic-like drafts for three major late works,
the Piano Sonata Op. 109, *Missa solemnis*, and *Diabelli* Variations.[39]

To promote his career, Felix sold Op. 11 and other works to Pietro
Mechetti. Through Delphine, Felix met J. B. Streicher, who placed at the
composer's disposal a piano from his firm, with its characteristic light,
bouncing action (*Prellmechanik*). But apart from playing quartets with
Mayseder, attending the Burgtheater, and conversing with musicians,
Felix appears to have kept a low profile, by visiting his patrician relatives, the Eskeles in Hitzing, and the Arnsteins and Ephraims in Baden,

where he performed on the parish church organ before a small circle of acquaintances.[40] Near the end of the Viennese sojourn, Felix traveled to Pressburg (Bratislava) to witness the coronation of the Crown Prince Ferdinand as king of Hungary, and was impressed by the colorful display of the Hungarian magnates, caparisoned horses of the nobility, and bands of gypsies and long-mustached commoners, all suggesting "oriental luxury, side by side with . . . barbarism."[41]

Felix intended to remain in Vienna for only a few weeks, but when news arrived in mid-September of instability in financial markets, he procrastinated and awaited his father's advice.[42] Counteracting the "frivolous dissipation" of the Viennese, Felix immersed himself in sacred music and conceived for the Singakademie a setting of the *Ave Maria*. His principal creative effort was a "grave, little sacred piece," a cantata on *O Haupt voll Blut und Wunden*, the Passion chorale treated prominently in the St. Matthew Passion. But the immediate stimulus for the work was visual: at the Alte Pinakothek in Munich, Felix had viewed a painting attributed to the Spanish baroque artist Francisco de Zurbarán, showing John escorting Mary home from Calvary.[43]

Felix now explored the tonal ambiguity of Paul Gerhardt's seventeenth-century chorale (based on a secular melody of Hans Leo Hassler) and admitted no one would be able to discern whether the cantata was in C minor or E♭ major.[44] Thus, in the first movement, with the chorale as a cantus firmus in the sopranos, the final choral strain reaches a cadence in E♭ major, diverted by a few orchestral measures to an ambiguous half cadence in C minor. The lyrical middle movement, a freely composed aria in E♭ major for Hauser, sets an unidentified text that elaborates Gerhardt's poetry; glosslike, the music too occasionally alludes to the chorale (**ex. 8.6**). The last movement, reviving the chorale to an accompaniment of pulsating string tremolos, adheres to C minor until the end, where the raised third (the *tierce de Picardie* of Baroque music) diverts the work to the major. By dividing the violas and cellos Felix gave the music an especially dark veneer, evidently to match the somber hues of the Munich painting. Musically the cantata is cut from a Bachian cloth; indeed, after examining the piece in 1841, the pedagogue Eduard Krüger assumed it was by Bach and caused a droll scene when Robert Schumann reported the misattribution to Felix.[45]

Ex. 8.6: Mendelssohn, *O Haupt voll Blut und Wunden* (1830), Second Movement

krönt!   Der   Schmer-zen   litt   und   Pla   -   gen   für mich am   Kreu - ze   hier,

II

Shortly before Felix departed for Italy, Hauser gave him a volume of Lutheran hymns, a fresh incentive for ruminating about Bach. Felix promptly jotted down several melodies and set five during the next two years, *Aus tiefer Noth, Vom Himmel hoch, Mitten wir im Leben sind, Wir glauben all' an einen Gott*, and *Ach Gott, vom Himmel sieh' darein*. From Graz he reported he was hard at work on his *Hebrides* Overture, now renamed *Ouverture zur einsamen Insel* (*Overture to the Solitary Island*).[46] But a few days later, after reaching Mestre, his senses were challenged by another island, when, in the dead, nocturnal calm, he was rowed across the sea and entered the Grand Canal of Venice.

La serenissima was a republic no longer, having been vanquished by Napoleon in 1797 and ceded to the Austrians, who administered it as a police state. Like Byron, Felix stood on the Bridge of Sighs and contemplated the history-laden edifices hovering on the water, rising "as from the stroke of the enchanter's wand" (*Childe Harold's Pilgrimage*, iv, 1), the remembrance of former glory. Truly alone, without acquaintances in the city,[47] Felix played the tourist, strolling on the Piazza San Marco, experiencing the bustling dockyards of the Arsenale, and visiting the Dominican (S. Giovanni e Paolo), Franciscan (Frari), and Jesuit (Gesuiti) churches, and, of course, San Marco, symbol of Venetian opulence and the meeting of Byzantium and the West. Above all, the city's art enticed the composer, who spent hours in the Accademia, the Scuole di S. Rocco, and other sites pondering the sixteenth-century masterpieces of Giorgione, Titian, Tintoretto, and Veronese. While Turner in 1819 had preferred the energetic brushwork of Tintoretto's *Miracle of St. Mark*, Felix was drawn to Titian's *Assumption* in the Santa Maria Gloriosa dei Frari and marveled at its dynamic upward thrust, the figure of Mary floating on the cloud, her awe as she approaches God, the waving motion of the painting, and the angelic musicians greeting her ascent.[48]

Felix may have had Titian's altarpiece in mind on October 16 as he put final touches on the motet *Ave Maria*, Op. 23 No. 2, drafted in Vienna. For eight-part chorus and organ continuo, the graceful Marian setting employs responses between a solo tenor and the choir and, in the middle section (*Sancta Maria, ora pro nobis*), a Baroque walking bass line. "I cling to the ancient masters, and study how they worked," Felix wrote of his veneration of Titian to Zelter;[49] the same sentiment applied to his musical models. The principal subject rises from a compact, four-note motive presented in three sequential transpositions, the second of which, the "Jupiter" motive (ex. 8.7), is familiar from the opening of the *Reformation* Symphony. Stylistically and spiritually the music harks back to

Ex. 8.7: Mendelssohn, *Ave Maria*, Op. 23 No. 2 (1830)

seventeenth-century Catholic sacred music, although Abraham later found some passages too intricate to "accord with the simple piety, and certainly genuine Catholic spirit, which pervades the rest of the music."[50] But on October 18, Felix reasserted his faith by finishing a somber setting of *Aus tiefer Noth*, Op. 23 No. 1, Luther's paraphrase of Psalm 130. Cantata-like, the score has a symmetrical, five-movement plan, with two homophonic statements of the chorale forming the endpoints of the penitential psalm. In the center a tenor aria paraphrases the last two phrases of the chorale; and on either side are contrapuntal elaborations, a fugue built upon the first phrase, and a Bachian movement in imitative counterpoint with the chorale placed in the soprano.

Memories of Delphine distracted Felix, and on October 16 he also composed two Lieder about their relationship. In the *Reiselied*, published as Op. 19a No. 6, a traveler bids the rushing waves to greet his beloved and to relate how he has lost all happiness since their parting. Probably not coincidentally, the song is in E major, the key of the *Rondo capriccioso* and Delphine's *Lied ohne Worte*. The second song is a *Lied ohne Worte* for piano solo, textless though no less evocative. It is Felix's first Venetian *Gondellied* (Op. 19b No. 6), invoking the genre of the barcarolle with lilting rhythms in $\frac{6}{8}$ for the lapping water, suffused in a muted G minor, with the melody doubled in thirds to suggest a love duet or, perhaps, a desired assignation among the canals. Felix dispatched the Lied to Munich, but Delphine never received it, for one night the police confiscated his manuscripts on suspicions they contained an encoded secret correspondence. Felix's travel plans nearly went awry when his wealthy Viennese cousins failed to send an *avviso* to Venetian bankers; Felix had to borrow 100 florins from a German acquaintance in order to continue the Grand Tour.[51]

From Bologna he crossed the Apennines in an open carriage and approached Florence on October 22, observing Brunelleschi's dome looming out of a blue mist suspended between the girding hills. During the next week he devoted himself to the city's art treasures in the Pitti and Uffizi, and compared the Medici *Venus* and Titian's seductively recumbent *Venus of Urbino* ("divinely beautiful," he wrote Paul, though "we can't speak of it in front of the ladies"[52]). Without succumbing to *stendhalismo*, the fainting spells that overwhelmed the French novelist when he visited the city, Felix explored the sixteenth-century Boboli

Gardens and fled to the hills to take in the sweeping views from Bellos-
guardo and visit the Torre de Gallo, the Ghibelline tower from which
Galileo reportedly made astronomical observations.

Felix arrived in Rome on November 1. Uncannily enough, his initial
experiences paralleled those of Goethe, who had reached the Eternal
City exactly forty-four years before. Felix first heard a requiem in the
Quirinal and then experienced the "tranquil, . . . solid spirit"[53] in the
Vatican described in Goethe's *Italienische Reise*. Eagerly Felix sought out
Raphael's final masterpiece, the *Transfiguration*, meticulously copied by
Hensel during his Roman sojourn, and assured his brother-in-law the
original was no more powerful than the copy. But before Felix's first
reports could reach Berlin, Zelter was writing Goethe about his pupil,
privately venting some anti-Semitic spleen: "Felix is probably now in
Rome, which makes me quite happy, since his mother has always been
against Italy, where she perhaps fears he will shed the last skin of his
Jewishness."[54]

Avoiding the cold air of the Capitoline, Felix secured lodgings at
Piazza di Spagna No. 5, flooded with morning sunlight and furnished
with a Viennese grand and scores of Palestrina, Allegri, and other Italian
composers. Nearby was that smoky haunt of artists, the Café Greco, and
the *pensione* by the one-hundred-and-thirty rococo Spanish Steps, where
Keats had succumbed to consumption in 1821. From the Piazza, Rome
lay "in all her vast dimensions" before Felix "like an interesting problem
to enjoy."[55] He found several solutions: exploring the Colosseum and
the ruins, losing all sense of proportion in St. Peter's, and experiencing
the incense and dim lighting of Santa Maria Maggiore, and the twelve
oversized, baroque Apostles in the nave of San Giovanni in Laterano.
There were relaxing walks in the Borghese Gardens and stunning views
of the Campagna from the Aqua Paola, the early Baroque fountain on
the Janiculum. And the chameleon hues of the Alban hills and fountains
of Tivoli offered alluring respites.

If Felix had lived largely incognito in Florence and Venice, he now
joined a circle of German and Italian officials, musicians, and artists.
His cicerone was the Prussian minister, C. K. J. Bunsen, a friend of the
Mendelssohns who had assisted Hensel in Rome. An avid musical amateur, Bunsen regularly performed Palestrina in his residence with members of the Papal Choir, led by their *camerlegno*, the priest Giuseppe Baini,
who in 1828 had published the first substantial biography of the leading
composer of the Counter-Reformation and "savior" of church polyphony.[56] Baini devoted himself to editing Palestrina's music but was
unequivocally opposed to modern instrumental music. Another priest,
the bibliophile Fortunato Santini, struck up a warm friendship with Felix,

whom Santini dubbed a faultless wonder (*monstrum sine vitio*).[57] For some thirty years Santini had faithfully scored Renaissance and Baroque Italian polyphony from parts and amassed a library of over a thousand items, to which Felix had free access. To Felix's amazement, the gregarious *Abbate* was interested in German music, translated into Italian the text of *Der Tod Jesu*, and arranged for the Passion cantata of the "infidel" Graun, as Felix called him, to be performed in Naples. Santini inquired too about the St. Matthew Passion, listened to Felix play Bach, and provided a copy of Handel's *Solomon* for his young friend, who began an arrangement of the oratorio.

Felix found Roman musical life severely lacking. Supporting the concerts of the Accademia Filarmonica, which made Felix an honorary member,[58] was a piano, not an orchestra, and the thirty-two aging members of the Papal Choir were almost "completely unmusical." With no prospect of a public Roman debut, Felix appeared in private gatherings. At Bunsen's, after the papal singers had rendered a grave work of Palestrina, the *brutissimo tedesco* improvised, and there was an awkward moment when he searched for an apt subject, as "a brilliant piece would have been unsuitable, and there had been more than enough of serious music."[59] But the musicians applauded and dubbed him *l'insuperabile professorone*.[60]

Felix spent his free time in the company of German artists who had congregated in Rome, including the young Eduard Bendemann, Theodor Hildebrandt, and Carl Ferdinand Sohn from Düsseldorf, and Julius Hübner from Berlin. Understandably Felix was curious about the Nazarene brotherhood that in 1816 and 1817 had executed the frescos for the drawing room of his uncle Jacob Bartholdy. There was the familial bond with Philipp Veit, son of Dorothea Schlegel, and Felix found the aesthetic judgments of Wilhelm von Schadow sensible and to his liking. But a few meetings with J. F. Overbeck, a founding Nazarene member, instilled in Felix "a particular aversion to this brood."[61] Seeking to revive medieval Christian art by uniting "Latin beauty and German inwardness,"[62] the majority of the society had embraced Catholicism and wore their hair and beards conspicuously long. They spoke condescendingly of Titian, and painted "sickly Madonnas, feeble saints, and milk-sop heroes."[63] The last straw for Felix came in February and March 1831, when the Nazarenes abruptly altered their external appearance. Fearing political unrest in the Papal States and the ire of the Roman populace, they shaved their beards and mustaches but intended to readopt their Christlike trappings once the danger had passed. Felix found the tonsorial adjustments hypocritical. As for the frescos in the Casa Bartholdy, he was able to view them at the end of January 1831 but under less than ideal conditions. The drawing room was now the bedroom of English ladies, detracting considerably from the Old Testament scenes of Joseph and his brothers, the interpretation of the Pharaoh's dreams, and the lunettes by Veit and Overbeck of the years of plenty and famine. In the middle of the room stood a four-post bed, which could do little more than allude to Veit's panel depicting Joseph and Potiphar's wife. Still, Felix found the frescos a "noble, regal idea."[64]

He was dutifully impressed with the Danish sculptor Bertel Thorvaldsen, celebrated for the Alexander frieze symbolizing Napoleon's triumphant entry into Rome (1812). Felix went weekly to the Quirinal Palace to study the panels depicting the vanquished Babylonians bringing tribute to Alexander, the whole a glorification of classical antiquity. Felix visited the artist's studio and offered piano improvisations while the leonine sculptor molded a figure in brown clay. It was a model of the Byron monument for Trinity College, Cambridge (1831), with the philhellene poet, "sufficiently gloomy and elegiac," seeking inspiration amid classical ruins, his feet resting upon the capital of a broken column.[65]

Another expatriate, Horace Vernet, enjoyed warm relations with Felix. The director of the French Academy in Rome since 1828, Vernet was known for rousing battle paintings glorifying the Revolution and Empire. But when Charles X forbade an official exhibition of Vernet's work, the flamboyant artist converted his Parisian atelier into a museum, transformed a crepe-covered table into a Napoleonic *tombeau*, and admitted pilgrims from "the debris of the *grande armée*."[66] In January 1831 Felix met Vernet at the French Academy, the Villa Medici on the Pincian Hill, and on learning of his admiration of Mozart's *Don Giovanni*, contrived to work its themes into an improvisation, so delighting the Frenchman that he painted Felix's portrait. It shows a young German gentleman wearing a black cravat and starched collar, with wavy dark locks and a somewhat bemused expression. Felix thought he appeared cross-eyed and that the portrait did not resemble him at all.[67] The same evening there was dancing, and Vernet's daughter took up a tambourine in the middle of a saltarello. "I wished I had been a painter," Felix reminisced, "for what a superb picture she would have made."[68] Instead, he incorporated the whirling leaps of the dance into the finale of a new work forming in his head, the *Italian* Symphony.

Through Vernet, Felix met a no less colorful personality, Hector Berlioz, who, having finally won the coveted Prix de Rome, arrived at the Academy on March 11, 1831. Since Berlioz's matriculation at the Paris Conservatoire in 1827, his unconventional scores had earned him the reputation of a hardened musical iconoclast. Three times he had competed for the prize and unsuccessfully submitted the required cantatas and stilted academic fugues. For the 1830 *concours d'essai*, the assigned text was *La Mort de Sardanapale*, treated by Byron and Delacroix, about the destruction of Nineveh and the debauched Assyrian king Sardanapalus. Here art approached life, for as Berlioz was finishing his score, the July Revolution erupted outside the Conservatoire and toppled the venal monarchy of Charles X. But by the time Berlioz found his hunting pistols, he was too late to join the uprising, which had transpired in three "glorious days." On August 25, a few days after the jury awarded the Prix de Rome, Ferdinand Hiller introduced Berlioz to Felix's father, who found the Frenchman "agreeable and interesting, and a great deal more sensible than his music." Abraham reported Berlioz's intention to seek permission to remain in Paris and forgo the five-year scholarship: "in all classes and trades here young people's brains are in a state of fermentation: they smell regeneration, liberty, novelty, and want to have their share of it."[69]

For a few short weeks in Rome Felix and Berlioz enjoyed almost daily contacts, discussed art and music, and explored the city and its environs together. Berlioz recognized in Felix one of the most formidable musical talents of the period. They visited Tasso's tomb at the convent of San'Onofrio,[70] and at the baths of Caracalla, the conversation turned to religion. According to Berlioz, Felix believed "firmly in his Lutheran faith."[71] When Berlioz contradicted Felix's piety with "outrageous" views, Felix slipped and fell on some ruins. "Look at that for an example of divine justice," Berlioz exclaimed, "I blaspheme, you fall."[72] While riding in the Campagna, they discussed the Queen Mab scene from *Romeo and Juliet* as a potential scherzo. Years later, Berlioz incorporated a "double attempt," a vocal scherzetto and orchestral scherzo, into his dramatic symphony on Shakespeare's play, but he dreaded that the composer of the *Midsummer Night's Dream* Overture had already preempted the subject.[73]

Felix's opinion of Berlioz mirrored that of Abraham. Personally Felix found Berlioz likable, a skilled conversationalist with stimulating ideas. The two shared an enthusiasm for Gluck, and they escaped the oppressive sirocco by reading arias from *Iphigénie en Tauride*, with Felix accompanying Berlioz's singing. Felix played Beethoven sonatas and shared a recently completed, "fine-spun yet richly colored work,"[74] the *Hebrides* Overture. But Felix could not abide the quirky, temperamental qualities of Berlioz's musical style. At their first meeting, Felix had declared the opening of *Sardanapalus* "pretty awful." He examined two Shakespearean works, the Overture to *King Lear* and the Fantasy on *The Tempest*, later redeployed as the finale of *Lélio*, sequel to the *Symphonie fantastique*. But Felix reserved his most acerbic comments for the finale of the symphony, the *Dream of a Witches' Sabbath* (*Ronde du sabbat*), with its extraordinary mixture of literary program, autobiography, and revolutionary orchestral devices. In a letter to Berlin he decried the "cold passion represented by all possible means: four timpani, two pianos for four hands, which are supposed to imitate bells, two harps, many large drums, violins divided into eight different parts, two different parts for the double basses which play solo passages, and all these means (which would be fine if they were properly used) express nothing but complete sterility and indifference, mere grunting, screaming, screeching here and there."[75] Felix found the intrusion of autobiography—here Berlioz caricatures his *idée fixe*, the Shakespearean actress Harriet Smithson, as a harlot—unseemly and demeaning. Felix was quite aware of Berlioz's emotional instability at this time in his life. When Lea hazarded the opinion that Berlioz's hyperbolic musical effects must have some purpose, Felix answered, "I believe he wishes to be married. . . . I really cannot stand his obtrusive enthusiasm, and the gloomy despondency he assumes before ladies,— this stereotyped genius in black and white. . . ."[76] In point of fact, Berlioz was desperate for news from his lover, the pianist Camille Moke. Upon learning of her infidelity, he left the Academy at the end of March and resolved to return to Paris to murder Camille, her new lover, and himself. By the time he abandoned the plot Felix had left for Naples. Upon his return in June, the two briefly renewed their friendship; not until 1843 did they cross paths again.

On November 30, 1830, Pope Pius VIII died after a brief reactionary reign. The day before Felix's twenty-second birthday, the conclave of cardinals elected Gregory XVI. Because much of the winter was devoted to the funeral rites of Pius and the enthronement of the new pope, "all music . . . and large parties" came to an end, and Felix turned his critical gaze to the ceremonies of the Church. He described how the construction of the hundred-foot-high catafalque drowned out masses offered for Pius, and how the conclave inspired satires about the cardinals' vices. From the farthest corner of St. Peter's Felix viewed the bier in diminished perspective through the spiraling columns of St. Peter's throne, as high as the palace in Berlin, and listened to the solemn chanting of the absolutions: "When the music commences, the sounds do not reach the other end for a long time, but echo and float in the vast space, so that the most singular and vague harmonies are borne towards you."[77] The elevation of the new pope coincided with the arrival of the Roman Carnival, and Felix now indulged in the liberating frivolity and commingling of the classes—the motley masks, horse racing on the Corso, and throwing of confetti, a carefree explosion of humanity when Romans threw "dignity and prudence to the winds."[78] The supplication of the Jews "to be suffered to remain in the Sacred City for another year" put Felix in a "bad humor," for he could understand neither the Jewish oration nor the Christian response. A week later, on February 12, he joined a horseback excursion around the walls of Rome, but on his return he found soldiers with loaded arms occupying the piazzas and no signs of merriment.[79] The July Revolution had triggered revolts in Modena and Parma (Paris was then the locus of the *carbonari*, the Italian revolutionary society), and sympathetic disturbances in the Papal States had prompted the suspension of the carnival.

There ensued some uneasy weeks while Felix assured his family of his safety. In March the Austrians suppressed the uprisings, and Felix decided to remain in Rome to witness Holy Week. He described services in St. Peter's and the Quirinal: the pope distributing twisted palms to the cardinals arrayed in a quadrangle on Palm Sunday; the psalmody alternating between two choirs during nocturns on Wednesday, culminating with the pope kneeling before the altar and the *Miserere*; the washing of the pilgrims' feet on Thursday; the adorning of the cross by the shoeless pontiff on Good Friday; the symbolic baptism of a child, representing Jews and Moslems, on Saturday at St. John Lateran; and the pope's High Mass on Sunday. In addition to the constant chanting (Felix detected eight different *formulae* for the psalms but found the Gregorian monophony a "mechanical monotony"[80]), there was sacred polyphony—Palestrina's *Improperia* (Reproaches) for the Adoration of the Cross and Victoria's St. John Passion (1585). Felix judged the latter, in which chant alternated with choruses for the *turba* scenes, abstract and unconvincing when compared to the dramatic cogency of Bach's St. Matthew Passion; Victoria offered neither "a simple narrative, nor yet a grand, solemn, dramatic truth."[81] Instead, the chorus ("very tame Jews indeed!" Felix observed) sang the same music for *et in terra pax* and *Barabbas*, and no musical distinction was drawn between Pilate and the Evangelist.

The legendary *Miserere* of Gregorio Allegri, a setting of Psalm 51 sung by the Papal Choir during Holy Week since the seventeenth century, especially piqued Felix's interest. A papal ban on copying this work had magnified its allure over the decades; when the fourteen-year-old Mozart visited St. Peter's in 1770, he summoned his prodigious memory to prepare his own copy. In 1831 Felix partially replicated this feat by recording some passages in letters to Berlin, including one striking refrain, in which the soprano part soared to an elevated C, transforming the male voices into "angels from on high." Perceptively, Felix surmised that underlying this sublime effect were elementary harmonic sequences, to which various embellishments had accrued over time, so that the work's beauty was fundamentally "earthly and comprehensible."[82]

III

During the Roman sojourn Felix composed a great deal of sacred music, alternating between Catholic and Lutheran texts that seemingly relived the narrative of the *Reformation* Symphony. He visited the Roman monastery where Luther had arrived a priest in 1511 and left a reformer. In the end, Felix remained a devout Protestant. Hauser's gift of Lutheran hymns proved a wellspring of inspiration. Felix's first setting, finished on November 20, was *Mitten wir im Leben sind*, based on the Reformer's reworking of a ninth-century antiphon. This powerful, stark composition—Felix wrote that it growled angrily or whistled darkly[83]—unfolds in three strophes, each concluding with "Kyrie eleison." Felix's music employs only the first two phrases of the chorale. Several choral techniques capture the grim images of mankind, encircled by the fires of hell, appealing to the Lord for salvation: dividing the eight-part ensemble into its male and female parts, combining the two for expressive homophony, and injecting compact imitative motives into the texture. A gem among Felix's sacred music (Johannes Brahms later prized the autograph), the motet is conspicuously un-Bachian, as if Felix temporarily ignored his penchant for complex linear counterpoint.

Far less imposing is *Verleih' uns Frieden*, the Lutheran *Da pacem Domine*. Felix conceived this work as a canon (the duetlike cellos at the opening are a vestige of this plan) but again avoided a contrapuntal display in favor of three direct supplications for the basses, sopranos, and full choir. The orchestral accompaniment supports the gradual swelling of registers, with low strings for the first, and winds and violins for the second and third, as the gentle prayer for peace becomes more fervent. Robert Schumann treasured this expressive miniature; "Madonnas by Raphael and Murillo," he mused, "cannot remain long from view."[84]

Two other Lutheran chorales, *Vom Himmel hoch* and *Wir glauben all' an einen Gott*, inspired full-scale cantatas that anticipated the grandeur of Felix's first oratorio, *St. Paul*. *Vom Himmel hoch*, dated January 28, 1831, falls into six movements, with the celebrated Christmas hymn featured in the first, third, and sixth; the intervening movements offer freely composed arias and an arioso. The brightly scored first movement—the music bursts forth with a descending violin figure from "on high"—suggests a fantasy on the first two phrases of the chorale (not unlike the finale of the *Reformation* Symphony), before the entire melody emerges at the end of the movement. Felix again eschews the Bachian prototype of weaving a web of imitative counterpoint around one voice that intones the chorale. In the finale, he accompanies the chorale with sweeping string arpeggiations and festive wind fanfares that take us farther from

Bach; indeed, Felix dispenses with the final phrase of the melody, to bring the work to a radiant conclusion in a freely composed coda.

Similarly, much of *Wir glauben all' an einen Gott*, finished in March 1831, employs only the first two phrases of the chorale, the Lutheran Credo. Respecting the tripartite division of the text, Felix apportioned his score into three movements, with successively faster rhythmic values: a walking bass line in quarter notes for the first, and eighth notes and triplets for the second and third. And, he coordinated the rhythmic crescendo with other means, bolstering the strings with winds and trombones for the last two movements, and setting off the imitative, fugal counterpoint of the first two with a forceful unison statement of the chorale in the last. Finally, in the closing pages he sprang one more surprise by supplementing the first two phrases of the chorale with his own, freely composed extension of the melody.[85]

Among the Catholic texts set in Rome are Felix's motets for female choir and organ, composed on the last two days of 1830 but not released until 1838, as the *Drei Motetten*, Op. 39. They were inspired by the fifteenth-century French church atop the Spanish Steps, the Trinità dei monti, where Felix enjoyed commanding views of the city at dusk, and studied the expressive singing of cloistered French nuns. He resolved to write sacred pieces they might perform for the "*barbaro Tedesco*, whom they also never beheld."[86] The motets include *Veni Domine* (No. 1), for the third Sunday in Advent, with barcarolle-like rhythms and responsorial singing. In 1837, Felix replaced *O beata et benedicta*, a short homophonic setting for the Feast of the Trinity,[87] by *Laudate pueri* (No. 2), a setting of verses from Psalms 113 and 128. Its euphonious melodic lines appear to recall the Kyrie of Palestrina's *Missa Assumpta est Maria*, which Baini may have introduced to Felix. *Surrexit pastor* (No. 3), for the second Sunday after Easter, treats Christ the Good Shepherd. Here Felix enlarges the chorus from three to four parts, not to accommodate imitative polyphony but to reinforce the largely consonant, diatonic harmonies that characterize these motets.

Arguably the most impressive of Felix's Roman sacred works is Psalm 115, *Non nobis Domine* ("Not unto us, O Lord"), finished on November 15, 1830, and scored for soloists, chorus, and orchestra. Felix had sketched the work in 1829 in England,[88] when he found inspiration examining the autograph of Handel's *Dixit Dominus* (composed during that composer's Roman sojourn of 1707). Here Felix discovered another cantata-like setting in G minor of a Vulgate text, Psalm 110. The two internal movements of Felix's composition, a duet with chorus and baritone arioso, give full expression to a warm, Italianate lyricism; embedded in the arioso ("The Lord shall increase you more and more") is the four-note psalm

Ex. 8.8: Mendelssohn, Psalm 115 (*Non nobis Domine*), Op. 31 (1830), Third Movement

intonation familiar from the opening of the *Reformation* Symphony. The finale ("The dead praise not the Lord") begins in the key of the arioso, E♭ major, as an eight-part, a cappella chorus sings the last two psalm verses in stately block harmonies. Felix redirects the "final" cadence to G minor, and now, in a subdued postlude, the chorus revives the text of the first verse. A few measures later, the principal theme of the first movement reappears, metrically transformed from the original $\frac{4}{4}$ to $\frac{3}{4}$ time, an eerie reminiscence that unifies the whole (**ex. 8.8**). For five years, Felix set aside the composition; when the Bonn firm of Simrock published it as Op. 31 in 1835, the Latin text appeared alongside a new German translation ("Nicht unserm Namen, Herr"), prepared by Felix himself, in order to render the Latin psalm marketable to German taste.

Felix's visit to the timeless city thus facilitated an immersion into sacred Catholic music, yet confirmed his identity as a Protestant German composer. But as he studied Gregorian chant in St. Peter's and admired Palestrina's mellifluous polyphony, Felix also took up several major works of a decidedly romantic and modern stance. He made progress on the *Scottish* Symphony, though the eruption of spring in March banished his "misty Scotch mood," and instead he took up the brightly hued *Italian* Symphony, of which he evidently sketched three movements in Rome. And, he began to compose the cantata *Die erste Walpurgisnacht* and conjured up vivid musical imagery for the clashes in Goethe's ballade between the early Christians and Druids on the Brocken. For Rebecka Felix drafted a wistful *Lied ohne Worte* in A minor, later subsumed into the first published set as Op. 19b No. 2. But the most significant accomplishment was the first draft of the *Hebrides* Overture, finished on Abraham's birthday, December 11, 1830. For some time Felix had struggled with the title, which he renamed *Ouverture zur einsamen Insel* (*Overture to the Solitary Island*).[89] He left no clues about the meaning of this revision: perhaps he was recollecting the bleak image of the tiny, windswept Staffa buffeted by the ocean; perhaps he was recalling the Ossianic poems, where Fingal's fleet is labeled "the ships of the lonely isles"; or perhaps he was alluding to the second canto of Sir Walter Scott's *Lady of the Lake*, which describes Ellen's refuge as "the lonely isle."[90] By December 16 Felix completed a second score of the overture that reverted to the original title, *Die Hebriden*.[91] Like *Die einsame Insel*, *Die Hebriden* was longer than the final, published version.[92] The hypercritical Felix was still not content and wrote Fanny that the noisy end of the exposition was lifted from the *Reformation* Symphony.[93] Temporarily banishing the seascapes of *Die Hebriden* from his mind, he instead prepared to visit the sun-drenched coast of Naples.

IV

In the company of German painters, Felix departed Rome on April 10, 1831, and followed the Appian Way south. Rapidly crossing the malaria-infested Pontine Marshes, they paused in Gaeta, where Grillparzer had written the poem that inspired Fanny's *Italien*. Recalling his sister's Lied, Felix now surrendered to sensual landscapes of fragrant lemon and orange groves, with Vesuvius and the Bay of Naples in the distance. On April 12 he stood on a balcony in Naples and could survey more clearly the dormant volcano, the islands of Ischia and Procida, and off the Sorrentine coast, the enchanting Capri. Though he renewed his friendship with Julius Benedict, conductor of Neapolitan opera, there were some disappointments. Felix regretted not finding smoke rising from Vesuvius and, at Abraham's bidding, abandoned a plan to emulate Goethe's itinerary by visiting Sicily. For nearly two months Felix indulged in a Neapolitan lassitude: he sketched the indescribable scenery, worked on his cantata, and read Sterne, Fielding, and his grandfather's *Phaedon*. He was critical of the social polarization he found: a sprawling underclass of desperate beggars and thieves, and a dissolute upper class. Felix felt keenly the lack of a prosperous middle class. The balmy atmosphere was "suitable for grandees who rise late, . . . then eat ice, and drive to the theater at night, where again they do not find anything to think about"; but also suitable for "a fellow in a shirt, with naked legs and arms, who also has no occasion to move about—begging for a few *grani* when he has literally nothing left to live on."[94]

Nor did Neapolitan musical life satisfy Felix. He compared the orchestra and chorus to those of provincial German towns and was annoyed to observe the first violinist at the opera beating time on a tin candlestick, the metallic tapping sounding "somewhat like *obbligati* castanets, only louder."[95] He deplored the quality of singing, for the best Italian soloists had left for London and Paris; only the *fiorituri* of the French soprano Joséphine Fodor, whom he heard in private, were tasteful. For several weeks the theaters were closed in honor of San Gennaro, patron saint of Naples, whose blood, preserved in a reliquary, was expected to liquefy in May.[96] Consequently, Felix left no description of the renowned Teatro San Carlo, although he did meet Donizetti, who had filled the vacuum caused by Rossini's departure in 1822 and was busily churning out operas, sometimes, Felix reported, in the space of ten days. If Donizetti's reputation fell into jeopardy, he might devote as much as three weeks to an opera, "bestowing considerable pains on a couple of arias in it, so that they may please the public, and then he can afford once more to . . . write trash."[97] (A few years later Felix reassessed this opinion and committed to memory much of Donizetti's *Lucia di Lammermoor* and *La Favorite*.) But Donizetti's lack of industry seems to have infected the critic as well: Jules Cottrau, son of the leading Neapolitan music publisher, reported that Felix was now "seized by idleness and somewhat abandoned music."[98]

Indeed, he devoted much time to tourism and the "tragedy" of the Present and the Past, by contrasting the colorful if grim reality of Naples with the constant reminders of Roman and Greek antiquity—Virgil's grave at Posillipo; the eerily preserved ruins of Pompeii ("as if the inhabitants had just gone out"[99]); the terraced villas and thermal baths of Baia, where Odysseus moored; the Sibyl's cave at Cumae and nearby Lake Avernus, entrance to the classical underworld; and, at the most southern point of Felix's tour, the majestic temples of Paestum. There were limitless opportunities for drawing with his companions, Wilhelm von Schadow, Theodor Hildebrandt, Eduard Bendemann, and Carl Sohn. Along the Gulf of Salerno Felix recorded a breathtaking view of Amalfi, later worked up into a vibrant water color (see p. 329): in the foreground, a languid fountain reflecting ruined columns; beyond, a dramatic drop to the medieval maritime town, its bleached buildings perched on the jutting cliffs of the gulf (**plate 11**). The islands, fabled in antiquity and modernity as sybaritic resorts, did not fail to entice Felix and his companions, though on Procida they found women wearing Greek dress, who did "not look at all prettier for doing so."[100] On Ischia, they ascended on mules the extinct volcano Monte Epomeo, and on the acacia-scented Capri they climbed in blistering heat five-hundred-and-thirty-seven steps to Anacapri, where Felix surveyed mosquelike churches with rounded domes. Above all, he yielded to the allure of the Blue Grotto, "rediscovered" only in 1826. Rather than a concert overture, the visit inspired a vivid description. The water resembled panes of opal glass; through the narrow aperture of the entrance the sun filled the cavern with refracting light, producing magical aquamarines on the dome of the cave. It was as if one "were actually living under the water for a time."[101]

On June 5 Felix began winding up his affairs in Rome. Writing to Thomas Attwood in polished English, Felix disclosed he had "finished" a new symphony, from which we might infer that his sketch of the *Italian* Symphony was completed during the Neapolitan sojourn. Still, he continued to lament the state of Italian music: "The fortunate circumstances which formerly made this country a country of arts seem to have ceased and arts with them."[102] He discussed with Berlioz the musical scene in Paris[103] and in letters home broached the possibility of returning to London, "that smoky place" fated to be his "favorite residence,"[104] where he intended to meet Paul, about to leave the parental nest to join a London banking firm. To Felix's concern, the family dynamic had been strained in February, when Rebecka revealed her desire to marry Dirichlet. Again Lea opposed the match, presumably because the young mathematician did not have sufficient means; not until November 5 was the engagement official.[105] Fanny endeavored to comfort her sister but also found joy in completing a cantata, *Lobgesang*, for Sebastian's first birthday. Based largely on scriptural texts, the composition celebrates childbirth and reaffirms Fanny's difficult pregnancy by drawing on John 16:21: "When a woman is in labor, she has pain, because her hour has come. But when her child is born, she no longer remembers the anguish because of the joy of having brought a human being into the world." The work opens with a Handelian pastoral for orchestra and contains a graceful soprano aria; still, Felix detected several infelicities in the orchestration and was unconvinced by the selection of texts, for "not everything in the Bible" is "suggestive of music."[106]

Departing Rome on June 18, 1831, Felix traveled via Terni and Arezzo to Florence, and again imbibed freely of the surfeit of art in the Uffizi. The Tribune Room became his observation post; with a few glances he could survey the *Venus de Medici* and masterpieces by Raphael, Perugino, and his preferred Titian. Later, in the 1870s, Samuel Butler targeted Felix's effusive description of these treasures. In Butler's scathing indictment of Victorian society, *The Way of All Flesh*, the Englishman George Pontifex, in the midst of a grand tour, endured three hours in the Uffizi succumbing to "genteel paroxysms of admiration." Felix claimed to have spent two hours in the Tribune Room and innocently provided grist for Butler's mill: "I wonder how many chalks Mendelssohn gave himself for having sat two hours on that chair. I wonder how often he looked at his watch to see if his two hours were up. . . . But perhaps if the truth were known his two hours was [*sic*] not quite two hours."[107]

Passing through Genoa, Felix reached Milan, capitol of Austrian Lombardy, in early July. At the Brera, he admired Raphael's *Marriage of the Virgin* (*Sposalizio*), later the inspiration for Franz Liszt's impressionistic piano piece. Felix finished a draft of *Die erste Walpurgisnacht* and pondered whether to add a "symphonic" overture or short introduction "breathing of spring." He met several foreign musicians, including the Russian composer M. I. Glinka, accompanied by the tenor Nicola Ivanov.[108] Then there was Carl Thomas Mozart (1784–1858), the elder surviving son of the composer, for whom Felix rendered the overtures to *Don Giovanni* and *The Magic Flute*. Mozart was among the very first to hear portions of *Die erste Walpurgisnacht*. And finally, Felix met the Baroness Dorothea Ertmann, an accomplished pianist to whom Beethoven had dedicated the Piano Sonata in A major, Op. 101. Felix and the Baroness played sonatas for each other, and she regaled him with anecdotes about Beethoven, how he used a candlesnuffer as a toothpick, and how, when she lost her last child, he comforted her by "speaking" in tones at the piano for over an hour.[109]

In Milan Felix took stock of Italy. To Devrient's insistence he write opera, Felix replied he would find a worthy libretto in Munich on his return journey, and that in Italy he had composed sacred music from inner necessity. He remained unrelenting in his criticism of Italian musical culture: a Bavarian barmaid, he opined, sang better than musicians trained in Italy, who "ape the little originalities, naughtinesses, and exaggeration of the great singers, and call *that* method." Italy was a "land of art, because it is a chosen land of nature, where there is life and beauty everywhere."[110] But the "land of the artist" remained Germany, and Felix now considered whether he should strengthen ties to London, Paris, and Munich, or return to the "stationary, unperturbed" life in Berlin. There, Felix acknowledged, after the revival of the St. Matthew Passion, he had been offered the directorship of the Singakademie. But after his return from England, there had been no further discussion; now, in order to accept it honorably, he felt compelled to stage another public event in Berlin, several concerts of his own music.[111]

V

Meanwhile, the Alps loomed before him. In the waning days of July he reached the Borromean Islands, of which Fanny had dreamed in 1822. At the baroque palazzo on the Isola Bella, he found lush gardens with recurring hedges of lemons, oranges, and aloes, "as if, at the end of a piece, the beginning were to be repeated," a technique of which Felix was fond.[112] He entered Switzerland via the Simplon Pass and, having made a diversion after Martigny to Chamonix to admire again Mont Blanc, reached Geneva on August 1. There he learned Abraham had sustained serious

Ex. 8.9a: Mendelssohn, *Die Liebende schreibt*, Op. 86 No. 3 (1831)

Ex. 8.9b: Mendelssohn, *Reiselied* (1831)

losses in a failed Hamburg bank.[113] But of immediate concern was the weather; as Felix began to retrace in reverse part of the 1822 Swiss holiday, from Vevay to Interlaken, the heavens opened up, flooding much of the countryside. Traveling became laborious or impossible; roads and bridges were washed out, and Felix often ventured forth on foot. Near Interlaken, on August 10, he worked on two Lieder, a setting of Goethe's *Die Liebende schreibt* (*The Lover Writes*), published posthumously as Op. 86 No. 3, and an unfinished *Reiselied* on verses of Uhland (**ex. 8.9**).[114] The texts poeticize Felix's separation from a beloved (Delphine?) and his identity as a romantic wanderer. Goethe's poem inspired a gentle series of pedal points in the accompaniment and avoidance of a stable tonic sonority until the end, where the female persona asks for a sign from her lover. Uhland's verses, about a traveler riding into a moonless, starless land beset by raging winds, prompted more insistent pedal points, as if Felix sought to recapture the mood of Schubert's *Erlkönig*, with its celebrated nocturnal ride. The choice of key, A minor, seems calculated to underscore the distance from Munich and Delphine, whose lyrical voice in *Die Liebende schreibt* sings in E♭ major.

In Engelberg, Felix visited the twelfth-century Benedictine Abbey and, a "very Saul among the prophets,"[115] participated in a Mass at the organ. At the end of August he ascended the Rigi and again witnessed a sublime dawn on the summit, before persevering through the inundations to Appenzell and St. Gallen. He left Switzerland a practiced yodeler and on September 5 crossed the Rhine to Bavarian Lindau. Finding an organ, he played J. S. Bach's hauntingly beautiful chorale setting of *Schmücke dich, O liebe Seele* to his heart's content. The shabby, rain-soaked pedestrian now changed into a "town gentleman, with visiting-cards, fine linen, and a black coat."[116]

He completed that transformation in Munich, but not before reading newspaper accounts of the advancing Asiatic cholera and longing to see his family. But Abraham insisted Felix adhere to his plan, and so he gave a concert of his own music on October 17 at the Odeon Hall. Once again he raised his English baton to direct the Symphony in C minor and the Overture to *A Midsummer Night's Dream*, premiered the Piano Concerto No. 1 in G minor, Op. 25, and, at the king's request, improvised on "Non più andrai" from Mozart's *Marriage of Figaro*. A few days before there was a private performance for the queen, who commented that Felix's extemporizing had transported the rapt royal audience, whereupon Felix "begged to apologize for carrying away Her Majesty, etc."[117] He enjoyed casual music making with several Munich acquaintances—the gregarious clarinetist Baermann, the diffident virtuoso pianist Adolf Henselt, and, of course, Josephine Lang and Delphine von Schauroth. In the year before his return to Munich, Josephine had made great strides in composition—her newest Lieder contained "unalloyed musical delight"; Felix offered daily lessons in counterpoint and recommended she study with Zelter and Fanny in Berlin.[118]

Delphine's musicianship too had improved; her playing displayed ease of execution and "sparkled with fire"—and she had become "very pretty," resembling a baby's soft pillow. But when King Ludwig played matchmaker and urged Felix to marry her, the flustered composer chose to sustain their relationship through piano music. On September 18 he finished a virtuoso solo piece in two movements, a lyrical Andante in B major joined to an impetuous Allegro in B minor.[119] Reminiscent of the *Rondo capriccioso*, the composition later appeared with orchestral accompaniment as the *Capriccio brillant*, Op. 22. Felix also completed and dedicated to Delphine the Piano Concerto No. 1 in G minor, Op. 25. Though Felix's Italian letters refer to ideas for the new concerto, he drafted most of the work and scored it hastily in Munich. One clear sign is that the autograph full score[120] does not contain the piano part, which Felix presumably performed from memory. Another is that on October 6, less than two weeks before the premiere, Delphine herself contributed a "deafening" passage,[121] presumably one of the noisy octave or arpeggiation passages in the first movement.

In three connected movements, Op. 25 is Felix's first concerto to observe the telescoped formal plan of Weber's *Konzertstück*. Thus, in the first movement he truncates the traditional opening orchestral tutti and enables the soloist to appear dramatically after a terse, crescendo-like introduction. The piano entrance resembles more a cadenza than a thematic utterance, and elsewhere too the music expresses a certain thematic freedom and formal spontaneity. For example, the second theme swerves from the expected mediant key, B♭, to the remote key of D♭. The luminous, nocturne-like Andante explores the sharp key of E, an unusual choice after G minor but not coincidentally the key of the *Rondo capriccioso* and Delphine's *Lied ohne Worte* for Felix. The effervescent finale erupts in a bright G major and, like the finale of Weber's *Konzertstück*, exploits two thematic ideas, the first doubled in octaves, the second a turning figure concealed in glittery virtuoso passagework. To tie the composition together, Felix recalls material from the first movement just before the jubilant coda. Popular through much of the nineteenth century, Op. 25 was gently caricatured in Berlioz's *Evenings with the Orchestra*, where thirty-one competing pianists perform it on an Erard, causing the instrument to ignite in a spontaneous *Da capo*, "flinging out turns and trills like rockets."[122]

Apart from the public concert, Felix's other goal was to secure a Munich opera commission. When it arrived at the end of October, he proudly sent a copy to Berlin,[123] as evidence of his new professional stature. Authorized to "negotiate with any German poet of renown," Felix began to search for a libretto—like so many of his operatic aspirations, an unfulfilled quest. In Stuttgart, he endeavored to consult Ludwig Uhland but missed the poet and proceeded to Frankfurt. There he shared his recent sacred music with Schelble, who suggested Felix compose a new oratorio, and thereby planted the seed for *St. Paul*. Felix enjoyed artistic exchanges with his cousin, Philipp Veit, director of the Städelsche Art Institute, but tactfully avoided mentioning the painter's mother, Dorothea Schlegel, in letters to Berlin. Declaring himself a German musician, Felix arranged to meet the dramatist/novelist K. L. Immermann (1796–1840) in Düsseldorf and arrived there late in November, having first visited the music publisher Simrock in Bonn to discuss the publication of Op. 23.

At the time of Felix's encounter with Immermann (November 27–December 4), the writer had yet to produce his novels *Die Epigonen* (1836), treating the decline of the Westphalian aristocracy, and *Münchhausen* (1838), about the madcap adventures of a baron later linked to a mental illness. In 1832 Immermann would become the director of the theater in Düsseldorf; a few months before, Felix, thirteen years his junior, approached him for a libretto. The composer and dramatist left conflict-ing accounts of their meeting. Felix, who had heard Immermann could be prickly, reported the dramatist received him with the greatest friend-ship[124] (Abraham was unimpressed and recommended that Felix find a French libretto and translate it into German). Immermann admired Felix's music, but detected in the unsolicited visit a "hook of egoism" and confided to his brother that the composer pursued him like a young maiden hanging onto her mother's skirts.[125] The dramatist read por-tions of his new trilogy, *Alexis*, about Peter the Great's son who was tor-tured to death in 1718, but the tragedy failed to inspire Felix's operatic muse (in 1834, he did set the gloomy "Death Song of the Boyars," from the first of the three plays, *Die Bojaren*). Instead, the two took up Shakespeare's comedy *The Tempest*. Felix then departed for Paris, confi-dent he had secured a librettist.

VI

On December 9, he found the metropolis seething politically, as Louis-Philippe consolidated his rule by aligning himself with the newly em-powered middle class (*juste milieu*). The failed Bourbon monarchy of legitimacy was exchanged for an experimental parliamentary monar-chy, and the "citizen king," donning galoshes and carrying an umbrella, mixed freely with his subjects. The relaxed restrictions on the press ren-dered him an easy target, and Honoré Daumier's caricatures depicted Louis-Philippe as a corrupt, pear-shaped monarch.

In letters home Felix alluded to the baneful effect of the *juste milieu* on French culture. Politics and sensuality were the "two grand points of interest, round which everything circles."[126] Felix attended sessions of the bicameral Chambers of Peers and Deputies. Euphoric from the revo-lution, *citoyens* were brandishing tricolored ribbons, and the parliament was reportedly preparing to debate whether all French males had the right from birth to wear the Order of the Legion of Honor. Egalitarian-ism swept over musical life as well. French pianos manufactured by Herz, Erard, and Pleyel all bore the inscription *Médaille d'or: Exposition de 1827*, and Felix's respect "seemed to diminish." And when Kalkbrenner, who specialized in "purloining" themes, embraced romanticism in a pi-ano fantasy titled *Der Traum* (*The Dream*), Henri Herz followed suit with an equally vapid programmatic piece, so that "all Paris" dreamed.[127]

Nowhere did Felix decry more harshly the philistinism of the bour-geoisie than in *Robert le diable*, which premiered in November 1831 and catapulted his countryman Giacomo Meyerbeer into the forefront of

French grand opera. Felix was particularly offended by a cloister scene in which nuns, including one played by the ravishing Italian dancer Marie Taglioni, attempted to seduce the hero; "I consider it ignoble," he wrote somewhat prudishly, "so if the present epoch exacts this style, . . . then I will write oratorios." Robert's father, the satanic Bertram, who attempted to lead his son astray, was a "poor devil." In Felix's view the work pandered to everyone, with ingratiating melodies for singers, harmony for the cultured, colorful orchestration for the Germans, and dancing for the French, but ultimately its plot, stretched thin over five acts, remained implausible.[128]

According to Ferdinand Hiller, Felix cropped his hair to avoid being mistaken for Meyerbeer.[129] Nor did Felix find much companionship among other German emigrés in Paris, including adherents of the Young Germany movement, such as Ludwig Börne and Heinrich Heine, who, like Felix, had converted from Judaism to Protestantism but had embraced more liberal political ideologies. Börne had made a career of attacking Goethe for not turning his pen to promote just social causes; Börne's unrelenting railing against Germany and his French "phrases of freedom" were repugnant to Felix, as was "Dr. Heine with everything ditto."[130] Felix saw little of Heine, who was "entirely absorbed in liberal ideas and in politics," and had infected Felix's friend Hermann Franck, who like a magpie, now chattered "abuse against Germany."[131] Matters were not helped when Felix learned of Goethe's death on March 22; seerlike, Felix predicted that Zelter would soon follow the poet.

Shortly after arriving in Paris Felix encountered his childhood friend Gustave d'Eichthal and Olinde Rodrigues, son of an acquaintance of Abraham. Both Jews, the two had joined the St. Simonians, a protosocialist-utopian sect founded in 1825 after the death of the philosopher Henri Saint-Simon. In the early days of the movement the disciples called for a redistribution of wealth based upon merit. By January 1832 they were recruiting artists and had attracted the interest of Balzac, George Sand, Heine, Berlioz, Hiller, and Halévy. During the 1830s Liszt toyed with the idea of the St. Simonian artist as a poet-priest of a new religion, and the impressionable composer Félicien David furnished music for the cult's rituals and later joined a band of apostles attempting to reenergize the movement in Egypt. Of all the musicians in Paris who flirted with the sect, Felix steadfastly resisted its proselytizing zeal; but when he began to attend meetings, his indifference quickly changed to abhorrence.[132]

Though founded on the ideal of mutual dependence (members wore garments buttoned in the back that required the assistance of a *confrère* to don), the St. Simonians had evolved into a doctrinaire cult, over which the clownish *père* of the movement, Prosper Enfantin, presided. Enfantin expended great energy searching for a *mère* with whom to lead the sect and preached the "emancipation of the flesh"—i.e., free sex, a revelation that disgusted Felix. But in the main, it was Enfantin's patronizing, authoritarian preaching that alienated the young Lutheran. Then, on January 22, 1832, the police summarily arrested the St. Simonians, an event witnessed by Hiller and Heine. Felix was there in spirit, for among the confiscated papers was a copy of his Piano Quartet in B minor, presumably performed at one of the sect's gatherings. Tongue in cheek, he mused that only the slow movement belonged to the *juste milieu*; the other, "revolutionary" movements would require a jury trial.[133]

As in 1825, Felix mixed with the French musical elite, though he again remained aloof from opera composers, excepting Cherubini, who examined Felix's *Tu es Petrus* and caviled about its dissonance treatment.[134] The virtuosi had strengthened their grasp on musical culture (Heine compared them to locusts descending upon Paris), and Felix now had contact with several, including Franz Liszt, whom he had met in 1825. Felix's earlier, unflattering estimation changed considerably when Liszt flawlessly sight-read the Piano Concerto in G minor, Op. 25.[135] Considerably less pleasant were Felix's dealings with the leading practitioner of salon music, Frédéric Kalkbrenner, who prided himself on dressing stylishly, his chest bedecked with medallions. In Berlin, Felix and Fanny had discovered that one of Kalkbrenner's piano "improvisations" had already been published; Felix came to regard the pianist as a charlatan. Heine had lampooned Kalkbrenner as a bonbon fallen in the mud, and Felix inserted unflattering comments in letters to Berlin, all judiciously deleted in nineteenth-century editions. Thus Kalkbrenner's intrigues against Felix's public appearances in Paris led him to contrast the pianist's impeccably groomed exterior with a coarse, soiled interior.[136] Moreover, Felix was livid when Kalkbrenner advised a newly arrived pianist, Frédéric Chopin, to submit to a three-year course of study.

On January 15, 1832, Chopin intended to make his Parisian debut under Kalkbrenner's aegis at the salon of the Pleyel firm. The program featured Chopin's Piano Concerto Op. 11 (accompanied by Baillot's string quartet)[137] and a *Grande-Polonaise* by Kalkbrenner for six pianists, including Felix, Hiller, and Chopin. But the event was postponed, and when it finally occurred on February 26, Felix was relegated to the audience. Still, he established an affectionate relationship with *Sciopino*, for whom Felix crafted a three-part canon, at the bottom of which he left room for his friend to embroider a freely composed bass line.[138]

Among Felix's new acquaintances in Paris was the young violinist Ole Bull, then introducing his Norwegian Hardanger fiddle to Paris, and the twelve-year-old prodigy Clara Wieck, escorted by her domineering

father, Friedrich, intent upon promoting her budding career as a pianist.[139] Felix especially enjoyed his reunion with Pierre Baillot; the two
played Felix's chamber works, Mozart piano concertos, and violin sonatas of Beethoven and J. S. Bach (on one occasion Felix improvised on
three subjects drawn from Bach). Felix performed his Op. 25 at Erard's
salon and Beethoven's Fourth Piano Concerto on March 18 before the
French court at a Conservatoire concert, where his pianism evinced a
"delicate talent, finished execution, and feeling deserving the highest
praise."[140] On February 19, after four rehearsals (at one Felix took up the
timpani part), Habeneck gave the French premiere of the *Midsummer
Night's Dream* Overture, but its success was tarnished by a dismal review
from Fétis, still smarting from his contretemps with Felix in London
nearly three years before.[141] No less disappointing was the failure to secure a performance of the *Reformation* Symphony; when Habeneck rehearsed the work, orchestra members rejected it as too learned (and,
perhaps, too Protestant). And finally, Felix endured an absurd spectacle
on March 26, at a memorial Mass for the anniversary of Beethoven's
death, when the scherzo of the Octet accompanied the priest's rituals at
the altar of L'Eglise de St. Vincent-de-Paul. The musicians indeed resembled Goethe's "cursed dilettantes," though the congregation considered the offering "very fine sacred music."[142]

VII

A number of old compositions haunted Felix during the Paris sojourn.
Two French firms requested him to retouch the Piano Quartet in B minor, Op. 3, for a new edition, and he revised and dispatched the Octet to
Breitkopf & Härtel on April 19. He was still unsatisfied with the *Hebrides*
Overture, for its development section exuded more counterpoint than
"train oil, gulls, and salted cod."[143] Finally, when Baillot's associates read
through the String Quintet Op. 18, they found it wanting a slow movement. On Felix's birthday in February, an unforeseen remedy materialized when he learned of the death of his boyhood friend and violin
teacher, Eduard Rietz. In a few days, Felix drafted for the work a memorial *Nachruf*. Parts of this expressive Andante feature the first violin in
its high register, including a second theme rising from the depths, as if
recalling the lustrous solo writing fashioned for Rietz in the Octet.
    Among Felix's new compositions were the Overture to *Die erste
Walpurgisnacht*, finished in February, and the *Sechs Gesänge*, Op. 19 (now
known as Op. 19a, to distinguish them from the *Sechs Lieder ohne Worte*,
Op. 19b). Felix's third collection of Lieder included three spring songs

(Nos. 1, 2, and the miniature No. 5), the folksonglike *Winterlied* (from the Swedish), the *Reiselied* written in Venice (No. 6), and, the most successful, *Neue Liebe* (*New Love*), on a poem of Heine. In this sprightly setting in F♯ minor (associated since *Der Freischütz* with the supernatural), the poet espies a train of elves in a moonlit landscape. The piano imitates their diminutive horn calls and bells, and all is couched in delicate Mendelssohnian tissues of sound. Seduced by the minuscule creatures, the poet wonders if they offer love or portend his death; the answer vanishes in a *pianissimo* puff.

Considerably more substantial is the cantata *Ach Gott, vom Himmel sieh' darein*, finished on April 5, 1832, for Schelble's Singverein. Like nearly all its siblings in the series begun in 1827, *Ach Gott* remained unpublished during Felix's lifetime. The subject is Luther's paraphrase of Psalm 12, with its contrasting images of a deceitful, vain world, and a responsive Lord, whose words are as pure as "silver tried in a furnace of earth, purified seven times." By far the most imposing movement is the first, which commences with rising chromatic lines and dissonant clashes, including duplicitous augmented triads that contravene our sense of tonal stability (**ex. 8.10**). Only well into the movement does the Lutheran melody appear, intoned by the chorus in a stark unison for the third verse ("The Lord shall cut off all flattering lips"). But in the majestic A-major conclusion Felix replaces the familiar chorale by his own chorale melody for the Lord's response to the oppression of the poor. The two, freely composed inner movements include a recitative (with verses from Psalm 103) and dark baritone aria in C♯ minor. The Lutheran melody reenters in the finale in full four-part harmony, initially in F♯ minor and then pivoting to A minor. As the composition concludes on a half cadence, the orchestra recalls phrases from the opening, giving the work a circular design. Fanny had misgivings about the tonal shifts in the finale,[144] and indeed, Felix's dramatic treatment of the chorale—delaying its appearance in the first movement, and partitioning it in the finale through transposition—gives the composition less the appearance of a Bachian cantata than part of an oratorio. Just at this time Felix was beginning to envision plans for *St. Paul*, for which *Ach Gott* impresses as a preliminary study.

Ex. 8.10: Mendelssohn, *Ach Gott, vom Himmel sieh' darein* (1832)

Felix's devotion to sacred music during the grand tour resonated with Fanny, who responded in 1831 with two more cantatas of her own. The first (*Hiob*), finished on October 1, possibly for her wedding anniversary, draws on verses from Job.[145] It begins with a troubled chorus in G minor on the searching question, "What is man, that thou shouldst magnify him?" (Job 7:17), stylistically indebted to the opening of Felix's Psalm 115. Fanny's middle movement exploits Handelian tone paintings for "Wherefore hidest thou thy face?" (13:24): pensive string tremoli and dark, chromatic harmonies recalling *Israel in Egypt*. In contrast, the third movement offers a buoyant finale in G major for "Thou hast granted me life and favor" (10:12). Here Fanny derives the head motive from that of the first movement, showing her ability to impose musical unity on a large form. But *Hiob* is overshadowed by another cantata composed between October 4 and November 20, 1831, on verses from the Old and New Testaments. Once considered an oratorio[146]—Fanny's most substantial composition, it divides into thirteen choruses, recitatives, and arias—it is in fact a cantata marking the abatement of the cholera epidemic in Berlin in 1831. The calamity claimed the life of Fanny's aunt Henriette (Jette) and the philosopher Hegel, who died days before Fanny completed her score.[147]

Drawing from the Psalms, Job, Isaiah, 2 Timothy, Revelation, and other scriptures, Fanny stitched together a three-part narrative, with a spiritual and emotional trajectory similar to that of *Hiob*, now expanded from the individual to a collective point of view. In the first part, God wreaks a catastrophic judgment on the faithless. The second culminates in a lament for the dead and a cappella chorus of the faithful confidently awaiting the Final Judgment. In the third, mankind confesses its sins, atones, and returns to God. The final chorus is a hymn of praise, culminating in the last verse of Psalm 150, "Let every thing that hath breath praise the Lord" (later adopted by Felix as the motto of his *Lobgesang* Symphony). Animating much of Fanny's cantata is the St. Matthew Passion; Fanny scores the work for orchestra, eight-part chorus, and four soloists, often attains an intensely dissonant, chromatic style, and resorts to fugue and chorale. But there is also clear evidence of Fanny's own awakening style and considerable advances in treating large forms. Much of the work is through-composed, and unifying the whole is a recurring, expressively drooping figure and taut tonal scheme, centered on G minor, but eventually progressing to C major. Most impressive is the range of choruses. In No. 6 the superimposed chorale melody "O Traurigkeit, O Herzeleid" recalls a similar technique in "O Mensch, bewein' dein' Sünde gross" from the St. Matthew Passion. In contrast, for No. 10, the chorus of the dead, Fanny conceptualized her own, "idealized" chorale melody in four-part hymn style for the famous verse from 2 Timothy, "I have fought the good fight."

No sooner did Fanny premiere the *Cholera* Cantata on Abraham's birthday in December 1831,[148] before she embraced dramatic composition and dispatched a setting of the mythological subject of Hero and Leander for soprano and orchestra.[149] The through-composed text, written by Wilhelm Hensel, divides into a recitative, aria, recitative, and finale.[150] The orchestra, bolstered by piccolo and serpent, revives the sound of Felix's *Calm Sea and Prosperous Voyage*, and indeed the basic conceptions of the two works are similar—both oppose tableaux-like visions of placid and dynamically charged, wind-swept seas. But the two psychological curves are reversed: in Felix's overture the terror of becalmed sailors gives way to jubilation with the return of the winds; in Fanny's scene, a peaceful, harmonious sea yields to a destructive storm, as Hero's lover, Leander, attempts to swim the Hellespont at night. Believing he has drowned, Hero plunges into the enveloping waves. At the end, Fanny recalls the serene opening gesture, a descending C-major triadic figure. Like *Calm Sea*, *Hero und Leander* thus leaves us with an image of an all-encompassing ocean.

As if emboldened by her new-found voice, Fanny around this time composed her sole work for orchestra, the Overture in C major.[151] She conducted the undated autograph "after two years for the first time" in June 1834, which suggests it dates from 1832.[152] Its design simulates that of *Calm Sea and Prosperous Voyage*—a slow, static introduction proceeds through a transition to an animated fast movement in sonata form. An effectively scored, worthy effort for a novice orchestral composer, the Overture occasionally leans heavily on Felix's *Prosperous Voyage*, as in the lyrical second theme, accompanied by wavelike gestures in the cello (**ex. 8.11**). Evincing clear signs of Fanny's talent, the Overture, cantatas, and *Hero und Leander* cap a remarkably productive period in her life. But outside the few private performances at her Berlin residence, Fanny's music fell into oblivion until its revival late in the twentieth century. The private, personal character of these scores again contrasts with the public career of Felix, who in April 1832 prepared for his second English sojourn and the international visibility of the annual concert season in London.

Ex. 8.11: Fanny Hensel, Overture in C (ca. 1832)

VIII

Felix was delayed by misfortune. What Klingemann had described as "humbug," and what one German correspondent thought could be withstood by musical study[153]—cholera—now devastated Paris. By April grim press bulletins were reporting eight hundred daily fatalities. An attempt to curb the epidemic by reforming sanitation services led to an uprising of *chiffoniers* (ragpickers), while more destitute Parisians, convinced they were being poisoned by the well-to-do, committed grisly murders.[154] Described by Heine as a "masked executioner," the scourge was a waterborne bacterium that killed its victims by acute dehydration. Felix contracted a relatively mild case but was compelled to remain in his room for days and have his back massaged and rubbed with vinegar by an old nurse. His thoughts turned to London, for in Paris the very social order was threatened, and one thought no longer of music, but of colic.[155]

His strength sufficiently revived, he departed for Calais and arrived on April 22 in London, where Klingemann again greeted him. Taking up quarters at 103 Great Portland Street, Felix saw Moscheles and Rosen daily and picked up threads of conversations severed by his departure in 1829. Augmenting the circle was Meyerbeer, with whom Felix attended the opera, and the baritone Franz Hauser. At the Philharmonic, Felix was touched by an unexpected reception. Recognized at a rehearsal on May 5, he had to acknowledge an ovation from the orchestra. The spontaneous demonstration was "more precious . . . than any distinction," as "it showed me that the *musicians* loved me, and rejoiced at my coming."[156]

For Moscheles Felix played recent compositions, among them the *Lieder ohne Worte*, Op. 19b, *Die erste Walpurgisnacht*, and new version of the *Hebrides*. Felix was confident enough of the overture to part with the original autograph, finished in Rome in 1830 (the proud recipient, Moscheles, could not understand why Felix had insisted on altering it). Partaking fully of the musical season, the two appeared at a variety of private functions. At one dinner party (May 7), when Felix declined to play, the Irishman John Field took his place. Suffering from alcoholism and cancer, the celebrated creator of the piano nocturne was a wraith and, Moscheles noted in his diary, a "poor substitute." At another soirée Felix agreed to perform and improvised on a glee by William Horsley. But Felix could not excuse the "eternal mawkishness" of the violinist who had preceded him—Paganini.[157]

As in 1829, Felix restricted his public performances to appearances at the Philharmonic and benefits for his friends. His music figured in three successive Philharmonic concerts, now at the King's Theatre: on May 14, Felix attended the premiere of the *Hebrides*, titled *The Isles of*

Fingal; on May 28 he was the soloist in his Piano Concerto No. 1, Op. 25; and on June 18 he encored the concerto and led the *Midsummer Night's Dream* Overture.[158] For concerts of the flutist Sedlatzek and violinist Nicolas Mori (May 21 and 25), Felix performed the Hummel Septet and premiered the *Capriccio brillant*, Op. 22. A few days later, on June 1, he participated fully in Moscheles's concert, by directing the *Midsummer Night's Dream* Overture and hearing Sir George Smart conduct the *Hebrides* Overture, performing with Moscheles Mozart's Concerto for two pianos, K. 365 (for which Felix designed new cadenzas), and even playing the bass drum in Moscheles's overture *The Fall of Paris*.[159] Through all these appearances, Felix maintained his dubious status as a musical amateur. Thus, in lieu of a fee from the Philharmonic he received a piece of silver, and when he departed from London, a silver inkwell and candelabra, presented by the Society in "admiration of his talents as a composer and performer, and their esteem for him as a Man."[160]

Apart from concert engagements, another venue enabled English music-lovers to witness Felix's extraordinary musicianship. At Attwood's invitation, he began to appear at St. Paul's, initially to offer the closing organ voluntaries for services but then to extemporize; Felix also tried the organs in Westminster Abbey; St. John's Chapel, Paddington; and St. John's, Waterloo.[161] In particular, his performances of J. S. Bach, which required a more extensive pedal board than that to which English organists were accustomed, was later credited by W. S. Rockstro with causing a "complete revolution in the style of English organ-playing."[162] (In 1832, the St. Paul's organ was the only London instrument that could accommodate the pedal parts of Bach's organ works "without destructive changes.")

Of Felix's "new" compositions, the *Capriccio brillant* was an orchestration of the solo piece written in Munich the previous year. Initially, Felix labeled it a rondo, leading to some confusion between the *Capriccio* and the *Rondo brillant*, Op. 29 of 1834. The telescoped design of the *Capriccio*, which links a slow introduction via a transition to a fast finale, recalls the *Rondo capriccioso* but ultimately derives from Weber's *Konzertstück*. Weberesque, too, are the opening of the introduction, where rolled chords accompany a sustained treble melody, and the second theme of the Allegro, a jaunty, marchlike theme that revives the third movement of the *Konzertstück*.

With *The Isles of Fingal* Felix brought to closure nearly three years of revision plagued by his perpetual self-doubts. The premiere on May 14 took place during a heady time in English politics, the crisis surrounding the Reform Bill, which encountered stiff opposition from the Tory party. The week before the premiere, Prime Minister Grey and his Whig cabinet abruptly resigned. When meetings were hastily convened at Guildhall (including one the day of the Philharmonic concert) to convince King William to overcome the resistance by creating a body of new peers, Felix attended.[163] Perhaps the politically charged atmosphere affected English musical sensibilities: Moscheles recorded that no one "seemed to understand" the overture, and the *Athenaeum* reported that, "as descriptive music, it was decidedly a failure."[164] Surely the title, *The Isles of Fingal*, caused some confusion, and the work's somber hues and dark melancholy were vitiated by its placement after an aria from Rossini's *Barber of Seville*. Nevertheless, William Ayrton cited Felix as one "of the most original geniuses of the age" and likened the music to an "angel's visits."[165]

Just a week before the premiere Felix was busily revising one of his most celebrated scores.[166] Capturing the desolate, remote Scottish seascape, he had crafted music well "removed" from the conventions of European art music. Thus, the opening, three-tiered theme is built upon a simple rocking motive, extended through repetition and sequential transposition, that in turn spawns its own accompaniment and the lyrical second theme (**ex. 8.12a, b**). The *Ur*-motive seems to simulate Scottish folksong and its gapped scales. Felix's treatment of sonata form is flexible: the exposition elides directly with the development, near the middle of which a static passage interrupts the thematic working-out, and the composition ends with a hushed recall of the first and second themes, giving the score a timeless circularity. Much of the overture is veiled in muted undertones. There are only three climactic *forte* passages, delayed until the ends of the exposition and development, and the coda; in each, a militaristic fanfare briefly conjures up some Ossianic saga but then disappears, as if a Hebridean mist has cloaked the music. The caliginous, indistinct orchestration led the Debussy scholar Edward Lockspeiser to compare the overture to Turner's *Staffa* and to label the work "one of the first examples of

Ex. 8.12a: Mendelssohn, *Hebrides* Overture, Op. 26 (ca. 1832)

Ex. 8.12b: Mendelssohn, *Hebrides* Overture, Op. 26 (ca. 1832)

musical Impressionism";[167] for Wagner, the music was the "masterpiece" of a "landscape-painter of the first order."[168]

Reading the overture as a musical landscape painting gained currency early on and remains attractive. The juxtaposition of Felix's 1829 drawing of Dunollie Castle and musical sketch of the opening (see p. 215) reveal the composer as a musical draughtsman translating Hebridean scenery into sonorous images. But broadening the avenue of critical inquiry admits other interpretations—for example, the overture as evincing Felix's Ossianic manner, a style manifest in works including the *Scottish Symphony*, *Scottish Fantasy* Op. 28, and concert scene *On Lena's Gloomy Heath*.[169] Most recently, Thomas Grey has proposed that the overture begins as musical landscape, before the second, *cantabile* theme injects a human element, a "viewer," like the *Rückenfiguren* (human figures seen from behind) of German romantic landscape paintings, who invite "us to imagine ourselves similarly inhabiting the depicted landscape and meditating on it from 'within' the scene."[170] For Grey the *Rückenfigur* contemplates not just a seascape but also Ossian's Dream, a *topos* established in early nineteenth-century French painting and music to support Napoleon's interest in Ossianic literature. The development of Felix's overture becomes a kind of dream sequence, in which the slumbering, blind bard conjures up visions of Fingal and his heroes (thus the emergence of the fanfares) that ultimately recede and vanish in the closing, crepuscular bars of the work. In a creative interpretation, Grey relates the phantasmagoric quality of Felix's music to the French vogue of *fantasmagorie*, a "magic lantern" technique that projected images appearing to hover in midair.

One other new composition that preoccupied Felix in London—the *Lieder ohne Worte*, Op. 19b—broached in a different way the ability of music to convey extramusical ideas. A few weeks before in Paris, he had arranged for Schlesinger and Simrock to publish the French and German editions, and now he sought an English firm. Of the six pieces, four had been composed between September 1829 and September 1831.[171] By January 1832 they were coalescing into a collection of Lieder paralleling the "texted" Lieder of Op. 19a. By mid-June Felix composed the missing two members, Nos. 3 and 5, and arranged the order of all six. The result balanced major- and minor-keyed pieces, and offered simulations of three vocal types, the solo Lied (Nos. 1 and 2), duet (No. 6), and partsong (Nos. 3 and 4). Felix conceived two more elaborate pieces (Nos. 3 and 5) as keyboard pieces in sonata form. Only one (No. 6), the *Venetianisches Gondellied*, bore a title, though No. 3, with its imitative writing and resounding horn calls, impresses as a *Jagdlied* (Hunting Song), and No. 4, which shares thematic material and the key of A major, as a *Jägerlied*

Ex. 8.13a: Mendelssohn, *Lied ohne Worte* in A major, Op. 19b No. 3 (1832)

Ex. 8.13b: Mendelssohn, *Lied ohne Worte* in A major, Op. 19b No. 4 (1832)

(Hunters' Song; **ex. 8.13**). Whether Felix had in mind specific texts for individual Lieder is unclear; Robert Schumann later imagined that the *Lieder ohne Worte* originated as songs, the texts of which were then suppressed.[172] More likely, Felix intended the pieces as abstractions of the art song, though he left tantalizing clues to encourage listeners to make the leap between the autonomous domain of piano music and German lyrical poetry.

The new genre, which blurred the lines between the song and character piece, later enjoyed great success and became synonymous with Mendelssohnism. But in 1832 the first volume had a difficult birth. Failing to place it with an English firm, Felix left the manuscript with Moscheles, who arranged for Vincent Novello, a choral-music publisher for whom Felix had promised to compose an Anglican Morning and Evening service, to print one hundred and fifty copies in August 1832. Curiously enough, the pieces appeared not as *Songs without Words* (a term Felix never used in English editions) but *Original Melodies for the Pianoforte*.[173] Moscheles himself corrected proof and paid the engraving expenses, for which Felix later reimbursed him. Though Novello added his imprint on the title page, he thus assumed no financial risk for the pieces, which were initially a dismal failure in England and sold only forty-eight copies by June 1833. In Paris the pieces appeared as *Romances sans paroles* and in Bonn, late in 1833, as *Lieder ohne Worte*, the official debut of the new term. But despite the initially tepid response to the new genre, Felix aligned his muse sufficiently with the character pieces to "sign" a pencil portrait, taken by Eduard Bendemann in 1832, with an incipit from Op. 19b.[174] Here he appears in an informal pose, his hair somewhat disheveled and eyes slightly askance, as he ponders the lyrical melody of the "first" *Lied ohne Worte*, Op. 19b No. 1, in E major.

After two months in London, on June 22, 1832, Felix departed for the Continent. Once again the "smoky nest" had restored his spirits and validated his standing as a significant new musical voice. His pocket diary and letters reveal a hectic social calendar and even plans to have another cast made of his skull, in order to examine whether the cranial bumps associated with his creativity had evolved during the past two years.[175] But the death of Zelter in Berlin on May 15 darkened the carefree happiness of his English interlude. When Felix received the news one week later,[176] he consoled himself by visiting Norwood to see Thomas Attwood, who, at age sixty-six, stood as another musical father figure. The question of Zelter's successor now weighed heavily upon Abraham in Berlin and upon his son returning from abroad, having reached a critical crossroads, the end of the Grand Tour.

Chapter 9
1832–1835

Düsseldorf Beginnings

You see I am thought infinitely more precious
when I am a little way from home.

—Felix to Berlin, October 26, 1833[1]

Even before enduring a second turbulent crossing of the English Channel and reaching Berlin late in June 1832, Felix was conflicted about his
homecoming. Abraham had urged his son to begin positioning himself
for the Singakademie directorship.[2] Felix was disinclined but regarded it
a solemn duty if Zelter "expressed this wish." Now, after his teacher's
death, Felix's reluctance stiffened. Recalling that a director, Lichtenstein,
had already promised him the post, Felix saw no need to apply. Rather,
as if foreseeing the imbroglio that would stretch into the early months
of 1833, he sequestered himself from the petty maneuvering that enveloped the choice of Zelter's successor.

The primary sources are silent about Felix's conversation with Lichtenstein, but presumably it had occurred in 1829, during the afterglow of
the St. Matthew Passion revival. By June 1832 Felix had been away from
Berlin for more than two years; in this period, Zelter had relied upon a
deputy assistant whose "creative gifts rarely rose above mediocrity,"[3] C. F.
Rungenhagen (1778–1851). Fifty-four at the time, Rungenhagen argued that
his seniority entitled him to the position (he had faithfully belonged to
the Singakademie since 1801, for nearly Zelter's entire tenure). Felix, in
contrast, appeared to some an arrogant youngster. In August the society
debated the issue of succession, but according to Eduard Devrient, an "animated knot" of members objected "it was an unheard-of thing to . . . thrust
a Jewish lad upon them for their conductor."[4]

After Devrient proposed a joint conductorship of Felix and Rungenhagen, a committee that included Devrient and Schleiermacher thrashed

out the details. Rungenhagen would serve as managing director, while Felix would have authority over musical decisions. Felix worked behind the scenes to promote the plan, as a note to Devrient (omitted from his published memoirs) reveals.[5] Here Felix urged Devrient to conceal that the committee's plan was advanced without a vote, lest Rungenhagen demand a ballot with absentee votes (i.e., proxies for his cause). But by October Rungenhagen rejected the proposal and called for an election. In the ensuing months he outflanked Felix, "too diffident and too proud" to canvass for votes. At the election on January 22, 1833, Felix was soundly defeated, with 148 votes for Rungenhagen, 88 for Felix, and 4 for Zelter's pupil Eduard Grell. According to Devrient, while Rungenhagen's majority accumulated during the tallying, there were outbursts of laughter as the clerk adopted an increasingly deprecating tone toward the Mendelssohn name. After the election, the directors endeavored to pacify Felix with the post of deputy director, but he "diplomatically" replied "they could go hang themselves,"[6] and Grell assumed the assistantship. Thus the Singakademie followed a "long course of mediocrity," and the Mendelssohn family, arch supporters of the institution for decades, re-signed in protest.[7]

Felix's letters project an increasingly despondent tone about Berlin. Shortly after his return, he retraced Eduard Rietz's final days and on July 3 found the emptiness of the Singakademie overwhelming; Zelter's death had undermined the foundation, exposing its very flaws.[8] To Horsley, Felix lamented Berliners' "tendency to criticism" and found music unimproved since 1830.[9] To Charlotte Moscheles he compared Berlin society to an "awful monster," and to Thomas Attwood decried Berlin philistinism at a Mozart commemoration, where an inebriated amateur played insipid gal-lopades and waltzes.[10] As an antidote, Felix offered the Englishman a short Kyrie eleison in a severe, fugal style.[11]

Now entering a fallow period, Felix lived like an asparagus, "very comfortable doing nothing."[12] He decided not to compose music for Im-mermann's libretto, since the playwright had not adequately distin-guished between the lyric, dramatic, and recitative; like Devrient, Felix found the action "even more dispersed than in the original."[13] A perfor-mance of Handel's *Solomon* at the Singakademie, for which Felix in-tended to rescore some numbers and recruited Klingemann to translate the text into German, fell through in December, and Felix's own composi-tional muse threatened to stagnate. Apart from two minor songs and a piano fugue,[14] the closing months of 1832 produced only the first Anglican setting for Novello, a Te Deum for chorus and organ finished in August. In five sections (Andante, Adagio, Andante, Allegro moderato, and An-dante), this contribution to the Morning Service betrays the anthems of

Ex. 9.1: Mendelssohn, *Te Deum* (1832)

William Croft and William Boyce Felix had examined in Attwood's library. Much of the score alternates between chordal and imitative styles; in the climactic "Make them to be number'd with thy Saints in glory everlasting," Felix unfurls an erudite double canon. The concluding Andante recalls the characteristic figure of *Ave Maria*, Op. 23 No. 2; the earlier invocation to the Virgin now broadens to a supplication for the Lord's mercy to "lighten upon us" (ex. 8.7, p. 234, and ex. 9.1).

Among Felix's private diversions from this time are two *Konzertstücke* in F and D minor for clarinet, basset horn, and piano, composed at the end of 1832 and beginning of 1833, and published posthumously as Op. 113 and 114. Written for two virtuosi, Heinrich Baermann and his son Carl, each has three compact movements, connected by transitions and exhibiting the telescoped forms of Carl Maria von Weber, who had produced several works for Baermann senior. Not surprisingly, Felix's music mimics Weber's dramatic gestures, and even approaches parody: the autograph of Op. 113 bears the saporific title *The Battle of Prague: A Great Duet for Noodles or Cream Pastry, Clarinet, and Basset Horn.*[15] The music exploits the full range of the two instruments. There are impetuous opening movements with wide leaps, tender, duetting slow movements, and vivacious finales with zesty *bravura* passagework. The use of basset horn, a kind of alto clarinet favored by Mozart but obsolete by the mid-nineteenth century, condemned these pieces to obscurity, though in the 1830s the instrument's deep, mellow tone was still in vogue, and Felix took the trouble to arrange Op. 113 with orchestral accompaniment.[16]

I

In Berlin he began to ruminate on an oratorio about St. Paul and rejoiced in securing the collaboration of A. B. Marx. For years the theorist had yearned to compose an oratorio about Moses, and during the summer of 1832 the two friends agreed to an exchange: Felix would draft the libretto for *Mose* and Marx that for *Paulus*, so that each could compose unencumbered by the task of selecting texts.[17] Sadly enough, this commendable act of friendship led ultimately to estrangement and the irremediable breakdown of their relationship in 1839. But in 1832 Felix avidly took up the task and on August 21 finished his assignment,[18] organized into three sections: "In the first part, the oppression of Israel up to Moses' conversation with God in the burning bush. In the second, Moses before Pharaoh, the plagues, exodus, the miracle at the Red Sea up to Miriam's Song of Triumph. In the third, the desert, the rebellions, the Golden Calf, the wrath of the Lord, finally the Ten Commandments."[19] Relying upon Exodus, Felix also drew from Numbers, the Psalms, Jeremiah, Job, Deuteronomy, and the Prophets, showing a thorough knowledge of scripture. Musically, Felix took as his models Bach's Passions and Handel's *Israel in Egypt*, and apportioned texts among choruses, arias, and a narrator, to whom he assigned a prominent number of recitatives.

Marx had fervently supported the revival of the St. Matthew Passion, but by 1832 his conception of oratorio had evolved—he now aspired to create a work conceived dramatically. Thus, as he recast Felix's libretto, Marx opted for chains of dramatic scenes instead of the narrator, which had lent the story of Moses and the exodus a certain objective, epic quality. In the end, Marx was unable to use Felix's offering:

> He had created the text as so many had before us, and as the great masters had adopted uncritically. The mixture of narrative, lyrical outpouring, and dramatic moments was the conventional procedure of Handel and Bach; our favorite work, the St. Matthew Passion, displayed the same plan. So Mendelssohn was totally beyond reproach. If one were at fault, it was I. Why had I neglected or was unable to show him clearly the new form I deemed necessary?[20]

Marx's comments are silent about another conflict between the two. Felix's selection of texts, as Jeffrey Sposato has argued, emphasized a Christological reading of Moses, who in nineteenth-century Protestant theology was understood to represent a kind of Old Testament Johannine Christ. Like Felix, Marx had embraced the Protestant faith but against the will of his "textbook rationalist" father, Moses Marx, who had turned to Voltaire's deistic philosophy. If Felix was a devout Protestant obediently promoting Abraham's agenda of assimilation (and turning away from the rationalist Judaism of Moses Mendelssohn), A. B. Marx "never attempted to disassociate himself from his Jewish heritage";[21] thus, he wished to imbue his oratorio with a distinctly Old Testament coloring. However impossible it is to penetrate the shadowy world of Felix's intentions, there is one valuable clue about his spiritual mindset in 1832: he concluded *Mose* by quoting the New Testament, "For this is the love of God, that we keep his commandments" (1 John 5:3), thereby linking the Ten Commandments to the New Covenant and building a bridge between the two faiths. Marx suppressed the quotation when he assembled the libretto.

While Felix fulfilled his part of the oratorio exchange, Marx initially balked at reciprocating. Several months before, Felix had enlisted Devrient's assistance and approached the Orientalist Julius Fürst.[22] *Paulus* was to be in three parts: the stoning of Stephen, the conversion of Saul, and "the Christian life and preaching," to include either Paul's departure from Ephesus or his martyrdom. But Marx tried to dissuade Felix from the plan: ". . . what should the musician do with the words 'It is hard for thee to kick against the pricks' [Acts 9:5]?" For Marx, Paul was the rationalist Protestant: "The thinker, the painter, perhaps the poet can base their work on Paul; but the musician, whose creation belongs most immediately to the sphere of the inner life and emotions?"[23] Failing to convince Felix that St. Peter was a more suitable topic, Marx to his credit finished a libretto for *Paulus* on March 15, 1833.[24] But the collaboration ran aground, for when Felix insisted on replicating the style of the St. Matthew Passion by inserting chorales, Marx detected an anachronism ("Chorales in Paul's time?" he reportedly challenged.) The theorist abandoned the project, and Felix turned to Julius Schubring for advice.

II

Despite the tedium of Berlin life, Felix maintained a high profile in concert life. On October 7, 1832, Moscheles arrived for two weeks, and though Felix admitted to bouts of depression, he entertained his friend sumptuously, loaned him an Erard piano that had just arrived, and hosted fêtes in his honor. The two improvised, darting around the keyboard "quick as lightning" on "each other's harmonies," in a kind of "musical blindman's buff."[25] When Moscheles departed on October 19, Felix gave him a special present, the Beethoven "Wittgenstein" sketchbook Felix had received from Aloys Fuchs in 1830.[26]

At concerts of Anna Milder-Hauptmann, Karl Möser, and Ferdinand Ries, Felix crafted cadenzas to Mozart's minor-keyed piano concerti (K. 466 and K. 491) and also played Beethoven's Violin Sonata, Op. 30 No. 2, and Triple Concerto, Op. 56.[27] But overshadowing these performances were three concerts for the widows of the royal orchestra. In quick succession, Felix presented at the Singakademie the *Midsummer Night's Dream* Overture, Piano Concerto No. 1, and premiere of the *Reformation* Symphony (November 15); *Meeresstille und glückliche Fahrt* and the *Capriccio brillant* (December 1); and the *Hebrides* Overture and premiere of *Die erste Walpurgisnacht* (January 10, 1833). As a pianist he rendered

Beethoven's *Waldstein* Sonata on the first concert, Beethoven's *Moon-light* Sonata and J. S. Bach's Concerto in D minor on the second, and Beethoven's Piano Concerto No. 4 and Weber's *Grand Duo concertant* (with Heinrich Baermann) on the third. Setting great stock in these concerts, which displayed his trifurcated talents as composer, pianist, and conductor, Felix believed the series would determine if he would live and work in Berlin.[28] An attempt to solidify his candidacy at the Singakademie, this effort nevertheless raised suspicions, and impressed some Berliners as a marketing campaign. Felix was offended when the widows' charity grudgingly accepted the proceeds from the first concert,[29] but the king supported the concerts,[30] and they were sold out. Felix was quite à la mode, even if regarded an "arrogant eccentric."[31] The royal Intendant, Count von Redern, offered to procure an opera libretto for Felix from the French dramatist Eugène Scribe, and the music critic Ludwig Rellstab solicited a biographical article for a lexicon. (Felix replied that other than his birth on February 3, nothing remarkable had transpired in his life.[32])

Press reports of the concerts were largely positive, though Rellstab challenged the program of the *Reformation* Symphony as extraneous and suggested Marx's aesthetics had led the composer astray.[33] *Die erste Walpurgisnacht* fared somewhat better; here Rellstab discovered "fantastic passages and bold combinations." A reporter from the Leipzig *Allgemeine musikalische Zeitung* found the score original, the choruses "frightening, bizarre, and energetic."[34] The path to the premiere of *Die erste Walpurgisnacht* had been especially arduous. After Felix's final visit to Weimar in 1830, the cantata gestated under Italian skies but was not "finished" until 1832 in Paris. In fact, years later it underwent thorough revision before its release in 1844 as Op. 60[35] and thus experienced the protracted process of re-composition visited upon so many of Felix's major works.

Goethe's ballad (1799, not to be confused with the witches' Sabbath in the *Walpurgisnacht* scene of *Faust*) concerns early medieval pagan rites in the Harz Mountains on May Eve. In Goethe's reading, the revelries originated as a defense against Christian zealotry. Attempting to scare off *dumpfe Pfaffenchristen* ("dimwitted Christian priests"), the Druids masqueraded as satanic figures to rout their oppressors by conjuring up the Christians' own, "fabricated" devil. Goethe's poem symbolized a recurring historical process—how something "old, established, tested, and reassuring" is repeatedly disarranged and displaced by innovation.[36] Though Felix excerpted Goethe's comment on the verso of the title page of the score published in 1844, Felix never disclosed his own interpretation of the ballade. Instead, twentieth-century scholars have advanced various readings. For Eric Werner, the poem was a "mild satire on medieval churchly

bigotry" that opposed a "pure monotheism, derived from natural philosophy, against the superstitious usages of the early European Church."
Lawrence Kramer found the "object of Mendelssohn's carnivalesque
flyting" not Christianity but "Phariseeism, the narrow, dogmatic, anti-
cosmopolitan cast of mind that Robert Schumann identified with the
Philistines." And Heinz-Klaus Metzger heard the score as a "Jewish protest against the domination of Christianity."[37]

Felix added one significant element not in the poem: an overture
depicting wintry "foul weather" and the transition to spring. The poet's
dialectic of tradition and innovation thus prompted naturalistic tone
painting, so that spring, season of renewal, became associated with an
uncontaminated form of druidism, uncorrupted by the encroachment
of civilization and reaffirmed after the raging elements of winter. The
basic motive of the overture, which reduces to the A-minor triad in second inversion (E–A–C), is already implicit in the unsettling sixteenth-
note accompaniment of the lower strings that agitates much of the
overture (ex. 9.2a). At the end of the development the bassoons and
horns interrupt the storm with a recitative based upon the motive, and
in the recapitulation, the turbulence eventually subsides, as the motive
serves as a harbinger of spring (ex. 9.2b). Now the blustery $\frac{3}{4}$ of winter
broadens to $\frac{4}{4}$, and soft wind tremolos propel a gently falling figure in
the strings and flutes, a passage Johannes Brahms surely later invoked in
his Second Symphony (ex. 9.3, 1877).

Through-composed, the nine numbers of the cantata fall into two
parts. In the first (Nos. 1–4), the Druids prepare their sacrificial fires, even
as they lament their suffering at the hands of the Christians and position
guards to ward off intruders. The opening chorus shifts to a bright A
major, with the elemental motive rearranged to the form A–C♯–D–E,

Ex. 9.2a: Mendelssohn, *Die erste Walpurgisnacht*, Op. 60 (1833), Overture

Ex. 9.2b: Mendelssohn, *Die erste Walpurgisnacht*, Op. 60 (1833), Overture

Ex. 9.3a: Mendelssohn, *Die erste Walpurgisnacht*, Op. 60 (1833), Overture

Ex. 9.3b: Brahms, Symphony No. 2 in D major, Op. 77 (1877), First Movement

affirming the triad in root position (A–C♯–E). The new permutation
returns in the chorus of Druid guards (No. 4), a lightly scored march in
E major punctuated by brisk chords and mock fanfares (ex. 9.4). In the
second part (Nos. 5–9), as the pagans hatch their plot, the music adopts
the tone of a macabre scherzo. Adding bass drum, cymbals, and piccolo,
a complement that revives the sound of Janissary music (associated with
military music but also "pagan," Eastern culture), Felix begins softly with
an ostinato-like figure in G minor, repeated through several variations
(No. 5). In No. 6 a chorus of pagans joins the guards, and the music attains
a new level of frenzy through an abrupt shift to A minor and boisterous
metrical displacements. Once again Felix rotates the *Ur*-motive, so that
its pitches outline the first-inversion form of the triad (C–E–A, ex. 9.5).
The increased dissonance level and reappearance of A minor revive the
discordant tone of the overture, as the howling pagans scatter the Christians with pitchforks and rattles. After they flee (No. 8), the Druids resume their sacrificial rites, and from the purifying smoke of fire rises a
glowing C major, and a motive outlining the second inversion of the triad

Ex. 9.4: Mendelssohn, *Die erste Walpurgisnacht*, Op. 60 (1833), No. 4

Ex. 9.5: Mendelssohn, *Die erste Walpurgisnacht*, Op. 60 (1833), No. 6

Ex. 9.6: Mendelssohn, *Die erste Walpurgisnacht*, Op. 60 (1833), No. 8

Die Flam - me   rei - nigt sich von   Rauch: so rei - nig   un - sern   Glau - ben!

(G–C–E), and returning us to the starting point of the original motive (ex. 9.6). "And if they steal our ancient rite," the chorus concludes, "who can rob us of thy light?"

Unifying this vision of pantheistic paganism is a taut network of motives, all based upon the *Ur*-motive of the overture, as if to suggest the immanence of the druidic *Allvater*. Felix later drew upon this thematic repository in another example of musical exoticism, the *Scottish* Symphony (see p. 430). In 1830, Felix had envisioned that work, the *Italian* Symphony, and *Die erste Walpurgisnacht* in southern climes. But in 1832 he was not yet ready to commit symphonic thoughts of the Scottish wilderness to paper. Rather, the counterestablishment abandon of the cantata and images of a pagan German past gave him respite from the stifling culture of Berlin.

III

Unexpected relief arrived with invitations from London and Düsseldorf. On November 5, 1832, the Philharmonic Society had offered Felix one hundred guineas for a new symphony, overture, and vocal piece.[38] The commission facilitated the twenty-four-year-old's passage from "amateur" to professional status in England and spurred the completion of the *Italian* Symphony. Between the middle of January and March he finished the score and dated it on March 13, 1833,[39] in time for the new London concert season. Another reason impelled him to return to England, to stand as godfather for his namesake, Felix Moscheles, born in February.

February brought a request from Immermann, who as the new director of the Düsseldorf theater planned to mount a series of classic plays, among them Calderón's *El príncipe constante*, after A. W. Schlegel's translation (*Der standhafte Prinz*). Abandoning the collaboration on Shakespeare's *Tempest*, Immermann secured instead Felix's commitment to provide incidental music for the seventeenth-century Spanish tragedy. Within a few weeks, four movements were ready.[40] The play concerns Prince Fernando, brother of the Portuguese king and hero of the *reconquista*, the war between the Christians and Moors on the Iberian Peninsula. Captured in 1438, Fernando died in captivity for refusing to

Ex. 9.7: Mendelssohn, Incidental Music to Calderón's *Der standhafte Prinz* (1833)

surrender the stronghold of Ceuta in exchange for his freedom. In the play, his martyred spirit leads the Portuguese to victory.

Though Immermann found Calderón's play operatic,[41] Felix was unable to insinuate much musical inspiration into the tragedy. Of the four modest numbers he provided, two are choruses of Christian slaves lamenting their captivity and voicing the hope that Fernando will free them. The most extended movement is the third (*Schlachtmusik*), an orchestral depiction of the raging battle. Here Felix resorts to stock figures of tone painting, including wind fanfares and a jagged G-minor string figure that plummets over chromatically descending tremolos; eventually the musical strife yields to a victory celebration in the major (**ex. 9.7**). The final piece is a short march to mark the appearance of the martyred Fernando exhorting his countrymen (*Geistererscheinung*).

Partly owing to a poorly rehearsed orchestra,[42] Felix's incidental music attracted scant attention when *Der standhafte Prinz* opened in Düsseldorf on April 9, 1833, and remains unpublished. Though Felix was unable to attend, he did arrive in the city one week later to discuss a more substantial invitation, to direct the fifteenth Lower Rhine Music Festival, scheduled for Pentecost in May. As early as February 1832 Felix had been approached about the opportunity; a formal invitation materialized in March 1833.[43] The fortuitous timing helped allay Felix's rejection by the Singakademie, and he eagerly accepted, despite his commitment to direct the Philharmonic in London in May.

En route to London, Felix reached Düsseldorf on April 17 to confer about the program with the festival committee, chaired by the appellate judge Otto von Woringen (1760–1838). There was consensus about the major work, Handel's *Israel in Egypt*, but when the committee proposed

Ex. **9.8**: Mendelssohn, *Responsorium und Hymnus*, Op. 121 (1833), No. 4

Beethoven's Fourth Symphony, Felix countered with the *Pastoral* and promptly played it from memory at the piano. Then, at a hastily arranged rehearsal at the concert hall, he conducted the ensemble without a score and filled in some missing parts by singing.[44] Immermann was impressed enough to wonder whether the young musician could be won permanently for the Düsseldorf orchestra and opera and, after advancing the idea during the April visit, confided to his diary that Felix was not "adverse to taking up such a post."[45] Conceivably, discussions had already begun. If so, the prospect of Felix's move to Düsseldorf might explain an unusual composition finished in Berlin on February 5, the *Responsorium und Hymnus* for male choir and bass line, published posthumously as Op. 121. The Latin Vespers text (twenty-first Sunday after Trinity), suggests Felix had in mind a Catholic service, such as he would encounter in Düsseldorf. Markedly Italianate, the setting revives his impressions of St. Peter's, with a "walking" Baroque bass line in the first movement, responsorial singing in the third, and imitations of psalmody in the second and fourth, where a chant appears in monophony and embellished by two tenor voices (**ex. 9.8**).

IV

From Düsseldorf Felix traveled to Rotterdam. There, on April 23, 1833, he finished a humorous male part-song, *Musikantenprügelei* (*Musicians' Fisticuffs*), for Robert Reinick, a pupil of Schadow who was planning an artists' festival on May 1.[46] Embarking for London, Felix arrived on April 25 and took up his familiar quarters at 103 Great Portland Street. Reunited with his German friends, he planned an extravaganza for two pianos

Ex. 9.9: Mendelssohn-Moscheles, *Variations brillantes* (1833), Theme

and orchestra for Moscheles's concert on May 1. The subject was the Gypsies' March from Weber's *Preciosa* (1821), based on a tale of Cervantes. The two pianists hastily fabricated four *bravura* variations, prefaced by an introduction and the theme, and culminating in a scintillating finale. Felix took the first two variations, Moscheles the third and fourth, and the two collaborated on a scherzo-like finale. An effective concert piece that bears comparison with Schubert's piano duets *à l'hongroise*, the collaboration captured the bohemian flavor of Weber's theme (**ex 9.9**). In 1833 the variations appeared in a version for two pianos as *Variations brillantes*, with an opus number (87b) from Moscheles's catalogue of works. Moscheles appears to have taken a heavy hand in editing the final product, for Felix later complained he hardly recognized a measure of the printed composition.[47] But at the concert, the audience marveled at the "intimate fusion of two musical minds"; for Moscheles the work was like "an ice *à la tutti frutti*" that dissolved "in one's mouth," and that one should savor for "the flavor it leaves behind."[48]

At private soirées Felix mixed with several celebrities, including Vincenzo Bellini, then under contract to produce his operas at the King's Theatre, and Hummel, who offered on May 6 such a monotonous improvisation that Felix "yawned an obbligato accompaniment."[49] No more fulfilling were his encounters with Paganini, whose "wretched quartet" almost put Felix to sleep again. The Italian violinist invited him to play Beethoven violin sonatas,[50] but their most celebrated appearance occurred on May 12 at a soirée of Dr. Billing, when Paganini premiered a *Trio concertante* for viola, guitar, and cello. Because a guitarist was lacking, Felix performed the part at sight at the piano, a feat cited in the *Morning Post*.[51] Among his English acquaintances, Felix socialized with J. B. Cramer, the Taylors, and the Horsleys, and again visited St. Paul's with Attwood. At Parliament, Felix attended the second reading of the Irish Church Reform Bill, and at the Royal Music Library examined the manuscript of *Israel in Egypt*, where he uncovered recitatives and arias missing in the printed version. Unable to conceal his delight, he reported the discoveries to Woringen and arranged to copy the recitatives; he also prevailed upon Klingemann to prepare a German translation of the libretto for use at the Düsseldorf festival.

Woringen's committee had been concerned about the lack of an overture for Handel's oratorio, so Felix pressed into service his old *Trumpet*

Overture, Op. 101. Shortly before leaving Berlin he had retouched the work, revised the ending, and, taking advantage of Handel's scoring for three trombones, added parts for those instruments.[52] Upon arriving in London, one of Felix's first acts was to present the "new" overture as partial fulfillment of the Philharmonic commission. Perhaps the disingenuousness prompted him to offer the institution's secretary, William Watts, a second overture.[53] What was its identity? Peter Ward Jones has argued convincingly for *Die schöne Melusine* (*The Fair Melusine*), Op. 32.[54] On February 27, 1833, Felix had attended a Berlin performance of Conradin Kreutzer's romantic opera *Melusine* and when its overture was encored, he determined to compose his own overture that "the people might not *encore*, but would cause them more solid pleasure."[55] Though Felix finished his autograph in November 1833, Ward Jones has suggested a first draft was advanced enough to share with the Philharmonic in April. Still, the directors selected the *Trumpet* Overture for performance on June 10, and shortly before Felix departed London on May 18, they granted permission for its use at the Düsseldorf festival.

The highpoint of Felix's third English sojourn came on May 13, when he conducted the sixth concert of the Philharmonic Society, relocated to the Hanover Square Rooms in the West End. Felix led the entire concert and underscored his new authority in English musical culture. Still, the evening ended in controversy: the orchestra, used to following the first violinist and not conductors, who usually merely turned pages, began the final work of the program while Felix was offstage.[56] Each program half was made up of a symphony, concerto (framed by two arias), and overture.[57] In the first half Felix performed Mozart's Piano Concerto in D minor K. 466 from memory and distinguished himself on an out-of-tune piano with two brilliant cadenzas that tied together the thematic threads of the outer movements. In the second half came the premiere of the *Italian* Symphony. As with *The Isles of Fingal* in 1832, reactions were somewhat mixed; at least one critic, John Ella, misheard the slow movement, which, when encored, reminded him of "some ancient Scotch melody."[58]

For nearly one hundred and seventy-five years, this masterful composition has symbolized Felix's perfectionism. After the premiere, he left the autograph with Moscheles, and in 1834 began its revision by preparing from memory a new score of the last three movements.[59] Dissatisfied with the first movement, he abandoned the task and left the final judgment of his symphony to posterity. Apart from a few performances in 1834, 1837, and 1838 conducted by Moscheles and Cipriani Potter, the work was not heard again during Felix's lifetime. Then, published posthumously as Op. 90 in 1851,[60] it entered the symphonic canon.

Ex. 9.10a: Mendelssohn, *Italian* Symphony, Op. 90 (1833), First Movement

Ex. 9.10b: Mendelssohn, *Italian* Symphony, Op. 90 (1833), First Movement

Ex. 9.10c: Mendelssohn, *Italian* Symphony, Op. 90 (1833), First Movement

The warm, southern character of the music breaks forth in the opening like a burst of Mediterranean sunlight: against pulsating wind tremolos and a pizzicato string chord, the violins convey an infectious, carnival-like melody in octaves (**ex. 9.10a**). The initial ascending third later emerges as a wind fanfare, anticipating the telltale *descending* third of the saltarello in the finale. Dancelike, the first movement prepares the topic of the finale, where, as we shall see, Felix juxtaposes two Italian folk dances. The euphonious second theme (**ex. 9.10b**), doubled in thirds in the winds, is also redolent of Italy. In the development Felix springs a surprise by introducing a third theme in a kind of mock fugato (**ex. 9.10c**). This intrusion of Germanic counterpoint is short-lived, banished by the reemergence of the fanfares. Especially memorable is the retransition to the reprise: against a high pitch in the first oboe, the fanfares gradually gain force, spilling over into the translucent wind tremuli.[61] In the ebullient coda, the third subject returns in A minor (presaging the finale) before its reunion with the lustrous A-major winds of the opening.

The haunting Andante impresses as a sacred procession, not unlike the *March of the Pilgrims* in Berlioz's *Harold en Italie* Symphony of 1834 (whether Felix shared parts of his symphony with the Frenchman during their Roman sojourns is unknown). But in 1963 Eric Werner, followed in 1987 by Wulf Konold, suggested that Felix's plaintive opening melody resembled Zelter's setting of Goethe's "Es war ein König in Thule" (**ex. 9.11a**) and was an homage to Felix's deceased teacher (or double homage to Zelter and Goethe).[62] Closer inspection casts doubt on the idea. First, Felix's melody does not replicate the interlocking fourths characteristic of Zelter's melody. Further, Felix may have conceived the slow movement in Rome a year or so *before* Zelter's death; the letter of June 11, 1831,

Ex. 9.11a: Zelter, "Es war ein König in Thule" (1796)

Es war ein Kö - nig in Thu - le, gar treu bis an das Grab,

Ex. 9.11b: Mendelssohn, *Italian* Symphony, Op. 90 (1833), Second Movement

Ex. 9.11c: Mendelssohn, *Italian* Symphony, Op. 90 (1833), Second Movement

Ex. 9.11d: Mendelssohn, *Italian* Symphony, Op. 90 (1833), Finale

Ex. 9.11e: Mendelssohn, *Italian* Symphony, Op. 90 (1833), Finale

to Attwood establishes the symphony was "finished" (i.e., conceived mentally though not written out in score) before he left Italy. And finally, a striking, though overlooked passage from the *Responsorium* of Op. 121 suggests Felix indeed intended the Andante to imitate the monophonic psalmody he had absorbed in Rome.

As we have seen, the second movement of Op. 121 features a monophonic intonation hovering around A, supported by B♭ and C above; the Andante begins by condensing this chantlike formula (see p. 274 and ex. 9.11b). In the symphony the winds then intone a modal melody against a walking bass line, a texture that vividly recalls the first movement of the *Responsorium*. When the violins answer the wind melody an octave higher, a pattern of responsorial chanting emerges. In m. 45, a new theme appears, bringing a shift from the modal D minor to the "modern" key of A major, so that the music now becomes tonally oriented (ex. 9.11c). But midway through the movement the intonation interrupts, *fortissimo*, and the chantlike melody and detached bass line resume. After the tonal melody reappears in D major, the intonation returns *mezzo forte* and then, echolike, falls to *pianissimo*. Broken up, the attenuated chant dies away, and the walking bass line expires in a few pizzicati. Taken as a whole, the alternating modal/tonal passages suggest a rehearing of monophonic chant through a modern, "tonal" perspective; the strategic placement of the intonation at various dynamics levels (*f*, *ff*, *mf*, and *pp*), an approaching and passing procession, the kind of spatial music Berlioz created in his *March of the Pilgrims* (**diagram 9.1**). It is difficult not to believe Felix's experience of sacred monophony in Rome informed this powerful movement.

The graceful third movement bears only the tempo marking *Con moto moderato* in the 1833 autograph, but when Felix revised the work in 1834 he labeled the movement a *Menuetto*, invoking the then obsolete court dance. His strategy was to contrast the aristocratic elegance of the minuet with the raucous finale, which begins with a saltarello modeled on folk dances he had heard in Rome. (In the 1834 score, the two worlds literally collide, for Felix added the inter-movement instruction, *attaca subito il Saltarello*.) The saltarello theme, doubled in thirds in the flutes, unfolds with a series of small leaps typifying the dance (ex. 9.11d; the word derives from the Latin *saltus*, for leap). The dance takes precedence over issues of form, for this restless movement resists ready analysis according to the sonata or rondo molds typically associated with finales.

Diagram 9.1: Mendelssohn, *Italian* Symphony, Op. 90 (1833), Slow Movement

A Modal	B Tonal	A Modal	B Tonal	A Modal
	(approaching)		*(passing)*	*(echo)*
f p	*p*	*ff p*		*mf* $>$ *pp*
reciting tone, responsorial, walking bass				
D minor	A major m. 45	A minor m. 57	D major m. 74	D minor m. 86

The monothematic "exposition," which moves to the dominant minor, is spun entirely from the saltarello melody. The putative "development" (m. 105) begins with a feigned repeat of the exposition but soon introduces a fresh *pianissimo* subject in imitative counterpoint (**ex. 9.11e**). Some commentators have regarded it as a second saltarello, but its profile, distinguished by conjunct motion and legato slurs, tells us otherwise. According to Felix's pupil William Rockstro,[63] the new melody is a tarantella, the southern Italian dance traditionally associated with tarantism, a nervous hysteria once thought caused by a tarantula's bite. Here Felix may have drawn upon not only his Italian experiences but also the finale of Weber's Piano Sonata No. 4, Op. 70 (1823), the first elevation of the folk dance into European art music.[64] In lieu of a recapitulation, Felix's finale culminates in a suspenseful juxtaposition of the two dances, built up over a prolonged pedal point.[65] Near the end, the music dies down to *pianissimo* (the traditional abatement of the hysteria) but flares up again with a few rousing, definitive chords.

V

Early on May 18, Felix left London[66] (the night before, he repeated the *Preciosa* Variations with Moscheles at a concert of Nicolas Mori). Two days later he was lodged comfortably at the Düsseldorf home of Wilhelm von Schadow, and he accepted a three-year appointment, from October 1, 1833, as the municipal music director.[67] According to the agreement, Felix was to direct music for church services and up to eight concerts per year. In compensation he received a salary of 600 thalers (around 800 thalers in Berlin currency) and a three-month annual leave. Abraham, who arrived from Berlin on May 23 to attend the festival, wholeheartedly approved, for while "so many others have titles without an office," [Felix] would have "a real office without a title."[68] In Düsseldorf there was "no court, no meddling influence from higher quarters, no General-Musikdirektor [i.e., Spontini], no royal this or that."[69] Annexed by Prussia in 1815 as part of the Rhine Province, Düsseldorf was administered by a mayor, with whom Felix executed his agreement, and protected by the garrison of Prince Friedrich, the Prussian monarch's nephew, with whom Felix dined.

In this unpretentious town of twenty thousand, he found haven from Berlin disappointments. Underscoring his new independence was his directorship of the Lower Rhine Music Festival, which, for fourteen years, had rotated between Aachen, Cologne, Elberfeld, and Düsseldorf, and developed into a relatively democratic form of public music making. In

1833 its participants included amateurs from surrounding communities, conveyed by "steamboats, diligences of every description, *Extraposten,* coaches," and "private carriages." To Abraham the scene was a "miracle, that 400 persons of all sexes, classes, and ages, blown together like snow before the wind, should let themselves be conducted and governed like children by one of the youngest of them all, too young almost to be a friend for any of them, and with no title or dignity whatever." Betraying liberal sympathies, Abraham found the occasion a "true public festival, for which I have not yet noticed either policemen or gendarmes."[70]

The openness of the festival infected its rehearsals, which commenced at 8:00 A.M. and resumed at 3:00 P.M. before the evening concert; the public could attend rehearsals for ten groschen, and nearly the same audience attended both. The musicians particularly welcomed one reform instituted by Felix. Earlier festival conductors had divided the personnel according to ability into "solo" and "tutti" groups, with the former playing in *piano* passages and the combined ensemble in *forte* passages. Felix argued that the less gifted musicians had not come to count rests and thus molded the combined forces into one orchestra.[71] Two concerts were given on Pentecost Sunday and Monday (May 26 and 27). The first began with the *Trumpet* Overture (imagined by the Düsseldorfers as composed for the festival) and featured Handel's *Israel in Egypt,* with an orchestra of 142 and chorus of 267. Felix added wind parts and entered corrections into the printed score, including recitatives from the London autograph he had examined.[72] The second concert brought Beethoven's *Pastoral* Symphony and third *Leonore* Overture, and cantatas by E. W. Wolf and Peter Winter. Owing to the success, the festival committee added for the first time a third, "impromptu" concert on the morning of May 28, in which the soloists performed arias, and Felix played Weber's *Konzertstück,* directed the *Fidelio* and third *Leonore* Overtures, and encored choruses from the oratorio. Then, at a festive evening ball, toasts were raised to Felix's health, and adulatory verses appeared in French and German in the *Düsseldorfer Zeitung.* Dubbed *le Prince de l'harmonie,* Felix was compared to his grandfather and likened to a young branch of an honored family that now blossomed on the Rhine, as Handel, Bach, and Beethoven looked on approvingly from high.[73] Schadow captured the enthusiasm of the moment in a commemorative coin and gold seal. Even Beethoven's former secretary, Anton Schindler, who later would reprove Felix's conducting,[74] publicly declared the festival had easily surpassed its fourteen predecessors.[75]

Flushed with triumph, Felix departed with Abraham for London, where they arrived on June 5. Now it was the father's opportunity to marvel at St. Paul's looming from the foggy metropolis of nearly one and a half million and to experience English weather: "This morning . . . the sun was just powerful enough to give a yellow tinge to the mist, and the air was just like the smoke of a great fire. 'A very fine morning!' said my barber. . . . 'Is it?' asked I. 'Yes, a *very* fine morning!' and so I learned what a fine summer morning here is like."[76] Abraham joined Felix in musical society and witnessed his son's improvisations and performances of Bach at St. Paul's and the eighth concert of the Philharmonic on June 10, when the *Trumpet* Overture, now expressly composed for the Society, was played. The next day Felix visited Alfred Novello and received royalties of £4 16s for the meager forty-eight copies of Op. 19b sold the previous year (deflating Felix's jesting boast that the proceeds would enable him to purchase a seat in the House of Commons and "become a Radical by profession").[77] In March Felix had composed an organ fugue in D minor (later subsumed in the third Prelude and Fugue of Op. 37) for Alfred's father, Vincent, and in July sketched in his album a chromatic, Bachian organ prelude.[78] But not until 1836 did the firm become Felix's principal English publisher, though within a few years, the relationship would sour.

On June 15 Felix stood as godfather at the christening of his namesake, Felix Moscheles, for whom the composer wrote the lullaby *Bei der Wiege*, later published as Op. 47 No. 6, on a text by Klingemann.[79] A few days later Felix again inspected Brunel's tunnel, presumably in Abraham's company. Felix's diary also records an excursion to Greenwich, where father and son visited the Royal Observatory and where a "thousand subjects for marine paintings"—the interminable commerce on the Thames—"followed each other."[80] At Somerset House, Abraham contemplated an exhibition of "living artists" but disagreed sharply with Felix about a canvas of David Wilkie depicting a young Capuchin at confession; in the father's view, the monk "must have taken an emetic for the occasion."[81]

At the beginning of July Felix and Abraham visited Portsmouth and the Isle of Wight. But while viewing English men-of-war at the Portsmouth naval dockyards,[82] Abraham injured his leg, and after only a day at Ryde on the Isle of Wight they returned to London. For weeks the invalid underwent a "therapy" of Bach fugues at 103 Great Portland Street from his doting son and Moscheles. Although Abraham's activities were restricted, he was able to attend a soirée featuring the ravishing mezzo-soprano Maria Malibran.[83] After performing a medley of Spanish songs, an English sea-song, and French tambour-ditty, she approached Felix: "Now, Mr. Mendelssohn, I never do *nothing* for *nothing:*—I have sung to please you—will you not play to please me?" Felix dexterously wove ideas from Malibran's songs into a *quodlibet*-like improvisation, impelling an incredulous Vincent Novello to exclaim, "He has done some things that seem to me to be impossible, even after I have heard them done."[84]

During the fourth London sojourn, Felix attended further sessions of Parliament. On July 23, he reported the passage in the House of Commons of the Jewish Civil Disabilities Act, which removed lingering policies of discrimination by permitting English Jews to vote and serve in public office. Ironically, just a few days before, Felix had read in the London *Times* about the Posen statutes, by which Frederick William III, "the new lawgiver of the Jews, with probably no chance of being reckoned their second Moses," had placed new restrictions on Polish Jews residing in the Prussian duchy of Poznań.[85] To his family Felix reacted to these events: "This morning they emancipated the Jews, which greatly amuses me, especially since a few days ago your wretched Posen statutes were rightly and justly put down."[86] As Jeffrey Sposato has shown, Felix's comments were retouched by Eric Werner, who cited the letter in 1955 and 1963 and then in the 1980 German edition of his biography.[87] Werner doctored the text, by replacing "which greatly amuses me" (*das amusirt mich prächtig*) with "which makes me proud" (*das macht mich stolz*), and, in a subsequent passage, extending Felix's summary, "This is totally noble and beautiful," to "This is quite noble and fills me with gratitude to Heaven." Werner appears to have fabricated evidence to strengthen Felix's identification with his Jewish heritage, whereas Felix's sense of "amusement" suggests a detached spectator, notwithstanding his clear concern for the plight of the Posen Jews. In 1833, as he began work on the libretto of *St. Paul*, Felix remained a devout *Neuchrist*, as if to confirm Devrient's observation that his friend usually "avoided all reference to his Jewish descent."[88] But Felix's father was considerably closer to the issue of emancipation and made this assessment to Lea: "at present there are only 27,000 Jews [in England], among them many rich, still more who are prosperous, and nearly all self-supporting, in a population of nearly 24,000,000, which admittedly permits a different action than do the Prussians in Posen." Abraham predicted that if the law passed the Upper House of Parliament, England would become the haven of Jews, who "since the birth of Christ have never experienced anywhere such a complete emancipation."[89]

Of new music, Felix finished relatively little during the summer of 1833. The exception is a graceful, through-composed setting of Byron's love poem "There be none of beauty's daughters," drafted on August 3, possibly for one of the Horsley daughters.[90] By this time, the Overture to the *Fair Melusine* was sufficiently advanced for Felix to render it at the piano, and he agreed to prepare a piano duet arrangement for Mary and Sophy.[91] A third, gestating composition was the *Rondo brillant*, Op. 29, for piano and orchestra, which Felix offered Breitkopf & Härtel on August 9, and tried out for the Horsleys later that month.[92] Meanwhile, at Great Portland Street, the convalescing Abraham received several English acquaintances. When the Horsleys arrived on July 20, the second daughter, Fanny, found a lachrymose, frenzied Felix rushing about Abraham's room ("But most geniuses are the same," she reflected, and "at any rate he is always delightful for he is always original").[93] Abraham was especially grateful to the family of Claud Alexander, a Scottish laird who had made his fortune in the East India Company and cotton industry. In London, the Alexanders resided in fashionable Hanover Terrace, Regent's Park, near Great Portland Street, where the unmarried daughters, garbed in black like the three ladies in Mozart's *Magic Flute*, arrived bearing gifts of arrowroot, port wine, and marmalade. Though Margaret, Anna-Joanna, and Mary were all older than Felix, he appears to have flirted with Mary, who, musically inclined and attractive, became infatuated with him.[94] Felix gave her a piano piece or song as a memento of their friendship, and shortly before he left London with Abraham, she reciprocated by sending a seal for use in his future correspondence. It bore a running hound and the prophetic words, *Je reviens*; in a note, Mary hinted that the short weeks since their meeting "made us better known to each other than years could have done passed in the usual frigid atmosphere of fashions."[95]

Eager to return to Germany, Felix and Abraham departed on August 25 and crossed the Channel to Rotterdam. Abraham longed to see his new grandson, Walter Dirichlet, born to Rebecka and Gustav on July 2, and to examine Hensel's imposing new canvas, *Christus vor Pilatus* (*Christ before Pilate*), about to be exhibited in Berlin. Concealing that Felix was accompanying him, Abraham notified his family he was traveling with a young painter named Alphonse Lovie.[96] When the two paused in Düsseldorf, Felix conferred with Immermann, who promoted his idea for a new municipal theater and won Felix's participation in a planning committee. Then, proceeding up the Rhine, Abraham and Felix visited Joseph Mendelssohn in Horchheim. Here, misfortune struck again: accidentally stepping on a nail, Abraham was laid up with a new foot injury. Not until September 13 did the two reach Berlin and unmask Alphonse Lovie as Felix.

The reunion was joyful but brief. On September 15, Felix performed his Piano Concerto No. 1 and J. S. Bach's Concerto in D minor at Fanny's Sunday musicale, then left the next morning for Leipzig. As he observed to Rosen, other than his family, he now had nothing to do with Berliners or Berlin.[97] Even his nomination to the Prussian Academy of Arts, along with Meyerbeer and Rungenhagen, had filled Felix with misgivings. When news of that honor had leaked in May, Meyerbeer wrote to his wife that the king might rescind the nomination because of his Jewish faith;[98] Felix was also potentially susceptible to this discrimination. The nomination went forward, though not until December, with prodding from Abraham, did Felix send his acceptance.[99]

Arriving in mid-September in Leipzig, Felix stayed with Franz Hauser; in pursuit of Bachiana, the two visited the Thomaskantor C. T. Weinlig, who two years before had instructed Richard Wagner in counterpoint. Felix also corrected proofs for the piano-duet arrangement of the *Hebrides* Overture, about to appear from Breitkopf & Härtel with the bilingual title *Ouverture aux Hébrides* (*Fingals Höhle*), the first public association of the work with Fingal's Cave. Through Hauser Felix met the deaf illustrator/musician J. P. Lyser (1803–1870), a member of Robert Schumann's new League of David, that artistic assemblage about to do battle with philistinism. Lyser had attended a reading of the overture and somehow perceived the "original" qualities of its ending,[100] though the effort cost him two days of headaches afterward. Deeply touched, Felix gave Lyser the proofs, in order to facilitate his acquaintance with the score.

VI

Days before his appointment began in October, Felix reached Düsseldorf. To Schubring he confided his purpose in moving there was to secure "quiet and leisure for composition,"[101] while to the authorities he announced his desire to revitalize the municipal musical life. In the early months of the new post, he endeavored to do both. His first official appearance was to conduct a Haydn Mass on October 13, the name day of the emperor Maximilian. For the occasion, Felix composed a processional march in E♭, which went awry when half the ensemble failed to repeat the first strain; still, the resulting cacophony was "of no consequence in the open air."[102] He uncovered more serious shortcomings in the library of the local choral Verein, limited to Masses in "modern dress." Recalling Thibaut's zeal for the "pure" a cappella style, Felix rummaged through the archives of neighboring Elberfeld, Bonn, and Cologne for sixteenth-century masses and motets by Palestrina and Lasso, including the *Improperia*, which Felix had heard in Rome during Holy Week. He also discovered seventeenth and eighteenth-century motets and settings of the *Miserere* and happened upon Handel's *Alexander's Feast*. Expediting his research in Elberfeld was the journalist A. J. Becher,[103] in Bonn the choral director and music scholar H. C. Breidenstein, and in Cologne the Intendant of cathedral music, E. H. W. Verkenius.[104] Felix made good use of what surely struck Düsseldorfers as museum curiosities: he performed Lasso's *Popule meus* on All Saint's Day (November 1, 1833), and Palestrina's setting of the Seven Last Words on Good Friday (March 28, 1834).

Laden with historical treasures, Felix returned to Düsseldorf, where preparations were underway for the visit of the crown prince, the future Frederick William IV. When the prince regretted Felix's decision to leave Berlin, he boasted to his family, "you see I am thought infinitely more precious when I am a little way from home."[105] Just how precious became evident on October 22, when Felix participated in a sumptuous multi-media fête at the Academy of Art before four hundred guests.[106] This private entertainment blended poetry, music, illuminations, and tableaux vivants in a three-part program introduced by verses of Robert Reinick, who appeared in medieval dress. In the first part, the royal visitor viewed three transparencies after Dürer and Raphael, while a concealed chorus performed works by Lotti and Carl Maria von Weber. In the second, Felix directed choruses from Handel's *Israel in Egypt*, behind which three tableaux designed by Eduard Bendemann and Julius Hübner appeared on a stage: the Children of Israel in bondage, Moses leading the exodus, and Miriam's song. A fourth tableau, designed by Schadow, depicted Lorenzo de Medici surrounded by Dante, Raphael, and Michelangelo, and this one concluded with a Haydn chorus. The third part featured illustrations by Academy painters of scenes from *A Midsummer Night's Dream*.

Unifying these disparate subjects was the implied homage to the prince, celebrated as patron of the arts (hence the allusions to Lorenzo de Medici and Theseus, Prince of Athens) and as a modern Moses preparing to lead the German *Volk* toward spiritual self-awareness. Though remembered today as the hapless monarch unable to withstand the revolutionary upheaval of 1848, in 1833 Frederick William entertained grandiose visions of completing Cologne cathedral, uniting the arts, and instilling in his future subjects a yearning for an idealized Gothic past.

From Felix's perspective, the fête underscored the interdependence of the musical and visual, especially in the third tableau, staged with the final number of Handel's oratorio (Miriam's solo, "Sing ye to the Lord," and the culminating choral fugue, "For He hath triumphed gloriously"): "—Miriam, with a silver timbrel, sounding praises to the Lord, and other maidens with harps and citterns, and in the background four men with trombones, pointing in different directions." Miriam's solo was sung "behind the scene, as if proceeding from the picture." Then, when the chorus broke in, real trumpets, trombones, and timpani appeared on stage and "burst in like a thunder-clap,"[107] effectively merging the musical and visual planes. Image thus became sound: the musical references of the tableau were realized by live music on stage; Handel's word paintings, mirrored by the imagery of the tableau.

On St. Cecilia's Day (November 22), Felix gave at his first public concert his Piano Concerto No. 1, Beethoven's *Egmont* Overture, and, appropriately, Handel's setting of Dryden's Ode to St. Cecilia, *Alexander's Feast, or the Power of Music*. At Felix's disposal were a choral Musikverein with one hundred and thirteen amateur singers and an orchestra of about thirty,[108] some of whom were Prussian military officers from the local garrison. Felix lavished special care on Handel's ode; unconvinced by K. W. Ramler's 1766 German rendering of the line "So Love was crowned, but Music won the cause" (*Heil, Liebe, dir! Der Tonkunst Ehr' und Dank*, or "Hail to thee, Love! Honor and thanks to music"), he revised the entire translation.[109] Meanwhile, in Berlin, Fanny Cäcilie also celebrated the feast day. In two days she composed a verset from the saint's Mass for soprano solo, chorus, and piano, and performed it with a tableau vivant and sets, designed by Hensel, with mock organ pipes to simulate Cecilia's preferred instrument. Pauline Decker, attired as Raphael's *Caecilia*, sang the solo, first concealed behind the scene and then joining the tableau, in imitation of Felix's rendition of Miriam for the Crown Prince.[110]

Felix now decided to support Immermann's "master" productions by mounting Mozart's *Don Giovanni*. Rehearsals began at the end of November but with a "thoroughly unmasterful cast"; according to Immermann, the conductor was still too young to win respect, and during the twenty rehearsals the cast began to bicker.[111] At the premiere (December 19) a scandal ensued when part of the audience protested the decision of the theater lessee to raise ticket prices. In the first act, the curtain fell three times, and catcalls that drowned out the opening duet of the second act nearly prompted Felix to lay down his baton. He maintained his composure, finished the opera, and then, after conferring with a dismayed Immermann, refused to direct another until apologies were received from the opposition, consisting "mainly of beerhouse keepers and waiters."[112] For three days the *Düsseldorfer Zeitung* ran articles about the affair, and a manifesto appeared from concerned members of the Musikverein voicing their support for Felix.[113] On December 23 he led a second, successful performance without incident and acknowledged fanfares from the orchestra. Having survived his first public performance of an opera,[114] Felix left for Bonn to spend Christmas with his cousin, the geographer Georg Benjamin Mendelssohn. From there Felix noted, "the singers who at first . . . were prejudiced against me personally, as well as against these classical performances, now say they would go to the death for me . . . ."[115]

Ex. 9.12a: Mendelssohn, *Fair Melusine* Overture, Op. 34 (1833)

Ex. 9.12b: Mendelssohn, *Fair Melusine* Overture, Op. 34 (1833)

Ex. 9.12c: Mendelssohn, *Fair Melusine* Overture, Op. 34 (1833)

Offsetting the scandal was the stimulation of creative composition. At the end of November he retouched yet again the *Hebrides* Overture and announced his intention to release it to the world.[116] But the major new work of the season was the *Ouvertüre zum Märchen von der schönen Melusine*, finished for Fanny's birthday and dispatched to London early in 1834. The fairy tale of Melusine, who must leave her knightly lover Raimund and human form once a week to change into a mermaid, inspired a finely wrought, delicate score. Concerned that his English audience would not know the German legend, Felix struggled over the title. When Moscheles premiered the overture at the Philharmonic on April 7, 1834, it appeared as *Melusine, or the Mermaid and the Knight*, hinting at the work's binary division between supernatural and real worlds. In brief, Felix adapted sonata form to accommodate a double exposition, double development, and double recapitulation. Thus, the first exposition introduces the mermaid's aqueous music in the winds (**ex. 9.12a**), based upon an ascending motive later adapted by Wagner to depict the Rhine in *Das Rheingold*. The $\frac{6}{4}$ meter and hypnotic, trochaic rhythms in the accompaniment (♩♩) invoke a ballad-like opening of "once upon a time." In contrast, the second exposition introduces the masculine world of Raimund, with an energetic theme descending through an F-minor triad (**ex. 9.12b**), and associated with its own distinctive rhythm (♪♪♪♪♩). A second, lyrical theme in A♭ (**ex. 9.12c**), accompanied by watery string tremolos, intimates the lovers or, perhaps, Melusine's human form. Like the dual exposition, the development and reprise alternate between music for the mermaid and the lovers, with the added feature that in the second reprise the two themes are reversed. A coda effects Melusine's final mermaid transformation, as the work returns to its fluid origins. Once again Felix bends a conventional sonata form to the needs of his subject to produce a circular, symmetrical design.

According to Moscheles, in rehearsals the Philharmonic overplayed, so that Felix suggested lowering the dynamics a degree. Still, the overture received only a lukewarm premiere, attended by Klingemann, who complained about Moscheles's stodgy tempo. Little surprise, then, that the hypercritical Felix subjected the work to thorough revision during the fall of 1835 before it finally appeared as Op. 32 in 1836.[117] Among its early admirers was Robert Schumann, who commented on the *pianissimo* B♭ in the trumpets near the beginning, "a tone out of the distant past."[118] But when Schumann read into the work images of pearls and magic deep-sea castles, Felix rejected the review as too fanciful. Asked about the meaning of his composition, he mused, "Hmm, a *mésalliance*."[119]

VII

In the Melusine legend, Raimund loses his bride when he breaks a vow and espies her changing into mermaid form. During the Düsseldorf period, amorous loss plagued Felix, who remained an eminently eligible bachelor. In September 1833 his old flame, Delphine von Schauroth, married the English clergyman Edwin Hill Handley, prompting Fanny Horsley to gossip to her aunt, "Mamma and Mary think Mendelssohn will never marry. I do, that is if he does not plague his mistress to death before the day arrives."[120] Though Fanny Hensel pressed for news about her brother's *amours*, Felix frustrated her with his characteristic reticence and alluded to an unnamed American with whom he had flirted and an Englishwoman who had lent him an English bible.[121] Still, he flew into a rage during a rehearsal of Beethoven's *Egmont* in January, when the musicians bungled the passage in Clärchen's Lied, *Glücklich allein ist die Seele die liebt* ("happy alone is the soul who loves"), and in April he admitted to Charlotte Moscheles he was still a "warm admirer" of Delphine, whom he likened next to her husband to a white mouse before a black tomcat, and vanilla ice next to roast beef.[122] Around this time Paul Mendelssohn-Bartholdy announced his intention to marry Albertine Heine, to whom he was secretly engaged; the idea met stiff resistance from Abraham, who had quarreled with her father, a Berlin banker. Undoubtedly the prospect of the younger Paul's marriage (the lovers did wed, on May 27, 1835) impressed upon Felix the relative solitude of his bachelor existence. But a more dramatic reminder came in April 1834 with the sensational news of K. A. Varnhagen von Ense's engagement to Marianne Saaling, less than a year after the widower *feuilletoniste* had lost his wife, Rahel. The scandal shocked Berlin society and distressed Marianne's cousin Lea, who suffered bouts of tachycardia and hypochondria. To her relief, within a few weeks the engagement was broken.[123]

Felix seems to have expressed his own feelings through music. When an anonymous poem urging him to marry arrived in January 1834, he improvised on a "Bachelor's Song," into which he introduced "Mir ist so wunderbar" from Beethoven's *Fidelio*.[124] A few days later, he composed three part-songs, ostensibly for Eduard Devrient's birthday, on love poems of Heine.[125] When they eventually appeared in the *Sechs Lieder*, Op. 41 of 1838 (Nos. 2–4), Felix combined them as three *Volkslieder*. The first invokes a lover to "flee with me and be my wife." In the second, an ill-fated elopement is like a spring frost that wilts flowers. And in the third, a lad rests by the grave of his beloved beneath a linden tree (a reworking of imagery in Wilhelm Müller's *Der Lindenbaum* in the cycle *Winterreise*). Then, in May 1834, Felix crafted four solo Lieder, of which one, published as Op. 34 No. 1, sings of a "tender maiden" whose eyes are brighter than the sun. Identified in the autograph as a *Mailied*, the song precedes an unpublished *Andres Mailied* that projects a more jaded outlook: "I know a fine and pretty maiden. Beware!"[126] The third setting (*Jagdlied*, released posthumously as Op. 84 No. 3) compares the hunter's game, three birds, to maidens. And the fourth, a wistful, incomplete setting of Heine's "Warum sind denn die Rosen so blass," revisits the imagery of its predecessors: why, the protagonist asks his lover, are the roses so faded, the violets so mute, and the lark's song so pitiful?

Perhaps the most compelling evidence that bachelorhood weighed heavily upon Felix was a comic opera he contemplated composing on Kotzebue's play *Pervonte*, based on a Wieland poem about a love affair between a commoner and a princess. As early as August 1833 Felix broached the subject with Klingemann and, during the spring of 1834, exchanged ideas before Klingemann began drafting the libretto. Their correspondence through January 1835[127] details several alterations; then, in a familiar pattern, Felix abandoned the project. In Kotzebue's comedy Princess Vastola, daughter of Prince Pumpapump, is a shrew who rejects all suitors. "Maidens rarely know what they want, and why they scold one day, and pout the next," opines a seneschal. But through a magic spell, she falls in love with Pervonte, transformed from an unassuming woodsman into a handsome youth. Eager to win her true love, he eventually renounces the spell.

Felix examined the character development through various scenarios. In one, Vastola's stubbornness is tamed; in another, a rival suitor, Astolfo, emerges to complicate the plot. Because he falls beneath her rank, Vastola's father bitterly opposes the match (echoes of Lea's and Abraham's opposition to their children's spouses?). Able to attract Vastola's love only through a spell, Pervonte renounces its potency, and she returns to Astolfo. In Felix's final version, Astolfo is lacking, Vastola again plays the shrew and Pervonte (Felix?) a simple woodsman uninterested in marriage. Through a fairies' spell the two fall in love; ultimately, Pervonte asks the spell be removed so the two can test their love. Framing the entire draft are scenes for the fairies, which, like the motto chords of the *Midsummer Night's Dream* Overture, might well have inspired from Felix evanescent *Feenmusik* and a delightful, Shakespearean confusion.

While Felix was pondering romantic relationships and the loss of Delphine, Mary Alexander was pining for him in England. Dutifully she studied German in order to correspond in his native tongue. Then, she translated three poems from Heine's *Heimkehr* into English for his review. He did not answer, though Fanny set the verses in March 1834. The first begins, suggestively, "Once o'er my dark and troubled life / There shone a ray of light; / But now that cheering ray's withdrawn, / Around me all is night."[128] Failing to elicit Felix's reply, Mary sent more urgent letters. Finally, in July, only weeks after Felix resumed their correspondence, she disclosed the news of her betrothal to a Yorkshire gentleman, an arranged marriage that secured her family's social standing but left her feelings for Felix painfully unresolved. Not until 1844 would she see him again.

VIII

Another, pressing family issue distracted Felix from his love life. Late in 1833 the Goethe-Zelter correspondence began appearing in installments, barely one year after their deaths. The editor was the classicist F. W. Riemer, whom in 1825 Felix had found corpulent and prelatelike in Weimar. The tactless Riemer failed to strike indelicate passages, including several that offended the Mendelssohns. "May God preserve us from our friends," was the reaction of Henriette (Hinni) Mendelssohn, who labeled some of Zelter's aperçus malicious (*hämisch*).[129] Because Abraham was suffering from cataracts, the family read aloud the correspondence to him and collectively experienced what Fanny described as at best "an unpleasantly awkward way of thinking," at worst the "trappings of self-interest, egotism, a disgusting idolizing of Goethe without a true, reasoned appraisal, and the most indiscreet exposing of everyone else."[130] Counting the indexed entries, Fanny found Felix was mentioned fifty-eight times; admittedly, many were laudatory, but there were also provocative comments, e.g., that Felix was the son of a Jew, but no Jew (here,

the Mendelssohns read Riemer's doctored text, since Zelter's original letter had informed Goethe that Felix was uncircumcised; see p. 30). Zelter
now emerged posthumously for the Mendelssohns as a pedestrian syco-
phant: "one of the numerous instances of Zelter's unbelievable lack of
knowledge is found when Zelter asks Goethe what Byzantium is and then
receives his answer. And for that one corresponds with Goethe!"[131]

Though Felix struggled to remain unruffled about the slights to his
family, Zelter's and Goethe's "arrogant" criticisms of Reichardt threw
him into such a rage that he planned to perform that composer's *Morgengesang* and vowed to get even with Riemer, whom he viewed as the
culprit in publishing material intended for Goethe's eyes only.[132] Abraham,
it seems, took umbrage at Goethe's criticism of Hensel's early paintings
for tending toward the Nazarene style (see p. 120). At least, that is what
Riemer believed, for he claimed to have received in 1834 an anonymous
letter, which he attributed to Abraham, demanding a retraction of the
passage. This sad affair had an even sadder postscript: in 1841, six years
after Abraham's death, Riemer crudely attacked his memory: "Meanwhile may the good father-in-law [of Hensel] have obtained his revenge
from what Heine and Börne poured out about G[oethe] before all of
Germany, or, as one might also say, have recognized his smell!"[133] (Ironically, Abraham numbered among Heine's most fervent detractors.[134])
Though Goethe in 1822 had promised never to throw his spear at Felix,
as Saul had at David, Zelter's letters now bristled with barbs that severely wounded Felix's memory of his teacher.

Various distractions in Düsseldorf assuaged his splenetic moods.
Felix purchased a horse from his cousin Benni and pursued equestrian
pastimes. He accepted some students, including a "pretty girl" from Aix-
la-Chapelle[135] and Hermann Franck's brother Eduard, with whom Felix
probed the sublime mysteries of J. S. Bach's *Art of Fugue*.[136] And there
was the companionship of the Academy painters, of whom several sang
in Felix's chorus. He resided in the same house as Wilhelm Schadow, the
former Nazarene, contributor to the frescos of the Casa Bartholdy in
Rome, and since 1826 director of the Academy. For Felix's twenty-fifth
birthday, in February 1834, Schadow arranged an evening ball during
which a military band serenaded the composer with Beethoven's Fourth
Symphony; a few months later, Schadow sketched Felix's portrait, capturing the young musician at the height of his Düsseldorf career (see
frontispiece). Among Schadow's pupils who had followed the artist from
Berlin to Düsseldorf were C. F. Sohn, Theodor Hildebrandt, Julius Hübner, and Eduard Bendemann; together with Schadow, "like a prophet
among his disciples,"[137] all numbered among Felix's close friends. Elise
Polko relates that during the Düsseldorf years Felix orchestrated move-

ments of Beethoven's sonatas for performance with tableaux vivants, designed by the painters.[138] Thus, for a representation in the Stadttheater on December 8, 1834, Felix scored the Andante and Funeral March from Beethoven's Piano Sonata in A♭, Op. 26, to accompany tableaux vivants designed by Sohn and Hildebrandt.[139] A more regular relationship developed with J. W. Schirmer, who specialized in landscape; on Sundays, Schirmer instructed Felix in watercolors and how to paint sunlight and use purple to suggest distance.

There was also the diversion of Felix's creative work. In February he succumbed again to revision mania and wrote out a new score of *Meeresstille und glückliche Fahrt*;[140] in April, he mused about the still unrealized *Scottish* Symphony; and in June he reworked the last three movements of the *Italian*. Among his new compositions were the *Rondo brillant* for piano and orchestra, Op. 29, finished on January 29, 1834, dedicated to Moscheles and premiered by the pianist in London in May, and the concert scene and aria *Infelice*, dated on May 3 and dispatched as the final installment of the Philharmonic commission. The *Rondo brillant* was an attempt to overcome what Felix described as his "poverty in shaping new forms" for the piano.[141] Though a premiere pianist of his age, Felix was conflicted about the encroachment of virtuosity on musical form; ultimately, keyboard acrobatics did not matter to him as much as the integrity of the composition. The *Rondo brillant*, cast in sonata-rondo form, betrays in its glittery passagework the influence of Carl Maria von Weber, especially in the vivacious, arpeggiated opening theme. Unfortunately, the contrasting second theme falls into square, predictable phrases and shows signs of the very "poverty" Felix lamented, only partially ameliorated by a third subject, an octave passage in mock counterpoint. Why Felix did not provide a slow introduction remains a mystery. Unlike the two-movement *Rondo capriccioso* and *Capriccio brillant*, the *Rondo brillant* commences with fanfares on the dominant, as if announcing a transition to a finale and encouraging us to imagine that Felix himself improvised an introduction when he performed this spirited, *bravura* piece.[142]

Less well-known is the concert aria *Infelice*, on texts cobbled together from four libretti of Metastasio to yield the "most beautiful nonsense" (*allerschönster Unsinn*).[143] The subject of a woman abandoned by her lover had a long ancestry in Italian opera, as evidenced by countless treatments of Dido and Aeneas (*Didone abbandonata*) and Beethoven's scene and aria *Ah! Perfido*, Op. 65, which may have offered a model for Felix. In *Infelice*, the unidentified betrayed enters with an agitated recitative (*Infelice! Già dal mio sguardo si diliguo!* "Unfortunate one! Already he has escaped my glance!"). The aria proper, introduced and accompanied by a sinuous violin solo (*Andante sostenuto*, ex. 9.13), is a plea for

Ex. 9.13: Mendelssohn, *Infelice*, Op. 94, First Version (1834)

the return of a golden age (*Ah, ritorna, età dell'oro*). A third, contrasting section (*Allegro vivace*) reminds the abandoned of her present torment; near the end, the solo violin briefly revives the Andante.

The coupling of an *obbligato* solo with the vocal line was not un-precedented; Felix would have known, for example, Italian concert arias of Mozart that use the technique. But Felix's duetlike scoring bore a hid-den meaning, for he disclosed to Lea that the violin solo was tailored for the Belgian musician C.-A. de Bériot, the illicit lover of the internation-ally acclaimed mezzo-soprano Malibran. Art thus (roughly) approxi-mated life. Still, when the work received its London premiere (May 1834), the soprano Maria Caradori-Allan, not Malibran, sang the solo. Less than two years later, Malibran and de Bériot wed in a clandestine ceremony. Tragically, within a few months, the young singer died. Felix withdrew the concert aria. In 1843 he would delete the violin solo and recast the work for the singer Sophie Schloss, who sang it at the Gewandhaus. Not until 1851 did this second version appear in print as Op. 94; the first version was forgotten until late in the twentieth century.[144]

Overshadowing these compositions and a handful of keyboard pieces[145] was Felix's progress on his oratorio. In October 1833 Schubring had returned the composer's second libretto draft with heavy annota-tions,[146] and he urged a division into two, not three parts, but approved Felix's plan to alternate between narrative and dramatic modes, and to leave the work open-ended with Paul's departure from the Ephesians. As for the issue of chorales, Schubring conceded they could not be used as in the St. Matthew Passion as signs of the collective, congregational awareness of the Passion. But Schubring also rejected Marx's argument that chorales were anachronistic for the early Christian apostle, since "every musical form that we know arose later." Indeed, Schubring ad-vised that many choruses of the oratorio were *choralmässig* and did not hesitate to recommend specific chorales.

Felix began composing *St. Paul* in earnest in April 1834. By the middle of July, he attained the midpoint of the first part and by November was conceptualizing music for the second, including choruses for Paul's first journey to Lystra, where the Gentiles mistake him as Mercury (Acts 14:12).[147] Around mid-November Felix paused to sketch the overture and hit upon the solution of coupling an instrumental chorale (*Wachet auf*) with a fugue to symbolize Paul's Christian awakening. Then, in December, he took up the music for the second part and responded to criticisms of his father, who had keenly followed the work, and awaited its premiere, scheduled for Schelble's Frankfurt Cäcilienverein in December 1835. Abraham found Stephen's defense too verbose and remarked about Saul's absence at the martyr's stoning. But Felix formulated worthy answers: he intended to compress Stephen's monologue into a recitative that would occupy only two or three minutes; he could find no words from Acts for Saul to utter at Stephen's martyrdom.

IX

Other than appearing in concerts of neighboring communities,[148] Felix remained in Düsseldorf through much of 1834. An exception was the sixteenth Lower Rhine Music Festival, which he attended in Aix-la-Chapelle in May 1834. For the occasion, conducted by the composer Ferdinand Ries, Ferdinand Hiller had arranged and translated Handel's *Deborah*. While Felix made the eleven-hour coach journey from Düsseldorf, Hiller left Paris with Chopin, who had to sell a new waltz to Pleyel to afford the journey. Soon the three pianists were celebrating their reunion. But Felix's dealings with Ries, with whom days before he had performed Beethoven's *Kreutzer* Sonata, were apparently less cordial. According to Fétis, the two had a falling out, owing to Felix's "impolite" criticisms of Ries's conducting.[149] Fétis's account may have been colored by his own strained relationship with Felix, who still remembered the 1829 affair at St. Paul's and now snubbed the Belgian critic at the festival by refusing to embrace him. After the festival, Felix, Hiller, and Chopin spent time together in Düsseldorf and Cologne. Felix's friends were probably among the first to hear him render portions of *St. Paul*. Felix found Chopin "quite a second Paganini," executing "all sorts of impossibilities which one never thought could be done."[150]

In Düsseldorf, Felix divided his responsibilities between the annual concert series, church services, and the opera. At the public concerts the instrumental and choral ensembles coalesced into a new *Verein zur Beförderung der Tonkunst* (Union for the Advancement of Music). But Felix complained that his musicians often appeared inebriated and could not play triplets clearly;[151] a disappointing performance of Handel's *Dettingen Te Deum* on August 17, 1834 earned Felix's private rebuke as *schändlich* (disgraceful).[152] His repertoire was almost exclusively German; he ignored French music, and of Italian composers performed only Cherubini and Mercadante.[153] Instead, Beethoven's symphonies formed the foundation:

Felix conducted at least five (Nos. 3, 4, 5, 7, and 8) during his tenure. Earlier music included oratorios of Handel (*Israel in Egypt, Samson, Judas Maccabeus*, and *Messiah*) and Haydn (*Creation* and *The Seasons*) and various works of Mozart. Of his own music Felix presented little, though he appeared as a pianist and occasionally improvised; a concert of May 3, 1834 ended with a *freie Fantasie* on the just heard Overture to Mozart's *Magic Flute* and selections from Handel's *Israel in Egypt*.[154] Of "modern" German composers, Felix offered works by Hummel, Weber, Spohr, and Marschner, and anticipated a practice later instituted in Leipzig—mounting concert versions of operatic excerpts. Finally, he promoted the native Düsseldorf composer Norbert Burgmüller and read his Piano Concerto and Symphony in C minor on May 3 and November 13, 1834. Burgmüller had been a rival for Felix's position in 1833 but soon became an unabashed admirer. When Burgmüller met an untimely death at twenty-six in 1836 (he had suffered from epilepsy), Felix composed the *Trauermarsch*, Op. 103, for his funeral.[155]

To the theologian Albert Bauer, Felix confided that, were he a Catholic, he would "set to work at a Mass this very evening."[156] In his view, composers of modern Ordinary settings no longer respected their sacred purpose; by the eighteenth century Pergolesi and Durante were introducing "the most laughable little trills" into their Glorias. As a corrective, Felix revived old Italian sacred polyphony, which affected him like incense,[157] and during Holy Week reintroduced the monophonic chant of the Lamentations of Jeremiah, for which he improvised organ interludes between the verses.[158] Felix also performed works of J. S. Bach in the Catholic city. During Lent, Felix began rehearsing the St. Matthew Passion but had to abandon the project on account of the ensemble's limitations.[159] Instead, he performed two cantatas (*Du Hirte Israel, höre* and the *Actus tragicus*, BWV 104 and 106) for the Feast of Peter and Paul (June 29, 1834).

Perhaps predictably, Felix relied upon Masses of Haydn, Mozart, and Beethoven; of Felix's own music only *Verleih' uns Frieden* was heard, and of contemporary composers only Cherubini and Moritz Hauptmann, a colleague of Spohr Felix met in Cassel. To accompany Beethoven's Mass in C on the feast of Corpus Christi (May 29, 1834), Felix composed another festive wind march for the procession into the church.[160] But after directing a Haydn Mass in October, Felix threatened to resign unless an incompetent organist was dismissed.[161] A performance of Mozart's Requiem the same month nearly precipitated another scandal. When the concertmaster, an outspoken critic, managed to disrupt the rehearsal, a Prussian general came to the rescue. Karl Emil von Webern relates how he replaced the concertmaster, a major then took up a cello part, and members of a regimental band replaced disaffected orchestral personnel, so that the performance could proceed.[162]

X

Winning Felix for Düsseldorf had been a mainstay of Immermann's plan to revitalize the municipal theater. To combat the provincial philistinism of the Lower Rhine, he instituted "master performances" of classic German plays by Lessing, Goethe, Schiller, and Kleist, and foreign plays of Shakespeare and Calderón. Felix supported these efforts with incidental music and by directing operas conducive to Immermann's reforms, including "classic" German works such as Mozart's *Don Giovanni, Die Entführung aus dem Serail,* and *Die Zauberflöte,* Beethoven's incidental music to *Egmont,* and Weber's *Der Freischütz* and *Oberon.* Into this repertory Felix also admitted Marschner's *Templer und die Jüdin* and a German version of Abraham's favorite Cherubini opera, *Les deux journées* (*Der Wasserträger*). Though Felix's tenure had begun inauspiciously in December with *Don Giovanni,* by late March 1834 he could report a successful revival of *Der Wasserträger,* after wearying nine-hour rehearsals in which he supervised "everything—the acting, scenery, and the dialogue."[163] A month later Immermann mounted his tragedy *Andreas Hofer,* about the Tyrolese patriot who led an uprising ruthlessly suppressed by the French in 1809. While researching the event, Immermann had drawn heavily upon the published account of Felix's uncle, Jacob Bartholdy,[164] and now turned to Felix for incidental music. But Immermann's popular drama stimulated only two minor pieces, a French march and folksonglike duet for two tenors.[165] Still, all these efforts promoted Immermann's fondest aspiration, the establishment of a new Düsseldorf theater, which he and Felix would direct.

To this end, in March 1834 the dramatist founded a Theater Verein and began raising funds. Somehow he cajoled Felix to serve as the "chief superintendent of the musical performances," even though he felt "no sympathy for actual theatrical life, or the squabbles of the actors and the incessant striving after effect."[166] Seeking to shield himself, Felix waived part of his salary in exchange for engaging a second conductor, on whom the "chief trouble" would devolve. Three letters to his preferred candidate, the cellist Julius Rietz (younger brother of Eduard), shed light on the arrangement.[167] Rietz would assume his post in September; Felix would manage the affairs of the company and conduct some of the operas, though the lion's share of rehearsals and performances would fall to Rietz. Somewhat duplicitously, Felix exhorted his friend, "You will like it here, I am convinced; it grows more agreeable to me with each day. . . ."

In reality, Felix soon had reason enough to regret his administrative role and agreement to devote part of his summer to recruiting and hiring singers. On August 29 he arrived in Berlin and spent a month auditioning candidates. Felix was ill-prepared for the endless negotiations: "To wrangle with a creature for two Thaler; to be severe with the good, and lenient with the good-for-nothing; to look grand in order to keep up a dignity that no one believes in; to seem angry without anger; all these are things which I cannot do, and would not if I could."[168] By the end of September he was fantasizing about operas without music, singers, or ballet dancers, in which only the sets would "perform."[169] On the afternoon of September 28 he performed Fanny's "wedding piece" on the organ of the Parochialkirche; two days later, he departed for Leipzig.[170]

His personnel search there also yielded slim results. Instead, he pursued Bachiana with Hauser, and attended a "majestic" rehearsal of *Calm Sea and Prosperous Voyage* at the Gewandhaus led by the concertmaster H. A. Matthäi. On this occasion, Felix was asked whether he would consider a position in Leipzig.[171] He visited the piano pedagogue Friedrich Wieck, who presented his most advanced student, a "quiet and shy" fifteen-year-old prodigy—his daughter Clara. On October 2 she played some Chopin, her own *Conzertsatz* (soon reworked as the finale of her Piano Concerto, Op. 7), and the virtuoso Toccata of another Wieck student, Robert Schumann.[172] Felix appears not to have met Schumann, then preoccupied with launching his music journal, the *Neue Zeitschrift für Musik*, but was dutifully impressed with Clara and promised to return (within a year, he would assume the directorship of the Gewandhaus and premiere her concerto). Continuing to Cassel, he saw Hauptmann and read through half of Spohr's new Passion oratorio, *Des Heilands letzte Stunden*.[173] With Spohr Felix now "moved stones" by singing through the score, heavily influenced by Bach and Handel, and stylistically akin to the forming music of *Paulus*.

Dreading the "singer storms" (*Sängerungewitter*), Felix assumed his duties as Intendant of the Düsseldorf Opera on October 9. At once the situation deteriorated. The very day he returned he was asked to travel to Aachen to engage singers. He refused but soon was issuing dozens of contracts, organizing rehearsal schedules, and attending to the bureaucratic realities of management. For Immermann the new theater represented the culmination of his life's work; for Felix it was an annoying intrusion into what mattered to him most—composing and making music. The two directors soon came to blows over hiring a stage manager for the opera. When Felix proposed a member of Immermann's troupe, the playwright balked. Letters were exchanged,[174] and Immermann, alarmed at what he took to be Felix's vanity, attempted to smooth over the affair.

On October 28, the new theater opened with Kleist's *Prinzen von Homburg*; Felix conducted overtures by Weber (*Jubel*) and Beethoven (presumably, *Consecration of the House*), and Immermann contributed a *Vorspiel* to which Felix fitted some incidental music.[175] Titled *Kurfürst Johann Wilhelm im Theater*, Immermann's prologue comprised a dialogue between the architect of the new theater and his assistants, interrupted by a "visit" from the municipal statue of Johann Wilhelm (1658–1716), Elector of the Palatinate. The somber knocking of the statue at the door inspired Felix to quote material from the Overture and Finale of Mozart's *Don Giovanni*, but this charming parody evidently failed to impress. The inauguration scored only a modest success, as did Marschner's *Templer und die Jüdin* two days later. Meanwhile, while preparing Weber's *Oberon*, Felix made new demands on Immermann. Dissatisfied with the elf king's garments, Felix required from the set designer a new "starry heaven" and sea. Immermann was unable to comply, and Felix began to believe resources needed for the Opera were being diverted to the theater. Even before *Oberon* opened on November 7, he declared his desire to be free of his role as Intendant. Three days later, and just two weeks after the theater opened, he took a *salto mortale*.[176] Felix compared his precipitous resignation to the abdication of Charles V, Holy Roman Emperor, who, weary of the religious wars of the Reformation, had abruptly renounced his throne in 1556.[177] The simile did not impress Devrient, who thought Felix had displayed a "snappish temper that one would hardly have suspected in him." Nor was Felix's father pleased by the dramatic upstaging of Immermann's authority; in one rash gesture, Felix had appeared unreliable and antagonized Immermann.[178] Still, Felix had won his freedom; the theater management granted him a dispensation, provided he would conduct an occasional opera. For all purposes, Julius Rietz now directed the Opera, and Felix, like "a fish thrown back into the water,"[179] could redouble his efforts on *Paulus*.

The New Year brought a regrettable epilogue to the affair. After Felix had shunned Immermann for more than two months, the playwright moved to repair the damaged friendship in a letter of January 18, 1835.[180] By January 26 Felix was reassuring Lea the two were resuming their friendly intercourse.[181] But Immermann's diary refers to an unpleasant meeting early in February and a "dreadful experience with the totally wild Mendelssohn" that prompted two lengthy reports to the directors of the theater.[182] Felix himself labored for two days on an account of the latest dispute for the same body and revealed some particulars to Abraham.[183] In a conciliatory gesture Immermann, it seems, had recognized Felix's release as Intendant, only to maneuver behind the scenes to persuade the directors to force Felix to resume the position. This double-dealing caused the final, irreconcilable rupture for Felix, and he severed all ties to the

Opera. For Immermann, the resignation wiped away the flowering of his cherished undertaking before its "buds" could even burst.[184] The hypersensitive Felix took the episode as a personal affront, even though a complex of issues was at work, including Abraham's long-standing desire to see his son succeed as a stage composer, and, of course, the painful memory of the *Camacho* debacle in 1827. But in 1870, the musicologist Friedrich Chrysander went farther.[185] After reviewing the Immermann episode, Chrysander took up Felix's lifelong failure to compose a major opera and expressed a sentiment that echoed in the Mendelssohn reception history: Felix's fortuitous childhood had not prepared him to apply his talents with "resignation," and he lacked the consummate mastery of the great opera composers.

XI

Embroiled with Immermann, Felix turned to others for companionship. At some point in 1835 Wilhelm von Schadow painted Felix's portrait[186] and on his birthday that year gave his friend another evening ball. Among the gifts that day was a Maezel metronome from an industrialist and music-lover from Solingen, so that Felix might specify precise tempi in his scores.[187] Early in the morning a regimental band serenaded the composer and made a droll effect by rendering with contrabassoons and bass drum the rustic drones of Chopin's Mazurka in B♭, Op. 7 No. 1.[188] But Felix found himself in an "all-devouring mood." Thus Chopin's mazurkas were "mannered"; Berlioz's *Symphonie fantastique* was a wearisome Philistine composition, despite its best efforts "to go stark mad"; there was no point to Liszt "with his two fingers on one key"; and Cherubini had succumbed to Parisian fads in his new opera *Ali-Baba*.[189]

Even Fanny did not escape unscathed her brother's criticism. Late in October 1834 she finished a major work, her String Quartet in E♭, and sent it to Felix.[190] It begins with two sororal allusions to his music, the openings of his own String Quartet in E♭, Op. 12, and *Calm Sea and Prosperous Voyage* (ex. 9.14). In January he rendered his judgment: of the four movements, Felix preferred the second, a capricious scherzo in C minor, but found much of the composition formally diffuse and tonally ambiguous. In the first, fantasia-like movement, the modulations to F minor and F major vitiated the stability of the tonic key and impressed as a mannerism; and the thematic contents were not strong enough to justify the formal freedom of the music.[191] Felix softened the blow by admitting his own music betrayed similar faults, but the damage was

Ex. 9.14: Fanny Hensel, String Quartet in E♭ (1834), First Movement

done. There now ensued a bit of sibling rivalry, with Fanny criticizing Felix's cantata *Ach Gott vom Himmel sieh' darein* for its tonal and formal latitude.[192] She observed that while Felix had experienced and lived through Beethoven's later style, she remained stuck in it and lacked the strength to sustain its nostalgic tenderness. Thus, her larger compositions died "in their youth of decrepitude," and she was in her element only in writing songs, for which "merely a pretty idea without much potential for development can suffice."

When not absorbed in *Paulus*, Felix turned out a quantity of smaller pieces. Among the most compelling is his setting of Byron's "Sun of the Sleepless" (published in 1836 along with "There be none of beauty's daughters"). Twenty years before, the Englishman Isaac Nathan had used Jewish cantorial melodies in setting Byron's popular collection of "ethnic" poems, *Hebrew Melodies* (1815–1819). Felix was acquainted with Nathan's songs and also Carl Loewe's *Die Sonne der Schlaflosen*, Op. 13 No. 6, on a German rendition by Franz Theremin of "Sun of the Sleepless.[193] Dissatisfied with the translation, Felix prepared his own (*Schlafloser Augen Leuchte*) and on December 31, 1834 set the poem in E minor, with a wistful, repeated high B to capture the image of the distant star (**ex. 9.15**).[194] Byron's

Ex. 9.15: Mendelssohn, "Sun of the Sleepless" (1834)

poem begins: "Sun of the Sleepless! Melancholy star! Whose tearful beam glows tremulously far." In Nathan's exegesis, the star referred to Balaam's third oracle (Numbers 24:17): "A star shall come out of Jacob." But, as Frederick Burwick has argued, the same passage was also "read as a prophecy of the Star of Bethlehem" and the coming of Christ[195]—a reading indeed familiar to Felix, who later used the same scripture in his unfinished oratorio *Christus*. Felix's decision to set Byron's poem in 1835 was probably not coincidental, coming as it did while Felix was fully engaged with *Paulus*. Byron's verses—"So gleams the past, the light of other days, which shines but warms not with its powerless rays," the second verse continues—offered another opportunity for Felix to mediate the space between his Jewish ancestry and Christian faith.

Late in the Düsseldorf tenure Felix began arranging several of his smaller pieces into groups for publication. To the three Heine *Volkslieder* he added two part-songs and prepared a *Reinschrift* of all five in May 1835[196] (they appeared with a sixth part-song as the *Sechs Lieder*, Op. 41, in 1838). He also pondered a cycle of piano etudes and fugues for Attwood,[197] an idea that gradually coalesced into the Six Preludes and Fugues, Op. 35 (1837). To that end, Felix asked Fanny to send his two E-minor fugues from 1827 (one became Op. 35 No. 1)[198] and in December 1834 composed a fugue in F minor and began one in A♭ (Op. 35 Nos. 5 and 4).[199] A contemporaneous organ fugue in D major, transcribed as an organ duet for Attwood,[200] was later reworked as Op. 35 No. 2.

A second series of piano pieces now evolved into the *Lieder ohne Worte*, Op. 30. Despite lackluster sales of Op. 19b in England, Felix had continued to craft piano Lieder, including Op. 30 Nos. 5 and 4, and Op. 38 No. 2.[201] Two new Lieder followed early in 1835, Op. 38 No. 3 and 53 No. 2, both composed for Clara Wieck.[202] Felix then paused to compile a discrete opus. The result, sent to Simrock on March 28, 1835 as Op. 30,[203] again juxtaposed examples of the lyrical solo Lied (No. 1), duet (No. 6), and part-song (No. 3) with character pieces (Nos. 2, 4, and 5). At least two Lieder were directly associated with women: No. 2 (B♭ minor) had celebrated the birth of Fanny's son, Sebastian, while No. 6 (F♯ minor) was inscribed in the album of Henriette Voigt, a Leipzig pianist and musical amateur,[204] as Felix's second Venetian *Gondellied*. Strengthening the association of the genre with the feminine, Felix dedicated the entire opus to Elise von Woringen, daughter of Otto von Woringen, one of Felix's principal supporters in Düsseldorf. The Lieder appeared from German, French, and English firms on May 1, 1835, a simultaneous effort that fell short of perfection: at least one piece, the etudelike No. 4, reveals discrepancies between the first editions. Felix, it seems, continued to revise the opus for Simrock, even after manuscript copies had been dispatched to Paris and London.[205]

XII

After Felix's visit to Leipzig in October 1834, the idea of attracting him to that city quickly gained momentum. The principals behind this effort were the music publisher C. F. Kistner, attorney and amateur singer H. K. Schleinitz, and founding editor of the *Allgemeine musikalische Zeitung*, Friedrich Rochlitz; all three belonged to the board of directors of the Gewandhaus Orchestra. Almost certainly Franz Hauser was involved in facilitating the negotiations. Curiously, the initial offer to Felix was for a professorship at the university, a proposal he declined early in January 1835, since he regarded himself a practical musician who had never left a colloquium about music without "feeling more unmusical."[206] By the middle of the month he had received a new offer, to direct the Gewandhaus concerts and choral society for an annual term of six months, and the Thomasschule, all for a yearly salary of 1000 thalers. Meanwhile, a proposal arrived from Munich offering the directorship of the Opera for a salary of 2000 florins.[207] To Schleinitz, Felix inquired if his acceptance of the Gewandhaus post would impel the resignation of another, and in early February, citing his principle not to write publicly about music, he declined an invitation from Breitkopf & Härtel to assume the editorship of the *Allgemeine musikalische Zeitung*.[208] But the prospect of an *Umzug* was alluring. From Leipzig Henriette Voigt forwarded scores of Ludwig Schunke, a talented young composer and pianist, who had died at age twenty-four, and also Schumann's *Carnaval*, which gave Felix great pleasure.[209] But in reply to Schumann's invitation to serve as a Düsseldorf correspondent for his journal, Felix again declined.

By April Leipzig negotiations were in final stages. Determining his acceptance would not jeopardize his predecessor, the choral director August Pohlenz, Felix agreed to direct the Gewandhaus concerts for a salary of 600 thalers (eventually raised to 1000) and an annual six-month leave. On May 1 he requested the termination of his Düsseldorf contract[210] and on June 13 formally accepted the new position, though only for the next concert season.[211] Thus began Felix's twelve-year association with Leipzig.

Before leaving Düsseldorf, Felix directed the seventeenth Lower Rhine Music Festival in Cologne (June 7–8). He was pleased at his selection over Ferdinand Ries, who had led the event seven times since 1825;

after the 1833 festival Felix had quipped the two were like a pope and anti-pope.[212] Breaking with Ries's precedent, Felix elected not to present his own works; he also realized his ambition to perform Handel's *Solomon* without modern wind parts. To that end, Felix fashioned a new organ part, after consulting with Sir George Smart about Handel's use of the organ as a continuo instrument. The performance was billed as an authentic recreation of Handel's performance practice. The program included Beethoven's *Consecration of the House* Overture and Eighth Symphony, Weber's *Euryanthe* Overture, a march and hymn for Charles X sent by Cherubini, and, finally, Reichardt's *Morgengesang* on a text by Milton, fulfilling the vow Felix had made in 1833 (see p. 292). The ensemble comprised musical amateurs from neighboring communities, who assembled to form a chorus of 427 and orchestra of 179.[213] Just how capably Felix presided over this army of musicians is evident from an account by Julius Benedict, who attended rehearsals of Beethoven's Eighth Symphony and other works: "nobody certainly ever knew better how to communicate—as if by an electric fluid—his own conception of a work, to a large body of performers. It was highly interesting, on this occasion, to contemplate the anxious attention manifested by a body of more than five hundred singers and performers; watching every glance of Mendelssohn's eye, and following, like obedient spirits, the magic wand of this musical *Prospero*. . . . Need I add, that he was able to detect at once, even among a phalanx of performers, the slightest error either of note or accent."[214] In appreciation of Felix's efforts, the organizing committee sent him thirty-two folio volumes of Samuel Arnold's Handel edition (1787–1797),[215] an acquisition Felix prominently displayed in his study, as had Beethoven toward the end of his life.

Among the altos in the chorus was Fanny, who attended the festival with her husband, sister, and parents, the last time the family enjoyed together a public performance by Felix. If Fanny was in awe of Felix, Rebecka struggled to convey the monumentality of the event and observed it was like a Swiss glacier that could be comprehended only if seen.[216] In Düsseldorf the Mendelssohns spent a few peaceful days before the Hensels departed for Paris, where Wilhelm lectured and met Horace Vernet and Gérard. The Hensels also saw Meyerbeer, who recorded privately some unflattering impressions: Wilhelm was an idiot of a husband, and Fanny indescribably plain.[217] Meanwhile, in Düsseldorf, where Felix played parts of *Paulus* for Abraham, Lea suffered recurring tachycardia. Felix now divided time between his rehearsals and tending to his parents. Sometime in June or July he encountered the publisher Heinrich Brockhaus, en route to Belgium, who confided to his diary,

"Felix Mendelssohn has now gradually become a man; he pleased me, and I hope to hear from him in Leipzig much that is good and beautiful."[218] Felix gave his final concert on July 2, on which he performed Beethoven's Seventh Symphony, his own *Calm Sea and Prosperous Voyage*, a capriccio, and his arrangement of Handel's *Dettingen Te Deum*. Then, after accompanying Abraham on a business trip to Cologne, Felix tied up his affairs and departed for Berlin with his parents on July 25, 1835. His last act was to inscribe for his successor, Julius Rietz, a haunting duet in B minor for piano and cello,[219] an open-ended offering that broke off inconclusively with a half-cadence. Though Felix had dissolved his first position, his association with Düsseldorf was not yet concluded.

Chapter 10
1835–1837

The Apostle's Voice

Res severa est verum gaudium.
(True joy is a serious matter.)
—Seneca, *Epistolae* I, 23

Escorting his parents to Berlin, Felix issued guarded bulletins about Lea to his siblings. Hardly were Lea, Abraham, and Felix relaxing on the evening of August 1, 1835, in the familiar comfort of Leipzigerstrasse No. 3, before an uprising erupted against the government. When the authorities forbade an unruly crowd to celebrate the king's birthday by firing rockets, one hundred and fifty "young ruffians" provoked the military and vandalized property on August 3 and 4 near Unter den Linden. Felix watched as protests broke out as the military killed innocent bystanders.[1] This disturbing scene turned his mind toward fleeing the "dreadful dump" (*abscheulicher Nest*). But the "model sick-nurse" stayed through most of the month, "preserved" Lea like an Egyptian mummy in the Berlin Museum,[2] and composed pieces well removed from the social unrest: a festive *Lied ohne Worte* in E♭ (published posthumously as Op. 85 No. 3), and a pensive setting of Eichendorff's poem *Das Waldschloss*, in which the sirenlike Lied of a *Waldfrau* perched on a rocky cliff seduces a young hunter.

On August 30 Felix arrived in Leipzig, a small city with a population nearing 45,000. He stayed for a few days with Hauser before securing quarters beyond the city ramparts in Reichels Garten, with a view of the Thomasmühle and Thomaskirche. On August 31 he heard the Gewandhaus orchestra rehearsing his *Meeresstille und glückliche Fahrt* and at once recognized the ensemble's decided superiority over the Düsseldorf orchestra. At the same rehearsal Henriette Voigt introduced him to a moody, retiring musician. This was Robert Schumann, who later recalled the meeting: "I told him I

306

knew all of his compositions well; he responded with something quite modest. The first impression was of an unforgettable man."[3]

For the next two weeks Felix settled into his residence, attended Bach performances at the Thomaskirche, and developed a new network of friends and colleagues. Schumann and Felix enjoyed frequent meetings,[4] as did Clara Wieck. On September 13 Felix played for her sixteenth birthday a Bach fugue and mimicked the styles of Liszt and Chopin; three days later he gave her the Capriccio in F♯ minor, Op. 5.[5] Earlier on Clara's birthday the Stadtrat K. W. A. Porsche and flutist Carl Grenser had offered Felix a hearty welcome to the Gewandhaus; after leading his first rehearsal, he had pronounced his satisfaction with the orchestra.[6]

From the previous director, C. A. Pohlenz, a vocal pedagogue who had also served as Thomaskantor, Felix inherited an honorable institution that had already celebrated its fiftieth anniversary. On November 25, 1781, J. A. Hiller had overseen the first concert in a new hall built within the Gewandhaus (Clothiers' Hall) on Universitätsstrasse. Seating an audience of about five hundred, the hall became the site of an annual series of twenty concerts that ran from early October, just after Michaelmas, to Easter, typically on Thursday evenings. (Supplementing the subscription series were extra concerts of visiting virtuosi, and benefit concerts for the ensemble's pension fund.) Hiller's orchestra comprised about thirty musicians: twelve violins, three violas, four celli and contrabass, double winds (without clarinets), double brass (without trombones), and timpani.[7] They performed in an acoustically resonant hall ornamented by ceiling frescos symbolizing the ousting of old music by new. Figures from Greek mythology appeared next to a "genius" holding a loose leaf with the name of Bach. A contemplative inscription above the organ case read *Res severa est verum gaudium* ("True joy is a serious matter"), from an epistle of the Roman Seneca. In half a century the ensemble had frequently reaffirmed this sobering asseveration, as in 1789, when Mozart performed a mammoth program featuring two each of his symphonies and piano concerti.

More recently, Paganini had played in 1829 to a sold-out audience that willingly paid three times the normal ticket price. Two years later, after hearing Chopin's Variations on *Là ci darem la mano*, Robert Schumann wrote his memorable review for the *Allgemeine musikalische Zeitung* in which he advised, "Hats off, gentlemen, a genius." The first movement of Schumann's early Symphony in G minor, reverberant with Beethoven's *Eroica*, received a reading at a concert of Clara Wieck in 1833, but Schumann remained in the shadow of Felix, whose fame had preceded him to Leipzig. Thus, three of Felix's overtures (Opp. 21, 26, and 27) had already echoed in the Gewandhaus.[8]

By 1831, the orchestral personnel had expanded to thirty-nine: sixteen violins, four violas, three celli, three contrabass, double winds (with clarinets), double brass (without trombones), and timpani.[9] In accepting his new post, Felix insisted upon a fundamental change: henceforth, he would direct all rehearsals and concerts with a baton, in contrast to the earlier division of labor between Pohlenz, who had overseen the choral music, and the concertmaster H. A. Matthäi, who had supervised the instrumental repertory.[10] There were some initial misgivings about the reform; in an otherwise enthusiastic review of the inaugural concert, Schumann quibbled, "I for my part was disturbed in the overture as in the symphony by the conductor's baton. I agreed with Florestan, who claimed that the orchestra in a symphony should stand like a republic which recognizes no sovereign."[11] But the improved results easily overcame any resistance to the new relationship between orchestra and director.

By late September 1835 preparations for the new season had begun in earnest, though pleasant distractions were a visit by Fanny and Wilhelm (September 22–26),[12] and the unexpected arrival of Chopin, who spent a few hours in Leipzig on September 27, en route to visit his parents in Karlsbad. Felix, then engaged with *Paulus*, played through the new work for his friend, who inserted etudes from his Op. 10 between the two parts of the oratorio. Chopin also offered a new "Notturno," possibly the *Andante spianato* (Op. 22, 1834), with which Felix was quite taken. The scene must have been remarkable—Felix's historicist oratorio, synthesizing in modern dress Bachian and Handelian strains, juxtaposed with Chopin's virtuoso studies that explored the very frontiers of modern piano technique. For Felix, the meeting was like a conversation between a Cherokee and a Kaffir, though he did not reveal who played which role.[13] But the weight of history prevailed that day: midway through their meeting Felix's reward for directing the Cologne Lower Rhine Music Festival arrived— the Arnold edition of Handel's collected works. Its sturdy volumes, including the imposing array of Handel's oratorios, served as a daily reminder for Felix to complete his most ambitious compositional undertaking to date.

At the beginning of October, just in time for the new season, Moscheles arrived in Leipzig. To his wife he reported, "[Felix] is idolized here, and lives on the most friendly terms with many musicians and notabilities, although he is intimate with but few, and reserved towards many."[14] With Schumann, Moscheles attended Felix's Gewandhaus debut on October 4, which featured his *Meeresstille und glückliche Fahrt* and Beethoven's Fourth Symphony. (Between them were three compositions featuring soloists: a scene and aria Weber had composed for Cherubini's *Lodoïska*, Spohr's Violin Concerto No. 11, and the introduction to Cherubini's new opera *Ali-Baba*.) The event inspired a fanciful *Schwärmbrief* from Schumann, who reviewed the concert in his journal. Listening to *Meeresstille*, he had visions of Venice from the sea at dawn, then (as if recalling the classical allusions in Goethe's poems) of a seductive daughter of Nereus (a marine divinity in Roman mythology), and finally, responding directly to Felix's music, perceived that "from the farthest horizon there came a tintinnabulation as though the little waves were speaking to one another in a dream."[15] Clara Wieck recorded in her diary a more straightforward assessment; Felix's overture, she observed, was "performed with a precision and refinement to which we have not been accustomed."[16]

For another week Moscheles and Felix regaled each other with music. Moscheles read his friend's new compositions, including *Paulus* and Lieder, such as the recently composed Heine setting, *Auf Flügeln des Gesanges* (Op. 34 No. 2). There was daily music making with a circle of musicians, among them Clara Wieck, Schumann, Hauser, the amateur tenor Konrad Schleinitz, and Henriette Voigt, who commissioned Theodor Hildebrandt to execute a formal portrait of Felix,[17] later used as a frontispiece for the first edition of *Paulus*. On October 6 the Wiecks hosted a reading of J. S. Bach's Triple Concerto in D minor (BWV 1063) from a manuscript in Hauser's possession, with Clara, Moscheles, and the young pianist Louis Rakemann taking the solo parts, while Felix condensed the orchestra at a fourth piano.[18] To support Moscheles's *Extraconcert* on October 9, Felix directed the *Hebrides* Overture and participated in his friend's piano duet, *Hommage à Handel*, about to be published by Kistner. At the second subscription concert (October 11), Moscheles reciprocated by performing his own Concerto in G minor, and encored his duet with Felix. In the audience that evening were the Dirichlets, returning from a vacation in Belgium. On the morning of October 13 they departed with Felix and Moscheles for Berlin.

After a sixteen-hour journey, they arrived late at night to a darkened house. The two pianists were unexpected, so the next morning Lea and Abraham awoke to a joyful reunion. Fanny joined Felix and Moscheles in performing for a nearly blind Abraham. At his request, Felix rendered at the piano the slow movement of Haydn's String Quartet, Op. 76 No. 5. Felix's expressive playing of the extraordinary Largo in F♯ major, marked *Cantabile e mesto*, brought the old man to tears.[19] With Moscheles Felix read Mozart's duet Sonata in D (K. 448) as Abraham delightedly mistook the playing of the one for the other. On their last day together (October 15), the two pianists collaborated on an improvisation, into which Felix cleverly worked horn calls announcing the departure of Moscheles's coach. Moscheles left for Hamburg, and Felix, promising to return at Christmas, departed early the next morning for Leipzig. Abraham's parting

words were, "Well, humanly speaking, we may hope to be spared till then."
He had embraced his son for the last time.[20]

Resuming a frenetic schedule, Felix now led four subscription concerts in as many weeks (October 22 and 29, November 5 and 12), and two
benefit concerts of Clara Wieck, and the pianist J. P. Pixis and his foster
daughter, the contralto Francilla Pixis (November 9 and 16). Among the
highlights were Felix's debut on October 29 as piano soloist in his Op. 25,
and on November 9 the premiere of Clara's Piano Concerto in A minor,
Op. 7, a work with a somewhat unusual gestation. In 1833 the fourteen-
year-old had composed a one-movement *Concertsatz*, orchestrated by
Schumann. Recasting it as a finale, she expanded the work to produce a
full-fledged concerto in three connected movements, like Felix's Op. 25.
The same concert also featured Felix's *Capriccio brillant*, which she played
"like a devil,"[21] and the J. S. Bach triple Concerto in D minor, with Clara,
Felix, and Louis Rakemann as soloists—remarkably enough, the very
first performance of Bach in the Gewandhaus.[22]

By this time Felix was preoccupied with the final choruses of *Paulus*;
he also crafted another example of his whimsical, tripping elfin style,
the *Scherzo a capriccio* in F♯ minor,[23] dispatched to Paris early in November for a new piano album. Then tragedy struck. On November 15
Abraham had a heated discussion with Varnhagen von Ense about the
Junges Deutschland movement, whose adherents, a loosely knit group of
young writers associated with the *emigré* Heine, were about to face pros-
ecution in Prussia for alleged blasphemy and immorality. Varnhagen
made the mistake of defending them and deprecating Lessing, venerated by Abraham as his father's constant friend. In a letter begun the
next day, after likening Lessing to a "sun in which dark spots may be
seen through smoked glasses," Abraham questioned Varnhagen's decision to champion "men who as yet have only shown spots, behind which
we are allowed to suppose a sun."[24] Two nights later, after listening to his
family reading Rousseau's *Émile*, Abraham fell ill. Though doctors found
no cause for alarm, the next morning, at 10:30 A.M., death "in its most
peaceful, beautiful aspect"[25] visited Abraham; to Schubring Felix reported
that his father slipped away serenely, as had Moses Mendelssohn.[26] Luise
Hensel had lost her mother only weeks before and had a premonition of
Abraham's passing; to Clemens Brentano she regretted not converting
him to Catholicism. She believed that despite his embrace of Protestantism, he had died, like his father, a deist.[27]

The afternoon of Abraham's death, Wilhelm Hensel journeyed to
Leipzig to break the news to Felix. Securing a deputy for the impending
concerts, Felix returned home the morning of November 21. Devastated
by the loss, he was initially unable to grieve. At the funeral (November

23) he found the violinist Ferdinand David, just arrived from Estonia, whom Abraham had taken under his wing when the young David had mourned his own parents' deaths.[28] David agreed to apply for the post of Gewandhaus concertmaster, newly vacated by Matthäi's death. The two friends proceeded together to Leipzig, where with a heavy heart Felix directed three more concerts, the last of which (December 17) again featured Clara Wieck. In the audience that night were Paul and Albertine Mendelssohn Bartholdy, who escorted Felix to Berlin on December 22. During the Christmas holidays, an "inexpressibly wretched," "purposeless"[29] Felix reviewed his parents' will and comforted Lea. The closing days of the year found him in Leipzig revising the Fugue in F minor, Op. 35 No. 5, for Clara Wieck,[30] while from Berlin, Fanny rued that her family was now in its seventh year of separation.[31]

<h1 style="text-align:center">I</h1>

Felix had lost his "instructor in art and in life,"[32] who had followed keenly the progress of the oratorio, and, like a conscience, urged Felix to finish it. Now, in the New Year, suffering from insomnia and avoiding society, Felix redoubled his efforts, even as Fanny, who perused the work in Berlin on Felix's twenty-seventh birthday, caviled about some recitatives she found "really pointless or too modern."[33] He had intended to premiere *Paulus* with the Frankfurt Cäcilienverein, but Schelble's debilitating illness rendered the plan impractical. An alternative venue emerged in January,[34] when Felix received an invitation to direct the oratorio at the eighteenth Lower Rhine Music Festival, scheduled for Düsseldorf in May 1836. By the end of February he was pressing to finish the piano-vocal score, so that Simrock, who bought the German rights for 60 Louis d'Or, could prepare choral parts for rehearsals under Julius Rietz. Felix dispatched the first half on February 27 and half of the second on March 12, the same day he agreed to direct the festival. The remainder followed on April 2.[35] Concurrently, the composer labored over the full score and was able to date its two parts on April 8 and April 18,[36] and thus brought to closure, or so it seemed, a prolonged, two-year effort.

The scores Felix released to Simrock had already undergone extensive revisions, for in assembling the draft the composer had deleted at least ten numbers. Happily, they have survived in volume 28 of the Berlin *Nachlass*. Four years after the 1836 premiere, Felix played through the rejected movements for Moscheles, who, noting their conspicuously dramatic treatment, judged them as "perhaps more adapted for isolated pieces in the concert-room than to be heard in connection with the oratorio itself."[37] Still unpublished, these movements were included in a 1998 commercial recording of the oratorio[38] that opened a new window into the tangled evolution of the work that catapulted Felix to the forefront of German music.

In several cases, he revised or replaced the rejected numbers. For example, following the opening chorus there was originally a three-fold statement of the chorale *Ach bleib mit deiner Gnade bei uns, Herr Jesu Christ* ("Ah, remain with us in Thy mercy, Lord Jesus Christ"), with an embellished tenor line woven into its second verse. Instead, Felix substituted a simple setting of the chorale *Allein Gott in der Höh' sei Ehr*, as if respecting Abraham's view about so-called figured chorales: "No liberties ought ever assuredly to be taken with a chorale. Its highest purpose is, that the congregation should sing it in all its purity to the accompaniment of the organ; all else seems to me idle and inappropriate for a church."[39]

Another discarded draft, "Herr Gott, dess die Rache ist," was Saul's original entrance aria in Part 1. Drawing upon Psalms 94 and 18 ("O Lord, you God of vengeance, shine forth!"), Felix drafted a solo for Saul in an agitated, though subdued C minor, with supporting interjections from a male chorus (**ex. 10.1**). But this attempt yielded to a much more compelling rage aria for Saul in B minor (No. 12,[40] "Vertilge sie, Herr Zebaoth," Psalm 59:13), preceded by a short recitative (Acts 8:3, "But Saul was ravaging the Church") that focused attention on Saul as persecutor of the early Christians.

Part 2 contained several movements Felix excised but did not replace. A recitative early in the second part, "Die unter Euch Gott fürchten," delivered part of Paul's sermon at Antioch (Acts 13), including verse 39, "by this Jesus everyone who believes is set free from all those sins from which you could not be freed by the law of Moses," and followed by a

Ex. 10.1: Mendelssohn, "Herr Gott, dess die Rache ist, erscheine," rejected movement for *Paulus*

Ex. 10.2: Mendelssohn, "Lobt ihn mit Pfeifen," rejected movement in *Paulus*

setting of the staple Lutheran chorale *Ein' feste Burg* ("A mighty fortress").
But Felix removed the dramatic presentation of the sermon and let stand
alone the concise, third-person recitative ("So he went in and out among
them in Jerusalem, speaking boldly in the name of the Lord," Acts 9:28).
A complex of discarded movements originally enhanced the scene at
Lystra, in which the gentiles worship Barnabas and Paul as Jupiter and
Mercury. Among three rejected "Gentile choruses" was a female chorus
in G with swaying, siciliano-like rhythms (Psalm 147, "Sing to the Lord
with thanksgiving"), a full, robust chorus in D on the unidentified text
"Danket den Göttern" ("Thanks to the gods"), and a "merry F♯-minor
chorus of pagans"[41] ("Lobt ihn mit Pfeifen," on verses from Psalms 150,
148, and 146), which erupts with clamorous woodwind trills and brass
tremolos (**ex. 10.2**). Alternating between the chorus and soloists, the
movement approaches stylistically the Druid choruses in *Die erste Walpurgisnacht*. Probably sensing he had given disproportionate weight to
the Greek pagans, Felix sacrificed all three choruses (later Fanny would
argue in vain for the reinstatement of "Lobt ihn mit Pfeifen").[42]

Finally, one other scene from Acts, the imprisonment at Philippi of
Paul and Silas, also originally figured in the oratorio. To that end, Felix
wrote a duet in E♭ for the two, "Gelobet sei Gott" ("Praise be to God," 2
Corinthians 1), and a recitative, "Suddenly there was an earthquake" (Acts
16:26), to narrate their miraculous release. The chorale *O treuer Heiland,
Jesu Christ* was to have rounded out this complex, but again, all three fell
by the wayside by the time of the première.

While hastening to finish his score,[43] Felix dispatched his duties at
the Gewandhaus. The year 1836 began with a festive concert featuring
Handel's anthem *Zadok the Priest*, for which Felix provided new wind
parts. The final concert (March 17) included works by Handel, Mozart,
Beethoven, and Weber. Typically in two parts, programs opened with a
symphony or overture, and concluded with a symphony or operatic finale. Between these substantial offerings Felix inserted solo concerti,

Lieder, or arias. Among the soloists of the 1835–1836 season were the violinists Ferdinand David and Léon de Saint-Lubin (rivals for the concertmaster vacancy), Viennese cellist Joseph Merk, and soprano Henriette Grabau, with whom Felix read Schubert's ballade *Erlkönig* and *Ungeduld* from *Die schöne Müllerin*.[44] Felix's own performance on January 28 of Mozart's Piano Concerto in D minor, K. 466, caused a sensation. Among the orchestral personnel was an elderly violinist who had heard Mozart render the same concerto in the Gewandhaus and averred that Felix's cadenzas rivaled Mozart's.[45] Departing from the license of the time, which emboldened soloists to admit into cadenzas all manners of extraneous virtuosity, Felix treated the improvised passage instead as a miniature composition thematically and harmonically integrated into the work, a "concerto within the concerto."[46] Thus, the cadenza for the first movement recalled Mozart's opening piano solo with its expressive octave leap, extracted Mozart's descending, sighlike figure, repeated the figure through a series of rhythmic accelerations, and then allowed it to dissolve into a series of dramatic trills.

Another less conventional soloist who came to Leipzig in 1836 aroused Felix's admiration. The Polish Jew M. J. Guzikow (1806–1837), a "phenomenon" "inferior to no virtuoso in the world,"[47] introduced a primitive version of the modern xylophone. Known as the *Strohfiedel* ("straw fiddle"), this instrument consisted of twenty-eight wooden bars arranged loosely in the shape of a trapezium and resting upon five rolls of straw. Fanny described how in Berlin the musician assembled the instrument before a bemused audience and then extracted sounds resembling Papageno's flute in Mozart's *Magic Flute*.[48] Guzikow's repertoire included original compositions based on Polish themes and transcriptions of concertos by Weber, Paganini, and others. In dress and habits an Orthodox Jew, Guzikow arrived with a retinue of bearded Polish Jews, who absorbed every positive comment Felix offered. For his part, Felix seems to have distanced himself from the assembly, for he could "not speak for laughing, seeing the small room crammed full of these bearded fellows."[49] Still, Moses Mendelssohn's grandson must have regarded the musician, who had risen from the ghetto to win fame on European concert stages, with a sense of distant familiarity.

At the Gewandhaus Felix drew largely upon classic and early nineteenth-century German repertoire and thereby reinforced the canonization of an increasingly familiar musical tradition. Thus, during his first season, Beethoven's music figured most prominently, with performances of the Violin Concerto, first finale of *Fidelio*, *Consecration of the House* and one of the *Leonore* Overtures, cantata *Meeresstille und glückliche Fahrt*, concert scene *Ah, Perfido*, and *Adelaide*, and all the symphonies except the First. Also prominently represented were Weber (several overtures and arias, and the first finale of *Oberon*), Mozart (last four symphonies, Piano Concerto, K. 466, and finales from *Don Giovanni, Così fan tutte,* and *La clemenza di Tito*), and Haydn (four symphonies). Of contemporary composers Felix drew principally upon Spohr (Third Symphony, Violin Concerto No. 11), Cherubini (several overtures and excerpts from *Ali-Baba*), and himself (Piano Concerto No. 1, and four overtures, Opp. 21, 26, 27, and 32).

In tandem with Felix, Ferdinand David, who held the post of concertmaster from February 1836 for thirty-seven years, instituted in January a series of chamber music concerts. Oversubscribed, the concerts were moved from the *Vorsaal* to the main hall of the Gewandhaus, to accommodate a second series of *Quartettsoirées* in February and March. The programming again underscored a distinctly German instrumental progression, with string quartets by Haydn, Mozart, and Beethoven, supplemented by works of Spohr and Felix (the Octet, in which Felix participated, and his String Quartet in E♭, Op. 12). Among the most memorable offerings was the friends' rendition of Beethoven's *Kreutzer* Sonata, performed from memory with a freshness and energy that captivated Leipzigers.

While Felix was experiencing a wintry January in self-imposed solitude,[50] the directors of the Gewandhaus were endeavoring to retain him. Only some three months after his arrival, they pressed to renew his contract (Felix replied he would decide by Easter). By the end of January he was acknowledging to his mother that unlike the petty bickering that had plagued his tenure in Düsseldorf, he had not spent a single irksome (*verdriesslich*) day in Leipzig.[51] In February came word that Frankfurt would offer him the directorship of the Cäcilienverein, which he interpreted as an unfortunate omen about Schelble's health. But Leipzig now prepared to award him a signal honor: on March 8, the faculty of the university voted to confer an honorary doctorate, which occurred on March 20 in a ceremony witnessed by Fanny and Lea, who visited Felix for a few days.[52] The diploma (**plate 12**) cited him as a "most illustrious man" (*vir clarissimus*) for his "contributions to the art of music."

In April Breitkopf & Härtel published the *Trois Caprices* for piano Op. 33, separately composed between 1833 and 1835. The release prompted reviews by Gottfried Fink in the *Allgemeine musikalische Zeitung* and Schumann in the *Neue Zeitschrift für Musik*.[53] Each caprice comprises a sonata-form movement prefaced by an introduction, ranging from a few, sketchy chords in No. 2 (E major) to more elaborate Adagios in Nos. 1 and 3 (A and B♭ minor) that bring the pieces into the realm of the fantasy (the

Ex. 10.3: Mendelssohn, Caprice in E major, Op. 33 No. 2 (1835)

beginning of No. 1, subdued arpeggiations over a descending chromatic bass, bears the label *Adagio quasi fantasia*). Schumann discerned three different affects in the caprices: the first expressed a "gentle grief," the second a seductive quality that could "make the most faithful of girls unfaithful for a few moments," and the third a "speechless, restrained wrath" that burst its boundaries at the conclusion. Schumann's favorite, the second, elicited a fanciful comparison to Jean Paul—its capricious turns and gossamer-like textures (**ex. 10.3**) conjured up one of Walt's "cross-country summer flights" in that madcap novel of adolescent awakening, *Flegeljahre*.

Another young composer also held Felix in high esteem. On April 11, 1836, the impecunious Richard Wagner, music director of a provincial theater in Magdeburg, sent Felix the score of a symphony in C major,[54] written in 1831 when Wagner was eighteen and performed at the Gewandhaus in 1833 by Felix's predecessor, Pohlenz. Heavily influenced by Beethoven, Wagner's youthful essay included as its centerpiece an Andante in A minor redolent of the soulful *Allegretto* of Beethoven's Seventh Symphony. By 1834 Wagner was assimilating Mendelssohnian features into his style. Thus, the E-major overture to his second opera, *Die Feen* (*The Fairies*), opens with *pianissimo* chords reminiscent of the *Midsummer Night's Dream* Overture. And in 1835, for his incidental music to Theodor Apel's drama *Columbus*, Wagner produced an overture strikingly indebted to another musical voyage, Felix's *Meeresstille und glückliche Fahrt*, which Wagner had conducted in Magdeburg (in 1879 Wagner would admit that he was guilty of plagiarism).[55] His letter of April 1836 makes it clear that the symphony was a gift; all that he requested was that Felix read through the score and offer suggestions, so that the two might become closer. But curiously, Felix never acknowledged the gift, and the score disappeared. Years later, in 1874, Wagner maintained to Cosima that Felix had deliberately destroyed the manuscript, "perhaps because he detected in it a talent that was disagreeable to him."[56] So began a strained musical relationship that would have profound consequences for German music and culture at mid-century.

II

Meanwhile, Felix made final preparations for the Lower Rhine Music Festival, scheduled for May 22 and 23, 1836. Because the concerts fell on Whitsuntide (Pentecost Sunday and Monday), the organizers had to petition the Prussian king for a special dispensation. While the premiere of *Paulus* formed the first concert, the repertoire for the second required more effort. Eventually Felix and the committee settled on Handel's ninth Chandos Anthem (with additional wind parts provided by Julius Rietz), Mozart's cantata *Davidde penitente*, K. 469, and Beethoven's Ninth Symphony and the then unpublished *Leonore* Overture No. 1, Op. 138. Securing the parts of the overture proved nearly impossible: when Woringen requested a copy from Anton Schindler, Beethoven's former amanuensis refused to lend the "holy relic" (*Heiligtum*), even if Mendelssohn offered his new oratorio in exchange.[57] But Felix circumvented Schindler's "rudeness" by appealing to the Viennese publisher Haslinger, who supplied parts by the middle of May, only days before the festival.

Departing Leipzig on May 1, Felix traveled first to Frankfurt, where he arrived the morning of May 4 to visit his cousin Philipp Veit and the ailing Schelble, for whom Felix had agreed to deputize that summer. His diary records meetings at the Cäcilienverein and with the Souchays,[58] a prosperous Frankfurt family to whom Felix gained an introduction from their cousin, the Leipzig attorney and amateur musician Fritz Schlemmer. One of the members of Schelble's chorus was Cécile Jeanrenaud, daughter of Elisabeth Jeanrenaud (née Souchay). To Klingemann, Felix later reported his first meeting on May 4 with his future fiancée,[59] said to have "luxurious golden-brown hair," a complexion of "transparent delicacy," and the "most bewitching deep blue eyes," with "dark eyelashes and eyebrows,"[60] a characterization supported by a family portrait of 1835 in the Frankfurt Historisches Museum,[61] and by a pencil portrait drawn by Felix's Frankfurt cousin Philipp Veit (**plate 13**). But Felix could not have progressed much beyond initial impressions; on May 6 he left for Mainz and Cologne, before reaching Düsseldorf two days later.

For the festival Julius Rietz had amassed an amateur chorus of 364 musicians (106 sopranos, 60 altos, 90 tenors, and 108 bass). As in previous years, they arrived via diligences from neighboring communities and steamboats on the Rhine (at least one vessel from Cologne conveyed sixty members singing festive part-songs). The orchestra, 172 strong, also comprised chiefly amateurs, though the concertmaster was Ferdinand David, who followed Felix from Leipzig. David led a contingent of strings that included 72 violins, 24 violas, 24 celli, and 12 contrabass.[62] The combined forces totaled 536 performers, a significant increase over the 420 dilettantes Felix had

directed in 1833 and an impressive, if unwieldy, symbol of the newly affluent, bourgeois mass music culture emerging in the Rhineland.[63] After
Rietz oversaw the initial rehearsals, Felix supervised the first general rehearsal on May 19. When the festival opened on Whitsunday, an audience of over one thousand crammed into the Rittersaal. It included
Ferdinand Hiller and three Londoners, among them Karl Klingemann
and the young pianist/composer William Sterndale Bennett, whom Felix
had met during the summer of 1833 at the Royal Academy of Music in
London and invited to Germany. The third was the future music critic
of the *Times*, J. W. Davison, at the time suffering from severe headaches.
Compassionately stroking his forehead, Felix offered in sympathy, "Poor
fallow, poor fallow," and earned a friend for life.[64] From Berlin came
Fanny, Paul, and his wife, Albertine. Lea, too, was eager to hear her son's
new oratorio, but Felix, concerned the strain might further injure her
health, discouraged her from traveling.[65]

The version of *Paulus* premiered on Whitsunday 1836 differed considerably from the piano-vocal and full scores published later that year
and in 1837 as Felix's Op. 36. After sending his manuscript to Düsseldorf
in April, the perfectionist had continued to polish the work, and, indeed, arrived from Leipzig with several new numbers for the soloists
only days before the performance.[66] At least one freshly written tenor
recitative for Ferdinand von Woringen prompted a humorous miscue in
rehearsal. The text, probably an early version of No. 31, which relates
Paul's healing of the lame man of Lystra, read in part "When the heathen
heard it they were glad." But Woringen misread the German *froh* as *frech*,
and inadvertently turned the elated into "saucy" Gentiles.[67]

Before leaving Leipzig, Felix had dispatched to Düsseldorf a piano-
vocal score for Rietz's choral rehearsals. This hastily prepared manuscript
survives with Rietz's note certifying it as the only "exemplar" transmitting
the version of the premiere.[68] A study of this neglected source awaits another occasion, but a cursory glance reveals some significant differences.
Thus, the numbering of the movements originally ran from 1 to 25 in
Part 1 and 26 to 46 in Part 2, instead of the nearly symmetrical 1 to 22 and
23 to 45 of the printed score. Part of the discrepancy concerns two solo
numbers inserted in Part 1, then removed for the publication of the work,
and eventually released by Simrock in 1868 as the *Zwei geistliche Lieder*,
Op. 112 No. 2, "Der du die Menschen lässest sterben" in F major (Psalm
90), was a soprano arioso that followed the chorale *Dir Herr, dir will ich
mich ergeben* after Stephen's burial (between Nos. 9 and 10 of the printed
score). For the fifth verse of the psalm ("Thou carriest them away as
with a flood") Felix inserted a meandering phrase that linked the arioso
to the chorale (**ex. 10.4**). No. 1, "Doch der Herr, er leitet die irrenden

Ex. 10.4a: Mendelssohn, "Der du die Menschen lässest sterben," Op. 112 No. 2 (ca. 1836)

Ex. 10.4b: Mendelssohn, *Paulus, Dir Herr, dir will ich mich ergeben* (1836), No. 9

recht" (Psalm 25:8, "Good and upright is the Lord; therefore will he teach sinners in the way"), for alto solo, appeared after the recitative of No. 13, just before Saul's blinding vision on the road to Damascus. Felix replaced this arioso with a more compact setting of "Doch der Herr vergisst der Seinen nicht" (No. 13; Psalm 115:12, "The Lord hath been mindful of us").

From all accounts the premiere was a triumph for the twenty-seven-year-old composer, even though during much of it he was lost in thought about his father, and the performance was marred by one unexpected blemish. When a "false witness" lost his way during the "testimony" against Stephen (No. 3), Fanny, singing as an alto in the chorus, stepped forward to help cue the soloist and momentarily left her choral anonymity to enter the limelight of her brother's public career. After the performance, Felix quipped, "I am so glad it was one of the *false* witnesses."[69] The press quickly accorded the composition the status of a masterpiece: the *Düsseldorfer Zeitung* labeled it a *klassisches Tonwerk*,[70] and Klingemann, who wrote a review for *The Musical World*, applied Winckelmannian attributes of "calm grandeur and pure beauty," and detected in the oratorio a certain timeless quality.[71] *Paulus* became Felix's most popular work during his lifetime, a favorite of music festivals and oratorio societies that reverberated throughout Germany, and in Denmark, Holland, Poland, Russia, Switzerland, and even the United States, where American audiences in Boston, New York, and Baltimore heard *St. Paul* between 1837 and 1839. We shall examine its music further when we consider the Leipzig premiere of the published version in March 1837.

The second day of the festival (May 23) featured Beethoven's Ninth Symphony, still relatively unknown in Germany. Fanny described it as "a gigantic tragedy, with a conclusion meant to be dithyrambic, but falling into the opposite extreme—the height of burlesque."[72] At the festival, controversy (and perhaps burlesque) visited the performance when the bass soloist, a Herr Fischer from Frankfurt, unilaterally elected to alter the epoch-making recitative in the finale and prompted a scathing rebuke from Anton Schindler in the Cologne *Zeitung*. Felix was implicated in this corruption of Beethoven's text and assailed for his fast tempi (Schindler later recalled, Felix "would chase whole orchestras in double quickstep through a piece of music").[73] Springing to his defense, a local music pedagogue and critic, L. F. C. Bischoff, challenged Schindler's authority as Beethoven's "alter ego" and placed the blame squarely on Fischer, who in rehearsal had not tampered with the recitative.[74] Schindler remained an outspoken opponent of Felix, and the criticism of fast tempi later returned to haunt discussions of his conducting.

On balance, though, little detracted from Felix's triumph. On May 24 he organized a third, impromptu concert that offered Mozart arias, Beethoven's first two *Leonore* Overtures, and a reprise of several numbers from *Paulus*. When a soloist fell ill, Felix and David entertained the audience with Beethoven's *Kreutzer* Sonata. Hiller reports that Felix was "in every way the center-point of the Festival, not only as composer, director, and pianist, but also as a lively and agreeable host."[75] He even found time to offer Sterndale Bennett instruction *gratis*, and shortly before the talented young Englishman departed, prophesied to Attwood that "if he does not become a very great musician, it is not God's will, but his own."[76] A few days later, toasts were raised to Felix as the successor of Handel and Bach, and on June 3, his last evening in Düsseldorf, the festival committee alluded to a special gift in preparation. A year later, after publication of the oratorio, it was ready: a special exemplar of the score fitted with illustrations of the life of St. Paul by several Düsseldorf artists.[77]

Announcing to Lea that he was now fairly established in Germany,[78] Felix returned to Frankfurt on June 7. There, he rekindled his friendship with Veit and his aunt Dorothea, a septuagenarian intellectually alert though in her declining years, and encountered his cousin Alexander, with whom he visited Mainz. There were daily conversations with Hiller, though Felix found his musical tastes too dispersed between the grave works of Bach and Beethoven on the one hand, and the buoyant operas of Auber and Rossini on the other. As it happened, Rossini himself arrived with the Baron Lionel de Rothschild to attend his arranged wedding with his cousin Charlotte,[79] and for several days Frankfurt society lionized the maestro. Now in retirement, the pensioned composer of *Guillaume Tell*, whom Felix described as a *lustiges Wundertier*,[80] had lost some of his celebrated girth and was a respected man of the world who dispensed witticisms about music and professed to admire J. S. Bach. But when Felix played his Capriccio in F♯ minor, Op. 5 (perhaps at one of the sumptuous Rothschild wedding receptions), he overheard the novice Germanophile react to its capricious leaps under his breath, *Ça sent la sonate de Scarlatti* ("that smells like a Scarlatti sonata"); what is more, Rossini advised his young colleague to adopt a more popular style of writing.[81] Among Felix's other musical diversions were a visit from the Swedish composer Lindblad, another concert by Guzikow, and an excursion to Offenbach to see the music publisher André.

Abandoning plans for a Swiss and Italian vacation, Felix replaced Schelble, who attempted to convalesce in the country. For some six weeks, Felix resided in his friend's Frankfurt residence that afforded a picturesque view of the Main River and its bustling traffic. On Wednesday evenings Felix fed the Cäcilienverein a traditional diet of Handel and Bach. The *Lieblingsstück* that summer was Bach's Cantata No. 106, the *Actus tragicus*, which, published in 1830, had been a favorite of Felix's father during his last years. Contrasting the certainty of death ("For the ancient sentence stands: You shall die," Sirach 14:17) and its transformation through Christ ("Even so, come, Lord Jesus," Revelation 22:20), the cantata now became a kind of requiem for Abraham. Though pressed again to accept the directorship of the Cäcilienverein, Felix declined, for he had already decided to accept another year at the Gewandhaus.

Laboring to revise his oratorio, Felix was able to finish the piano-vocal score in late July; but his "awful reverence for print" necessitated so many changes that the choral parts, prematurely printed for the Düsseldorf premiere, had to be re-engraved.[82] He spent more and more time visiting Cécile Jeanrenaud and her family, who resided in a mansion known as Am Fahrtor, after an adjacent gatehouse on the Main. Initially, Felix was quite discreet in displaying his affection; indeed, Cécile herself imagined that the object of his attention was her mother Elisabeth, an attractive forty-year-old who conducted vivacious conversations in an elegant Frankfurt patois. But as he relaxed on Ferdinand Hiller's couch, Felix poured out his heart about the "chosen one" in the "most charmingly frank and artless way," without, Hiller assures us, any "exaggerated sentimentality or uncontrolled passion."[83] Meanwhile, Felix maintained his reserve to his family and tantalized Lea, Fanny, and Rebecka in July by referring to a *wunderschönes Mädchen*, and admitting that he was "dreadfully in love."[84]

Not long after Felix arrived in Frankfurt, Cécile left to visit relatives in Heidelberg; during a two-week separation, she haunted his mind, for on June 27, he composed an endearing piano piece, a *Duett ohne Worte* in A♭ major, that he later inserted into her autograph album.[85] When this nocturne-like composition appeared in 1837 as the sixth of the *Lieder ohne Worte* Op. 38, Felix appended the instruction, "*N.B.*: Both voices must always be brought out clearly," underscoring again its function as a

Ex. 10.5: Mendelssohn, *Lied ohne Worte* in Ab major, Op. 38 No. 6 (1836)

duet. Undoubtedly, he conceived the piece as an instrumental love duet. Its $\frac{6}{8}$ meter and delicate, lapping accompaniment conjured up the barcarolle, though Frankfurt and the Main replaced Venetian lagoons as the *locus* of this idealized assignation. Felix enriched the texture of the music to accommodate four distinct elements: two melodic strands in the soprano and tenor parts, separated by triplet arpeggiations and supported by a bass line (**ex. 10.5**). In the first two thirds of the composition the lyrical melody unfolds as a dialogue between the soprano and tenor, before the two, united, sing together. The conceit was familiar enough; Felix would have known precedents in Mozart's *duettino* "Là ci darem la mano" in *Don Giovanni*, in which the Don seduces Zerlina, and in Carl Maria von Weber's (text-less) depiction of courtship through the medium of the waltz in the piano composition *Aufforderung zum Tanze* (1819).

Felix's euphonious Lied could almost stand as a musical metaphor for his idyllic courtship of Cécile, and for what traditional biographers, following Sebastian Hensel, have depicted as a stable, blissfully happy marriage. In a similar way, Cécile herself appears in idealized tones in nineteenth-century accounts. Thus, according to Sebastian Hensel she exercised an "influence as soothing and refreshing as that of the open sky or running water."[86] And for Eduard Devrient, "Cecilia was one of those sweet, womanly natures, whose gentle simplicity, whose mere presence, soothed and pleased. She was slight, with features of striking beauty and delicacy; her hair was between brown and gold; but the transcendent luster of her great blue eyes, and the brilliant roses of her cheeks, were sad harbingers of early death. She spoke little, and never with animation, in a low, soft voice. Shakespeare's words, 'My gracious silence,' applied to her no less than to the wife of Coriolanus."[87]

For Devrient, Cécile thus played to Felix's Coriolanus the minor role of Virgilia, the doting wife who brought out the tender side of the patrician general as he plotted to lead the Volsci against the early Roman Republic. Taciturn and "unable to express all she felt," Cécile became known as the "Goddess of Silence" next to Felix, who "never could be silent, but was always bubbling over like champagne in a small glass."[88] Though Cécile sang in Schelble's chorus, she was not especially gifted musically and indeed was reluctant to play the piano for Felix, whom she had imagined as a "stiff, disagreeable, jealous old man, who played dull fugues with a velvet cap on his head."[89] But she was quite skilled in drawing and painting, and during the summer of 1836 her favorite pastimes provided pretexts for social engagements with Felix. Thus, on July 9 he recorded in his diary a gift from Cécile, an album he was soon filling with drawings taken in her company, including views of the river from her residence.

At Christmas 1835, Felix had promised Fanny he would look for a bride that summer and put to rest Abraham's concern that his son's "censoriousness" (*Mäkelei*) would prevent him from finding a wife or an opera libretto.[90] As the last of his siblings to marry, Felix probably did not imagine he would choose someone whose family bore certain striking resemblances to his own. Like Lea, Cécile's mother, Elisabeth Souchay (1796–1871) belonged to a patrician family. Her father, Cornelius Carl Souchay (1768–1838), had amassed a fortune of two million florins from an import-export firm dealing in English wares, with principal offices in Frankfurt, London, and Manchester.[91] During the Continental Blockade, Souchay profited from smuggling activities and speculating, and, like the Mendelssohns, seems to have run afoul of the French authorities. Then, during the Restoration, he expanded his business, Schunck, Souchay & Co., into the most successful German merchant house in England. Although a highly successful capitalist, Souchay was also a music lover somewhat oblivious to the "spirit of capitalism" his famous great-grandson, Max Weber, would formulate in 1905 when he traced the rise of capitalism to the Protestant work ethic. Weber's wife, Marianne, characterized Souchay as a "cheerful, amiable and cultured man, who by his own efforts and marriage acquired considerable wealth, which he spent generously"[92]—a description just as easily applicable to Felix's father.

Through intermarriages with other prominent families the Souchays rose to the highest social levels of the Frankfurt patriciate. The center of German-English trade, Frankfurt reemerged as a city-republic after its brief, forced realignment as a Napoleonic duchy and flourished independently until annexation by Prussia in 1866. An unabashed Anglophile, Souchay favored the marriage in 1826 of his daughter Henriette to

Friedrich Wilhelm Benecke (1802–1865), who in 1813, two years after the Mendelssohns had surreptitiously left Hamburg, fled that city and arrived in England, where he later managed a successful chemical enterprise. During the summer of 1836, Felix came to know the Beneckes well and even composed for Friedrich Wilhelm an Allegro in E minor for piano,[93] published posthumously in 1859 and then incorporated into the composer's catalogue as Op. 117. Like Op. 38 No. 6, the Allegro is nocturne-like and animated by an accompaniment of flowing arpeggiations. But its opening thematic idea is now angular, dissonant, and masculine. Only the central part in the major inclines toward the *Duetto*, with murmuring arpeggiations and the suggestion of a soprano-tenor duet.

Cécile Jeanrenaud's paternal side was of more modest means. Her father, Auguste (1788–1819), was a French Huguenot minister whose ancestors, like the Souchays, had emigrated in 1685, when Louis XIV revoked the Edict of Nantes, and settled in Switzerland, near Neuchâtel, where they were goldsmiths. At his ordination in 1808 Auguste promised to "further the honor and glory of God," and to "eschew schism, dissensions and plots."[94] Two years later, he moved to Frankfurt, succeeded Pastor Jean-Daniel Souchay (Cécile's great-grandfather) as the minister of the French Reformed Church, and married Elisabeth Souchay in 1814. The issue of religious tolerance loomed large in their families, even in Frankfurt, where with their fellow Huguenots they congregated on "an island of Calvinism in the very heart of the Lutheran country."[95] Indeed, before the French Revolution the Huguenots were compelled to worship outside the city walls of Frankfurt, and full equality with other citizens came only in 1806. Thus, like the Mendelssohns, Cécile's relatives remembered their identity as a distinct class of citizens not yet fully assimilated in German culture.

In the marble-appointed Reformed Church on the Goetheplatz, where Felix and Cécile would wed in 1837, Jeanrenaud preached French sermons for a few years before declining health compelled him to seek more moderate climates in Lyon. There, in 1817, Cécile-Sophie-Charlotte Jeanrenaud was born. The next year the family returned to Frankfurt, but within a year the pastor died of consumption, leaving a widow of twenty-two to support four children. Elisabeth moved her family from the pastor's apartment above the sanctuary to the elegant, quayside mansion of the Souchays in the Louis XVI style, Am Fahrtor, where Felix courted Cécile during the summer of 1836.

Felix had promised to accompany Wilhelm von Schadow on a Dutch holiday in August and, as the departure date drew near, may have determined to use the separation from Cécile to gauge his feelings for her. There was little doubt in Berlin about how he should resolve the issue.

As early as July 28, Rebecka was referring to his fiancée, and Fanny, imagining herself as Sancho Panza to Felix's Don Quixote, offered a host of maxims that might "hasten a favorable decision."[96] Even Lea approved the union at the end of July, well before she ever met the Souchays. And so, after finishing his stint with the Cäcilienverein, Felix departed Frankfurt with Schadow for Mainz. Boarding a steamship, they continued on to Horchheim and Bonn, where Simrock met Felix for a short conference about *Paulus*. In Düsseldorf Schadow's son Rudolph, whom Felix had promised to tutor in Latin, joined the party. Steaming down the Rhine, they reached The Hague at the beginning of August.

On his doctor's advice, Felix decided to take a "minor" cure at the nearby resort of Scheveningen. The therapy required three weeks of bathing in the ocean. Each morning, Felix and the Schadows traveled to the beach, where, recalling *Meeresstille und glückliche Fahrt*, Felix pondered a new overture about the ocean, for he found the "straight green line" as "mysterious and unfathomable as ever." But the low horizon and dreary sand dunes were prosaic, so that any music they inspired would be in a minor key and *traurig*.[97] After two weeks, Schadow and his son departed; Felix remained behind "in the deepest solitude" to complete the cure. He sketched and painted, and finished a watercolor, *Der klyne Groenmarkt*, begun under the supervision of Schadow, who had offered advice about drawing figures. The lively urban market scene, populated by stiff human shapes that seem cut out, betrays for once Felix's unsure hand,[98] an insecurity he acknowledged by informing Elisabeth Jeanrenaud he was "no learned painter" (*kein gelehrter Maler*).[99]

Between daily ablutions Felix wrote to the Jeanrenauds; after his death Cécile destroyed his letters to her but those from Felix to her mother survive. Thus, in a rather servile letter of August 13, he asked Elisabeth if he was vulgar for daring to write without receiving her permission.[100] In correspondence to Berlin he begged his family not to visit Frankfurt and described Cécile as fluent in French and German and unmusical but talented in drawing; to Lea, he promised after returning to Frankfurt to send a flood of details or, if his suit proved futile, nothing at all.[101] To Hiller, Felix pined for news about the Fahrtor and despaired of his isolation.[102]

As it happened, he was not completely cut off. Through J. H. Lübeck, director of the Royal Conservatory in The Hague, Felix met the young Dutch composer Johannes Verhulst (1816–1891), and found his Overture in B minor Op. 2 promising.[103] The English publisher J. Alfred Novello, eager to secure English rights to *St. Paul*, tracked down Felix in The Hague and visited him the very day he finished revising the final chorus.[104] Preparations were now made for the English premiere under Sir George Smart in Liverpool in October, with Malibran as the leading soprano. Felix asked

Klingemann to prepare an English translation, authorized his friend to emend the recitatives as necessary, and even considered collaborating with him on a second oratorio. Among the proposed subjects was Elijah.[105]

During his cure, Felix managed to sprain his foot severely enough to warrant medical "attention" upon his return trip up the Rhine, when he paused in Coblenz to visit his uncle. There, on August 27, Felix had leeches applied to the affected area. He may have recovered by drafting the tremulous love duet "Ich wollt' meine Lieb' ergösse sich," Op. 63 No. 1, to some suggestive verses by Heine. The final strophe reads: "And if in nightly slumber, you have scarcely closed your eyes, my image will still pursue you, into the deepest dreams."[106] Animating the graceful vocal lines are quivering piano tremolos, which create an aura of expectant longing. On the last day of August, having disembarked in Mainz and completed the last leg of his trip by carriage, Felix was once again at the Fahrtor.

III

Frankfurt society had already begun to stir with gossip about Felix and Cécile. On September 9, during a daylong excursion to the spa of Krontal in the Taunus hills north of the city, he proposed to her beneath a canopy of trees and, giddy with excitement, sent word that evening to Berlin of their engagement. Yielding to the matronly will of Cécile's grandmother, Hélène Souchay, the couple withheld a public announcement until they could pay the mandatory social calls.[107] By September 13 some fifty relatives and friends were endeavoring to maintain the secret.[108] Among the confidantes may have been Chopin, who passed through the city on the 14th. A few days later, it was time for Felix to return to Leipzig to prepare the new season. Dorothea Schlegel saw him off on the 19th and reported that her nephew departed a cheerful bridegroom, untroubled by the new separation from Cécile.[109]

Still, in Leipzig Robert Schumann found Felix utterly bewitched (*behext*) by his fiancée and pursued by his sister Rebecka, who had arrived for a visit. He was able to read at sight Schubert's Piano Trio in B♭ major at a soirée hosted by Henriette Voigt.[110] Within days Felix was ready to plunge into the new concert season, which opened on October 2 with a featured performance of Beethoven's Seventh Symphony; according to Rebecka, the *Allegretto* "droned and sighed with an unbelievable tenderness."[111] But the landmark event that week took place on October 7 in Liverpool, where Sir George Smart presided from the organ of St. Peter's Church in the English premiere of *St. Paul*. Among the soloists were J. Alfred Novello, who sang one of the false witnesses, and Maria Caradori-Allen, who replaced Malibran after she died from complications suffered from a riding accident weeks before in Manchester (on learning of the tragedy, Felix contemplated composing a Requiem for her[112]). The performance caused a sensation and grossed receipts in excess of £8000.[113] Novello secured the English copyright for 30 guineas and announced the publication of the piano-vocal score, with an English text adapted by William Ball, in mid-November. The full score, a bilingual edition with German and English texts, appeared from Simrock in Bonn.[114]

In Leipzig the new season attracted its share of visiting virtuosi, among them K. J. Lipiński, first violinist of Tsar Nicholas I, and the young pianist Theodor Döhler (1814–1856), then at the start of his international career. On October 29 another pianist, the twenty-year-old William Sterndale Bennett, arrived. Bennett brought his Third Piano Concerto and two lithesome Mendelssohnian overtures, *The Naiades* and *Parisina* (after Byron); all three were premiered at the Gewandhaus in the first three months of 1837. In particular, the classical sprites of *The Naiades* impressed as cousins of Melusine, and Bennett now became perhaps the first of many English composers to emulate Felix's music. In Leipzig, Bennett joined a circle that enjoyed billiards and daily lunches with Felix, Schumann, and David, and a growing list of Felix's students. Among these were Camille Stamaty, a Kalkbrenner pupil whom Felix inculcated with German double counterpoint; Walther Goethe, grandson of the poet; and Eduard Franck, younger brother of Hermann.[115]

To Eduard, Felix entrusted a special task—the registration and execution of an organ part newly written for a performance of Handel's *Israel in Egypt* in the Paulinerkirche on November 7. Some two thousand Leipzigers crowded into the cold sanctuary to hear this work, for which the various Singvereine of the city united into a chorus three hundred strong (among the choristers were Clara Wieck[116] and Paul Mendelssohn Bartholdy, then visiting his brother). Since the late eighteenth century, Handel arrangements had proliferated with added wind parts that effectively replaced the organ continuo (e.g., Mozart's arrangements of *Acis and Galatea, Messiah, Alexander's Feast*, and *Ode for St. Cecilia's Day*, 1788–1790; and I. F. von Mosel's arrangements of *Israel in Egypt, Samson*, and *Jephtha*, 1815–1832). By removing the supplemental winds and reinstating the organ, Felix endeavored to restore Handel's music; the press seized on the event as reviving a historically informed, authentic performance tradition. From Berlin Fanny observed, "organ and church together in a Handel work haven't been heard since time immemorial."[117] And G. W. Fink argued colorfully for the instrument's revival:

"The organ belongs to Handel's oratorios. It is well known that Handel himself played it splendidly; his colossal build, full of health and vigor, and his uncommonly large hands enabled him to play as long as necessary coupled manuals without tiring."[118] Sterndale Bennett was not convinced by the performance, for he found "the orchestra wanted point, and the organist was continually lugging."[119] But the Berlin *Vossische Zeitung* hailed Felix for restoring Handel's score,[120] and the performance was encored on November 17. What is more, Felix's success motivated the Gewandhaus directors to renew his contract, and raise his salary to 1000 thalers. In exchange, he agreed to add to his yearly duties two church performances. Pleased, Felix wrote Lea that he could not imagine finding for himself a better position elsewhere.[121]

At the subscription concerts Felix introduced several new compositions during his second season, including Ferdinand Hiller's Overture on Shakespeare's *As You Like It*, and symphonies by the Dresden *Hofkapellmeister* K. G. Reissiger and two Stuttgart musicians, P. J. von Lindpaintner and Bernhard Molique. There were performances of "prize" symphonies by Franz Lachner and the violinist Johann Strauss (Sr.), then undertaking European and Russian tours to establish himself as a composer of dance music. Perhaps the most unusual offering was a "symphony" based upon Beethoven's *Kreutzer* Sonata, a work Felix knew especially well. The score of this oddity, premiered on March 2, 1837, has not survived, but its Hamburg creator, Eduard Marxsen, later won fame as the teacher of Johannes Brahms. Of Felix's own music only two overtures (Opp. 21 and 27) and the Piano Concerto, Op. 25 received performances, although he also appeared as the soloist in J. S. Bach's Concerto in D minor and Beethoven's Fourth and Fifth (*Emperor*) Piano Concertos. The last was not without rehearsal difficulties, especially in the closing bars, where Beethoven limited the orchestral accompaniment to *pianissimo* timpani strokes. Dissatisfied with the ensemble playing, Felix dismissed the timpanist Grenser in favor of the theology student E. G. B. Pfundt, who subsequently joined the orchestra and, indeed, became the "first timpanist in all of Germany."[122]

While Felix was preoccupied at the Gewandhaus, Fanny returned to serious composition. Citing Goethe's "demonic influence" that she claimed Felix held over her, she began composing in the spring of 1836 several piano pieces, of which she finished seven by late October and dispatched with Paul and Albertine to Leipzig.[123] Songlike, they approach the tuneful lyricism of Felix's *Lieder ohne Worte*. By November she was contemplating publication but came into conflict with the two most important men in her life: "With regard to my publishing I stand like the donkey between two bales of hay. I have to admit honestly that I'm rather neutral about it, and Hensel, on the one hand, is for it, and you, on the other, are against it. I would of course comply totally with the wishes of my husband in any other matter, yet on this issue alone it's crucial to have your consent, for without it I might not undertake anything of the kind."[124] On Fanny's birthday Felix praised her new compositions[125] and, as we shall see, later alluded to some in his own piano miniatures but could not bring himself to support her entering the lists as a "professional" composer. This issue would haunt the final ten years of Fanny's life.

Eager to see Cécile, Felix gave on December 12, 1836, his last concert of the year, which culminated with the finale of Beethoven's *Fidelio*. Having kept silent about his fiancée, Felix now sat down at the piano and gleefully improvised on Beethoven's music for Schiller's lines "Wer ein holdes Weib errungen, stimm' in unsern Jubel ein" ("He who has won a virtuous wife, may he join in our rejoicing"), which erupts in a festive choral Allegro midway through the finale. As Max Müller, son of the poet and a chorus member, explained, "That was his confession to his friends, and then we all knew."[126] The next day Felix departed for Frankfurt and soon was making the rounds of the Jeanrenauds' relatives and friends. Incredibly, he counted 170 such obligations; Fanny calculated that at twenty a day, the "superhuman task"[127] would consume more than an entire week. At the Fahrtor Felix celebrated a joyful Christmas, in contrast to the dark depression of the previous year. He gave Cécile an album teeming with autographs of literary and musical celebrities, including Goethe, Haydn, Mozart, and Beethoven,[128] and thus brought her to the threshold of his world of art. Hiller contributed a love duet, Spohr a short Lied, and Fanny two Lieder decorated with vignettes by her husband.[129] Felix offered a watercolor of Amalfi (inspired by his 1831 Italian sojourn, **plate 11**), and four compositions, including three Lieder from Op. 34, then being readied for publication, and, appropriately, the *Duet ohne Worte* for piano, Op. 38 No. 6. On the last day of the year, he wrote from Leipzig to Lea of his complete contentment with Cécile and genuine happiness reminiscent of his childhood years.[130]

IV

Early in 1837 Felix put the finishing touches on two new works for Breitkopf & Härtel, the six *Gesänge*, Op. 34, and six Preludes and Fugues for piano, Op. 35. At least four of the songs (Nos. 1, 2, 3, and 5) had been composed before Felix met Cécile, and he now reordered them into a collection on themes of idealized love, separation, and yearning that anticipated the lovers' imminent marriage. To suggest his new familial bonds, Felix dedicated the opus to Cécile's older sister Julie and opened it with a simple, Old German *Minnelied* that G. W. Fink recognized was more appropriate for domestic music making than the concert hall.[131] The text addresses a "tender maiden" whose eyes shine more brightly than the sun. The song must have been a favorite of Cécile; on a copy inserted into her album, Felix appended a note commemorating the evening of December 22, 1836, spent blissfully with the Jeanrenauds in Frankfurt.

Among the other *Gesänge* are two Klingemann settings, a robust *Frühlingslied* (No. 3, Spring Song), with images of swelling buds, and *Sonntagslied* (No. 5, Sunday Song), in which a protagonist hears wedding bells from the solitude of his room. Far and away the most successful songs are two Heine settings (Nos. 2 and 6) and Felix's rendition of one of the *Suleika* poems attributed to Goethe, but now known to be by Marianne von Willemer (No. 4). In December, Fanny had set the same poem for Cécile, which may have inspired Felix to craft his own. Suleika, separated from her lover, implores the moist west wind, depicted by restless arpeggiations in the piano, to convey the message that his love is her life, his presence a joyful feeling (suggested by a turn from E minor to E major). Of the Heine settings, No. 2, *Auf Flügeln des Gesanges* ("On Wings of Song") became Felix's most celebrated song. Here the piano arpeggiations impress as tranquil ripples, as the lilting vocal line transports a beloved to the Ganges and to dreams beneath its shading palm trees. The *Reiselied* (No. 6) also speaks of dreams, in this case deceptive musings. A nocturnal rider gallops to his beloved's house only to be brought back to reality by an oak tree. The dramatic narrative of the horseman, the imagined wind, baying dogs, and reunion with his lover is no more than "a pleasant self-delusion taking place within the framework of a continuous, stormy reality."[132] The energetic opening piano figure, a dissonant, biting chromatic tremolo, serves as musical metaphor for naturalistic tone painting but also the errant imagination of the protagonist (**ex. 10.6**).

Ex. 10.6: Mendelssohn, *Reiselied*, Op. 34 No. 6 (1837)

Der Herbst - wind rüt - telt die Bäu - me, die Nacht ist feucht und kalt;

In the case of Op. 35, Felix produced his most substantial piano work. To create this homage to the *Well-Tempered Clavier*, he first compiled five separate fugues from 1827 to 1835 (Nos. 1–5). Early in 1835 he wrote Thomas Attwood of a plan to dedicate to him a cycle of etudes and fugues[133] and began coupling the fugues with prefatory, etudelike pieces. But by October 1836 Felix had adopted Bach's term, *Praeludium*, and was crafting preludes for the fugues. It appears that he rewrote at least three preludes (Nos. 2, 3, and 6) and left the rejected pieces for posthumous publication as the *Drei Präludien*, Op. 104a.[134] In November 1836 he finished the missing sixth prelude and fugue, and on January 22, 1837, played through the complete set for Schumann.[135]

The decision to preface the fugues with preludes reinforced the Bachian character of the opus, as did perhaps the contribution of a somewhat improbable ally. In March 1836 Felix received the dedication of Carl Czerny's Op. 400, a collection of preludes and fugues with a rather leaden, academic title—*The School of Playing Fugues and of Performing Polyphonic Compositions and of Their Particular Difficulties on the Pianoforte in 24 Grand Exercises*.[136] Here Felix found twelve paired Bachian preludes and fugues, in order of increasing complexity, from two- to three- and four-part writing. Like Czerny, Felix explored Bach's technique of linking individual preludes to fugues by means of motivic and harmonic references. Thus in No. 1, the melodic line of the prelude adumbrates the contours of the fugal subject; and in No. 4, the melodic leap of a fourth in the prelude (E♭–A♭) likewise prepares the return of that interval in the fugue (ex. 10.7a, b). Like Bach, too, Felix arranged his compositions in a tonal plan, though not the traditional pairing of parallel major and minor keys. Instead, Felix devised an innovative scheme alternating between minor and major tonalities, with three sharp keys followed by three flat keys (e–D–b–A♭–f–B♭).

Early reviewers[137] recognized immediately the weight of Felix's debt to Bach, perhaps most evident in No. 1, in which an artful fugue culminates in a chorale with a "walking" bass line imitating an organ pedal part, and thus offers three allusions to the Thomaskantor. The fugue of No. 2, originally for organ, employs a subject that simplifies that of the more ornate Fugue in D from the *Well-Tempered Clavier* I (ex. 10.7c, d). No. 3 offers a learned fugue that presents a neo-baroque subject in its "prime" and inverted forms and then combines the two. And the poignant fifth Prelude, with its throbbing tremolo chords and surprise ending in F major (using the raised third), affords one more reference to the Bachian Baroque.

But all this unabashed historicism represents one side of a dialectic that operates in the opus between the musical past and present. Thus,

Ex. 10.7a: Mendelssohn, Prelude in A♭ major, Op. 35 No. 4 (1836)

Ex. 10.7b: Mendelssohn, Fugue in A♭ major, Op. 35 No. 4 (1835)

Ex. 10.7c: J. S. Bach, Fugue in D major, *Well-Tempered Clavier* I (1722)

Ex. 10.7d: Mendelssohn, Fugue in D major, Op. 35 No. 2 (1835)

Ex. 10.7e: Beethoven, Piano Sonata in A♭ major, Op. 110 (1822), Finale

Ex. 10.7f: Mendelssohn, Prelude in B♭ major, Op. 35 No. 6 (1837)

Ex. 10.7g: Fanny Hensel, *Allegretto grazioso* in B♭ major (1836)

Ex. 10.7h: Fanny Hensel, Andante in B♭ major (1837)

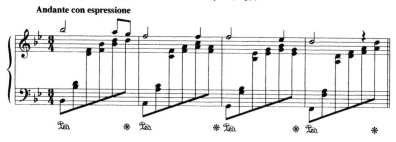

Ex. 10.7i: Mendelssohn, Prelude in E minor, Op. 35 No. 1 (1835)

the fourth fugue, in A♭, draws upon a more recent memory than Bach by alluding to the fugal finale of Beethoven's Piano Sonata. Op. 110 (1822), with which Felix's fugue shares its key and the distinctive feature of an accelerating tempo (ex. 10.7b and 10.7e). Moreover, the original pairing of fugues with etudes encouraged Felix to explore conspicuously "modern" keyboard idioms. For instance, the third prelude, a staccato study that mimics Felix's trademark elfin style, ultimately evaporates in another *pianissimo* conclusion. The lyrical fourth prelude is a *Duett ohne Worte* stylistically akin to Felix's Op. 38 No. 6. Similarly, the sixth prelude has songlike qualities that have more to do with the modern German Lied than Bach's prelusive ruminations. Here Felix produced music rather close to an *Allegretto grazioso* by Fanny in the same key, composed in 1836 (ex. 10.7f, g).[138] Then, on Felix's wedding day, March 28, 1837, Fanny composed an Andante, also in B♭ major, with striking similarities to Felix's prelude (ex. 10.7h).[139] In June, Felix was writing Fanny about the coincidental similarities between the two and thanking her for "your Prelude No. 6 in B♭ major to my Fugue in B♭, for it really is the same inside and out, and delights me by the neat coincidence. Is it not strange that sometimes musical ideas seem to fly around in the air and come to earth here and there?"[140]

Felix's engagement with contemporary piano styles is most evident in the first prelude, conceived as an etude in the so-called three-hand technique, in which he enveloped a melody, sculpted by the two thumbs in the middle register, by "all sorts of arpeggios and artful figurations in the same harmony" (ex. 10.7i).[141] The origins of this harplike device are unclear, but it became associated with the virtuoso Sigismond Thalberg (1812–1871), at the height of his career early in 1837, when he participated in a celebrated musical "duel" with Liszt in Paris.[142] The French cartoonist Jean-Pierre Dantan caricatured Thalberg as a superhuman apparition with ten hands; Thalberg's novel device of thickening keyboard textures caught the fancy of Felix, who used it in an etude in B♭ minor in June 1836 (Op. 104b No. 1), in the presumably contemporaneous E-minor Prelude, and in several other works. Op. 35 thus juxtaposed technical and contrapuntal studies that blended the new and old, and filtered the increasingly outmoded art of fugue through the prism of keyboard modernity and novelty. The goal was not a lifeless reenactment of an earlier age but a revitalization of modern music through exemplary historical models.

V

While the Jeanrenauds planned an elaborate Frankfurt wedding for March, a curious drama played out in Leipzig and Berlin as Felix endeavored to arrange for his mother to meet Cécile and her family. First he proposed the newlyweds travel to Berlin that summer, *after* the wedding. No doubt he was concerned about the strength of Lea's constitution, but perhaps he also remembered her strong opinions about his siblings' engagements. Meanwhile, on January 28 he met Elisabeth and Cécile in Weimar and escorted them back to Leipzig for a visit. Mother and daughter now planned to travel to Berlin, but on February 17 Elisabeth fell ill with influenza. Felix entertained his guests with part-songs written for the Leipzig Liedertafel; and he composed a tender *Gondellied* in A major for piano, with amorous duetlike thirds, presumably for Cécile. In 1841 Schumann published it in a supplement to the *Neue Zeitschrift für Musik*.

At the Gewandhaus, Cécile had ample opportunities to witness Felix in his element. According to Heinrich Brockhaus, her eyes "reflected her joy about the triumphs of her beloved," then in possession of a "rich, great talent, and universally loved and honored."[143] She likely attended a benefit concert on March 6 of the soprano Henriette Grabau, whom Felix accompanied in several of his own songs, Schubert's *Erlkönig*, and Fanny's Hölty setting, *Die Schiffende*.[144] Felix had requested a copy of the last for Cécile's album, and Fanny had obliged. Without his encouragement, she had published the song under her name in an 1836 album[145] and thus embraced official authorship. Still, he thanked her "in the name of the public of Leipzig and elsewhere" for releasing the song "against my wish."[146] The album also contained Felix's duet "Wie kann ich froh und lustig sein?" on a poem by Philipp Kaufmann. Folksonglike, this setting treats a lovers' separation from a feminine point of view: the unnamed protagonist (Cécile) yearns through the winter for her beloved to return during a springtime of renewal. Unlike Felix's Opp. 8 and 9, which had silently assimilated six of Fanny's Lieder under his authorship, the Schlesinger album marked the only occasion when the siblings' music appeared together under their own names.[147]

By early March, Elisabeth had decided to attend the Leipzig premiere of *Paulus* (March 16) in the Paulinerkirche; reversing his earlier view, Felix now urged Lea to visit as soon as possible, before Elisabeth changed her mind and returned to Frankfurt.[148] Braving the winter, Lea arrived on March 8 and finally met Elisabeth and Cécile, whom Schumann described as a "blooming, highly exotic rose."[149] We do not have Lea's reaction to her new relatives, although she appears to have intimidated Elisabeth by looking at her in a "penetrating way."[150] Overshadowing their forming relationship were the preparations for the oratorio, promoted to associate it with Handel's *Israel in Egypt*, which Felix had performed in the same church only months before.

On March 7, the successful London premiere of *St. Paul* under Joseph Surman had occurred at Exeter Hall; now it was Felix's turn to introduce the revised, published version in Germany. Once again the brightly illuminated church filled to capacity as enormous forces presented the work in the spirit of a music festival. Among the three-hundred choristers was W. A. Lampadius, author of an early biography of the composer, who reminisced, "Mendelssohn understood as no other director has how to enlist his singers' whole enthusiasm; it was owing to his splendid leading that we accomplished such marvels in the crescendo, diminuendo, whispered tones and the like."[151] In the *Allgemeine musikalische Zeitung* Gottfried Fink published a glowing report and deferred a critical appraisal for later.[152] But in the *Neue Zeitschrift für Musik*, Robert Schumann went considerably further.[153] As it happened, a few weeks after the performance, on April 9, came the Leipzig premiere of Meyerbeer's French grand opera *Les Huguenots*; Schumann seized on the two works as the most significant of his time and illustrative of diametrically opposed tendencies. While the oratorio began with the chorale *Wachet auf* as a symbol of the apostle's Christian awakening, Meyerbeer's work opened with the Lutheran chorale *Ein' feste Burg* (*A Mighty Fortress Is Our God*) as the rallying call of the French Huguenots, persecuted by the Catholics during the St. Bartholomew's Massacre (1572). But Meyerbeer's colorful score earned Schumann's reproving rebuke for what he regarded as crass musical sensationalism. The work played alternately "in the brothel and in church," and the bloodiest episode in the history of Protestantism was "degraded to the level of a farce at a fair for the purpose of raising money and applause." The consecration of the swords in the fourth act before the massacre amounted to a "revamped *Marseillaise*" that confirmed Meyerbeer's "motto"—"to strike dumb or to titillate."[154]

In contrast, *Paulus* offered a "verdant landscape" of palm trees, where one could turn to "faith and hope" and once more "love mankind." Schumann recognized the oratorio was the effort of a "young master," and he alluded to certain controversial issues—e.g., the use of chorales, the revelation of Christ to Saul on the road to Damascus by a female choir, the concentration of the dramatic action in the first part, and the depiction of Paul as a "convert rather than a converter."[155] But he left no doubt about his positive judgment of the work, and praised it in an overflowing sentence for its "deep religious feeling," its "masterly musical perfection, its prevailing lyricism of the most noble kind, the marriage of word and tone, of language and music, which cause the depths to wax eloquent—the charming grouping of figures, the grace that seems to have been breathed over the work, the freshness, the indelible colorfulness of the instrumentation, the perfectly articulate style, not to mention the masterly play with all forms of composition."[156] Felix was the prophet of a "glorious future"; his path led to happiness, that of Meyerbeer, to evil.

VI

In 1836 and 1837 *Paulus* entered a crowded field. The production of nineteenth-century German oratorios was at its zenith, with manifold examples by Friedrich Schneider (*Das Weltgericht, The Last Judgment,* 1819), Louis Spohr (*Die letzten Dinge, The Last Judgment,* 1826; and *Des Heilands letzte Stunden, The Savior's Last Hours,* 1835), Carl Loewe (several, including *Die Zerstörung von Jerusalem, The Destruction of Jerusalem,* 1829), and others disseminated through burgeoning, popular choral societies.[157] Between 1824 and 1835, three German composers—Eduard Grell, Heinrich Elkamp, and Carl Loewe—fabricated oratorios about St. Paul. Though they rapidly fell into oblivion, Felix's first oratorio quickly became an international symbol of the revival of the genre. A host of factors explains its extraordinary popularity, ultimately eclipsed only by *Elijah.* First of all, oratorios were compatible with Restoration politics: they supported the new social stability after Napoleon and the emergence of a new German nationalism. As we have seen, Felix was centrally involved with the revival of Bach and Handel, and *Paulus* was understood to descend from these authoritative staples of the old musical order: "The work is so manifestly Handelian, Bachian, and Mendelssohnian," G. W. Fink wrote, "that it appears as if it really exists to facilitate our contemporaries' receptivity to the profundities of these recognized tone-heroes...."[158] In effect, Felix's oratorio offered a blend of historicism and contemporary musical idioms, of baroque chorales and fugues with modern orchestration suffused with a Lied-like lyricism, that popularized the complexities and severities of Bach and Handel for a newly empowered, middle-class musical culture. *Paulus* was a concerted attempt to solve, in Abraham's words, the "problem of combining ancient conceptions with modern appliances."[159]

By performing the work in St. Paul's (University) Church, Felix underscored the distinctly Christian message of his oratorio. The story of the apostate Saul turned apostle Paul and his miraculous conversion from Judaism to Christianity had appealed to Abraham, intent upon distancing his family from his father's faith. By heeding Abraham's encouragement

338 ✦ THE ROAD TO DAMASCUS

Ex. 10.8a: J. S. Bach, St. Matthew Passion, Part II, No. 39 (1729)

Ex. 10.8b: Mendelssohn, *Paulus*, Op. 36 (1836), No. 4

to complete the oratorio, Felix fell into the position of embracing scriptures harshly critical of traditional Judaism. In a painstaking analysis of
Felix's libretto drafts, Jeffrey Sposato has shown how the composer did
little to soften the negative, stereotypical depiction of the Jews in his
first oratorio (ten years later, in *Elijah*, his theological stance would change
considerably).[160] Of several examples we can adduce, three stand out. In
No. 4,[161] for the false testimony against Stephen (Acts 6:11), Felix devised
a wooden imitative passage that mimicked the mocking counterpoint
of the false witnesses against Jesus in Bach's St. Matthew Passion (**ex.
10.8**). In both works the Jews appear bound by strictures rather than the
spirit of their laws. Similarly, the *turba* (crowd) scenes surrounding the
stoning of Stephen (Nos. 5, 6, and 8) and in Part II the persecution of
Paul (Nos. 28 and 29) recall the highly charged, dissonant choruses in
Bach's Passions before the Crucifixion. And finally, in Stephen's impassioned speech to the Sanhedrin (Acts 7), the martyr's recitative spills
over into a turbulent Allegro for "Ye hard of heart! Ye always do resist
the Holy Ghost."

From the earliest stages of work on *Paulus*, Felix seems to have regarded it as confirming his own Protestant faith; in 1831, he announced
to Klingemann that the work would form a sermon (*Predigt*).[162] The
completion of the oratorio and its successful reception were critical steps
toward achieving Abraham's cherished agendum—full assimilation of
his family into Prussian society. But ironically the very success of the
oratorio—Lampadius, commenting on its rapid recognition, labeled 1837
and 1838 the *Paulusjahre* in music history[163]—was met with prejudice at

mid-century from those prepared neither to recognize Felix's conversion nor to accept him as standing at the forefront of German music. Thus, the Christian Felix fell victim to anti-Semitism, even though he "was willing to pay the price of assimilation."[164]

The overarching theme of the oratorio—the Christian awakening of Paul and his missionary work—plays out in a series of crescendo-like intensifications operating throughout the composition. We can identify as examples four broadly applied styles and techniques, two of which, the chorale and fugue, emerge already in the overture as unifying structural devices. The five chorales Felix selected, all familiar emblems of collective Protestant worship from the sixteenth and seventeenth centuries, enhance the sermonlike quality of the work and articulate its essential dramatic segments. According to Klingemann, the chorales serve as "resting points" and remind us of the Greek chorus, "pointing . . . from the individual occurrence to the general law, and diffusing a calmness through the whole."[165] They include, in Part 1, *Wachet auf* (Overture), *Allein Gott in der Höh' sei Ehr* (No. 3), *Dir, Herr, dir will ich mich ergeben* (No. 9), a repetition of *Wachet auf* (No. 16), and, in Part 2, *O Jesu Christe, wahres Licht* (No. 29) and *Wir glauben all' an einen Gott* (No. 36). Notably, the chorales appear in scorings and settings designed to reinforce the idea of *Steigerung* (intensification). Thus, they range from the wordless, instrumental chorale of the Overture, which uses only part of the melody of *Wachet auf*, to homophonic choral settings, more complex settings with instrumental interludes (the return of *Wachet auf* in No. 16, now complete with text and intervening, bright brass fanfares anticipating the return of Saul's sight; and No. 29, fitted with instrumental interludes in imitative style), and, finally, as the climactic culmination, the Lutheran Credo *Wir glauben all'* (No. 36) to suggest the Paulinian doctrine of justification by faith alone, which Felix presents as part of a complex chorale fugue.

Steigerung informs too his use of fugues and fugal passages, a factor in eight of the forty-five numbers of the oratorio. The partial presentation of *Wachet auf* in the Overture gives way to an energetic four-part fugue in A minor on a subject derived from the opening of the chorale (ex. 10.9a, b). Dissonant in character, the fugue symbolizes Saul's struggle for spiritual reawakening, leading to a culminating juxtaposition of the fugue and chorale. In Nos. 2 and 15 fugal passages accompany verses from Acts ("The Heathen furiously rage, Lord") and Isaiah ("Behold, now, total darkness covereth the kingdoms"), while in No. 20 Saul's aria ("I praise Thee, O Lord, my God," Psalm 86) introduces a choral fugue that suggests a meditative recasting of the fugal subject from the overture (ex. 10.10). Then, in the concluding number of Part 1, Felix intensifies

Ex. 10.9a: Mendelssohn, *Paulus*, Op. 36 (1836), Overture

Ex. 10.9b: Mendelssohn, *Paulus*, Op. 36 (1836), Overture

Ex. 10.10: Mendelssohn, *Paulus*, Op. 36 (1836), No. 20

his fugal applications by crafting a double fugue on verses from Romans. The protracted "Amen," which introduces the second subject, and the uplifting, compact entries of the first ("Sing His glory for evermore") betray the influence of Handel, as do word paintings for "O great is the depth of the riches of wisdom and knowledge of the Father," the expansive exordium that prefaces the fugue. A final stage of contrapuntal intensification is achieved in Part 2, which begins and ends with fugues (Nos. 23 and 45), and includes two five-part double fugues (Nos. 23 and 36). Of these, No. 36 combines five-part counterpoint with the Lutheran chorale *Wir glauben all' an einen Gott*, and thus returns us to the genre of the chorale fugue, with which the oratorio begins.

Two other techniques—the accelerando and crescendo—support the effect of intensification in directly perceptible ways. Several numbers employ shifts toward faster tempi, including the Overture and No. 22, cast as accelerando fugues. No. 6, Stephen's defense, progresses from *Andante sostenuto* to *Andante, Allegro,* and *Allegro molto*. Preparing these shifts is a refrainlike phrase sung by Stephen at progressively higher transpositions (ex. 10.11). Similarly, several numbers employ dramatic crescendi, as in the broad orchestral passages that introduce the chorus "Rise up! Arise! Rise and shine!" (No. 15) and the soprano recitative "And there fell from his eyes like as though it were scales" (No. 21) that announces the restoration of Saul's sight. In a related technique, Felix augments the orchestra with the organ at crucial structural points to suggest crescendo-like expansions.

Ex. 10.11: Mendelssohn, *Paulus*, Op. 36 (1836), No. 6

A - ber sie ver - nah - men es nicht

Each part of *St. Paul* subdivides into three dramatic segments: in Part 1, the martyrdom of Stephen (Nos. 4–9), Saul on the road to Damascus (Nos. 10–16), and the restoration of his sight and baptism in Damascus (Nos. 17–22); in Part 2, the commissioning of Paul and his preaching with Barnabas among the Jews (Nos. 23–29), Paul and Barnabas among the Gentiles (Nos. 30–36), and Paul's departure from the Ephesians (Nos. 37–45). An initial complex including the first chorus and chorale *Allein Gott in der Höh' sei Ehr* (Nos. 2–3) introduces us to the early Christian community and, like the "opening prayers of a religious service, in which the audience is a congregation,"[166] enhances the sermonizing quality of the whole. The story of Stephen unfolds principally through a series of recitatives, divided between a soprano narrator and a tenor part for the martyr and accompanied by the orchestra. Although the use of the *testo* derives from Bach's Passions, not infrequently the recitatives take on a modern, songlike quality, as in Stephen's plea, "Lord! Lay not this sin to their charge." The chorus now becomes the *turba* in a series of increasingly dissonant responses to Stephen's vigorous defense. Interrupting the drama is the first aria, No. 7, for soprano ("Jerusalem! Jerusalem! Thou that killest the prophets"), which links the stoning of Stephen to Christ's prophetic words in Matthew 23:37. Here Felix departs from baroque models to produce a meditative Lied that became a staple of Victorian parlor-room music making. Its gently percussive triplets (♩♩♩) adumbrate the militant figure of the following *turba* chorus (♫♫), "Stone him to death."

The second section presents Saul of Tarsus as a zealous persecutor of the Christians in the "rage" aria No. 12, "Consume them all, Lord Sabaoth," on texts from the Psalms. The emotional and spiritual high point of the oratorio follows in No. 14— Saul's blinding revelation on the road to Damascus. Introduced by a tenor recitative, a female chorus delivers Christ's words ("Saul! Why persecut'st thou me?") in a scoring that cost Felix considerable effort and controversy. Schubring informs us that Felix rejected the idea of employing a "very powerful bass voice" and instead originally intended the passage for a soprano solo. When Schubring countered with the idea of a four-part mixed chorus, Felix responded, "Yes, and the worthy theologians would cut me up nicely for wishing to deny and supplant Him who arose from the dead."[167] Whether or not Felix also considered Louis Spohr's preference, a strong male choir to convey the shattering impact of Christ's intervention,[168] is unknown. Felix's solution, a four-part female chorus, prompted criticism from G. W. Fink, who "wanted the *vox humana* to be omitted entirely, and only indefinite sounds of the trombone heard."[169] Accompanied by softly repeated chords in the brass and high winds, the result produces a strikingly ethereal, otherworldly effect as the divine message descends from on high.

Having fallen to the earth, Saul now "rises" as an orchestral crescendo emanating from the bass register ushers in the majestic chorus "Rise! Up! Arise!" (No. 15, Isaiah 60), and the chorale *Wachet auf* reappears (No. 16). In the third section of Part 1 the blind Saul, having journeyed to Damascus, encounters Ananias, sent by an angel to restore his sight (No. 19; the music recalls Christ's appearance in No. 14). Saul sings two contemplative arias on Psalm texts. No. 18 ("O God, have mercy"), in B minor, forms a pendant to his earlier rage aria, while No. 20 ("I praise thee, O Lord my God") is a hymn of praise that prompts the choral response "The Lord, He is good." A dramatic recitative (No. 21) relates the laying on of hands by Ananias, the restoration of Saul's sight, and his baptism. The majestic chorus "O great is the depth" (No. 22) ponders the unfathomable divine mysteries as Part 1 concludes.

Part 2 commences with a large-scale chorus on verses from Revelation. The idea of spiritual discovery, and the purpose of Paul's missionary work, is conveyed through the celebratory fugue "For all the Gentiles come before Thee, and shall worship Thy name." Its subject (**ex. 10.12**) revives the centuries-old psalm formula used by Mozart in the *Jupiter* Symphony, and is thus one more example of Felix's efforts to tether his oratorio firmly to historical tradition. Paul and Barnabas as ambassadors of Christ is the subject of two, pastoral-like numbers in G major, the duet No. 25 and chorus No. 26. Counterbalancing them are the two dissonant *turba* choruses, Nos. 28 and 29, in which the Jews reject their proselytizing efforts.

In the central portion of Part 2 Paul announces his intention to preach to the Gentiles. The duet No. 31 ("For so hath the Lord Himself commanded, behold, I have made thee a light to the Gentiles") revives the "Jupiter" motive of the opening fugue, before the dramatic action resumes in No. 32, as Paul heals the lame man of Lystra. There follows a

Ex. 10.12: Mendelssohn, *Paulus*, Op. 36 (1836), No. 23

group of three numbers (33–35), into which Felix insinuated the "most delicate fragrance of classical Hellenism."[170] The Gentiles now offer sacrifices to Paul and Barnabas as Mercury and Jupiter, and in No. 35 sing a disarmingly naive chorus; presumably Felix crafted its unidentified text ("O be gracious ye Immortals! Heed our sacrifice with favor!"), not drawn from the Bible. Rending his garments, Paul rejects the false idols, for "God dwelleth not in temples made with hands." At this point the chorus responds with the fugue "But our God abideth in Heaven" (No. 36), the climax of which is the appearance of the Lutheran chorale *Wir glauben all'*. Here the sophisticated counterpoint and dense textures seem calculated to revive something of the grandeur and complexity of the opening chorus of the St. Matthew Passion.

The concluding section of the oratorio begins with the assault of the Jews and Gentiles upon the apostles. The last *turba* chorus (No. 38) literally recalls music from No. 8 and thus completes Paul's spiritual trajectory from a persecutor of the Christians to a persecuted Christian. In the final numbers the dramatic element recedes more and more into the background in favor of deliberative music that reflects on his life's work. Thus, Felix carries the account of Paul in Acts only to his departure from Ephesus and omits his return to Jerusalem, imprisonment and transfer to Caesarea, and final journey to Rome. Instead, Paul's imminent journey is compared to Christ's return to Jerusalem and crucifixion. A pensive, sparsely scored chorus (No. 42) cites Peter's response in St. Matthew after Christ predicts the Crucifixion: "Far be it from thy path! These things shall not be unto thee!" The final recitative (No. 44) brings closure with the well-known verses from Paul's second epistle to Timothy, "I have fought a good fight, I have finished my course, I have kept the faith," and leads directly to the concluding chorus (No. 45), which crowns the oratorio with a brisk fugue of praise to the Lord (Psalm 103).

Scholars have debated whether Felix intended *St. Paul* as concert music, "imaginary" or, indeed, in some sense "real" church music, thereby reversing the historical progression by which the baroque oratorio had left the oratory of the church for the concert hall.[171] Certainly the incorporation of familiar Protestant chorales and devotional, prayerlike arias (regarded by later critics as overly sentimental) contribute to a pervading mystique of Christian piety. Among Felix's articles of musical faith was his father's notion that "every room in which Sebastian Bach is sung is transformed into a church."[172] By using Bachian models in *St. Paul*, and, indeed, by linking Stephen and Paul to Christ's words in St. Matthew, Felix probably viewed his oratorio as a modern rumination about Bach's immortal Passion. *St. Paul*, the work that launched Felix as a truly international celebrity, also dispatched his deeply felt sense of filial obligation to his father. Abraham's agendum of assimilation was now triumphantly achieved, or so it seemed, in a major oratorio whose subject matter treated symbolically his family's spiritual journey. The apostle's voice thus resonated on several levels—to a German Restoration public intent upon discovering nationalist, cultural symbols, to a German Protestant community reaffirming its religious roots, and to a twenty-eight-year-old composer tapping into the wellspring of Protestant music and seeking his own spiritual growth.

Part III

Elijah's Chariot

Chapter 11
1837–1839

Musical Biedermeier

"After all, I prefer the German Philistine, with his
nightcap and tobacco."[1]

Palm Sunday 1837 (March 19) found Felix returning with Elisabeth and
Cécile to Frankfurt, little more than a week before the wedding. In the
expiring days of his bachelorhood, he nervously awaited the delivery of
documents, including a certification he was "unusable" (*unbrauchbar*)
for the Prussian military service. On the 23rd papers finally arrived from
Konrad Schleinitz in Leipzig attesting Felix was neither a vagabond nor
already married.[2] Five days later, several flower-festooned barouches arrived at the French Reformed Church. Chains were drawn across the
Allée to restrain curious onlookers. Inside the sanctuary, the Frankfurt
elite witnessed Auguste Jeanrenaud's successor, Pastor Paul Joseph Appia,
perform the wedding ceremony in French at 11:00 A.M. and preach a sermon on Psalm 92: "It is a good thing to give thanks unto the Lord, and to
sing praises unto thy name, O Most High; to show forth thy loving kind-
ness in the morning, and thy faithfulness every night, upon an instrument of ten strings, and upon the psaltery; upon the harp with a solemn
sound."

Declaring Felix and Cécile's marriage "an unceasing song in praise
of the Lord" (*une continuelle louange à la gloire du Seigneur*), Appia acknowledged their lives were "destined to be untroubled by the material
needs and interests which govern those of most men and women." Art
would embellish their union, Felix would use his genius to "influence
beneficially" Cécile's soul, and Cécile, stirred by memories of her father
and grandfather, would adopt the "incorruptible purity of a tranquil
and gentle heart which is of great value in the eyes of God."[3] The music

included an organ work by Felix, perhaps the processional envisioned
for Fanny's 1829 wedding. Then the carriages returned to the Fahrtor for
a reception and dinner in a grand room overlooking the Main. To greet
the newlyweds, Ferdinand Hiller composed a festive wedding song. At
5:30 P.M. Felix and Cécile departed for Mainz on their honeymoon in a
new blue and brown carriage.

Most of these details come from *Le mariage de Mendelssohn*, published in 1937 by a descendant of the Souchays, Jacques Petitpierre, to
mark the event's centenary. We cannot confirm his entire, euphoric account; although a transcript of Appia's sermon is preserved,[4] none of
Felix's surviving letters describes the ceremony. The only Mendelssohn
to represent Felix seems to have been Dorothea Schlegel; no immediate
family member attended. We might read much into his mother's and
siblings' absence, although the reasons are not difficult to ascertain. Lea
was still in ill health and could not make the journey, Paul was acquiring
a bank in Hamburg,[5] and Rebecka and Fanny were pregnant (late in March,
Fanny would suffer her second miscarriage).[6]

In Mainz, where more than a thousand years before Boniface had
consolidated the conversion of Germanic tribes to Christianity, Felix
and Cécile spent their wedding night at the Rheinischer Hof, an elegant
hotel with a balcony overlooking the Rhine. Their accommodations were
considerably less satisfactory at Worms, site of Luther's defense of his
teachings at the Diet of 1521. The inclement weather, too, did not cooperate, but in their wedding diary Cécile recorded there was "one agreeable thing which I will refrain from mentioning!"[7] Farther up the Rhine,
at Speyer, they climbed to the gallery of the Romanesque cathedral. She
sketched the Heidenturm, last remnant of the town's medieval wall, while
Felix turned to organ music. He tried out an instrument, probably at the
Protestant Trinity Church, which Cécile dismissed as a "wretched box of
whistles,"[8] and between April 2 and 6 quickly drafted three preludes.
After pairing them with earlier fugues in the same keys,[9] he later dedicated the collection in 1837 to Thomas Attwood as the *Drei Praeludien
und Fugen* Op. 37—the first significant contribution to the organ repertoire since its steep decline after the monuments of J. S. Bach.

Like its counterpart for piano (Op. 35), Op. 37 offers in part an uncompromising return to the German baroque and its rigorous counterpoint. Thus the first prelude, with its undisturbed pedal points and gentle
trochaic rhythms, suggests a pastoral, while the second fugue, animated
with leaps and in compound meter, exudes the character of a baroque
gigue and revives the Thomaskantor's favored association of that dance
with erudite counterpoint. The subject of the third fugue, with its dis-

Ex. 11.1a: Mendelssohn, Fugue in D minor, Op. 37 No. 3 (1833)

Ex. 11.1b: J. S. Bach, Fugue in B♭ minor, *Well-Tempered Clavier* I (1722)

Ex. 11.1c: Beethoven, Piano Sonata in C minor, Op. 111 (1822)

tinctive pause and expressive ascending ninth, traces its parentage to the antepenultimate fugue of the *Well-Tempered Clavier*, Book I (ex. 11.1a, b). Still, as in Op. 35 and *St. Paul*, fidelity to baroque models informs only part of Op. 37, in which Felix juxtaposed Bachian traits with modern expression. Thus, songlike elements permeate the second prelude, and the improvisatory characters of the first and third evince a certain formal freedom. The third prelude, regulated by distinct rhythmic shifts from eighth notes to triplets and sixteenths, reveals cadenza-like passages that anticipate the first movement of his second piano concerto, Op. 40 in D minor, begun during his honeymoon. The Bachian third fugue also recalls the fugal subject of Beethoven's final piano sonata, Op. 111 (**ex. 11.1c**), though its energetic anacrusis has fallen by the wayside, leaving a subject more subdued and reflective.

In Strasbourg, where the newlyweds arrived on April 8 after crossing the French border, Felix explored the magnificent Gothic Minster, with its lacelike, open tower penetrated by the blue sky. The organ (1713–1716) was an imposing instrument, with three manuals, thirty-nine stops, and thirty-two-foot pipes, the culminating opus of the Alsatian builder Andreas Silbermann. In the unheated sanctuary Felix played with "blue hands" and "chattering teeth."[10] The wedding diary contains his new impressions of Abraham's favorite country, and the culinary "*charmes*" of Strasbourg—roquefort, potage à la Julienne, and omelette soufflée. Within a few days, Felix and Cécile recrossed the border and reached Freiburg im Breisgau.

Here, on the edge of the romantic Black Forest, they paused for three weeks. In the surrounding countryside they visited an old Carthusian monastery, the paper mills built along the waters of the Dreisam, and the dramatic scenery of the Höllenthal (Valley of Hell), with its precipitous rock walls punctuated by waterfalls. To alleviate Elisabeth Jeanrenaud's fear that the exertion was too great for Cécile, the newlyweds wrote pacifying letters; Felix assured Elisabeth "there is no trace of illness or weakness in her entire being."[11] The lovers had their first quarrel when Felix flirted with a peasant woman; he apologized by playing Cécile's favorite piano pieces and gathered for her bouquets of violets. His floral offering inspired an affectionate *Allegretto* in A major for piano, a symbol of domestic consonance, with the soprano and tenor voices singing together in harmony.[12] Around this time, Felix accepted an invitation to direct the Birmingham Musical Festival in September, and in anticipation he began to teach Cécile English.[13]

The honeymoon diary, published in a meticulously documented edition by Peter Ward Jones, chronicles not only these domestic affairs but also Felix's ability to envision several compositions simultaneously. Thus in April he sketched a string quartet (Op. 44 No. 2, in E minor) and the opening chorus of Psalm 42 (Op. 42), and gathered ideas for a new piano concerto for Birmingham. He also put the finishing touches on the third installment of his *Lieder ohne Worte*, Op. 38, forwarded to Simrock on April 25.[14] As with Opp. 19b and 30, Felix culled together the new volume from separately composed Lieder, at least four of which were in place before the honeymoon. He finished the final piece, No. 5 in A minor, in Speyer on April 5.[15] Emphasizing again the feminine, domestic quality of the opus, Felix dedicated it to a daughter of Otto von Woringen, Rosa. (At least three Lieder were originally gifts for women: No. 2, for the soprano Henriette Grabau;[16] No. 3, for Clara Wieck; and No. 6, the "duet" for Cécile, in which, as Schumann noted, a pair of lovers conversed "softly, intimately, and trustfully.")[17]

Though Felix titled only the sixth Lied (*Duetto*), Julius Schubring did not hesitate to speculate about the extramusical meanings of other pieces. In particular, he ascribed to the fourth, part-songlike Lied in A major a certain "comfortableness" (*Behaglichkeit*) and imagined it originated after Felix's wedding as an expression of marital contentment (Felix disabused his friend by revealing that the piece preceded his engagement).[18] As for the duet, Schubring observed tongue in cheek that the woman had the final say in the closing bars but then modified his opinion—her closing phrase was rather an echo of the masculine motive, to which she ultimately deferred. Another piece that might have aroused Schubring's extramusical musings, No. 5, exceeded his abilities as a pianist. It stands out for its compound meter $\frac{12}{8}$, agitated syncopations, insistent repeated pitches, and dramatic crescendi and pedal points. It has, in short, all the markings of a narrative-like ballade,[19] with its text suppressed. Felix owned a copy of the *Première Ballade* in G minor of his friend Chopin (Op. 23), the first composer to apply the term to a piano composition; indeed, when that work appeared in 1836, G. W. Fink labeled it a *Ballade ohne Worte*.[20] But Op. 38 No. 5 impresses more as a response to Schubert's texted ballade *Erlkönig*. The static, reiterated pitches, rising bass figures, and opening motive recurring like a refrain throughout the composition (ex. 11.2a, b) conjure up the nocturnal ride in Schubert's masterpiece, performed by Felix with Henriette Grabau on March 6, only a month before he composed the *Lied ohne Worte*.

From Freiburg Felix and Cécile proceeded to Heidelberg, where they spent a week (May 7–13) visiting the bride's cousins, including the lawyer and amateur organist Fritz Schlemmer, who entertained Felix on the instrument in the Heiliggeistkirche. There were walks along the serpentine Philosophenweg across the Neckar River and a visit to the castle on the Königstuhl, partly in ruins from lightning and French efforts in the seventeenth century to blow it up. Felix rekindled his friendship with Justus Thibaut, whom he had met ten years before. With Schlemmer the newlyweds made an excursion to Mannheim, where the men seem to have overindulged in champagne. Then, heeding Elisabeth's summons, they returned to Frankfurt on May 13.

Ex. 11.2a: Mendelssohn, *Lied ohne Worte*, Op. 38 No. 5 (1837)

Ex. 11.2b: Schubert, *Erlkönig* (1815)

I

Their social calendar was full. Alexander Mendelssohn and his family arrived from Berlin, and Felix conversed with the crown prince of Sweden, the future Oscar I, who later accepted the dedication of Felix's Op. 44 string quartets. With Hiller, who performed *Paulus* twice at the Cäcilienverein in May, Felix resumed daily meetings. Verkenius arrived from Cologne, and from Leipzig Sterndale Bennett, who had just published his Piano Sonata in F minor, Op. 13, dedicated to Felix. The eccentric Swiss composer Xaver Schnyder von Wartensee (1786–1868), accomplished on several instruments, including the glass harmonica, entertained the couple with mathematical magic squares.[21] Beethoven's former pupil Ferdinand Ries, Felix's rival in the Lower Rhine Music Festivals, read through his new oratorio, *Die Könige in Israël*, based upon the account of Saul and David in I Samuel. The newlyweds were not impressed: Cécile dismissed Ries as a "desiccated clover leaf."[22]

Of his own work, Felix finished the String Quartet, Op. 44 No. 2, sketched Psalm 42, and began the String Quartet, Op. 44 No. 3. But the arrival of Cécile's grandmother, the matronly Hélène Elisabeth Souchay, interrupted the halcyon days, for she decided to renovate the Fahrtor. The dust and noise disturbed Felix's inspiration, which flagged in the middle of his new piano concerto for England; "it is a misery," he informed Klingemann, "with the piano and its 100,000 little notes."[23] Seeking escape, he returned with Cécile on June 7 to Krontal, the site of their engagement. Commemorating the visit, Cécile entered in the diary that "new, young life has come to the trees and meadows, and also to her who today stood beneath them,"[24] and confirmed she was pregnant. The couple determined that Felix would travel alone to England in August, though the death of William IV on June 20 initially jeopardized the festival.

Meanwhile, Felix endeavored to deal with two sensitive family issues. The first concerned Fanny's continuing aspirations to publish her music. On June 7 Lea pressed him for assistance: "For about a year she's been composing many excellent works, especially for the piano. . . . That *you* haven't requested and encouraged her to do it—this alone holds her back. Wouldn't it therefore be appropriate for you to encourage her and help her find a publisher?"[25] But Felix replied firmly that authorship implied a "series of works, one after the other," for which Fanny had "neither inclination nor vocation"; she was now too much the *Hausfrau* to justify exposing her to public scrutiny. If Fanny chose this course of her own volition, he of course would support her, but "to encourage something that I do not consider right, that I cannot do."[26] Rather disingenuously—he had already sent positive comments to Fanny about her piano pieces—he asked Lea to share his views neither with his sister nor Wilhelm.

Sebastian Hensel, ever the perfect bourgeois, later glossed over the issue in *The Mendelssohn Family*; his mother, who "had herself no desire to appear in print, and had yielded only to please her husband, readily gave up the idea."[27] But the evidence of her manuscripts does not necessarily support this assertion. At some point, probably during the winter of 1837, Fanny took the trouble to prepare a fair copy of ten piano pieces composed since the spring of 1836.[28] Not only does the revised order suggest a coordinated scheme of key relationships but the individual movements appear with numbers, as if she envisioned a coherent group of pieces. Moreover, the manuscript bears markings of staff and page breaks, as if an engraver tinkered with the manuscript to prepare it for publication. Possibly, Fanny intended to print privately some copies for her friends, but she may have responded to an initiative from Schlesinger, after the successful publication of her song *Die Schiffende*.

Many of Fanny's pieces replicate unabashedly the refined lyricism of Felix's *Lieder ohne Worte*, but there are also supple, original turns of phrase and adventuresome harmonic progressions that move effortlessly between sharp and flat keys. *Cantilena*-like treble lines predominate, though a few technically more demanding pieces impress as etudes. And the collection ends with a spirited Capriccio in F♯ minor, the only titled work of the set. Its principal subject patently derives from Felix's *Scherzo a capriccio* in the same key (**ex. 11.3a, b**). For some reason, Fanny abandoned the project of publishing her work until 1846, when she elected to release only the second piece, an Andante in G major, as the first of the four piano Lieder, Op. 2. In 1837, she was not yet ready to break free of Felix's "demonic" influence.

From Alexander Mendelssohn Felix learned of a second family issue, the hurt he had caused his sisters by not bringing his bride to Berlin to meet them. To repair the damage, he sent mollifying letters to Rebecka and Fanny but a few days later received Fanny's regrets that it was "no

Ex. 11.3a: Fanny Hensel, Capriccio in F♯ minor (1837)

Ex. 11.3b: Mendelssohn, *Scherzo a capriccio* in F♯ minor (1835)

longer possible to see Cécile as a girl."[29] Matters were not helped by Felix's decision, after some seven weeks in Frankfurt, to accompany Elisabeth, Cécile, and her sister Julie on an extended summer holiday to Bingen before he departed for England and returned to the Gewandhaus in the fall, which effectively barred Cécile from meeting her relatives that year.

For nearly a month (July 5 through August 2) the four tourists explored the environs of Bingen, where the cloistered twelfth-century Benedictine abbess Hildegard had recorded her mystical prophecies and produced hagiographic and scientific tracts, poetry, and monophony. At Eibingen near Rüdesheim, Felix sketched the ruins of a convent founded by Hildegard and encountered an old nun caring for the moldering graves. The *Mäuseturm* (Mouse Tower), on an island in the Rhine just north of Bingen, prompted another, fanciful drawing, this one of Hatto, tenth-century Bishop of Mainz, being devoured by mice after he had imprisoned the destitute during a famine in a barn and set it afire.[30] West of Bingen Felix and Cécile followed a challenging path to the pilgrimage site of the Rochuskapelle, where, in 1820, the boy Felix had played the organ inside the chapel. Morning sickness restricted Cécile's activities; the athletic Felix swam across the Rhine, but on one occasion evidently suffered cramps and had to be rescued by boatmen.[31] Felix and Cécile socialized with Gottfried and Wilhelm Schadow and attended a ball at Bad Kreuznach with Franz Bernus, a wealthy Frankfurt senator and merchant, and his wife, Marie. For her birthday (July 13) Cécile made a floral garland, and Felix composed the tender song *Die Freundin*, on verses ascribed to Goethe but in fact by Marianne von Willemer.[32] Felix may have intended the Capriccio for piano in E minor, Op. 118, finished on July 11,[33] for Franz Bernus; it comprises a nocturne-like Andante in E major coupled to an energetic, masculine sonata-form movement in the minor.

More imposing projects now stimulated Felix's imagination. Since breaking off work on *Pervonte* in 1835, he had continued to search for an opera libretto; he corresponded with J. P. Lyser, the Frankfurt *Theater-repetitor* Karl Gollmick and the light dramatist Karl von Holtei, who determined that Felix's judgment was "much too acute" for him ever to secure a libretto.[34] In February 1837 Felix had asked Klingemann to prepare a libretto for a new oratorio about Elijah.[35] But impatient by July, Felix turned to Schubring for assistance with a new oratorio for the Lower Rhine Music Festival at Düsseldorf, scheduled for Pentecost 1839. Felix envisioned coupling *St. Paul* with a pendant work about St. Peter, so as to "bring the two chief apostles and pillars of the Christian Church side by side in oratorios," and again focus on the "outpouring of the Holy Ghost, which must form the central point, or chief object."[36]

Early in August 1837 Felix's party proceeded to Coblenz, at the confluence of the Rhine and Mosel. Near St. Goarshausen upstream, they marveled at the echo effects of the Lorelei and took in the scenic views of the Rhine, its surrounding hills articulated by a patchwork of vineyards and studded with medieval castles. By crossing a bridge of boats at Coblenz, they reached Ehrenbreitstein, where they stayed at the Weisses Ross (White Steed).[37] From there they traversed the short distance to Horchheim and made nearly daily visits to the estate of Felix's uncle and aunt, Joseph and Henriette Mendelssohn. On Joseph's birthday (August 15), Felix played a river god in a dramatic skit. He now found leisure time to finish the orchestral score of his new piano concerto and the motet *Laudate pueri*, completing Op. 39, which appeared in 1838.

Felix's party proceeded by steamer on August 16 to Bonn, where he read through Czerny's duet arrangements of the *Lieder ohne Worte* and learned of Schelble's death. The next day the travelers visited the Cologne Cathedral, unfinished after construction had ceased in the sixteenth century and yet an enduring symbol of the Gothic Revival. Pausing for a week in Düsseldorf, they enjoyed an exhibition of the Akademie painters, and Felix received from Julius Rietz the exemplar of *St. Paul* illustrated by his friends. Eduard Steinbrück drew Felix's portrait, and Felix read the *Kreutzer* Sonata with Rietz; an inquisitive creature, either a mouse or spider, joined the spellbound audience and somewhat upstaged Beethoven's dramatic music.[38] From the deck of a steamer bound for Nijmegen on August 24, Felix watched Cécile wave goodbye from the dock, then saw only her white handkerchief, and finally "nothing more."

II

At Rotterdam on the morning of August 26 he embarked on the *Attwood*, the vessel that had conveyed him to London in 1829, but now "unloved by all on account of its decrepitude."[39] There was the same steward with whom he had practiced English for the first time, and another uncomfortable thirty-hour crossing that left him seasick. When he arrived at the Custom's House near the Tower of London, he spied Klingemann approaching in a small rowboat. Klingemann's residence in Eaton Square became the base of Felix's fifth London sojourn. There, on August 30 and 31, the two began to draft an outline of *Elijah*. In the original conception, the oratorio began with a chorus on verses from Jeremiah (48:33): "And joy and gladness is taken from the plentiful field, and from the land of Moab."[40]

Though he missed Moscheles, then on holiday in Hamburg, Felix visited his many London friends, including Rosen, the Horsleys, Alexanders, and Taylors, the engineer I. K. Brunel (recently wedded to Mary Horsley), George Hogarth, William Ayrton, and Charles Neate. Through Sir George Smart, Felix met an "attractive slim lady,"[41] the contralto Mary Shaw, who had sung in the Liverpool premiere of *St. Paul* and would appear at the Gewandhaus during the 1838–1839 season. He was less impressed with the soprano Clara Novello, and when he sought to sell to her brother, the publisher J. Alfred Novello, the new piano concerto, Psalm 42, and the organ preludes and fugues for £40, Felix found his reluctance "churlish."

Since the concert season had ended, Felix discovered another outlet in several churches. On September 8 he offered organ fugues of J. S. Bach on a two-manual instrument in St. John, Paddington. Two days later, after evensong in St. Paul's, he threaded his way through worshipers to the organ and attacked Bach's Prelude and Fugue in A Minor, BWV 543. In order to disperse the thronging crowd, a Dickensian beadle excused the organ blower, so that at the climactic pedal passage near the end of the fugue the instrument gave out, leaving Felix to "exhibit the glorious ideas of Bach in all the dignity of dumb action"[42] and nearly precipitating a riot among the exasperated audience. On September 12 Felix was able to perform the complete work on a three-manual instrument at Christ Church, Newgate Street and improvised several fantasias.

Henry John Gauntlett, who witnessed the event, reported that in the Bach prelude Felix "amplified and extended the idea of the author, in a manner so in keeping and natural, that those unacquainted with its details could not by any possibility have discovered the departure from the text."[43] An accomplished organist (Gauntlett was Felix's choice to play the organ part at the premiere of *Elijah* in 1846), Gauntlett recorded several comments that testify to Felix's mastery on the instrument. Thus, Felix was unfazed when he had to adapt Bach's demanding pedal part to "suit the scale of an ordinary English pedal board." And Felix's touch was "so even and firm, so delicate and *volant*, that no difficulties, however appalling, either impede or disturb his equanimity." Another witness was the septuagenarian Samuel Wesley, nephew of the founder of Methodism and a devoté of Bach's music, who had just composed for Felix a fugue on the subject of a canon written for Wesley's daughter Eliza.[44] Suffering from depression, Wesley had not played in public in years, but Felix now convinced the "trembling and bent" musician to extemporize. His daughter was so overcome with emotion that she fainted, and when Felix praised Wesley's efforts, he replied, "Oh, Sir, you have not heard me play; you should have heard me forty years ago."[45] He died one month later.

Upon arriving in London, Felix was drawn into a controversy attending the performance of *St. Paul* by the Sacred Harmonic Society on September 12. Joseph Moore, benefactor and organizer of the Birmingham Musical Festival, was displeased that Felix intended to conduct the performance and protested through the organizing committee in the strongest terms. Felix withdrew from the performance but attended the rehearsals; when he ventured to correct one of the parts, the musicians recognized him and broke into spontaneous cheers. But this joyful recognition was offset by the suddenly deteriorating health of Rosen, who was suffering from a malignant tumor. Between engagements, Felix hastened to his friend, who urged him on September 11 not to visit, for there was "no joy to be gained from me." The next day the Alexanders escorted Felix to Exeter Hall in the Strand to hear Joseph Surman perform *St. Paul* with the amateur chorus and orchestra of the Sacred Harmonic Society. When Felix took his place in the gallery, he found Julius Benedict and the scrupulous Sir George Smart, prepared to time the performance with his watch. Also in the audience was the American hymnodist Lowell Mason, author of "Nearer My God to Thee," who left an ambivalent judgment in his journal: "There is too much narrative—and recitative—Choruses are good—some magnificent."[46] Still, between the two parts, Felix had to acknowledge a prolonged ovation, and several numbers were encored. After the performance, he reached Rosen's residence at midnight. But he was too late; his friend had passed away in Klingemann's arms during the oratorio.[47]

Having experienced "one of those days in the world, with its mysterious, incomprehensible ways,"[48] Felix left the next morning by coach for Birmingham. His host, Joseph Moore (1766–1851), who owned a die-sinking business, was the driving force behind the triennial festival and had promoted the construction of its site, the new Town Hall, modeled on a Greek temple. Here Felix tried out an imposing four-manual organ and also a piano sent by the London firm of Broadwood (in the end, Felix elected to play on an Erard). The festival committee had collapsed seven performances into four days (September 19–22) but incredibly scheduled only one day for rehearsals. "That is how calves are led to the slaughterhouse," Felix noted in his diary.[49] At the rehearsal for *St. Paul*, part of which was allotted to Sigismund Neukomm's Ascension oratorio *Christi Himmelfahrt*, Felix offered trilingual curses in English, French, and German. Somewhat more successful was the preliminary reading of the new piano concerto, which prompted a bidding contest for its rights between J. Alfred Novello and Nicolas Mori of Mori & Lavenu.

At the second concert (September 19), Felix directed the *Midsummer Night's Dream* Overture without rehearsal and improvised an organ "concerto" on themes from Handel's *Solomon* and a Mozart symphony performed on the same concert.[50] There were considerable difficulties with *St. Paul*, presented the morning of the 20th before an audience that included Klingemann and several of the Souchays and Beneckes, among them Cécile's grandfather, who had arrived from Manchester. Clara Novello sang the aria "Jerusalem" "atrociously," in the middle of which the organist (James Turle of Westminster Abbey) "groped around on full organ, and created a devilish noise," instead of the *pianissimo* pedal entrance. And the length of the program caused the curtailment of at least three numbers.[51] Still, the oratorio enjoyed an enthusiastic reception, as did the Piano Concerto No. 2, premiered the evening of September 21. Having balked at paying £40 for Opp. 37, 40, and 42, Novello now paid £42 for the concerto alone.[52] By then, Felix was packing for his return to Frankfurt. On the final day of the festival, he began the seventh concert with J. S. Bach's "St. Anne" Prelude and Fugue in E♭ (BWV 552) before departing in a coach waiting at the door, as members of the audience waved their handkerchiefs.

Felix's fifth English sojourn consolidated his remarkable popularity in the musical life of the British Isles. There were invitations to conduct *St. Paul* in Dublin and attend a festival in Edinburgh. The publisher William Chappell was prepared to offer Felix £300 for a new opera.[53] But on September 22, Felix's principal thought was of Cécile. Arriving in London late that evening, he received a silver snuffbox from the Sacred Harmonic Society and then boarded the mail coach to Dover. The tempestuous crossing blew his steamer off course, so that he arrived in Boulogne instead of Calais. Composing a canon to pass the time, he continued in a rattling diligence to Brussels, Liège, and Cologne, and then up the Rhine by steamer, until it became fogbound near Horchheim. For the last leg, he hired a special coach and reached Cécile in Frankfurt the afternoon of September 27. They departed the next day for Leipzig and arrived October 1. Having traveled for nearly ten days, he had only a few hours to spare before conducting Beethoven's Fifth Symphony in the opening concert of the new season.

III

Waiting to move into a renovated apartment in Lurgensteins Garten, with views of the city walls, promenade, and J. S. Bach's quarters near the Thomaskirche,[54] the couple resided near Julie Louisa Schunck, a great-aunt of Cécile. Advanced in her pregnancy, Cécile was transported in a sedan chair. Between concerts, they entertained several visitors. First to appear were Fanny, Wilhelm, and Sebastian. Early in October, Fanny had written candidly to Cécile: "when anybody comes to talk to me about your beauty and your eyes, it makes me quite cross. I have had enough of hearsay, and beautiful eyes were not made to be heard."[55] Two days after Cécile's twentieth birthday (October 10), Fanny finally met her sister-in-law and was won over: "I consider Felix most fortunate," she wrote Klingemann, "for though inexpressibly fond of him, she does not spoil him, but when he is capricious treats him with an equanimity which will in course of time most likely cure his fits of irritability altogether."[56] And to her diary Fanny confided how happy she was that he had found a wife who exercised such an agreeable, calming influence on him.[57]

On October 23 the Novellos arrived—Vincent, his wife, Mary, and their daughters Emma and Clara. They had tea with Felix and Cécile, and heard Felix and Fanny play duets. Something of a prig, Clara found the Gewandhaus "small and frightfully painted in yellow, the benches arranged that one sits as if in an omnibus—and no lady and gentleman ever are allowed to sit together here or in their churches."[58] Nevertheless, the soprano's appearances, including her debut on November 2, with an aria from Mozart's *Clemenza di Tito* and "Casta diva" from Bellini's *Norma*, created a sensation. Felix praised her "purity of intonation" and "thoroughbred musical feeling."[59] And two weeks later, Clara won acclaim as a soloist in Mozart's arrangement of Handel's *Messiah*, conducted by Felix in the Paulinerkirche.

One week before (November 7), Charles and Adelaide Kemble paid Felix and Cécile a visit. Avoiding bankruptcy by promoting the acting career of his daughter Fanny—she married an American plantation owner in 1834—the celebrated Shakespearean now endeavored to launch a singing career for Adelaide. Felix judged her a dilettante but after an hour of singing was impressed by her passion and appearance (less charitable, Clara found her "like an Abbé in her black cassock dress—hair brushed away from thin face. All nose").[60] But when Felix arranged a dinner party for thirty and prevailed upon the famous actor to recite *Hamlet*, Adelaide flung herself at her father's feet and then insisted upon singing—in Cécile's phrase, *à casser les vitres* (to break the windowpanes).

During the winter of 1837 the Gewandhaus welcomed two other virtuosi of note. On November 13, the seventeen-year-old Henri Vieuxtemps performed a new violin concerto,[61] probably No. 2 in F♯ minor, Op. 19, designed to emulate Paganini's technical brilliance. And on December

29, the pianist Adolf Henselt presented Weber's *Konzertstück* and solo pieces. Subject to nervous anxiety, Henselt was known for the uncommonly wide span of his hands, which may explain his decision that day to perform Chopin's first etude, Op. 10 No. 1, bristling with treacherously spaced arpeggiations that sometimes exceed a tenth. Felix found Henselt's playing "exquisite" but doubted he would return to Leipzig; the moody pianist, who typically expended his energies the day of a concert in practicing, could not control his nerves.[62]

Felix himself appeared as soloist on October 19 to introduce the Piano Concerto No. 2 in D minor to a German audience. After returning from Birmingham, he fussed over the score before dispatching it to Breitkopf & Härtel in December. Its three connected movements replicate the external stylistic features of the G-minor Piano Concerto—in the first movement, the early entrance of the piano and telescoped orchestral *tutti*, in the second, a quiescent, nocturne-like *Lied ohne Worte*, and in the third, brilliant "piano fireworks" illuminating a scherzo-like rondo.[63] The outer movements balance the demands of virtuosity and the artistic integrity of the work. Thus, the piano initially enters with a series of cadenza-like passages that interrupt the orchestra as it attempts to "discover" the principal theme—a conceit later exploited powerfully by Liszt in his first piano concerto (1849). The head motive of Felix's first theme later reemerges in a canonic elaboration in the development, a bit of counterpoint that suggests almost a symphonic elaboration. On the other hand, Felix's concessions to virtuosity include a "three-hand," Thalbergian second theme (**ex. 11.4a**), and a related texture in the finale, where the second theme appears in the soprano (fourth and fifth fingers of the right hand), beneath which the two hands divide a stream of harplike arpeggiations, while the left provides a bass line in octaves (**ex. 11.4b**).

From Cologne, Felix received an invitation to direct the 1838 Lower Rhine festival; from Vienna, a diploma citing him as an honorary member of the Gesellschaft der Musikfreunde (Society of Friends of Music).[64] Tending to Cécile, arranging his wine cellar, and reading Dickens' new novel *Pickwick Papers*, Felix relaxed in his comfortable surroundings. The birth of Rebecka's second son, Felix Dirichlet, reinforced his contentment, and his domestic bliss found expression in several minor works, including the sentimental love song *Im Kahn*, sent to Charlotte Moscheles on December 12.[65] The intimate genre of the part-song stimulated his creativity, as he readied his first volume, the *Sechs Lieder im Freien zu singen* (Six Songs for Singing Outdoors, Op. 41) for publication.[66] But the principal new work of the winter was Psalm 42, Op. 42, sketched during the honeymoon. In October, Felix gathered some friends (Cécile

Ex. 11.4a: Mendelssohn, Piano Concerto No. 2 in D minor, Op. 40 (1837), First Movement

Ex. 11.4b: Mendelssohn, Piano Concerto No. 2 in D minor, Op. 40 (1837), Finale

took a soprano part and Felix the alto),[67] who, fortified by Rheinwein, made a "wondrous bellowing" as they read the manuscript. He recast the work in December and premiered it on New Year's Day 1838, with Clara Novello as the soprano soloist.

During his lifetime Op. 42 became one of his most popular sacred choral works. For Robert Schumann, it attained the "highest summit" available to "modern church music,"[68] but the twentieth century criticized the composition for excessive sentimentality. Philip Radcliffe found the restrained chordal accompaniment of the opening chorus "dangerously near that of a slow waltz,"[69] and Eric Werner attributed to the concluding fugue, on a doxology added by Felix, an "unpleasantly unctuous character which reminds us of bad preachers."[70] Early on, Ferdinand Hiller recognized that the work's "tender and longing pathos . . . is based on a foundation of perfect trust in God, and the subdued sentiment . . . may well harmonize with the blissful feelings of deep happiness which penetrated him at the time."[71] In its revised form the work achieved a symmetry that indeed seems to mirror his marital harmony: seven movements, anchored by choruses at the end and midpoints (Nos. 1, 4, and 7), and balanced by soprano recitatives and solos (Nos. 2–3 and 5–6), supported by female and male choruses (Nos. 3 and 6). Tying the euphonious complex together is the unifying head motive of the opening chorus (**ex. 11.5a**). Its gentle stepwise motion and ascending fourth are reworked in No. 4 (**ex. 11.5b**), where the rising figure is reversed downward to adumbrate the fugal subject of No. 7.

Ex. 11.5a: Mendelssohn, Psalm 42, Op. 42 (1837), First Movement

Wie der Hirsch schreit nach fri-schem Was - ser, so schreit mei-ne See - le, Gott, zu dir.

Ex. 11.5b: Mendelssohn, Psalm 42, Op. 42 (1837), No. 4

Har - re auf Gott! har - re auf Gott! denn ich wer - de ihm noch dan - ken,

Rather than depicting a soul in distress, the serene beginning ("As the hart panteth after the water brooks, so panteth my soul after thee, O God") projects an idealized approach to God through carefully regulated dissonances. The aria "My soul thirsteth for God" individualizes the struggle through alternating phrases in the oboe and soprano and suggests a "religious drama expressed in music."[72] But the addition of female and male choruses and return of the full chorus for the refrainlike fifth and eleventh verses ("Why art thou cast down, O my soul? And why are thou disquieted in me? Hope thou in God") expands the scope from the particular to the general. The composition ends with a broadening, universal song of praise—an addition buttressed by trombones and the organ—that traces, as in *St. Paul*, a course of emotional and spiritual *Steigerung*.

Under less than ideal conditions Op. 42 received its premiere. Clara Novello was suffering from a severe cold, as was Felix, who lost hearing in one ear for several days. But he maintained the concert schedule (at least five appearances in January alone) and presided over Novello's farewell concert on January 8, when he performed Beethoven's Third Piano Concerto. As the time for Cécile's confinement approached, Felix remained immersed in professional concerns. He reviewed four potential opera subjects, reacted with alarm when he received an unsolicited text for *Elijah* from the Reverend J. Barry,[73] published two Lieder in a supplement to Schumann's *Neue Zeitschrift für Musik*,[74] and released the six part-songs Op. 41 to Breitkopf & Härtel.

Designed for performance outdoors, the choral songs fall into two groups. The first four are strophic and reuse music for successive verses. Only the last two songs introduce contrasting music for internal stanzas. Throughout the opus the music aspires toward folksong; indeed, Felix sequestered the three Heine settings (Nos. 2–4) as *Drei Volkslieder*. The texts celebrate nature as a colorful canopy that envelops human realms, and the music responds by suggesting a communion with the natural world: in No. 1 (*Im Walde*), twittering birds are oblivious to human sorrows; in No. 4 (*Auf ihrem Grab*), a linden tree grows above the grave of deceased lovers; in No. 5 (*Mailied*), spring erupts in May; and in No. 6 (*Auf dem See*), a traveler finds nourishment and new blood in the "free" world. We are to imagine the music as a spontaneous reaction triggered by various naturalistic settings. There is a freshness about these compositions and at times a sweetness (e.g., reliance on subdominant harmonies) that some twentieth-century commentators found maudlin.

Shortly after celebrating his twenty-ninth birthday, Felix finished the String Quartet in E♭ major, Op. 44 No. 3. The following day, February 7, Cécile gave birth to their first child, Carl Wolfgang Paul, named after Zelter and Klingemann (Carl), Goethe (Wolfgang), and St. Paul. The proud father described his son as a strong, stout child who had his mother's blue eyes and snub nose.[75] Now Felix eagerly invited Lea to attend the baptism, scheduled for her birthday, March 15. But Lea remained in Berlin, as did Rebecka and Fanny, and Paul and Albertine made the twelve-hour journey to Leipzig and stood as godparents. Instead, Fanny represented her brother's interests by attending the rehearsals for a Singakademie performance of *Paulus* (she was appalled to find a tuba had replaced the organ part). And she performed Felix's Piano Concerto in G minor at a charity concert on February 19—one of her few documented public appearances as a pianist.[76] A critic for the English *Athenaeum* found her playing "bore a strong family resemblance to her brother's in its fire, neatness, and solidity," and opined that had she "been a poor man's daughter, she would have been known throughout the world . . . as a female pianist of the highest order."[77]

In February and March Felix directed a series of historical concerts, arranged according to the "succession of the most famous masters from one hundred or more years ago up to the present time." The impetus for this musicological programming may have been an ambitious concept the Dresden musician Carl Kloss had shared with Felix during the summer of 1835[78]—a plan for concert cycles encompassing pre-Christian and Christian eras. Kloss contemplated reviving Egyptian, Hebraic, Greek, and Roman music (how is not clear), and then, after leaping over the Middle Ages and Renaissance, examining baroque music of early eighteenth-century composers such as Alessandro Scarlatti and Durante. Bach was positioned as the culmination of the fugal style; Chopin, the epitome of the new romantic school. Far more circumscribed, Felix's series began with Bach and continued through Beethoven. On the first concert (February 15), Felix directed Bach's orchestral Suite in D (BWV 1068) and performed the Violin Sonata in E (BWV 1016) with David. The balance of the program included Handel's *Zadok the Priest*, an overture and scene of Gluck, and a violin concerto by Viotti. The second program (February 22), built around Haydn, offered a piano trio, selections from *The Creation*, and a "curiously melancholy piece" in which the musicians finished by extinguishing the candles on their stands—the *Farewell* Symphony. The third concert (March 1) featured works by Mozart (among them the Piano Concerto in C minor, K. 491, for which Felix crafted a brilliant cadenza in the first movement), his "nemesis" Salieri, and the Frenchman E. N. Méhul, composer of the dark, exotic Ossianic opera *Uthal* (1806). And the fourth (March 8), introduced by compositions of Abbé Vogler and Carl Maria von Weber, culminated with Beethoven's Violin Concerto and *Pastoral* Symphony. Felix then devoted the last two subscription concerts of the season (March 22 and 29) to "all possible modernities,"[79] chiefly selections from Italian operas of Bellini, Rossini, and Mercadante, but, significantly, no works by himself.

Today these concerts seem utterly naive—Handel and Bach challenged by Viotti, Haydn by Righini, Mozart by Salieri, and Beethoven by the eccentric, (perhaps) charlatan, Vogler. The coupling of musical giants and now largely forgotten figures as "the most famous masters" in fact betrays the beginnings of European canon formation in music. Discernible in Felix's programming is a main line of German music descending from Bach and Handel through Mozart and Haydn to Weber and Beethoven. Also implicit is the recognition of distinct historical styles—the baroque, classical, and modern (romantic), and, further, the notion of a classic-romantic dialectic, under development in the intellectual discourse of the 1830s before it became a conceptual commonplace.

IV

Felix's own muse remained restless in the early months of 1838. He procured from Droysen a text on the subject of the Nausicaa episode in *The Odyssey* (Book VI), but feared its length approached an oratorio rather than the shorter choral work he envisioned.[80] Meanwhile, in London, the librettist of Weber's *Oberon*, J. R. Planché, agreed to write an opera libretto for Felix, and the two began a correspondence.[81] Felix preferred a serious opera in two or three acts (not the five of French grand opera) on a historical subject, with contrasting light roles and many choruses. Planché was to avoid subjects drawn from current popular operas; Felix suggested the ideal lay somewhere between Beethoven's *Fidelio*, centered on a "virtuous, heroical deed," and Cherubini's *Les deux journées*, with the sinister figure of Cardinal Mazarin, who could "remind us of history . . . and . . . of our present time." Planché thought a suitable topic was

Edward III's Siege of Calais in 1347 and forwarded a sketch in April. But Felix's characteristic captiousness now prevailed: his probing uncovered problems with the plot, and the principal characters seemed to act as men bound by the action rather than "their own human feeling, as real living people do." By October 1839, the project had run aground.

Felix closed the winter 1838 season with a special appearance. When the Bohemian contralto Caroline Botgorschek implored him to perform on her benefit concert (April 2), he conceived in two days the *Serenade und Allegro giojoso* for piano and orchestra, Op. 43, and left fifteen bars in the piano blank, for completion during the performance.[82] Introduced by a plaintive piano solo in B minor, this work joins a pensive *Lied ohne Worte* to a festive rondo in D major built around two alternating subjects, a staccato, *scherzando* figure and a contrasting lyrical theme supported by rippling arpeggiations. The ease with which Felix dispatched this *bravura* piece is underscored by another remarkable deed: he also composed at this time a *Festgesang* for chorus and piano, commissioned in the middle of March by the Tyrolean music dilettante Anton Christanell for the birthday of the Austrian emperor Ferdinand I (April 19). Discovered in a Russian archive by Christoph Hellmundt in 1996,[83] the *Festgesang* was finished on March 30, 1838, amid work on the *Serenade*. Though a minor occasional piece, the *Festgesang* bears scrutiny: Felix later recast its ceremonial subject (**ex. 11.6**) in the opening of the *Lobgesang* Symphony of 1840 (see **ex. 12.2**, p. 398).

Early in April, he finished a setting of Psalm 95, revised in 1839 and 1841 and released in 1842 as Op. 46. Then, bowing to family pressure, he escorted Cécile and Carl to Berlin, so that Rebecka at last could meet his wife. For several weeks, the family enjoyed a happy reunion (only Paul, pursuing business in Hamburg, was away). Felix and Cécile indulged in what Fanny described as a "double counterpoint" of music and painting, imitating her own lifestyle with Wilhelm.[84] Felix brought Bach cantatas to share with Fanny and prepared for the twentieth Lower Rhine Music Festival in Cologne, where he arrived on May 25. After negotiations with the festival committee, he succeeded in introducing Bach's

Ex. 11.6: Mendelssohn, *Festgesang* (1838)

music on the program for the first time. The two-day Pentecost festival (June 3–4, 1838) began with a symphony by Ferdinand Ries, followed by the obligatory Handel oratorio, in this case, *Joshua*. On the second day Felix performed a Mozart symphony, an overture by Cherubini, Beethoven's patriotic cantata *Der glorreiche Augenblick*, and what Felix billed as an Ascension Day cantata by J. S. Bach. This work was in fact a fabrication consisting of movements chosen from the Ascension Cantata No. 43 (*Gott fähret auf mit Jauchzen*), an aria and chorale from No. 25 (*Es ist nichts gesundes an meinem Leibe*), and the opening double chorus from No. 50 (*Nun ist das Heil und die Kraft*). Insisting on using organ for the Handel and Bach, Felix prepared parts for the oratorio and cantata. The orchestral and choral forces for this gargantuan spectacle totaled some seven hundred musicians.

Returning to Berlin on June 10, Felix resumed private life with his family; but because everything in Berlin hung together "with the sand," he did not regret his decision to pursue his career elsewhere.[85] For several months the family circle was weakened by the departure of Hensel, who traveled to London to attend a fairy-tale event. On June 28 the young Queen Victoria, attired in medieval dress, arrived in a golden carriage, supported by trident-bearing Tritons, for her coronation at Westminster Abbey. Hensel managed to have an audience with Victoria, who purchased his painting of Miriam's song of praise after the crossing of the Red Sea (among those rejoicing in the painting were likenesses of Fanny, Rebecka, and Paul's wife, Albertine).[86] Hensel received commissions from the Duchess of Sutherland and Lord Egerton but cut short his sojourn when news came of a measles epidemic in Berlin.

Now more a spectator of Berlin musical life than active participant, Felix avoided the public light to take up several new compositions, including preliminary ideas for a symphony in B♭ major.[87] The opening of a violin concerto in E minor began to haunt him,[88] and on June 15 he finished a draft of the Violin Sonata in F major, intended for Ferdinand David, but rejected as a "wretched sonata." In three movements, it included a *Lied-ohne-Worte*-styled slow movement and a *perpetuum-mobile* finale. Dissatisfied with the expansive first movement, Felix began to revise it in 1839 but then abandoned the effort. (It remained virtually unknown until 1953, when Yehudi Menuhin published the score in an edition that conflated the two versions of the first movement.) For Breitkopf & Härtel, Felix dispatched a piano work, the *Andante cantabile e Presto agitato*, that appeared late in 1838 for an 1839 album. Recalling the *Rondo capriccioso* and *Serenade und Allegro giojoso*, he reapplied the well-worn scheme of the two-movement concert piece, with a nocturne-like introduction linked to a lively rondo finale. The figuration betrays some concessions to keyboard fashions—thickened textures in the *Andante* and rapidly repeated notes in the *Presto*, an effect facilitated by the double-escapement action of Felix's Erard piano. But the prevalent foursquare, symmetrical phrasing gives the work a certain predictability that vitiates the dramatic contrast between the two movements.

Robert Schumann detected in Felix's music of the later 1830s a propensity toward the Mozartean. Of the Cello Sonata No. 1, Op. 45, conceived during the summer of 1838 but not finished until October, Schumann observed: "A smile hovers round his mouth, but it is that of delight in his art, of quiet self-sufficiency in an intimate circle. . . ."[89] Indeed, a classical tranquility envelops this music, which avoids dramatic contrasts within and between movements, and favors balance and structural stability. Thus, Felix reworks the opening unison figure of the first movement, with its characteristic dissonant leap (A–E♭), into the principal theme of the rondo finale, where the leap is smoothed out by stepwise motion (**ex. 11.7**). In the middle movement, he minimizes contrast between the *scherzando*-like A section in G minor and Lied-like B section in G major by recalling the characteristic dotted figure of A in the accompaniment of B. "Especially fitting for the most refined family circles," was Schumann's judgment of this composition, written for Felix's brother, as if a celebration of fraternal harmony.

The major new work of the summer was the String Quartet in D major, Op. 44 No. 1. Its completion on July 24 facilitated the release of all three in 1839 with a dedication to the crown prince of Sweden. Op. 44 displays in abundance the new classicizing tendencies. The joyful outer movements of No. 1, with thrusting, rising themes in the first violin, recall something of the Octet, though the music now seems comparatively restrained and well mannered. Whereas the Octet begins by charting a melody rising irrepressibly some three octaves from a tremolo accompaniment, the opening theme of the Quartet, spanning only a tenth, unfolds in three symmetrical phrases for the violin placed securely

Ex. 11.7a: Mendelssohn, Cello Sonata No. 1 in B♭ major, Op. 45 (1838)

Ex. 11.7b: Mendelssohn, Cello Sonata No. 1 in B♭ major, Op. 45 (1838), Finale

above the tremolos. The phrases fall tidily into four-bar units, and little disturbs the equipoise of the movement. Probably not coincidentally, the second movement is a minuet (the only one among Felix's mature string quartets), and here the classical attributes of grace and clarity achieve an even greater prominence. Thus, the first part of the minuet divides, in a question-and-answer fashion, into two mirroring eight-bar periods on the tonic and dominant, of which the second is nearly an exact transposition of the first. The songlike Andante contains occasional hints of Felix's *scherzando* style, as in its trills and *leggiero* writing, but the capricious, vaguely sinister element of his earlier scherzi is absent; Puck has matured, as it were, into a respectable, complacent *Bürger*.

The beginning of the second quartet, in E minor, complements that of the first. Again, the violin projects a rising, arpeggiated theme, but accompanying it are syncopated chords, and the mood, subdued and elegiac, anticipates that of the Violin Concerto Op. 64, also in E minor. With a burst of repeated, staccato notes the second movement ushers in a frolicsome, delicate scherzo in E major, brimming with delightful effects: the opening eight-bar period, for example, divides not into predictable groups of four but three groups of three, three, and two bars, injecting a playful asymmetry into the music (**ex. 11.8**). The more serious Andante in G offers another extension of the *Lied-ohne-Worte* style into the domain of chamber music. The weakest of the four movements is the finale, the *perpetuum-mobile* Presto that runs on too long, despite its contrast between the agitated first and lilting second themes.

The bustling finale of the third quartet, in E♭ major, also suffers from undue length, but offsetting this shortcoming is the meticulous workmanship of the first three movements. The quartet begins with an upbeat figure, repeated through a process of concision to achieve a motivic intensity reminiscent of Haydn. The inner movements again pair a scherzo and *Lied ohne Worte*. The infectious scherzo in C minor is a delightful masterpiece that unfolds as a complex rondo built upon three themes (**ex. 11.9**). The first asserts a stubbornly repeated note against rapid staccato work in the accompaniment. The *sotto voce* second theme also employs repeated pitches, now articulated by rests that inject hiccupping gaps into the coursing music. The third enters in fugal and canonic style, though its contrapuntal elaboration evaporates into the whirling, delicate textures of sound.

Ex. 11.8: Mendelssohn, String Quartet in E minor, Op. 44 No. 2 (1837), Scherzo

Allegro di molto

Ex. 11.9: Mendelssohn, String Quartet in E♭ major, Op. 44 No. 3 (1838), *Assai leggiero e vivace*

When the third subject later reappears, Felix adds a fresh countersubject, a descending chromatic tetrachord, and playfully invokes a traditional, Baroque fugal subject. This late addition prepares the poignantly chromatic flavor of the slow movement, which begins by progressing from the tonic major to minor subdominant, and establishing a strident cross relation between the cello and first violin.

Often the Op. 44 quartets are thought to evince a stylistic retrenchment, as if in 1837 and 1838 Felix stepped back from the "progressive" threshold of the Octet and Opp. 12 and 13 to revalidate a reactionary classical aesthetic. In 1963 Eric Werner went so far as to seek a causal effect in Felix's domestic happiness: his "wish to please and impress Cécile weakened his artistic integrity."[90] Somehow her calming, moderating influence cured Felix of his compositional irascibility and led him to produce undemanding "armchair" music. But the reasons for Felix's compositional retrenchment are much more complex. That he overlaid his music of the late 1830s with a classical veneer was probably a deliberate choice. The surface clarity and balance of Op. 44 may indeed reflect his stable domestic life and the adoption of a conservative compositional outlook—understandable enough for a new husband and father. But the cultural temper of the *Restaurationszeit*, which in German realms promoted political and domestic stability, surely played a role as well. Then there was the increasingly demanding regimen of duties at the Gewandhaus, which more and more required Felix to confine composition to the summer months and thus rely upon well-tested compositional models. Finally, notwithstanding his assertion that unless he was "made" for popularity he could not strive toward it,[91] at some level Felix may have been responding to Rossini's suggestion that he adopt a more accessible style. But Felix's minimizing of romantic *Angst* and his elevation of the enjoyable in the quartets does not mean *per se* a decline in quality. The inner movements of the third quartet, for example, offer anything but complacent music and can stand with Felix's best work.

V

In August 1838 the measles epidemic abruptly interrupted the Berlin holiday. When Felix Dirichlet contracted the disease, Felix and Cécile returned to Leipzig in an attempt to safeguard Carl's health. But after their arrival on August 20, Cécile and Felix fell ill with the measles, so that in September David had to substitute for Felix in a performance of *Paulus* and the first subscription concert. Felix took up the new season with the second concert (October 7) and conducted five more before tragedy struck his family. On November 17, Rebecka's son Felix died of complications from the measles, and Felix hastened to Berlin to comfort her. He found his sister still suffering from the disease and so delirious that she had to be restrained in bed.[92] Hensel endeavored to console her with some idealized drawings of the lifeless child.

At the Gewandhaus, the closing months of 1838 featured several virtuosi, including the contralto Mary Shaw, engaged for several appearances during the 1838–1839 season, and soprano Clara Novello, who, after her "farewell" concert in January offered an *Extra-Konzert* on October 23. With Mary Shaw Felix introduced on November 15 a new arrangement of a familiar Scottish folksong, "O dinna ask me" (**ex. 11.10**). Its successful reception convinced the publisher Friedrich Kistner to request more arrangements. Felix obliged and produced five more in December; they appeared in February 1839 as the *Sechs schottische National-Lieder*, with Felix's editorship suppressed.[93]

Ex. 11.10: Mendelssohn (arranger), "O dinna ask me" (1839)

Among the visiting pianists was Clara Wieck, recently returned from Vienna, where she had acquired the title of *Kaiserliche-Königliche Kammervirtuosin*. Clara appeared in a benefit concert on September 8 and with Felix on the ninth subscription concert (December 6). Her repertoire included some of Liszt's modish piano transcriptions of Schubert Lieder, which prompted a revealing comment from Fanny, who viewed the wordless songs as the inversion of a game she had played with Felix years before—contriving texts to fit his piano Lieder. Now the "jokes that we, as mere children, contrived to pass the time," she mused, were "adopted by the great talents and used as fodder for the public."[94] Two other virtuoso pianists captivated Leipzig audiences in December. Sigismond Thalberg entranced Felix with a fantasy on Rossini's opera *Donna del lago* (*The Lady of the Lake*), crammed with three-hand effects and astounding technical difficulties. While Thalberg was in Leipzig, an unknown Czech pianist, Alexander Dreyschock (1818–1869), managed to secure his own solo concert at the Gewandhaus, where he executed a stentorian rendition of Chopin's *Revolutionary* Etude, with the left-hand part in or doubled by tempestuous octaves.[95]

If the virtuoso wars entertained Felix, they did not convince him to alter his own artistic agenda. Instead of appearing as a soloist, he pondered an invitation to direct the next Lower Rhine Festival in Düsseldorf, and conducted two weighty symphonies of Louis Spohr, the Fifth and Fourth, on October 25 and December 20. The Fourth, titled *The Consecration of Sound* (*Die Weihe der Töne*), came with a program, for distribution to the audience, about the nature of musical sound, ranging from birdsong to dance, military, and funeral music.[96] During the closing months of 1838 Felix also revisited the gestating libretto for *Elijah*. When Klingemann faltered in developing a suitable text, the composer turned again to Schubring, who set to work in October. But Schubring expressed misgivings about parts of *Paulus* and urged Felix to elevate the devotional character of his next oratorio. Felix, however, announced his preference for a dramatic treatment of the Old Testament prophet, and the collaboration fell apart early in 1839, not to be revived until 1844.

VI

"We are living a pleasant life" (*Wir leben ein angenehmes Leben*), Felix announced to Rebecka on her birthday in 1839.[97] His letters to Berlin bespeak a domestic coziness—counting Carl's teeth, receiving installments of *Oliver Twist* (regrettably, we do not have Felix's reaction to Dickens' stark novel of social protest), and admiring an alabaster bust of

Shakespeare sent by Fanny for his birthday. The delivery of a new Erard grand early in the new year stimulated Felix's return to performance, and at the Gewandhaus, he offered the "Moonlight" Sonata on Mary Shaw's farewell concert (January 28), an improvisation on Beethoven's *Adelaide* (February 14), Moscheles's new *Pastoral* Concerto (March 14), and Felix's *Rondo brillant*, Op. 29, with a new improvised introduction (April 4). Other highlights of the season included appearances by Sterndale Bennett, who premiered two of his own works—another Mendelssohnian overture, *The Wood-nymphs*, and the Piano Concerto No. 4 in F minor; following Felix's suggestion for its slow movement, Bennett substituted a barcarolle, destined to become one of his most popular compositions. The signal event came on March 21, when Felix directed the premiere of a hitherto unknown symphony in C major, the "Great" of Schubert.

The credit for this rediscovery, the prime mover in the nineteenth-century Schubert revival, is usually assigned to Robert Schumann, who had moved to Vienna in 1838 with the aim of transferring the *Neue Zeitschrift für Musik* and settling there with Clara.[98] But Metternich's censors balked at approving the journal, and on New Year's Day 1839 Robert took up another pursuit, the music of Schubert. Visiting the deceased composer's brother Ferdinand, Robert examined several unpublished symphonies from the *Nachlass*. At the end of the month Ferdinand dispatched the two C-major symphonies (Nos. 6 and 9, D589 and 944) to Breitkopf & Härtel and a letter to Felix, who examined the scores. Though the score for No. 9 had its gatherings out of order, forcing the busy Felix to spend time deciphering the confused music, he elected to have parts made of the "Great," so that he could perform the work on the final concert of the season. Largely on its success Breitkopf & Härtel decided to engrave the score, and Felix made efforts to have the work performed by the Philharmonic Society in London. Accounts of the Leipzig premiere make clear that Felix performed the symphony without cuts, so that it lasted nearly an hour, later inspiring Robert to wax rapturously about its "heavenly length," like a Jean Paul novel in four volumes. Felix thus took the decision to resuscitate the "Great," and effectively transformed Schubert from a respected "ballad" composer to a symphonist of stature.[99] There were other ramifications of the revival: the Viennese publisher Anton Diabelli brought out Schubert's Piano Sonata in A minor D784 with a dedication to Felix, who around this time began work on a Piano Sonata in G major, subsequently abandoned, that betrays clear signs of Schubertian influence.[100]

The early months of 1839 found Felix preoccupied with several works. For Simrock he revised the *Harmoniemusik* Overture from 1824, for release in piano-duet and full wind-orchestra arrangements as Op. 24. In

February he dispatched two modest hymn settings of English psalms (Nos. 5 and 31), commissioned by Coventry & Hollier; the texts, "Lord, hear the voice of my complaint" and "Defend me, Lord, from shame" were derived from the seventeenth-century *New Version of the Psalms of David*, assembled by Nicholas Brady and Nahum Tate, librettist of Purcell's *Dido and Aeneas*.[101] But a setting for soloists, chorus, and orchestra of Psalm 95 required considerably greater effort. At a charity concert on February 21 Felix premiered the first version of the work in six movements, completed the previous year. A reviewer found the composition displayed a "pure, inward piety" and praised the composer for his perceptive grasp of the text.[102] Almost at once Felix began to revise the work. In April he drafted a new setting of the majestic fifth verse ("For His is the sea"),[103] and assigned the German rights to Friedrich Kistner. But then he succumbed to nagging self-criticism, and the work began to unravel, like Penelope's web.[104] A fundamental issue seems to have been how to impose musical unity upon a psalm text divided into two disparate parts, a call to worship and praise God, and an admonition not to disregard God's law. Not until 1841 would Felix discover a satisfactory solution.

In marked contrast to this indecision was the relatively effortless creation of the concert overture *Ruy Blas* for a production of Victor Hugo's play to benefit the pension fund of the Leipzig Theater. Felix was approached in February to compose an overture and a chorus for the second act. But on reading the play, set in seventeenth-century Madrid, he found it "detestable" and "utterly beneath contempt."[105] Apparently its intrigues—the grandee Don Salluste seduces the Spanish queen's lady-in-waiting, and his valet, Ruy Blas, falls in love with the queen—offended Felix's sensibilities. Declining to write an overture, he finished instead on February 14 an unassuming Romance for a chorus of washerwomen ("Wozu der Vöglein Chöre"). The theater management pressed him again for an overture; he now took up the task as a personal challenge and completed it in three days (March 5–8), just in time for the copyist to prepare parts and Felix to rehearse the piece before premiering it on March 11. Then, on the final Gewandhaus concert of the season (March 21), after premiering the Schubert "Great" Symphony, Felix performed the overture again but without reference to the play—it was announced simply as an overture for the *Theater-pension-Fond*.

His eagerness to divorce the overture from the play might imply he conceived the score without meaningful links to Hugo's drama. After all, the celebratory C-major climax of the overture, with its vivacious amphibrachs (♩♩♩), seemingly has little to do with Hugo's "horrific" conclusion, in which Ruy Blas, having won the queen's intimacy by masquerading as a nobleman, murders Don Salluste and commits suicide when the disguise is finally exposed. But, there is evidence Felix responded musically to Hugo's metaphor of the servant as "an earthworm enamored with a star." Felix captured the mixing of classes by juxtaposing distinctly different, high and low musical styles. The solemn, slow opening, fortified by trombones and stated three times, uses majestic dotted rhythms, by 1839 a cliché for an elevated style (ex. 11.11a). The restless, agitated first theme of the Allegro suggests intrigue and deception, while the contrasting second theme, accompanied by clipped staccato chords, connotes a popular idiom (ex. 11.11b, c). Tying the whole together is the recurring use throughout the overture of various forms of a descending tetrachord (C–B♮–B♭–A♮–A♭–G), traditional symbol of a lament. But was all this posturing in earnest or in jest? In the 1930s Sir Donald Tovey suggested that the infectious second theme was a response to Hugo's affected, if virtuoso twelve-syllable Alexandrines,[106] and recently Thomas Grey has heard the overture as a "perfectly straight-faced 'parody' of a melodramatic overture in the modern Franco-Italian idiom."[107] Whatever Felix's intention, the overture is a testament to his prodigious abilities; nevertheless, after the two performances he set the work aside and left it for posthumous publication as Op. 95 in 1851.

With the end of the concert season, Felix prepared to direct the twenty-first Lower Rhine Musical Festival in Düsseldorf before enjoying his annual leave. Just before departing Leipzig on April 24, he forwarded

Ex. 11.11a: Mendelssohn, *Ruy Blas* Overture, Op. 95 (1839)

Ex. 11.11b: Mendelssohn, *Ruy Blas* Overture, Op. 95 (1839)

Ex. 11.11c: Mendelssohn, *Ruy Blas* Overture, Op. 95 (1839)

to Breitkopf & Härtel a new collection of six Lieder;[108] they appeared in November as Op. 47, with a dedication to Constanze Schleinitz, wife of Konrad Schleinitz. The opus comprised new and old songs. On April 17 and 18, Felix created the buoyant setting of Lenau's *Frühlingslied*, Op. 47 No. 3, animated by reverberant harplike effects in the piano, and the simple but dignified *Volkslied* No. 4. Two days later he again captured a folksong quality for Uhland's *Hirtenlied* (*Shepherd's Song*), which he arranged the same day as a part-song but elected to withhold for his next *Liederheft* (it appeared as Op. 57 No. 2, and, posthumously, as the part-song Op. 88 No. 3). Among the older songs of Op. 47 were Nos. 5 and 6, fashioned in 1832 and 1833 on Klingemann texts. No. 6, the gentle *Wiegenlied* (*Lullaby*), with its characteristic rocking figure, had been composed on the birth of the Moscheles' son Felix. Perhaps the most successful Lieder were the first two. The *Minnelied* (No. 1), on a text by Tieck, compares a beloved to a murmuring stream, represented in the piano by gently meandering, sixteenth-note figuration. Heine's poem *Morgengruss* (*Morning Greeting*, No. 2) inspired simple but effective music that again aspired toward folksong. A shepherd tending his flocks greets his beloved, who does not answer. For Oswald Lorenz, Felix's music displayed the "beautifying power of a good engraving, which can lend to an insignificant locale . . . a bright, attractive appearance."[109] Felix conceived the songs for the growing market of domestic music making; impeccably crafted, they indeed show great polish but in the main impress as an undemanding supplement to the earlier Op. 34 set.

En route to Düsseldorf, Felix, Cécile, and Carl paused in Frankfurt to visit her family. There they learned of the death in Berlin of Eduard Gans, the Mendelssohns' intimate *Hausfreund* and former suitor of Rebecka, eulogized by Felix as a "worthy, irreplaceable man."[110] Fanny reported that he was buried next to Fichte and Hegel. The shock of Gans's passing (added to Rebecka's depression following the death of her son) raised new concerns about her health, so that later that summer Fanny escorted her to the Baltic resort of Heringsdorf for a cure.

Arriving in Düsseldorf on May 11, Felix plunged into rehearsals. The festival opened on Pentecost Sunday (May 19), with Handel's *Messiah*. Since no organ was available, Felix employed the 1789 arrangement by Mozart with supplemental wind parts. The event marked the debut of the young alto Sophie Schloss, whom Felix subsequently engaged for the next Gewandhaus season.[111] The next day featured Beethoven's *Eroica* Symphony and Mass in C major, an overture by Felix's successor in Düsseldorf, Julius Rietz, and Felix's own Psalm 42. The soloists included the sopranos Auguste von Fassmann from the Berlin opera and Clara Novello, who imbibed the local *Maitrank* with Felix and performed "Heil dir im

Siegerkranz," the German version of "God save the Queen" for Prince Frederick, governor of the Prussian Rhine Province.[112] Despite Felix's desire to mount a staged production of Gluck's *Alceste* on the third day, the final concert was devoted to the soloists, who sang arias and operatic excerpts; Felix played his Piano Concerto in D minor, Op. 40. With combined forces of 574 participants, the orchestra and chorus made an impressive spectacle: hundreds of dilettantes playing nearly to perfection, according to the critic of the *Kölner Zeitung*, Ludwig Bischoff. Only Novello was gently chastised for adding too many embellishments (*Schnörkeleien*) to her parts.[113]

VII

By late May 1839 Felix and family were once again enjoying the good life in Frankfurt, where they remained through the middle of July. To Lea he revealed Cécile was expecting their second child,[114] and on June 4 he happily performed organ music at the wedding of Cécile's sister Julie to Julius Schunck. Felix considered traveling to Vienna in the fall to conduct *Paulus*, and he accepted an invitation from the critic W. R. Griepenkerl to direct the Brunswick Music Festival in September. Among the diversions that summer was performing canons, including one designed to accommodate three voices and "sung" *ad infinitum* by Felix, Cécile, and Carl.[115]

To honor Felix, patrician Frankfurters organized a *fête champêtre* on the evening of June 19, when a party of forty (among them Dorothea Schlegel, her son Philipp Veit, and the writer Heinrich Hoffmann) crossed the Main and journeyed by omnibuses into the adjacent hills. There, amid beech trees softly lit by lanterns, an ensemble of twenty performed Felix's part-songs, including three newly composed, the canonic *Lerchengesang* (*Song of the Lark*), Op. 48 No. 4, *Hirtenlied*, Op. 88 No. 3, and, appropriately, *Im Wald* (*In the Forest*), Op. 100 No. 4. The guests drank champagne and supped on strawberries before returning to Frankfurt in the early morning hours.[116] Felix recorded the scene in a drawing[117] and came away appreciating how songs ought to sound in the open air; "it does seem the most natural of all music," he wrote to Klingemann, "when four people are rambling together in the woods, or sailing in a boat, and have the melody all ready with them and within them."[118] Later that year, the experience inspired Felix to complete his second collection of part-songs for mixed voices, Op. 48, and to begin his first collection for male chorus, Op. 50.

A somewhat more intimate occasion occurred near the end of June, when Cäcilienverein members organized an evening of tableaux vivants, for which Felix's music provided the inspiration and accompaniment. In the last illustration Fritz Schlemmer struck a humorous pose to imitate Felix absorbed in composition. Despite this merriment, Felix did produce serious music that summer, including three organ fugues in E minor, C major, and F minor.[119] Of these, the second eventually reappeared in the finale of the second Organ Sonata, Op. 65 No. 2, and Felix later considered redeploying the third in Op. 65 No. 1.[120] The occasion for the three fugues is not known, but Felix's Bachian studies may have prompted them, for in June the Frankfurt Kapellmeister, K. W. F. Guhr, showed Felix several Bach manuscripts, including autographs of the Passacaglia and chorale preludes.[121] Felix's C-major fugue is not unlike that of BWV 545, and the chromatic lines of the E-minor fugue recall something of the "Wedge" Fugue, also in E minor (BWV 548). In Frankfurt Felix found an unusual way to sharpen his organ playing through Fritz Schlemmer, who provided a pedal piano,[122] an odd invention that coupled a pedal board to a piano keyboard and thus allowed the musician to approximate the dense textures of an organ in a private residence (in 1845 Robert Schumann composed several studies for the instrument).

Undoubtedly the most impressive accomplishment of the summer was the Piano Trio No. 1 in D minor, Op. 49, drafted in June and July and revised in the fall before its release to Breitkopf & Härtel in January 1840. This was the work that prompted Schumann to label Felix the Mozart of the nineteenth century, the "most brilliant" of modern musicians who had reconciled the "contradictions" of the time.[123] Exactly which contradictions Schumann had in mind is unclear, but Ferdinand Hiller shed light on at least one issue of paramount importance to Felix—the tension between modish virtuoso display and the structural integrity of the work. When Felix played a draft of the trio for Hiller, he found the piano figuration too traditional:

> Certain pianoforte passages in it, constructed on broken chords, seemed to me—to speak candidly—somewhat old-fashioned. I had lived many years in Paris, seeing Liszt frequently, and Chopin every day, so that I was thoroughly accustomed to the richness of passages which marked the new pianoforte school. I made some observations to Mendelssohn on this point, suggesting certain alterations, but at first he would not listen to me. "Do you think that that would make the thing any better?" He said, "The piece would be the same, and so it may remain as it is." "But," I answered, "you have often told me . . . that the smallest touch of the brush, which might conduce to the perfection of the whole, must not be despised. An unusual form of arpeggio may not improve the harmony, but neither does it spoil it—and it becomes more interesting to the player." We discussed it and tried it on the piano over and over again, and I enjoyed the small triumph of at last getting Mendelssohn over to my view.[124]

Ex. 11.12a: Mendelssohn, Piano Trio in D minor, Op. 49 (1839), First Movement (first version)

Ex. 11.12b: Mendelssohn, Piano Trio in D minor, Op. 49 (1839), First Movement (final version)

According to Hiller, the exchange convinced Felix to rework the entire piano part, and give it a more brilliant polish. An examination of the original version[125] reveals that Hiller exaggerated somewhat, for the changes affected primarily the first movement. Even so, the retouches added a modern veneer to a work steeped in the classical tradition. Ex. 11.12a, b shows how Felix recast a passage from the closing group of the first movement, replacing routine triplets in the bass with thickened, cascading arpeggiations in the treble and syncopated chords in the bass.

What Felix did not alter was the thematic content and harmonic design of the work, and its measured formal proportions. With the exception of the scherzo, thematically unpredictable and delightfully quirky, the composition generally displays symmetrical phrase structures, sometimes in tension with the underlying affect of the music. The first thirty-nine measures of the first movement offer a case in point. The noble, opening cello melody falls into a sixteen-bar period that unfolds evenly in four-bar phrases (ex. 11.13). To create an undercurrent of rhythmic tension (the tempo is marked *Molto Allegro agitato*), Felix accompanies the theme with syncopated, *pianissimo* chords in the piano. Now the violin answers in two four-bar units, broadening the ascending fourth of the cello to an expressive sixth. In the third stage, all three instruments join in the thematic statement, which reaches its climax with an octave leap. The phrases again fall into predictable four-bar segments, as if Felix intends to balance the opening sixteen-bar period of the cello with one for the ensemble, to yield a readily apprehensible design: 16 + 8 + 16 bars. But the final phrase is cut short one bar, so that we have in-

Ex. 11.13: Mendelssohn, Piano Trio in D minor, Op. 49 (1839), First Movement

stead 16 + 8 + 15 bars, thus slightly disturbing the perfect symmetry and reconciling, as Schumann might have it, the needs of formal clarity and romantic unpredictability. When the recapitulation enters, Felix makes some adjustments to avoid routine repetition: the cello theme now appears against a new countermelody in the violin, and the symmetrical four-bar phrases momentarily yield to a five-bar, piano cadenza that again mars the symmetry. If a Mozartean grace suffuses the whole, there are nevertheless signs that mark the work as modern and romantic.

The B♭-major slow movement (in ternary ABA song form) begins as a gentle *Lied ohne Worte* for piano solo, answered by a duet for violin and cello. The contrasting middle section in the parallel minor introduces a new theme and accompaniment, in which the supple sixteenths of the opening give way to more insistent triplet chords. The return of the opening underscores the abstract vocal model of the genre, as the piano pauses to allow the violin and cello to execute two "vocal" cadenzas. Then the strings take up the sixteenth-note accompaniment and leave the piano to draw this enchanting movement to its murmuring close.

The third and fourth movements employ similar rondo designs, anchored by recurring refrains, and two statements each of two contrasting sections, to produce the scheme ABACABCA'. The puckish scherzo in D major begins with an asymmetrical refrain, an impish seven-bar figure that divides into three plus four and injects an element of playful whimsy. Animating much of the movement are the bustling sixteenth notes of the piano, which knit together the delicate tissues of the ensemble. Near the end an attenuated version of the refrain appears and dissolves into another telltale *pianissimo* puff, as the piano executes an ascending flourish that vanishes into delicate chords.

The weighty finale begins quietly with a restless theme that destabilizes the tonic D minor by dwelling on its Neapolitan, E♭ major. Though the music adopts a serious tone reminiscent of the agitated first movement, there is a subtle link to the scherzo: the defining rhythmic figure of the refrain, a quarter and two eighths (later at work too in the B section), derives from the scherzo, which springs from a rhythmic kernel of an eighth and two sixteenths. Proceeding farther into the finale, we realize that its function is to summarize the whole composition. Thus, the lyrical C section in B♭ major recalls the slow movement, and near the end, the metamorphosis of the brooding D minor into the parallel major recaptures something of the effervescent scherzo. The result is a masterful trio with subtle relationships between the movements, and a psychological curve that incorporates the agitated brooding of the first, subdued introspection of the second and the playful frivolity of the third. The finale combines all three moods, before reconciling them in the celebratory D-major ending.

The ink was hardly dry on the autograph of Op. 49 before Felix and his family left Frankfurt on July 19 to visit Horchheim for three weeks. There, near the vineyards of Uncle Joseph's estate, he settled into a quiet, uniform (*einformig*)[126] routine: composition in the morning, and swimming or drawing, piano practice, and walks in the afternoon. Drawing on his memory, he completed with Cécile the entries of their honeymoon diary. In the middle of this summer idyll came news of the death of Dorothea Schlegel, which Felix related to Lea: after an eight-day illness, his favorite aunt had succumbed, having lost her strength, "but not the consciousness, cheerfulness and spirit that always accompanied her in life."[127]

In Horchheim Felix penned the sentimental song *In dem Wald*, eventually released as Op. 57 No. 1. The major new effort was a magisterial setting of Psalm 114, for double chorus and orchestra. Little is known about the origins of the score, other than that Felix produced it in about two weeks, between the closing days of July and August 9.[128] In 1840 it inaugurated the New Year's Day Gewandhaus concert; later that year Felix revised the work and added a dedication to the Düsseldorf painter J. W. Schirmer, before publishing it in 1841 as his Op. 51.

The choice of text, a psalm in eight verses about the wonders of the Exodus (and one of the Hallel psalms sung before and after the Passover meal), prompted Sir George Grove in his landmark *Dictionary of Music and Musicians* of 1880 to hear the score as reaffirming Felix's Judaic roots: "The Jewish blood of Mendelssohn must surely for once have beat fiercely over this picture of the great triumph of his forefathers. . . ."[129] But, as Wolfgang Dinglinger has argued, Groves's conjecture was not based upon any statement from the composer himself.[130] Even so, it is difficult to imagine the Protestant Felix oblivious to the significance of the text for his family history. Here the positive imagery of the Exodus—e.g., the second verse, "Judah became God's sanctuary, Israel his dominion"— contrasts notably with the decidedly negative depiction of the Jews in *Paulus* as a "stiff-necked" race. Op. 51 may point to Felix's attempt to reconcile his Jewish ancestry and Christian faith by adopting what Jeffrey Sposato has termed a "dual perspective,"[131] a process that would ultimately reach its goal in *Elijah*.

From a musical point of view, Op. 51 owes much to Handel, especially *Joshua*, which Felix had performed at the Lower Rhine Festival in Cologne in 1838, and *Israel in Egypt*. Handel's word painting for the turning back of the Jordan in the eighth number of *Joshua* ("In wat'ry heaps affrighted Jordan stood, and backward to the fountain roll'd his flood") was not lost upon Felix, who devised similar watery imagery for the third verse of the psalm, "The sea looked and fled; Jordan turned back" (**ex. 11.14**). The reliance upon eight-part chorus (there are no soloists in Op. 51), too, suggests the grand double choruses of *Israel in Egypt*. But in conception and design, from the exordium-like opening to the culminating fugue on a celebratory verse added by Felix ("Hallelujah! Sing to the Lord

Ex. 11.14: Mendelssohn, Psalm 114, Op. 51 (1839), No. 2

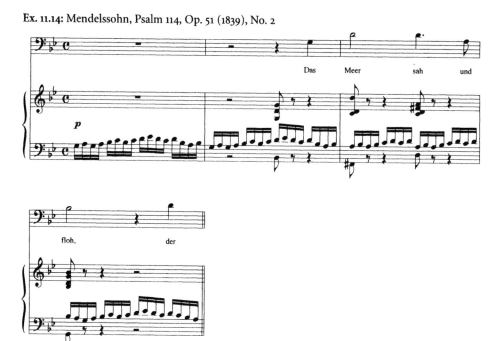

in eternity"), the composition is a product of nineteenth-century sensibilities and aesthetics. The eight verses of the psalm fit into four connected movements, according to this scheme:

1. Verses 1–2, *Allegro con moto maestoso*, G major
2. Verses 3–4, *Allegro moderato*, G minor
3. Verses 5–6, *Grave*, E♭ major (a cappella chorus)
4. Verses 7–8, *Allegro maestoso e vivace*, C major

To round out the work Felix added a fifth movement in G major, which
begins by recalling the music for the first two verses and continues with
the fugue on the supplemental text. The result is a circular, organic design centered on the powerfully moving third movement, in which the
hushed chorus asks, without orchestral support, "Why is it, O sea, that
you flee? O Jordan, that you turn back?" The shattering answer, "Tremble,
O earth, at the presence of the Lord," comes in the radiant fourth movement and then is intensified in the extrapolated fugue. The musical design thus resembles a protosonata form, in which the fifth movement,
restoring the key of G major, functions as recapitulation and coda.[132]
But the liberties Felix took with the text came at a cost: a review in the
Allgemeine musikalische Zeitung pondered why Felix had treated the culminating seventh and eighth verses as a mid- or turning point, instead
of the natural conclusion (no intensification was possible, the reviewer
noted, after the eighth verse),[133] and Schumann, who preferred Felix's
setting of Psalm 42, found that the second half of Psalm 114 reminded
him of music his friend had already composed.[134]

From Horchheim the Mendelssohns retraced their itinerary via
Frankfurt to Leipzig, where they arrived the evening of August 20, 1839.
One week later they were hosting Fanny, Wilhelm, and Sebastian, who
visited from Berlin en route to a yearlong Italian sojourn.[135] The happy
reunion was cut short by Felix's departure at the end of the month to
direct the Brunswick (Braunschweig) Music Festival. During the first
week of September, the citizens of the lower Saxon city and its ducal
court spared little effort to honor Felix as an international celebrity. On
the evening of his arrival, there was a torch-lit serenade outside his villa,
and thousands jostled into the Aegydien Church (the "fragment of a
large Gothic building, . . . sorely despoiled of much of its old ornaments
by time or violence")[136] to attend the rehearsals. We owe eyewitness reports of the gala concerts to the music critic of the *Athenaeum*, Henry
Fothergill Chorley, an anonymous correspondent for the *Allgemeine
musikalische Zeitung*, and Felix himself.[137] The orchestra, Chorley in-

forms us, comprised "unequal materials," members of the *Hofkapelle* and amateurs unused to rehearsing together. Despite the presence of the duke on a raised dais and the ban on applause during Felix's *Paulus*, the festival was vaguely egalitarian and promoted the mingling of the classes, so that elegant ladies primmed for a ball sat with "gypsy-colored, hard-handed peasant women."

Brunswick was the home of the progressive W. R. Griepenkerl, playwright, contributor to Schumann's music journal, and author of the recently published *Das Musikfest, oder die Beethovener* (*The Music Festival, or the Beethovenists*, 1838). In this *novella*, in which Felix directs a rehearsal of the Ninth Symphony, Griepenkerl celebrated Beethoven's final symphony as capturing the temper of the time and reading Schiller's "Ode to Joy" as a yearning for freedom.[138] Now, it seems, Griepenkerl's liberal sentiments were put to the test at the Brunswick Festival, as art imitated art, and Felix presented two Beethoven Symphonies (Nos. 5 and 7) to heterogeneous audiences on the second and third concerts.

The festival began on September 6 with a performance of *Paulus*, which inspired the *Allgemeine musikalische Zeitung* correspondent to compare Felix to a priest led by the muses to the invisible realm of Bach, Handel, Mozart, and Beethoven. The more prosaic Chorley regretted the lack of an organ to buttress the choruses and found the soloists wanting in feeling, but the chorus (some 440 strong) clear and precise and impressive in its sibilating effects. The highpoint of the second concert (September 7) was Felix's performance of Beethoven's Fifth Symphony, after which some ladies showered Felix with a *feu de joie* of floral bouquets. The evening continued with a ball, culminating in a ceremonial apotheosis of the composer. On a stage draped in white, with columns to imitate a temple, a female *geni* placed a crown of laurels upon his head while an ensemble softly sang a chorus from *Paulus*. The final concert (September 8) offered Beethoven's Seventh Symphony and featured Felix as a soloist in his D-minor Piano Concerto and *Serenade und Allegro giojoso*. According to Chorley, Felix's pianism lacked the "exquisite *finesses*" of Moscheles, the "spiritual seductions of Chopin," and the "brilliant extravagances of Liszt." "And yet," Chorley continued, "no one that ever heard Mendelssohn's pianoforte playing could find it dry, could fail to be excited and fascinated by it, despite of its want of all the caprices and colorings of his contemporaries. Solidity, in which the organ-touch is given to the piano without the organ ponderosity; spirit . . . animating, but never intoxicating, the ear; expression, which, making every tone sink deep, required not the garnishing of trills and appoggiature, or the aid of changes of time,—were among its outward and salient characteristics."[139]

VIII

Basking in the triumph of the festival, Felix returned to Leipzig about a month before the opening of the new Gewandhaus season on October 6. There was little time for rest. After a protracted correspondence with Vienna, Felix withdrew his earlier agreement to conduct *Paulus* at the Gesellschaft der Musikfreunde. His Viennese hosts had been unable or unwilling to reimburse his traveling expenses, and the issue had been bruited about in the Austrian press, much to Felix's displeasure.[140] Instead he took up a new "hobby"—advocating for the working conditions of the Gewandhaus orchestral personnel. After "no end of letter-writing, soliciting, and importuning," he managed to secure a salary raise for his musicians. "You see I am a regular small-beer Leipziger," he wrote to Moscheles. "But really you would be touched if you could see and hear for yourself how my good fellows put heart and soul into their work, and strive to do their best."[141] Felix was now deluged with visits from "foreigners," including musicians, dilettantes, and nobility, so that on September 10 he began keeping a *Fremdenliste*, scrupulously maintained until the end of the concert season in April 1840 (by the beginning of 1840 he had recorded 116 names).[142] The closing months of 1839 brought the Bach enthusiast and conductor J. T. Mosewius from Breslau; the Danish nationalist composer J. P. E. Hartmann from Copenhagen; Chorley from London; Clara Wieck, now visiting from Berlin and engaged, against her father's vehement opposition, to Schumann; Felix's old friends Droysen, Bendemann, and Hübner; Meyerbeer's brother Heinrich Beer; and Ferdinand Hiller, who arrived on December 6. During the stream of visitors, Cécile gave birth on October 2 to Marie Mendelssohn Bartholdy, and Felix began posting daily bulletins to Berlin about his daughter, whom he described as having dark hair in abundance and blue eyes. Near the end of October, Lea, Paul, and Albertine arrived from Berlin to attend the baptism.

The new concerts featured the Leipzig debuts of the Belgian soprano Elisa Meerti and mezzo-soprano Sophie Schloss, who appeared to perform Italian operatic excerpts, chiefly cavatinas by Spontini, Rossini, Bellini, Donizetti, and Mercadante. Because full scores were not readily available, Felix had orchestral arrangements prepared from piano scores by a copyist, who cleverly introduced "bold orchestral effects" that required slight retouches by Felix.[143] Among the other soloists was the pianist Marie Pleyel (née Moke), erstwhile fiancée of Berlioz, who had severed the engagement in 1830, after he left for Italy, to marry Camille Pleyel. The noteworthy performances included the premiere on October 30 of Felix's *Verleih' uns Frieden* of 1831, which Breitkopf & Härtel had published in June 1839 as a supplement to the *Allgemeine musikalische*

Zeitung, a lithographed facsimile of an autograph Felix prepared on specially ruled paper.[144] According to Chorley in 1839 the Gewandhaus was "infinitely too small for the audience who crowded it, paying their sixteen *groschen* (two shillings) for entrance, with no vainglorious notions of exclusiveness . . . to trouble their brains, but from a sheer thoroughgoing love of the art, and a certainty that they should be gratified."[145]

As 1839 drew to a close, Felix returned in earnest to the part-song and produced several new euphonious examples, among them *Abendständchen,* Op. 75 No. 2 and the drinking song *Ersatz für Unbestand,* published in the *Deutscher Musenalmanach* for 1839.[146] By year's end he had finished his second volume for mixed chorus, Op. 48; the first volume for male voices, the *Sechs Lieder* Op. 50, followed one month later. In these settings, inspired by the open-air parties of Frankfurt and the Leipzig Liedertafel (twelve male friends who met regularly for music, conversation, and wine), Felix explored the cozy domain of the musical *Biedermeier.* Gracefully melodious and entertaining, the choral songs project again those attributes of moderation, contentment, and domesticity we have detected in other works from the early years of Felix's marriage. Harmonically straightforward and unchallenging contrapuntally,[147] the music inevitably serves the texts, which offer escapist images of nature and convivial drinking songs. Among the latter is Op. 50 No. 5, *Liebe und Wein* (*Love and Wine*), to be sung in an intoxicated tone. Hiller reports that for the amusement of the Liedertafel, the two friends composed the same text and offered their creations like a blind musical wine tasting to the Liedertafel. Only one member, Schleinitz, was able to distinguish correctly their authorship.[148]

Several of Felix's part-songs (e.g., the marchlike *Der Jäger Abschied* [*Hunters' Farewell*], Op. 50 No. 2, to which he added optional brass parts) attained great popularity in nineteenth-century Germany and reveal his abiding appeal to the burgeoning middle-class culture of Leipzig. Indeed, some of the melodies were assimilated into folksong collections. But as the pendulum of the twentieth-century swung, these pleasant miniatures were dismissed as superficial utterances. Thus Philip Radcliffe found the choral songs "liable to cloy in too large quantities," and Eric Werner detected "Old Boys Philistinism" in a part-song from Felix's last year, *Comitat,* Op. 76 No. 4.[149] The former popularity had become a liability, and the music fell to an elitist argument. But Felix himself probably never viewed these pieces as anything more than a rapprochement with middlebrow culture; hence the "everyday," formulaic harmonic progressions that announce the coming of spring in Op. 48 No. 1 (*Frühlingsahnung* [*Presentiment of Spring*]) and its anticipated return at the conclusion of No. 6 (*Herbstlied* [*Autumn Song*]). Similarly, the use of humor in Op. 50 Nos. 1

Ex. 11.15: Mendelssohn, *Wasserfahrt*, Op. 50 No. 4 (1840)

and 5 progresses nearly to pastiche, as if parodying the bourgeois mentality. The part-songs, however, are not altogether devoid of artistic merit and originality. Op. 48 shows signs of a cyclic design in its coordinated key relationships and subtle manipulation of spring imagery, from the gentle stirring in No. 1 (*süsser Hauch*) to the forest rustling of No. 6 (*Waldesrauschen*).[150] And the barcarolle-like Op. 50 No. 4, *Wasserfahrt* (*Water Journey*), on a poem of Heine, successfully captures the seductive rhythms and veiled undertones of the piano Venetian *Gondellieder* (**ex. 11.15**). Nevertheless, by 1839 Felix could convincingly play the contented bourgeois and produce music designed to appeal to middle-class sensibilities. But his accommodation to *Biedermeier* values and lapse into *Behaglichkeit* was only one side of a multifaceted, versatile genius.

Chapter 12
1840–1841

Leipzig vs. Berlin

Berlin—one of the sourest apples one can
bite, and yet it must be bitten.

—Felix to Klingemann,
July 15, 1841[1]

The new decade began unpropitiously for Felix: debilitated by a severe
cold, he arrived on a *Portechaise* at the Gewandhaus to direct the New
Year's Day concert. The winter season, among the most memorable of
his tenure, was soon in full swing. For the next concert (January 9), he
made a virtue of necessity when the featured violinist, Carl Stör from
Weimar, disappeared after his first solo, leaving a gap in the second half.
On the program were Beethoven's first two *Leonore* Overtures; Felix now
added the third and *Fidelio* Overtures—both unrehearsed, according to
the *Allgemeine musikalische Zeitung*[2]—so that for the first time Leipzigers
heard all four together. Felix's choice of repertoire again underscored
his effort to promote new music, including symphonies by Friedrich
Schneider of Dessau, J. F. Kittl of Prague, and J. W. Kalliwoda of Donau-
eschingen, and a new overture by Julius Rietz. But an attempt to encore
the Schubert "Great" Symphony on March 12 failed when a false fire
alarm emptied the hall; Felix reprogrammed the symphony on the final
concert of the season two weeks later.

The concerts also featured works for soloists other than the custom-
ary singers, violinists, and pianists. A series of wind players, many drawn
from the orchestra, took the stage to perform pieces featuring the flute,
oboe, clarinet, bassoon, natural horn, and trombone. And on February
6, there was an unusual, late addition to the fifteenth concert: the cavatina
"Casta diva" from Bellini's *Norma*, rendered by Herr Toselli of Ferrara

on a glass harmonica. This entertaining contraption, comprising "tuned" glasses that could be struck or rubbed, had appeared in the eighteenth century. In the 1760s, captivated by the glasses' otherworldly resonance, Benjamin Franklin began tinkering with the instrument, which subsequently enjoyed a new vogue. In 1791, Mozart composed a quintet that employed the instrument (K. 617). Toselli's instrument boasted several octaves of glass disks struck with a cork hammer. Their eerie high partials and silvery tones must have created a sensation among an audience accustomed to a coloratura soprano playing Bellini's Druid priestess.

Compensating for this unusual fare was a diet of Haydn, Mozart, and Beethoven; as a soloist, Felix chose to appear with a classical work and on January 30 performed the Mozart Double Piano Concerto in E♭, K. 365. Felix's partner was Ferdinand Hiller, in Leipzig to finish his new oratorio, *Die Zerstörung Jerusalems* (*The Destruction of Jerusalem*). As in the 1832 performance of the concerto with Moscheles in London, Felix produced two brilliant cadenzas for the outer movements, performed in the spirit of a "free double fantasy" extemporized on the spot.[3] But Felix took the time to notate his contributions, designed as two tautly unified miniature compositions that recalled, developed, and rewove the diverse themes of the concerto,[4] and thus harnessed the virtuoso display to buttress the artistic integrity of Mozart's composition.

In tandem with the orchestral concerts was the expanded series of six chamber-music concerts (January 25–March 7), again organized by Ferdinand David and benefiting from the participation of Felix, who accompanied David and played piano duets with Hiller. Formerly described as *Quartettsoiréen*, these performances were rebilled as *Abendunterhaltungen* ("evening entertainments"). The repertory, chiefly "classical" violin sonatas, piano trios, and string quartets, drew heavily upon Haydn, Mozart, and Beethoven; representing contemporary music were works by Cherubini, Spohr, Onslow, Hiller, and Felix. The season stood out for several memorable events. The final concert introduced Schubert's "Death and the Maiden" String Quartet and culminated in two octets, Spohr's Double Quartet in D minor and Felix's own genial Octet, in which he took up one of the viola parts. Equally noteworthy was his effort to enrich the classical and modern repertory by presenting little-known music of J. S. Bach. Thus, on February 29, 1840, Felix performed a work destined to become a staple of twentieth-century pianists, the *Chromatic Fantasia and Fugue*, BWV 903. Felix managed to unravel its fugal complexities and achieve clarity of interpretation, and almost entranced a correspondent into imagining Felix had composed the work, among Bach's most harmonically audacious and contrapuntally involved creations.[5]

A few weeks before, on February 8, Ferdinand David performed two solo violin works of Bach: the Prelude from the Partita in E major, and the formidable *Ciaconna* from the Partita in D minor, BWV 1006 and 1004. Both had been in print since 1802 but not yet entered the modern violinist's repertory, on account of their uncompromising technical difficulties and the public's lack of interest in Bach's austere, contrapuntal music. The 1840 Gewandhaus performance changed the common perception: ". . . Herr Dr. Mendelssohn Bartholdy accompanied both works on the piano with a harmonic reduction freely executed in contrapuntal style. These Bach solo pieces were originally for violin alone, without a bass line or figured bass, ... To be sure, this [manner] suffices for artists, who are in a position to recognize and evaluate the harmonic progressions and artful design. But the public requires in addition an aid, a kind of commentary, to render the whole work more graphic and to facilitate its understanding."[6]

In the main, Felix simply added a bass line and modest chordal accompaniment, and thereby modernized Bach's Baroque masterpieces by extracting from the violin part its implied harmonic underpinnings. But in the magisterial Chaconne variations, Felix took the process somewhat farther. J. Michael Cooper has shown that whereas Bach's conception grouped several variations in pairs, Felix's conceptualization reinforced a broader division of the work into three movements (D minor, D major, and D minor), with Bach's arpeggiated variations near the end of the first and third sections, performed without the crutch of the keyboard, serving as virtuoso cadenzas. The effect was to transform a previously inaccessible solo violin work into a *Konzertstück* for violin and accompaniment,[7] a genre music-loving Leipzigers fully appreciated. In this way Felix rendered a Baroque masterpiece meaningful to his contemporaries. His arrangement, published in 1847, triggered a rash of transcriptions of the Chaconne for the next hundred years (including examples by Schumann, Brahms, Busoni, and the American conductor Leopold Stokowski[8]) and gave renewed impetus to the nineteenth-century Bach Revival.

Curiously, Felix's arrangement appeared first not in Germany but in England, where Ewer & Co. brought it out only months before the composer's death. The manager of this firm was Edward Buxton, a London wool merchant of German descent, who in 1840 began to vie with Novello for the English rights to Felix's music. Several issues had strained Felix's relationship with J. Alfred Novello and led to a final rupture in 1841, when Alfred organized an English performance of the *Lobgesang* Symphony, despite Felix's desire to withhold the work for revision.[9] First, Alfred had tried to advance the career of his sister, Clara, by urging Felix to dedicate to her his setting of Psalm 42. Then, in 1838, Alfred pressed the internationally acclaimed composer of *St. Paul* to enter a choral competition in Dublin. And finally, in February 1840 the publisher declined the Piano Trio No. 1, Op. 49, for he feared "such a work would command a very small sale amongst our ignorant public."[10] In Alfred's defense, he was not the only publisher unconvinced by the trio. Breitkopf & Härtel's Parisian agent, Heinrich Probst, encountered difficulty securing a French publisher and reported, "Mendelssohn is not yet moving here. Perhaps he will do better in the future. He is too learned to be popular."[11] Still, the French firm of Simon Richault paid 200 francs for the Trio, and Buxton readily bought the English rights for 10 guineas.[12]

In the middle of the concert season Felix pondered several invitations to direct music festivals that year. The first was the brainchild of John Thomson, the Scottish composer Felix had befriended in 1829 and, ten years later, recommended for a professorship of music at the University of Edinburgh. From his new post Thomson aspired to mount oratorios of Handel, Haydn, and Mendelssohn. But the plan foundered when Felix urged instead a performance of the St. Matthew Passion—not possible in Presbyterian Edinburgh, Thomson explained, for "having Christ as one of the dramatic personae would be a fatal objection to its performance in this country."[13] And so Felix declined the invitation and accepted engagements to direct *Paulus* in Weimar (May), the North German Musical Festival in Schwerin (July), and the Birmingham Musical Festival (September). In addition, he began a composition for a Leipzig festival in June commemorating the 400th anniversary of Gutenberg's invention of movable type; by February the work was still not advanced enough to determine whether it would be "a kind of smaller oratorio or larger psalm."[14]

Another project dear to Felix's heart slowly coalesced when the Leipzig publisher Brockhaus inquired why there was no reliable modern edition of Moses Mendelssohn's writings. In February, Felix wrote to Joseph Mendelssohn and set in motion a train of events that ultimately produced a new *Gesamtausgabe*, edited by Joseph's son Benjamin, with a biographical sketch of the philosopher by Felix's uncle.[15] Joseph's literary interests also extended to a volume published that year about Dante and his time, on which Felix labored, translating into German sonnets by Boccaccio and other *trecento* poets. But according to Hiller, Felix's nagging self-criticism delayed the timely completion of his work, and Joseph, with "an uncle's want of consideration," availed himself of other versions.[16]

The resounding acclaim for *St. Paul* encouraged Felix's search for a new oratorio libretto, even though discussions with Klingemann and

Schubring in 1837 and 1838 had failed to produce a viable option for *Elijah*. Other admirers of the composer had begun to volunteer their services. Thus, from Moscow the Lutheran pastor Karl Sederholm sent in November 1838 a collection of texts from Milton, Metastasio, and the Roman Breviary for a large church piece that "would envelop *all* the principal moments of Christendom."[17] Nothing came of this unsolicited contribution, though its striving for monumentality seems to have intrigued Felix: by the summer of 1839 he was discussing with Karl Gollmick an oratorio provisionally titled "Earth, Heaven and Hell" (*Erde, Himmel und Hölle*), to concern the "three highest principles of moral existence."[18] At some point Felix took up the concept with Chorley, who by November 1839 had devised a new proposal to concretize the vague "floating vision of Earth, Hell, and Paradise"[19]—the chiasmic Lucan parable of Dives and Lazarus. But Felix found Dives only "very rich" and Lazarus "very poor"; Chorley's *scenarium* failed to explain why one ended up in Hell, while the other received comfort in Abraham's bosom.[20] Felix now turned to Schubring, who advised him to consult the apocryphal Gospel of Nicodemus, which contained a "really poetic depiction of Christ's descent into Hell" and might provide a unifying element for the oratorio.[21] Felix even committed himself to reading the gospel in Greek but then became distracted by the thought of writing an oratorio about John the Baptist. Possibly, this new subject was a response to the commission for the Gutenberg Festival, for its first day, June 24, was not only the name day of the printer but also the Feast of John the Baptist, the traditional initiation day for printers' apprentices.[22] Lack of time dissuaded Felix from this effort, and instead he developed sketches he had made in 1838 and 1839 for a symphony in B♭ major. In short, his oratorio needs found a partial outlet in what became the *Lobgesang* Symphony.

I

Amid Felix's oratorio ruminations, the 1839–1840 season came to a tumultuous climax in March, when Franz Liszt made his Gewandhaus debut (March 17–24 and 30–31). Initially, there were no signs of the sensational *Lisztmanie* that would sweep over staid Berliners late in 1841, when swooning female admirers fought over his cigar butts and locks of hair. Indeed, the first Leipzig concert nearly caused a fiasco.[23] The German tour began auspiciously enough in Dresden, where on March 16 Liszt dazzled a capacity audience, including members of the Saxon court, with transcriptions of Schubert Lieder and fantasy-like paraphrases of Meyerbeer and Donizetti. Present that evening was Robert Schumann, who covered the event for the *Neue Zeitschrift für Musik* and found himself overwhelmed by sensations ranging from tenderness to madness.[24] The next day, Schumann accompanied the virtuoso on a train to Leipzig and witnessed with Felix an extraordinary chain of events. Owing to a scheduling miscue, Liszt's first engagement with the Gewandhaus orchestra had to be rearranged at the last minute as a solo concert, but what truly enraged music-loving Leipzigers were the actions of his concert manager, Hermann Cohen ("Puzzi"), who ignored Gewandhaus protocols by hiking the ticket prices, adding a surcharge for reserved seating, and disallowing complimentary passes. When the elegantly dressed Liszt strode onto the stage "as lithe and slender as a tiger-cat," and with flowing, long locks, he was booed. Felix made a telling aside to Hiller, "There's a novel apparition, the virtuoso of the nineteenth century."[25]

Unlike most concert pianists of the time, Liszt was accustomed to presenting solo recitals, unassisted by an orchestra or other artists; but his choice of repertoire on the evening of March 17 failed to win over the audience. Although half the audience stood on their chairs to witness Liszt's electrifying rendition of Schubert's *Erlkönig*, in the same hall where Felix had performed Beethoven's nine symphonies Liszt now dared to offer a transcription of the last two movements of the *Pastoral* Symphony, the pictorial thunder storm and shepherd's song of thanksgiving. The Leipzig audience, familiar with the genuine article, found the striving toward orchestral effects comparatively pale (Liszt's assertion, that the modern piano could successfully reproduce orchestral effects, failed to convince Felix, who reacted, "Well if I could only hear the first eight bars of Mozart's G minor Symphony, with that delicate figure in the [violas], rendered on the piano as it sounds in the orchestra,—I would believe it").[26] The next day Liszt fell ill with a fever and canceled his second concert. Schumann evidently believed the illness was a "diplomatic" malady;[27] still, he joined Felix and Hiller in tending to the artist in his sick room. Of the three, Felix most impressed Liszt; writing to his mistress Marie d'Agoult, he praised Felix's drawings and violin and viola playing, and noted that he read Homer in the Greek and spoke four or five languages fluently.[28]

Though comfortable conversing in German, Liszt insisted on using French, so that Felix complained that social intercourse with him was like sitting in the middle of Paris.[29] Schumann found Liszt's bearing overly aristocratic—the middle-class culture of Leipzig was apparently not to the liking of the artist, who complained about the lack of toilets and nobility.[30] Sensing a need to heal a growing rift, Felix, Hiller, and Schumann arranged a series of private musicales, from which the general public was excluded. At one musical matinée given by Felix, Liszt ap-

peared in Hungarian uniform and played a series of pyrotechnical variations on a Hungarian folk melody. Then, insisting his host reciprocate,
Liszt watched incredulously as Felix replicated the Hungarian melody,
executed one variation after another, and managed to imitate Liszt's
"movements and raptures" without offending him.[31] The culmination
of Liszt's visit was a grand soirée at the Gewandhaus on March 23 for 250
guests, which Felix organized in two days, complete with an orchestra,[32]
chorus, and three English grand pianos. Between mulled wine and crêpes,
Felix directed the Schubert "Great" Symphony, Psalm 42, *Meeresstille und
glückliche Fahrt*, and choruses from *Paulus*. Then, Felix, Liszt, and Hiller
performed the Bach Triple Concerto in D minor (the parts arrived from
Dresden at the beginning of the concert), and Liszt concluded with some
solo numbers.[33]

Felix's goodwill facilitated Liszt's successful return to the public stage.
On March 24 he gave his second public concert, which featured Felix's
favorite *Konzertstück* of Carl Maria von Weber, and Liszt's fantasy on
Meyerbeer's *Les Huguenots* and transcriptions of Schubert's *Ständchen*,
Ave Maria, and *Erlkönig*. A reviewer in the *Allgemeine musikalische Zeitung*
marveled at Liszt's fast tempi, precision, and monstrous technique, and
Schumann found the Weber the "crown" of Liszt's accomplishments.[34]
But the reviewer also noted Liszt's habit of introducing novelties into
Weber's score, including doublings to render relatively easy passages more
difficult, and a superabundance of ornaments to give the work a more
brilliant veneer. If, the critic admitted, these changes accorded with the
spirit of the original, there was nevertheless the danger that younger
pianists would attempt similar modifications, with more pernicious results. No doubt Felix found Liszt's willful tampering a violation of the
integrity of Weber's score and expressed further reservations about Liszt's
compositional abilities. In his colorful fantasies and transcriptions, all
based on other composers' works, Felix detected a lack of original ideas.
Liszt's performance was "as unpremeditated, as wild and impetuous, as
you would expect of a genius, but then I miss those genuinely original
ideas [that] I naturally expect from a genius."[35]

On March 30 Liszt concluded his Leipzig tour with a benefit concert
for the orchestral pension fund. Seeking to acknowledge the hospitality
of Felix, Hiller, and Schumann, he featured works by the three, including Felix's Piano Concerto No. 2, some etudes by Hiller, and Schumann's
Carnaval. But the performance of the concerto, which Liszt had learned
only a few days before, was technically imperfect. Still, Felix admired
Liszt's standing as a pianist without peer and his musical feeling that
found "its way to the very tips of his fingers."[36] The two would meet
again in 1841 in Berlin.

II

Recovering from the Lisztian tumult, Felix returned to the sobering world of German oratorio. On April 2 came the premiere of *Die Zerstörung Jerusalems*, about the destruction of Jerusalem by Nebuchadnezzar's Babylonians. Hiller had struggled to create the work, and Felix was heavily involved with it, which remained popular with German choral societies for a few decades. A few months before the premiere, on Christmas Eve 1839, he surprised Hiller with a cleanly written revision of the libretto. The music was not far removed from the Handelian choruses of *Paulus*, though Hiller preferred to view his score as anticipating *Elijah*.[37]

On April 9, 1840, Felix entered in his *Fremdenliste* a visit by a Marx of Berlin, almost certainly Adolf Bernhard Marx, at the time also laboring over an oratorio. Undeterred by his failed earlier collaboration with Felix (see p. 267), Marx had pressed on and finished *Mose* in 1839 (in 1853, Joachim Raff, impressed by the attempt to bridge the gulf between oratorio and opera, described *Mose* as a "music drama in evening dress").[38] Now Marx turned to Felix for assistance in promoting his *magnum opus*. According to Marx's widow, Therese, after playing through the work Felix curtly announced he could do nothing for it, whereupon Marx closed the score and returned to Berlin. A few days later, from a bridge in the *Tiergarten* he threw Felix's letters into the water and thus severed the final bond of friendship.[39] Embittered, Marx now became an implacable foe of Felix. Instead of a triumphant Leipzig performance, he settled for a premiere in Breslau in 1841, while the musical press debated the merits of the oratorio.[40] At mid-century, Liszt revived it in Weimar, but it failed to enter the repertory.

After the end of the concert season Felix celebrated Easter in Berlin with Lea, Rebecka, and Paul. Traveling by carriage with Carl, Marie, and Cécile, now pregnant with their third child, Felix spent the night in Potsdam and then on April 10 used the new train service to Berlin, which brought his family nearly to the front door of Leipzigerstrasse No. 3.[41] Clara Wieck and Robert Schumann were then in Berlin (in June Schumann would bring a slander suit against her father) and enjoyed intimate musical parties with Felix.[42] He also encountered the French composer Adolphe Adam, returning from St. Petersburg to Paris and about to create his most popular work, the ballet *Giselle*.[43] With Cécile and the children safely resettled in Leipzig, Felix proceeded to Weimar, where, after three rehearsals, he directed *Paulus* on May 26. The resources were considerably smaller than those of the grand music festivals over which Felix had presided. The orchestra consisted of only sixty musicians; the chorus, one hundred and forty-five. Still, the performance was a success, and in the town of Goethe, Schiller, and Hummel, Felix was treated like a dignitary, escorted everywhere by doting cicerones.[44]

Two civic projects now underscored Felix's role as the arbiter of Leipzig musical culture. In February 1839 the Oberhofgerichtsrat Dr. Heinrich Blümner, a Gewandhaus director, had died, bequeathing to the Saxon king 20,000 thalers to support the establishment of an institute for art or science. Felix began a determined campaign to win the funds for a new music conservatory. Writing on April 8, 1840 to the king's Kreisdirektor, J. P. von Falkenstein, Felix outlined the proposed academy and made the case for Leipzig, where music had long been inextricably woven into the social fabric.[45] The Thomaskirche and its cherished Bachian traditions, the flourishing concert life at the Gewandhaus, and the established university were prominent symbols of a municipal musical culture that had "struck its roots deep." Lacking was a local institute to consolidate the artistic triangulation and to facilitate the musical training of students from the various classes. Felix sketched a vision of the school: it would admit local and foreign students supported by scholarships and offer a three-year course in the practical and theoretical sides of music. The faculty would include instructors in theory (thoroughbass, counterpoint, and fugue), singing, piano, violin, and cello. Students would sing in a chorus and play in an orchestra. Overseeing the governance of the institution would be directors including the Leipzig mayor and the royal Kreisdirektor.[46]

A more immediate demonstration of Felix's civic-mindedness came in June, when he participated in the three-day Gutenberg Festival. Many German cities held celebrations, but those in Leipzig struck an especially resonant chord: as epicenter of the German book trade, Leipzig had long been associated with publishing, and the anniversary thus offered a nostalgic occasion to celebrate the centuries-old trade and its guilds. The festival honored more than printing: the Gutenberg Bible was championed as the lamp that disseminated enlightenment, the means by which German realms had progressed from ignorant superstition to enlightened wisdom. Gutenberg's technological advance was linked to Luther and the spread of the Reformation; as it happened, the second day of the festival, June 25, coincided with the commemoration of the Augsburg Confession, one of the signal events in the Protestant calendar.

Preceding the festivities was the premiere on June 23 of Albert Lortzing's new comic Singspiel about the life of Hans Sachs, the legendary sixteenth-century *Meistersänger* from Nürnberg whom Richard Wagner repopularized in his music drama of 1868. Then, on June 24, the bustling Leipzig Marktplatz became the site of several ceremonies, including a church service, dedication of a new statue of Gutenberg, and speech by Raymund Härtel, who likened the inventor to the "John the

Baptist of the Reformation."[47] For the occasion, Felix composed a *Fest-gesang* for male chorus and double brass band (trumpets, horns, trombones, ophicleide, and timpani), spatially separated to generate echo effects in the square. Performed by a chorus of two hundred, with sixteen trumpets and twenty trombones, the composition made quite an impression; Felix assured Lea that not even Spontini, never one to resist fustian effects, would have been able to say, *encore deux violins*.[48] The text, by a Gymnasium teacher from Freiberg, Adolf Proelss, summarized in rather insipid verses the principal metaphors of the festival—Gutenberg as a German hero who had lit a symbolic torch, the victory of light over darkness through the dissemination of printing, and the role of the festival as a *Lobgesang*, or hymn of praise. While the *Festgesang* resounded over the square, members of the printing guild plied their trade, and printed copies of a Lied were distributed from a local press and sung as the new statue was unveiled.[49]

To underscore the ceremonial, quasi-sacred function of the *Festgesang*, Felix framed the work with well-known Lutheran chorales, *Sei Lob und Ehr der höchsten Gut* and *Nun danket alle Gott*, to which he fitted Proelss's verses. The two internal movements included antiphonal effects for "The Lord spoke, let there be light!" (No. 3) and a Lied destined to become one of Felix's most famous compositions (No. 2, ex. 12.1). Sung largely in unison to an accompaniment of brass chords, Felix's melody extolled Gutenberg and the *Vaterland*. One year later the melody was pressed into service for the unveiling of a monument to Hermann, who centuries before had defeated the Romans in the Teutoburger forest.[50] Then, in 1843, Felix corresponded with Buxton about a suitable text for an English edition: "If the right [words] are hit at, I am sure that piece will be liked very much by the singers and the hearers, but it will *never* do to sacred words. There must be a national and merry subject found out, something to which the soldierlike and buxom motion of the piece has some relation. . . ."[51] Felix never found a suitable English text, but in 1856, the young organist William H. Cummings discovered that the words of Charles Wesley's Christmas hymn, "Hark! the Herald Angels Sing," readily fitted the melody.[52] By 1861, the new *contrafactum* had appeared in a hymnal, and begun its second life as a Christmas carol.

Ex. 12.1: Mendelssohn, *Festgesang* (1840), No. 2

Va - ter - land, in dei - nen Gau - en brach der gold' - ne Tag einst an,

The culmination of the festival came on June 25, when Felix conducted three ceremonial works in a crowded Thomaskirche: Weber's *Jubel Overture*, which cited the Saxon anthem *Gott segne Sachsenland* (to the melody of "God save the King"), Handel's *Dettingen Te Deum*, and the premiere of the *Lobgesang*, published the following year as Op. 52. Employing biblical texts, principally from the psalms, the symphony tied together the principal threads of the festival into a patriotic offering of thanksgiving. The work, three orchestral movements chain-linked to a cantata of nine movements, traced the triumph of light over darkness and celebrated Gutenberg's invention as the disseminator of God's word through the printed Lutheran Bible. (For the first edition of the score, Felix appended as a motto a quotation from Luther's sacred song book of 1525: "Rather I wished to see all the arts, especially music, serving Him who gave and created them.") But though the initial response was overwhelmingly favorable, the composition would enjoy a curiously mixed reception—among the most popular of Felix's works during his lifetime, it also prompted vigorous debate about its hybrid genre (part symphony, part cantata), insertion of chorales into the concert hall, and transparent reliance on Beethoven's Ninth Symphony.[53]

Some of its detractors were not completely objective. In 1847 Felix's estranged colleague A. B. Marx published a substantial essay in the *Allgemeine musikalische Zeitung* in which he dismissed the work as an ill-conceived imitation of the Ninth. Whereas in his finale Beethoven had opposed instrumental and choral forces for different ends, in the *Lobgesang* Felix allied two statements of the same idea: an abstract, instrumental hymn of praise prepared a (redundant) vocal utterance of that praise. The result was a pale imitation of Beethoven that lacked inner necessity.[54] Punning on Felix's name, Fétis rejected the *Lobgesang* as an "unhappy" conception,[55] while in the essay *Das Kunstwerk der Zukunft* (1849) Wagner mocked the "full-throated" choral hymn of praise as unoriginal and, without identifying Felix, derided him as an example of "this or that composer" emboldened to write a choral symphony.

Even some of Felix's friends expressed public and private reservations. After comparing the soprano duet "Ich harrete des Herrn" (No. 5, "I waited for the Lord," Psalm 40:1) to a glimpse of heaven adorned with Raphael's Madonnas, Robert Schumann recommended the separation of the symphonic and choral movements, to their mutual advantage.[56] In a letter to Franz Hauser, Moritz Hauptmann wondered whether the symphonic movements were an "accessory" to the whole, and Hans von Bülow, who as a young boy had met Felix in April 1840 and later had piano instruction from him, found several parts pale and uninspired, though others not smudged by the stamp of genius.[57] The central issue

concerned the work's generic identity, and, indeed, the composer himself labored over this problem. Months before its premiere, Felix announced to Klingemann the work would probably be a small oratorio
or large psalm setting. But the composer then quashed rumors that he
was writing a major oratorio for the festival and labeled the work a symphony. After performing the *Lobgesang* at the Birmingham Musical Festival in September, self-doubt again tormented him, and, at Klingemann's
suggestion, Felix subtitled the work a *Symphonie-Kantate*.[58] By the end
of November, he had finished revising the score,[59] which mainly involved
adding three new solos to the cantata (Nos. 3, 6, and 9) and an organ
part. In its final form the work then appeared from Breitkopf & Härtel
in September 1841.

If Beethoven emphasized in the Ninth the divide between the orchestral movements and choral finale (it begins, of course, by rejecting
the themes of the three preceding movements), Felix aimed in the
Lobgesang at a unified whole, in which the addition of text served to
complement and explicate (but not disavow) the abstract symphonic
form. Binding the binary complex together is the *Ur*-motive announced
at the opening by the trombones (ex. 12.2) and answered by the orchestra
in ceremonial responsorial style. Related to the "Jupiter" motive and the
intonation employed in Felix's setting of Psalm 42, the figure is prominent
throughout the first movement and anticipates the later addition of text.
The symphonic movements contain other clear references to vocal models. Thus, a clarinet recitative links the first movement to the second, an
expressive *Allegretto* in G minor, in the Trio of which Felix introduces a
freely composed chorale melody in G major (ex. 12.3). Intoned in the winds
like a call to worship, the pseudochorale sounds vaguely familiar and prepares the third movement, in a devotional tempo marked *Andante religioso*.
The cantata then begins by reasserting the intonation, to which the chorus adds the final verse of Psalm 150, "All that has life and breath, sing to
the Lord." Finally, the composition concludes with a recall of the motive,
thus returning us to its opening and reaffirming its wholeness.

Ex. 12.2: Mendelssohn, *Lobgesang* Symphony, Op. 52 (1840), No. 1

Ex. 12.3: Mendelssohn, *Lobgesang* Symphony, Op. 52 (1840), Allegretto

The formal designs of the wordless and vocal parts also reinforce that unity through a series of structural parallels, key relationships, and links between movements (**diagram 12.1**). The three symphonic parts chart a tonal descent, from B♭ major to G minor/major and D major. Similarly, the first half of the through-composed cantata (Nos. 2–5) unfolds a downward tonal spiral, this one by thirds (B♭–g–E♭–c), to suggest a symbolic plunge into darkness. The midpoint, No. 6 ("The sorrows of death had closed all around me," Psalm 116:3), presents Felix's most dissonant vein. In a tenor recitative based on Isaiah 21, the question "Watchman, will the

Diagram 12.1: Mendelssohn, *Lobgesang* Symphony, Op. 52 (1840)

Sinfonia, No. 1

Maestoso	**Allegro**	**Allegretto**	**Andante religioso**
motto	(recitative)	Trio (chorale)	
B♭ —	B♭	g / G / g	D

(B♭—B♭ bracketed) (g/G/g bracketed)

Cantata, Nos. 2–10

2		3	4	5 ⌢	6 ⌢
Allegro	**Moderato**	**Recitative, Allegro**		**Andante**	**Allegro**
motto					
Chorus (organ)	Sopr., Chor.	Tenor		Chorus	Sopr. duet, Chor.	Tenor
B♭ —	B♭	g	—	g	E♭	c

(tonal descent by thirds)

7	8	9	10	
Allegro	**Chorale**	**Andante**	**Allegro**	**Maestoso**
Chorus (organ)	*Nun danket alle Gott* a cappella, orch.	Sopr./Ten.	Chorus fugue (organ)	motto
D	G	B♭ —	B♭ —	B♭

(reversal of *Sinfonia*)

night soon pass?" is posed three times, at successively higher pitch levels, in a dramatic technique reminiscent of Stephen's recitative in *Paulus*. A soprano heralds the lifting of darkness, celebrated in the radiant D-major chorus, "The night is departing" (No. 7, Romans 13:12). Then the chorale *Nun danket alle Gott* appears in G major (No. 8, the very chorale and key Felix had employed in the *Festgesang*) and gives meaning to the voiceless chorale in the *Allegretto* of the *Sinfonia*. The final two movements, which culminate in a celebratory fugue, return us to B♭ major and thus reverse the tonal descent of the symphonic movements to suggest the triumph of light over darkness.

Much of the debate that swirled around the *Lobgesang* concerned its relationship to Beethoven's Ninth Symphony. For some critics, the *Lobgesang* failed because it imitated that colossus too directly; it flew, Icarus-like, too "close to the center of the musical solar system."[60] But the response to Beethoven was only part of Felix's strategy. Mark Evan Bonds has shown how Felix's score invokes a variety of historical models, and "relativizes" the Ninth by incorporating references to other composers, including Handel (the anthem *Zadok the Priest*) and Schubert (the "Great" Symphony).[61] We might note too that references to Beethoven are not limited to the Ninth; in the first movement, for example, the second theme is remarkably similar to one from Beethoven's Piano Sonata Op. 22, in the same key (**ex. 12.4**). And certainly the heralded chorales betray Felix's urge to extend the symphonic tradition into the domain of Protestant church music. The result is a broad historical review that relates the German past to the present and summons various musical icons—symphony, cantata, oratorio elements, responsorial psalmody, and chorale—into the service of praising God. If the *Lobgesang* failed, it did so not by emulating the Ninth but by aspiring toward an unattainable comprehensiveness—a symphony-*cum*-cantata with the trappings of a sacred service, a concert piece created for a specific occasion but reaching toward musical universality.

Ex. 12.4a: Mendelssohn, *Lobgesang* Symphony, Op. 52 (1840), No. 1

Ex. 12.4b: Beethoven, Piano Sonata in B♭ major, Op. 22 (1802), First Movement

III

Days after the Gutenberg Festival, Felix left Leipzig with David for Schwerin in Mecklenburg. At the Second North German Musical Festival (July 8–10, 1840), Felix directed *Paulus* and Haydn's *Die Schöpfung*, and the two performed a piano and a violin concerto. On their return trip, they paused in Berlin and indulged in chamber music with Paul before reaching Leipzig on July 17. Seeing no rest in sight, Felix formally accepted the invitation to Birmingham in September and gave serious thought to a new concerto for David; to Chorley, Felix wrote he was now finishing the work,[62] though, in fact, the path to the Violin Concerto in E minor, Op. 64, would prove circuitous indeed. By the end of the month, Felix was distracted by another project, an ambitious solo recital in the Thomaskirche of Bach organ works. To prepare he practiced for a week—so diligently, he reported to Lea, that on the streets of Leipzig his gait betrayed several awkward pedal passages.[63]

The goal of the concert (August 6, 1840) was to support Felix's effort to place a new Bach monument near his residence adjacent to the Thomasschule. The program represented the primary genres associated with Bach's organ music, the prelude and fugue (the "St. Anne" Fugue in E♭, BWV 552, and the Prelude and Fugue in A minor, BWV 543), chorale setting (*Schmücke dich, O liebe Seele*, BWV 654), the rhapsodic toccata (BWV 565), the monumental Passacaglia in C minor (BWV 582), and also the Pastorella in F major, BWV 590.[64] Framing the two parts of the program were two improvisations, Felix's "modern" entry point into and departure from the baroque splendor of Bach's music. While we know little about the first, labeled an "Introduction" to the Fugue in E♭, Schumann identified the second as a *Freie Phantasie*.[65] Based on the Passion chorale *O Haupt voll Blut und Wunden*, the improvisation culminated in a fugal passage and included Bach's musical signature, the motive B♭–A–C–B♮. The artful combination of these three elements impressed Schumann as a "finished composition." Felix never published the improvisation, though he may have considered doing so: an undated autograph folio in the Bodleian Library transmits part of an organ composition that, after a harmonization of the chorale, leads to the beginning of a series of variations on the familiar melody.[66] The choice of key for the chorale, D minor, emphasizes the pitches B♭ and A, the first two letters of Bach's name, which appear no fewer than four times in the melody (**ex. 12.5**). If the page represents Felix's unfinished attempt to preserve the improvisation, only a small leap is needed to imagine how he would have insinuated the Thomaskantor's name into the music. Felix's homage encouraged Robert Schumann's own Bachian deliberations for organ: in

Ex. 12.5: Mendelssohn, Sketch of organ improvisation on *O Haupt voll Blut und Wunden* (1840?)

BACH

1845, he composed the Six Fugues on BACH, Op. 60, thus trying to perpetuate something of Felix's "twofold mastery," that of "one master emulating another."[67]

Physically depleted by the full summer schedule, Felix sought respite by visiting art galleries in Dresden with Cécile. But on his return he
fell violently ill while swimming in a cold river and possibly suffered a
stroke. Unconscious and in convulsions for hours, he was confined to
his bedroom and endured debilitating headaches for two weeks. His trip
to England in doubt, Felix conceded he understood what it meant to be
seriously ill.[68] He recovered his strength and on September 6 joyfully welcomed the Hensels, returning from their yearlong Italian sojourn. Fanny
found her brother weakened and pale but in good spirits.[69]

After departing from Leipzig in September 1839, Fanny and Wilhelm
had met in Munich Felix's old flame Delphine von Schauroth, now
Delphine Hill Handley. Fanny found her improvisations and performance of one of Felix's piano concertos especially impressive.[70] At Lake
Como, where the snow-encrusted Alps yielded to a botanical paradise
of aloes and figs, Fanny beheld Italy in all its beauty. By October they
had reached Venice, ten years after Felix's visit there, and followed his
advice to contemplate Titian's *Assumption*. Arriving in Rome on November 26, they found an apartment near the Monte Pincio and settled
in for a six-month residence. Their connections gained them access to
the private apartments, appointed in red damask and green curtains, of
Pope Gregory XVI. But at the Sistine Chapel, Fanny was obliged to sit
behind a grate with other women and, because of her astigmatism, could
not see much of the services. Still, her acute ear compensated. Drawing
on perfect pitch, as had Felix, she recorded portions of Allegri's *Miserere*
during Holy Week but was appalled at the quality of the singing. Formerly eighty strong, the papal choir now had shriveled to only nineteen
voices that could not stay in tune; with each verset of the *Miserere* they
dropped about a third of a pitch, so that the composition began in B
major but sank to G.[71]

At the Villa Medici, the Hensels met the old and new directors of the
French Academy, Horace Vernet, attired in Arabian dress, and the painter

J.-A.-D. Ingres, an amateur violinist who knew Fanny's brother Paul as a cellist,[72] and now played piano trios with her. A group of artists formed around Wilhelm, including the Prussians F. A. Elsasser, A. T. Kaselowsky, and Eduard Magnus, who later painted Felix's portrait (see p. 500), and Ingres's pupil Charles Dugasseau. Two young recipients of the Prix de Rome, Georges Bousquet and Charles Gounod, completed the circle. The impressionable Gounod, contemplating the priesthood and drawn to the liberal theology of the Dominican Père Lacordaire, was overwhelmed by Fanny's talents. She seems to have inculcated him with a heavy dose of German music, including Bach concerti, Felix's piano works, and the sonatas of Beethoven (*Beethoven est un polisson*—"Beethoven is a rascal"— Gounod exclaimed[73] after hearing Fanny play parts of *Fidelio* and a sonata, probably the *Waldstein*). Armed with a letter of introduction from Fanny, Gounod later visited Felix in Leipzig and emulated his style in several works, including the vivacious First Symphony (1855).

Continuing south in June 1840 the Hensels visited Naples, where they encountered the singer Pauline Viardot, sister of Marie Malibran. After exploring the Sorrentine coast, the Hensels made a fatiguing excursion to Vesuvius on Sebastian's tenth birthday. By horseback they reached lava flows, still warm from the eruption of the preceding year; then, for the final ascent, Fanny was carried up one of the cones to "Satan's headquarters." After Wilhelm visited Sicily in July, the family proceeded to Genoa and Milan, and met Ferdinand Hiller near Lake Como before their reunion with Felix. Fanny shared her musical impressions of Italy, some of which were recorded in her piano cycle of 1841, *Das Jahr*; Felix reciprocated by playing the *Lobgesang*. He announced his intention to spend a year in Italy after the end of the next concert season, when his contract expired. On September 10 Felix "signed" a newly drawn portrait by Hensel that revealed a slender, pensive composer with thinning hair and, perhaps, traces of his recent illness.[74] The following day, he left for England, while the Hensels departed for Berlin.

One week later, Felix reported his safe arrival in London; happily, he had not succumbed to seasickness during the crossing from Calais.[75] After a day in London, he traveled with Moscheles via the new train service to Birmingham, where Joseph Moore again greeted him as an honored guest. In the three years since Felix's last visit, the pace of industrialization had accelerated, and he now recorded a view of the city dominated by smokestacks (**plate 14**), like so many harbingers of Dickens' Coketown, that town of "tall chimneys, out of which interminable serpents of smoke trailed themselves for ever and ever."[76] During the four-day festival (September 22–25), Felix made several appearances. He conducted the *Lobgesang*, in which the aging tenor John Braham sang, performed the Piano Concerto in G minor, and offered works by Bach and an improvisation on the new organ in Town Hall. Between concerts Felix also regaled a smaller group of friends with private demonstrations of his organ playing. The *Lobgesang* did not fail to impress Victorian tastes; Moscheles reported that at the entrance of *Nun danket alle Gott* the audience "rose involuntarily from their seats—a custom usually confined in England to the performance of the Hallelujah Chorus."[77] After spending an extra day in Birmingham so as not to offend his host, Felix returned to London on September 26.

For a week he enjoyed shopping with Charlotte Moscheles and visited the Alexanders, who showed him a portrait Hensel had drawn of his father. Unusually, Felix transacted little professional business. To Novello he sold the English rights to the *Lobgesang*, and from an eccentric pupil of Moscheles, C. B. Broadley, Felix accepted a commission for an anthem based on Psalm 13. His friend H. J. Gauntlett again led Felix to the organ at Christ Church, Newgate Street, with its expanded compass and pedal board, and on September 30 he tried out an instrument at St. Peter's Church, Cornhill. The organ, installed under Gauntlett's supervision, also had the German C-compass; the black keys had inlaid tortoiseshell, and the stop knobs, mother-of-pearl rosettes. On this instrument Felix played his own Prelude and Fugue in C minor, Op. 37 No. 1, and the Fugue in F minor, a Bach prelude and fugue in E minor, and the Passacaglia. The organist of the church was the talented young woman Elizabeth Mounsey (1819–1905); although too shy to play for the visiting celebrity, she became a devoted Mendelssohnian.[78]

Accompanied by Chorley and Moscheles, Felix left London in early October. At Aix-la-Chapelle they encountered a gaunt, Don Quixote-like figure, Anton Schindler, whose greeting Felix returned with "some mental reserve."[79] Arriving in Leipzig late on October 9, the two pianists enjoyed ten days of robust music making and companionship. Having missed the first concert of the new season, for which David had deputized, Felix now had only a day to prepare for the second (October 11), which featured Beethoven's Fourth Symphony. For a week the Gewandhaus directors urged Moscheles to perform publicly, but he relished instead the small, private gatherings with Felix and Cécile, whom he found "very unassuming and childlike,"[80] and their circle, including the newlyweds Robert and Clara Schumann. Finally, Moscheles relented and on October 19 he and Felix gave a private concert for an audience of three hundred. Felix directed the *Hebrides* Overture, Psalm 42, and the first two *Leonore* Overtures of Beethoven, and performed with his friend the duet *Hommage à Handel*. Moscheles offered some studies and his Concerto in G minor; then, with Clara Schumann, the three pianists played the Bach Triple Concerto in D minor.

The concerts featured two singers engaged for the new season, Elise List and Sophie Schloss, and two visiting violinists. The first was the Russian A. F. L'vov, Generaladjutant of Nicholas I and composer of the Russian anthem "God save the Tsar" (1833). Because of L'vov's high rank, he did not perform publicly; instead, Felix arranged an "extraordinary" morning concert on November 8 and invited a select audience.[81] Social protocol did not limit the audience of the sensationally popular violinist Ole Bull, who appeared with Felix at the Gewandhaus on November 30 and performed a concerto, a Mozart Adagio, and some variations on a Bellini aria.[82] In Paris, where Felix had first met him, the Norwegian had introduced the Hardanger folk fiddle and adapted its relatively flat bridge and heavy, long bow to his modern violin, which enabled him to dispatch challenging passages rivaling the feats of Paganini.

Felix complemented his arduous conducting schedule with solo appearances in piano trios by Haydn and Beethoven, and Mozart's Piano Quartet in G minor, K. 478, at David's chamber music series (November 14 and December 12). A score from Felix's library, possibly used for the Mozart, has survived, with markings that may divulge clues about how he performed this masterwork.[83] The edition Felix owned was the *Oeuvres complètes* of Mozart, issued by Breitkopf & Härtel between 1824 and 1840. Lacking fingerings and spare in articulation markings (phrasings, dynamics, and the like), Felix's score encouraged him to pencil in liberal markings. For the most part his fingerings tend to facilitate a legato style of playing, but there are also some surprises, including the dramatic final thirteen bars of the first movement, marked *forte* in the edition, but vividly articulated by Felix into four segments: a *forte*, then two crescendi from *piano* to *forte* leading to a climactic *fortissimo*.

During the closing months of 1840, the magnet of Leipzig continued to attract celebrities. On November 11 a young Danish writer attended the Gewandhaus rehearsal of Beethoven's Seventh Symphony, scheduled for performance the following evening.[84] A few years before, Hans Christian Andersen had begun defining a new literary genre— original fairy tales for children—in such stories as "The Princess and the Pea," "Thumbelina," "The Little Mermaid," and "The Emperor's New Clothes." But Felix knew him principally as a novelist. During his recent illness, he had read Andersen's third novel, *Only a Fiddler* (1837), and Felix now made a point of discussing it with the author. Exploring deeply felt issues of alienation, it concerns two childhood playmates, Christian and Naomi, both outsiders—Christian (i.e., Andersen) is a gifted but insecure violinist, while Naomi is a Jewess who confronts issues of sexual identity. Christian dies a pauper, while Naomi acquires wealth through marriage, but both remain rootless in a modern world. Unable to spend much time with Felix, Andersen exchanged album entries (Felix offered a rather severe two-part canon in C minor). The two would meet again in 1841 and 1846.

In December Leipzig received a royal visitor, the music-loving Saxon king, Frederick Augustus II, who had ordered a special performance of the *Lobgesang*. After the Birmingham Festival, Felix continued to struggle over the score, which he finished revising on November 27.[85] One week later he performed the new version at a charity concert for pensioned musicians of the orchestra and on December 16 presented it before the king. The concert fell on a Wednesday, breaking the traditional Thursday venue for subscription concerts. On the first half of the program, after Felix and David performed Beethoven's *Kreutzer* Sonata by royal request, the king deigned to receive Felix, who walked from his podium through the double rows of ladies to the king, and conversed at length with him about the music. But after the *Lobgesang*, the two exchanged roles: incredibly, the king processed through the audience to Felix's podium, thanked the composer and musicians, who did their best to bow, and then left, causing a commotion in the hall Felix likened to Noah's Ark.[86]

IV

The successful command performance encouraged Felix to imagine Frederick Augustus would bestow the Blümner bequest on a new Leipzig conservatory; but just then another monarch was endeavoring to secure Felix's services. On June 7, 1840, Frederick William III had died; his son Frederick William IV acceded to the throne with visions of transforming Berlin into a center for the arts. Convinced his monarchy was divinely ordained, the new king still struggled to respond to changes rapidly altering the Prussian social/political landscape—the quickening pace of industrialization, strengthening middle class, and increasing demands for a constitutional monarchy. In part Frederick William IV sought to reinforce his authority by creating what David Barclay has termed a "chivalric tradition"—appealing to pseudomedieval constructs (he founded a romantic Order of the Swan, dismissed by Fanny as sentimental nonsense[87]) and projecting the monarchy as a sacred, Christian institution.[88] During the "honeymoon" months of his reign, the king enjoyed great popularity with his subjects. He made efforts to resolve tensions with Catholics in the Rhineland and vague promises of constitutional reform, emboldening the Jewish doctor Johann Jacoby (in the pamphlet *Vier Fragen*,

Four Questions, February 1841) to assert the right of citizens to participate in the government. Felix privately endorsed its arguments and reflected that such a publication could not have appeared one year before.[89] In September 1840 some 60,000 Berliners delivered oaths of fealty before the enthroned monarch. Then, too, a wave of pan-German nationalism bolstered the king when France, responding to the secret Treaty of London (July 15), threatened to seize the Rhine. After the jurist Nikolaus Becker penned the jingoistic poem *Der deutsche Rhein*, a host of composers, including Robert Schumann, Kreutzer, and Marschner, scurried to set its vapid verses.[90] Felix found the whole affair childish and declined to compose music, even though Härtel estimated he could sell six thousand copies in two months.[91]

Soon after the king's accession, his ministers began to consider reorganizing the Academy of Arts. Ludwig Tieck and Peter Cornelius were invited to direct the theater and painting, and the Grimm brothers, lately associated with the prosecuted group of liberals known as the Göttingen Seven, were "rehabilitated" by a summons to Berlin. By the end of October 1840 the king was conferring with C. K. J. Bunsen about attracting Felix to the capitol. From the beginning, defining his exact duties proved vexing, but Bunsen and the king shared the hope Felix would eventually direct a new musical institute, compose sacred music for the reformed Prussian liturgy, and perform oratorios as a branch of the theater. "Is that not enough for one man, one master?" Bunsen mused. "I believe it is rather too much for any one other than Felix Mendelssohn."[92]

On November 23 Geheimrat Ludwig von Massow communicated the king's desire for Felix to serve the fatherland by returning to Berlin and "raising music in all its scope."[93] Paul traveled to Leipzig to deliver the letter. Another missive followed on December 11 with some particulars: Felix was to head the musical class of the academy, receive a generous salary of three thousand thalers, and direct concerts by royal command. Still not swayed, he diplomatically deferred a decision for a more exact definition of his duties; meanwhile, he confided his situation to Schleinitz and David.[94]

Massow's second letter found Felix contemplating an intriguing proposal from Fanny—that he write an opera about the *Nibelungenlied*[95]; the chief difficulty was imagining how, with the slaughter of so many Teutonic heroes, the whole affair would end. More easily dispatched was the setting of Psalm 13 for alto solo, chorus, and organ, finished on December 12.[96] Felix apportioned Broadley's five quatrains (the first reads "Why, O Lord, delay for ever / smiles of comfort to impart? / Oh, if Thou forget me—never / more shall gladness cheer the heart") into three movements. Following the tradition of the English verse anthem, each

Ex. 12.6: Mendelssohn, Chorale (Psalm 13), Op. 96 (1840), No. 2

Dei-nes Kind's Ge - bet er - hö - re, Va - ter, schau' auf mich he - rab;

alternates between a solo and chorus, but there are some German features as well. The second movement offers a freely composed chorale
(ex. 12.6), and in the third Felix lapsed into his habitual fugal writing (two
years later, he made an expanded orchestral arrangement, published
posthumously as Op. 96). The work appeared in England as an anthem,
but in Germany as *Drei geistliche Lieder*; Felix himself may have prepared the German translation.

Early in 1841 Felix corresponded with Paul about the Berlin situation.
Finding von Massow's communications increasingly vague, the composer
requested a copy of the statutes of the Berlin Academy of Arts. Furthermore, Felix was not pleased when two Berliners passing through Leipzig
openly discussed the proposal, even though the negotiations were supposedly confidential[97] (Felix had refrained from mentioning the potential move to Lea and Fanny, so as not to raise prematurely their hope of
a family reunion[98]). The statutes confirmed what Felix feared—that little
thought had been given to coordinating the various arts in Berlin. To
that end, in May he drafted a *Pro Memoria*.[99] He advised concentrating
the various musical resources of the capitol and allying them with the
Musical Academy; the new musical conservatory would need faculty in
composition, singing, choral singing, and piano (as in his proposal for
Leipzig, Felix again recommended a three-year course of instruction for
students, admitted *gratis*). But the project encountered bureaucratic
obstacles: the Academy of Arts was regulated by a royal *Ministerium* of
science, instruction, and medicine, and Felix had to confer with the official in charge, Minister K. F. Eichhorn. And so, May 5 to 25 found Felix
in Berlin, where Eduard Devrient prevailed upon him to have patience
with the *odiosa* of court ceremoniousness and pedantry.[100]

Because Eichhorn was unwilling to restructure the Academy on short
notice, von Massow resorted to compromise. Felix would move to Berlin for a year, during which Eichhorn would expedite the desired reorganization. Felix would enjoy the benefits of his salary and new title, without
immediately having to undertake specific duties. As early as mid-May,
Felix was inclined to accept, though not until early June did he reveal his
final decision to Paul and Lea (to Moscheles, Felix wrote that he would
rather remain in Leipzig).[101] But the terms continued to shift; Eichhorn
recommended that the king grant the title of Kapellmeister only upon

the implementation of the academy reorganization. Felix now compared Berlin to a sour apple into which he had to bite; he was to become a school-master to a conservatory that did not yet exist.[102] On the evening of July 28, 1841, members of the Gewandhaus serenaded him with his *Volkslied*, Op. 47 No. 4; Felix joined in singing its refrain, "When people separate, they say, 'Auf Wiedersehen.'" Without giving up his apartment in Lurgensteins Garten,[103] he left Leipzig the following day with his family. Initially they resided in Rebecka's quarters (she was again on vacation in Heringsdorf). Later, Felix secured rooms across the street from his child-hood home.

Meanwhile the Saxon king endeavored to strengthen ties to the com-poser through the minister J. P. von Falkenstein. In March came word that Frederick Augustus II would support the foundation of a Leipzig conservatory, and in April Felix visited Dresden. His purpose was to ex-amine a model Bendemann had prepared of the new Bach monument, but it seems likely Felix discussed the conservatory as well. Having re-quested permission to dedicate the *Lobgesang* to the king, Felix sent a copy of the newly published piano-vocal score to Dresden in June; Frederick Augustus acknowledged the gift on July 1 and conferred on Felix the title of Saxon Kapellmeister.[104]

Despite the prospect of moving to Berlin, Felix maintained an unre-lentingly hectic schedule at the Gewandhaus. Between New Year's Day and Palm Sunday (April 4) he appeared as soloist on three subscription concerts, directed eleven in addition to the St. Matthew Passion, and participated in the chamber-music *Abendunterhaltungen*, the highlight of which came on January 20, when Felix performed the *Kreutzer* Sonata with Ole Bull, who used a rare violin by the sixteenth-century Brescian maker Gasparo da Salò. But when the Norwegian indulged in some "taste-less" gestures in other solos, Felix became "progressively more disturbed and agitated," so that the publisher Heinrich Brockhaus bade Felix not to expect everyone to "regard art as sacred," to which Felix rejoined that "one should not also act as if it were."[105] Felix supported visits to Leipzig by several other artists, including Sigismond Thalberg, Sophie Schloss, Wilhelmine Schröder-Devrient, and appearances by Clara Schumann. In the midst of all this music making, Cécile gave birth on January 18 to their third child, baptized on February 15 and named after three Men-delssohns, Paul Felix Abraham Mendelssohn Bartholdy (1841–1880), and destined later to found the chemical firm Agfa.

Among the offerings of the season was the Leipzig premiere on Janu-ary 7, 1841, of Spohr's Sixth Symphony (*Historical*), which reinforced the canonization of German music then underway. The four movements offered a chronological review, beginning with a fugue and pastoral to depict the *Bach-Händel'sche Periode* (1720) and continuing with a graceful *Larghetto* in the style of Haydn and Mozart (1780), a Beethovenian scherzo employing an additional third tympanum (1810), and a finale meant to depict the "most recent period" (1840). Felix and others questioned the finale;[106] instead of a serious example of Spohr's mature style, the audience heard a caricature of Italian opera, with a surfeit of garish diminished-seventh harmonies, trivial melodies, and a noisy percussion complement enlarged to include a triangle, bass drum, snare drum, and cymbals.

The musical past continued to haunt Felix, who reexplored the terrain of Spohr's symphony by launching a series of four historical concerts (January 21 and 28, and February 4 and 11). In contrast to the earlier 1838 cycle (see p. 363), in which titans of German music had dominated several minor composers, the second began by pairing Bach (the Chromatic Fantasy and Fugue, motet *Ich lasse dich nicht*, Violin Chaconne, and three movements from the B-minor Mass) and Handel (Overture and aria from *Messiah*, Variations on *The Harmonious Blacksmith*, and choruses from *Israel in Egypt*), and continued with three concerts devoted to Haydn, Mozart, and Beethoven. Representing Haydn were selections from the oratorios *Die Schöpfung* (including the extraordinary overture depicting chaos) and *Die Jahreszeiten*, the *Emperor* String Quartet, Op. 76 No. 3, an a cappella motet, and a Symphony in B♭. Robert Schumann, still recovering from the passacaglia in the *Crucifixus* of Bach's Credo—Schumann wrote that masters of all ages must bow before it—compared Haydn to a familiar house guest, politely received but no longer of interest for the present time.[107] For Mozart, Felix chose the Overture to *La clemenza di Tito*, Piano Concerto in D minor K. 466, *Jupiter* Symphony, the aria with *obbligato* violin solo, *Non più, tutti ascoltai* (K. 490), and some Lieder, sung by Sophie Schloss. Now unable to contain his enthusiasm, Schumann wished that all Germany could have attended. No less impressive was the Beethovenian finale, including the Third *Leonore* Overture, movements from the Mass in C, the Violin Concerto, and the Ninth Symphony. When the engaged tenor fell ill and abandoned the cycle *An die ferne Geliebte*, Felix saw in the audience the soprano Wilhelmine Schröder-Devrient, just arrived from Dresden, who took off her bonnet and pelisse and performed with Felix the Lied *Adelaide*.[108]

As if imitating the trajectory of Spohr's symphony, Felix devoted the next two concerts (February 18 and 25) to the lighter fare of modern music, including a new symphony by Kalliwoda, virtuoso pieces by the violinists Molique and Lipiński, and operatic excerpts from Bellini, Donizetti, and Meyerbeer. Though Sophie Schloss's rendition of an aria from *Robert le diable*, which had raised Felix's ire in 1832, resonated with the Leipzig audience, he could only liken the shift in repertoire after the Beethoven concert to a precipitous descent from Adam to the populist writer Holtei.[109] A more serious attempt to champion contemporary music came on March 31, when Clara Schumann presented a benefit concert for the orchestral pension fund. On that evening Felix gave the premiere of Robert Schumann's First Symphony (*Spring*), Op. 38, catapulting the composer into the ranks of estimable modern symphonists. In an intense, four-day burst of creativity late in January 1841, Schumann had sketched the work, inspired by a poem by Adolf Böttger (in April, Felix would set the same poet's verses in the tenderly melancholy song, *Ich hör ein Vöglein*[110]). By early March Robert was sharing the full score with Felix, who offered suggestions before recommending its performance. Beginning with a brass fanfare and in B♭ major, like the *Lobgesang*, Schumann's symphony reflected Schubert's epic "Great" Symphony, yet betrayed Schumann's genius in several quirky features[111]—for example, its episodic, narrative approach to form, colorful orchestration, and thematic unpredictability.

The concert marked Robert and Clara's professional debut together as husband and wife. Regrettably, their wedding on September 12, 1840, (the day after Felix's departure for England) had not resolved tensions with Friedrich Wieck, and the lovers now awaited the judgment of a slander suit Robert instituted against his father-in-law. The concert was Felix's way of supporting the couple and elevating Robert's relatively low profile as a music journalist and creator of eccentric piano music. (Sadly enough, only a few months before, in November, Robert had shared with Clara in their diaries some anti-Semitic comments about Felix, whom Robert still regarded as a Jew.[112]) In the days leading up to March 31 Felix hastily composed for Clara a piano duet, which the two performed on the concert. It consisted of a "singing" Andante in the style of a *Duett ohne Worte* coupled to a brisk *Allegro brillant* in Felix's trademark scherzo idiom, with a patter of staccato work and brilliant, darting figurations.[113] Felix thus revived for Clara the paradigms he had employed in the *Rondo capriccioso* for Delphine von Schauroth and the *Duett ohne Worte* for Cécile. But when, four years after his death, Breitkopf & Härtel published the piece as the *Allegro brillant* Op. 92, the firm omitted the Andante; not until 1994 were the two movements rejoined and the composition once again made whole.[114]

The culmination of the concert season came on Palm Sunday 1841 (April 4), when Felix directed the St. Matthew Passion in the Thomaskirche with an amateur chorus. Since Bach's premiere of his masterwork in the same church on Good Friday 1727, it had lain dormant in Leipzig; incredibly, Felix revealed to Paul, not a single note was known in the city,[115] despite the Berlin revival in 1829 and its ripple effect throughout Germany.

To realize the performance Felix had to borrow parts from the Sing-akademie and the estate of Eduard Rietz. In place of piano, Felix employed two cellos and a double bass for the continuo, and he made other modifications as well, including reinstating four of the ten arias cut from the 1829 performance.[116] The receipts from the performance were dedicated to the Bach monument. Felix again stirred the German musical consciousness, but now it was the internationally acclaimed composer of St. Paul, not the twenty-year-old prodigy, who reclaimed for Leipzig Bach's masterwork. Though Felix never conducted it again, the Passion became a traditional fixture for Good Friday services in the city.

V

Less than two weeks later Felix directed an encore performance of *Paulus* in Weimar. Half an hour before the concert (April 15), he was nonchalantly putting finishing touches on an orchestral piece to celebrate the Dresden visit of the painter Peter Cornelius.[117] The result was a festive march in D major, published posthumously as Op. 108. Of greater concern that day was the tenor soloist for the oratorio, who fell ill during the dress rehearsal. Regrettably, his replacement also became indisposed during the performance and struggled to complete Part 1; during the intermission, Felix hurriedly initiated a third singer into the tenor arias of Part 2 and managed to salvage the concert.[118]

With the end of the concert season Felix resumed active composition. Concentrating on keyboard music, he finished during the spring and summer of 1841 the *Lieder ohne Worte*, Op. 53, three sets of piano variations (Opp. 54, 82, and 83; a fourth set, envisioned for orchestra, did not materialize), and one piano and one organ prelude. The fourth volume of piano Lieder included three older pieces: from 1835, No. 2 in E♭, composed for Clara Wieck; and, from 1839, No. 1 in A♭, for Sophy Horsley, and No. 3 in G minor.[119] To these three he added the final three Lieder in April and May, and sent the finished *Heft* to Simrock in June, with a dedication to Sophy, daughter of the glee composer and a gifted pianist. Just at that time her younger brother, Charles Edward Horsley, was in Leipzig to study piano and composition with Felix. Charles reports that the technically challenging No. 6, in A major, may have been in response to Sigismond Thalberg's visit in February 1841, when the pianist presented a caprice on themes from Bellini's *Sonnambula*.[120] Into this *bravura* display Thalberg had introduced clamorous chromatic octaves alternating between the hands; impressed by the device, Felix began imitating it on the piano in his study. Op. 53 No. 6 has a distinctive texture

Ex. 12.7: Mendelssohn, *Lied ohne Worte* in A major, Op. 53 No. 6 (1841)

in which chords embellished by chromatic pitches are rapidly exchanged between the hands (**ex. 12.7**), yielding piquant chromatic juxtapositions somewhat reminiscent of Thalberg's virtuoso effect.

Only one Lied, Op. 53 No. 5, appeared with a title, though extramusical ideas inspired at least two others, the third and fourth. The composing autograph of No. 3 bears the title *Gondellied*, but apart from the meter ($\frac{6}{8}$) and telltale rhythms (♩♪), the piece has little in common with Felix's other Venetian barcarolles. Instead of a dreamy Andante with a duet accompanied by lapping arpeggiations, we find an agitated Presto with the melody in three-part harmony supported by turbulent broken chords. The tranquil No. 4 was originally titled *Abendlied*[121] (*Evening Song*), though Felix suppressed it too for the first edition. He did release the fifth as a *Volkslied*, conceived as a colorful imitation of Scottish folksong; the principal theme is not unlike that of the *Scottish* Symphony, completed early in 1842 (**ex. 12.8a**). Felix's piano Lied seems to have inspired in turn the young Brahms, who in 1853 conjured up Scottish folksong in the finale of his first piano sonata, in a passage suspiciously similar to Op. 53 No. 5 (**ex. 12.8b**).

Though Brahms revealed to his colleague Albert Dietrich the textual source of the passage was Robert Burns's "My Heart's in the Highlands," Felix remained reluctant to tie his piano Lieder publicly to specific poems. Still, the published and suppressed titles of Op. 53 suggest he conceived

Ex. 12.8a: Mendelssohn, *Lied ohne Worte* in A minor, Op. 53 No. 5 (*Volkslied*, 1841)

Ex. 12.8b: Brahms, Piano Sonata in C major, Op. 1, Finale (1853)

the pieces as abstractions of familiar categories of German romantic lyrical poetry, if not, as Schumann had imagined, songs with their texts simply removed. That is to say, in Op. 53 No. 4, Felix sought to abstract the
musical essence of an *Abendlied*. As the *Lieder ohne Worte* grew in popularity, Felix seems to have stiffened his resolve not to allow poetic ideas
to influence unduly the appreciation of the music. There was a practical
reason for this aesthetic stand. By 1840 pirated editions of the Lieder
were beginning to appear, forcing Simrock to take legal action. Moreover, in July 1841, not long after Felix finished his Op. 53, his friend, the
attorney Konrad Schleinitz, brought a claim against Schuberth & Co. for
reissuing some of the Lieder with texts freely added by Karl Christern, a
minor Hamburg editor and composer.[122] But Schleinitz's efforts proved a
rear-guard action, for later nineteenth-century publishers did not hesitate
to adorn the Lieder with vacuous titles, all in an effort to bolster sales.

Felix's crowning achievement in the summer of 1841 was the *Variations sérieuses* in D minor, Op. 54, finished on June 4, 1841,[123] and generally regarded as his masterpiece for piano. In March Pietro Mechetti had
pressed him to participate in a new Beethoven Album, the proceeds from
which were to support the raising of the famous monument in Bonn. Ad-
vertised in January 1842 as *Dix morceau brillants*, the album included
contributions from nine other pianists: Chopin, Czerny, Döhler, Henselt,
Kalkbrenner, Liszt, Moscheles, Taubert, and Thalberg.[124] Excepting
Chopin's soulful Prelude in C♯ minor, Op. 45, Felix's variations were the
most substantial and original contribution. By labeling them "serious," he
intended to distinguish his effort from the superficial variations of the
virtuosi then in vogue. The theme, a brooding, chromatic creation, begins with two dissonant suspensions—emblems of an elevated, earnest
style—and rising melodic leaps of the dissonant tritone (G♯–D) and
diminished fourth (C♯–F; **ex. 12.9**). The solemnity and grandeur of the
composition recall Beethoven's epic thirty-two Variations in C minor;
its grave affect, something of Beethoven's *Serioso* String Quartet Op. 95.

Felix arranged his eighteen variations into crescendo-like waves of
increasing dramatic tension. The first nine build in intensity through
faster rhythmic values and the rigorous application of canon in the
fourth. The tenth and eleventh variations mark a structural pause; the
tenth, a fugato, forms a contrapuntal pendant to the fourth, while in the

Ex. **12.9**: Mendelssohn, *Variations sérieuses*, Op. 54 (1841), Theme

Ex. 12.10: Mendelssohn, *Variations sérieuses*, Op. 54 (1841), No. 14

eleventh, the theme is transformed into a Schumannesque *rêverie*: an outline of the theme now appears against *pianissimo* syncopated chords. In succeeding variations, the theme descends from the soprano to the tenor register, first in a dramatic, *martellato* explosion (No. 12), then in a demonstration of the Thalbergian three-hand technique (No. 13), and finally in a contemplative, hymnlike variation in the major (No. 14; **ex. 12.10**). In No. 15, the theme is fractured and displaced among several registers (**ex. 12.11**). The increasingly agitated Nos. 16 and 17 build to a climax in which the reconstituted theme returns in the soprano over a tremolo in the bass. The stretto-like No. 18 serves as a coda. Here the theme appears in unrelenting syncopations, interrupted, near the end, by a sweeping arpeggiated flourish. Then, a few quiet D-minor chords bring this work to its subdued close.

The serious tone of Op. 54 informs a contemporaneous pencil drawing of Felix by J. H. Schramm, dated June 14, 1841,[125] which shows a somber, bearded composer only weeks before his departure to Berlin. Two lesser compositions from the period, the Prelude in E minor for piano and Prelude in C minor for organ, also project grave affects, but not so the keyboard Variations in E♭ and B♭, Opp. 82 and 83. All four date from July or early August 1841 and were dispatched after Felix again received Hans Christian Andersen, who visited Leipzig from July 4 to 6. The piano prelude offers another application of Thalberg's three-hand technique; Felix coupled the piece with a fugue from 1827 and published the two in the album *Notre temps* of 1842. The organ prelude fulfilled a request from the musical amateur Henry E. Dibdin of Edinburgh for a

Ex. 12.11: Mendelssohn, *Variations sérieuses*, Op. 54 (1841), No. 15

"long measure psalm tune."[126] Instead, Felix obliged with a short, im-
promptu-like piece in a severely chromatic and disjunct style reminiscent of the *Variations sérieuses*.[127] In decided contrast are the two variation
sets, published posthumously in 1850, which he described to Rebecka as
"sentimental" and "graceful."[128] Less ambitious than Op. 54, Opp. 82 and
83 comprise a theme with five and six variations, the last of which serve
as extended codas. Brahms may have had in mind Op. 82 when, late in
life, he composed the finale of the Clarinet Sonata in E♭, Op. 120 No. 2
(1894). It has a "sentimental" theme, not unlike Op. 82, that emphasizes
the dominant harmony through "weak," "feminine" half cadences and
five variations, the last of which is considerably expanded.

Before moving to Berlin Felix completed one other major work, the
revision of Psalm 95, Op. 46. Since its premiere in 1839, his nagging self-
doubts had hindered its publication. Although Kistner had already begun engraving the score, Felix withdrew the composition and set it aside
for nearly two years. Only in August 1841 was he able to release it, together with an apologetic canon for Kistner on the text *Pater, peccavi*
("Father, I have sinned").[129] The final form of the psalm comprised five
movements, with a structural break between the fourth and fifth to reflect the division of text between the joyful call to worship (verses 1–7a)
and sobering admonition to the faithful not to harden their hearts against
the Lord (7b–11). Felix underscored the division by pairing two major
and minor tonalities. The first four movements describe a cycle of keys
centered on E♭, while the fifth movement, linked to the fourth through
an orchestral transition, introduces the dark coloration of G minor.

To lessen the severe emotional descent from the first to the second
part of the psalm—for C. F. Becker, the "downward sinking of the
whole"[130]—Felix took liberties with the order of the verses. The first movement begins with the reverent verses 6–7a ("O come, let us worship and
bow down"), introduced by a tenor soloist to which the chorus responds.
The second movement, a bright chorus energized by wind chords in
dotted rhythms, employs the celebratory opening verses ("O come, let
us sing to the Lord; let us make a joyful noise to the rock of our salvation!"), but changes in texture to a somber canon for the third verse
("For the Lord is a great God," **ex. 12.12a**). The third movement, a lyrical
duet for two sopranos, treats the fourth verse ("In His hand are the depths
of the earth") but also briefly cites the text of the sixth. And the fourth
movement, a broad choral fugue for the fifth verse ("The sea is His, for
He made it"), recalls the music of the opening chorus and the sixth and
seventh verses, thus completing the first part.

Felix allotted the verses of the second part (7b–11) to a dark-hued
finale in G minor. Divided violas doubled by bassoons introduce a plain-

Ex. 12.12a: Mendelssohn, Psalm 95, Op. 46 (1841), No. 2

Denn der Herr ist ein gro - ßer Gott und ein gro - ßer Kö - nig ü - ber al - le Göt -

Denn der Herr ist ein gro - ßer Gott und ein gro - ßer Kö - nig

Ex. 12.12b: Mendelssohn, Psalm 95, Op. 46 (1841), No. 5

Heu - te so ihr sei - ne Stim - me hö - ret so ver - stok - ket, eu - er Herz_ nicht

tive melody (**ex. 12.12b**), sung by the tenor soloist, to which the sopranos and altos, and then the full chorus, reply. At the warning of the eighth verse, "Do not harden your hearts, as at Meribah, as on the day at Massah in the wilderness, when your ancestors tested me" (a reference to Exodus 17:1–7), the music becomes increasingly agitated and falls into a dramatic recitative for the Lord's oath, "Therefore in my anger I swore, 'They shall not enter my rest.'" The composition ends with hushed, *pianissimo* chords, a subdued musical effect that C. F. Becker compared to the music of the spheres.

VI

With no small apprehension Felix arrived with his family in Berlin at the end of July 1841. Under his direction during the previous six years, the Gewandhaus had developed into one of the premiere musical institutions of Europe. "With such a devoted orchestra," the flutist Carl Grenser wrote on behalf of the orchestra, "you have won a victory for German music, and set a distinguished example for all Germany. The Fatherland will thank you!"[131] As composer, conductor, pianist, and organist, Felix had flourished and now, an internationally recognized figure with few peers, stood at the very forefront of his art. In Leipzig he had enjoyed more or less complete artistic freedom and had embraced the positive aspects of the dominant, middle-class musical culture. Now he was to give up not only the stability of his position at the Gewandhaus for the long desired reunion with his family but also for the uncertainty of Berlin and its court. The exchange would exact a significant price.

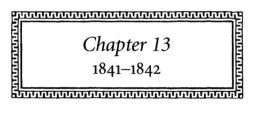

Chapter 13
1841–1842

From Kapellmeister to
Generalmusikdirektor

... we are children no longer, but we have
enjoyed what it really is to be so.

—Felix to his brother, Paul,
December 22, 1842[1]

Overshadowing the happiness of Felix's homecoming was the frustrating uncertainty of his position at the court, the topic of a stream of letters from August and September 1841. To Ferdinand David, who directed
the Gewandhaus in Felix's absence: "You wish to hear news about the
Berlin Conservatory; I do as well, ... but there is none." To Verkenius in
Cologne: "all the causes which formerly made it impossible for me to begin ... my career in Berlin ... still subsist, just as they formerly did, and are
likely, alas! to subsist to the end of time." In a second, "hypochondriacal"
letter to the same, Felix groused about the lack of professionalism in the
royal orchestra, which he ascribed to Spontini's vainglory (in July, Felix's
old nemesis had been convicted of lèse majesté and dismissed). To Klingemann Felix caviled that after six months he still did not know what the
court expected of him, and to Rebecka, he eagerly awaited the opening of
the Leipzig-Berlin railroad, so that he could invite her to Leipzig concerts
and imagine no longer serving the monarch.[2] Somehow the wondrous
new mode of travel, beginning to etch indelibly the German terrain, would
provide a ready-made escape for his professional predicament.

Though Felix's duties were ill-defined, the press readily publicized
his call to Berlin. The *Neue Zeitschrift für Musik* reported his salary as
3000 thalers and convinced some he now enjoyed a cosseted existence as
royal Kapellmeister.[3] As if justifying the effort to bring him to the capital, the king finally ordered in September a dramatic production shared

by Felix and Ludwig Tieck. The aging poet, summoned from Dresden as the monarch's *Vorleser*, or chief court reader, would undertake a revival of classical and Shakespearean drama, for which Felix would compose music. The collaboration began with the *Antigone* of Sophocles, available in a new, metrically reliable German translation by the Stuttgart Gymnasium-director J. J. C. Donner. For Tieck, the final play of the Oedipus trilogy was "nearer in feeling to modern Christian associations"[4] than any other Greek tragedy. A favorite in German letters, *Antigone* crystallized a fundamental issue confronting the new monarch's vision of modern Prussia—the relationship between individual and state. The play treats the moral dilemma of Oedipus's daughter, determined to provide a proper burial for her brother Polynices. He has led an insurrection against Thebes, and, in a double fratricide, died fighting against his brother. The regent Creon assumes power and decrees that Polynices's corpse lie disgraced on the battlefield, without burial rites. Antigone disobeys the edict and is condemned to death. But her end precipitates further tragedies—the suicides of her betrothed, Haemon (Creon's son), and Eurydice (his wife). Thus, Creon's "high and mighty words and ways / are flogged to humbleness, till age, / beaten to its knees, at last is wise."[5]

Though Tieck was unconvinced by the wisdom of adding "autonomous" music to Sophocles,[6] Felix was eager to pursue the project and dispatched music for the choruses in less than three weeks.[7] Rehearsals began at the end of September for the private premiere before the court in Potsdam on the evening of October 28. Present were the royal family and other nobility, ministers, military officers, diplomats, clergy, and Berlin intelligentsia—some two hundred invited guests, including Fanny and Meyerbeer[8] (only a month before, he had left Berlin for a three-week cure in order to avoid encountering Felix).[9]

Felix described the performance to his old friend, the philologist Droysen, as a "private amusement,"[10] but the play resonated with timeless themes relevant to Frederick William's reign. Thus, the court, intent upon bolstering the post-Napoleonic Restoration and resisting constitutional reform, viewed sympathetically Creon, who upheld the legitimacy of the state and restored Thebes after Polynices's insurrection. Whether, as Michael P. Steinberg has suggested, Felix's score betrayed his identification with the Antigone-Creon, outsider vs. state conflict— his relationship to German Jewry, on the one hand, and state-validated Protestantism, on the other—remains open to debate,[11] but one point bears emphasis. Now essentially forgotten, Felix's *Antigone* enjoyed extraordinary popularity during his lifetime. After a second Potsdam performance on November 6, the king authorized its public premiere at the

Berlin Schauspielhaus on April 13, 1842—"thus long the authorities had hesitated to bring the work before the general public," Devrient recalled in his memoirs of 1869. Within three weeks, a broad public enthusiastically received six more performances: the "solemn and religious tone" of Felix's score "delighted and edified even the lower strata of the public,"[12] who no doubt sympathized with Antigone, not Creon. Frederick William had a medallion commemorating the production struck,[13] and performances burgeoned throughout Germany and abroad. In Leipzig, where *Antigone* reached the theater as early as March 5, 1842, a philhellenic craze took hold, parodied in Albert Lortzing's comic opera *Der Wildschütz* (1842), in which the provincial schoolmaster Baculus masquerades as a classicist versed in Sophocles. By 1845 the English were mounting a production at Covent Garden, where forty-five consecutive performances occurred that year alone. One distinctive feature of the English version— the addition of "ballet girls" during the Dionysos chorus—must have exasperated Felix, though he found amusing two *Antigone* caricatures in an issue of *Punch* for January 18, 1845, one of which presented the "Chorusmaster, with his plaid trousers shewing underneath."[14]

Along with Tieck, Felix conferred with the classicist P. A. Böckh, who rented rooms at Leipzigerstrasse No. 3 during the 1840s, and Eduard Devrient, who played Haemon. Modern music now engaged classical erudition, a rapprochement Felix found stimulating. With Böckh Felix reviewed the Greek prosody and retouched Donner's translation. Felix himself rendered into German some choruses, including the first ode, sung to celebrate the end of the Theban civil war; and even after the premiere, Böckh continued tinkering with the German, to respect as precisely as possible Sophocles's dactyls and internal choriambs.[15] The whole project must have seemed vaguely familiar: some fifteen years before, Felix had fidgeted over his translation of Terence's *Andria*, though there was then no prospect of composing music for the Latin comedy.

According to Devrient, Felix seriously thought of approximating the putative musical practices of antiquity by restricting the chorus to singing in a chantlike unison or recitative and limiting the instruments to modern "counterparts" of the aulos, salpinx, and lyre—the flute, tuba, and harp. He soon abandoned the plan, as Devrient explains, lest the choral chant became "tedious and unmusical," and the "accompaniments for so few instruments" made "the whole appear as a mere puerile imitation of the ancient music, about which after all we knew nothing."[16] Instead, Felix scored for a modern orchestra (double winds, brass with paired horns and trumpets, three trombones, timpani, harp, and strings) that could be applied in whole or in parts.[17] He assigned the choral odes to an ensemble of sixteen men (divisible into two groups of eight), of whom one served as the *coryphaeus*, or leader.

The actors delivered most of their lines without music; but a few passages, in which Sophocles specified interaction between the actors and chorus, required other solutions. Felix resorted here primarily to melodrama, in which a muted orchestral backdrop supported the spoken text. But in a few passages, he experimented with a novel form of rhythmic speech, by bending the musical accompaniment to the natural inflections of the text. Devrient reports the experiment may have been inspired by a technique in Prince Radziwill's incidental music to *Faust* (1831). Felix intended a type of delivery in which the text approached musical expression, at least rhythmically. No. 4, which follows Haemon's plea to Creon to spare Antigone's life, illustrates the technique. The section begins with the third ode, in which the chorus sings in the style of a male part-song of "love untamed / lighting on largess / with spoils / all night upon a maiden's cheek." Guards now escort the condemned Antigone onstage, as the chorus turns from major to minor mode. The orchestra imitates its dirgelike strains (**ex. 13.1a**) and pauses with sustained chords; then, Antigone declaims, "See me friends and citizens, / Look on this last walk." For the lines, "No wedding march, no bridal song / Can cheer my way, / whom Hades Lord of the dark lake weds," she shifts to rhythmic speech, softly supported by *pianissimo* winds (**ex. 13.1b**). In a letter to George Macfarren, Felix clarified that the winds were to follow Antigone, and not vice versa, in this eerie meeting of music and spoken text.[18]

In contrast to musical concessions to modernity, Tieck and Böckh made efforts to replicate a historically "authentic" performance space. The Neues Palais theater was rebuilt according to theories of the neoclassical architect H. C. Genelli. The proscenium, the arena of the actors,

Ex. 13.1a: Mendelssohn, *Antigone*, Op. 55 (1841), No. 4

Ex. 13.1b: Mendelssohn, *Antigone*, Op. 55 (1841), No. 4

was raised five feet above the orchestra, which, accommodating the musicians and the chorus, remained visible from every seat in the house. In the middle of the orchestra was the *thymele*, or Dionysian altar. Justified by Böckh as necessary for the sixth choral ode, the paean to Bacchus, the *thymele* was in fact *ungriechish*, for it concealed the anachronistic *souffleur*, or prompter. Connecting the stage to the orchestra were two descending sets of stairs. There was no curtain, so that the actors and chorus entered from the sides, and in lieu of sets a back wall to represent Creon's palace (through a door, opened near the end of the play, the audience could see soldiers bearing the body of Eurydice—for Böckh an incomparable image[19]). In visual terms, the audience experienced a tragedy of antiquity; in musical terms, Felix's score mediated between modern genres (e.g., the overture, the male part-song) and antique musical representations (e.g., metrical choral odes, and recitatives, familiar to audiences from an operatic tradition ultimately based on Greek drama).

Felix's score comprises a short orchestral overture and seven numbers—the first choral *stasimon*, or ode, in which the chorus enters the orchestra, five additional *stasima* that articulate the dramatic segments of the tragedy, and the concluding lines, in which the chorus exits. Instead of a full overture, Felix wrote a compact, bipartite introduction to establish the conflict between Creon and Antigone. We hear first ceremonial music in majestic dotted rhythms (ex. 13.2a) and imitative counterpoint, symbols of the Theban state. As this solemn exordium approaches a cadence, the music swerves to a passionate Allegro, harmonically unstable, and featuring a widely flung, agitated melody in the violins, evidently Felix's depiction of Antigone, who does not bow to Creon's edict (ex. 13.2b). The choral odes follow more predictable plans; strophically organized, they observe Sophocles's regular division between strophes and antistrophes. Conceiving the music for the odes to highlight the shifting responses of the chorus to the unfolding drama, Felix identified seven *Stimmungen*:

Ex. 13.2a: Mendelssohn, *Antigone*, Op. 55 (1841), Overture

Ex. 13.2b: Mendelssohn, *Antigone*, Op. 55 (1841), Overture

"victory and the dawn of day, restful contemplation, melancholy, love, mourning, song to Bacchus, and, at the end, serious warning."[20]

The music ranges from the celebratory entrance ode, with rising, optimistic triadic figures, to No. 2, a calming, pastoral reflection about the nature of man; No. 3, a melancholy comment, alternating between a soloist and the chorus, on the house of Labdacus, beset by calamity; and No. 4, an ode to love, scored for alternating brass choir and chorus in block chords. In No. 5, the chorus recounts in unison other Greek figures who shared Antigone's fate. In No. 6, encored at the Potsdam premiere, the chorus begins its appeal to Bacchus in a festive mood that becomes more desperate, with pleas to the divinity to save his favorite city, "shadowed by plague," from impending calamity (ex. 13.3). The final number,

Ex. 13.3a: Mendelssohn, *Antigone*, Op. 55 (1841), No. 6

Allegro maestoso

Ex. 13.3b: Mendelssohn, *Antigone*, Op. 55 (1841), No. 6

Hör   uns,   Bach - chus! Die Stadt, die du stets   hoch vor al - len Städ-ten ver - ehrst,

Ex. 13.4a: Mendelssohn, *Antigone*, Op. 55 (1841), No. 7

Andante con moto maestoso

Ex. 13.4b: J. S. Bach, St. Matthew Passion (1727), "Wir setzen uns mit Thränen"

which commences as Creon's lament before turning to the choral admonition against "high and mighty words," ends in C minor, reviving the key of the orchestral introduction and thus completing the tragic circle. But the sobering pedal points and inexorably descending lines of the closing seem to recall the poignancy of another final chorus. Was Felix alluding to the last movement of Bach's St. Matthew Passion (ex. 13.4), also in C minor, and a powerful link to the German past and Christian adumbrations Tieck detected in Sophocles? It seems plausible that Felix used modern means not to reclothe a timeless drama in modernity but to reconcile what Franz Brendel in 1845 described as the "most extreme antitheses, the inwardness of Christian music and the 'externality' of the Greek-plastic principle."[21]

I

On October 13, 1841, three days after the completion of *Antigone,* the king appointed Felix royal Prussian Kapellmeister[22] but issued no other musical commissions. Instead, Felix worked on a piano arrangement of the *Lobgesang* for the queen and began to realize a symphonic project that had haunted him for years—the *Scottish* Symphony.[23] He also continued the search for a suitable opera libretto. Early in 1841 Felix had received a proposal that he write a new opera with Eugène Scribe for the Paris Opéra but declined, unable to meet the condition that Felix attend the premiere;[24] when pressed by the Mainz music publisher Schott, eager to secure the rights to the collaboration, Felix replied that he would write for the German, not the French stage.[25] From England the chemist, amateur musician, and floral illustrator William Bartholomew (1793–1867) sent two libretti. *Titania, or the Christmas Night's Dream* was an attempt to inspire the creator of the *Midsummer Night's Dream* Overture to conceive "similar picturesque strains."[26] Unconvinced, Klingemann found the piece lacked "dramatic interest" and suggested "the time for fairy-operas is gone"[27]; Felix believed the fairies "would come out much better if a real earthly life would have been opposed to their fanciful one."[28] Undeterred, Bartholomew then sent Felix a manuscript for an opera on Sappho, not "as the lascivious creature she is said to have been, but rather a noble soul struggling with a passion working strongly upon her too sensitive mind, until reason fails, wrought upon by superstition, and in the frenzy self destruction by 'the lover's leap' ensues."[29] The work would begin with a "choral symphony," and Bartholomew imagined that the English text Felix would set would readily adapt to German without the need to alter much of the music.[30] Though nothing came of the plan—in June 1842 Felix replied that the text was more suitable for melodrama than opera[31]—the correspondence marked the beginning of a significant friendship: Bartholomew provided the translations for several of Felix's major choral works, including *Elijah*. Yet another potential librettist emerged in the poet Adolf Böttger, who proposed the legend of St. Genoveva. Here too Felix chose to avoid the subject, for "our interest in Genoveva arises more from what she suffers . . . than from what she does, or from any dramatic business or action on her part."[32] In this case, his instincts were justified; when Robert Schumann produced his *Genoveva* at mid-century, it enjoyed only a *succès d'estime*.

After the second Potsdam performance of *Antigone*, Felix escaped the royal indecision for a few weeks by visiting Leipzig, where he arrived on November 12 and was joined by Cécile, Paul, and Albertine on the 21st. Greeting Felix were David, the Dutch composer Johannes Verhulst, and Robert and Clara Schumann, among the first to hear the composer render the *Scottish* Symphony at the piano.[33] At the Gewandhaus Felix conducted two subscription concerts (November 13 and 25) and a benefit concert for the orchestral pension fund (November 22), and appeared on one of David's *Abendunterhaltungen* (November 27). The major works performed were the Overtures to Weber's *Oberon* and Cherubini's *Wasserträger*, Beethoven's Seventh Symphony, Fourth Piano Concerto, and Violin Sonata in C minor, and Felix's own Op. 51, selections from Op. 53, the revised version of Op. 46, Opp. 54 and 49, and selections from the first part of *Paulus*. On the 29th he returned to Berlin, to await the king's pleasure. An invitation to direct the Lower Rhine Musical Festival in Düsseldorf in May 1842 stimulated correspondence with Julius Rietz, but otherwise the quietude of domestic life momentarily contrasted with the usually frenetic pace of his professional affairs.

As it happened, in December Felix found Fanny finishing a substantial composition, *Das Jahr*, piano character pieces on the twelve months, thirty-five years before Tchaikovsky completed a similar project in *Les saisons*. Composed between August 28 and December 23, 1841, Fanny's cycle remained all but forgotten until late in the twentieth century.[34] Fanny herself saw through the press only one of the twelve, *September* (subtitled *Am Flusse, By the Stream*), which she incorporated into her *Vier Lieder für das Pianoforte*, Op. 2 (1846), without reference to its temporal or aquatic imagery. A triplet figure, introduced in the middle register and flowing throughout the composition, provides the essential musical metaphor. Blended between it and a simple bass line is a haunting, meandering melody apportioned between the hands, an application of Thalberg's three-hand technique (**ex. 13.5a**). Songlike, the piece has several imaginative harmonic turns, as it flows and ebbs effortlessly from B minor to B major and back, and remains among Fanny's most inspired creations.

Ex. 13.5a: Fanny Hensel, *Das Jahr* (1841), *September*, published as Lied, Op. 2 No. 2 (1846)

Ex. 13.5b: J. S. Bach, St. Matthew Passion (1727), "Kommt, ihr Töchter"

Ex. 13.5c: Fanny Hensel, *Das Jahr* (1841), *Nachspiel*

Ex. 13.5d: Fanny Hensel, *Das Jahr* (1841), *März*

Ex. 13.5e: Mendelssohn, *Serenade und Allegro giojoso*, Op. 43 (1838)

Ex. 13.5f: Fanny Hensel, *Das Jahr* (1841), *April*

Ex. 13.5g: Mendelssohn, *Capriccio brillant*, Op. 22 (1832)

Whether she envisioned publishing the entire *Das Jahr* is unknown, although the manuscripts clearly reflect her aspirations to produce an estimable cycle transcending the limitations of the short character piece. Thus, she revised the work and prepared a handsome *Reinschrift* in which she recast *June* and tightened the cycle considerably through excisions and a bridge connecting *April* and *May*.[35] Her husband illustrated each month with a vignette, and together the couple provided descriptive verses that offer clues about the programmatic contents of the music. Thus, *March*, retitled *Präludium und Choral*, begins with muffled bells anticipating Easter, while *October*, resounding with horn calls, celebrates the hunt. Instead of twelve unrelated pieces we find a tautly organized collection with a clear key sequence (proceeding from sharp to flat keys, and concluding in the "neutral" C major and A minor), the use of thematic links (the dreamlike sequence *January* foreshadows material from *February*, *May*, *June*, and *August*), and an overarching programmatic design organized around the Protestant calendar. Anchoring the cycle are March and December—Easter and Christmas—with chorales treating Christ's resurrection and birth, *Christ ist erstanden* and *Vom Himmel hoch*. In addition, Fanny appended a short postlude (*Nachspiel*) in A minor that cites the chorale *Das alte Jahr vergangen ist* and thus reflects on the "year" that has transpired. But between the subdued chorale phrases we hear a rising soprano figure and chromatically descending bass line, emblem of a lament. The forceful contrary motion and surprise turn to the major for the final cadence unmistakably betray their origins in the monumental opening of J. S. Bach's St. Matthew Passion, "Kommt, ihr Töchter, helft mir klagen" ("Come, ye daughters, help me lament," ex. 13.5b, c). Fanny's cycle thus ends by looking ahead to Christ's Passion, and the repetition of the cycle.

The powerful Bachian allusion links *Das Jahr* to Felix's youthful deed, the 1829 revival of Bach's masterpiece.[36] The cycle also betrays other ties to her brother. On one level are allusions to styles and genres associated

428 ❖ ELIJAH'S CHARIOT

with Felix, including the *Lied ohne Worte* (most notably *June*, subtitled
Serenade, which imitates the Venetian *Gondellieder*), part-song (*May*,
subtitled *Frühlingslied*), and elfin scherzo (*February* and the first part of
December, where a blurry sixteenth-note figure creates the impression
of a snowstorm). Then there are specific quotations and transforma-
tions of themes from Felix's music, which occasionally intrude into the
private, diarylike utterances of Fanny's cycle. In *March* Fanny prepares
the Easter chorale *Christ ist erstanden* by a dissonant phrase drawn from
the *Serenade und Allegro giojoso*, Op. 43 (**ex. 13.5d, e**), while in *April* she
reworks the second theme from the *Capriccio brillant*, Op. 22 (**ex. 13.5f,
g**). Even the culminating variations on *Vom Himmel hoch* in December,
which extend the chorale into a freely composed coda, recall similar techniques in Felix's effulgent cantata on the same chorale (1831).

Some scholars have read *Das Jahr* as a musical travelogue, in which
Fanny recorded experiences from her Italian sojourn of 1839–1840.[37] But
in contrast to Felix's *Italian* Symphony, little in *Das Jahr* is specifically
Italianate, unless we hear the frolicsome *February* as carnival-like,[38] or
the wistful *June* as depicting a Venetian lagoon. Like Felix, Fanny had
attended services at St. Peter's and was an acute student of Catholic
monophony and polyphony; yet, she chose not to incorporate her impressions into *Das Jahr*. Thus, there is no chantlike procession, as in the
slow movement of Felix's symphony. Indeed, as if to affirm Fanny's
Lutheran faith, Protestant chorales identify Easter and Christmas. A thoroughly Germanic spirit permeates *Das Jahr*, which conjures up idealized images of Fanny's spiritual and musical identities, as a fully
assimilated Protestant and aspiring member of Felix's musical confra-
ternity. The musical memories of this annual cycle, related through the
feminine perspective of a talented composer seeking increasingly challenging creative outlets, inevitably bring us back to Berlin.

II

Before the old year expired, Berlin was gripped by Lisztian frenzy late in
December 1841. Since his Leipzig visit in March 1840, the virtuoso had
traveled to England (where he introduced the term "recital" to describe
his solo concerts) and performed for the ducal nobility of Weimar, where
in 1848 he eventually would settle, ending his peripatetic concert life.
Before departing Berlin early in March 1842, Liszt concertized at a mara-
thon rate, performing some eighty compositions in twenty-one appearances,[39] initially at the Singakademie, and then, to accommodate the
swelling audiences, at the Schauspielhaus. Felix, Spontini, and Meyerbeer

greeted Liszt when he arrived in Berlin, and at his first concert (December 27), he used an English piano "owned by a famous composer resident in Berlin, himself a great pianist"—in other words, Felix.[40]

In contrast to the Leipzigers, who had to be won over to Liszt, stolid Berliners readily succumbed to the mass hysteria Heinrich Heine dubbed *Lisztmanie*. A faddish cult surrounded the pianist, with female admirers swooning before him and collecting his personal effects like so many relics, and the Prussian court treating him as an *Ersatz*-nobleman. But privately, Felix vented his rage at Liszt's musical licenses: ". . . Liszt pleases me here not half as much as in other locales, and has forfeited a good deal of my deep respect through all the silly tomfoolery he perpetrates not only on the public (which doesn't hurt) but on the music itself. Here he has played pieces of Beethoven, Bach, Handel and Weber so wretchedly and inadequately, . . . that renditions by average performers would have given me much greater pleasure. Here he added six bars, there omitted seven; here he made false harmonies, and later introduced other similar corruptions, and there in the most gentle passages made a dreadful *fortissimo*, and, for what I know, all pathetic nonsense."[41] Not surprisingly, when Liszt again asked to use Felix's piano, he declined.[42] Still, the Hungarian's triumph was complete: the Berlin Academy of Arts elected him a member, and later Frederick William awarded the pianist the *Ordre pour le mérite*, a new class of civilian distinction also conferred upon Felix and Meyerbeer. When Liszt left the Prussian capital on March 3, he departed in a carriage drawn by six white horses, accompanied by thousands of well-wishers.

Though upstaged by the virtuoso, Felix performed *Paulus* by royal command on January 10 in the Schauspielhaus, with soloists from the royal opera; the chorus, two hundred strong, included amateurs and members of the Singakademie, selected by a committee appointed by the king.[43] The receipts went to charity, and a newly composed sonnet commemorated Felix's "magical waves of sound" that summoned the audience to a second (Christian) life.[44] The success was great enough to justify a second performance at the Singakademie on February 17, though the *Allgemeine musikalische Zeitung* alluded to a division among that institution's ranks, and Devrient reported that "some disagreeables" and sarcastic comments had emerged during the rehearsals that further embittered Felix.[45] Even his reception as an honorary member of the Singakademie on March 15[46] did not assuage the strained relationship to the academy.

On January 15, Felix completed a minor work for another society, *Die Stiftungsfeier*, a part-song for male chorus. More or less neglected in the literature, the work calls upon the society's members to perpetuate

Ex. 13.6: Mendelssohn, *Die Stiftungsfeier* (1842)

Auf, Freun-de, lasst das   Jahr__ uns sin-gen,   das un-sern Bun - des Wie - ge war,__

the memory of those who established an "asylum of friendship" (**ex. 13.6**). From the correspondence of Giacomo Meyerbeer, who also contributed to the undertaking, we learn the purpose—to commemorate the fiftieth anniversary of the Society of Friends (*Gesellschaft der Freunde*),[47] which Joseph Mendelssohn and other liberal Jews had founded in 1792 to promote mutual toleration and respect, and challenge Orthodox Judaism. "Though many have already departed," the text reads, "their great, beautiful work endures. Let us lean on their teachings, that their work never perishes."

Somehow the return to Berlin brought closure to the *Scottish* Symphony, Op. 56, which Felix dated on January 20, 1842,[48] and played through at the piano several times to Sterndale Bennett, who arrived in the Prussian capital the following day.[49] Felix decided to premiere it in Leipzig, and dispatched a score to the city on February 13.[50] Two days later, the two friends embarked on the eight-and-a-half-hour train ride to Leipzig. On February 28, Felix presided over the Gewandhaus concert of the English harpist Elias Parish-Alvars, sometimes credited with developing layered tissues of sound that anticipated Thalberg's harplike, "three-hand" technique on the piano.[51] Then, at the nineteenth concert on March 3, Sterndale Bennett offered his Fourth Piano Concerto, and Felix premiered the *Scottish* Symphony. Finally, on March 5, he introduced in the municipal theater his music for *Antigone*. Initially, the new symphony caused some bewilderment, for Felix had specified its four movements be performed *attacca*, without pauses. But at its second performance, on March 17 by Karl Bach (the Leipzig theater Kapellmeister), the audience energetically demarcated the movements with bursts of applause.[52]

The exact chronology of Felix's final symphony has long vexed scholars. At Holyrood Palace in 1829, he had easily conceived the somber Andante opening, notated in piano score with instrumental cues for the orchestration. The moldering, ivy-covered ruins of Queen Mary's chapel stimulated simple but powerfully evocative musical imagery: a rising figure, doubled at the octave, and gloomily scored for oboes and violas, that unfolded the A-minor triad in its form, E–A–C (**ex. 13.7**). Despite Felix's sporadic efforts to work on the composition during the 1830s, the symphonic kernel appears to have lain dormant until his return to Berlin in 1841.[53] In the meantime, the figure found an expressive outlet in another context:

Ex. 13.7: Mendelssohn, *Scottish* Symphony, Op. 56 (1842), *Andante con moto*

the wintry *schlechtes Wetter* of the overture to *Die erste Walpurgisnacht* (1832, see p. 270). Felix thus seems to have associated Goethe's medieval Druids on the Harz Mountains with their Scottish cousins.

At the premiere Felix performed the symphony without reference to its extramusical inspiration; still, for a reporter of the *Allgemeine musikalische Zeitung*, much of the score displayed a folk character.[54] Somehow Robert Schumann confounded the composition with the unpublished *Italian* Symphony, and, in a critical misfire, imagined in its opening "ancient melodies sung in lovely Italy."[55] But the Leipzig audience would have had little difficulty relating the symphony to Scotland, for its musical style recalled Felix's then well-known *Fingal's Cave* Overture. Thus we find examples of open-spaced chords, dronelike fifths, rough-hewn harmonic progressions, darkly hued scorings, and sequential repetitions, all reminiscent of the overture and what might be termed Felix's Ossianic manner.[56]

Around this time another composer was drawing upon the *Fingal's Cave* Overture to create an explicitly programmatic, Scottish work. Late in 1840 the young Dane Niels Gade (1817–1890) had composed the *Echoes of Ossian* (*Nachklänge von Ossian*) Overture and submitted it to a competition of the Copenhagen Musikforeningen. Its director, the composer J. P. E. Hartmann, had secured the services of three German musicians to judge the entries—Louis Spohr, Friedrich Schneider, and Felix. But at the end of 1840, owing to his mounting workload, Felix had withdrawn.[57] In March 1841 his colleagues awarded the prize to Gade; later that year Gade's overture appeared in Copenhagen and Leipzig, and it received its German premiere at the Gewandhaus on January 27, 1842, one week after Felix finished the *Scottish* Symphony in Berlin.

Although Felix did not meet Gade until 1843, *Echoes of Ossian* may have left its mark on the new symphony. Felix's copy of the 1841 first edition of Gade's overture survives at Oxford,[58] though admittedly, we do not know when Felix acquired the score. Especially intriguing are several musical similarities between the overture and first movement of the symphony, both of which employ a framing device, a brooding A-minor passage that recurs as an epilogue to the movements. Gade's overture begins with some melancholy chords that introduce a folksonglike melody, evidently intended to connote an ancient, bardic song (**ex. 13.8**). As does Felix, Gade animates the tempo for the primary theme of his

Ex. 13.8: Gade, *Echoes of Ossian* Overture (1840)

sonata-form exposition, a militaristic figure with brass fanfares. Its dissonant harmonies indeed resemble the bridge section in Felix's movement,
which also bristles with fanfares. The similarities may be coincidental, but
possibly by January 1842 Felix was aware of Gade's overture; its emulation
of the *Fingal's Cave* Overture may have influenced, in turn, certain features of the symphony.

As we know, Gade sketched a private program for his overture, based
upon excerpts from a Danish translation of Ossian.[59] *Echoes of Ossian*
adopts a narrative approach—it tells a story, in a ballade-like tone, of Celtic
exploits. Thus, when we read in Gade's program "The warriors strike
their shields" (a quotation from Macpherson's *Temora*), we can pinpoint
that portion of the program in the fanfares of his score. To underscore
the mythic voice of the bard, Gade employs a harp—the traditional instrument with which Ossian accompanies his recitations—that figures
intermittently throughout the overture. Felix's *Scottish* Symphony too
displays narrative features but expands its compass to incorporate other
extramusical strategies. As a result, the symphony lies somewhere between the poles of programmatic and absolute music and, like the *Fingal's
Cave* Overture, admits a rich variety of interpretations.

In a probing analysis, Thomas Grey has argued for multiple, inter-
secting readings in the symphony.[60] The framing introduction suggests
an "epic-narrative prelude" that "mimics the gestures . . . of storytelling,
without telling the story." Using Felix's prefatory note to the first edition
(1843), which identified the characters of the movements (*Introduction
und Allegro agitato, Scherzo assai vivace, Adagio cantabile,* and *Allegro
guerriero und Finale maestoso*), Grey proceeds to sketch out a narrative
sequence, "loosely summed up as 'balladic invocation/chivalric sortie,
country dances, prayer, battle and victory tableau.'" But the symphony
embraces too techniques that bring us from the realm of the narrative
into the pictorial. For instance, Grey finds allusions to the traditions of
landscape and historical painting—the celebrated storm sequence in the
coda of the first movement, the battle (*guerriero*) scenes of the finale,
with its dissonant fugato and military fanfares—but also sees the connected movements as a series of musical tableaux vivants, in which im-

ages successively fade, one into the other. Grey also invokes the Parisian "diorama" spectacles popularized by L. J. Daguerre in the 1820s, in which screens and filters manipulated illustrations of natural and historical landscapes to suggest different viewings of the same object, as if striving toward a "protocinematic" reality. As Grey points out, one of Daguerre's most successful series was of Holyrood Chapel, as seen at various times of day and night. Could Felix, who had viewed these popular entertainments in 1832, have recalled the diorama sequence in his final symphony? Be that as it may, the appeal of the composition lies in its ability to stimulate alternate modes of analytical inquiry—musical, literary, and pictorial, all of which penetrate each other.

Thus the celebrated second movement, a scherzo that begins with a delicate staccato stirring in the strings, introduces in the clarinet a pentatonic melody (**ex. 13.9a**), surely meant to imitate folk music Felix

Ex. 13.9a: Mendelssohn, *Scottish* Symphony, Op. 56 (1842), Scherzo

Ex. 13.9b: Mendelssohn, *Scottish* Symphony, Op. 56 (1842), First Movement

Ex. 13.9c: Mendelssohn, *Scottish* Symphony, Op. 56 (1842), Third Movement

Ex. 13.9d: Mendelssohn, *Scottish* Symphony, Op. 56 (1842), Finale

Ex. 13.9e: Mendelssohn, *Scottish* Symphony, Op. 56 (1842), Finale

had heard in Edinburgh at the Highland Games. In contrast, the main body of the first movement, with its $\frac{6}{8}$ meter and pronounced rocking rhythms, projects the character of a ballade (ex. 13.9b). The details of its story come somewhat into focus in the third and fourth movements. The regal dotted rhythms of the Adagio and dirgelike procession in the winds over a descending, "lament" bass plausibly allude to the tragic figure of Queen Mary (ex. 13.9c). And the breathless, energetic finale, with its jagged dissonances and contrapuntal strife, generalizes the topic of conflict in Scottish history (ex. 13.9d).

We are left with the coda-like *Allegro maestoso assai* in A major; after nearly four hundred bars of the stormy finale, a new melody rises from the violas and clarinets in a fourfold crescendo. Nearly pentatonic, the melody suggests a new folksong, closely modeled on the primary theme of the first movement (exs. 13.9e and b), and thus affirming the tight-knit thematicism of the symphony, a quality early critics noted. But what is the purpose of this appendage? Too short to form an independent movement like the fifth-movement finale of Beethoven's *Pastoral* Symphony, the *Allegro* nevertheless recalls that model by resolving the dissonance of the fourth movement and projecting tonal stability and closure. Felix himself offered a clue about the coda when he recommended the passage begin like a *Männerchor*[61] (to that end, after the premiere he retouched the scoring, lest the timpani obscure the part-song texture). Drawing on this statement, Peter Mercer-Taylor has argued that the coda in fact alludes to the German genre of the male part-song, so that the symphony ends as a German symphony celebrating the German present and its memories of a distant Scottish past.[62]

Other readings of the symphony remain for consideration. In 1979 Ludwig Finscher labeled it a "Walter Scott symphony,"[63] as if to suggest a line of influence from the poetry and novels of Scotland's most famous writer, translated and widely read by the German middle class. In Scott's *The Abbot* (1820), for instance, Felix would have found a historical romance about Mary's flight to England after the Battle of Langside (1568). On the other hand, the novel's sequel, *Kenilworth* (1821), which focused on Mary's adversary Elizabeth, left Felix unimpressed. In 1840 he rejected a libretto for an opera on the subject, because of his "irrepressible aversion to the novel and its material."[64] But given the German perspective of the symphony, perhaps Felix had in mind a source closer to home: Schiller's tragedy *Maria Stuart* (1800), which treats the final days of the queen's life before her execution, and which almost certainly Felix had discussed with Goethe during the visits to Weimar. Perhaps this play too had a role in the unwritten "program" of the symphony, which concerns a German's perspectives on Scotland as a musical, literary, and historical theme.

III

From Berlin in March 1842, Felix finalized his plans for the summer. He convinced the committee of the Lower Rhine Music Festival, scheduled for May, to program Handel's *Israel in Egypt*; he determined to visit London, this time with Cécile, for the conclusion of the English concert season, for which he contemplated composing a third piano concerto.[65] The couple then intended to return to Frankfurt before embarking on a Swiss holiday.

If the public premiere of *Antigone* in April scored an unqualified success—six performances occurred between April 13 and 29—Berliners' memories of Liszt's tour overshadowed Felix's other appearances. On April 16 and 21 he participated in two *Quartett-Soiréen* in the Singakademie. With the Moravian violinist H. W. Ernst, celebrated for imitating Paganini's pyrotechnical feats, Felix performed his Piano Trio, Op. 49 and Beethoven's *Kreutzer* Sonata. Then, on April 25, he directed a lavish concert in the Schauspielhaus that offered one of Beethoven's *Leonore* Overtures, Handel's *Zadok the Priest*, Felix's Piano Concerto No. 2, and the *Lobgesang*. But the reception was "not cordial," and when Felix again inquired about plans for the new Berlin music academy, he was put off with vague assurances.[66] Around this time Felix received an importunate visitor, Richard Wagner, then attempting to secure the premiere of *The Flying Dutchman* in Berlin. Wagner reported that he "struck up rather friendly relations" with Felix,[67] though there is no mention of Wagner in Felix's contemporaneous letters. It seems unlikely Felix did more than observe social amenities, although he appears to have revealed his determination to leave Berlin to Wagner.[68] In the end Meyerbeer, not Felix, promoted the new opera, premiered not in Berlin but Dresden, where Wagner became a Kapellmeister early in 1843.

The beginning of May 1842 found Felix in Leipzig, where he again concertized with Ernst. Separating from Cécile and his children in Frankfurt, he proceeded to Düsseldorf, and en route learned of the calamitous fire that for three days (May 6–8) had consumed sizable areas of his birthplace, Hamburg (experiencing the firestorm firsthand, Paul and Albertine had to flee their Hamburg residence[69]). The Pentecost music festival opened on Sunday, May 15, with *Israel in Egypt* and Beethoven's Fifth Symphony, followed on the 16th by the *Lobgesang* Symphony and other works. The organizers were able to amass a chorus of 403 and orchestra of 170.[70] On the morning concert of the third day (May 17), when Ernst, scheduled to appear, fell ill, Felix performed without rehearsal Beethoven's *Emperor* Concerto, and then continued with some *Lieder ohne Worte*, and an improvisation on works heard at the festival, including Beethoven's Fifth.

A reminiscence of the festival has come down to us from Karl Schorn, who reports that during rehearsals Felix quietly glided from his rostrum to musicians' stands to correct their parts without interrupting the ensemble, and that he beat time calmly, while encouraging the orchestra with energetic glances.[71] Felix's improvisations created such a stir among female admirers that they seized his handkerchief and shredded it into so many mementos of the event. Schorn closed with a sketch of Felix's appearance that revealed as much about Schorn as Felix: "He was . . . a delicate little man with distinguished, elegant manners and fastidious grooming, so that one recognized the subject had not been cradled next to a loom. On his refined, black-curled head he wore a high top hat tilted somewhat toward the right ear, which made a smart, cheerful impression. His facial features—dark, flashing eyes, Roman nose, and pronounced sideburns hanging down on each cheek—did not disown his oriental extraction, but conveyed absolutely nothing of its often unpleasant aftertaste. This was a personality who won love and respect from everyone coming into contact with him."[72]

Felix convinced the festival committee to donate its proceeds to the Hamburg relief efforts and to that end waived his fee and travel expenses. Unhappily, despite these gestures, the festival closed its books with a deficit. Still, he continued his philanthropic efforts by giving concerts in Bonn (May 21) and Cologne (May 22, Haydn's *Die Schöpfung*) that raised over one thousand thalers.[73] Then the composer met Cécile in Bonn; alone for the first time since Carl's birth, the couple made a leisurely trip by way of Aachen, Liège, Antwerp (where they viewed paintings of Rubens), and Ghent to Ostende.[74] On May 29 they experienced a calm crossing of the English Channel. Two days later, in Berlin, the Prussian king announced the appointment of thirty distinguished men to the new *Ordre pour le mérite*; along with Liszt and Meyerbeer, Felix was cited in music.[75]

In London Felix's hosts were Cécile's aunt Henriette and her husband, the merchant F. W. Benecke, who had settled near the south edge of the city on Denmark Hill, Camberwell. By 1842 their family had grown to seven children ranging from an infant to fourteen years (Victor, eleven, later married Marie, Felix and Cécile's first daughter, and Victor's first cousin, once removed). At Camberwell Felix enjoyed musical entertainments with Moscheles and charades, in which Klingemann acted out Sir Walter Scott. To Klingemann Felix later wrote of his affection for the Beneckes[76] and their children, with whom he cavorted in the garden. On June 1, after the other adults left to visit Windsor, Felix found himself alone with his young charges, who teasingly pulled on his hands as he worked on two new *Lieder ohne Worte* at the piano. If the elegiac Op. 102 No. 1, in E minor, betrayed nothing of these pranks, the famous "*Frühlings-*

Ex. 13.10: Mendelssohn, *Lied ohne Worte* in A major, Op. 62 No. 6 (1842)

lied" in A major, Op. 62 No. 6, depicted them through clipped staccato notes exchanged between the hands (**ex. 13.10**).[77] On July 11, the day before his departure, Felix inscribed a humorous *Bärentanz* (*Bears' Dance*), dedicated to the "gooseberry eaters at Benecke castle" (a reference to Felix's favorite fruit in the garden). Resembling a caricature, this sketch opposes a lumbering, ursine pedal point in the bass and shrill, fifelike figure in the high treble.[78]

Felix sought to capture in both pieces a childlike naiveté, a quality he explored more thoroughly in eight keyboard miniatures recorded in sixpenny music books of two of the children, Teddy and Lilly.[79] The composer prepared six of the pieces for publication as *Kinderstücke* in 1846, but their release was delayed until December 1847, one month after Felix's death, when they appeared in England from Ewer & Co. as Op. 72, with the surely unauthorized title "Six pieces for the Pianoforte, composed as a Christmas present for his young friends, by Felix Mendelssohn Bartholdy." Less ambitious than Robert Schumann's *Kinderscenen* (*Scenes of Childhood*, 1838), Felix's Op. 72 nevertheless shares the same compositional strategy of self-reflective juvenescence, as the mature composer seeks to reclaim musically his childhood. Unlike Schumann, however, Felix did not fit descriptive titles to his pieces; still, little imagination is required to apprehend their refreshing innocence, projected through a tuneful, melodious style with repetitive rhythms and straightforward harmonies. But Felix suggests too the topsy-turvy world of childhood, as in No. 5 in G minor, which re-explores his elfin, scherzo idiom, and No. 6 in F, in which the inversion of the parts and canonic imitation suggests a helter-skelter chase.

At the height of the concert season Felix made at least six public appearances, including three as organist. On June 12, 1842, he returned to St. Peter's Cornhill, where he found the congregation appropriating Haydn's "Emperor's Hymn" as an English hymn.[80] The young organist Elizabeth Mounsey prevailed upon Felix to improvise on the melody for the concluding voluntary.[81] Four days later, at Christ Church, he reexplored the melody but added an extemporized fugue. One of his young English admirers, W. S. Rackstraw (later the well-known musical pedagogue Rockstro), recalled how before the fugue Felix introduced a "long treble A... on the swell," and developed it into "an inverted organ-point of prodigious length, treating it with the most ingenious and delightful harmonies, his invention of which seemed to be inexhaustible."[82] A third organ performance followed the next day, June 17, at a Sacred Harmonic Society Concert at Exeter Hall, where Felix rendered Bach's "St. Anne" Fugue and improvised on Handel's *Harmonious Blacksmith*. Arriving to attend another concert there, Felix was greeted by a spontaneous ovation led by the prime minister, Sir Robert Peel.[83]

Of Felix's other engagements, we know little about the last, on June 24, when he participated in a benefit concert Moscheles organized for victims of the Hamburg fire. But Felix's two other appearances, at the Philharmonic Society, are well documented. On June 13 he led the seventh concert, which began with Haydn's "Clock" Symphony (No. 101) and included overtures by Beethoven and Weber, two piano fantasies performed by Thalberg, and the English premiere of the *Scottish* Symphony. From the audience, the young composer G. A. Macfarren decided to hiss Thalberg and flirt with his female admirers, but then discovered in Felix's symphony an overwhelming pathos, "that deep, intense, and soulful feeling which dives down to the bottom of the human heart."[84] At the eighth and final concert Felix performed his D-minor Piano Concerto and directed the *Fingal's Cave* Overture. The reception was so positive that the directors gave a dinner in his honor at Greenwich on July 9, a few days before Felix and Cécile left London,[85] and offered him a small sum, despite the Society's constrained treasury.[86]

To his brother Paul Felix reported that on average he received three to four invitations a day,[87] many of which he declined. There were "dull" dinners with Frederick William's minister von Massow and ambassador C. K. J. Bunsen, dramatic readings from *Antony and Cleopatra* by Fanny Kemble, meetings with the banker George Grote, preoccupied with his *History of Greece* (twelve volumes appeared between 1846 and 1856), viewings with Cécile of private art galleries, and an excursion to Manchester to visit her uncle and aunt, Jean David and Thekla Souchay. The English bass Henry Phillips secured Felix's agreement to write an Ossianic *scena* (unfulfilled until 1846),[88] and the blind organist J. G. Emett brought him a manuscript of "the XLVIII," which Felix certified as an autograph of Bach's *Well-Tempered Clavier*.[89] The dandified M.P., Sir Edward Bulwer, author of *Rienzi, the Last Tribune of Rome* (on which Wagner based his opera of 1842) and *The Last Days of Pompeii*, flirted with Cécile.[90] But Felix's most celebrated engagements were his visits with Queen Victoria and Prince Albert.

Within days of arriving in London, Felix forwarded a letter to Prince Albert from his cousin, Frederick William IV, and awaited "his Royal Highness's command."[91] The first audience, which likely occurred the morning of June 14, was with the prince alone.[92] The following evening the Queen and the Consort received Felix in Buckingham Palace, where he entertained them with piano music and improvisations. He reported about the meeting in a well-known letter to Lea and an unpublished one to Paul;[93] cited here are the Queen's own recollections, recorded in her journal on June 16:

> After dinner came Mendelssohn Bartholdy, whose acquaintance I was so anxious to make. Albert had already seen him the other morning. He is short, dark & Jewish looking—delicate—with a fine intellectual forehead. . . . He is very pleasing & modest, & is greatly protected by the King of Prussia. He played first of all some of his *"Lieder ohne Worte"* after which, his Serenade [Op. 43] & then, he asked us to give him a theme, upon which he could improvise. We gave him 2, "Rule Britannia" & the Austrian National Anthem. He began immediately, & really I have never heard anything so beautiful; the way in which he blended them both together & changed over from one to the other, was quite wonderful as well as the exquisite harmony & feeling he puts into the variations, & the powerful rich chords, & modulations, which reminded one of all his beautiful compositions. At one moment he played the Austrian Anthem with the right hand he played "Rule Britannia", as the bass, with his left! He made some further improvisations on well-known themes & songs [including Lützow's *Wilde Jagd* and *Gaudeamus igitur*, later popularized by Brahms in the *Academic Festival* Overture]. We were all filled with the greatest admiration. Poor Mendelssohn was quite exhausted, when he had done playing.[94]

Another audience followed on Saturday, July 9, when Felix tried out Prince Albert's chamber organ.[95] After performing a chorale, Felix began "How lovely are the messengers" from *St. Paul*, to which Victoria and Albert joined in, while Albert pulled the stops for Felix. Augmented by the arrivals of the Prince and Princess of Gotha and Duchess of Kent, the party adjourned to the Queen's sitting room, so that she might perform a Lied accompanied by Felix. But first she ordered the royal parrot removed, lest the creature screech louder than she could sing, and to the servants' astonishment, Felix proceeded to carry out the cage. After the Queen rendered Fanny's *Italien* and sustained its last high G more purely than "any amateur," he confessed that Fanny had composed the song. The Queen then essayed *Pilgerspruch*, Op. 8 No. 5, and Albert sang the *Erntelied*, Op. 8 No. 4. To summarize the meeting, Felix improvised on the royal performances and wove together various elements into a kind of quodlibet. After securing the Queen's permission to dedicate the *Scottish* Symphony to her and receiving a ring engraved "V.R., 1842," he took his leave, walked through the rain to Klingemann's residence, and gave him and Cécile a "piping-hot account."

IV

By mid-July 1842, Felix and Cécile had returned to Frankfurt, where they met Paul and Albertine; late in the month, the couples departed for Switzerland. They planned to attend a performance in Lausanne of the *Lobgesang* by the Allgemeine Schweizerische Musikgesellschaft, which had mounted *Paulus* in 1838 and elected Felix an honorary member.[96] Sparing little effort, the Society had prepared a French version of the text, augmented the personnel of the orchestra and chorus to 706, and modified the venue to accommodate an audience of 2500.[97] But, owing to Cécile's indisposition, the couples tarried in Basel and arrived in Lausanne on August 4, the day after the monster concert, in time only for the concluding ball.[98] On August 7 Felix recorded a view of the city from the promenade de Montbenon, and captured the cathedral spires soaring above a dense counterpoint of buildings and city walls. The sketch was one of his first entries in a new album, one of three used during the third Swiss sojourn.[99] For the next month, drawing became Felix's preoccupation; indeed, as he later confessed to Klingemann, "In all Switzerland I composed not even a bit of music, but rather drew entire days, until my fingers and eyes ached."[100]

From Lausanne the party crossed the lake on the steamer *Helvétie* to Geneva and then proceeded southeast to Chamonix, where Felix worked up a dramatic view of *les Aiguilles*, the imposing mountains with needle-like peaks north of the resort. The Weimar actor Eduard Genast now joined the party, which grew to eleven with the arrival of the Preussers from Leipzig. Genast left this vignette of Felix leading a climbing expedition: "The elder ladies used sedan-chairs, the younger ones sure-footed mules, and we men, our *Alpenstöcke*. Always in front of everyone, Felix sprang like a chamois from rock to rock. His costume consisted of an Italian straw hat, black coat and breeches, white vest and collar. Apart from his hat and alpine shoes, he could have appeared straightaway at court."[101]

From Martigny the party followed the Rhone valley to Leuk and then crossed the Gemmi Pass to the Bernese Alps. Felix recorded most of his sketches in situ, but he elaborated from memory a "reminiscence" of the Gemmi in Interlaken, which he reached on August 17. "Time is, time was, time is passed," he wrote to Lea the next day[102] and recalled how in 1822 his father had admired from an Interlaken inn the sprawling, gnarled walnut trees, and how, when Felix himself returned in 1831, the same innkeeper was reluctant to serve him because of his shabby appearance. Now he resided there as a person of consequence. For three days he labored over a romantic scene, composed partly in his imagination: a monk seated with a child on a bench encircling an ancient tree, its foliage extending beyond the walls of a monastery.[103]

Enjoying the panorama from the Wengern Alp, the travelers continued on to Meiringen, where Felix had a reunion with his carefree guide
of 1831, Peter Michel, now the sedate landlord of the inn Die Krone. Eleven
years before, Michel had entertained Felix by yodeling a *ranz des chèvres*,
or goatherd's song, and Felix now revived and fixed the bucolic tune in
his memory.[104] Near the Lake of the Four Cantons, in Altdorf, he separated from his companions, crossed the Surenen Pass, and reached the
secluded twelfth-century Benedictine abbey at Engelberg, where, in 1831,
he had assisted in a Mass. By the end of August he was filling the last pages
of his two albums and beginning a third,[105] before rejoining his family in
Lucerne. En route to Zurich they encountered another trusted companion, Dominic Jutz, who had served as the Mendelssohns' guide in 1822
and now regaled Felix with accurate memories of his father.[106] At Basel
they boarded a steamer bound for Mainz and returned to Frankfurt early
in September with happy memories of their idyllic journey.

Though the concert season was officially finished, Felix's arrival in
Frankfurt generated new music making, much of it for private gatherings. He played the organ at St. Catherine's Church, and at a matinée
organized by Ferdinand Hiller, he performed his recently finished piano-
duet arrangement of the *Scottish* Symphony. Unknown to Hiller, Felix
urged Simrock to publish his friend's music,[107] and he composed an
Eichendorff setting ("Es weiss und räth es doch Keiner," Op. 99 No. 6)
for Hiller's wife, a Polish singer. When she arranged for the painter Carl
Müller to sketch Felix's portrait, he agreed on condition she sing Lieder,
sixteen of which she executed while Müller drew. The sketch shows Felix,
sporting sideburns, sitting with his hands crossed and listening attentively.[108] When the young German pianist Charles Hallé visited the city,
Felix joined him and Hiller to perform J. S. Bach's Triple Concerto in D
minor and gave unstintingly of his time. Hallé left this account of his idol's
prodigious memory: "The greatest treat . . . was to sit with him at the
piano and listen to innumerable fragments from half-forgotten beautiful
works by Cherubini, Gluck, Bach, Palestrina, Marcello, '*tutti quanti*.' It was
only enough to mention one of them, whether it was a Gloria from one of
Cherubini's Masses or a psalm by Marcello, to hear it played to perfection,
until I came to the conclusion that he knew every bar of music ever written, and, what was more, could reproduce it immediately."[109]

After a late night serenade by his many admirers,[110] Felix and his
family departed Frankfurt and arrived in Leipzig on September 26. They
stayed for only about a week, time enough for Felix to become acquainted
with Robert Schumann's three new String Quartets, Op. 41. Here Felix
would have discovered several deft allusions to his own music—e.g., the
mischievous scherzo style (Nos. 1–3), lyrical *Lied ohne Worte* (No. 1), and

perpetuum-mobile finale (No. 2). A grateful Schumann dedicated the opus to his friend and recorded in his diary that of all living musicians, Felix had the most astute critical eye.[111] To the delight of his audience, Felix lingered in Leipzig to direct the first concert of the new season on October 2, in a Gewandhaus now festively illuminated by gas; the featured works were Beethoven's Seventh Symphony and Weber's *Konzertstück*, performed by Clara Schumann. Three days later, Felix was once again in Berlin, determined to resign his untenable position in the service of the Prussian king.

V

Writing to Hiller, Felix quickly fell into his "old Berlin strain": there was nothing worse, he groused, than "traveling north in the autumn," where one ate "sour grapes and bad nuts."[112] While waiting for an audience with the king, Felix considered a proposal from the royal Intendant, von Küstner, to compose music for the choruses of Euripides's *Medea*, but declined[113] (instead, Felix's colleague Wilhelm Taubert undertook the commission in 1843). At this time Felix also received an inquiry from Cécile's cousin Marc André Souchay, Jr., about the meaning of the *Lieder ohne Worte*. As a child, this musical dilettante had pondered these "masterful paintings," and now was emboldened to imagine their extramusical contents. Thus, Souchay determined that Op. 19b No. 1 concerned resignation, and No. 2, melancholy. In Op. 30 No. 1 he uncovered a "depiction of a devout and thankful person," while in Op. 38 No. 1, his unleashed imagination beheld nothing less than "boundless but unrequited love, which therefore often turns into longing, pain, sadness, and despair, but always becomes peaceful again."[114] Replying to these musings, Felix crafted what is sometimes taken as a defense of the absolutist position in musical aesthetics—the notion that music can stand by itself, unsupported by extraneous ideas. In composing a *Lied ohne Worte*, Felix only intended the song as it stood. If he had thought of specific words or texts for any of the songs, there was no point in revealing them, because the verbal ambiguities would engender confusion for listeners. Music, on the contrary, was far more precise, and filled the soul with a thousand things better than mere words.[115]

Curiously enough, two days after answering Souchay, Felix finished two new Lieder—*mit Worten*.[116] What is more, these texted songs represented genres already familiar to Souchay in the *Lieder ohne Worte*. Thus, Felix's fourth *Venetianisches Gondellied*, Op. 57 No. 5 employed the lap-

Ex. 13.11: Mendelssohn, *Venetianisches Gondellied*, Op. 57 No. 5 (1842)

Wenn durch die Piaz - zet - ta die A - bend - luft weht,

ping water imagery, softly dappled minor-keyed sonorities, and barcarolle rhythms familiar in its three predecessors for piano solo, but now Felix did "disclose" the text, Thomas Moore's poem about an amorous assignation on the Venetian lagoons (ex. 13.11). Similarly, the *Volkslied*, a duet for two sopranos, Op. 63 No. 5, characterized by rustic drones, adopted elements of Felix's Scottish manner already explored in a variety of instrumental works. The text was drawn from Robert Burns's sentimental poem, "O wert thou in the cauld blast." Felix's remonstrations to Souchay notwithstanding, a wealth of subtly reflecting musical and literary ideas bridged the gap between the texted and wordless Lieder, a fertile testing ground for the definitude of musical expression.

On Sunday, October 16, 1842, Felix emerged from an intense, two-hour meeting with a perturbed Prussian monarch, who declined to release his subject from royal service. Frederick William began to lay out plans for reorganizing music in the capital, a task he could not imagine finishing without Felix. But, the king conceded, until its implementation, Felix was free to travel. Writing immediately to Schleinitz, Felix announced his impending return to Leipzig to resume the Gewandhaus concerts, but also that he was duty bound not to accept a position from the Saxon king.[117] There ensued more discussions with von Massow and Eichhorn, who proposed that Felix take charge of sacred music in Berlin. Felix replied that "such a situation, if considered *practically*, must either consist of a general superintendence of all the present organists, choristers, schoolmasters, etc., or of the improvement and practice of the singing choirs in one or more cathedrals"[118]—exactly the kind of bureaucratic post that gave him no joy. Now deciding to force the issue, Felix determined to tender his resignation and requested a second royal audience, which occurred on October 26. The evening before, he tried to break the news gently to his mother but succeeded only in upsetting her at the prospect of losing her son a second time.

The second audience lasted only about an hour but produced results Felix could not have envisioned. Searching for a solution, the king
offered to found a new court chapel, consisting of thirty singers and a
small orchestra, all drawn from the best musicians of the city. Felix would
conduct the ensembles in church music on Sundays, and oratorios and
other works on other occasions, and compose music for them. Until the
new ensembles were in place, he was free to return to Leipzig ("It appears
you are fond of traveling," the monarch observed repeatedly). Here, finally, was an idea that could take root; charmed by the king's efforts,
Felix acquiesced, prompting a relieved von Massow to react, "You will
never dream of leaving us now!" After informing his overjoyed family,
Felix summarized the main points of the conversation in a letter to the
king[119] and announced his wish, during the organization of the new ensembles, to waive half his salary and return to Leipzig. A few days before
leaving Berlin, he conferred with Tieck and agreed to compose incidental music to Shakespeare's *A Midsummer Night's Dream* and Sophocles's
Oedipus at Colonos, and thus recommitted himself to the king's service.[120]

In Leipzig, where Felix arrived the evening of November 8, he plunged
into the hectic municipal concert life and, between November 12 and
December 21, directed or participated in eight concerts, including six
subscription concerts and two added events for the orchestral pension
fund and the aging actress Sophie Schröder. Among the highlights were
Spohr's Fourth Symphony (*Die Weihe der Töne*), a Moscheles piano duet
performed with Clara Schumann, and Beethoven's Fourth Piano Concerto (described by Felix as his *cheval de bataille*[121]) and Seventh Symphony. The benefit concert for Sophie Schröder (November 26) renewed
Felix's fledgling relationship with Wagner, who directed excerpts from
Rienzi, performed by the actress's daughter, Wilhelmine Schröder-Devrient
and the *Heldentenor* Joseph Tichatschek, creators of the roles of Adriano
and Rienzi at the Dresden premiere of *Rienzi* in October. Felix himself
performed his *Ruy Blas* Overture and Piano Concerto in D minor. At the
residence of the publisher Friedrich Brockhaus, Felix accompanied
Schröder-Devrient in some Schubert songs[122] and had an unusual encounter with Wagner, who happened to play the seductive Venusberg theme
from *Tannhäuser*, on which he was then at work. When Felix asked, "What
is that?" Wagner replied, "Do you think I am going to reveal it to you?"
whereupon Felix at once reproduced it himself at the piano.[123]

Among Felix's first concerns in Leipzig was to arrange an audience
with the Saxon king, Frederick Augustus II. This occurred in Dresden
on November 13, when Felix respectfully declined his appointment as
Kapellmeister but successfully urged the establishment of the new conservatory in Leipzig.[124] When the king granted final approval a week later,

Felix scrambled to prepare a prospectus for opening the institution in the spring of 1843. Writing to Moscheles, he pondered the idea of his friend moving to Leipzig to direct the new school and held talks with the Schumanns to solicit their support. By December he had formed a nucleus of instructors to include himself, the Schumanns, the organist C. F. Becker, C. A. Pohlenz (Felix's predecessor at the Gewandhaus), and Moritz Hauptmann (the new Kantor of the Thomasschule). But while these plans were underway, Frederick William made fresh demands on Felix's energies. There was now talk of music for Shakespeare's *Tempest* and Racine's *Athalie*, in addition to the other commitments for incidental music. And on November 22, the king signed a Supreme Cabinet Order appointing Felix *Generalmusikdirektor für kirchliche und geistliche Musik*, and stipulating the establishment of a new institute for "the improvement of sacred singing and sacred music in general."[125] Centered on the Berlin court and cathedral, the institute was to provide a model for the reform of sacred music throughout Prussia—and a specific sphere of influence for Felix. Embarrassed by this new distinction and reluctant to count among musicians who possessed "a greater number of decorations than they have written good compositions," Felix obediently acknowledged the new title.[126]

As 1842 came to a close, Felix took up composition with rededicated efforts. He made significant progress on the ebullient Cello Sonata in D major, Op. 58, and overhauled his old cantata *Die erste Walpurgisnacht*, which he wished to program early in the New Year. By December 11, his father's birthday, Felix was conceptualizing music for *A Midsummer Night's Dream* and *Oedipus at Colonos*. On that "hallowed" day, he wrote Lea of his intention to bring the new pieces to Berlin to share with his family over the Christmas holidays,[127] but she never received the letter. In the middle of a festive dinner party on December 11 she fell ill, after merrily urging her guests to dance, and suffered a stroke. She died the next morning.[128] The same day an obituary, probably written by Varnhagen, appeared in the *Vossische Zeitung*: "Her death will be deplored not only by her gifted children and near relations, but by a large circle of friends and acquaintances, for she had gathered round her a society as select as it was brilliant, and as sociable as it was animated."[129]

Overcome again by grief, Felix appears to have commuted to Berlin between the closing concerts of the year. On the morning of the 13th, after receiving a letter from Paul written before Lea's death, he hurriedly took a train to Berlin, only to arrive too late.[130] The last subscription concert (December 21) required his presence in Leipzig, because the Saxon king was in attendance. The concert began by commemorating Friedrich Rochlitz, founder of the *Allgemeine musikalische Zeitung* and a stalwart member of the Gewandhaus directors, who had died just days before. It continued with the *Eroica*, a solo by David, and Felix's *Midsummer Night's Dream* Overture. But the most difficult work for him was his setting of Psalm 42; during rehearsal, its imagery of the soul thirsting after God caused the composer to flee the hall in tears.[131] "We are children no longer," Felix wrote ruefully to Paul. Lea's unexpected death had severed one of the last ties to Berlin and left the children parentless. To be sure, at the height of his fame, Felix enjoyed the company of monarchs and now served as Prussian Generalmusikdirektor, but of what still remained unclear.

Chapter 14
1843–1844

Portrait of a Prussian Musician

What made me specially cling to Berlin . . .
no longer exists now.

—Felix to Hiller, January 19, 1843[1]

Felix had grieved before. Upon the death seven years earlier of his "instructor in art and life," the bachelor composer had fulfilled Abraham's ardent wish by completing *St. Paul*. Now, in 1843, Felix mourned with his family, drew windmills for his children, and alleviated headaches by reading Dickens' *Pickwick Papers*.[2] New creative work was difficult; instead, he reorchestrated *Die erste Walpurgisnacht* and rewrote the concert aria *Infelice*. But on January 19, he drafted a new *Lied ohne Worte* in E minor, assimilated the next year into the fifth volume as Op. 62 No. 3.[3] Though untitled, the Lied eventually became known as the *Trauermarsch* (*Funeral March*);[4] its dirgelike fanfares and somber processional effects made musically palpable his grief (**ex. 14.1**).

Felix was now content to stay in Leipzig. Paul handled the affairs of Lea's estate, estimated as a fortune of 160,000 thalers.[5] Meanwhile, his

Ex. 14.1: Mendelssohn, *Lied ohne Worte* in E minor, Op. 62 No. 3 (1843)

brother went through the motions of conducting the Gewandhaus concerts, four of which fell in January alone, and promoted the new conservatory. Instruction would be offered to Saxons and foreign students in composition, violin, piano, organ, and singing, supplemented by lectures in music history and training in chamber music and choral singing. Tuition was eighty thalers a year; each student would enjoy free admission to concerts at the Gewandhaus, where classes would be held; to Hiller Felix confided he would have to lecture about $\frac{6}{4}$ chords three or four times a week in a small room adjacent to the hall, but he was willing for "love of the cause." By early March thirty-four students had applied; among the inquiries was a letter from a young American, E. B. Oliver, whom the composer pledged to help, noting that he was far from his home—Boston.[6]

By late January Felix's mood had improved. His uncle Joseph sent him a lithograph of Moses Mendelssohn and a biographical essay for inclusion in the new edition of the philosopher's writings that the publisher Brockhaus began to bring out that year. Felix, Joseph wrote, was "the first to give new life to the brilliance of your grandfather's name. . . . About the biography I can only say to you, *it is* true, the gulf between the conditions of the grandfather's life and that of the grandson will astonish you. If the moral world were always to make such giant steps, it would be inconceivable that it has not progressed further in 5000 years."[7]

Felix was touched by the dedications of Ludwig Spohr's Piano Sonata in A♭, Op. 125, and Niels Gade's First Symphony in C minor, Op. 5, then in rehearsal at the Gewandhaus.[8] When Hector Berlioz, embarking on his first German tour, inquired about a Leipzig concert, Felix affably offered to assist.[9] Berlioz arrived on January 28 with his mistress, the mezzo-soprano Marie Recio, and proceeded to the Gewandhaus, where he found Felix, who "behaved like a brother" toward him,[10] rehearsing *Die erste Walpurgisnacht*. Impressed by the score's fire and passion, Berlioz prevailed upon Felix to exchange batons, the Frenchman's "heavy oak cudgel" for an elegant marshal's baton.[11] Accompanying Berlioz's offering was a mock note, in the style of James Fenimore Cooper's *Last of the Mohicans*, that concluded, "when the Great Spirit sends us to hunt in the land of souls, may our warriors hang our tomahawks side by side at the door of the council chamber."[12] According to Fanny, Berlioz's "odd manners gave so much offense" that Felix continually had to smooth ruffled feathers. Indeed, the baton exchange itself caused a misunderstanding. Fanny described Felix's as a "pretty light stick of whalebone covered with white leather," while Berlioz's rated only "an enormous cudgel of lime-tree with the bark on."[13] Berlioz's note compared the two in an indelicate *double entendre*—*Le mien est grossier, le tien est simple* ("Mine is coarser, yours is simple").

On February 2, 1843, Berlioz attended the sixteenth Gewandhaus concert, an all-German program, with works by Haydn, Beethoven, Mozart, Weber, and Henselt, culminating in the premiere of the revised *Erste Walpurgisnacht*. Berlioz wrote rhapsodically about Felix's cantata, praising its "impeccable clarity, notwithstanding the complexity of the writing," the "whirling momentum and sweep" of the finale, and inter-weaving of voices and instruments "with an apparent confusion" that was "the perfection of art."[14] The next day Felix devoted part of his thirty-fourth birthday to rehearsing Berlioz's concert and resolving last-minute glitches. In particular, the unusual scoring of the *Symphonie fantastique* strained the resources of the Gewandhaus. First, Berlioz requested twenty-four instead of the usual sixteen violins. The cor anglais, needed for the shepherd's song in the slow movement, was in such disrepair that a clarinet had to replace it. The ophicleide was declared "null and void" and supplanted by a fourth trombone. And when an amateur harpist bungled the decorative arpeggiations of the waltz in the second move-ment, Felix sight-read the part on the piano. Despite these obstacles and only two rehearsals, on February 4 the orchestra performed Berlioz's symphony and other works to his satisfaction.

Critical reaction was far from positive; indeed, the concert "threw musical Leipzig into a state of agitation."[15] In the *Allgemeine musikalische Zeitung* an anonymous reviewer, probably the new editor, Moritz Hauptmann, inveighed against the "unpleasant" harmonies and disso-nances of Berlioz's music, many of a previously unheard intensity. Com-pared to the symphony, the "Wolf's Glen" scene of Weber's *Der Freischütz* was a barcarolle; instead of pleasing the audience, Berlioz pursued a willful musical iconoclasm, and so forth.[16] Felix remained above the fray, though his private opinion of Berlioz had not changed since their meeting in Rome. When the flamboyant Frenchman departed for a Dresden en-gagement, Felix returned to less controversial fare—a benefit concert for Sophie Schloss (February 9) that featured his *Infelice* and Robert Schumann's new Piano Quintet, and the seventeenth subscription con-cert (February 16), on which his old friend Carl Baermann performed some virtuoso clarinet variations. Around this time Felix made a short trip to Berlin (February 5–6)[17] and then entertained relatives in Leipzig, first Paul and Albertine, followed by Wilhelm and Fanny, who arrived just in time to meet Berlioz returning for his second appearance, a char-ity concert of February 23.

Impressed by the Leipzig musicians, Berlioz now programmed the formidable finale of his "dramatic symphony" *Roméo et Juliette*, for or-chestra, bass solo, and triple chorus. Copyists hastily fitted a translation to the parts but failed to observe proper German prosody, so that Felix had to make corrections. When the bass engaged to sing Friar Laurence's aria muttered "gross Teutonic imprecations," Berlioz summarily withdrew the work. The morning of the concert, Felix organized a final rehearsal, and Berlioz was able to substitute in the eleventh hour his *King Lear* Overture and a movement from his Requiem, which inspired the taciturn Robert Schumann to comment, "This *Offertorium* surpasses everything."[18]

The final month of the season brought four more concerts for Felix to direct (March 2, 9, 23, and 30). Among the attractions was the premiere of Niels Gade's First Symphony, in C minor, Op. 5, which aroused Felix's admiration for the young Dane. Its stylistic proximity to the *Scottish* Symphony notwithstanding, Gade's symphony delighted the German audience by evoking a distant Danish past, already vaguely familiar through Felix's Ossianic musings in the *Fingal's Cave* Overture. One week later, on March 9, the Gewandhaus celebrated its centenary in a *Jubiläumskonzert.* The first part offered seven works by the principal musicians associated since 1743 with the Gewandhaus and Thomaskirche—J. F. Doles, J. S. Bach, J. A. Hiller, J. G. Schicht, H. A. Matthäi, Moritz Hauptmann, and Felix—all stitched together by a flowery poem recited between performances. It closed by extolling the future to be faithful to the motto enshrined in the hall, *res severa est verum gaudium.*[19] The second half then capped the commemoration with Beethoven's Ninth Symphony.

While Felix turned his thoughts to Leipzig's past, fresh dispatches affecting Berlin's future arrived. On March 21 Frederick William approved a plan establishing the royal *Hof- und Dom-Chor* (court and cathedral choir). Unconvinced of its viability, Felix grumbled that in Berlin "nobody knows, nobody cares, but everybody rules, from the King down to the meanest porter and the pensioned drummer."[20] Still, the bureaucratic machinery began to grind, and on March 27 von Massow was able to predict the choir would be ready for Felix by winter.[21] Developed by a Major Einbeck, who had organized military choruses after Russian prototypes, the new ensemble was initially directed by H. A. Neithardt and Zelter's former pupil Eduard Grell. Its personnel was made up of seventy singers: twenty-three boy sopranos, twenty-three boy altos, nine tenors, and fifteen basses. Though Einbeck thought the choir might require a year to mature, it began singing in sacred services on May 7, so that once again Felix had to ponder returning to royal service in Berlin.[22]

The pull between Berlin and Leipzig intensified in April, when four events in quick succession tested Felix's Saxon loyalties. First, on April 2, 1843, the new conservatory opened its doors to twenty-four students.[23] Among those matriculating were the composer/organist Theodor Kirchner; Emil Naumann, later known for his popular illustrated music history; and Wilhelm von Wasielewski, Robert Schumann's "first" biographer.[24] At this time Felix also knew and possibly offered lessons to Gustav Nottebohm (1817–1882), who during the 1870s developed the study of Beethoven's sketches into the new scholarly discipline of compositional process.[25]

The original faculty included Hauptmann (harmony and counterpoint), Robert Schumann (piano and composition), David (violin), C. F. Becker (organ), and Henriette Bünau (née Grabau, voice), who replaced the recently deceased Pohlenz. Felix himself offered instruction three times a week in "solo singing, instrumental playing, and composition."[26] Though the guiding force behind the institution, he scrupulously avoided assuming its directorship. No doubt his Düsseldorf experiences still haunted him, and he was bound to respond to Frederick William's summons to Berlin, whenever that occurred. Instead, the management of the school was entrusted to a Directorium of five (all Gewandhaus directors), including the Saxon minister von Falkenstein, Felix's close friend H. K. Schleinitz, the music publisher Kistner, Stadtrat Moritz Seeburg, and Hofrat J. G. Keil. Within a year, the student roster expanded to sixty-three, requiring additional faculty; eventually a two-story building was erected in the courtyard of the Gewandhaus to house the new school.

Scarcely had the conservatory opened before Felix hastened to Dresden to direct *Paulus* on Palm Sunday, April 9, 1843. (Cécile was unable to accompany him, on account of her advanced fourth pregnancy.) In gratitude, the Saxon king sent the composer a handsome rococo clock of Meissen porcelain.[27] Ironically, among Felix's most ardent supporters was Richard Wagner, recently installed as the new Dresden Kapellmeister and author of a short but glowing review.[28] Praising the oratorio as a classical masterwork, Wagner regretted only that *Paulus* was not joined to a Protestant service, so that its true religious import could reach the hearts of the faithful.

Four days later (April 13), Felix received the honorary freedom of Leipzig in "recognition of his great services for the musical culture of this city."[29] Bolstering those efforts, the fourth event then followed on April 23, bringing to culmination his efforts to restore the legacy of J. S. Bach. At a morning Gewandhaus concert Felix presented an all-Bach program: the orchestral Suite in D, the motet *Ich lasse dich nicht*, the Keyboard Concerto in D minor, an aria from the St. Matthew Passion, a free fantasy and cantata, the E-major Prelude for violin performed by David, and the Sanctus from the B-minor Mass.[30] The finale was a remnant of Felix's original intention to perform on this day the entire Mass, which, like the St. Matthew Passion, had lain unrecognized in Leipzig for over a century.[31]

After the concert, a select audience reconvened before Bach's former residence in the Thomasschule. There, in a simple ceremony, the Thoman-erchor sang two chorales and the motet *Singet dem Herrn ein neues Lied*, interspersed with short speeches. Then the Bach monument, three years in planning and the first such remembrance of the Thomaskantor, was unveiled. Designed by Felix's friend Eduard Bendemann in consulta-tion with Julius Hübner (both professors at the Dresden Academy of Art) and the sculptor Ernst Rietschel,[32] the sandstone monument rested upon a cluster of columns, and spiraling, free-standing columns at the four corners. They supported a four-sided monument protected by a "Gothic covering" and a cross. The principal side featured a colossal bust of Bach; the other three sides, bas-reliefs symbolizing Bach's work as organist, teacher (this side faced the Thomasschule), and composer of Christian music. After an advance viewing in December, Felix had de-scribed the effect in the last letter he wrote to his mother: "The monu-ment for old Sebastian Bach has become wonderfully pretty. . . . The many columns, little columns and scrollwork, above all the bas-reliefs and the old, splendid wig-adorned countenance shone freely in the sun-light, and gave me great joy. With its many decorative ornaments the whole really recalled the old Sebastian."[33] At the dedication at least one other member of the audience, who had traveled from Berlin to attend the ceremony, wholeheartedly agreed. An infirm octogenarian with snow-white hair, this mysterious person had served as Kapellmeister to the queen of Prussia until his retirement in 1811, and now was a forgotten, impoverished pensioner. He was Wilhelm Friedrich Ernst Bach (1759– 1845), son of J. C. F. Bach (the "Bückeburg" Bach), and sole surviving grandson of J. S. Bach.[34]

I

Late in the evening of May 1, 1843, Cécile gave birth to a boy, named Felix. Sadly, the composer's namesake did not prosper; sickly and frail, he succumbed to scarlet fever at age seven, in 1851. On May 2 , however, the father joyfully announced the birth of his third son and thanked God.[35] The concert season finished, Felix looked forward to a restful summer. His only public engagement was with the Milanese violinist An-tonio Bazzini (May 14).[36] The next day he received the composer Charles Gounod, who had visited Fanny in Berlin after the conclusion of his Prix de Rome fellowship. Felix reportedly greeted the young Frenchman with the salutation, *Ah, c'est vous le fou dont ma soeur m'a parlé* ("Ah, it's you, the madman of whom my sister has spoken"). For four days Felix entertained Gounod, reviewed his compositions, arranged a reading of the *Scottish* Symphony at the Gewandhaus, and played Bach organ works at the Thomaskirche.[37] But on May 25 Felix again had to return to Berlin for a conference. Industriously, he had finished in piano score the choruses for the projected production of Racine's *Athalie* and brought the manuscript with him. His principal purpose, though, was to gauge the quality of the new Domchor.[38]

In June the infant Felix was baptized in a ceremony witnessed by Fanny, Wilhelm, and Sebastian.[39] At last Felix anticipated the leisure time to finish new compositions, even though another royal commission intruded upon his time. On June 7, in the baroque courtyard of the Dresden Zwinger, he attended the unveiling of Rietschel's new statue of Frederick Augustus I. For the celebration Felix contributed a setting of the Saxon national anthem, *Gott segne Sachsenland*[40]—as it happened, the same melody as "God Save the King," which Carl Maria von Weber had used in his *Jubel-Ouvertüre* of 1818 for Frederick Augustus's jubilee.

Conducting Felix's offering was the thirty-year-old Richard Wagner, who himself composed an a cappella male part-song for the festivity (*Der Tag erscheint*, WWV 68) and assembled a chorus of some two hundred and fifty. Felix scored the anthem, reminiscent of the 1840 Gutenberg *Festgesang*, for two, spatially separated male choirs, each singing in unison, and supported by an array of brass instruments—trumpets, horns, trombones, and ophicleides for the "Chorus of Singers," and horns and trombones for the "Chorus of the People," which carried the melody of the anthem. To the first chorus, Felix assigned a new countermelody. Fearing the anthem would dissolve in the welter of sound, Wagner judged this arrangement a miscalculation and wrote to Felix for clarification.[41] A series of documents reveals that Wagner now saw himself as Felix's rival. While adopting a polite, solicitous tone to Felix, Wagner privately boasted to his half-sister Cäcilie Avenarius: "it was *universally* agreed that my own piece, which was straightforward & uplifting, knocked Mendelssohn's over-elaborate & artificial composition into a cocked hat."[42] Ex. 14.2 illustrates part of Felix's setting that Wagner found overwrought; here fussy, chromatic harmonies envelop the anthem, which momentarily yields to the countermelody. We do not have Felix's reaction to the performance, though an earlier letter suggests his estimation of his younger colleague. "Talent he has most certainly," Felix wrote, but also that "a great deal becomes exaggerated in that quarter," and that Wagner had managed to make many enemies in his early weeks as a Dresden Kapellmeister.[43]

Ex. 14.2: Mendelssohn, *Gott segne Sachsenland* (1843)

By July 1843 three new works were ready for the publishers. The *Sechs Lieder*, Op. 57, was Felix's first *Liederheft* to appear simultaneously in Germany, England, and France, where Breitkopf & Härtel, Wessel & Stapleton (London), and Benacci & Peschier (Lyon) paid forty *Louis d'Or*, ten guineas, and three hundred francs, respectively, for the rights.[44] Containing songs from 1839 to 1842, the collection included imitations of folksongs (Nos. 1 and 4) and drew upon texts representing stock types of lyric poetry (No. 2, *Shepherd's Song*; No. 5, *Gondellied*; and No. 6, *Wanderer's Song*). In the center of the collection stood the throbbing *Suleika* setting (No. 3, "Was bedeutet die Bewegung?"), widely known from Goethe's collection of exotic poetry *West-östlicher Divan* (though in fact by Marianne von Willemer). Here the feminine *persona* imagines the stirring east wind bears her lover's tidings and kisses, but only his amorous breath (*Liebeshauch*) can renew her life. The palpitating piano tremolos (**ex. 14.3**) connect these images. Most of the other Lieder, too, treat love texts, though from a masculine point of view—for example, in No. 2 (also arranged as the part-song, Op. 88 No. 3), a shepherd compares winter and spring as seasons of separation from and reunion with his beloved, while in No. 5, a masked protagonist, consumed by *Sehnsucht*, anticipates an assigna-

Ex. 14.3: Mendelssohn, *Suleika*, Op. 57 No. 3 (1843)

tion in the Venetian lagoons. The selection of songs may have depended to some degree on the English edition, for which the music critic J. W. Davison made the translations. Felix dedicated that edition to the English contralto Charlotte Helen Dolby, with whom, Davison confessed, he was hopelessly in love.[45]

With the Cello Sonata in D major, Op. 58, written for Paul but dedicated to the Russian patron and cellist Count Mateusz Wielhorski, Felix made a substantial contribution to the instrument's repertoire. Of the four movements, the outer two overflow with a sparkling, effervescent virtuosity that features, in the first, a soaring cello theme against pulsating piano chords (later recalled by Schumann in the finale of his Piano Trio in D minor, Op. 63, 1847) and, in the finale, frolicsome scales and arpeggiations. The two inner movements reveal contrasting facets of Felix's mature style. The second movement (*Allegretto scherzando*) begins as a subdued scherzo in B minor, with staccato articulations in the piano answered by hollow cello pizzicati. A warmly lyrical second theme then emanates from the cello, and the rest of the movement unfolds in a dramatic crescendo and decrescendo based on the alternation of the two ideas. The third movement opens with a freely composed chorale for piano solo, performed in an arpeggiated style (**ex. 14.4**) that injects a spiritual element into the chamber medium. The cello answers with an impassioned recitative, and the remainder of the movement combines the two. At the end the piano takes up the recitative in a retrospective passage with chromatic arabesques that link Felix's chorale to J. S. Bach's expressive harmonic language.

Felix's third volume of part-songs for mixed chorus, dedicated to Henriette Benecke, appeared during the summer of 1843 as the *Sechs Lieder*, Op. 59. Nos. 2–5 came from a group of eight composed that year,[46] to which Felix added a setting of Helmina von Chézy's *Im Grünen* from 1837. Like their predecessors, designed for performance in the open air, the Lieder celebrate natural settings—No. 1 (Helmina von Chézy) the freedom of the outdoors, No. 2 (Goethe) an early spring, No. 3 (Eichendorff)

Ex. 14.4: Mendelssohn, Cello Sonata No. 2 in D major, Op. 58 (1843), Third Movement

the departure from a forest, No. 4 (Goethe) a nightingale that sings old songs, No. 5 (Uhland) the quest for a valley of peace (*Ruhetal*), and No. 6 (Eichendorff) a hunt. The set betrays Felix's preference for straightforward strophic settings in a popular idiom, though the final song, filled with descriptive horn calls and animated rhythmic patterns to suggest galloping horses, employs a modified strophic arrangement and turns unexpectedly in the final couplet from a restless B minor to a euphonious B major. No. 3 (*Abschied vom Wald*) attained the status of a folksong in the nineteenth century.

II

By July 1843 Friedrich Wilhelm's ministers were placing fresh demands upon Felix, who for the next few months commuted between Leipzig and Berlin. The king had kept his promise and created the musical institute, the "instrument" on which Felix was to play. On July 10 Felix joined the ministers von Küstner and Redern, Wilhelm Taubert (Kapellmeister of the royal orchestra), and Meyerbeer (Generalmusikdirektor of opera) to discuss arrangements for the fall. The new choir, thirty-six strong, would sing chorales and the Te Deum on high feast days; Felix would direct two oratorios a year and several orchestral concerts.[47] But when, a week after the meeting, new conditions were imposed, *viz.*, that Felix and the institute would report to von Küstner, Felix refused to agree. He wrote to Paul of the "tedious everlasting affair" and "shook off" his anger in a defile near Naumburg,[48] southwest of Leipzig, where he made a brief excursion with Cécile's relatives.

Meanwhile, the king had decided to revise the Prussian liturgy to enhance the musical treatment and increase congregational participation in the singing. To that end, von Massow sent Felix a new order of worship.[49] Among the reforms was the introduction of Introit psalms at the beginning of the service, sung antiphonally by the choir and congregation. There was to be a revival of the Reformed metrical Psalters of the sixteenth and seventeenth centuries, and Felix was to provide settings of the traditional melodies. Of course, all these changes necessitated further consultations in Berlin, as did yet another royal assignment, which abruptly materialized on July 14. "By the most high command of his Majesty the King," von Massow wrote, "I request, esteemed sir, the favor that you set *as quickly as possible Herr Gott dich loben wir* in a score for four-part chorus, and an instrumental accompaniment for the 36 members of the *Kapelle* and organ."[50] Obediently, Felix dispatched in two days an arrangement of the Lutheran Te Deum—two hundred and thirty seven measures long—scored for two four-part choirs, four trombones, strings, and organ.[51]

The occasion for the Te Deum, traditionally sung on the battlefield as a victory hymn, was the millennium of the German Reich, established in 843 by the Treaty of Verdun. Felix was summoned to Berlin to conduct his medieval revival in the Berlin Cathedral on August 6, 1843, with all due ceremony—reinforced by volleys from one hundred cannons.[52] Tingeing the whole affair was Frederick William's attraction to a romanticized medieval past, which some took to betray his "catholicizing" tendencies. Felix was to apply the ancient Ambrosian modal melody as a cantus firmus and write in a "pure" style, with minimal intrusions from the instrumental accompaniment. But he found the assignment unavoidably tedious[53] and struggled to diversify his treatments of its thirty odd verses of praise. Among his solutions: combining vocal and instrumental resources for the outer sections, and applying smaller ensembles (e.g., the first or second choir with strings, the two choirs singing *alternatim* in unison, the first choir and trombones vs. the second choir and strings, and a cappella writing) to the interior of the work. For the most part Felix respected the modal attributes of the melody, which hovered around the pitch A and occasionally sank to its *finalis*, E, characteristic of the fourth (hypophrygian) church mode. But Felix could not avoid introducing some modern tonal harmonies into his setting, as if to render the austere chant palatable to its modern audience (**ex. 14.5**).

In Potsdam Felix was "commanded" to hear Taubert's music for *Medea* but found the score boring, the foundation "rotten."[54] Instead, he reapplied himself to his own music for *A Midsummer Night's Dream* and *Athalie*. By early September, both were essentially finished except the overture to the latter. Having returned to Leipzig on August 9, Felix completed a minor diversion, a Capriccio for string quartet in E minor, which paired a melancholy, *Lied ohne Worte*-like Andante with a studious mirror-inversion fugue (it appeared after his death as Op. 81 No. 3).[55] Felix enjoyed billiards with Robert Schumann, and appeared with Clara on a concert of the soprano Pauline Viardot, sister of Malibran (August 19). The same event featured the twelve-year-old prodigy Joseph Joachim,[56]

Ex. 14.5: Mendelssohn, *Herr Gott dich loben wir* (1843)

already possessing a fully developed violin technique (Felix took the boy under his wing and dubbed him alternately *Posaunenengel*, "trombone cherub," and *Teufelsbraten*, "devil"[57]). A few weeks later, Felix celebrated Clara's twenty-fourth birthday by playing the so-called *Frühlingslied*, Op. 62 No. 6 (dedicated to her when the entire opus appeared the following year). The occasion reunited Felix with the musician Heinrich Dorn. After a thirteen-year separation, Dorn witnessed an extraordinary demonstration of Felix's memory. When Dorn performed some "new" Lieder, Felix announced he already knew one and played derivative passages from an unpublished melodrama Dorn had composed in 1827. Felix then observed to the astonished Dorn, "It is only good melodies we should endeavor to retain."[58]

After the Prussian king had approved the terms of Felix's position, he began to plan his family's second move. First, though, he hastened to Berlin for a command performance of *Antigone* on September 19 (changes in the king's travel plans caused the postponement of *Oedipus at Colonos* and *Athalie*).[59] Then, only a week before rehearsals for *A Midsummer Night's Dream*, Felix returned to Leipzig to greet his deputy Ferdinand Hiller, who inaugurated the new Gewandhaus season on October 1, with assistance: Felix performed his First Piano Concerto and some *Lieder ohne Worte* and, to the audience's delight, wove together into a free improvisation themes from works heard on the concert.[60] The same day Felix finally met Niels Gade, who had traveled to Leipzig to direct his First Symphony. After endorsing a petition to improve working conditions of the orchestral personnel, Felix departed for Berlin on October 4[61] and began eleven grueling rehearsals for the new Shakespeare production.

The premiere of *A Midsummer Night's Dream*, in celebration of the king's birthday, occurred on October 14, 1843, at the theater of the Neues Palais in Potsdam. Several sold-out public performances followed at the Berlin Schauspielhaus. Among the audiences were the aging Sarah Levy, Fanny, Paul, Anton Schindler,[62] and several musicians from Leipzig, including Hiller, David, the young Joachim, and Gade. (Fanny invited the Dane to Leipzigerstrasse No. 3, where he became acquainted with her music and noticed the telling stylistic similarities between the two siblings.[63]) Three accounts of the production survive from Eduard Devrient (who played Lysander), Hiller, and Fanny.[64] Unlike the earlier collaboration on *Antigone*, Felix and Tieck now worked independently, so that while Felix composed music for the Schlegel translation, which retained Shakespeare's five acts, Tieck compressed the comedy into three, by conjoining acts 2–4, all set in the forest near Athens. As a result, two of Felix's entr'actes, Nos. 5 and 7 (falling between the second, third, and fourth acts) were heard with the curtain raised, forcing the use of a dramatic expedient to introduce the pieces without dropping the curtain. "This could be done," Devrient recalled, "with the *agitato* in A minor (No. 5), to accompany Hermia's seeking after her lover, especially if filled by the actress with grace and variety; but with the *notturno* in E major (No. 7), the long contemplation of the sleeping lovers was rather a painful effort, and Tieck's escape from the dilemma, by pushing forward some pieces of scenery to screen the lovers, was rather coarse and stagy, and of doubtful effect."[65]

There were other difficulties. Fanny was unconvinced by Tieck's costumes in seventeenth-century Spanish style, and during the Mechanicals' performance of *Pyramis and Thisbe* in the final act, a dog bit Lion. More disturbing, Felix was unable to realize his vision of a unified production, uninterrupted from the four chords of the opening of the overture to their recall at the very end of the finale. The king's retinue required a grand pause, "to offer all kinds of refreshments to the people in the front rows belonging to the Court, so that a full half-hour was taken up with loud talking and moving about, while the rest of the audience . . . had to beguile the time as best they could."[66]

Shakespeare's play mirrored the political/cultural reality of Potsdam/ Berlin, with its divide between the private and public, the court and the general populace. In the concluding act Frederick William would have identified with Theseus, who deigns to hear the Mechanicals' uncouth adaptation of *Pyramis and Thisbe*—the play within the play, which unfolds as a humorous clash between high- and lowbrow culture. Endeavoring, like Theseus, to perceive the "concord of this discord," Felix designed two different kinds of music. Framing the complex was the celebrated Wedding March in C major, in regal, ceremonial style with dotted rhythms befitting Theseus and Hippolyta. The march functions as entr'acte between the concluding acts and returns in No. 12 as a recessional for the court, retiring at midnight and making way for the elves, who bless the house in the finale. Between the stately appearances of the march occur three short pieces for the bumptious Mechanicals (Nos. 10a, 10b, and 11), in a decidedly rough-hewn style. First we hear a flourish of trumpets and drums, in which the timpani enter one measure late, to introduce the Ovidian playlet. Then, in the Dead March for Pyramis, the winds commit parallel fifths in a flagrant violation of voice-leading rules (Fanny found the morsel a caricature, like the "mock preludes" Felix played when one could not "get him to be serious").[67] And finally, in the Dance of Clowns Felix revives the colorful ninths from the Overture to depict Bottom's ungainly braying.

Sprinkled throughout the incidental music, like drops of Puck's magical juice, are persistent reminiscences of the overture. After a fermata of seventeen years, the mature master successfully reharnessed the inspiration of his adolescence. In particular, the tetrachordal motive, unifying idea of the overture (see p. 163), resurfaces in many movements. To trace its peregrinations is to marvel at a kaleidoscope of variations on a common idea (ex. 14.6). Thus in the breathless Scherzo (No. 1) that transports us to the second act and introduces Puck, that "merry wanderer of the night," an ascending chromatic scale assimilates the tetrachord (14.6a), while in the Fairies' March (No. 2) the descending pizzicato strings retrace its descending form in the key of the overture (14.6b). Prefacing the second strophe of "You spotted snakes" (No. 3)—the "roundel" Titania requests as a musical sedative—is a descending tetrachord. And in the ensuing melodrama (No. 4), when Oberon administers the juice to Titania, Felix reduces the music to little more than bare ascending tetrachords (14.6c), later answered by *descending* tetrachords in the mirroring counterpart (No. 8), when Oberon releases the queen from the spell (14.6d). The Intermezzo in A minor (No. 5), depicting Hermia's errant pining for Lysander, couples a fractured theme, divided between the winds and violins, with a descending chromatic scale (14.6e).

At the midpoint of the score (No. 6), a descending tetrachord languidly unfolds in the winds (14.6f); and as the entranced Titania encounters the transformed Bottom, Felix revives the motto chords of the overture and their latent tetrachord in a droll reharmonization (14.6g). A few bars later we hear a more accurate quotation from the close of the overture; then, in the serene Nocturne (No. 7) between the third and fourth acts, Felix begins the calming horn melody with the fourth B–E (14.6h), thus reviving the interval of the original tetrachord (in the closing bars, it is filled in by pizzicato violins, in the form E–D♯–C♯–C♮–B; 14.6i). No. 8 contains two quotations from the overture: the nimble elves' music in E minor and, announcing the arrival of Theseus's hunting party, the fanfares from the end of the exposition. We reach the entr'acte to the fifth act, the Wedding March, and the ensuing numbers that transfer us to the Athenian court.

Only when Theseus's party retires to attenuated strains of the march does the elves' diminutive motive reappear, to prepare the finale. Like a miniature re-enactment of the overture, the finale begins and ends with the motto chords and borrows its material from the dainty elves' figure and quiescent closing bars of the overture. But here a chorus of elves obeys Oberon's and Titania's directive to bless Theseus's house and thus gives verbal substance to the familiar music (14.6j). At the end, Puck muses about "this weak and idle theme, no more yielding than a dream"; his final seven lines are apportioned between the motto chords. The last sonority stands alone, as it must, our final passage from fairyland. It is,

Ex. 14.6a: Mendelssohn, Incidental Music to *A Midsummer Night's Dream*, Op. 61 (1843), No. 1

Ex. 14.6b: Mendelssohn, Incidental Music to *A Midsummer Night's Dream*, Op. 61 (1843), No. 2

Ex. 14.6c: Mendelssohn, Incidental Music to *A Midsummer Night's Dream*, Op. 61 (1843), No. 4

What thou seest, Do it for thy Love, and languish Be it ounce, or Pard, or boar, with In thy eye that When thou wak'st, Wake, when some
when thou dost wake, truelove take; for his sake! cat, or bear, bristled hair: shall appear it is thy dear; vile thing is near.

Ex. 14.6d: Mendelssohn, Incidental Music to *A Midsummer Night's Dream*, Op. 61 (1843), No. 8

Be, as thou wast wont to be; Dian's bud o'er Hath such force and Now, my Titania:
See, as thou wast wont to see; Cupid's flower blessed power. wake you, my sweet Queen!

Ex. 14.6e: Mendelssohn, Incidental Music to *A Midsummer Night's Dream*, Op. 61 (1843), No. 5

Ex. 14.6f: Mendelssohn, Incidental Music to *A Midsummer Night's Dream*, Op. 61 (1843), No. 6

What hempen home-spuns have So near the cradle of What, a plan An actor too, perhaps,
we swaggering here the fairy queen? toward? I'll be an auditor; if I see cause

Ex. 14.6g: Mendelssohn, Incidental Music to *A Midsummer Night's Dream*, Op. 61 (1843), No. 6

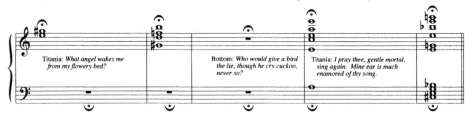

Titania: What angel wakes me from my flowery bed?

Bottom: Who would give a bird the lie, though he cry cuckoo, never so?

Titania: I pray thee, gentle mortal, sing again. Mine ear is much enamored of thy song.

Ex. 14.6h: Mendelssohn, Incidental Music to *A Midsummer Night's Dream*, Op. 61 (1843), No. 7

Con moto tranquillo

p

Ex. 14.6i: Mendelssohn, Incidental Music to *A Midsummer Night's Dream*, Op. 61 (1843), No. 7

pizz.

Ex. 14.6j: Mendelssohn, Incidental Music to *A Midsummer Night's Dream*, Op. 61 (1843), Finale

Tro' this house give glim' - ring light by the dead and

pp

of course, the E-major chord, with a slight swell and diminuendo, the same inflection Felix specified for its first appearance in the fourth bar of the overture. With a fine ear for nuance, Felix has retouched the scoring, adding low trumpets, horns, strings, and a timpani roll. Thus the chords continue to metamorphose[68] and capture that fleeting, dreamlike state essential to the play. When Robert Schumann reviewed an 1844 performance,[69] he thought that perhaps Felix had overstated the "fairy parts" (*Feenparthien*) and by recalling the overture had missed an opportunity to create something new. But Felix viewed play and overture as interdependent, and the incidental music as organically connected— its characteristic thematicism and coloration derive from the elves. The incidental music thus elaborates Felix's earlier reading of the play in the overture. Devrient was so bold to conclude, "The originality of his portrayal of fairy life has become typical; all later composers have, in similar subjects, followed in his footsteps."[70]

III

In her brother's shadow, Fanny too had composed music for elves but of a less mischievous sort. On October 29, 1843, after a lapse of a year and a half, she resumed her fortnightly Sunday musicales and premiered her music for Goethe's *Faust*, Part 2.[71] She set only the opening lines of the first act, in which Ariel, appropriated from Shakespeare's *Tempest*, instructs a "circle" of "charming little creatures" (*anmutige kleine Gestalten*) to lull to sleep Faust, tormented by memories of Gretchen's death at the end of Part I. For soprano solo, women's chorus, and piano, the score has four sections linked by piano interludes and employs Felix's preferred elfin keys, E major and minor. But whether Fanny's music, composed in March, benefited from any knowledge of Felix's incidental music is unclear.

During the fall of 1843 she also composed a substantial Piano Sonata in G minor.[72] Its four linked movements (G minor/major–B minor–D major–G major) mirror and invert the key scheme of Felix's contemporaneous Cello Sonata Op. 58 (D major–B minor–G major–D major), which also inserts a scherzo and slow movement between weightier endpoints in sonata and rondo forms. The exuberance of Felix's Op. 58 washes over Fanny's finale, which features thickened "three-hand" textures, typically with the right hand divided between a descant theme and busy figuration, while the left provides a bass line and chordal support. Though Fanny does not seem at ease with the sonata principle—thus, in the first movement she avoids securing the contrasting second theme in the contrasting relative major key—the work contains impressive music worthy of revival: the plaintive scherzo has a contrasting trio with shimmering tremolos in the high soprano, and the Adagio impresses as a warm Italianate serenade reminiscent of *Juni* in *Das Jahr*.

By late October 1843, Felix had returned to Leipzig and was intent upon enjoying a few weeks of music making before moving to Berlin. On October 26, he directed the fourth Gewandhaus concert, where he performed Gade's First Symphony and introduced the *Chevy Chace* Overture of George Macfarren. Then, at a benefit concert for the orchestral pension fund (October 30), Felix participated in the Bach Triple Concerto with Hiller and Clara Schumann. In November Felix arranged a concert in honor of the Grand Duchess Hélène of Russia, and at the first *Abendunterhaltung* of the season (November 18) he took up a violin part in his Octet. Around this time Felix met the young German composer Carl Reinecke, who submitted a sheaf of manuscripts, among them a string quartet. When Reinecke returned the next day, Felix astonished him by playing from memory passages of the quartet. Flustered, he returned to his room and recorded every word—as good as gold, he noted—Felix had uttered.[73]

After a farewell party with the Schumanns, Felix traveled on November 25 with his family to Berlin. Four days later he directed the first orchestral soirée at the Singakademie, which featured Mozart's *Magic Flute* Overture, a Haydn symphony, Beethoven's Seventh Symphony, and the *Emperor* Concerto, with Taubert as soloist. Further appearances followed at the second and third soirées (December 6 and 20), at which Felix directed symphonies of Mozart and Beethoven and a Weber overture, and played his First Piano Concerto,[74] and at a chamber music concert of the violinist Bernhard Molique, with whom Felix performed Beethoven's *Kreutzer* Sonata. Ludwig Rellstab found the orchestral concerts nearly on the level of the Paris Conservatoire, a view not shared by Felix, who caviled, "unless they improve very much they will never be worth anything."[75] For a moment, an escape seemed at hand: on behalf of the Philharmonic Society Sterndale Bennett offered Felix lucrative terms to direct the entire 1844 season in London,[76] but Felix hesitated to accept, discouraged by the prospect of prolonged separation from his family.

At long last, in December, Felix appeared as the new director of sacred music. But when the revised liturgy was introduced in the cathedral, confusion reigned. Varnhagen von Ense, who worshiped on December 10, struggled to apprehend the many Kyries and Amens apportioned between clergy and laity, and reported, "the people were dumbstruck."[77] In preparation, Felix had received from the cathedral officialdom a list of psalms for the principal liturgical days between Advent and the first Sunday of Lent.[78] The goal was to revive the Genevan (Huguenot) Psalter, translated into German by the humanist Ambrosius Lobwasser in 1565. In 1843 the Lobwasser revival was part of the king's strategy to unite the Reformed and Lutheran divisions of German Protestantism. By November 13 Felix had drafted simple harmonizations of seven psalms, including Psalm 24 for Advent,[79] but there is no evidence he ever used them.

Instead, he focused attention on new music for Christmas and New Year's Day.[80] For the Christmas Introit he composed Psalm 2, for double chorus and organ,[81] paired not with the Lesser Doxology but with "For unto us a child is born" from Handel's *Messiah*, for which Felix prepared an organ part.[82] Before the Alleluia the congregation heard the a cappella verse "Frohlocket ihr Völker" ("Rejoice, ye people"), posthumously published in 1849 as the first of the six *Sprüche*, or "proverbs," Op. 79. Also used were new harmonizations of the chorales *Vom Himmel hoch* and *Allein Gott in der Höh' sei Ehr*, and the German *Te Deum*, for which Felix presumably pressed into service his setting from the previous summer. If the compact verse shows signs of haste—its opening mimics that of the Overture to *Athalie*—Psalm 2, revised in 1845 and published posthumously in an a cappella version as Op. 78 No. 1, fully tests the expressive range of the eight-part double choir. First, the two choirs answer each other and mass together in tight formations to depict the raging of the nations. For "I have set my king on Zion, my holy hill" (verse 6), the texture changes to alternating trios of soloists, while at "You shall break them with a rod of iron" (verse 9), the dramatic antiphonal effects of the two choirs resume. At the other extreme, subdued voices in unison admonish the kings to "be wise" (verse 10); in the final section, turning from G minor to a translucent G major, soloists appear against the choir, which hovers on a chantlike figure for "his wrath is quickly kindled." The full choir then comes together for the comforting final cadence, "happy are all who take refuge in him." Fanny found the effect "very Gregorian, and reminding one of the Sistine."[83]

The Viennese *Allgemeine Musik-Zeitung* ran a brief report of the service, as did the Leipzig *Allgemeine musikalische Zeitung*, which commented, "As edifying as this version of the sacred service is, its musical portion is still fragmented, and one would hope that in the future . . . entire, even if shorter, vocal works are performed. . . ."[84] Felix himself groused about the new liturgy; after all the protracted discussions between king and clergy, "the great, much discussed church music" had shriveled up to "one piece before the beginning of the service."[85] As if to circumvent those restrictions, Felix now attempted an ambitious introit psalm with orchestral accompaniment. On Christmas Day he was still composing this new setting (of Psalm 98), rushed into rehearsal the next day, and premiered at the New Year's Day service. For the verse before the Alleluia, Felix produced a short a cappella setting of the opening of Psalm 90 ("Lord, you have been our dwelling place, in all generations"), Op. 79 No. 2. The other musical portions included the chorale *Wachet auf* from *Paulus*, and again *Allein Gott in der Höh' sei Ehr* and the *Te Deum*.

According to Fanny, Psalm 98 was marred by the sermon—"miserable beyond description"[86]—of the minister F. A. Strauss, who appears to have held strong views about the role of music in the liturgy. While the king and his advisers sought to reinstate Palestrinian a cappella music as an ideal, Felix contrived to introduce instrumental forces into the services, in what must have seemed like the thin end of a wedge toward ever increasing musical demands upon the liturgy. Psalm 98 led Felix to develop an especially cunning strategy. For the first three verses he limited himself to eight-part choral writing, with the full ensemble initially responding to the short invocation of the bass solo, "Sing to the Lord a new-made song," in a radiant D major, before dividing into antiphonal four-part choirs (**ex. 14.7**). Then, for "The Lord hath made known his salvation," Felix alternated groups of soloists and the ensemble. But the imperatives of the fourth, fifth, and sixth verses—to make joyful noises to the Lord with instruments—induced him to add a harp, trombones, and trumpets in a discrete accompaniment to the chorus, now realigned to unfold a two-part canon. The imagery of the seventh and eighth verses, in which the roaring sea and rejoicing hills join the praise, inspired a full orchestral accompaniment, leading to the final section, "He then shall judge the world with righteousness." Here Felix recalled the opening of the work in a triumphant Handelian finale for orchestra and chorus with compact points of imitation and wind fanfares. At its conclusion on New Year's Day, in lieu of the Doxology, Felix then launched into the "Hallelujah" chorus from Handel's *Messiah* (like the psalm, in D major), further reinforcing the crescendo effect from an a cappella beginning to the joining of chorus and orchestra. But all this festive music ran counter to Strauss' ascetic tastes; Felix later referred to "orders" and "counter orders" concerning the *Psalmodieren*, and Fanny averred that "to hear Felix talk of his dealings with the cathedral clergy" was "as good as a play."[87]

Ex. 14.7: Mendelssohn, Psalm 98, Op. 91 (1843)

From January and February 1844 dates music for two more services, Passion Sunday and Good Friday, which fell in March. For the two introits Felix set Psalms 43 and 22 (Op. 78 Nos. 2 and 3) and for the verses composed two more *Sprüche* (Op. 79 Nos. 4 and 6). But in contrast to his earlier offerings, Felix avoided instruments and contented himself with double choirs. He arranged the five double verses of Psalm 43 into four sections, of which the first and third (verses 1–2 and 4) placed the tenors and bases in unison against the sopranos and altos in harmony. For the second section (verse 3, "O send out your light and your truth"), the ensemble blossomed into concordant eight-part harmony, revisited in the final section (verse 5), where Felix indulged in a rare instance of self-quotation. Here the text, "Why are you cast down, O my soul," cited a refrain from the psalm's predecessor, Psalm 42, already composed by Felix as the concert cantata Op. 42 (1837). He now adapted the earlier setting of the passage (**ex. 14.8**), with its characteristic four-note psalm intonation, and thus effectively bridged the gap between concert and liturgical music.

Felix's music for Psalm 22, which opens with Christ's words uttered on the cross ("My God, my God, why have you forsaken me?"), approached most compellingly the Prussian monarch's ideal of a cappella responsorial psalmody. Here the composer collapsed the psalm to fit into three broad sections (verses 1–8, 14–18, and 19–28) and in the process truncated several verses, probably to restrain the length of the composition. A fair amount of the music alternates between expressive chantlike intonations, floating around a tone recited by a solo tenor acting as cantor, and

Ex. 14.8a: Mendelssohn, Psalm 43, Op. 78 No. 2 (1844)

Ex. 14.8b: Mendelssohn, Psalm 42, Op. 42 (1837)

muted choral responses, first in four-part harmony and then expanding to eight. For "I am poured out like water" (verse 14) the texture shifts to four soloists answered by the chorus, in a series of poignant, rising chromatic lines. The closing section, in which the psalmist's cry for help is heard, turns from minor to major and revives the responsorial patterns of the opening. "All the ends of the earth shall remember," the soloists intone, answered in hushed reverence by the chorus, "and all the families of the nations shall worship before him."

Two other psalms—Nos. 55 and 100—occupied Felix at the beginning of 1844. Neither achieved the expressive power of the Op. 78 settings, yet the anthem *Hear My Prayer* would enjoy extraordinary success in England. Set to William Bartholomew's paraphrase of the opening verses of Psalm 55, the score, for soprano solo, chorus, and organ, was written for the newly renovated Crosby Hall on Bishopsgate Street, where Elizabeth Mounsey (later Bartholomew's sister-in-law) organized sacred concerts during the 1840s. (An impressive fifteenth-century timber and stone edifice, the Hall had been the residence of Richard Plantagenet, before his coronation as Richard III.) Felix modeled his composition on the English verse anthem, with its alternating solo and choral writing, and had studied seventeenth- and eighteenth-century examples of Purcell, William Croft, and others. Still, Felix was not reluctant to introduce German color into the work, as in the chromatic recitative for "My heart is sorely pain'd within my breast" and the involved organ part, which interacts with and accompanies the soloist. But the very popularity of the anthem in England (it entered the cathedral repertoire during the last quarter of the nineteenth century) and its gentle tunefulness later exposed it to charges of superficiality from those contemptuous of Victorian mores. The English success (in contrast, the 1845 German version, dedicated to Wilhelm Taubert, attracted scant attention on the Continent)[88] gave credence to the idea Felix had accommodated his style to English tastes; indeed, the English scholar Wilfrid Mellers went so far as to inveigh against Felix's "spurious religiosity which reflected the element of unconscious humbug in our morality and beliefs."[89]

We know vexingly little about Felix's a cappella setting of Psalm 100, for four-part chorus, completed on January 1, 1844.[90] In 1963 and 1984 Eric Werner maintained it was a commission of the New Israelite Temple of Hamburg.[91] Indeed, among the thousands of letters the composer preserved in the so-called Green Books are five (November 14, 1843 to April 12, 1844) from the director of the temple, Dr. Maimon Fränkel,[92] conveying the request that Felix, "dear to every German Israelite," compose several psalms, among them Nos. 24, 84, and 100, for the temple, about to celebrate its twenty-fifth anniversary.

Fränkel's letters of March 29 and April 12 reveal he eagerly awaited the delivery not of Psalm 100 but Psalm 24. Felix could well have intended to compose Psalm 24, or perhaps sent a setting, now lost, but the work in question was surely not Psalm 100, since he had already set it on January 1.[93] The straightforward, popular style of the music and its Lutheran version indicates it was written for the Berlin cathedral. When the work was published in 1855, it appeared in *Musica sacra*, a three-volume series of psalms for the use of the Berlin Domchor throughout the liturgical calendar. The king had desired that Felix compose the entire cycle, but on February 14, 1844, he sought release from this assignment, no doubt wary of its scope and tiring of the restricted a cappella medium.[94] Instead, he proposed that a committee of composers, including Spohr, Carl Loewe, and Moritz Hauptmann, collaborate to accomplish the task.

Less than two months after returning to Berlin, an increasingly embittered Felix was predicting his imminent departure.[95] But first the royal Musikdirektor shared with Wilhelm Taubert the orchestral concerts, where Felix presided over his own Psalm 114 and Handel's *Israel in Egypt* at the Garnisonkirche on Palm Sunday (with personnel of four hundred and fifty), and Beethoven symphonies, including the Ninth on the last concert, March 27. A rehearsal of the Eighth convinced Richard Wagner that Felix was guilty of taking overly fast tempi and of glossing over passages, though during rehearsal he polished some details with a "certain obstinacy."[96] At private musicales Felix improvised, performed humdrum waltzes of the English ambassador, Lord Westmoreland, and accompanied several visiting artists—the soprano Schröder-Devrient, the Italian tenor Napoleone Moriani, and the Belgian cellist A. F. Servais, whose grimaces Felix slyly studied.

On January 7, 1844, Felix attended the Berlin premiere of Wagner's *Flying Dutchman*, which played before the king to a packed house. According to Wagner, Felix embraced him after the performance.[97] Though the German aesthetician Karl Werder judged the opera an "unprecedented masterpiece,"[98] Felix publicly maintained his reserve; still, a tantalizingly brief diary entry of Robert Schumann reveals Felix was "totally indignant" about Wagner's music.[99] And when Raymund Härtel considered publishing the work and pressed Felix for his judgment, he procrastinated, preferring to speak to the publisher personally about the matter.[100] Felix afforded quite a different reception for the Schumanns, who arrived in Berlin on January 25, en route to embarking upon their Russian sojourn. Not only did Felix urge Edward Buxton to publish Robert's new oratorio after Thomas Moore, *Das Paradies und die Peri*, he also dedicated to Clara the fifth volume of the *Lieder ohne Worte*, Op. 62.[101]

Ex. 14.9a: Fanny Hensel, Andante in G major, Op. 2 No. 1 (1836)

Ex. 14.9b: Mendelssohn, *Lied ohne Worte* in G major, Op. 62 No. 1 (1844)

Ex. 14.9c: Mendelssohn, *Lied ohne Worte* in A minor, Op. 62 No. 5, *Venetianisches Gondellied* (1841)

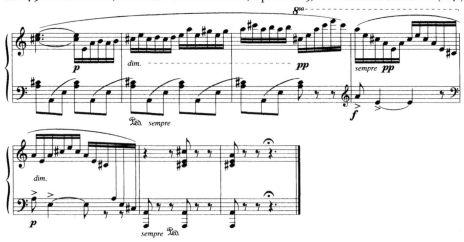

Three of the new Lieder already had ties to Clara, including the second and third ("Trauermarsch"), and the sixth ("Frühlingslied"), which Felix had presented to Clara a few months before on her twenty-fourth birthday.[102] In compiling the opus, Felix continued to exploit the genre of the piano Lied to explore the feminine qualities of parlor-room music making. Thus, No. 1 (*Andante espressivo*), which begins unassertively on the dominant with a drooping, sighlike figure, paraphrases material from an Andante in G major of Fanny from 1836 (**ex. 14.9a, b**).[103] The part-song-like No. 4, also in G major, is to be performed with much *Innigkeit*, a word, difficult to translate, that connotes depth of feeling and intimacy. And No. 5, in A minor, is yet another *Gondellied*, with broken chords generating lapping cross rhythms against the subdued love duet in the treble. The surprise ending in A major, where the melodic thirds disappear into blurry arpeggiations, subtly prepares the opening of the "Frühlingslied," which, in the same key, perhaps suggests yet another song of desire and love (ex. 14.9c and p. 437).

Felix would have shared the new piano Lieder with Fanny, who was then revitalizing her fortnightly musicales. After a pause of several weeks, the series began anew on February 11, 1844, with Felix's participation. The day before, as he copied out a duet arrangement of his Variations, Op. 83, Fanny took the sheets one by one to the piano and began to practice; on Sunday, the two premiered the new work, playfully described on the autograph as *composto per la musica delle Domeniche in casa Hensel dalla (vechhia) Vedova Felice*[104] (why Felix dubbed himself an "old widow" remains a mystery). A more brilliant gathering took place a month later (probably on March 10), when twenty-two carriages filed into the courtyard of Leipzigerstrasse No. 3. In the audience were eight princesses and a young, slender man whose eyes "had something surprising, even subjugating about them"[105]—Franz Liszt. The program featured Pauline Decker and Felix performing songs, the young Joachim some virtuoso variations of Ferdinand David, and Fanny directing her brother's *Erste Walpurgisnacht*, in which Felix helped her render the overture at the piano—adding bits of material in the bass and treble[106]—before "disappearing" into the audience.

IV

With the end of the concert season Felix longed to relax in Leipzig before traveling to London, where he had agreed to direct several concerts in an effort to bolster the precarious finances of the Philharmonic. On February 22 Felix had managed to slip away from Berlin to attend a Gewandhaus concert and had heard Hiller conduct the *Scottish* Symphony. But "social susceptibilities"—Felix's alarm at the deterioration of the orchestra under Hiller's interim leadership—had caused a falling out between the two friends and ended their correspondence.[107] Now, in April, Felix and Cécile arrived after the concert season, to take up a quiet life at Lurgensteins Garten. Only the arrival of the cellist A. F. Servais, who gave a late concert on April 24, brought Felix before the public eye to perform Beethoven's *Archduke* Trio.[108] Otherwise, Felix spent his time working on the final chorus of the incidental music to Racine's *Athalia* and planning a new piano concerto for England.[109] Shortly after arriving in Leipzig, Cécile fell ill with an alarming cough; "I believe we must take it very seriously in hand, lest worse should be in store,"[110] Felix reacted, no doubt concerned the symptoms suggested consumption, to which Cécile's father had succumbed (Cécile would die of the disease in 1853). The trip to England now in jeopardy, Felix brought Cécile and his children at the end of April to Frankfurt and rented a country house for her convalescence, carefully supervised by her mother. By early May Cécile's recovery was sufficiently advanced to permit Felix to depart for London; there he arrived on May 8 and took up quarters with Klingemann.

Once again Felix enjoyed an unusually warm reception.[111] In contrast, he had left Berlin in some controversy. When the king asked him to provide music for the *Eumenides* of Aeschylus, Felix replied he would attempt the project even though he thought it at best difficult; his lack of enthusiasm was viewed as a refusal. Indeed, Bunsen questioned the composer's loyalty to the monarch by comparing Felix to Brutus in *Julius Caesar*.[112] The *Eumenides* affair posed yet one more irritant to Felix's professional concerns in Berlin. But in England, he enjoyed unbridled artistic freedom and again flourished in the vibrant concert life and high society of the city.

The center of his efforts was the Philharmonic, where between May 13 and July 8 he directed the final five concerts of the season. Felix's presence added much luster to the society; the *Musical World* characterized his stewardship as "the wisest thing that has ever been done since the society came into existence."[113] He programmed several notable English premieres—the *Scottish* Symphony and Beethoven's first *Lenore* Overture (May 13); selections from the incidental music to *A Midsummer Night's Dream* (May 27); Overture to Schubert's opera *Fierrabras* (June 10); Bach's orchestral Suite in D (June 24); and *Die erste Walpurgisnacht* and Beethoven's *Ruins of Athens* (July 8). Nevertheless, Felix's leadership was not without controversy. On the morning of the last concert (July 8), when Felix arrived late for a rehearsal, a disgruntled violist began to hiss him, and Felix was accused of neglecting to program works by English composers.[114] Moreover, Felix's efforts to introduce Schubert's music fell on deaf ears. Felix had planned to perform the "Great" C-major Symphony, of which he had sent the parts to London several years before,[115] but at a rehearsal the strings bridled at the superabundance of repeated triplets in the finale, and he substituted the overture to *Fierrabras* (1823), a grand opera then utterly unknown. Nevertheless, the critic J. W. Davison rejected this work as "literally beneath criticism": "[Schubert] has certainly written a few good songs, but what then? Has not every composer that ever composed written a few good songs?"[116] (Not until 1856 did the symphony receive its English premiere.)

At the fifth Philharmonic concert (May 27), Felix presided over the English debut of Joachim, who, circumventing a regulation against the appearance of prodigies on the series, performed Beethoven's Violin Concerto to acclaim.[117] Preparations for the concert, which included selections from the *Midsummer Night's Dream* music, were painstaking. Felix supervised at least one seven-hour rehearsal, which gave him a severe headache, forcing him to decline an invitation from Charles Babbage, the cantankerous mathematician then developing his futuristic calculator known as the Difference Engine.[118] Two other Philharmonic concerts attracted considerable attention. On June 24 the Italian cellist Alfredo Piatti performed a concerto on a seventeenth-century Amati cello given by Liszt, and on the same concert Felix rendered Beethoven's Fourth Piano Concerto. From Rockstro we have an amusing anecdote about the cadenza for the first movement, which gave the orchestra difficulty in finding the cue for its reentry. In rehearsal Felix made no fewer than three attempts, each a freshly improvised cadenza, only at the performance to reject all three in favor of a fourth cadenza.[119] No less spectacular was the concert of June 10, at which the *Midsummer Night's Dream* music was encored before a royal audience that included Queen Victoria, Prince Albert, the Saxon king, and the Duke of Wellington, all of whom sat ten steps away from Felix.[120]

Throughout the eighth English sojourn Felix maintained a harried calendar of engagements; he confessed that in two months he had experienced more music than elsewhere in two years.[121] Among his performances were: (1) the First Piano Trio on May 21 (when the violinist Ernst missed a page turn, Felix improvised a few bars, causing a banker in the audience to banter there were more notes in "circulation than allowed by printed authority");[122] (2) Bach's Triple Concerto in D minor with Moscheles and Thalberg on June 1 at the Hanover Square Rooms (according to C. E. Horsley, Felix unleashed an "electrical" cadenza that culminated in a "storm, nay a perfect hurricane of octaves, which must have lasted for five minutes");[123] (3) an improvisation at a Crosby Hall concert on June 3, when Felix wove together themes from Mozart's String Quintet in G minor and Schubert's *Ave Maria*, heard earlier on the program;[124] (4) again the First Piano Trio on June 5 (by mistake, only the string parts were placed on the music stands, so that Felix had to play from memory; still, he insisted a colleague occasionally turn the pages of some other music on the piano, lest Felix's memory become the center of attention);[125] (5) a "monster" morning concert organized by Julius Benedict with twenty-three works performed by Felix, Thalberg, Jacques Offenbach (then celebrated not for operettas but as a cello virtuoso), the harpist Parish-Alvars, Joachim, and several leading singers;[126] (6) an appearance at a concert of

the Society of British Musicians given in Felix's honor on June 15, where
after hearing for the first time a piano trio by William Horsley and
canzonet by George Macfarren, Felix improvised on their themes;[127] (7)
a morning concert of Sterndale Bennett on June 25 (when members of
the orchestra were tardy, Felix began the concert by fabricating the instrumental accompaniments himself on the piano[128]); and (8) two performances of *St. Paul* at Exeter Hall before Prince Albert (June 28) and
the Duke of Cambridge (July 5).

Felix's correspondence reveals a composer at the height of fame, lionized by English society. Among the celebrities he met were Charles
Dickens, who, having finished *Martin Chuzzlewit*, was about to embark
for the Continent; Felix recorded in his diary that on June 16, at 3:00, the
two dined together.[129] Possibly during this sojourn Felix met Dickens's
friend and fellow novelist Thackeray, who after breakfasting with the
composer recalled that his face was "the most beautiful face I ever saw,
like what I imagine our Savior's to have been."[130] Felix enjoyed private
audiences with the Queen and the Consort, and on June 9 inscribed to
them a new four-hand piano arrangement of seven *Lieder ohne Worte*,
including Op. 62 and the as yet unpublished Op. 67 No. 1.[131] Aristocratic
ladies requested private piano lessons, and the widow of the chemist Sir
Humphry Davy, who had isolated potassium and sodium, sent a note
asking for a meeting. It was delivered by the wife of George Grote, who
wryly commented, "If I did not know your vanity was fairly used up, it
might serve to rekindle it, at least till you beheld the fair Lady, after which
I fear her flatteries would fall pointless."[132] Somewhat more serious was
the importuning of Mary Alexander, now Mary Crompton, but still enamored of Felix and desperate to see him after an absence of ten years.
Her letters betray the depth of her feelings, hint at a spark of romance, and
suggest that Felix was not at all the prude he was later portrayed to be.[133]

Among Felix's other social engagements was a "musical *séance*" on
May 19 at the residence of the music critic Thomas Alsager, who organized private performances of Beethoven's late string quartets.[134] A few
days before, Felix experienced English eccentricity in the form of a peculiar invitation to join the Contrapuntists' Society, a musical club
founded by G. F. Flowers to advance the most rigorous discipline of music.
Felix was to review the "rules" of the Society and to compose exercises
for potential candidates; his fame, Flowers hoped, would win royal patronage for the organization. But Felix found more pedantry than art
and penned a Pickwickian reply: "I thank you for the Rules, notices etc.
concerning the Contrapuntists' Society which you kindly sent me. I perused them with much attention and as I always think it my duty to tell
my sincere opinion, particularly when it relates to matters of art, I must

confess to you that I cannot agree with those rules that have been fixed for the exercises to be composed by the Candidates for the Contrapuntist Society; . . . ." He thus declined the honor of "entering this Society."[135] In June came another unusual request, this one from the patriotic Englishman Boyman Boyman, who reasoned that the army of the "greatest nation in the world" should have a national song, written by the "greatest composer,"[136] that might compete with the Royal Navy's *Rule Britannia*. Boyman sent Felix some verses and even offered to give him two thirds of the profits, but nothing came of the scheme.

Declining another request caused Felix much regret. In June, Charles Graves, a mathematician at Trinity College, Dublin, invited him to Ireland to receive an honorary doctorate in July, and Felix was asked to deliver a letter to John O'Connell, the imprisoned leader of the Irish emancipation movement.[137] Felix's many commitments made the plan impractical; indeed, he was able to venture out of London for only a few days (June 17–20), to visit Cécile's relatives in Manchester and Joseph Moore in Birmingham. Otherwise, there was no end of fresh demands upon his time. From Berlin came a directive to complete the overture to *Athalie*, urgently needed for a royal production; Felix complied, but the performance was postponed until December 1845. And the Handel Society, founded in June 1843 to promote "a superior and standard edition" of the composer, enlisted Felix to edit *Israel in Egypt*, a task he completed on July 4, only one week before his departure.

The history of this project, which involved Felix in some controversy, can be sketched here. In April 1844, George Macfarren, secretary of the Society's Council, invited Felix to edit *Messiah*.[138] Instead, Felix settled on *Israel in Egypt* and, after his arrival in London, began work in earnest, comparing a printed edition with Handel's autograph in the Queen's Library. Felix's duties were to enter corrections and dynamics, tempo, and metronome markings, prepare a keyboard reduction of the orchestral parts for a piano-vocal score, complete the figured bass for the organ part of the full score, and write a preface discussing the "historical particulars" of the oratorio. But the Society's editorial practices ran counter to Felix's musical priorities: while the Society expected to blend Felix's editorial alterations into the score, Felix intended to prepare a text faithful to the autograph. He thus envisioned the full score as an *Urtext*, at the time a novel notion in music editing, and insisted on introducing alterations only in the orchestral reduction of the piano part, printed beneath the score in small notes, so that readers could separate the two. Achieving this result required a protracted, heated correspondence with the Handel Society that delayed publication until 1845 and 1846; an exasperated Felix wrote to Moscheles that "it would be no slight evil if the edition did not clearly distinguish between Handel's and the editor's views."[139]

Concerning the organ part, which also appeared in small notes beneath the score, Felix clarified his intentions in his preface: "I have written it down in the manner in which I would play it, were I called upon to do so at a performance of this Oratorio. These works ought of course never to be performed without an Organ, as they are done in Germany, where additional wind instruments are introduced to make up for the defect. In England the Organist plays usually *ad libitum* from the Score, as it seems to have been the custom in Handel's time, ..."[140] Felix conceived the part as "a genuine improvisatory continuo realization, entirely free from the pedantically rigid observance of four-part playing required in theoretical books of Handel's time. . . ,"[141] and thus introduced a variety of textures and settings—for example, the organ in four-part harmony or two- or three-part imitation, and the organ simply doubling the bass line (*tasto solo*). Felix's musical "liberties" later collided with the pedestrian views of Friedrich Chrysander, a musicologist who in 1856 founded a German Händel Gesellschaft, and in 1867 published a damning study of Felix's organ part.[142] Chrysander's conclusion, that the greatness Handel achieved in *Israel in Egypt* was "despite Mendelssohn, rarely with him and never through him," smacks of pettiness. The longer view of history has recognized Felix's considerable efforts on behalf of modern Handel scholarship and Chrysander as a hidebound and arbitrary scholar.

Of Felix's new compositions, time allowed the completion of only the Six Duets, Op. 63, released later that year. In their final form, they included two earlier duets, the *Volkslied* after Burns (No. 5, 1842, see p. 443) and the Heine setting, "Ich wollt' meine Lieb'" (No. 1, 1836), in which Felix again used pulsating piano chords (cf. *Suleika*, Op. 57 No. 3) to suggest a wind bearing tidings of love. Among the newer settings was the wistful *Abschiedslied der Zugvögel* (von Fallersleben, No. 2), with its image of migrating birds mourning the passing of summer ("after joy came sorrow," the text reads), the tender *Gruss* (No. 3, Eichendorff), which greets an idealized lover, and the playful *Maiglöckchen und die Blümelein* (No. 6, von Fallersleben), in which lilies of the valley summon spring flowers to a miniature round dance, lightly syncopated in Felix's brisk scherzo idiom. While all these duets employ simple strophic or modified strophic schemes, the *Herbstlied* (Autumn Song, No. 4, Klingemann) required a more complex, through-composed solution. The piece had begun its existence in October 1836 as a *Duett ohne Worte* for piano, not long after Felix had parted from Cécile to return to Leipzig (**ex. 14.10a**).[143] Whether he already had in mind a generalized text of separation is un-

Ex. 14.10a: Mendelssohn, *Duett ohne Worte* in F♯ minor (1836)

Ex. 14.10b: Mendelssohn, *Herbstlied*, Op. 63 No. 4 (1844)

clear, but when, in 1844 (presumably during the London sojourn) Klinge-mann fitted his autumnal verses to the piano miniature,[144] the piano song metamorphosed into a poignant expression of loss and transience, and mirrored verbal images from the other duets—fleeting memories of the round dance, and the turning of spring to winter, of joy into sorrow (ex. 14.10b).[145] This curious experiment, with its text subordinate to the original musical inspiration, tests the definiteness of musical expression and offers tantalizing evidence to support Fanny's claim that as children the siblings had indulged in the "game" of adding texts to Felix's "instrumental *Lieder*."[146]

V

After a rapid crossing but disquieting return through Antwerp, where Felix had passport difficulties, he reached the Frankfurt spa of Bad Soden on July 13, 1844, and found Cécile fully recovered and his children, with whom he cavorted in the garden, "brown as Moors."[147] In contrast to the din of London, Felix now enjoyed a bucolic existence, with quiet walks along the Taunus hills overlooking Frankfurt. Among his companions were the poets Lenau and Hoffmann von Fallersleben, author of the nationalistic *Deutschland, Deutschland über alles*. Pressed by the Baroness Bunsen, Felix agreed to read a new version of Aeschylus's *Oresteia* trilogy that collapsed the three plays into one act, but he remained skeptical of conceiving music for such concentrated choruses.[148] Meanwhile, two new projects, brainchildren of the English publisher Charles Coventry, piqued Felix's interest. Capitalizing on his reputation as a peerless organist, Coventry invited the composer to edit J. S. Bach's organ works and write several voluntaries for the instrument. By late August Felix had amassed all he possessed of Bach's organ chorale settings,[149] including forty-four of the little preludes of the *Orgel-Büchlein*, BWV 599–644, fifteen of the larger *Choral-Vorspiele*, BWV 651–668, and the variations on *Christ, der du bist der helle Tag* and *Sei gegrüsset Jesu gütig*, BWV 766 and 768. Felix drew upon his own library, and collections of at least two other Bachians, Franz Hauser and F. X. Gleichauf, a local music pedagogue whom Felix visited in Frankfurt.[150] Setting a fee of thirty guineas,[151] he dispatched the edition to Coventry & Hollier, who released it in four volumes in 1845 and 1846; a German edition followed from Breitkopf & Härtel, further accelerating the Bach Revival.[152]

Coventry's second commission initially perplexed Felix, uncertain about the boundaries of the voluntary, generally understood as freely composed or improvised organ pieces used within English church services. But on July 21 he made a start with an Andante in F major, and within days finished three more pieces, a scherzo-like Allegretto in D minor, theme and variations in D major, and Allegro in D minor that culminated in a freely composed, "imaginary" chorale and fugue in four parts.[153] On July 25 he asked Fanny to send him the old *Orgelstück* in A major written for her wedding, but then interrupted work to attend the eleventh Palatinate Music Festival in Zweibrücken (July 31–August 1), where he conducted *Paulus* and *Die erste Walpurgisnacht*. Felix later recalled that nearly as much socializing took place as serious music making— rehearsals began at 7:00 A.M., and drinking at 8:00—and he had to hold his baton in front of at least one soloist's nose.[154] En route to the festival, he learned of the attempted assassination of Frederick William IV by a disgruntled Brandenburg burgomaster. The jaded royal Generalmusikdirektor experienced a range of emotions, from shock and disbelief to relief the monarch had suffered only slight wounds. Recalling some reassuring verses from Psalm 91 ("For he will command his angels concerning you to guard you in all your ways"), Felix dispatched to Berlin upon his return to Soden an a cappella motet for eight soloists. Later incorporated into the oratorio *Elijah*, *Denn er hat seinen Engeln befohlen über dir* approached the ideal of "pure," contemplative church music favored by the king, with antiphonal blocks of euphony, clear syllabic declamation of the text, and careful control of dissonances (**ex. 14.11**), and it became a staple of church choirs.[155]

Ex. 14.11: Mendelssohn, *Denn er hat seinen Engeln befohlen über dir* (1844)

Meanwhile Coventry's organ commission continued to gestate; by early September Felix had finished several new pieces, which he began to group together according to keys.[156] A concern for the unity of the collection led him to conceptualize the new opus as a series of organ sonatas, a redefinition to which Coventry acceded.[157] Felix began to tie his pieces to the legacy of Bach's organ music, most notably by extending the A-major wedding processional for Fanny to accommodate a learned chorale fugue on *Aus tiefer Noth*. By September 24 he was able to announce the commission was "finished," though in fact a good deal of revision and new composition ensued before the collection emerged in 1845 as the Six Organ Sonatas, Op. 65.

During the restful summer of 1844 Felix did "complete" one other major work, over which he had long ruminated—the Violin Concerto in E minor, Op. 64, for Ferdinand David. As early as July 1838 its haunting, elegiac beginning had "given him no peace," and a year later he was still brooding about the high E's of the first solo.[158] Then the work disappeared in his correspondence, presumably because he set it aside. By March 1842 he had turned instead to a new piano concerto and two years later was still "finishing a piano concerto" for England.[159] An undated autograph with several pages in full score and piano draft conveys the first two movements of what almost certainly would have been Felix's third mature piano concerto.[160] Significantly, he chose the key of E minor for this torso, which betrays a telling stylistic proximity to Op. 64. There were to have been three movements connected by transitions (*Allegro molto vivace* in E minor, *Andante* in A minor, and a finale in E major—Felix sketched only the transition to the finale before breaking off work). The opening *tutti* of the first movement, marked by vigorous leaps, resembles the close of the first movement of Op. 64, while the placid second theme sounds like a preliminary sketch for that of the violin concerto (**ex. 14.12a–d**). As with the *Andante* of Op. 64, Felix designed the piano *Andante* as a *Lied ohne Worte* in three parts (ABA), though here he had in mind a wistful barcarolle-like duet, along the lines of his earlier *Gondellieder* (**ex. 14.12e**). We can only speculate about

Ex. 14.12a: Mendelssohn, Piano Concerto in E minor (1842–1844), First Movement

Ex. 14.12b: Mendelssohn, Violin Concerto in E minor, Op. 64 (1844), First Movement

Ex. 14.12c: Mendelssohn, Piano Concerto in E minor (1842–1844), First Movement

Ex. 14.12d: Mendelssohn, Violin Concerto in E minor, Op. 64 (1844), First Movement

Ex. 14.12e: Mendelssohn, Piano Concerto in E minor (1842–1844), Second Movement

the finale, but in all likelihood it was to have offered a brilliant virtuoso conclusion, perhaps in the brisk scherzo idiom of Op. 64.

Exactly when Felix resumed work on the violin incarnation of the concerto[161] is unclear, but in September 1844 he easily finished the orchestral score of Op. 64; the autograph shows only a few alterations, for the most part concerned with the finer seams of the orchestral accompaniment and details of solo violin figuration but not major structural or thematic changes.[162] Nevertheless, scarcely had Felix finished the manuscript before a plague of self-doubt beset him, and he corresponded with David about a host of details—extending the cadenza into a more florid display, reassessing issues of balance between the soloist and orchestra, and the like. By year's end Felix was entering fastidious corrections into a second score prepared by his principal copyist, Eduard Henschke.[163] In

Ex. 14.13: Mendelssohn, Violin Concerto in E minor, Op. 64 (1844), First Movement

this form Ferdinand David premiered the work in Leipzig on March 13, 1845, with Niels Gade conducting.

Beloved of generations of violinists, Op. 64 achieved early on an honored place in the canon of European "masterworks" and served as a model for later composers, "many of whom would be horrified at the notion of confessing a debt to anything so old-fashioned," but, upon hearing their work, would admit that "like *Hamlet*, it was full of quotations."[164] Felix's first movement contains two structural innovations, of which one, the inversion of the traditional *tutti-solo* arrangement, affects the very opening, where the soloist presents a pensive first theme high above tremulous, rustling strings and timpani strokes (**ex. 14.13**). The music then builds to the delayed orchestral *tutti*. The lyrical second theme in G major, of almost naive simplicity, reverses the roles of soloist and orchestra: now the winds present the theme, while the soloist defers by sustaining its open G-string (**see ex. 14.12d**). The second innovation comes at the end of the development, where a brilliant solo cadenza unexpectedly interrupts the transition to the recapitulation. Beginning with triplets sweeping across the instrument's strings, the cadenza intensifies and eventually shifts to florid sixteenth-note arpeggiations to accompany the reentrance of the first theme in the orchestra. By displacing the cadenza from its traditional place near the end of the movement, Felix minimized the break between movements and underscored the continuity of the entire composition. Later composers imitated this experiment, perhaps most notably Jean Sibelius, who in his brooding Violin Concerto (1903) employed an expanded cadenza in lieu of a development.

After culminating in a turbulent presto, Felix's first movement undergoes transformation through a succinct transition. First, the bassoon emerges from the final *fortissimo* chord and rises by step from B to C; after a few deft chromatic touches, Felix effaces E minor and replaces it with a calming C major. He abandons the passionate yearning of the Allegro to explore a warmly lyrical *Lied ohne Worte* that gently impels the violin to its high register. Only the contrasting middle section of the Andante, tinged by a turn to the minor mode, recalls in the quivering accompaniment something of the earlier agitation (**ex. 14.14**). When, in the transition to the finale, the pitch C descends to B, and when the solo violin

Ex. 14.14: Mendelssohn, Violin Concerto in E minor, Op. 64 (1844), Second Movement

searches for a new theme, Felix seems intent upon reinstating the E minor and dactylic rhythms of the first movement. Instead, he introduces bright wind fanfares to announce another fleet-footed scherzo in his trademark capricious style—this one in E major. The whirlwind finale then unfolds as a rondo based upon two alternating themes—the first a delicate, major-keyed cousin to the principal motive of the *Rondo capriccioso* (see p. 229), the second a festive march that conjures up the mood of the *Midsummer Night's Dream* wedding march (ex. 14.15a, b). From these allusive materials Felix spins a finale of irrepressible zest, an emotional pendant to the drama of the first movement. Further probing reveals that the key sequence of the finale reverses the tonal trajectory of the first movement, and it gives the entire composition an overarching symmetry and balance that indeed stamps this delightful work as the most classical of the great romantic violin concerti (see **diagram 14.1**).

Ex. 14.15a: Mendelssohn, Violin Concerto in E minor, Op. 64 (1844), Third Movement

Ex. 14.15b: Mendelssohn, Violin Concerto in E minor, Op. 64 (1844), Third Movement

Diagram 14.1: Mendelssohn, Violin Concerto in E minor, Op. 64 (1844)

Allegro   Andante   Allegro molto vivace

Sonata Form   Ternary Song Form   Rondo

Exp.	Dev.	Recap.	Trans.	A	B	A	Trans.	A	B	A	A	B	A
Solo Tutti	cad.*		(B - C)				(C - B)						
e	G↝B	e E	e	C	a	C		E	B	G	E	E	

* Cadenza

VI

On September 23, 1844, Felix finished drawing a cozy domestic scene in Bad Soden (**plate 15**).[165] Resting on a sofa, Felix and Cécile take tea while maids attend their children; enveloping the group is a protective garland of lush vines and flowers at the borders of which Felix sketched some Frankfurt landmarks. The only disruptive element intrudes near the bottom, where Felix set two symbols of modern conveyance, the railroad and steamship, in opposite directions, signifying his restless, uprooted existence. Indeed, only two days later, after securing quarters for his family in Frankfurt, he departed for Berlin, via Leipzig and Dresden, and arrived in the Prussian capital on the last day of the month, with the intention of seeking his release from the king's service.

Felix's diary records a visit to Potsdam on October 7,[166] when he may have had an audience with Frederick William IV. Somehow the two reached an amicable understanding: Felix was no longer obliged to live in Berlin or perform fixed duties; in exchange, his salary was reduced to 1000 thalers, and he agreed to fulfill royal commissions. A dismayed Fanny realized she would not be able to grow old together with Felix and Cécile, for Felix announced his decision to Devrient "never again to stay" in Berlin; to Klingemann, he described the resolution as if a heavy stone had fallen from his heart.[167] Through the end of November he lingered in Berlin to conduct two orchestral soirées (October 31 and November 14) and, at the king's pleasure, *Paulus* at the Singakademie (November 28). He polished *Athalie*, composed choruses for *Oedipus at Colonos*, began a collection of twelve *Studien für die Orgel* for Fanny's birthday,[168] sat for an oil portrait by Wilhelm Hensel,[169] and, on October 21, through the sculptor Ludwig Wichmann, met the young "Swedish nightingale," then about to take the Berlin opera stage by storm—Jenny Lind. Her debut, in Bellini's *Norma*, was postponed until December, but her fame had preceded her; Felix, who had not yet heard her sing, remarked about her "great talent." When she challenged him to explain, he replied, "all who have heard you are of one opinion only, and that is so rare a thing that it is quite sufficient to prove to me what you are."[170]

Around this time Felix corresponded with Griepenkerl about potential opera libretti; to his proposals for subjects such as the Destruction of Jerusalem or Shakespeare's *Tempest*, Felix replied that he rather wished to discuss with the librettist not the *what* but *how* of a collaboration.[171] But there was little time to contemplate new creative projects, as Felix hurriedly wound up his affairs in Berlin and arranged to move his possessions. To that end, he made detailed inventories of his library, music, and personal belongings, as if to impose a superficial order over the disruption in his life. Perhaps most revealing was his list of books; Peter Ward Jones has demonstrated that less than ten percent concerned music: the majority were standards of the literary canon, including Greek and Roman classics; editions of Lessing, Moses Mendelssohn, Goethe, Schiller, Jean Paul, and Hegel, Shakespeare, Burns, Byron, Cervantes, and Boccaccio; lyric poetry of Uhland, Eichendorff, Tieck, and Rückert; and novels of Sterne, Sir Walter Scott, and Dickens.[172] There were foreign-language lexicons, Bibles, hymnals, the *Graduale Romanum*, and various guidebooks Felix had accumulated during his travels, including a copy of *Bradshaw's Railway Companion*.

On November 24 Felix took his musical leave of Berlin, as it were, by copying two part-songs he had composed earlier on texts of Eichendorff, the high poet of German romanticism, whose works are filled with images of *Wanderlust*. *Der frohe Wandersmann* (*The Happy Wanderer*), on popular verses from the novel *Ahnung und Gegenwart*, projected a carefree, optimistic view of restless wandering. The darker *Abschiedstafel* (*Farewell Banquet*) sings of failed deeds along life's path but trusts in God's protection.[173] A few weeks before, Fanny had set two poems of Eichendorff in a solo song titled *Traum* (*Dream*). On the autograph Wilhelm Hensel drew a vignette of a dreaming shepherd, who recalls happier times, and the mountain from which in past spring times he had surveyed the land, with thoughts of his mother, friends, and brethren.[174]

On November 30, 1844, Felix left his family home. For the first time in more than ten years, his career was unencumbered. Away from the court intrigues of Berlin and the frenzied music making of Leipzig, he chose the relative tranquility of Frankfurt for rest and recuperation. For the moment, he could breathe freely and rediscover his muse in the company of his wife and children.

Chapter 15
1844–1846

The Noon of Fame:
Years of Triumph

Felix Mendelssohn comes sometimes to
Berlin, and I have often been in his company.
He is a *man*, and at the same time he has the
most supreme talent. Thus should it be.

—Jenny Lind[1]

During his return trip, Felix visited Dresden to see Eduard Devrient, who
had accepted a position at the Saxon Royal Theater. The two discussed
opera subjects, including the Lorelei legend, for which Felix began to
compose music in 1847, only to die before he could realize his final operatic ambition.[2] Another issue drew him to Dresden: Frederick Augustus
II sought to entice Felix to move there, or at least resume his Leipzig post.
Still nominally in the employment of Frederick William, Felix was obliged
not to serve another monarch. Private entertainments were another
matter, and so at the Saxon court on December 4, 1844, Felix performed
a Beethoven piano sonata and regaled the court with improvisations.
The Leipzig physician C. G. Carus left an account. From a grand duchess
Felix solicited as his theme a march from Spontini's *La Vestale* and, after a
quiet introduction, introduced the march as if from afar. Then, manipu-
lating the theme to render its "approach" increasingly festive, Felix insinuated into the fantasy the *Midsummer Night's Dream* Overture and wove
the two together into a delightful musical garland, before he finished with
some *Lieder ohne Worte*.[3] In gratitude the king sent two vases of Meissen
porcelain.[4]

Arriving in Leipzig on December 5, Felix found a worrisome letter
from Cécile about their son Felix, perilously ill with the measles, and
from Florence came word that Rebecka, expecting her second child, was

suffering from jaundice. The composer hastily rejoined his family in Frankfurt and throughout December sent medical bulletins to Paul in Berlin. By December 18 young Felix had improved considerably,[5] but Rebecka's condition was so disquieting that Fanny and Wilhelm planned to leave at the New Year for Italy. Felix spent a quiet Christmas with Cécile in Frankfurt and gave her a special present, an album filled with autographs of political, musical, and literary celebrities. Among its treasures: signatures of Frederick the Great and other monarchs, letters of Moses Mendelssohn, Heinrich von Kleist, and the Schlegels, verses by Victor Hugo, the opening pages of Chopin's Fourth Ballade, Op. 52, and a pencil drawing by Felix of the Frankfurt woods, from the period of his courtship of Cécile in July 1836.[6]

For the moment, family took precedence over career. Felix tutored his children in reading and arithmetic, but when he attempted to teach Marie the C-major scale, he erroneously had her turn her thumb under the fourth instead of third finger.[7] Uncharacteristically, Felix now declined professional invitations, including a flattering proposal from the United States. In November Ureli Corelli Hill, president of the fledgling New York Philharmonic Society and director of the Sacred Music Society, had entreated Felix to come to New York to direct a "Grand Musical Festival." A student of Spohr, Hill had served as a violinist in the orchestra at the 1836 Düsseldorf premiere of *Paulus* and witnessed Felix's magnetic charisma as a conductor. Hill's terms were generous and included Felix's trans-Atlantic passage (a journey of fifteen days from Berlin, via a Liverpool steamer), $1000 in cash, and a comparable amount for an additional benefit concert. Felix would have at his disposal an orchestra of 250 and chorus of 500; his role would be that of a "musical missionary," to provide the "means of stimulating and advancing the musical art"[8] in the United States. But Felix declined, citing poor health: "a journey like that to your country, which I would have been most happy to undertake some 3 or 4 years ago, is at present beyond my reach" (to Paul, Felix described the undertaking as "no more possible than a trip to the moon").[9]

For the better part of 1845 Felix remained in Frankfurt and directed his newly found leisure toward composition. Among his tasks was the completion of the English organ "voluntaries," for which he quickly drafted seven new movements in December and January. Succumbing to a need to impose an overarching unity, he gradually culled and molded the movements into six sonatas that cohered through key relationships and various unifying devices. By sonata Felix had in mind not the classical paradigm, dependent upon sonata form and thematic development, but a conception more familiar to J. S. Bach—a multimovement instrumental work that might encompass a variety of genres and styles, such as the fugue, toccata, or fantasia. Dissatisfied with the Fourth Sonata in B♭ major, Felix finished on April 2 a new fugal finale, the last piece composed.[10] He then revised and polished his work,[11] and arranged its simultaneous international publication on September 15, 1845, as Op. 65 by four firms: Coventry & Hollier in London, Breitkopf & Härtel in Leipzig, Maurice Schlesinger in Paris, and Giovanni Ricordi in Milan. The new opus was quickly embraced for giving fresh impetus to the instrument and reviving its rich historical legacy. In England, where generations of organists had worked largely ignorant of Bach's music, one hundred and sixty musicians—among them eleven cathedral musicians—subscribed in 1845 at a cost of one guinea per copy.[12] What Felix feared would have a limited market in fact encouraged a rash of composers to write for the "King" of instruments, including Robert Schumann, who in 1846 published his erudite *Sechs Fugen über BACH*, Op. 60, and Joseph Rheinberger, who later in the century produced twenty organ sonatas.

Felix envisioned Op. 65 as a "kind of Organ-school,"[13] and even before its publication Coventry & Hollier was avidly marketing its pedagogical utility. To Breitkopf & Härtel, Felix described the work as illustrating his personal way of handling the instrument.[14] Not surprisingly, he affirmed his Bachian proclivities through the prominent placement of chorales and fugues. Four of the sonatas employ chorales, including *Was mein Gott will, das g'scheh allzeit* (No. 1), *Aus tiefer Noth* (No. 3), and *Vater unser in Himmelreich* (No. 6); in No. 5 Felix frames the sonata with the strains of a freely composed chorale. Every sonata except No. 5 has fugal writing or full-fledged fugues. Among them are a chorale fugue in No. 3 that, like the *St. Paul* Overture, employs an accelerando; a fugue on a wedge-shaped subject in No. 4; and a fugue culminating the last sonata, designed as a chorale partita, or variations, on *Vater unser*.

At least two sonatas draw on compositions from Felix's early maturity. The second movement of No. 2, a majestic Allegro, reuses a festive postlude (*Nachspiel*) composed in Rome in 1831.[15] And the opening of No. 3, in a radiant A major, was probably a reworking of the processional Felix sketched in 1829 for Fanny's wedding (**ex. 15.1a**). This sonata, which continues with the chorale fugue on *Aus tiefer Noth*, betrays a connection to one other work of Felix—the initial fugal subject quotes a recitative from the *Lobgesang* Symphony (**ex. 15.1b, c**).[16] Against this dissonant subject, Felix intones in the pedals the chorale *Aus tiefer Noth* (Psalm 130); eventually the return of the bright opening music dispels the symbolic darkness and tribulation, and the sonata concludes with a reflective Andante as a postlude.

Ex. 15.1a: Mendelssohn, Organ Sonata in A major, Op. 65 No. 3 (1844), First Movement

Ex. 15.1b: Mendelssohn, Organ Sonata in A major, Op. 65 No. 3 (1844), First Movement

Ex. 15.1c: Mendelssohn, *Lobgesang* Symphony, Op. 52 (1840), "Hüter, ist die Nacht bald hin?"

This unabashed revival of baroque forms, chromatic part-writing, active pedal parts (as in Bach's organ works, Felix called upon the feet "to do everything that the hands were asked to do"),[17] and immersion in fugal science imbue the music with a distinctly Bachian coloration. Nevertheless, Felix tempered his revival of the German baroque in Op. 65 by referring to contemporary styles of writing, an approach he had already exploited in keyboard works such as the *Sieben Charakterstücke* Op. 7, Six Preludes and Fugues, Op. 35, and Three Preludes and Fugues, Op. 37. Thus the slow movements of Nos. 2 and 4 impress as a Lied and *Duett ohne Worte*, while the *Andante con moto* of No. 5, with its peculiar staccato work in the pedal part, suggests a lumbering scherzo. Beyond these examples, the sonatas exude a spontaneous invention and formal freedom—for example, nowhere do they illustrate a conventional sonata form—reminding us that Felix was especially celebrated for his organ improvisations and suggesting that some of the movements may have originated as private improvisations.

The first sonata in particular reveals Felix at his most spontaneous and innovative mode: here elements of fugue and chorale (first movement), *Lied ohne Worte* (second), recitative (third), and toccata (fourth) combine to form a flexible, variegated composition bordering on the

Ex. 15.2a: Mendelssohn, Organ Sonata in F minor, Op. 65 No. 1 (1844), First Movement

Ex. 15.2b: Mendelssohn, Organ Sonata in F minor, Op. 65 No. 1 (1844), First Movement

Ex. 15.2c: Mendelssohn, Organ Sonata in F minor, Op. 65 No. 1 (1844), First Movement

realm of the fantasia. The sonata begins with a brief exordium for full organ, a series of chords embedded in which is the expressive motive (A♭–E♮–F; ex. 15.2a). A few bars later, above an organ pedal point Felix introduces a chromatic fugato derived from this motive (ex. 15.2b). But then, rising from a different manual, we hear the calming, opening strains of the chorale *Was mein Gott will, das g'scheh allzeit*, which now alternates with the unfolding fugue (ex. 15.2c). In the second half of the movement Felix applies the fugal subject in mirror inversion before combining the two and reintroducing the chorale in the closing bars.

The unusual shape of the movement suggests a model in the pathos-laden recitative from Bach's St. Matthew Passion (No. 25), in which, as Jesus arrives in Gethsemane to pray, an agitated, disjunct tenor recitative alternates with the chorale *Herzliebster Jesu, was hast Du verbrochen?* (ex. 15.3).[18] Not only is Bach's movement in the same key, F minor, but the motive A♭–E♮–F saturates the recitative in imitative counterpoint and even appears over a pedal point, as in the sonata. As for the chorale, Bach does employ *Was mein Gott will* a few movements later in the Passion (No.

Ex. 15.3: J. S. Bach, St. Matthew Passion (1727), No. 25

31), appropriately, in response to Jesus' prayer, "My Father, if this cannot pass unless I drink it, your will be done." All in all, the first movement of Felix's sonata impresses as a musical reading, or improvisation, on Bach's music and uses Bach's preferred instrument to penetrate the spirit of the Passion. Elsewhere the sonata returns us stylistically to the 1840s, as in the Lied-like Adagio or the resplendent *moto-perpetuo*-like arpeggiations of the finale. Ultimately, the sonata, and Op. 65 as a whole, remains paradoxically Janus-faced, eyeing the baroque splendors of Bach through the lens of Felix's own stylistic identity.

Shortly after moving to Frankfurt in December 1844 Felix also began to plan the sixth volume of *Lieder ohne Worte*, Op. 67. He assembled the new collection primarily from earlier piano songs, but a fresh stimulus was his creation on December 12 of a colorful new piece, titled in a later copy *Reiterlied*. Largely a canonic repartee in octaves between treble and bass, Felix's *Reiterlied* unfolds as a crescendo and a diminuendo that suggest the approach and passing by of riders on horseback; presumably the implied subject is a romantic text of the hunt (**ex. 15.4**).[19] By December 24 Felix had assembled six Lieder as a present for Cécile's cousin Fritz Schlemmer (to whom Felix would dedicate the Organ Sonatas); it comprised Op. 67 Nos. 1, 5, and 6, two posthumously published piano songs, Op. 85 Nos. 1 and 2, and the *Reiterlied*. In mid-January Felix prepared a similar volume for Klingemann, who had obtained leave to visit Frankfurt. And, Felix sent copies of *Lieder ohne Worte* (possibly similar volumes) to the painters K. F. Lessing and Julius Hübner.[20] Then he set

Ex. 15.4: Mendelssohn, *Reiterlied* in D minor (1844)

the work aside until April, when he hit upon the idea of dedicating the collection to Klingemann's new fiancée, Sophie Rosen.[21] Further rumination inspired several new pieces, including Op. 85 Nos. 4 and 5, Op. 102 No. 2, and Op. 67 No. 4.[22] But excepting the last, the celebrated "*Spinnerlied*," Felix rejected all, as well as the *Reiterlied*. By May 21, the opus was in final form[23] and released on September 1.

Op. 67 was the last volume of *Lieder ohne Worte* Felix saw through the press. Unlike the previous *Hefte*, each of which included at least one titled Lied, the six new pieces stood by themselves, without programmatic labels. Even so, they are among his most evocative utterances. No. 1 in E♭ major, which Felix had arranged in June 1844 as one of seven piano duets fashioned for Queen Victoria and Prince Albert, concludes by superimposing above its lyrical melody intermittent, belllike pitches in the soprano. The whimsical No. 2 in F♯ minor begins as a solo Lied but evolves into a graceful *Duett ohne Worte*. No. 3 in B♭ major, is mottled with impressionistic, softly syncopated harmonies (**ex. 15.5**). The brilliant No. 4 in C major inevitably became known as the *Spinnerlied* (*Spinning Song*), on account of its whirling figurations and recurring, refrainlike opening that lends the design a mesmerizing circularity. The volume concludes with two pieces of sharply contrasting characters. No. 5 in B minor, prefaced by drones that conjure up a folksong, actually borrows a somber figure from the First Organ Sonata (cf. **exs. 15.6** and **15.2b**), while No. 6 in E impresses as a sentimental waltz.

Ex. 15.5: Mendelssohn, *Lied ohne Worte* in B♭ major, Op. 67 No. 3 (1844)

Ex. 15.6: Mendelssohn, *Lied ohne Worte* in B minor, Op. 67 No. 5 (1844)

Some larger works also piqued Felix's interest during the Frankfurt sojourn. The idea of a second oratorio tantalized him, although his correspondence with Schubring about *Elijah* had broken off early in 1839. References to an oratorio crop up in Felix's letters from the first half of 1845, and on June 10 he announced he had begun the new work.[24] Almost certainly it was *Elijah*, for on January 28, Edward Sartoris, husband of Adelaide Kemble, had inquired "whether Elijah (with imitative music for the ravens in the desert) is progressing," revealing that Felix had begun to conceptualize music for the prophet's exile to Cherith's brook (1 Kings 17:4).[25] Still, other oratorio subjects were in circulation. In August 1844 he had declined a proposal for an oratorio about Luther[26] and a few months later rejected one from the Reverend John Webb, whom Felix had met in Birmingham in 1837, for an oratorio titled *Rachel in Ramah*.[27] Then, in June 1845, the Birmingham Musical Festival committee, chaired by Joseph Moore, resolved to invite Felix to compose a new oratorio for the 1846 festival, to which he provisionally agreed in July. This commission provided the impetus for him to resume serious work on *Elijah*.

Meanwhile, in February Felix finished the score for *Oedipus at Colonos* and awaited the Prussian monarch's order for its premiere. When the minister Eichhorn inquired if Felix would be prepared to direct a new school of composition in a reorganized Academy of Arts, Felix sidestepped the issue by requesting clarification about the administrative relationship of the school to the academy. And when the Privy Minister Müller again raised as a royal *desideratum* the production of Aeschylus's *Oresteia* with Felix's music, the composer responded that instead he had sketched music for *Oedipus Rex*, which, along with his scores to *Oedipus at Colonos* and *Antigone*, effectively completed a Sophoclean trilogy. Whether Felix was being disingenuous is unclear; in any event, no music for *Oedipus Rex* has survived.[28]

The early months of 1845 also found Felix planning a new symphony, as references in letters from February, March, and April attest. We may identify it as the *Sinfonia* in C major, for which he drafted material for the exposition and development of the first movement and sketched a subject for a second movement.[29] The broadly conceived inaugural theme, unfolding in three wavelike statements rising from bass to treble, recalls the *Eroica* Symphony, though Felix rejected Beethoven's militant, steely opening in favor of a balanced, classical beginning (**ex. 15.7**). While Felix was contemplating this new symphonic foray, Ferdinand Schubert sent from Vienna the sketches for his brother's own unfinished Symphony in E major (D729). "Believe me," Felix wrote Ferdinand, "I know how to value the full worth of this splendid present. . . . It is as though I have gotten to know your brother more closely and reliably through the incompletion

Ex. 15.7: Mendelssohn, Symphony in C major (1844–1845), First Movement, Sketch

of the work, through its unfinished comments scattered here and there, than would have been the case through any of his finished compositions."[30] But while later musicians, including Sir Arthur Sullivan, tinkered with completing Schubert's draft, Felix's autograph has remained to this day a torso.

Felix enjoyed a comparatively private existence in Frankfurt but scrupulously maintained his correspondence, of which he preserved nearly six hundred incoming letters from 1845 alone.[31] There were offers of honorary membership from singing societies in Freiburg and Mainz (in June Felix traveled to Mainz to acknowledge the award). Among the more unusual requests was a commission from the Belgian musician H.-G.-M.-J.-P. Magis for a setting of the sequence *Lauda Sion* to celebrate the six hundredth anniversary of the Feast of Corpus Christi in Liège (1846).[32] From considerably closer to home, Dresden, came a special request. Owing in part to Richard Wagner's efforts, in December the remains of Carl Maria von Weber had been transferred from London to Dresden and reinterred in the Catholic cemetery. Wagner now wished to memorialize Weber with a new monument and, deferentially signing his request "your most sincere admirer," turned to Felix for assistance in raising funds.[33]

A stream of visitors sought him out in Frankfurt. Among them was the young English student W. S. Rockstro, on his way to Leipzig to matriculate at the Conservatory. With Ferdinand David, Felix read through parts of his new Piano Trio in C minor, Op. 66, and at St. Catherine's Church played through all six sonatas of Op. 65, of which Rockstro remembered especially the "wonderfully delicate staccato" of the pedal part in the second [fifth] sonata, executed "with all the crispness of Dragonetti's most highly-finished pizzicato."[34] A few weeks before, the American J. Bayard Taylor, who, in the tradition of James Fenimore Cooper and Washington Irving, authored several European travelogues, met the composer: "He received me with true German cordiality, and on learning I was an American, spoke of having been invited to attend a musical festival in New York. . . . I have rarely seen a man whose countenance bears so plainly the stamp of genius. He has a glorious dark eye, and Byron's expression of a 'dome of thought' [*Childe Harold's Pilgrimage*, ii.6] could never be more appropriately applied than to his lofty and intellectual forehead, the marble whiteness and polish of which are heightened by the raven hue of his hair. He is about forty years of age, in the noon of his fame and the full maturity of his genius. . . . [He] is now the first living composer of Germany."[35]

Taylor later penned a fuller description of Felix's physical appearance, as did the American's traveling companion, Richard Storrs Willis,[36] who found Felix to be a "man of small frame, delicate and fragile looking; yet possessing a sinewy elasticity, and a power of endurance, which you would hardly suppose possible. His head appeared to have been set upon the wrong shoulders,—it seemed, in a certain sense, to contradict his body." The head was not "disproportionately large, but its striking nobility was a standing reproof to the pedestal on which it rested"—perhaps a reference to Felix's relatively short height, which according to Sir George Grove measured less than five feet, six inches.[37] What struck Taylor in particular were the composer's "dark, lustrous, unfathomable eyes." "They were black, but without the usual opaqueness of black eyes, shining, not with a surface light, but with a pure, serene, planetary flame. His brow, white and unwrinkled, was high and nobly arched, with great breadth at the temples, strongly resembling that of Poe. His nose had the Jewish prominence, without its usual coarseness: I remember, particularly, that the nostrils were as finely cut and as flexible as an Arab's. The lips were thin and rather long, but with an expression of indescribable sweetness in their delicate curves."

Taylor's visit to Frankfurt coincided with a grave natural calamity. On March 28 the Main flooded, inundating its banks and the alleyways and residences near the river, including the Fahrtor of Cécile's family (at the time, Felix and Cécile were living in an apartment on the Bockenheimer Gasse near the highest part of the city and were thus spared the destructive energy of the deluge). The water crested some seventeen feet above flood stage. "They were using a rowboat in Frau Souchay's vestibule," Felix related to Paul, "and had to try to jump out of it onto the stairs"; Felix likened the chaotic destruction to the malice of "badly behaved children" who "had been playing with everything and ran off in the middle of their games." Once again he offered his services for charity, and performed a Beethoven sonata at a relief concert in the Cäcilienverein.[38]

I

The Frankfurt period produced two major chamber works, of which one, the Piano Trio in C minor, appeared early in 1846 as Op. 66 with a dedication to Louis Spohr, while the other, the String Quintet in B♭ major, was left for posthumous publication in 1851 as Op. 87. The Trio, finished on April 30 and presented to Fanny on her birthday that year,[39] opens with an alluring passage: a sinuous, mysterious figure rises sequentially in three tiers (mm. 1, 3, 5) above a brooding pedal point in the cello (ex. 15.8a). Recalling the *Hebrides* Overture, the *pianissimo* nebulous passage creates an aura of instability and expectation. From this material Felix constructs an expanded exposition with three thematic groups, the opening complex in C minor, a lyrical second group in E♭ major, and a dramatic closing group in G minor. On a second level, he manipulates several rhythmic layers throughout the movement: first the restless eighth notes of the opening give way through diminution to sixteenths that invert the contours of the *Ur*-motiv (15.8b); then, in the development, a series of chromatic modulations unfold to an accompaniment of rippling triplets in the piano; and finally, in the culminating coda, the *Ur*-motiv returns in augmented quarter notes against its original form (ex. 15.8c).

The two internal movements offer ingratiating examples of Felix's tuneful *Lied ohne Worte* and capricious scherzo idioms. In the gentle *Andante espressivo* the piano introduces a rocking, lullabylike melody in

Ex. 15.8a: Mendelssohn, Piano Trio No. 2 in C minor, Op. 66 (1845), First Movement

Ex. 15.8b: Mendelssohn, Piano Trio No. 2 in C minor, Op. 66 (1845), First Movement

Ex. 15.8c: Mendelssohn, Piano Trio No. 2 in C minor, Op. 66 (1845), First Movement

chordal style suggestive of a choral part-song. Soon the violin and cello enter and, against a piano backdrop, transform the music into a sentimental *Duett ohne Worte*. Propelling the frolicsome scherzo, which Felix described as "a trifle nasty to play,"[40] is a crisp anacrusis that impregnates an ingenious rondo design—first, in the opening material, with cascading imitative entries in the violin, cello, and piano (**ex. 15.9**), then in the strings accompanying the dizzying second subject of the piano, and finally in the bass of the piano, against the playful third subject in the strings. Reminiscent of Felix's earlier scherzi, this scurrying, evanescent movement dissolves at the end into blurring figurations and crisp, pizzicato chords.

The weighty finale projects a rondo scheme also based upon three subjects, of which the third, a freely composed chorale, injects a spiritual idea into a musical narrative of high drama and reconciliation. Here the dissonant opening cello theme, impelled by an unusual (for Felix) leap of a ninth (**ex. 15.10a**), yields to the calming strains of the chorale (**ex. 15.10b**), which eventually reemerges in the celebratory conclusion in C major. To lend the chorale a semblance of familiarity, Felix begins by alluding to *Gelobet seist Du, Jesu Christ*, though the succeeding strains diverge into his own melodic invention. The idea of a culminating, free chorale later appealed to Johannes Brahms, who fitted a similar device into the finale of his third Piano Quartet, Op. 60, also in C minor (1875). Underscoring his reliance on Op. 66, Brahms's finale begins with a subdued, winding figure in the piano, an allusion to Felix's first movement (**ex. 15.10c**).

Why Felix chose to return to the genre of the string quintet in his Op. 87, dated in Soden on July 8, 1845, is not known. Its four movements

Ex. 15.9: Mendelssohn, Piano Trio No. 2 in C minor, Op. 66 (1845), Scherzo

Ex. 15.10a: Mendelssohn, Piano Trio No. 2 in C minor, Op. 66 (1845), Finale

Ex. 15.10b: Mendelssohn, Piano Trio No. 2 in C minor, Op. 66 (1845), Finale

Ex. 15.10c: Brahms, Piano Quartet in C minor, Op. 60 (1875), Finale

include an exuberant *Allegro vivace* that, with its soaring theme for the first violin ascending against energetic tremolos, recalls the optimistic élan of the Octet. The interlude-like Andante, a subdued scherzo in G minor, acts as a foil to the Adagio in D minor, cast in Felix's most serious vein, with majestic dotted rhythms and intensely chromatic progressions. Toward the end, the first violin again attains its high register, accompanied by agitated tremolos. But the music breaks through to a radiant D major, and the violin eventually reaches a climactic high pitch, a ray of sunlight that disperses the chromatic dissonance of the movement. The finale, much of which impresses as a restless *perpetuum mobile*, caused difficulty for Felix, who reported his displeasure to Moscheles.[41] The issue seems to have concerned the formal imbalance of the movement, a sonata-rondo framework in which Felix elected not to recapitulate the second subject and thus left the bustling material of the opening "overtaxed"[42] and the composition as a whole, unfinished.

The same day he dated the Quintet, Felix also fulfilled a request of Friedrich Aulenbach, a law student from the Palatinate who had sung under the composer's baton at Zweibrücken in 1844. Aulenbach had recently lost a friend and asked Felix to set some sentimental verses, in which an angel's touch releases the spirit of the departed. Felix obliged by rapidly composing a somber *in memoriam* for chorus, published in 1869 as the *Trauergesang* Op. 116.[43] Yet even this minor occasional piece inspired two different versions from the composer, then about to surrender the tranquility of Frankfurt for the resumption of his professional career.

By early July 1845, Frederick William IV had ordered the premiere of *Oedipus at Colonos* for the fall, so that the composer had to forego participating in a Beethoven festival in Bonn in order to supervise rehearsals in Berlin.[44] Further complicating Felix's affairs, around this time he entered into negotiations with the Saxon court concerning the resumption of his duties at the Gewandhaus and Leipzig Conservatory. Eager to strengthen Felix's ties to Dresden, the king proposed through his minister J. P. von Falkenstein that Felix would direct occasional royal concerts and music for Catholic services, "regardless of the responsibilities" of the other Saxon Kapellmeister, who included Richard Wagner.[45] Further, Eduard Devrient was authorized to explore with Felix the possibility of moving the Conservatory to Dresden and joining it to a new school of drama.[46] Wary of court intrigue, Felix declined an "official" position and also the directorship of the Conservatory. Instead, he agreed to serve on the faculty of the institution, to share direction of the Gewandhaus concerts with Niels Gade, who had conducted during Felix's absence, and to appear occasionally at the Dresden court. Though nominally in the service of the Saxon king, he demanded no official title. His salary was set at 2000 thalers, of which the royal exchequer provided three fourths, the directors of the Gewandhaus, one fourth. Coupled with the 1000 thalers from the Prussian king, Felix now thus earned the handsome annual sum of 3000 thalers. But in exchange, he served two monarchs and began again a taxing double life.

In mid-July Rebecka, Fanny, and Wilhelm returned from Italy. Devotedly Fanny had nursed Rebecka back to health in Florence after the birth of her daughter, Flora, in February. Now Felix arranged a joyful family reunion in Freiburg im Breisgau, where on July 12 the Freiburg Liedertafel gave a concert in his honor,[47] and the travelers joined Felix and Paul for a few restful days (Cécile, pregnant with her fifth child, remained in Soden). There was music making, for the Woringens from Düsseldorf augmented the party, and Felix notated part-songs for open-air entertainments.[48] Then the "Felicians" proceeded down the Rhine and, en route to Soden, encountered Varnhagen von Ense at the picturesque Roman spa of Bad Homburg, just north of Frankfurt. After a fortnight together with Cécile in Soden, Rebecka, Paul, Fanny, and Wilhelm returned to Berlin, and Felix prepared to move to Leipzig.

II

Only days after arriving in Leipzig on August 13, Felix was on his way to Berlin to consult with Tieck about *Oedipus at Colonus*. Returning to Leipzig, the composer then visited Dresden to finalize his agreement with the Saxon king; the formal contract appeared on September 18, permitting Felix to begin his "service" on October 1. A search for new quarters in Leipzig came to fruition on September 4, when the family moved into the second floor of a stately building just off the Promenade, Königsstrasse Nr. 3—Felix's final residence (**plate 16**).[49] But two days later, he left for Berlin and, having returned to Leipzig after nine days, again commuted to Dresden. In the midst of this *Unruhe*, the family's furnishings arrived from Berlin, and Cécile gave birth on September 19[50] to Elisabeth (Lili) (1845–1910), who later married the jurist Adolf Wach.

To trumpet fanfares and stormy applause in the Gewandhaus, Felix inaugurated the new concert season on October 5.[51] The program, which included the Overture to Weber's *Der Freischütz*, solos by Clara Schumann, and Beethoven's Fourth Symphony, won acclaim in the *Allgemeine musikalische Zeitung*, a veritable Mendelssohnian organ that greeted the composer's return as the "greatest security for the true enjoyment of art."[52] Once again Felix presided over the refined musical life of Leipzig's art-loving burghers. At the first chamber-music *Unterhaltung* (October

18), he accompanied the charming French cellist Lisa Cristiani, for whom he composed that year a tender *Lied ohne Worte* in D major, posthumously published as Op. 109. And at the Conservatory, he drafted detailed reports of the students' progress. W. S. Rockstro merited Felix's general approbation, while Otto Goldschmidt, Jenny Lind's future husband, received not only praise for his piano skills but also encouragement to avoid the superficial (*Äusserliche*) in favor of a more serious tone in his compositions.[53] Alternating with Gade, Felix then directed the third Gewandhaus concert (October 23), which featured Robert Schumann's First Symphony and Felix's Violin Concerto, Op. 64, performed for the first time under the composer's direction by Ferdinand David. The concert also marked the debut of the English contralto Helen Dolby (Sainton-Dolby), who left an amusing anecdote about Felix. Preoccupied with preliminary work on *Elijah*, Felix arrived late one evening for a dinner party hosted by Raymund Härtel. When Felix blamed his tardiness on the contralto part of the oratorio, Miss Dolby exclaimed, "'do tell me what that will be like, because I am specially interested in that part.' 'Never fear,' he quipped, 'it will suit you very well, for it is a true woman's part—half an angel, half a devil,'"[54] revealing the part's division between angelic voices and Queen Jezebel.

Not quite extricated from his Leipzig commitments, Felix arrived in Berlin on October 24 to oversee *Oedipus at Colonos*. Within days he was sitting for a new oil portrait by his old friend Eduard Magnus, subsequently widely copied and disseminated, and later judged by Sir George Grove as a "good representation," though it was "deficient in that lively speaking expression which all admit to have been so characteristic" of the composer.[55] Somehow, Albert Lortzing had secured Felix's agreement to compose a choral work for the annual Leipzig celebration of Friedrich Schiller's birthday (November 11). Between final rehearsals in Berlin, Felix drafted a spirited part-song for mixed chorus, *Die Frauen und die Sänger* (*The Ladies and the Minstrels*), on stanzas from *Die vier Weltalter* (*The Four Ages of the World*).[56] By filling this commission, Felix revealed liberal sympathies, for in Leipzig before the 1848 Revolution, political clubs intent upon promoting a pan-German, constitutional monarchy championed Schiller's verses. In 1831 Felix had written a rapturous letter to his parents about Schiller's egalitarian play *William Tell*;[57] he now chose two stanzas from Schiller's 1802 poem that, in a reworking of Ovid's Four Ages, divided the world into eras of shepherds, dragons, and heroes, and a final utopian vision of beauty. Early in 1846, Felix added two more stanzas, expanding the composition into a paean to the union of art and life that Schiller had glorified in his optimistic vision of classical antiquity.

On November 1, 1845, Felix directed the long-delayed premiere of *Oedipus at Colonos*, held, like *Antigone*, before Frederick William IV in the Neues Palais at Potsdam. The first "public" performance followed in Berlin at the opera house on November 10. But unlike the popular wave of philhellenism that followed *Antigone* in 1841, *Oedipus at Colonos* failed to excite the Berlin public. A correspondent for the *Allgemeine musikalische Zeitung* confessed to being utterly bored by the play and found the production's scholarly trappings as tedious as a doctoral exam in philology.[58] Minna Meyerbeer, wife of the composer, reported that the king did not attend the second performance, that Felix was neither acknowledged nor called for, and that only one chorus received applause.[59] No doubt his newly diminished relationship with the king explains in part the *succès d'estime* of the Berlin performances. Unfortunately, Frederick William never ordered a production of *Oedipus Rex*, which, had Felix composed the music, would have completed his Sophoclean trilogy and placed *Oedipus at Colonos* in the context of the whole. For his part, Felix abandoned further attempts to bridge classical Greece and modern Germany: he made no effort to perform *Oedipus at Colonos* in Leipzig or publish the score (premiered in Leipzig after Felix's death by Julius Rietz in 1850, it appeared posthumously as Op. 93 in 1851).[60] Indeed, since 1845, the work has remained among Felix's most obscure, unknown compositions, though a fresh appraisal reveals some compelling music, suggesting its fate was not entirely justified.

In the first play of the trilogy, *Oedipus Rex*, we learn how the proud Theban King had unknowingly murdered his father and married his mother; the revelation of these horrific acts caused him to put out his eyes and exile himself. As the second play opens, he has wandered for years with his daughter Antigone and reached a grove sacred to the Eumenides at Colonos, near Athens. Here, through a rite of purification, he is reconciled with the avenging goddesses and given asylum by the Athenian king, Theseus. Summoned by divine thunderclaps, Oedipus prepares to enter Hades. His painless passing, "of human exits the most marvelous," transforms him into a heroic protector of the Athenian state; in death, the gods receive and exalt him.

Like its sibling *Antigone*, the score to *Oedipus at Colonos* describes a closed, musico-dramatic circle, now circumscribing an overture and nine numbers, including episodes in melodrama (with the orchestra providing a musical backdrop to dramatic action), portions in which the chorus interacts with the actors, and several reflective choral odes. Felix intensifies the expressive range of the chorus by testing the extremes of a barren, recitative style, with the chorus singing in unison and, in the odes, opulent eight-part harmony that invokes the lush sonorities of German part-songs. The overture, reduced (in contrast to *Antigone*) to a spartan Introduction of thirteen bars, establishes as a dissonant melodic and harmonic element

the interval of the tritone, symbol of Oedipus's defilement as an incestuous parricide (ex. 15.11a). This dissonant agent remains in force until
his ultimate heroic transformation. Examples 15.11a–f summarize several
variants of the unifying motive, including: (1) the revelation of Oedipus's
identity to the Athenians and Antigone's response (15.11b, c); (2) the chorus's
view of Oedipus as a victim of fate, and the ensuing thunder peals summoning him to Hades (15.11d); and (3) the final choral ode, a lament for
Oedipus (15.11e). Only in the closing bars does the dissonant metaphor
yield to majestic dotted rhythms in D major (15.11f), symbolizing
Oedipus's heroic transformation.

The spirit of Greek tragedy also imbued Felix's incidental music to
Racine's *Athalie*, premiered privately one month after *Oedipus at Colonos*,
on December 1, 1845, at the royal Berlin palace of Charlottenburg. In this
case, Felix focused primarily upon the choruses in the neoclassical French
drama, which, in a relaxed imitation of their Greek counterpart, comment about the impious reign of the Old Testament queen of Judah (ca.
843–837 B.C.). In 1690 Racine had written his tragedy for the Maison Royale
de Saint Louis in St.-Cyr, a school founded by the wife of Louis XIV for
daughters of impoverished nobility. The playwright's theme—"that in
heaven kings have a severe judge, innocence an avenger, and the orphan
a father"[61]—struck a resonant chord in Prussia. Frederick the Great reportedly confessed that instead of winning the Seven Years' War he would
have preferred to write *Athalie*,[62] and in 1783 J. A. P. Schulz, Kapellmeister
to the Prussian monarch's brother, composed incidental music for a Berlin production. Though the young Abraham Mendelssohn hummed favorite choruses from this score,[63] Schulz's music failed to impress, and
in 1785, Princess Anna Amalia refused its dedication.[64] By the 1840s, of
course, Schulz's choruses, stylistically somewhere between Gluck and
C. P. E. Bach, were woefully obsolete. By commissioning Felix to compose new music, Frederick William IV remedied this inadequacy and
furthered his own neoclassical project.

According to 2 Kings and 2 Chronicles, when Athaliah, daughter of
Ahab and Jezebel (soon to figure in Felix's oratorio *Elijah*), seized the
throne, she attempted to purge all eligible male heirs. But the high priest
Jehoiada (Joad) and his wife Jehosheba sequestered Athaliah's grandson
Joash in the Temple for six years, then crowned and anointed him king,
and mounted an uprising against the queen. Her demise led to the destruction of Baal idolatry and the renewal of the Old Covenant. These
are the main elements on which Racine based his play, delivered in the
elevated style of French alexandrines typically with twelve syllables per
line, divided more or less evenly by a caesura midway. Felix's fluency in
French facilitated his setting the choruses in the original language, though

Ex. 15.11a: Mendelssohn, *Oedipus at Colonos*, Op. 93 (1845), Introduction

Ex. 15.11b: Mendelssohn, *Oedipus at Colonos*, Op. 93 (1845), No. 1

Ex. 15.11c: Mendelssohn, *Oedipus at Colonos*, Op. 93 (1845), No. 1

Ex. 15.11d: Mendelssohn, *Oedipus at Colonos*, Op. 93 (1845), No. 8

Ex. 15.11e: Mendelssohn, *Oedipus at Colonos*, Op. 93 (1845), No. 9

Ex. 15.11f: Mendelssohn, *Oedipus at Colonos*, Op. 93 (1845), No. 9

for the Berlin premiere a new German translation by Ernst Raupach was introduced. Early in 1846 Felix fulfilled another royal request by dispatching a copy of the score with a French dedication to Queen Victoria;[65] the work received its English premiere, in French, at Windsor Castle on New Year's Day, 1847, and was published the following year with an English text by William Bartholomew.

Though Felix designed his score as incidental music, after his death the religious drama enjoyed a second life as a kind of oratorio, with the choruses stitched together by a narrative in lieu of stage action. Both Bartholomew and Eduard Devrient fashioned connecting texts to facilitate concert versions of the work. In part, they were motivated to read *Athalie* as a preliminary sketch for the more monumental *Elijah*, with which *Athalie* shared a common subject, the struggle against Baalism. On general stylistic grounds, *Athalie* indeed approaches *Elijah*. Thus, prefacing the score is a full-scale overture that depicts the essential dramatic conflict. The orchestra begins with a majestic rising figure later associated with God's wrath, and the just rebellion against the queen (**ex. 15.12a**). Next, we hear a yearning wind melody, accompanied by harp and pizzicato violins, evidently meant to remind us "of the temple service and the psalms," and to superimpose over the whole a "kind of Oriental cloud of fragrance" (**ex. 15.12b**).[66] Trumpet fanfares herald a third musical figure, symbolizing the military uprising. From these three elements Felix constructs his overture, which culminates in a reprise of the wind-harp melody, transformed into a victorious, festive march.

As a musical topic, marches figure three more times in Felix's score, first in the opening chorus, as the Levites prepare a sacred procession from the Temple with a song of praise: "Heaven and earth display, His grandeur is unbounded" (**ex. 15.12c**). The same music returns at the end of the work, so that the idea of musical ritual frames the score (in an early version of the conclusion Felix expanded the chorus to include a fugue[67] but excised it to preserve the marchlike character of the finale). Finally, between the third and fourth acts Felix inserted the celebrated *War March of the Priests* (**ex. 15.12d**), which in the nineteenth century fairly rivaled in popularity the Wedding March from *A Midsummer Night's Dream*. But this entr'acte march was purely Felix's invention, to suggest the bellicose stirrings of the priests as they prepare to reveal Joash's identity and overthrow Athaliah.

Other passages of the score show Felix as a creative interpreter of Racine's play, by gradually strengthening musically a Christological interpretation of the Old Testament drama. Preparing this process is the first chorus (I:iv), commemorating the delivery of the Ten Commandments

Ex. 15.12a: Mendelssohn, *Athalie*, Op. 74 (1845), Overture

Ex. 15.12b: Mendelssohn, *Athalie*, Op. 74 (1845), Overture

Ex. 15.12c: Mendelssohn, *Athalie*, Op. 74 (1845), No. 1

Ex. 15.12d: Mendelssohn, *Athalie*, Op. 74 (1845), No. 5

Ex. 15.12e: Mendelssohn, *Athalie*, Op. 74 (1845), No. 1

Ex. 15.12f: Mendelssohn, *Athalie*, Op. 74 (1845), No. 2

and the establishment of God's law. In No. 2 (II:ix), attention turns to the young Eliazin (Joash), who, "like Elijah, boldly stands forth undismay'd by this Jezebel's [Athaliah's] wrath," and is praised in a lyrical soprano duet as an "ever blessed child, by heav'nly love protected." When the chorus of the faithful asks in distress, "How long shall we see the godless against Thee arise?" Felix unexpectedly inserts the Lutheran chorale *Ach Gott vom Himmel sieh' darein*, to the text *Qu'ils pleurent, O mon Dieu, qu'ils frémissent de crainte*, which Bartholomew rendered as "They, Lord, who scoff at Thee, who scorn, while we adore Thee" (**ex. 15.12e**). Within a few measures, the famous melody dissolves into a freely composed chorale tune, but the reference, relating the Old Testament story to modern Lutheran worship, is clear enough. And the choice of the chorale—Luther's paraphrase of Psalm 12—is particularly apposite. Like the psalm, Racine's chorus is a plea to God for assistance in a time of evil. The final stage in Felix's "reading" of Racine follows in the melodrama of No. 3 (III:vii). With the Temple doors closed, Jehoida now prophesies the destruction of Jerusalem and, in its place, a "new Jerusalem" that "appears in yonder desert, darting brilliant rays." Felix supports Racine's allusion to the advent of Christianity by introducing the Lutheran Christmas chorale *Vom Himmel hoch* (Luke 2) in a striking setting: against harp arpeggiations and shimmering *pianissimo* wind and string tremolos, the melody appears in the trumpet (**ex. 15.12f**), as if from on high. Felix symbolically reconciles his family's history by joining the Old and New Testaments in an optimistic Christian vision: the anointing of Joash is understood to reestablish the rightful line of David, which will culminate in the Messiah—as Matthew informs us, the "son of David, the son of Abraham."

III

Between *Oedipus at Colonos* and *Athalia*, Berliners were transfixed by the return of Jenny Lind, who triumphed in the title role of Bellini's *Norma*, and as Donna Anna in *Don Giovanni* and Agathe in *Der Freischütz*, where, Ludwig Rellstab noted, her "voice seemed to float upwards, like a cloud of incense."[68] Felix now experienced her supple, natural voice firsthand: an unpublished record of his Berlin engagements reveals he attended all three operas on November 9, 19, and December 2, and saw the soprano on at least five other occasions (November 17, 21, 22, 27, and December 1).[69] Mendelssohn's biographers have sometimes sought in the artistic friendship a romantic liaison, though the question of an affair remains speculative.[70] Hans Christian Andersen, who was smitten by Jenny and in "The Nightingale" allegorized her voice as the pure expression of art,[71] reports an extraordinary comment from Felix, who asserted, "There will not be born, in a whole century, another being so gifted as she."[72] Clearly, Felix was quite taken by her talent, so much so that his thoughts turned again toward opera. He began discussing seriously with Emanuel Geibel a libretto on the Lorelei legend. By early December, Felix was responding positively to a draft, several passages of which he found already finished, though the whole still lacked a continuous dramatic thread.[73] Almost certainly he intended the bewitching title role of the opera, now to occupy him until his death, for the Swedish nightingale.

Two days after the *Athalie* premiere, Felix and Jenny departed Berlin together for Leipzig. She had agreed to sing in the Gewandhaus and did not disappoint. Anticipating her debut, the concert management doubled the ticket price and suspended the students' privileged *gratis* admission (the young Otto Goldschmidt led an unsuccessful protest). When she appeared at the eighth subscription concert (December 4), she came forward, Elise Polko informs us, as "a slender girlish form with luxuriant fair hair, dressed in pink silk, and white and pink camellias on her breast and in her hair, in all the chaste grace of her deportment, and so utterly devoid of all pretension. . . ."[74] She sang arias from *Norma* and *Don Giovanni*, a duet from Bellini's *I Capuleti e i Montecchi* with Helen Dolby, and songs of Felix, with the composer at the piano. She closed with a Swedish national air in which she accompanied herself, captivating the audience with a sustained, *pianissimo* F♯, described by the press as utter magic.[75] (Felix took note of the effect, and later designed the soprano aria of *Elijah* "Hear ye, Israel!", which features a high F♯, for her voice.) The publisher Heinrich Brockhaus recorded in his diary, "a song sung by her goes straight to the heart."[76]

The next day, Jenny and Felix collaborated in an extra concert for the orchestral pension fund. Before an audience of a thousand, the two appeared in alternation, with Felix performing his Piano Concerto in G minor, Op. 25 and two *Lieder ohne Worte*, Op. 67 No. 1 in E♭ and the "*Frühlingslied*," Op. 62 No. 6 in A major. Felix connected them with a masterly improvisation that modulated between the two distantly related keys, and somehow transformed the belllike B♭'s of the first into the "feathery" arpeggiations of the second.[77] Jenny offered selections from Mozart's *Marriage of Figaro*, Weber's *Der Freischütz* and *Euryanthe*, Felix's Lieder, and again Swedish folksongs. That evening, grateful members of the orchestra serenaded her, and she asked Felix to acknowledge their hospitality. "Gentlemen," he exclaimed from a balcony. "You think that the Kapellmeister Mendelssohn is speaking to you, but in that you are mistaken. Fräulein Jenny Lind speaks to you, and thanks you for the beautiful surprise that you have prepared for her. But now I change myself back again into the Leipzig Kapellmeister, and call upon you to wish long life to Fräulein Jenny Lind."[78]

When Jenny returned on December 6 to Berlin, Felix accompanied her as far as Dessau; an unpublished letter refers to an interrupted conversation there about Swedish customs and the Berlin court.[79] Most likely, Felix traveled to his grandfather's birthplace to consult Schubring about *Elijah* (only a week later the composer was sending his friend a complete draft of the libretto[80]). Having returned to Leipzig, Felix took up his baton to direct the ninth Gewandhaus concert, on December 11; he also par-

Ex. 15.13: Mendelssohn, "Wenn sich zwei Herzen scheiden," Op. 99 No. 5 (1845)

ticipated in the tenth, one week later, when he directed with brisk tempi some ensembles from Mozart's *Così fan tutte*.[81] But Felix continued to dwell on Jenny; in his letter of December 10 (using the formal *Sie*), he had asked her to remember him, either in the billiards room, when children played piano duets, or when another composer approached her with songs. At Christmas, Felix exercised the third option, by sending her as a present a *Liederheft*.[82] Among its contents was the *Schilflied* (*Song of the Reeds*) of 1842 to a text of Lenau, destined to appear in 1847 as Op. 71 No. 4. Though not composed for Jenny, the song concludes with a "sweet remembrance of you" (*ein süsses Deingedenken*, with the intimate *Dein*), and thus, perhaps, alludes musically to their friendship. But another song, Op. 99 No. 5, composed on December 22 to a text of Geibel and included in the *Liederheft*, was considerably more suggestive. "When two hearts part," it begins, "that once were in love, that is a great sorrow, for which there is no greater" (**ex. 15.13**). And in his letter of December 23, which accompanied the songs, Felix concluded, "As far as I am concerned, you know that at *every* happy Festival and on *every* serious day, I think of you, and you have a share in them, whether you like it or no— But you wish it, I am sure, and you know from me that it is the same with me and never will be otherwise."[83]

IV

Writing to the Frankfurt senator and merchant Franz Bernus in October 1845, Felix revealed his grueling Leipzig schedule was taking its toll: "As soon . . . as I have won the right to live solely for my inward work and composing, only occasionally conducting and playing in public just as it may suit me, then I shall assuredly return to the Rhine, and probably . . . settle at Frankfurt."[84] But in the meantime, Leipzigers rejoiced at his renewed commitment to their musical life. In addition to the Gewandhaus concerts, he participated fully in the concurrent *Unterhaltungen*, by performing his two piano trios, Beethoven's Cello Sonata in A major, Op. 69, and a new piano quintet by Louis Spohr. The season brought the Leipzig premiere of Beethoven's unfathomable String Quartet in C♯ minor, Op. 131, encouraging Felix to explore Beethoven's transcendent, then little understood, late style. Thus, at the Königstrasse residence on New Year's Eve, Felix rendered the Piano Sonata in E major, Op. 109, in a private performance attended by the Schumanns (though Clara also performed, Robert was suffering from nervous exhaustion and depression, and "with his usual custom took no active part in the proceedings"[85]). At the second, public *Unterhaltung*, Felix offered Beethoven's final piano sonata, the Op. 111 in C minor. According to Otto Goldschmidt, the ineffable variations of the second movement "came out more clearly in their structure and beauty than I have ever heard before or since."[86] The young journalist Franz Brendel, who in 1845 had assumed the editorship of the *Neue Zeitschrift für Musik* after Robert Schumann sold the journal, gave Felix's effort a mixed review. If his conception of the variations in the second-movement finale was compelling, Brendel found Felix's touch in the first movement "too light and fleeting" to convey the "painful disunity" of the composition.[87] Brendel's criticism, a rare, dissenting voice in a city that lionized the composer, marked the beginning of a divide in German music journalism that would widen considerably after the Revolution of 1848. For Brendel, Felix's classical propensities (and his refined pianism) were increasingly incongruent with the political and artistic aspirations of a modern Germany.

The beginning of 1846 brought Felix little respite. On January 1, Clara Schumann gave the premiere of her husband's Piano Concerto in A minor, Op. 54, expanded, just months before, by the composer from a one-movement *Phantasie* to a three-movement concerto. When, two days later, Fanny arrived from Berlin for a visit, Felix organized an evening party with the Schumanns and possibly took up the viola part in Robert's Piano Quartet Op. 47.[88] At the farewell concert of Helen Dolby on January 15, Felix played his old *Rondo brillant* Op. 29, prefaced by a free improvisation as a slow introduction. Then, in rapid succession, came three subscription concerts, with selections from the incidental music to *A Midsummer Night's Dream* (January 22), Beethoven's *Ruins of Athens* (January 29), and Beethoven's Ninth Symphony (February 5), a performance attended by Devrient, who now "understood the strange colossal work for the first time."[89]

Especially memorable was the concert given for the benefit of the orchestral pension fund on February 12. According to Ludwig Rellstab, the "pearl of the evening" was Felix's performance of Beethoven's 32 Variations for piano in C minor,[90] which may well have inspired this account by Otto Goldschmidt of Felix's approach to the instrument: "His mechanism . . . was extremely subtle, and developed with the lightest of wrists (never from the arm); he therefore never strained the instrument or hammered. His chord-playing was beautiful, and based on a special theory of his own. His use of the pedal was very sparing, clearly defined, and therefore effective; his phrasing beautifully clear."[91] The program also included three contemporary works. If Louis Spohr's Concerto for String Quartet and Orchestra (1845) was the least provocative, Robert Schumann's "genial" Overture, Scherzo, and Finale Op. 52 (1841, revised 1845) came across as something of a lightweight miscalculation. The press, however, reserved its strongest criticism for Richard Wagner's *Tannhäuser* Overture, which elicited only lukewarm applause. The opera had received its premiere in Dresden in October 1845, when Schumann reported to Felix: "Wagner has just completed an opera—he's certainly an ingenious fellow, full of the most extravagant ideas and immeasurably audacious, but believe me, he can hardly set down and think out four measures either beautifully or correctly." But after a second performance, Schumann reversed himself, noting that "from the stage everything appears quite differently" than from a piano-vocal score.[92] Presumably the two friends discussed the work when the Schumanns visited Leipzig in January. Be that as it may, the Leipzig press reacted in a decidedly negative tone. In particular, Rellstab complained about the descending, two-note sigh figure in the violins with which Wagner "over satiated" the audience: the "groaning, sighing, and whimpering" was interminable, so that one had to doubt the taste of a composer who put his listeners in such a painful mood.[93] According to Hans von Bülow, the Gewandhaus reading was in response to the realization, after the Dresden premiere, that Wagner had broken new ground in his opera, but the Leipzig performance was "unpleasant beyond all measure—an execution, in the particular sense of the word." And, von Bülow asserted, Felix's "morose demeanor" (*missmuthige Miene*) while he conducted only encouraged the audience to reject the work.[94] For whatever reason, Felix's sole performance of Wagner's music reinforced in Leipzig a general antipathy toward the Dresden Kapellmeister, a rejection Wagner later did not hesitate to ascribe to Felix's influence.

Among the audience that night was Hans Christian Andersen, who, after visiting Jenny Lind in Weimar (she was "extremely fond of Mendelssohn-Bartholdy," he noted in his diary), had proceeded to Leipzig to discuss with publishers a new, collected German edition of his works. When the overture "met with opposition," he applauded, for he recognized within the music "an entire painting." For a week Andersen enjoyed daily meetings with Felix; the writer attended a *selskab*, or evening musical party, arranged by Felix, and heard the harpist Parish-Alvars at one of the concerts.[95] In exchange, Andersen delighted his Leipzig admirers with readings from his works and endured teasing from the composer about the prevalence of storks in the fairy tales.[96]

Early in March Felix found a brief respite from his Gewandhaus duties in Berlin, when he attended the baptism of his brother's daughter Katharine and confirmation of Fanny's son, Sebastian.[97] Felix heeded a royal summons to appear in Dresden (March 28), where he privately entertained the court.[98] The following day, he participated in a morning musicale, organized by Eduard Bendemann and attended by the widow of Carl Maria von Weber. With Clara Schumann, Felix shared the task of performing Beethoven's *Appassionata* Piano Sonata and also selected movements from the *Midsummer Night's Dream* music, arranged for piano duet. Robert Schumann later recorded that on this occasion, the last time he heard his friend as a pianist, Felix described Liszt as a "constant exchange between scandal and apotheosis."[99] Possibly during this visit too Felix attended a production of *Tannhäuser*, though the only passage for which he was able to compliment Wagner was some canonic imitation in the second finale.[100]

Welcoming Moscheles's decision to join the faculty of the Conservatory that fall, Felix remained the guiding force of the institution and took an active role in examining students.[101] On January 3, 1846, he began two classes in piano and one in composition, which met on Wednesday and Saturday afternoons. For more than two months, the aspiring pianists strove to master the pearly virtuosity of the Hummel Septet in D minor, and then etudes of Chopin and fugues from the *Well-Tempered Clavier*, before Felix allowed them in March to approach an old staple of his repertoire, Weber's *Konzertstück* Op. 79. Rockstro informs us that Felix instilled a respect for the authority of composers' scores, and rarely treated "questions of simple technique," which were referred instead to other faculty. Rather, he was more concerned with "special forms of expression" and recommended his pupils emulate good singers. "You will learn far more from them," he advised, "than from any players you are likely to meet with."[102]

In composition Felix accepted pupils advanced in music theory. His method of instruction was to correct their work in class, by adding comments about how to improve particular passages. If a student recommitted a mistake made several weeks before, Felix would draw upon his memory to reproduce the earlier faulty passage at the piano.[103] He devoted not a few classes to the intricacies of counterpoint, revealed on a large blackboard bearing eight red staves. On one Felix would write a cantus firmus and then invite students to generate additional parts, until all were filled. "The difficulty of adding a sixth, seventh, or eighth part to an exercise already complete in three, four, or five," Rockstro noted, "will be best understood by those who have most frequently attempted the process." Often, it was impossible to finish the exercise, but Felix "would never sanction the employment of a rest, as a means of escape from the gravest difficulty, until every available resource had been tried, in vain."[104] Sometimes the exercises led to "checkmate," with even the composer of the Octet unable to complete the final part without transgressing some rule of voice leading.

During the early months of 1846 Felix spared little effort to further his contacts with Jenny Lind, who visited Leipzig at the end of January, en route to Berlin to prepare for her debut as Valentine in Meyerbeer's *Les Huguenots*. But when Jenny sprained her foot and was confined to quarters for several weeks, Felix comforted her from Leipzig with a long, chatty letter.[105] He discussed rehearsals for Gade's new Ossianic cantata *Comala* ("Fingal, with his warriors, and harps, and horns, and spirits, plays an important part in it") and Swedish folksongs. A few weeks later a recuperated Jenny returned to Leipzig. Once again her concert, announced for April 12, was sold out within hours. Because the orchestra was engaged the same day to perform an opera,[106] Felix undertook to accompany her arias of Pacini, Mozart, and Weber, one of Felix's *Suleika* settings, and three Swedish *Nationallieder*, and performed Beethoven's *Moonlight* Sonata and the Violin Sonata, Op. 30 No. 3, with Ferdinand David. But when Felix was about to begin some *Lieder ohne Worte*, he turned to the audience and escorted Clara Schumann, visiting from Dresden, to the piano. Leipzigers were thus treated to appearances by four of the most eminent musicians of the day.

In January Felix had agreed to direct the twenty-eighth Lower Rhine Musical Festival, scheduled for Pentecost in Aachen (Aix-la-Chapelle), and he looked forward to making "a little music together"[107] with Jenny, who like himself had the "love of Art so deeply implanted" in her soul. Even the prospect of this collaboration did not satisfy him, and he also actively pursued the idea of writing an opera for her. Though already corresponding with Geibel about *Die Lorelei* (in May Felix would ask Devrient to assist the poet),[108] Felix hedged his bets by approaching another potential collaborator. His choice was Charlotte Birch-Pfeiffer, a writer and actress with whom Jenny had studied German. Between April 1846 and February 1847, Felix and Charlotte exchanged ideas about numerous subjects;[109] Felix himself mentioned Joan of Arc, the Lorelei, Goethe's *Faust*, and the *Nibelung* saga, though the discussion centered chiefly on the Peasants' War of 1524—unknown to Charlotte, Devrient had forwarded a libretto on the same subject to Felix in May 1846— Achim von Arnim's story *Die Kronenwächter*, and the legend of Genoveva. Only the last produced a tangible result, a *scenarium* Charlotte sent to Felix on May 19.[110] But the composer's habitual reservations derailed the project: in Felix's view, she had strayed too far from the popular legend

by introducing secondary figures and had invented too many motiva-
tions for the characters' actions. Charlotte's work came to a grinding
halt, Felix rejected Devrient's libretto for its excessive "historical bal-
last,"[111] and Geibel's *Lorelei* remained the only viable option.

Of new compositions, Felix finished his commission for Liège, *Lauda
Sion*, on February 6 and dispatched it to Belgium two weeks later.[112] The
composer had delayed completing the score, he explained, owing to his
decision to set Thomas Aquinas's entire text, and the work had grown to
nearly half an hour in length. A new work commissioned for the German-
Flemish Singing Festival in Cologne, the part-song *An die Künstler*, Op.
68, offered considerably less resistance and was ready on April 19.[113] There
is some evidence that around this time Felix considered fashioning a
seventh volume of *Lieder ohne Worte*. In December, he had composed
two piano *Kinderstücke* (published posthumously as Op. 102 Nos. 3 and
5), and in April he sent a manuscript of six *Lieder ohne Worte*, with Op. 85
Nos. 1, 2, 3, and 5, the *Reiterlied*, and Op. 102 No. 2, to Frau von Lüttichau,
wife of the Dresden theatrical Intendant.[114] Felix never saw the new volume into print; rather, after his death, it devolved to Simrock to cobble
together the seventh and eighth volumes, Opp. 85 and 102, from piano
pieces left in the composer's estate.

All these projects did not distract Felix from his chief effort—*Elijah*.
Though much of the libretto for the second part remained in a tentative
state, Felix plunged into the music for the first part in the early months
of 1846. He does not appear, however, to have composed the numbers of
the oratorio in any particular order. Thus, when Eduard Devrient visited Leipzig early in February, the actor found that Felix had begun, "un-
consciously, to copy older masters, especially Sebastian Bach, and that
his writings exhibited certain mannerisms,"[115] an assertion Martin Staehelin has used to date around this time Elijah's aria from the second
part, "Es ist genug" ("It is enough, O Lord," No. 26), closely modeled on
"Es ist vollbracht" from Bach's St. John Passion. By March, Felix could
report he was "now very busy at my Oratorio," and at the end of the
month Robert Schumann recorded in his diary that Felix was in the "full
fire" of inspiration.[116] By mid-May, as Part 1 neared completion, Felix
optimistically wrote to Jenny: "Sometimes, in my room, I have jumped
up to the ceiling, when it seemed to promise so very well."[117] He made
arrangements for William Bartholomew to begin fitting English words
to the score, composed to the German text. On May 23, just days before
he was due in Aachen, Felix sent to London the whole of Part 1.[118]

Incredibly, only one month later, after "toiling day and night,"
Bartholomew had produced the English version, a paraphrase kept "as
scriptural as possible," and also copied the choruses, so that they could

be engraved for rehearsals.[119] For the next seven weeks composer and translator kept a brisk correspondence, with Felix sending portions of the second part as they were ready, Bartholomew returning the newly fabricated English texts, and Felix responding with a multitude of meticulous revisions. Their letters reveal indeed that he scrutinized Bartholomew's work "bar by bar, note by note, syllable by syllable, with an attention to detail which might be termed microscopic."[120] For Felix, this *modus operandi* was a matter of course; "a little more trouble" would be amply repaid by a "little improvement!"[121]

V

Interrupting his labors on *Elijah*, Felix departed Leipzig for Frankfurt, to rendezvous with Jenny Lind, returning from a triumphant Viennese tour. Delayed, she did not reach Der weisse Schwan, the fashionable hotel where Felix waited fretfully an entire day, until midnight the evening of May 26. The next day, accompanied by friends and Jenny's chaperone, the musicians embarked at Mainz on a steamboat down the Rhine. According to Emil Naumann, a Conservatory student who partook of the *Rheinfahrt*, Felix sought to entertain Jenny by comparing to composers the islands dotting the river and peaks dominating its sloping banks. Thus, the Johannisberg, with its Benedictine monastery and eighteenth-century castle, was the "Mozart among the vineyards"; the craggy rocks near Rüdesheim, Beethoven.[122] Safely established in Charlemagne's old Kaiserstadt, Felix threw himself into the remaining rehearsals for the Aachen festival. May 30, the day before the first concert, proved especially exhausting. At 7:00 A.M., he spent an hour discussing *Elijah* with Simrock, who had arrived from Bonn. Then the general rehearsal began, interrupted at 2:00 P.M. by an obligatory dinner, followed by another monumental rehearsal from 5:00 to 9:00. During the day, Jenny received an unexpected visitor: her friend E. G. Geijer (1783–1847), a history professor from the University of Uppsala, who had traveled from Sweden with his wife to attend the Musikfest, surprised her at the rehearsal. Felix had a piano sent to his room and late that evening played some *Lieder ohne Worte* and the *Moonlight* Sonata at an impromptu musical gathering.[123]

The festival began under Felix's baton on Pentecost Sunday, May 31, with a Mozart symphony and Haydn's *Creation*, performed by a chorus of 487 and orchestra of 139 before an audience of 1200 in the municipal theater. Jenny sang the roles of Gabriel and Eve.[124] The highpoint was the third part of the oratorio, when she "threw the whole poetry of her womanly nature into the part of Eve."[125] The next day, she appeared in

Handel's *Alexander's Feast*, for which Felix had tinkered with the German of Ramler's translation, in order to render Dryden's poem more intelligible.[126] In addition, Felix conducted works by Weber, Cherubini, and Mozart, but generated a special excitement by an announcement prior to performing Beethoven's Fifth Symphony. A letter from Beethoven to his publisher, Felix explained, had emerged that disclosed an error in the printed score of the third-movement scherzo. Just after the C-major trio, at the return of the opening C-minor motive, Beethoven had originally included two bars (for use in an expanded version of the movement, with full repeats of the scherzo and trio). Somehow, in 1809 and again in 1826, when the parts and score were printed, the superfluous bars had evaded the engraver's attention.[127] Now, in 1846, Felix undertook to excise the bars for his Aachen performance and rectify a nearly forty-year-old error in the performance tradition of the familiar masterpiece.

Though Breitkopf & Härtel published Beethoven's letter in the *Allgemeine musikalische Zeitung*,[128] and revealed the composer clearly had labeled the questionable passage an error, a controversy erupted among musicians and the press, with Berlioz and Habeneck in Paris defending the redundant bars. Beethoven's former secretary Anton Schindler, no friend of Felix, admitted that the "noble creator of the work" had "put a curse on these two measures"; still, Schindler endeavored to rationalize their inclusion. And a Viennese critic sought to demonstrate that none of the printed parts from Beethoven's time suppressed the measures; therefore, they must be legitimate.[129] Nevertheless, Beethoven scholarship subsequently endorsed Felix's revision, putting the "cursed" measures to rest.

On the morning of June 2, the Aachen festival closed with the "Artists' Concert," at which portions of Haydn's *Creation* were encored and Felix's String Quartet Op. 12 and an overture by Georges Onslow performed. Onslow, who reviewed the festival for the *Revue et gazette musicale de Paris*, received Felix's baton as a memento.[130] But the star attraction was again Jenny, who sang Felix's Lieder so successfully that the entire three-day event was remembered as the *Jenny-Lind-Fest*, probably the first public music festival dominated by one virtuoso. Felix was moved to add another song to the *Liederheft* he had sent her for Christmas. Then, the two spent a day visiting Cologne and the lore-encrusted Drachenfels (Dragon's Rock) south of Bonn. When they parted, Jenny left for Hanover and Felix for Düsseldorf, where on Trinity Sunday (June 7) he participated in a concert of Julius Rietz, which "would have been a fine one if Jenny Lind had been there."[131] Still, two competing singing societies serenaded Felix, and at a friend's residence he had access to a new Erard piano and discovered *Veuve Clicquot* to be an "excellent woman."[132]

Four days later, Felix was in the Church of St. Martin of Liège, for the premiere of *Lauda Sion* on Thursday, June 11, 1846, the six hundredth anniversary of the feast of Corpus Christi, first observed in the Belgian city in 1246. He had intended to assist with the rehearsals but not to direct the performance. What he found were musical forces woefully inadequate to the task, as two accounts by the English critic Chorley and the choral director John Hullah, who journeyed from London, disclose. The church was "one of those buildings which swallow up all sound, owing to the curve of the vaults and the bulk of the piers; the orchestra was little more powerful, when heard from below, than the distant scraping of a Christmas serenade far down the street; the chorus was toneless, and out of tune; and only one *solo* singer, the *soprano*, was even tolerable. . . . Mendelssohn gave up the matter in despair. 'No; it is not good; it cannot go well; it will make a bad noise,' was his greeting to us."[133] Somewhat offsetting the poor preparation was the solemn pageantry of the event, attended by fourteen bishops, "magnificently vested in scarlet, and purple, and gold, and damask—a group never to be forgotten."

Following a sermon on the mysteries of the Eucharist, Felix's score was read by a "scrannel orchestra, and singers who could hardly be heard."[134] Hullah found the chorus "most inefficient," owing to a bishop's refusal to allow women to sing the soprano and alto parts.[135] But in the final movement, at *Ecce panis angelorum, factus cibus viatorum* ("Behold the bread of angels, made the food of pilgrims"), came a "surprise of a different quality." The Host was suspended "in a gorgeous gilt tabernacle, that slowly turned above the altar, so as to reveal the consecrated elements to the congregation. Incense was swung from censers; and the evening sun, breaking in with a sudden brightness, gave a fairy-like effect to curling fumes as they rose, while a very musical bell, that timed the movement twice in a bar, added its charm to the rite." Chorley felt a grasp at his wrist. "Listen!" Felix said. "How pretty that is! It makes me amends for all their bad playing and singing, —and I shall hear the rest better some other time."[136]

Felix's most substantial Catholic setting, *Lauda Sion* draws upon a rich tradition extending back to the thirteenth century, when Thomas Aquinas composed the text as a sequence[137] for the liturgy of the newly instituted Feast of Corpus Christi. Falling predominantly into trochaic dimeters (*Láuda Síon sálvatórem, láuda dúcem ét pastórem*), the twelve-odd stanzas of the poem employ a modal chant originally used for twelfth-century Parisian sequences. During the Renaissance and Counter-Reformation composers such as Brumel, Victoria, Lassus, and Palestrina wrote polyphonic motets that paraphrased or cited the chant. A sure sign of its popularity was the decision of the Council of Trent (1545–1563) to remove from the liturgy all sequences save a small handful, including *Lauda Sion* and *Dies irae*. Whether Felix had access to early polyphonic settings is unclear (he reported to Robert Schumann that old Italian church music came over him like incense[138]); in any event the Latin verses, inextricably associated with the doctrine of transubstantiation, and thus removed from Felix's own Protestant tradition, inspired him to create a major, unjustly neglected composition.

From the outset the score radiates euphonious, Italianate warmth foreign to the chromatic, Bachian austerities usually characteristic of Felix's sacred music. The work begins with an ascending, incalescent C-major figure announcing a chorus of praise (ex. 15.14a). In the second movement, the figure reappears in a minor-keyed incarnation against pulsating string tremolos, solemnly linking the Eucharist to the Last Supper. The theme of praise returns in the third movement, which, like a response, alternates between a soprano soloist and chorus. We now approach the three central movements, the core of the composition, in which Felix allies the mysterious ritual of Holy Communion with the centuries-old art of counterpoint. In No. 4, the text refers to the New Covenant replacing the Old and to truth chasing shadowy appearance. Here Felix crafts a series of canons for pairings of four solo voices. Then, in the culminating fifth movement, he celebrates the sacerdotal "dogma given to Christians" by unveiling the modal chant of *Lauda Sion* as a cantus firmus. Felix's exact source for the melody is unknown, but significantly he transformed it from its original, mixolydian church mode into a version compatible with the more modern aeolian, or natural minor, a technique that rendered the melody at once exotic yet vaguely familiar (ex. 15.14b, c).

Three times the chorus sings the opening strain in unison, a reference to the Trinity, as the celebrants, "learned in the sacred institutions" (*docti sacris institutis*), consecrate the bread and wine as the Host of salvation. At the fourth repetition, the text extols Christ's presence through living faith and "different signs, not things" (*sub diversis speciebus, signis tantum, et non rebus*); here the chorus abandons its stark unison declamation in favor of a free harmonization, with the chant transposed to the bass. The sixth movement explores the same text by means of a chorale fugue (ex. 15.14d), in which trumpets and trombones intone the chant between expositions of the fugal subject. Curiously, when *Lauda Sion* appeared in 1848 as Op. 73, the first of Felix's posthumous works, the fugue was omitted; it disappeared until a Belgian scholar published the movement in 1954.[139] Clearly Felix intended to include it, although "it is a bit strict and *although* it is a fugue and *although* it is too long."[140] Taken with the canonic and cantus-firmus techniques of the fourth and fifth

Ex. 15.14a: Mendelssohn, *Lauda Sion*, Op. 73 (1846), No. 1

Ex. 15.14b: *Lauda Sion Salvatorem*

Lau - da Si - on Sal - va - to - rem, Lau - da du - cem et pas - to - rem, In hy - mnis et can - ti - cis.

Ex. 15.14c: Mendelssohn, *Lauda Sion*, Op. 73 (1846), No. 5

Do - cti sa - cris in - sti - tu - tis pa - nem, vi - num in sa - lu -

Ex. 15.14d: Mendelssohn, *Lauda Sion*, Op. 73 (1846), No. 6

Sub di - ver - sis spe - ci -

Sub di - ver - sis spe - ci - e - bus si - gnis tan - tum, et nos

movements, the fugue completes the association of high counterpoint with the ineffable ritual of the Eucharist.

Next, a soprano aria (No. 7) reminds the communicants that the breaking of bread does not divide Christ but "accepts Him whole." The final movement begins dramatically, as the thousands of good and evil receive communion. While the text hints at the Last Judgment, Felix reinforces the idea by alluding to another sequence, the *Dies irae*, as set by Mozart in the *Rex tremendae* of his Requiem. But Felix's *fortissimo* chords in majestic dotted rhythms subside to a calming transition that returns us to the "bread of the angels," and the music of the opening movement. The score ends *pianissimo* with a vision of Christ the Good Shepherd (*bone Pastor*) and the bread that nourishes the faithful.

VI

Felix's next musical experience contrasted starkly to the high solemnities of Corpus Christi. From June 14 to 17, 1846, he attended the first (and only) German-Flemish Singing Festival (*Deutsch-Vlaemisches Sängerfest*) in Cologne. An orotund mass, some two thousand men—"everything in Belgium, the Rhine Land, and Baden, that could bear a part in a part-song"[141]—convened to sing concerts and compete for a prize. The rowdy participants crammed into Gürzenich Hall, an old, turreted building festooned with the colorful banners of the various *Liedertafel* societies. Here, Felix directed "O Isis und Osiris" from Mozart's *Magic Flute* and the premiere of *An die Künstler* (*To Artists*), Op. 68, for male choir and brass band, to a text of Schiller. Similar in style to the Gutenberg *Festgesang* of 1840, Op. 68 celebrates the power of art to guide its sacred magic to the "great ocean of harmony" (**ex. 15.15**) and to preserve "human worthiness." Also heard on the concert was the Bacchus chorus from *Antigone*, "no bad prelude to the drinking bouts"[142] that followed. Both works were encored, and at a second concert one of Felix's part-songs was sung from memory. Late that night, a procession of torch-bearing musicians serenaded the composer. During the festival, Felix met the young composer Joachim Raff (later Liszt's assistant at Weimar), whose music Felix had recommended to Breitkopf & Härtel in 1843.[143] On June 16, there was more singing, this time atop the Drachenfels, after a leisurely *Liederfahrt* up the Rhine. And on June 17, Felix and his party toured the unfinished cathedral to inspect the "hives upon hives of Gothic ornaments ready to be placed—hundreds of grotesques, thousands of crockets, canopies, and finials."[144] With the head architect Felix imagined composing music for the nave, though he reported to Moritz Hauptmann that the acoustics were less than desirable.[145]

Ex. 15.15: Mendelssohn, *An die Künstler*, Op. 68

Still len - ke sie zum O - ce - a - ne der gros - sen, gros - sen Har - mo - nie

Hardly had Felix returned to Leipzig before he was playing host to Louis Spohr, who arrived from Cassel on June 22 for a six-day visit. Each day culminated in intense music making, and at the Gewandhaus Felix organized a surprise concert (June 25) dedicated to Spohr's compositions.[146] But the unrehearsed reading of his Fourth Symphony (*Die Weihe der Töne*) nearly led to an embarrassing moment. When Felix invited the esteemed visitor to conduct the third movement, he neglected to inform Spohr of a substantial cut entered into the parts but not the score. After receiving the news with an "Olympian calm" from Ferdinand David, Spohr revealed that in Cassel he had instituted the same cut, for the work was "too long."[147] At the Thomaskirche Moritz Hauptmann read choral works of Spohr and J. S. Bach, and at private dinner parties Felix took up three instruments in his guest's chamber works: piano in the Piano Trio Op. 119, viola in the Third Double String Quartet Op. 87, and violin in the new String Quartet Op. 132.[148] Felix also performed, Spohr informs us, with "monstrous *bravura*," an "unheard of difficult and most highly idiosyncratic composition of his own,"[149] the *Variations sérieuses*. Among the listeners was Richard Wagner, who had come to Leipzig to meet Spohr, and impressed him with his liberal political sympathies. Regrettably, Felix seems not to have recorded in his letters his impressions of Wagner in what was probably their last meeting.

After Spohr's departure Felix took up the second part of *Elijah*, interrupted only by a memorial concert for the trombonist C. T. Queisser on July 19, when the composer performed Beethoven's *Kreutzer* Sonata with David.[150] Prior to leaving for the engagements in the Rhineland, Felix had sought Schubring's assistance with the libretto of the second part, still in a tentative, disorganized state. Among Felix's concerns were how to connect Jezebel's threat against Elijah (1 Kings 19) with the prophet's flight into the wilderness, whether to have Elijah sing at his ascension, and whether to introduce his disciple Elisha. The last point led to a droll exchange: when Felix imagined Elisha as a child and asked if a soprano could sing the part, Schubring responded by alluding to *Paulus*: "Such a question should not be put by one who has set Christ's words for a chorus. . . . One who ploughs with twelve yoke of oxen (1 Kings 19:19) is no child."[151]

In the end, Elisha did not have a role in the oratorio, nor did Elijah sing at his ascension, represented instead by the chorus No. 38, "Then did Elijah the prophet break forth like a fire" (Sirach 48). How to conclude the oratorio remained a difficult issue. Schubring had argued for giving the work an avowedly New Testament flavor and recommended a final trio of Peter, John, and James. When Felix found this stratagem "too far removed from the grouping of the (Old Testament) story," Schubring replied, "I see most distinctly that the oratorio can have no other than a New Testament ending; the Old Testament (Malachi) and also the New Testament demand this in terms of the most definite kind. Elijah must help to transform the old into the new covenant—that gives him his great historical importance."[152] By alluding to Malachi 3 ("The messenger of the covenant in whom you delight—indeed, he is coming, says the Lord of hosts"), a passage Handel had incorporated into the first part of *Messiah*, Schubring sought to reaffirm a common Christian reading linking the Gospels to the prophets Isaiah and Malachi and interpreting Elijah as a precursor to John the Baptist and Christ.

As the summer of 1846 advanced and the deadline approached, Felix "lived the life of a marmot,"[153] scrambling to finish the second part while refining Bartholomew's English translations. Not until the middle of June did the chorus master, James Stimpson, begin receiving the choruses of Part 1, which, though printed, were filled with enough alterations in black, red, and blue ink to render their decipherment taxing. The final chorus of Part 2 arrived only nine days before the festival. Even before "finishing" the oratorio, on August 11, 1846 (**plate 17**),[154] Felix began implementing revisions, some at Bartholomew's suggestion. As early as June he had encouraged Felix to write an overture, but the composer had intended to begin the work with Elijah's solemn recitative announcing the drought and could not imagine what an overture "should or could mean before that curse."[155] Bartholomew then devised a creative solution: the overture, "descriptive of the misery of famine," could immediately follow the recitative, and thus prepare the opening chorus, "Help, Lord! Wilt Thou quite destroy us?" Felix acceded to the request and early in August hastily composed the orchestral movement.

Another recommendation by Bartholomew nearly induced Felix to remove the alto aria, "O rest in the Lord" (No. 31; Psalm 37:7), sung by an angel to accompany Elijah's journey to Mt. Horeb. The translator had detected a nagging resemblance between the opening phrase and the Scottish air "Robin Gray," which begins "Young Jamie lov'd me well, and ask'd me for his bride." Fearing the similarity would expose Felix to "the impertinence of the saucy *boys* of the musical press,"[156] Bartholomew alerted the composer, whose first instinct was to delete the movement.

But after arriving in London, Felix retouched the phrase slightly to disguise the similarity and spared the aria. Not so a chorus originally incorporated into the penultimate No. 41, "He shall open the blind eyes" (Isaiah 42:7). Eighty-six measures in length, the movement unfolded as a four-part canon with orchestral accompaniment.[157] But after trying it out at a rehearsal in Leipzig on August 5, Felix informed Bartholomew of its excision: "Pray let the choral people at Birmingham know this *directly*; it will spare them much time, as the *Alla breve* is not easy, and as I am sure I will not let it stand."[158]

VII

Prior to departing for London, Felix answered an important letter of Fanny that revisited an old issue in their relationship. In the spring of 1846 she had met a young musician, Robert von Keudell (1824–1903), about to join the diplomatic corps (in 1873, during Bismarck's term as chancellor of the newly unified Germany, Keudell would become German ambassador to Rome[159]). Fanny found in him a skilled pianist who possessed a fine ear for music and impressive memory comparable to Felix's. By July, she and Hensel were seeing the young man on a nearly daily basis: "Keudell keeps my music alive and in constant activity, as Gounod did once. He takes an intense interest in everything that I write, and calls my attention to any shortcomings; generally he is in the right too."[160] Keudell's and Hensel's encouragement rekindled Fanny's interest in publishing her music, and she accepted an attractive offer from the Berlin firm of Bote & Bock to bring out six Lieder as her *opus primum*.

Eager to have her brother's approbation, she broke the news to Felix on July 9, but with some apprehension:

> ... I'm afraid of my brothers at age 40, as I was of Father at age 14—or, more aptly expressed, desirous of pleasing you and everyone I've loved throughout my life. And when I now know in advance that it won't be the case, I thus feel *rather* uncomfortable. In a word, I'm beginning to publish. . . . And if I've done it of my own free will and cannot blame anyone in my family if aggravation results from it (friends and acquaintances have indeed been urging me for a long time), then I can console myself, on the other hand, with the knowledge that I in no way sought out or induced the type of musical reputation that might have elicited such offers. I hope I won't disgrace all of you through my publishing, as I'm no *femme libre* and unfortunately not even an adherent of the Young Germany movement. I trust *you* will in no way be bothered by it, since, as you can see, I've proceeded completely on my own in order to spare you any possible unpleasant moment, and I hope you won't think badly of me.[161]

For more than a month, Fanny waited for a reply. When it finally came in mid-August, after Felix had met Keudell in Leipzig and a few days before Felix's departure for London, she finally received her brother's blessing for her decision "to enter our guild": ". . . may you taste only the sweets and none of the bitterness of authorship," he wrote; "may the public pelt you with roses, and never with sand; and may the printer's ink never draw black lines upon your soul."[162] Felix drolly signed his letter, "The journeyman tailor," and thus somewhat facetiously recalled Zelter's symbolic *Gesellensprechung* of 1824, when Felix had "graduated" from his apprenticeship. Abraham's pronouncement, that music would be an ornament to Fanny's life, was no longer valid; the curtain concealing her private musical thoughts was about to be raised. While Felix departed to premiere *Elijah* in Birmingham, Fanny decided to seek more public recognition of her music, and perhaps enter the lists as a professional composer. Reading between his lines a stinting approval, she recorded in her diary: "At last Felix has written, and given me his professional blessing in the kindest manner. I know that he is not quite satisfied in his heart of hearts, but I am glad he has said a kind word to me about it."[163]

The Prophet's Voice:
Elijah's Chariot

Wait, let us see whether Elijah will come to take Him down.

—Mark 15:36

Reunited in London with Klingemann by August 18, 1846, Felix attended that day a concert in his honor by the Beethoven Quartet Society. Among the participants were the violinists Henri Vieuxtemps and Joachim, and cellist Alfredo Piatti, who joined five other musicians in what was billed as the English premiere of the Octet.[1] Felix improvised and played the piano part of his Second Piano Trio. But excepting this appearance, he devoted all his energies toward *Elijah*. On the 19th Moscheles heard him play from memory the newly composed overture and read through the arias with the principal soloists, Maria Caradori-Allan (soprano), Maria Hawes (alto), Charles Lockey (tenor), and Joseph Staudigl (bass). The women proved *prime donne*: the soprano asked Felix to transpose down a step the aria "Hear ye, Israel," as it was not a "lady's song"; and the alto dared introduce an extraneous trill at the close of "O rest in the Lord."[2] On the 20th and 21st Felix led two orchestral rehearsals in the Hanover Square Rooms but lost considerable time proofing and collating the hastily produced parts, spread out on benches in the hall. Then, at 2:00 on August 23, he boarded a special train at Euston Station for Birmingham. Among the passengers were the soloists, members of the orchestra and chorus, and a press contingent. The reporters included the young critic J. W. Davison, recently hired by the *Times* and on assignment from London.

One of the singers who traveled to Birmingham was the bass Henry Phillips, who sang in the chorale-like "Regard thy servant's prayer" (first version of No. 15). Around the time of the 1842 English premiere of the *Scottish* Symphony, Felix had agreed to compose for Phillips a *scena* for bass and orchestra and, on August 22, 1846, finally made good on his word by delivering the manuscript of *On Lena's Gloomy Heath*.[3] Though Macpherson's eighteenth-century Ossianic forgeries had long been exposed, Phillips still thought to exploit the fascination with the pre-Christian bard and cobbled together two unrelated texts from the fourth and third books of Macpherson's *Fingal*. In the first, a vision of Ossian's deceased wife, Everallin, stirs him to rescue their son, Oscar, trapped in an ambush. In the second, Ossian girds himself for battle to a text actually designed for another Celtic hero, Calmar.

Phillips's choices inspired from Felix a three-part setting, with a dreamy, tonally evasive recitative centered on G minor followed by Everallin's plea and a martial march in the major. The haunting iambic rhythms and dark imagery of Macpherson's prose (*On Léna's glóomy héath the vóice of músic díed awáy*) encouraged Felix to revisit the brooding Ossianic style of earlier works such as the *Fingal's Cave* Overture and *Scottish Symphony*. Thus, the *scena* begins with several soft wind fanfares, fleeting visions of an exotic, distant past, accompanied by a series of blurred trills in the bass line that distort our sense of tonal stability (**ex. 16.1a**). From this phantasmagoric atmosphere emerges Ossian's voice in a subdued passage reminiscent of the *Scottish* Symphony (cf. **ex. 16.1b** and p. 430). Everallin's plea is delivered over a chromatically agitated, rising sequence. Then, at the moment of truth, the fog disperses, and Ossian sings a square-cut march tune, a transformation of his opening material into the major mode. But after all the fine, atmospheric music, the march is rather banal, perhaps betraying the haste with which Felix produced the work and explaining why he chose not to keep a copy for himself. According to Phillips, after reviewing the score, Felix was dissatisfied and offered to write another work, a proposal he was unable to fulfill.

Ex. 16.1a: Mendelssohn, *On Lena's Gloomy Heath* (1846)

Ex. 16.1b: Mendelssohn, *On Lena's Gloomy Health* (1846)

Instead, Phillips premiered *On Lena's Gloomy Heath* in London at a Phil-harmonic concert of March 15, 1847,[4] after which it fell into obscurity.

Not so, of course, *Elijah*, which even before its premiere received fa-vorable press attention that marked the oratorio as a momentous musical milestone. After hearing two "naturally imperfect" rehearsals at the Han-over Square Rooms, a reporter for *The Musical World* declared the work the masterpiece of Felix's genius, though, in contrast to *St. Paul*, its "es-sentially dramatic" character caused some to wonder why Felix had not written an opera.[5] In the London *Times* Davison published a fairly de-tailed analytical survey, commented on the surprising paucity of fugues from the "most accomplished living musician," and labeled the oratorio the "greatest achievement of Mendelssohn's genius" and a "great event in the present dearth of serious purpose."[6]

The festival offered no fewer than six concerts, of which *Elijah* formed the zenith on Wednesday, August 26. Rehearsals in Town Hall began Monday morning and continued Tuesday evening, after the first morn-ing concert, which featured Haydn's *Creation*. When Moscheles, sched-uled to conduct several concerts, fell ill, Felix graciously took over a rehearsal Monday evening of Beethoven's *Missa solemnis*, possibly the only occasion on which Felix explored that monumental composition. Of the rehearsals the *Birmingham Journal* commented on Felix's "re-markable power over the performers"; "molding them to his will, and though rigidly strict in exacting the nicest precision, he does it in a man-ner irresistible—actually laughing them into perfection."[7] By then the town was "in a state of great bustle and excitement" in anticipation of *Elijah*, now elevated in the *Times* as "the cynosure of universal interest" on which depended "the *entire* prestige of the festival."[8]

On Wednesday morning, nearly four hundred musicians filled the stage of Town Hall, behind which the organ with "its thirty-two-foot pipes, looking like gigantic rolls of oil-cloth, rose up from behind till its head touched the roof, like some vast animal of mysterious form."[9] The orchestra numbered 125 musicians, principally members of the London Philharmonic and opera orchestras (when Joseph Moore had attempted to exclude a few Philharmonic members who in 1844 had treated Felix rudely at a rehearsal, the composer protested against the "spirit of vin-dictiveness," and insisted they be engaged[10]). The chorus, 271 strong, was allotted to 79 sopranos, 60 "bearded" male altos, 60 tenors, and 72 basses. Shortly before entering the hall, filled with an audience of some two thousand—among them clergy, earls, members of Parliament, and Felix's friends Sterndale Bennett and Charles Horsley—the composer requested of Henry Chorley, music critic for the *Athenaeum*, "Now stick your claws into my book. Don't tell me what you like, but tell me what you *don't* like." When Felix reached the conductor's rostrum, "the forms of etiquette were unanimously laid aside, and one loud and universal cheer acknowledged the presence of the greatest composer of the age."[11]

By all accounts,[12] the performance was an unqualified triumph, with eight numbers (four arias and four choruses) encored. The close of the final chorus was "drowned in a long-continued and unanimous volley of plaudits, . . . as though enthusiasm, long checked, had suddenly burst its bonds, and filled the air with shouts of exultation." *Elijah* was hailed as not only Felix's masterpiece but also "one of the most extraordinary achievements of human intelligence."[13] Felix himself noted to his brother that no other premiere of his music enjoyed such an enthusiastic reception.[14] The festival committee had hedged its bets by adding music to the concert; it stretched the program to accommodate (after the oratorio) arias of Mozart and Cimarosa, sung by the fashionable Italian couple Giulia Grisi and Giovanni Mario, and a chorus of Handel. Following the concert, Felix led Chorley and other friends on the "prettiest walk in Birmingham"— the banks of the canal, where, amid piles of coal and cinders, he hit upon the idea of transforming the duet "Lift thine eyes" (No. 28, Psalm 121) into an a cappella trio.[15] Then, after a few hours respite, he returned to the hall for the third concert, which featured Moscheles's unrehearsed performance—time had not permitted rehearsals—of Beethoven's Seventh Symphony, among other works.

The fourth and fifth concerts followed on Thursday morning and evening, August 27. Heard first was Handel's *Messiah*, completing (with Haydn's *Creation*, and *Elijah*) a triptych of oratorios. But *Messiah* too was unrehearsed, and the addition of "two serpents, three trombones, and an ophicleide" made an "absolutely ridiculous" effect.[16] At the evening concert Felix performed with Moscheles the latter's piano duet *Hommage à Handel* and directed the overture and some of the incidental movements to *A Midsummer Night's Dream*. In lieu of a rehearsal, there had been "a sort of scramble" over the scherzo, "Ye spotted snakes," and final chorus, so the performance was less than ideal.[17] Thus, in the overture, which Felix took at an unusually fast tempo, he had "no small difficulty in checking the *rallentandi*, in the middle and at the end, which he never dreamed of when he made the score, but into the habit of which our London orchestras have, by some mistake, been led." But the Wedding March was encored, and "in some measure redeemed previous inaccuracies."

Felix had no official role in the sixth, final concert of Friday morning, yet an unusual circumstance compelled his participation. The "monster" program included among other works an overture by Méhul, a psalm setting by Moscheles, arias of Marcello, Stradella, and Handel, a trio from a Cherubini Mass, selections from Beethoven's *Missa solemnis* and *Christ on the Mount of Olives*, a solo by the festival organist, H. J. Gauntlett, and a hymn of Spohr. Its crowning conclusion, Handel's *Zadok the Priest*, was jeopardized just before the performance. The distributed program book included the words of a recitative, introduced when the coronation anthem had been given during the 1837 festival celebrating Queen Victoria's accession. "The Lord God Almighty, who ordereth all things in heaven and on earth, hath anointed His handmaid," the text read. Unfortunately, no music could be found for this Victorian accretion, until Felix withdrew to an anteroom and, during the performance of the anthem, composed in a few minutes a convincing Handelian simulation. Parts of the new recitative were hastily generated and, with the ink barely dry, inserted into the performance, so that no one save "those who were in the secret" realized the movement was not the "genuine" article.[18] "That's the way a Mendelssohn manages," Moscheles recorded in his diary.[19]

Largely owing to Felix's celebrity, the festival earned a surplus of some £4800, donated to the charitable work of the Birmingham General Hospital.[20] Having declined to direct two concerts in Manchester, Felix returned to London with Moscheles and recuperated with the Beneckes at Ramsgate, where Felix's only tasks were to take sea air and eat crab. The Sacred Harmonic Society was eager to perform *Elijah* in London, but objections from Birmingham foiled the scheme. On September 6 Felix departed London with Joseph Staudigl for Ostende and made a leisurely return trip, visiting the vineyards of his uncle Joseph in Horchheim and stopping in Frankfurt before reaching Leipzig.

Felix now had sufficient leisure time to complete one minor and two more significant commissions, all for sacred works. In May 1846 Pastor Appia, officiant at Felix and Cécile's wedding in Frankfurt, requested a contribution to a new edition of hymn tunes for the French Reformed Church.[21] Since the mid-eighteenth century, a growing repertory of *cantiques*, freely composed melodies set to new devotional poems, had supplemented the largely sixteenth-century corpus of French psalm harmonizations. Felix now composed for Appia *Venez et chantez les louanges de ce Christ* ("Come and sing the praises of this Christ").[22] Its verses, probably by the Huguenot minister D. A. Touchon of Hanau, proved difficult, as Felix struggled to fit "weak," feminine endings into the phrases of a chorale-like setting. In 1849 his melody, but not the supporting harmonization, appeared in the Huguenot hymnbook *Recueil de cantiques chrétiens* without attribution of authorship; not until 1997 was the complete *cantique*, Felix's sole work for the Huguenots, finally published.[23]

In May 1846 Frederick William IV had issued two commissions to Felix for the Berlin Domchor.[24] First, he was to compose two additional

Sprüche to follow the reading of the Epistle in the Prussian liturgy (*Agende*). By joining the new pieces to the four written in 1843 and 1844 (see pp. 465, 467), Felix completed in October 1846 a cycle of six a-cappella miniatures for high feast days—Advent, Christmas, New Year's Day, Holy Week, Good Friday, and Ascension Day. Each piece concluded with a short, cadential "Alleluia," reflecting the placement of the verse before the Alleluia in the *Agende* of 1829 (still observed by Frederick William IV) and also Felix's interest in imbuing the music with a cyclic, timeless quality. That he intended to publish the music is clear from a letter of October 17, 1846, dispatched with the manuscript to Bote & Bock, then preparing to bring out Fanny's Opp. 1 and 2.[25] But for unknown reasons, a month later Felix withdrew the work, and it did not appear until 1849, when Breitkopf & Härtel published it posthumously as the *Sechs Sprüche*, Op. 79.

Curiously, the first edition reshuffled the pieces into an incongruous order, with Ascension Day preceding Passion Week, and Advent before Good Friday, a realignment Felix surely would have rejected. But when placed in the proper sequence,[26] the opus coheres with considerably greater clarity. Thus, the pieces for Advent and Christmas share the key of G major and similar, rising triadic figures (**ex. 16.2**), while those for New Year's Day, Passion Week, and Good Friday form a sobering group related by minor keys and use of an elementary motive with a repeated pitch. Standing somewhat apart is the *Spruch* for Ascension Day, exalting Christ in majestic dotted rhythms. All six pieces require eight-part double choirs, yet Felix employs their resources sparingly, alternating translucent passages of imitative Palestrinian counterpoint with more densely sculpted block harmonies. Terse, epigrammatic utterances, the *Sprüche* range in length from only twenty to forty measures, yet they manage through simple means to convey an expressive beauty and spiritual power that ranks high among Felix's sacred works.

Ex. 16.2a: Mendelssohn, *Sechs Sprüche*, Op. 79, *Im Advent* (1846)

Ex. 16.2b: Mendelssohn, *Sechs Sprüche*, Op. 79, *Weihnachten* (1846)

Much the same could be said of his music for Frederick William's second commission, a setting of the standard musical portions of the Prussian liturgy, for the weekly Sunday services of the Berlin Cathedral. Felix finished his version of the *Deutsche Liturgie* at the end of October and dispatched a copy to Berlin on November 6.[27] Though recalling his earlier, disagreeable experiences with the cathedral choir and clergy, he lavished special care on the ten movements, fitted delicately like so many musical pieces into the liturgical puzzle apportioned among the minister, chorus, and congregation. No fewer than six were short responses or Amens. The four more substantial pieces included an "Ehre sei dem Vater" (composed earlier for the Domchor), and three new movements, the "Kyrie," "Ehre sei Gott in der Höh," and "Heilig," the Protestant counterparts to the Kyrie, Gloria, and Sanctus from the Ordinary of the Catholic Mass. Felix again restricted the scoring to double choir, from which he selected various textures: four-part harmony expanding to eight full parts ("Ehre sei dem Vater"), antiphonal exchanges between the two choirs ("Kyrie" and "Ehre"), and eight-part imitation ("Heilig"). Throughout he set the text with one note per syllable, to render the declamation as clear as possible. Once again Felix envisioned his work as a cycle and thus placed all the pieces in related keys, centered on A major with three sharps, possibly a reference to the Holy Trinity. Arguably the most impressive setting is the "Heilig," impelled by a cascading series of thirds. Descending from the soprano, they complete a sequence beginning and ending on D, as the texture increases in density from one to eight voices. The effect is of suspended heavenly voices eventually "grounded" in a radiant major sonority (**ex. 16.3**). Along with the "Kyrie" and "Ehre sei Gott in der Höh," the "Heilig" was published separately in the 1850s, but not as part of a liturgical cycle.[28] Indeed, not until 1998 did all ten parts of the *Liturgie* appear in a collected edition that rescued this little-known gem from its unjustified oblivion.[29]

Ex. 16.3: Mendelssohn, *Die deutsche Liturgie* (1846), *Heilig*

I

For the new Gewandhaus season Felix and Gade again shared the twenty subscription concerts. By directing the first five odd-numbered and final five even-numbered concerts, Felix inaugurated and closed his last year at the Gewandhaus. His first two appearances (October 4 and 22) featured the pianists Louise Dulcken (Ferdinand David's sister) and Clara Schumann, who performed the Beethoven Fourth Piano Concerto and works by Chopin and her husband. Attending that evening was Ignaz Moscheles, recently established as "Head of the Department for Playing and Composition"[30] at the Conservatory. There were private entertainments and speeches in Moscheles's honor, and Felix arranged for his friend a recital by the best piano pupils of the school. The most important performance of this period was the highly anticipated premiere on November 5 of Schumann's Second Symphony, Op. 61, but the work's placement at the end of the program minimized its impact. When the audience demanded Felix first encore a rousing work heard earlier, Rossini's *William Tell* Overture, Schumann's symphonic fortunes suffered further. An oversatiated audience could not appreciate the majestic beauty of the new symphony, and its unusual chains of high string trills in the slow movement gave some listeners pause.[31]

To make amends, at an *Extra-Konzert* on November 16, Felix read the work a second time, when it appeared at the beginning of the program. Still, his relationship with Robert seems to have suffered a considerable strain. The details of this episode remain mysterious, but exacerbating it was an ugly, anti-Semitic report in the *Leipziger Tageblatt*, where Felix's encore of the Rossini was somehow taken as a "Mosaic" plot to undermine Robert's symphony.[32] Schumann's biographer Berthold Litzmann assures us Robert had nothing to do with the article, but the atmosphere was sufficiently poisoned to dampen Felix's enthusiasm for helping the moody composer.[33] Still, Robert's memoirs of Felix contain no reference to a falling out; Robert recorded their last meeting, a few months later on March 25, 1847, in Leipzig, without revealing the nature of their conversation.[34]

In mid-November 1846 Felix spent several days in Dresden visiting the art galleries with Cécile and her Frankfurt relatives. He may have entertained Frederick Augustus II at the Saxon court, but a special reason for the trip was to procure parts to J. S. Bach's monolithic Mass in B minor, so that Felix could correct his own error-ridden score of that masterpiece.[35] According to Eduard Devrient, Felix's Dresden friends were "struck by his excessive touchiness, which approached the quarrelsome testiness of his father." In particular, the political ferment of the day distressed him;

he "predicted evil of it from every one of its exaggerations, which were certainly numerous enough."[36] Though Felix did not live to see the eruption of revolution in March 1848, his apprehension betrays his political views during the prerevolutionary Vormärz. Like many educated German Bürger, he was a constitutional moderate, eager to see reform "effected by lawful authority,"[37] not by radical excesses.

While the post-Napoleonic Restoration enjoyed its final year of stability, the composer's family suffered a personal loss. The night of their return to Leipzig (November 22), Felix witnessed the death of his loyal servant Johann Krebs. To Devrient the composer related an especially affecting scene—how Krebs, in the final weeks of his illness, had insisted on managing the family's social events from his bedside and incessantly rang his bell to supervise subordinates in the finer details of dinner protocols. When a summoned doctor declined to treat a gravely ill servant, Felix insisted on care in his residence, for "to refuse him medical attendance was to refuse it to his household." After Krebs's death, Felix found among the deceased's papers his last will, in which Felix read: "I also ask Herr and Frau Doctor to forgive and pardon my faults, and thank you a thousand fold for all the goodness you have shown me. I wish you also much happiness and blessings for the children, and hope that some day we will meet again, where we are no longer separated."[38]

Shortly after returning to Leipzig, Felix took up revisions to *Elijah*. To Klingemann he reported satisfaction with the new, more "solemn" version of the widow's scene (No. 8), vindication for withholding the score until it could be "improved" no further.[39] In mid-December he visited Berlin for a week, and there played for Fanny parts of the oratorio;[40] he may also have shared with her his *Kinderstücke*, readied for publication but not released until late 1847 as Op. 72, the last opus Felix saw through the press. No doubt, too, at this last meeting with his sister he discussed her recent publications, issued by Bote & Bock by early December.

First to appear were Fanny's *Sechs Lieder* Op. 1 and *Vier Lieder für das Pianoforte* Op. 2. By April 1847 Bote & Bock also brought out six *Gartenlieder* Op. 3 for mixed chorus;[41] meanwhile, in January, their competitor Schlesinger released the first half of the *Six Mélodies pour le piano* Op. 4. In the final months of her life Fanny prepared three more works—for Schlesinger, the second installment of the *Six Mélodies* as Op. 5; for Bote & Bock, a second volume of *Vier Lieder für das Pianoforte* Op. 6, and the *Sechs Lieder* Op. 7—but they appeared between June and October 1847, after her death.[42] Felix had at his disposal advance exemplars of these publications; in February she sent him as a birthday present the *Gartenlieder*,[43] and around the same time he played her piano pieces, presumably including Op. 2, for Moscheles, who found them "treated in a genuine musical spirit," even if "close imitations" of Felix's *Lieder ohne Worte*.[44] But there is no evidence to suggest he offered her advice or read proof. What is more, her Op. 1 reached him during the closing months of 1846 through the "mediation" of Cécile, as Fanny explained, revealing that for all her artistic independence, she remained intimidated by her brother: "Why didn't I address my Lieder to you? In part I know why, in part I don't. I wanted to enlist Cécile as a go-between because I had a sort of guilty conscience toward you. To be sure, when I consider that ten years ago I thought it too late and now is the latest possible time, the situation seems rather ridiculous, as does my long-standing outrage at the idea of starting Op. 1 in my old age. But since you're so amenable to the project now, I also want to admit how terribly uppity I've been, and announce that six four-part Lieder [Op. 3], which you really don't know, are coming out next."[45]

For her "professional" debut in Op. 1 Fanny selected settings of Heine, Eichendorff, Goethe, and Geibel that displayed her clear melodic gifts and sensitivity to textual nuances. The most striking include two wistful Heine settings (Nos. 1 and 3), and the *Gondellied* (No. 6) of Geibel. All three share a $\frac{6}{8}$ meter and gently rocking, trochaic rhythms. The barcarolle-like *Schwanenlied* (No. 1, *Swan Song*) compares the course of love to a descending star, the deciduous leaves of an apple tree, and dulcet song of a swan plunging into a watery grave. The closing *Gondellied*, with its gently undulating arpeggiations and clandestine rendezvous, revisits a genre explored by Felix in his own *Gondellieder* with and without texts. *Warum sind denn die Rosen so blass?* (No. 3, "Why, then, are the roses so pale?"), composed in 1837 and copied in 1838 for Cécile's album,[46] explores the plight of an abandoned lover, expressed through images of pale flowers, a lark's lament, and the gravelike earth. Fanny emended one verse of Heine's poem she found too trenchant: "Why, then, does the scent of a corpse rise from the fragrant foliage?" became "Why, then, does the scent of withered flowers rise from the fragrant foliage?"[47] Despite this poetic sanitizing, her music captures the urgent questioning of Heine's poem by opening with a nagging, first-inversion dominant harmony and by delaying the establishment of the tonic key, A minor (**ex. 16.4**).

In her Opp. 2, 4, 5, and 6 piano pieces, the lyrical impulses of a songwriter again reign supreme. For all purposes these are *Lieder ohne Worte* that closely approach the exemplars of Fanny's brother, a feature not lost upon one of the early reviewers of her work.[48] Thus, Op. 6 No. 4 (*Il Saltarello Romano*) summarizes Fanny's impressions of Rome by recalling the piquant A-minor finale of Felix's *Italian* Symphony.[49] And in Op. 6 No. 3, Fanny appears to revive a phrase from his *Lied ohne Worte*, Op. 53 No. 4, though the allusion is distorted by the change of key (F to F♯)

Ex. 16.4: Fanny Hensel, "Warum sind denn die Rosen so blass," Op. 1 No. 4 (1846)

and meter ($\frac{9}{8}$ to $\frac{3}{4}$), and by a harmonic excursion that leads Fanny's passage to A♯ major (**ex. 16.5**). To her credit, the result shows not so much a crutchlike dependence upon her brother as an imaginative melodic spontaneity that increasingly diverges from Felix's style. As we have seen, Op. 2 No. 1, which begins as a solo Lied and then evolves into a duet, may have influenced Felix's Op. 62 No. 1 in the same key (see p. 470). No. 2 in B minor, originally conceived as *September (Am Flusse)* in *Das Jahr* but released in Op. 2 without extramusical headings, is a deeply felt, poignant composition that easily stands alongside Felix's best *Lieder ohne Worte* (see p. 426).

Ex. 16.5a: Mendelssohn, *Lied ohne Worte* in F major, Op. 53 No. 4 (1841)

Ex. 16.5b: Fanny Hensel, *Vier Lieder für das Pianoforte*, Op. 6 No. 3 (1847)

With the *Gartenlieder* Op. 3, Fanny symbolically moved from the "feminine" genres of domestic music making—the Lied and piano character piece—to the more masculine "open-air" part-song and thus vied with Felix's four popular volumes, Opp. 41, 48, 50, and 59. There is compelling evidence that she approached the new genre with an eye to publication and determined to make the part-songs "as good as possible."[50] Thus, between February and September 1846 she composed seventeen examples for mixed chorus, all rehearsed or performed at the Sunday musicales in the Gartenhaus—hence their title, *Gartenlieder*—of Leipzigerstrasse No. 3. After revising her work, she shaped six into the new opus and even made preliminary notations for a second, unfinished volume. Unlike Opp. 1 and 2, drawn from songs and piano pieces composed over a span of many years for private use, Op. 3 thus benefited from the start from the composer's critical editorial eye. The result is a cohesive sequence of six songs, organized by a cycle of predominantly sharp keys (B–e–A–D–a–A) that, like Felix's part-songs, celebrate nature and the open air through the poetry of Eichendorff and Uhland, among others. Though Fanny's songs undoubtedly lean heavily on Felix's stylistic "authority," they contain some well-turned phrases, including one from *Im Herbste* (*In Autumn*), Op. 3 No. 3, cited in a review published the very day of Fanny's death, May 14, 1847.[51] Here Uhland's poetic soul has a presentiment of spring songs, captured by Fanny in a rising, yearning sequence that moves from the minor to major mode (**ex. 16.6**).

Initially, the *Gartenlieder* enjoyed some success. In Dresden, Robert Schumann read them with a newly formed choral Verein in 1848, while in Bonn, Johanna Kinkel, who had attended some of Fanny's Berlin musicales, performed the opus with an amateur chorus.[52] The American hymnist William B. Bradbury, arriving in Leipzig late in 1847 to study with Moscheles, incorporated one of Fanny's part-songs into his anthology *The Alpine Glee Singer* (N.Y., 1850). And in England J. J. Ewer brought out five songs in the series *Orpheus: Collection of Glees of the Most Admired German Composers*.[53] The pieces were still available in Germany after 1871, although a curtain of silence descended soon thereafter on Fanny's music, not to be lifted until late in the twentieth century.

Ex. 16.6: Fanny Hensel, *Gartenlieder*, Op. 3 No. 3 (1847)

Ahn - est du,＿ O See - le wie - der sanf - te süs - se Früh - lings - lie - der?

II

Preoccupied at the close of 1846 with revising *Elijah*, Felix paid little attention to a parcel received that summer from an admirer of *St. Paul.* In July 1845 the young Belgian composer César Franck requested a critique of his Op. 1, three piano trios, of which the first contained a more or less clear allusion to the scherzo from Felix's own youthful Piano Quartet Op. 3. Oddly enough, the parcel disappeared in the mail for nearly a year, so that in June 1846 Franck wrote again. Only on December 22 did Felix reply in French, offering to meet and make music with Franck and "chat" (*causer*) about positive and negative features of his trios.[54] The meeting never took place, much to Franck's regret.

By the end of 1846, Felix had revised Part I of *Elijah* and was about to begin sending Simrock installments of the piano-vocal score. The new year brought increased urgency. Both Simrock and Edward Buxton (Ewer & Co.), Felix's English publisher, were concerned about pirated copies of the score, especially since *Elijah* had already been circulating in the public musical consciousness for months after the Birmingham premiere.[55] Moreover, Felix had acceded to the Sacred Harmonic Society's request to perform the revised version in April[56] and intended to oversee the second, London premiere himself. Thus began the familiar, obsessive process of revision—an interminable mixture of recasting, reorchestration, retouching of text, and wholesale recomposition. To prepare Buxton, who had already engraved the choral parts for Birmingham, Felix offered his apology: "I was sorry to see that you will have to make so many alterations in the choral parts; but I think I told you before, that I was subject to this dreadful disease of altering as long as I did not feel my conscience quite at rest, and therefore I could not help it, and you must bear it patiently."[57] When Moscheles, incredulous that Felix expended so much effort redesigning successful music, asked if *Elijah* was "to become still more beautiful," Felix merely replied, "Yes."[58]

On February 14 he could announce he had written the last note for the work;[59] yet, three days later, he was dispatching the "final" version of the widow scene (No. 8). This time, to "reconcile" Buxton "to the trouble you had for my and my alterations sake,"[60] Felix enclosed two additional manuscripts—a recently completed orchestration of the anthem *Hear My Prayer* for the Irish baritone Joseph Robinson, whom Felix had met during his last visit to London,[61] and an arrangement of the Overture to *Elijah* for piano duet.[62] The latter was a response to a special request of Buxton, shrewd businessman that he was, for a version of the overture with a concert ending to permit its separate sale. But after attempting unsuccessfully to divorce the overture from the elided opening chorus, Felix opted for the duet arrangement to be published in the vocal score, which at least rendered the fugue of the overture easier to realize at the keyboard.

With Bartholomew, Felix renewed the frenzied correspondence about the English translation; their exchanges again yielded significant musical alterations. Thus, at the end of the recitative No. 25, to represent Elijah's flight to the wilderness, Bartholomew suggested adding a short "instrumental interlude" before the prophet's aria of resignation, "It is enough, O Lord."[63] Felix added four Adagio bars for the orchestra. But then came a setback: in March, he learned that Joseph Staudigl would not be able to sing the bass solos. When Felix suggested postponing the performance until the fall, Bartholomew hurriedly replied, "I can tell you twenty reasons why *you should come*, and not one why *you should not come*."[64] Preparations continued apace; on March 18, Felix sent off the revised organ part for the oratorio and, early in April, the final missing piece—metronome markings for all the movements.[65]

Such a schedule would have taxed most musicians, yet Felix accomplished the revisions while carrying out his duties at the Conservatory and Gewandhaus. Thus, on January 10, he detailed a report about fifteen negligent students: Cécile's relative Alfred Jean Petitpierre from Neuchâtel rated only a mediocre appraisal ("very moderately diligent and comes irregularly"), while the Londoner Alfred Albert Suggate, faring somewhat better, avoided a *strenge Mahnung* ("sharp warning") for missing one of David's classes.[66] Felix's final appearances at the Gewandhaus began on January 14 with the twelfth concert, when he conducted his *Meeresstille und glückliche Fahrt* Overture. For the fourteenth (January 28), which featured the Czech virtuoso pianist Alexander Dreyschock, Felix accompanied the young Elise Vogel in Schubert Lieder and also performed Mozart's Symphony in G minor, K. 550, with a tempo, according to Moscheles, moderate enough that the chromatic modulations of the finale emerged "much more clearly than I have been accustomed to hear them."[67]

The sixteenth concert (February 11) culminated with the *Scottish* Symphony; then, with Gade, Felix shared a series of four historical concerts (February 18 and 25, March 11 and 18), interrupted by a royal summons from Dresden. On February 24 the minister Falkenstein had admonished Felix about his rare appearances in the Saxon capital; three days later, he was entertaining Frederick Augustus II with piano music, obtaining leave to direct *Elijah* in England in April, and discussing his concerns about Geibel's *Die Lorelei* with Eduard Devrient.[68] Meanwhile, in Leipzig the final four concerts explored a historical progression from J. S. Bach and Handel to Haydn and Mozart, to Beethoven and Weber, and on to modern times. Sparing little effort to program lesser-known works of eighteenth-century composers, Felix searched out for the second concert a symphony of C. P. E. Bach and orchestrated a trio from

Cimarosa's comic opera *Il matrimonio segreto* (1792).[69] But this time his historicizing efforts earned mixed reviews in a Leipzig on the threshold of the cataclysmic Revolution of 1848. If Franz Brendel ostensibly supported the return to "the old, healthy times," he effectively treated some of the compositions as museum curiosities. And an anonymous reviewer in the *Allgemeine musikalische Zeitung* went farther, criticizing the repertoire as beholden to the conservative past and present but neglecting the future. Thus the critic could only wonder why Marschner's formerly popular *Der Vampyr* (1827)—its overture was the final work Felix conducted in the Gewandhaus—had fallen from the operatic repertory, and why future-minded composers such as Berlioz were excluded.[70] If anything, Felix's performance of *Paulus* on Good Friday (April 2) at the Paulinerkirche ignored the reviewer's "progressive" agendum, though neither he nor his contemporaries could have imagined that its final chorus, resplendent with Bach, Handel, and the "old, healthy times," was Felix's very last public performance in Leipzig.

To summarize Felix's achievement at the Gewandhaus, W. A. Lampadius observed that he was "as great as a conductor, as he was as virtuoso and composer," and that he perfected "three gifts which are usually granted only singly to men." In an age when the role of the virtuoso conductor was taking shape and finding its definition, Felix's contributions were indeed of seminal importance:

> When once his fine, firm hand grasped the *bâton* the electric fire of Mendelssohn's nature seemed to stream out through it, and be felt at once by singers, orchestra, and audience. We often thought that the flames which streamed from the heads of Castor and Pollux must play around his forehead, and break from the conductor's staff which he held, to account for the wonderful manner with which he dissipated the slightest trace of phlegm in the singers or players under his direction. . . . As soon as he had given the first beat, his face lighted up, every feature was aflame, and the play of countenance was the best commentary on the piece. Often the spectator could anticipate from his face what was to come. The fortes and crescendos he accompanied with an energetic play of features and the most forcible action; while the decrescendos and pianos he used to modulate with a motion of both hands, till they slowly sank to almost perfect silence. . . . He had no patience with performers who did not keep good time. His wondrously accurate ear made him detect the least deviation from the correct tone, in the very largest number of singers and players. He not only heard it, but knew whence it came.[71]

III

Felix's correspondence from his last year betrays a markedly wistful quality as he struggled with issues of loss, imagined and real. As early as

October 1846, he disclosed to Jenny Lind his intention to leave Leipzig: "in two or three years, at the utmost, I think I shall have done my duty here, after which I should scarcely stay any longer. Perhaps I might prefer Berlin; perhaps, the Rhine; somewhere where it is very pretty, and where I could compose all day long, as much as I liked. But really, you would have to sing to me, sometimes."[72] For a brief moment, the parental home held a special appeal: when Gustav Dirichlet, concerned at the social unrest in Berlin, considered moving to Heidelberg, Felix urged his brother-in-law to remain. A change of residence could accomplish no more against the gathering political crisis than Felix's Gewandhaus concerts. Indeed, Felix now felt compelled to leave Leipzig, to "rejoin those with whom I enjoyed my childhood and youth, and whose memories and friendships and experiences are the same as my own." He desired to secure "one pleasant united household, such as we have not seen for long, and live happily together (independent of political life or *non-life*, which has swallowed up *all* else)."[73] And yet, a day trip to Berlin at the end of March burst the illusion of his idealized childhood home—to Droysen, Felix confessed how "almost each and every thing that in our day was fresh and young had disappeared, and was stultified, obsolete, and in decline!"[74]

In Leipzig he found other ways to preserve distant memories. For Klingemann, Felix made careful copies of the drawings from their Scottish sojourn of 1829.[75] And on February 3, 1847, he celebrated his last birthday with the Moscheles's and Cécile's relatives. Encircling the cake and its "candle of life" were thirty-seven tapers, to which Charlotte Moscheles attached comments reviewing Felix's life, "from the cradle to the piano and the conductor's desk; from his first attempt at composition to *Saint Paul, Elijah*,"[76] and the hoped-for opera. The principal entertainment was a theatrical representation of the word "Gewandhaus." First, a wig-adorned Joachim played a fantasy *à la* Paganini on the G (*Ge*) string. The Pyramis and Thisbe scene from *A Midsummer Night's Dream*, with the lovers communicating through a chink in a makeshift wall, represented *Wand* (wall). And to convey *Haus*, Charlotte Moscheles delivered a domestic soliloquy on "the foibles of female authoresses," interrupted by her husband impersonating a female cook. Then a children's symphony, directed by Felix's godson, Felix Moscheles, and performed on toy instruments, parodied the orchestra and reinforced musically the entire word.[77]

A much more serious distraction was the career of Jenny Lind, who naively had entered into conflicting engagements with two London opera impresarios. Early in 1845 Alfred Bunn, lessee of Drury Lane Theatre, had pursued Jenny to Berlin, where she was featured in Meyerbeer's *Ein Feldlager in Schlesien*. Between the acts of the opera, Bunn convinced her to sign a London engagement for the next season. Though the terms were generous, Jenny later reneged, partly because Bunn required her to sing Meyerbeer's opera in English, a language still unfamiliar to her. Then, in 1846, Benjamin Lumley, director of the Italian opera at the King's Theatre, saw the fortunes of his company decline when a succession of musicians, including the conductor Michael Costa, left to establish the Royal Italian Opera at Covent Garden. Lumley attempted to salvage the situation by engaging Jenny, and appealed for assistance to Felix, who encouraged her in October 1846 about the prospect of a London debut. No disinterested spectator, Felix had discussed with Lumley writing an opera for the King's Theatre and no doubt cherished the idea that Jenny would sing at its premiere. All Felix lacked was a suitable libretto; "in the meantime," he wrote, "I have music-paper and finely-nibbed pens lying on the table—and wait."[78]

Lumley rejoiced when the same month Jenny signed an exclusive agreement with his company. But now events took a legal turn. Foiling her attempt to win release from the earlier Drury Lane engagement, Bunn threatened an action for breach of contract. The soprano conceived "so inordinate a dread of Mr. Bunn's vengeance" that she remained on the Continent.[79] Felix's opera fell through as well. After initial discussions, he had provisionally settled on Shakespeare's *Tempest* as a subject, and the enterprising Lumley had persuaded the French dramatist Eugène Scribe to draft a libretto. Receiving it near mid-January 1847, Felix at first was favorably inclined: early in February he wrote Paul that the first half was quite promising.[80] But by February 21, the captious composer had decided not to compose Scribe's opera; the book was "too French," he later explained to Henry Chorley, and the third act "thoroughly bad."[81] An exasperated Lumley summed up the difficulty: "it was impossible to reconcile their peculiar idiosyncrasies. The German and French natures were in conflict. The more strictly logical and analytical spirit of the former seemed strangely hypercritical to the latter. The facile imagination of the Frenchman, however fertile in scenic resources . . . found no response in the less flexible tenets of the German."[82] Scribe's *féerie* inspired no suitable *Elfenton*.

Another factor helped trigger Felix's refusal. When Lumley prematurely announced the Scribe-Mendelssohn collaboration in the English papers, the publicity, far from encouraging Felix to compose the score, acted as a disincentive. First, Emanuel Geibel, engrossed with his own libretto for Felix, got wind of the proposed opera and, coolly asking for an explanation, suggested the composer return *Die Lorelei*.[83] Meanwhile, the *Morning Chronicle*, favorable to Covent Garden, challenged the legitimacy of Jenny's engagement to Lumley and denounced Felix's new opera as "a mere fabrication." Wondering whether instead of *The Tempest* the whole affair was "much ado about nothing," Felix asked Klingemann to clear up the confusion, but when new announcements of the opera appeared, the composer himself wrote in March to the *Morning Chronicle* and returned Scribe's libretto to Lumley, thus ending the "opera fuss."[84] By then Felix had resumed serious discussions with Geibel about *Die Lorelei*[85] and also rejected new libretti from the Bavarian writer Konrad Philipp Lattner.[86]

Somehow, in the midst of this confusion, Felix left for London with Joachim on April 8, 1847. In the composer's baggage were the revised score of *Elijah* and also a setting of the *Jubilate Deo* (Psalm 100) for four-part choir and organ, completed just days before, on April 5[87]—apparently with some difficulty (on the margins of the draft manuscript Felix toyed with an unrelated canon to the Virgilian moral *per aspera ad astra*). The *Jubilate Deo* complemented Felix's old setting of the *Te Deum* (1832)— originally written for Novello but issued by Edward Buxton's firm, Ewer & Co., in 1846—and thus completed the Anglican Morning Service. Buxton had requested the new composition in January 1847,[88] and in the hurried days before he left Leipzig Felix was able to comply. But Buxton's additional request for the Evening Service would remain unfulfilled until Felix's return from England.

While Felix was in transit to London, some six hundred members of the Prussian *Landtag* (United Diet) were assembling in Berlin from the provinces at the behest of Frederick William IV. Privately the king regarded the convocation as a grudging concession to "the principles of popular representation, which have laid hold of so many states and ruined them since the French Revolution";[89] he had no intention of granting the Diet legislative powers, let alone a popular constitution. And so the king severely curtailed the Diet's authority and called out the military to quell food riots that erupted in Berlin in April. Fanny, whose last portrait was drawn by her husband during the final months of her life (**plate 18**), silently joined her voice in her diary to that of the growing opposition; "Now politics will for a time take the lead," she noted, "and absorb all other interests."[90] But at Leipzigerstrasse No. 3, sequestered from the unrest, she continued her Sunday musicales and on April 11, the opening day of the Diet, premiered her last major work, the Piano Trio in D minor, written for Rebecka's birthday.

Following the *Gartenlieder*, and published posthumously in 1850 as Op. 11, the trio represented for Fanny another step toward the larger musical forms and the public world of her brother. Its key, D minor, inevitably prompts comparisons with Felix's Piano Trio in D minor, Op. 49; indeed, Fanny's first theme, asserted by the violin and cello against a

Ex. 16.7: Fanny Hensel, Piano Trio in D minor, Op. 11 (1847), First Movement

piano accompaniment, begins with the same upbeat figure (see **ex. 16.7**), but the effect differs markedly: Felix's subdued melancholy yields to an explosive, passionate opening, with a turbulent undercurrent in the piano. For the second theme, later recycled in the finale, Fanny offers a more lyrical gesture, preparing us for the two, connected inner movements, in which she retreats into her familiar, private world of the Lied. Thus the Andante begins with a *Lied-ohne-Worte*-like piano solo, answered by a duet for the strings. The third movement (*Allegretto*), actually titled *Lied*, strengthens the reference to vocal models by seemingly alluding to Obadiah's aria in *Elijah*, "If with all your hearts ye truly seek me" (**ex. 16. 8**).[91] The finale then begins with a cadenza-like improvisation that restores the D minor of the first movement and gradually articulates a new, noble theme enveloped by lush arpeggiations. Through the course of the movement a second, rhythmically distinct subject alternates with

Ex. 16.8a: Fanny Hensel, Piano Trio in D minor, Op. 11 (1847), *Allegretto*

Ex. 16.8b: Mendelssohn, *Elijah*, Op. 70 (1846), No. 4

the first before the recall of the second theme from the opening movement. This conceit ties the whole together and clarifies its underlying cyclical progression, in which the outer, extroverted movements are balanced by the more intimate inner movements. The music exudes an irrepressible spontaneity and harmonic freshness that begin to suggest what she could have achieved as a professional composer. Clara Schumann, for one, was impressed enough to plan to dedicate her own piano trio to Fanny, who died before she could receive this honor.[92]

IV

A wearied Felix arrived in London on April 12. His former pupil Rockstro was startled by his "worn look, quite foreign to his usual expression—a look of pain"[93] and concluded the composer was working himself to death. On the 16th Felix met the soloists, Charlotte Ann Birch, Helen Dolby, Henry Phillips, and Charles Lockey, and rehearsed in Exeter Hall with performing forces, according to Phillips, of some five hundred.[94] The performance two days later, attended by the Duke and Duchess of Cambridge, inspired a full-column article in the *Times*, though it labeled the ensemble an "unfinished and clumsy exhibition" inferior to the Birmingham premiere. The reviewer, probably Davison, attributed the deficiency to the lack of sufficient rehearsal; the superfluous custom of the "leader," George Perry, of beating time with his "fiddlestick, in such a manner as to obstruct the views of the conductor"; and the amateur status of many of the musicians. Though membership in the Sacred Harmonic Society entitled them to participate, their "worthy" efforts threw "a kind of fogginess over the general effect" of *Elijah*.[95]

There now ensued an unrelenting schedule through the end of April, with Felix conducting five more performances of the oratorio in three cities. On April 20, he was in Manchester to introduce *Elijah* with the Hargreaves Choral Society at the Free Trade Hall;[96] on April 27, in Birmingham to conduct the work at a benefit concert for the chorus master James Stimpson, for which Felix accepted no fee. On the 23rd came the second performance at Exeter Hall, prefaced by the national anthem, since Queen Victoria and Prince Albert were in attendance. This time the results were far more satisfying; indeed, although the royal presence normally obviated encores, etiquette was ignored to allow the repetition of three numbers ("Baal, we cry to thee," "Lift thine eyes to the mountains," and "O rest in the Lord"); many other pieces "would have been encored, had it not been for respect to the Queen."[97] The next day Prince Albert penned in his program book an appreciative note in German, validating the "Noble Artist who, surrounded by the Baal-worship of debased art, has been able, by his genius and science, to preserve faithfully, like another Elijah, the worship of true art."[98] In the days before Felix received this royal tribute on May 8, the Sacred Harmonic Society secured a facsimile copy, lithographed and widely circulated after his death. Of the two final performances of *Elijah* on April 28 and 30 in an Exeter Hall "crowded to suffocation," the second aroused great excitement when Staudigl, bass soloist in Birmingham, did agree to sing. Perhaps this was the performance the young Mary Ann Evans—later canonized as George Eliot—described as a "glorious production," a "sacramental purification of Exeter Hall, and a proclamation of indulgence for all that is to be perpetrated there during this month of May,"[99] an allusion to the boisterous annual meetings of the Church of England Missionary Society that soon followed.

Felix's final performance at the Philharmonic Society, on April 26, was again graced by the presence of the Queen and Prince Albert, and heard by Jenny Lind, who, to the composer's delight, had arrived in London nine days before. During the concert he played Beethoven's Fourth Piano Concerto and directed the *Scottish* Symphony and selections from the *Midsummer Night's Dream* music. As in 1844 and on other occasions, he executed the concerto from memory and crafted his own cadenzas, "displays of extemporaneous invention and mechanical facility that would have astonished Thalberg, Leopold de Meyer, or Madame Pleyel herself."[100] Felix's conducting prompted comparisons with that of the new Philharmonic director, Michael Costa, who presided over the first part of the concert. If the Italian led like an "admirable" though soulless metronome, Felix made the orchestra "express all the modifications of feeling that an imaginative soloist would give a tongue to on a single instrument." Still, the *Times* reported that in the Wedding March the brass "sinned on the side of coarse obstreperousness," though Felix's position in English musical life was unambiguous: he was "the greatest musician of his time—one upon whose shoulders the mantle of Beethoven has descended, and who wears it worthily." And *Elijah*, composed by Felix at the zenith of his fame, had "no parallel but in the greatest monuments of art."

Through the first week of May Felix lingered in London and kept a full social calendar. Presumably around this time he met the nine-year-old boy William Beatty-Kingston, who played a Bach Prelude and Fugue for the composer and then listened in astonishment as Felix improvised twenty variations on "The Blue Bells of Scotland." Among the various "amazing feats" were two treatments of the theme in canon, two different harmonizations in the minor mode, a left-hand etude-like variation in the style of Chopin, a four-part fugue with the inversion of the melody, a chorale and free cadenza in which Felix "notoriously delighted to 'let himself go,'" and culminating march.[101] On April 30 Felix joined the Baroness Bunsen, wife of the Prussian ambassador, for lunch and performed Lieder; on May 5 and 6 the Bunsens hosted at the embassy two musical gatherings, attended by London high society and the future prime minister, Gladstone, at which Felix also performed.[102] On May 1 he spent an hour alone with Victoria and Albert in Buckingham Palace; Felix played some new compositions, with "that indescribably beautiful touch of his," and the Queen sang three of his songs. The new offerings apparently included parts of *Die Lorelei* and a third oratorio, about which Felix was already ruminating, as Victoria's journal reveals: "For some time he has been engaged in composing an Opera & an Oratorio, but has lost courage about them. The subject for his Opera is a Rhine Legend & that for the Oratorio, a very beautiful one depicting Earth, Hell, & Heaven, & he played one of the Choruses out of this to us, which was very fine. . . ."[103] When the Queen offered in exchange to fulfill a wish, Felix asked to see the "Royal children in their Royal nurseries," and, personally escorted by Victoria, discussed with her "homely subjects that had a special attraction for both."[104]

On May 4 the Beethoven Quartet Society gave another concert in Felix's honor. He delighted his listeners with a memorized rendition of Beethoven's 32 Variations in C minor, though the other repertoire was drawn from Felix's works, including one of his piano trios, the String Quartet, Op. 44 No. 1, and Octet, in which Alfredo Piatti took up a cello part. Possibly at this time Felix shared with Piatti the first movement of a new cello concerto sketched or composed for the Italian sometime after the two met in 1844.[105] Source material for this work has yet to materialize; in Piatti's estimation, it "did not come up to the violin concerto by a long way."[106] After the Quartet Society concert Felix joined the throngs of

Londoners crowding into Her Majesty's Theatre to hear the London debut of Jenny Lind, who triumphed in Meyerbeer's *Robert le diable* as Alice, a "fine histrionic study," the *Times* reported, "of which every feature is equally good."[107]

Before leaving England, Felix enjoyed another meeting with the Prince Consort. On May 5, at a Concert of Ancient Music organized by Albert for the Hanover Square Rooms, Felix improvised and performed a Bach organ prelude and fugue on an instrument, according to Anna Joanna Alexander, that "seemed a little loathe to do so at first"[108] (more blunt, the *Times* noted that Felix "had to wrestle with the inconvenience of an organ that may reasonably be pronounced one of the worst in the metropolis"[109]). The next day, Felix made a four-hand arrangement of the *Lied ohne Worte* in B♭ major, Op. 85 No. 6, which he sent to Albert with a note of appreciation on May 8, the day of his departure.[110] When a friend regretted Felix could not extend his stay, the exhausted composer replied, "One more week of this unremitting fatigue, and I should be killed outright!"[111] That evening he left the city with Klingemann, who accompanied him across the Channel before bidding farewell in Ostende.

V

English-speaking realms early on identified *Elijah* as Felix's principal masterpiece and, indeed, emblematic of Mendelssohnism. The English embrace of the work—long a staple of oratorio societies, it stood only behind *Messiah* in popularity—is not difficult to explain. Unlike *St. Paul*, written for the Lower Rhine Musical Festival, *Elijah* was designed for Birmingham and English tastes. In contrast to the cumbersome translation thrust upon *St. Paul*, *Elijah* benefited from Bartholomew's expert paraphrase of the German libretto, meticulously polished in collaboration with the composer. And the linkage of the revised version with Victoria and Albert—and with Albert's pronouncement of Felix as a second Elijah—bolstered the composition's claim as a Victorian masterpiece. But in the end, the heightened status was a two-edged sword. If in 1847 H. F. Chorley asserted, "*Elijah* is not only *the* sacred work of our time, ... but it is a work 'for our children and for our children's children,'" by the 1880s George Bernard Shaw was decrying Felix's "despicable oratorio mongering,"[112] and reversing Albert's metaphor—Felix was no longer a courageous prophet contending with musical Baalism, but a sanctimonious musician exuding a "kid glove gentility" that concealed a flawed Victorian culture. In the critical tradition *Elijah* has thus traversed, pendulum-like, the vast, uneven terrain between these extremes.

In many ways though, the oratorio was the crowning achievement of Felix's career. Standing upon the shoulders of *St. Paul*, *Elijah* reflects Felix's lifelong love of Handel and Bach through a historicism now blended subtly into the composer's mature style. Thus, in comparison to *St. Paul*, we find a reduction of Bachian counterpoint—of forty-two numbers only a handful of fugues (principally to anchor the work at its endpoints), fugal passages, and chorales. Felix himself identified No. 15, "Cast thy burden upon the Lord," as the "only specimen of a Lutheran Chorale in this old-testamential work."[113] In addition, unlike *St. Paul*, *Elijah* does not employ the traditional narrator to advance the action; rather, the principal characters serve this purpose, lending the oratorio the dramatic immediacy of opera and partially fulfilling Felix's lifelong quest to achieve a large-scale dramatic conception. (His efforts failed to convince the Mozart biographer Otto Jahn, who maintained the inviolability of the oratorio as an intrinsically epic, not dramatic genre.[114])

A survey of Part 1 illustrates the dramatic nature of the oratorio, which unfolds as a series of scenes framed and supported by reflective choruses. At the outset, Elijah solemnly appears in a recitative to pronounce the seven-year drought and introduces two motives, melodically and harmonically active throughout the oratorio[115]: a consonant, rising triadic figure (D–F–A–D), associated with the prophet as servant of the Lord, and a series of grating, descending tritones (C–F♯, G–C♯, D–G♯), symbolizing the curse (ex. 16.9). The subsequent overture expresses the time of tribulation through a fugue, the fanlike subject of which contains a tritone (ex. 16.10). Intensified by a shift to faster rhythms and use of mirror inversion, the overture spills over into the opening chorus, designed as a vocal fugue on the lamenting text from Jeremiah, "The harvest now is over, the summer days are gone, and yet no power cometh to help us!" In response to Obadiah's consoling aria (No. 4),

Ex. 16.9a: Mendelssohn, *Elijah*, Op. 70 (1846), *Einleitung*

Ex. 16.9b: Mendelssohn, *Elijah*, Op. 70 (1846), *Einleitung*

Ex. 16.10: Mendelssohn, *Elijah*, Op. 70 (1846), Overture

which shifts the tonal center to E♭ major, the agitated following chorus initially recalls the curse motive but then gives way to a consoling passage for "His mercies on thousands fall." Connecting the two parts of No. 5 is a short section in chorale style, presaging the later use of a chorale in No. 15. The next complex of movements (Nos. 6–9) introduces Elijah and the widow. After the prophet appeals three times to the Lord, the widow's lifeless son miraculously revives. Framing this scene are two choruses drawn from psalm verses to represent angelic hosts. No. 7, "For he shall give his angels charge over thee," is a re-scoring of the 1844 a cappella chorus composed after the assassination attempt on Frederick William IV. No. 9, "Blessed are the men who fear Him," recalls with clear points of imitation and acclamations "For unto us a Child is born" of Handel's *Messiah*, in the same key of G major.

At the midpoint of Part 1 (No. 10) Felix revives the opening of the Introduction, now transposed a step above to E♭ major, to mark the passage of three years, after which Elijah decides to confront Ahab and the priests of Baal. The prophet challenges them to slay a bullock and invoke their deities to light a sacrificial fire. When their pleas in successively higher keys and faster tempi fail (Nos. 11–13), Elijah addresses the "Lord God of Abraham, Isaac, and Israel" in a soothing aria in E♭ major (No. 14), joined to the chorale "Cast thy burden upon the Lord" (No. 15). The fire appears in No. 16, a powerful chorus that ends in another chorale-like passage, in which the people recognize the Lord; the energetic flames, symbolized by broken arpeggiations in the strings, then carry over to Elijah's aria (No. 17), "Is not His word like a fire?" It remains for the prophet to lift the drought, accomplished dramatically in No. 19, with Elijah's implorations to the Lord set against terse reports of a soprano, who looks out to the sea for signs of rain. When the inundation finally arrives, the chorus erupts into No. 20 ("Thanks be to God! He laveth the thirsty land!"), which brings Part 1 to its triumphant close in E♭ major. Animating much of this chorus are wavelike arpeggiations in the strings, but the music begins with a majestic rising triad, another reference to the opening measures of the work, and a final unifying gesture.

The second part similarly features several dramatic scenes in the prophet's life: his confrontation with Ahab and Jezebel (Nos. 23–24), flight to the wilderness (25–29), journey to Mt. Horeb and encounter with the Lord (30–36), and ascension to heaven (38–40). The final two numbers

Ex. 16.11a: Mendelssohn, *Elijah*, Op. 70 (1846), No. 4

Ex. 16.11b: Handel, *Messiah*, No. 53 (1742)

Ex. 16.11c: Mendelssohn, *Elijah*, Op. 70 (1846), No. 42

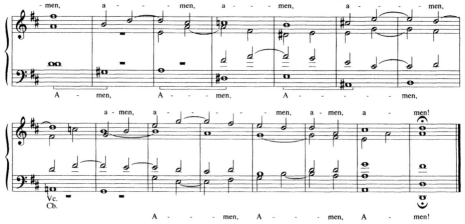

(41–42) form an epilogue linking Elijah through texts from Isaiah to the coming of the Messiah. That Felix expected his English audience to discover in the conclusion a Christian message of salvation is evident in the music of the ultimate chorus—a majestic fugue in D major on a subject derived from the final "Amen" fugue of Handel's *Messiah* (ex. 16.11a–b).[116] But the closing bars offer something else—the resolution of the curse motive, presented near the final cadence in the bass (ex. 16.11c). Examination of the fugal subject shows too how the clashing, descending tritones are now replaced by a sequence of ascending perfect fourths, a consonant motive that gradually has gained currency in the second part. A sequence of fourths appears first at the close of the chorus No. 22, and in No. 37, the pastoral aria Elijah sings after the passing by of the

Ex. 16.12a: Mendelssohn, *Elijah*, Op. 70 (1846), No. 22

Ex. 16.12b: Mendelssohn, *Elijah*, Op. 70 (1846), No. 37

Lord ("For the mountains shall depart"), the fourths appear in a bass line initially reminiscent of a baroque chaconne. In both examples (ex. 16.12) the fourths preserve the downward spiral of the original curse motive, but in the culminating fugue, to reinforce the image of the "fiery chariot" that takes Elijah "away to heaven," the fourths ascend.

Like *St. Paul*, *Elijah* raises critical issues that touch on Felix's own spiritual identity. His choice of an Old Testament subject sometimes has been viewed as a late-in-life reaffirmation of his Judaic roots and has encouraged some to search for signs of "Jewishness" in the music. Thus, in 1956 Jack Werner labeled a descending minor triad in Felix's music a "Mendelssohnian cadence."[117] Werner traced the figure in a variety of compositions, including the *Variations sérieuses*, *Lieder ohne Worte* and part-songs, *Antigone*, and two movements of *Elijah*, where it concludes the chorus "Lord, bow Thine ear" (No. 2) and Elijah's aria "It is enough" (No. 26). To Werner's ear, the figure resembled a cadence sung during Passover, when the congregation receives a blessing of verses from Numbers (6:24–25). Werner assumed that before converting to Christianity, the boy Felix had accompanied his parents to a synagogue service and been impressed by the "plaintive oriental chanting." Furthermore, Werner believed the musical examples adduced established beyond doubt the influence of the composer's "Jewish origin and of traditional synagogue music on Mendelssohn." But there is no evidence young Felix ever attended a synagogue, or that he construed the descending minor triad, common enough in nineteenth-century music, as Jewish.

In 1963 Eric Werner argued that the chantlike opening of No. 34, "Behold, God the Lord passed by," which Ferdinand Hiller claimed was

Ex. 16.13a: Melody of Thirteen Divine Attributes

A - DO - NAI,　A - DO - NAI,　EL　-　RA - CHUM　VE　-　HA-NUN, etc.

Ex. 16.13b: Mendelssohn, *Elijah*, Op. 70 (1846), No. 34

Der　Herr　ging　vor - ü　-　-　-　ber!
Be - hold,　God　the　Lord　pas - sed　by!

the original inspiration for the oratorio, recalled a "variant of the melody to which the 13 Divine Attributes (Exodus 24:6–7) have been sung since the fifteenth century in all German synagogues on the High Holy Days."[118] Indeed, similarities between the two led Werner to suppose the old melody "must have impressed itself upon the boy and associated itself with the representation of the Divine." In this case the resemblance (**ex. 16.13**) is perhaps striking enough to suggest that Felix, in depicting Elijah's journey to Mt. Horeb, sought to capture musically the idea of the old Mosaic covenant and somehow (through Joseph Mendelssohn or other relatives who professed Judaism?) had access to the melody.

But if Felix pursued here a "purely historical," Jewish perspective,[119] thorny problems still remain for the oratorio's exegesis. He did not follow strictly the account of the Old Testament prophet in 1 and 2 Kings but selected certain episodes, loosely strung together with devotional, biblical texts, and culminating with pre-Messianic texts from Isaiah. (Thus, he ignored Elijah's disciple Elisha, who received a double portion of the prophet's spirit upon his ascension to heaven, and instead effectively turned Obadiah into a servant of Elijah.)

The result, for Eric Werner, was a "weak potpourri of religious fanaticism and sanctimonious preacher's piety whereby both elements are torn out of their respective contexts." It did not matter whether the theological standpoint was Jewish or Christian; the libretto was "not only insultingly naïve, but really untenable."[120] An alternate reading, at which Otto Jahn hinted as early as 1848, may extricate us from this difficulty. For Jahn, *Elijah* explored a territory that "is rendered symbolic by its preparation for Christianity. . . . This symbolic element in the Old Testament, as a subject for Christian contemplation, is found through *Elijah*. . . ."[121]

In a careful analysis based upon the drafts of Felix's libretto, Jeffrey Sposato has extended Jahn's comments through a Christological interpretation of *Elijah*, not limited to the epilogue but embracing the whole.[122] For Sposato, Felix utilized the precedent of Handel's *Messiah*, in which a series of Old Testament prophecies reminded listeners of their "fulfill-ment in the Gospels." When a Christological perspective is applied to *Elijah*, Werner's criticisms of the libretto "begin to fall away, and the work takes on a new coherence—one more concerned with the long-term impli-cation of events, than with their historical accuracy."[123] Sposato argues that Felix shaped the libretto to underscore parallels between Elijah and Christ, in part to heed Schubring's advice that Elijah helped to "transform the Old into the New Covenant."[124] Thus, Obadiah's call to the people to "re-turn to God" (No. 3, Joel 2) finds its New Testament counterpart in John the Baptist's call to repentance; Elijah's raising of the widow's son (No. 8), Jesus's similar miracle in Luke 7: 1–15; Queen Jezebel's plot to kill Elijah (Nos. 23–24), the Pharisees' plot to kill Jesus; Elijah's journey to the wilderness (Nos. 25–29), Jesus's prayer vigil at Gethsemane; Elijah's encounter with the Lord at Mt. Horeb (No. 34), Jesus's Transfiguration; and Elijah's ascension (No. 38), Jesus's ascension.

We may find some support for Sposato's interpretation in Felix's re-vealing comment to Bartholomew about No. 15, the free-standing chorale heard just before Elijah calls upon fire to descend from heaven to answer the Baalites' vain entreaties. "I *wanted* to have the *color* of a Chorale," Felix wrote, "and I felt that I could not do *without it*, and yet I did not like to have *a* Chorale."[125] His solution was to adapt the hymn *O Gott, du frommer Gott*, from the Meiningen *Gesangbuch* of 1693 and fit to it verses from four different psalms (**ex. 16.14**).[126] The first (Psalm 55:22) Bartholomew quoted as "Cast thy burden upon the Lord, and He shall sustain thee." The result was a melody that sounded familiar but adopted its own shape and text, and thus occupied middle ground between an established Protestant cho-rale and a freely composed melody. It suggested the *color* of a chorale, without being *a* chorale. Elsewhere, too, in the oratorio Felix inserted hymnlike passages, as in Nos. 5 ("For He, the Lord our God, He is a jealous God") and 16 ("The Lord is God: O Israel hear!"), where freely composed chorale phrases abruptly appear in the middle of two choruses, as if to interpret the Old Testament drama through the lens of Christianity and, indeed, adumbrate the trappings of modern Protestant worship.

Ex. 16.14: Mendelssohn, *Elijah*, Op. 70 (1846), No. 15

In the plaintive aria No. 26, sung by Elijah in Part 2 after his flight to
the wilderness, Felix made special efforts to advance a Christological reading. Though he could have related Elijah's words from 1 Kings 19, "It is
enough, O Lord, now take my life, for I am not better than my fathers,"
to Moses's lament in Numbers 11, instead Felix designed the aria to fore-
shadow Christ's final words in John (19:30), "It is finished," and the references linking the crucified Christ to Elijah in Matthew (27:47) and Mark
(15:35, 36). To clarify this reading, Felix modeled the aria on "Es ist vollbracht" from Bach's St. John Passion (No. 58), a similarity occasionally
noticed in the literature but not examined until 1986 by the German scholar
Martin Staehelin.[127] The resemblances are indeed striking. Preceding both
arias are recitatives with two soloists, Obadiah and Elijah in the oratorio, the narrator and Jesus in the Passion. Both arias are scored for strings
with a solo line in the lower register (cellos in "Es ist genug," viola da
gamba in "Es ist vollbracht"), both arias fall into a ternary ABA form in
which an opening Adagio yields to a contrasting middle section in a
faster tempo, and both arias begin with a descending melodic line spanning a sixth (ex. 16.15). Staehelin interpreted Felix's aria as evidence of
his desire to give the Old Testament prophet a "New Testament coloration," and to bolster "Elijah–Christ correspondences." And to clinch the
argument, Staehelin demonstrated that Felix was familiar with a series
of popular lectures by the preacher F. W. Krummacher, *Elijah the Tishbite*,
where Felix would have found a comparison between Elijah's juniper
bush in the wilderness and the Cross, a "juniper covered with thorns
and barbs that pierce the soul."[128]

Ex. 16.15a: Mendelssohn, *Elijah*, Op. 70 (1846), No. 26

Ex. 16.15b: J. S. Bach, St. John Passion (1724), "Es ist vollbracht"

In 1848 Otto Jahn noted that at the time of *Elijah* Felix was already working on a third oratorio, *Christus*, unfinished at his death; Jahn speculated the two were to form a "complementary whole, so that in a certain sense the prophet of the Old Testament was to precede Christ."[129] Almost surely the oratorio fragments, published in 1852 as Op. 97, were what remained of Felix's collaboration with Gollmick on a work titled *Erde, Himmel und Hölle* (*Earth, Heaven, and Hell*, see p. 391), parts of which Felix played for Queen Victoria in May 1847. Because the thirteen surviving movements—a trio, several recitatives and choruses, and a chorale setting—treat the birth and Passion of Christ, Paul Mendelssohn Bartholdy, who examined the untitled autograph in Leipzig after his brother's death, labeled it *Christus*, the title that has come down to us. But more likely, the fragments belonged to the *Erde* segment and were to precede a second and third for Christ's Resurrection and the Last Judgment.[130]

Though we risk over interpreting what remains a torso, Felix's selection and treatment of the biblical texts suggest he was designing the new oratorio to complement *Elijah*. Perhaps the most compelling evidence occurs in the chorus "Es wird ein Stern aus Jakob aufgeh'n," in a radiant E♭ major that recalls the prominence of that tonality in the first part of *Elijah* (ex. 16.16a). The opening text, Numbers 24 ("A star shall come out of Jacob"), can be understood to prophesy the rise of King David but also to refer to the Messiah and, in a Christological sense, the star of Bethlehem. Felix clarifies the last interpretation in the closing portion of the chorus, where he introduces a chorale, at first a cappella and then

Ex. 16.16a: Mendelssohn, *Christus*, Op. 97 (1847), "Es wird ein Stern"

Ex. 16.16b: Mendelssohn, *Christus*, Op. 97 (1847), "Es wird ein Stern"

supported by the orchestra, to promote a Protestant reading of the text. Unlike *Elijah*, the chorale that intrudes here is no altered or freely composed melody but Philipp Nicolai's famous 1599 hymn, *Wie schön leuchtet der Morgenstern* ("How brightly gleams the morning star," ex. **16.16b**), which in a cantata of 1725 J. S. Bach had associated with the Annunciation. Felix thus employed the shared image of the star, captured in shimmering string tremolos, to link the Old and New Testaments.

With the movements devoted to Christ's Passion, Felix employed the traditional narrator and discordant choral *turba* scenes and thus reverted to the style of *St. Paul* and its models, the Bach Passions. But here again, Felix's treatment of the scriptures is revelatory: Sposato has suggested that Felix removed references to the Jews in passages from Luke and John, apparently to "reduce the oratorio's anti-Jewish content." Instead, Felix may have designed this portion of the work to uphold the "Lutheran tradition of universal blame for sin." The final movement is a setting of the chorale *O Welt, sieh' hier dein Leben*, set by J. S. Bach in the St. Matthew Passion, as a sobering reflection on Christ's disclosure that one of the apostles would betray him. While Bach set the fourth and fifth verses, Felix chose the sixth ("He takes upon his back the burdens that oppress me"), according to Sposato, to "convey the same sense of universal guilt."[131]

What are we to make of Felix's pairing, in the last year of his life, of *Elijah* and *Christus*, the Old and New Testaments, the faith of his grandfather and his own professed Christianity? The conclusion, developed by Sposato in the epilogue of his study, is that Felix's attitude toward the oratorio—traced from his revival of the St. Matthew Passion in 1829, through the libretto drafted for A. B. Marx's *Mose* in 1833, and the three oratorios of 1836, 1846, and 1847—shifted during his career as he struggled with issues of his Jewish ancestry and adopted Christian faith. If *St. Paul*, with its depiction of the Jews as a "stiff-necked people" resisting the Holy Spirit (Acts 7:51), proclaimed (with Abraham's encouragement) Felix's avowed Protestantism, *Elijah* and *Christus* explored areas of reconciliation by embracing what Sposato terms a "strategy of dual perspective." Thus, for all its Christological imagery and ending oriented toward the New Testament (the tenor aria No. 39, sung after Elijah's ascension, cites verses from the parable of the weeds in Matthew 13), *Elijah* was performed in 1937 in a Berlin synagogue, whose members, Leon Botstein has observed, "believed they were hearing a Jewish work written by a German Jew affirming the greatness of Judaism."[132] Though all evidence suggests Felix was a sincere, devout Protestant, in the eyes of his contemporaries at some level a "Jewish identity had been etched indelibly into his being, character, and life."[133] By forging links in *Elijah* between that identity and an adopted Lutheran worldview, Felix in a way continued the project of assimilation advanced by his grandfather Moses, which had "focused on the compatibilities between religion and eighteenth-century rationalism."[134] In a sense, then, the dual perspective emerging in *Elijah* completed Felix's life's work.

VI

Felix's final return to German soil did not begin auspiciously. On the Belgian border, authorities detained him after mistaking him for his cousin Arnold Mendelssohn (son of Nathan Mendelssohn), wanted for a petty theft in a scandal of the Count and Countess of Hatzfeld.[135] In Frankfurt on May 12, the exhausted Felix began to contemplate a much-needed rest in Switzerland. Meanwhile in Berlin, Fanny composed on May 13 her last work, the Lied *Bergeslust*, on verses of Eichendorff destined to generate her epitaph—incredibly, its concluding line reads "Thoughts and songs are heaven bound" (*Gedanken geh'n und Lieder bis in das Himmelreich*).

The next day she began a rehearsal of Felix's *Erste Walpurgisnacht*, scheduled for a Sunday musicale two days later. But in the opening chorus, her hands lost sensation, a symptom she had experienced before. After washing them with warm vinegar and recommencing the rehearsal, she suffered a more serious reverse; "It is probably a stroke," she commented, "just like mother." When Paul arrived forty-five minutes later, she was already unconscious and died several hours later, at 11:00 P.M. on May 14.[136] On Sunday Fanny's flower-adorned coffin replaced the piano in an eerily quiet Gartensaal. Wilhelm struggled to sketch the scene and, according to his son, Sebastian, "never painted anything worth having during the fifteen years that he survived her."[137] On Monday, she was interred in the cemetery of Trinity Church, not far from her parents; among the mourners was Giacomo Meyerbeer.[138] The following day, May 18, a memorial service was held in the Singakademie, and an obituary appeared in the *Vossische Zeitung*, where Ludwig Rellstab eulogized her for having attained a level of artistic cultivation of which few professional musicians could boast.[139] The same day, Felix learned in Frankfurt of his sister's death through a brother of Paul's wife, who relayed the tragic news; shrieking, the composer fell fainting to the ground.

He had lost his Minerva, his Thomaskantor with the dark eyebrows; "if the sight of my handwriting checks your tears, put the letter away," he wrote Wilhelm, "for we have nothing left now but to weep from our inmost hearts."[140] Unable to bear a journey to Berlin and uncertain how to take up his newly saddened life, Felix sought refuge with his family and by the end of the month had escaped to the resort of Baden-Baden in the Black Forest, where Paul's family joined them. Initially, Felix could do little more than draw, but on June 12 and 13, he was able to complete the two canticles for the Anglican Evensong, the *Magnificat* and *Nunc dimittis*.[141] A few days later his party departed for Switzerland; at Schaffhausen, where they waited for Wilhelm, Felix worked on three watercolors of the famous *Rheinfall*. Its churning cataracts mirrored the torment within his soul.[142]

Through July and August Felix rested in Switzerland and centered his activities in Interlaken, site of happy memories once shared with Fanny and his parents. With Paul, Felix enjoyed the "*old* familiar mountain-summits, which look as hoary as five or twenty-five years ago, and on which Time makes little impression!"[143] He sublimated his grief through a remarkable series of watercolor landscapes "such as no artist need have been ashamed to own." Compared to his earlier efforts, they were "broader in design," according to Sebastian Hensel, with "the same minute treatment and correct drawing and observation of detail, but a much greater freedom of handling, and force and harmony of coloring."[144] The paintings celebrate a panoramic natural world into which diminutive signs of mankind have tentatively encroached. Thus, in Lucerne Felix captured an inspiring view of the cathedral, symbol of salvation, with its two spires piercing the sky, as the Rigi looms in the background over the serene, glassy lake. Traversing the water diagonally in the foreground is the covered bridge, within which were concealed centuries-old murals of the *Totentanz* (Dance of Death); surely not coincidentally, Felix positioned the bridge to lead directly to the cathedral (**plate 19**).

Writing to Fanny Horsley from Thun on July 9, Felix confessed a desire to return to the routine of composition; to dig and turn like a worm, he observed, was preferable to human brooding.[145] In his diary he began to draft the strident scherzo of a string quartet in F minor.[146] His chief concern, though, was to dispatch to London the three choral pieces, which included the Evensong canticles composed in Baden-Baden—"perhaps a little longer & more developed than usual in your Cathedral style," Felix commented to Buxton[147]—and the *Jubilate Deo* for the Morning Service. The manuscript, published later that year by Buxton,[148] included an organ part and English text, and thus was intended for Anglican services; when the Ewer firm brought out the three motets, it reissued the companion *Te Deum* at the same time. But when the first German edition appeared from Breitkopf & Härtel in 1848 as the *Drei Motetten*, Op. 69, with dual, German-English texts, there were significant changes. Whether the composer approved, we shall never know. Most conspicuous was the deletion of the organ accompaniments, transforming the motets into a cappella compositions that approached the German ideal of "pure" church music. No less important was the replacement of the *Gloria Patri* for the *Jubilate Deo* (Op. 69 No. 2). In place of the spare, somewhat severe A-minor conclusion in Felix's manuscript,[149] Breitkopf & Härtel inserted the eight-part *Gloria Patri* from Felix's unpublished *Deutsche Liturgie*, transposed up a step from E to F major, so that the four-part motet culminated in an opulent final cadence.

Like the Psalms, Op. 78 and *Sechs Sprüche*, Op. 79, Felix's final sacred works evince transparent textures that highlight the text declamation. Compressed points of imitation, typically on motives spanning expressive fourths or fifths, alternate with homophony, as Felix weighs a delicate balance between counterpoint and harmony. Only in the multipartite *Magnificat* (Op. 69 No. 3), the most ambitious of the three, does he indulge in learned counterpoint: the final section of Mary's canticle, "As he promised to our forefathers, Abraham and to his seed forever," blossoms into a fugato on two subjects, combined and intertwined with skillful applications of mirror inversion. Throughout the opus, dissonances occur generally on weak beats; indeed, in the *Nunc dimittis* (Op. 69 No. 1) the prevailing Palestrinian euphony seems to support the affirming sense of resolution in Simeon's canticle (Luke 2), "Lord, now lettest Thou Thy servant depart in peace" (**ex. 16.17**).

Toward the end of July, after Felix's relatives returned to Berlin, he reengaged his creative muse. By July 24, he was again industrious, painting watercolors, reading Disraeli, and composing.[150] There were the interminable proofs for the first edition of *Elijah* to correct, and several invitations to ponder. Helmina von Chézy sent yet another opera libretto

Ex. 16.17: Mendelssohn, Motet, Op. 69 No. 1 (1847), *Nunc dimittis*

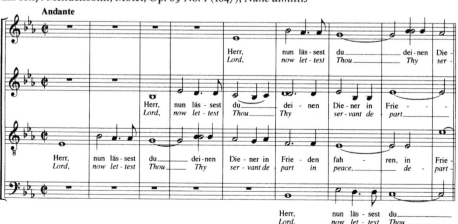

that Felix declined, this time because it contained considerable dialogue; he preferred to write through-composed music.[151] From Cologne came a request for music to consecrate the opening of the cathedral nave,[152] and from Liverpool a commission for an occasional work, communicated by Henry Chorley and the Swiss conductor Jakob Zeugheer Herrmann, whom Felix had met in Zurich. In 1848 the new Liverpool concert hall would open, and Felix was asked to write a cantata, not "sacred, but rather illustrative of the Science of Music, to which art the building will be dedicated, with perhaps some reference to the commercial greatness of the Town."[153] Chorley recommended Wordsworth's poem "The Power of Sound," but Felix reached an early impasse when he recalled that Handel had already explored the subject in *Alexander's Feast*.

Though isolated amid the scenic beauties of Interlaken, Felix received several visitors during his last Swiss sojourn. Early in August the English historian George Grote arrived, followed by Heinrich Hoffmann, who found the composer simultaneously orchestrating and doing arithmetic exercises with his children.[154] A few weeks later he was discussing publishing Fanny's music with Hermann Härtel[155] and spent the last three days of the month in the company of Henry Chorley, who recorded some details of his final meeting with the composer, now "aged and sad," and "stooped." The two took in views of the Jungfrau and visited a remote church near Lake Brienz where, while a peasant boy operated the bellows, Felix performed organ works of Bach, improvised, and, as Chorley, citing Milton (*Il Penseroso*, 166), recalled, brought "all heaven before the eyes." The friends discussed Rossini, Donizetti, and Verdi, whose *I masnadieri* had premiered in Covent Garden with Jenny Lind in July—Lumley's replacement for Felix's aborted opera on Shakespeare's *Tempest*. When pressed by Chorley to consider a libretto based on *The Winter's Tale*, Felix confessed that "something very merry could be made with Autolycus," but reaffirmed his intention to finish *Die Lorelei*. "But what is the use of planning anything? I shall not live," Felix mused. Chorley last saw Felix trudging alone on a road to Interlaken, "looking none the younger for the loose dark coat and the wide-brimmed straw hat bound with black crape which he wore. . . ."[156]

By the end of August, the music for nearly entire first act of *Die Lorelei* was already "on paper."[157] Despite this assertion, only some fragments have survived, of which three—the finale, an *Ave Maria*, and *Winzer-Chor* (Vintners' Chorus)—appeared in 1852 as Op. 98. In addition, Felix's composing score contains a draft of a duet and a significant amount of music for the penultimate scene, including a festive orchestral march and quartet.[158] Still, the very incompleteness of the manuscript has remained a metaphor for his lifelong inability to find success in opera. For Chorley, Felix "may have been much too curious in waiting for the faultless *libretto* which never would have come, as Rossini was too ready in setting any book and every book, which contained a few airs, duets, and a *finale*."[159] The actor Eduard Devrient, who at Felix's bidding revised *Die Lorelei* with Geibel, echoed Chorley with a sense of the dramatic: "There is a Hamlet-like tragedy about Mendelssohn's operatic destiny. During eighteen years he could not make up his mind firmly to adopt any subject and work it out, because he wanted perfection; and when at last he overcame his scruples and determined upon a poem, though far from what it should have been, he sank with his fragment into the grave."[160]

In German literature, the popularization of the *Lorelei* legend effectively dates from 1802, when Clemens Brentano inserted a poem about the enchantress into his novel *Godwi*. Geibel's libretto, published *in memoriam* to Felix in 1861, concerns the transformation of Leonore from mortal to supernatural seductress. The daughter of a Bacharach innkeeper, she has fallen in love with the Pfalzgraf Otto, betrothed (unknown to Leonore) to a countess. To seek revenge, she climbs the cliffs above the Rhine and invokes its spirits to grant her a "men-blinding beauty" (*männerverblendende Schönheit*); then, casting a ring into the water, she plights her troth as the river's bride. Ultimately, two acts later, an infatuated Otto plunges from the cliff into the hissing water, while the Lorelei joins the spirits through a gaping archway in the rocks.

For Eric Werner, Felix succumbed to a charming lyricism in conceiving Leonore; she was a "mixture of Cécile and Jenny Lind," but no "Malibran, whose wild charm and sexual magnetism would have been necessary here."[161] More recently, John Warrack has found that Felix's Rhinemaidens have "none of Wagner's magic," and "suggest not so much the gathering of a host of spirits as girls joining a new school."[162] But to prejudge Felix's opera on the basis of a few fragments is surely problematic. Rather, all we can realistically offer are preliminary observations about the general tone of the fragments, which no doubt would have undergone revision, possibly wholesale recomposition, before Felix completed the score, let alone released it. The surviving music suggests he intended to distinguish the mortal and supernatural realms through different musical colorations, with an earthen, folksonglike idiom for the peasants (*Winzer-Chor*) and bright, regal music for the nobility (e.g., the unpublished march, ex. 16.18a) and darker shades for the Rhine spirits. Connecting the two was a certain "churchly tone," as evidenced by the softly lit *Ave Maria*, in which Leonore hears the distant pealing of bells, conveyed by a syncopated pedal point in the horns. The most substantial fragment, the through-composed finale (ex. 16.18b), shows that in 1847 Felix could not escape the influence of Weber—in particular, the

Ex. 16.18a: Mendelssohn, *Die Lorelei*, Op. 98 (1847), March (BJ, *MN* 44)

Ex. 16.18b: Mendelssohn, *Die Lorelei*, Op. 98 (1847), Act I, Finale

Wolf's Glen scene culminating the second act of *Der Freischütz*. But there are some admirable qualities of the music, which, chainlike, describes a complete cycle of keys by descending thirds (e–C–a–f♯—the key of Weber's Wolf's Glen, for Leonore's appearance—D–b–G–E). Felix effects several of the linking modulations by means of so-called deceptive cadences[163] and thus uses a stratagem also employed by Robert Schumann in his famous Eichendorff setting *Waldesgespräch* (Op. 39 No. 3), in which a traveler encounters the Lorelei in a forest, to suggest harmonically her seductive magic.

Though *Die Lorelei* remained a torso, early in September 1847 Felix completed another major work that preoccupied him during the Swiss sojourn—the String Quartet in F minor, Op. 80. Its thoroughly discordant affect, arguably a major stylistic departure at the end of Felix's life, is usually viewed as his creative response to Fanny's death; in 1961 the Marxist scholar Georg Knepler went farther and labeled this work of the

pre-Revolution Vormärz the "requiem of an era."[164] Friedhelm Krummacher has argued that, though the quartet awaited posthumous publication in 1850, Felix had essentially completed the score.[165] The quartet
challenges, through unrelenting stylistic discontinuities and motivic dis-
integration, the smooth polish and classical veneer of the Op. 44 quartets.
Like a tonal opprobrium, the key of F minor hangs over its emotionally
charged four movements—only the lyrical third movement Adagio asserts a contrasting key, A♭ major, though the beginning, with its descending figure in the cello (A♭–G–F–E♮–F), clearly invokes the F minor
of the first two movements. Unifying all four movements is the cyclic use
of a basic *Urmotiv* incorporating the dissonant interval of the diminished fourth, E♮–A♭, traditionally associated with the stronger, darker
emotions (**ex. 16.19**). Thus, in the first movement, the first violin outlines
in agitated tremolos the motive F–E♮–F–G–A♭. The macabre scherzo,
erupting *in medias res* with jarring syncopations on the dominant, unfolds the diminished fourth in a rising, chromatic bass line, as if Felix
sought to fulfill his earlier prediction that Fanny would compose a
"*scherzo serioso*."[166] And the finale, which revives the tremolos of the first
movement and syncopations of the third, also highlights the diminished
fourth in its opening bars.

Ex. 16.19a: Mendelssohn, String Quartet in F minor, Op. 80 (1847), First Movement

Ex. 16.19b: Mendelssohn, String Quartet in F minor, Op. 80 (1847), Second Movement

Ex. 16.19c: Mendelssohn, String Quartet in F minor, Op. 80 (1847), Finale

VII

On September 18, Felix's family resumed their domestic life in Leipzig, first at the guest house Zum grossen Blumenberg, while some renovations were undertaken at Königstrasse No. 3.[167] Gathering his courage, he traveled to Berlin for the last week of the month. There, he planned the Berlin premiere of *Elijah*, set for October 18, and envisioned the lyrical numbers of the second and third acts of *Die Lorelei*. But the sight of Fanny's unaltered rooms at the family residence utterly unnerved him and, according to his nephew, "destroyed all the good effects produced by the journey to Switzerland."[168] Returning to Leipzig at the beginning of October, Felix enjoyed trying out a new Broadwood grand piano sent from London[169] but shunned most society. On October 3, Gade inaugurated the new season at the Gewandhaus; secluded in an anteroom near the gallery, Felix may have heard Joachim perform the Violin Concerto Op. 64, though a report reveals that after an aria the composer stormed out in an irritable mood.[170]

One colleague who saw him nearly daily was Ignaz Moscheles. His diaries, edited by his wife, chronicle in detail Felix's last weeks.[171] The friends walked in the Rosenthal, discussed "low" and "high" art—polkas Felix had heard in Frankfurt and Bach gigues—and examined Conservatory applicants, who labored over figured-bass exercises while Felix sketched landscapes on scraps of paper. With Julius Rietz, the new Kapellmeister at the Stadttheater, they played chamber music. Moscheles was among the first to see Felix's last compositions, including that "agitation of painful feelings," Op. 80; Moscheles also reports perusing the first movement of a string quartet in D minor—a theme and variations, "less gloomy, somewhat more cheerful, and harmonically quite tasteful."[172] No such work survives, though among Felix's manuscripts were two string-quartet movements, released posthumously as Op. 81 Nos. 1 and 2. The first, variations in E major that, save their key, resemble Moscheles's description, begin with a graceful, classical theme, from which Felix progressively departs in five subsequent variations. Of these, the ultimate erupts as a turbulent Presto in E minor that dissolves all traces of the theme. Similarly, the scherzo in A minor follows a course that eventually fragments its theme, so that the movement ends with two empty, pizzicato chords.

Felix devoted his final creative efforts to the *Sechs Lieder*, Op. 71, of which three (Nos. 4, 2, and 1) date from 1842 and 1845. To these he added three finished after Fanny's death, on allusive Lenau and Eichendorff texts: Nos. 5, from the Swiss sojourn, and 3 and 6, written after the final return to Leipzig. On October 7 Felix drafted a seventh, his last surviving composition,[173] and considered its inclusion in the opus (instead, it appeared in 1850 as Op. 86 No. 6). Its text, from an old German spring song, begins "Bleak winter is over, the swallows return, now all bestirs itself afresh, the springs multiply." Gently coursing through the music is a sinuous sixteenth-note figure, a soft undercurrent of aquatic imagery, interrupted by the final, telling lines, "only I suffer pain, I will suffer without end, since, most beloved, you must part from me, and I from you."

On October 9, Felix described his mood to Charlotte Moscheles as *grau in grau* (gray on gray), equally applicable to his final *Liederheft*. That afternoon, he visited Livia Frege, to try out the songs. Excepting the *Frühlingslied* (No. 2), on a Klingemann text of springtime renewal, the soprano found the others suffused with melancholy. Thus, in No. 3 (*An die Entfernte*, "To the Distant One") the poetic image is of withering roses, while No. 4 (*Schilflied*, "Song of the Reeds"), cast in a haunting, barcarolle-like F♯ minor, concludes with a turn to the major for a "sweet thought of you, like a quiet evening prayer." In No. 5 (*Auf der Wanderschaft*, "Wandering") a wanderer confronts the cold wind for snatching away his beloved's last greeting. The opus closes with the funereal *Nachtlied*, composed on October 1 for the birthday of Felix's friend Schleinitz, though yet another musical vessel for the composer's grief (ex. 16.20): against syncopated, tolling bells in the piano, the singer asks, "Where now has the merry joy gone, the comfort of friends and faithful breast, the beloved's sweet appearance?" "The whole book is serious," Felix observed to Livia Frege, "and serious it must go into the world."[174]

After reading through the Lieder several times, Felix suffered a stroke and appears temporarily to have lost sensation in his hands. He described the affliction as if "a foreign body wanted to impress itself forcefully into his head"[175] and later compared the symptoms to less severe ones he had experienced in 1840 (see p. 402). Somehow he managed to walk home, where a terrified Cécile found him stretched out, shivering, on a sofa. Two Leipzig physicians, Ernst Hammer and J. C. A. Clarus, now began

Ex. 16.20: Mendelssohn, *Nachtlied*, Op. 71 No. 6 (1847)

to "treat" Felix, and he passed a first fretful night with a few hours of sleep interrupted by severe headaches. On October 10 Dr. Hammer ordered leeches, applied unfortunately by an unskilled barber, who "tormented" Felix for several hours. Still, during the following week he rallied and received friends, including Julius Benedict, who arrived from London. Postponing the Berlin performance of *Elijah*, Felix still intended to conduct the oratorio in Vienna on November 14. When exemplars of the first edition of the full score arrived from Simrock, he sent a copy to Frederick William IV, with regrets that illness prevented him from personally delivering the score to the monarch.[176] By October 19 Felix was able to visit a newly dedicated obelisk commemorating the Battle of Leipzig (1813) and examine copper engravings of Albrecht Dürer, including the well-known *Ritter Tod und Teufel* (1513). But these reminders of death did not oppress him; when his headaches abated, Rebecka sent from Berlin a cheering letter about his improvement, and Felix could write that he was again "among the living."[177]

In the evenings he played cards with Cécile, and by the last week of October had resumed daily two-hour walks. On October 25 he sent Op. 71 to Breitkopf & Härtel and began to think of rescheduling the Viennese premiere of *Elijah*. But after embracing Cécile three days later, he suffered a second stroke that rendered him speechless for fifteen minutes. The intense headaches resumed, and leeches were again applied, this time by a skilled surgeon. Paul, having received a disquieting bulletin from Cécile, now hastened from Berlin with another doctor—but to no avail. Felix began to slip from lucidity into incoherence; his mind wandered, and, according to Moscheles, his speech mixed English and German. On the afternoon of November 3 he suffered a third stroke and became unconscious, as Paul futilely rubbed his brother's temples with vinegar. By the next morning his facial gestures seemed to imitate the percussive rhythms of a march, perhaps the music that the American correspondent William B. Bradbury, in a dispatch to the *New-York Tribune*, reported that Felix was composing on his deathbed.[178] At times, he could still recognize Paul and Cécile, and to her inquiries Felix replied he was "tired, very tired" (*müde, sehr müde*). These were among the final words he uttered. By then, crowds of Leipzigers had gathered outside and nervously awaited reports. The exhausted Cécile slept for a few hours but was awakened by a commotion among those attending her husband— he had suffered a final paralysis, his breathing became slow and shallow, and Moscheles was reminded now of a passage from the funeral march of Beethoven's *Eroica* Symphony; Moscheles's torpid friend resembled a model for a sculpture of Canova or Thorwaldsen. Surrounded by Cécile, Paul, David, Schleinitz, Moscheles, and his doctors, one of whom held a watch, Felix expired at 9:24 P.M. on November 4, 1847. Probably within a few months of his death, Cécile drafted a detailed report of his last twenty-seven days, which corroborated and augmented more cursory eyewitness accounts of Moscheles, David, and Benedict.[179] Handed down through generations of family members, Cécile's report remained neglected until 2000, when its contents were finally examined and published by Peter Ward Jones.[180] It provides the basis for our summary of Felix's final days.

News of Felix's death spread rapidly throughout Leipzig; soon the entire city was in mourning and preparing for a solemn funeral.[181] As if in anticipation, on November 4 the Gewandhaus directorate cancelled the fifth subscription concert, scheduled for that evening—according to the *Allgemeine musikalische Zeitung,* the composer passed away exactly when the concert would have ended.[182] At the deathbed Cécile placed five flowers upon her husband's body for their children. Wilhelm Hensel, arriving from Berlin, decorated Felix's coffin and sketched his countenance (**plate 20**).[183] To accompany the drawing, which captures a certain seraphic expression, Hensel added a quotation from *Elijah* (No. 34): "And after the fire there came a still small voice, and in that still voice, onward came the Lord." The Dresden painters Eduard Bendemann and Julius Hübner also executed deathbed sketches, and Hermann Knaur made a mask of the deceased.[184] For two days hundreds of mourners kept a wake-like vigil at the residence. Eduard Devrient found his friend resting "in a costly coffin, upon cushions of satin, embowered in tall growing shrubs, and covered with wreaths of flowers and laurels."[185]

Late in the afternoon of November 7, a procession of thousands formed and slowly wound its way through the Leipzig streets from the Königstrasse to the Paulinerkirche. Before the bier members of the Gewandhaus orchestra and Thomanerchor, and the faculty and male students of the Conservatory assembled. The casket, an "isle of peace in the midst of a surging crowd,"[186] was draped with silver-embossed velvet and adorned with palm branches. Four horses covered in black drew the hearse, escorted by six pallbearers—Moscheles, David, Hauptmann, Gade, Rietz, and, from Dresden, Robert Schumann. Behind them walked Paul as the chief mourner, then members of family, clergy, faculty of the university, civic and military officials, and the public. Among the mourners was Otto Jahn, director of the archaeological museum in Leipzig. Grieving "the early loss of a master, whose cultivation, self-discipline, and endeavors after the good and beautiful had exercised a truly beneficial influence over the art of our time," Jahn turned his thoughts to Mozart and conceived the idea for a new, multivolume biography of the composer to whom Felix had often been compared.[187] During the procession a

wind band played a funeral march by Beethoven, and Moscheles's hastily prepared arrangement of Felix's *Lied ohne Worte*, Op. 62 No. 3, which
had served, a few years earlier, as Felix's lament on the death of his mother.

In the Paulinerkirche the open coffin was placed on a catafalque illuminated by six tall candelabras. Before it the senior Conservatory student
placed a cushion bearing a laurel wreath and the *Ordre pour le mérite*,
awarded the composer by the Prussian monarch. As the mourners entered the church, an organist performed a movement from *Antigone*, the
marchlike music heard when Creon appears with the corpse of his son
Haemon. Then, a chorus of four hundred sang chorales, including *Jesu
meine Zuversicht*, before Pastor Samuel Rudolf Howard of the Reformed
Church preached a sermon on Job 1 ("The Lord gave and the Lord has
taken away"). Then came the chorus from *Paulus* that follows the stoning of Stephen, "Siehe, wir preisen selig," and the final chorus of the St.
Matthew Passion. After the church had emptied, Cécile entered alone
and prayed by the side of her husband.

In the evening the students accompanied the casket to the train station in a torch-lit procession. At 10:00 P.M. an *Extrazug* departed for Berlin. At Cöthen the local singing society turned out to pay homage to the
composer. By 1:30 A.M. the train had reached Dessau, the birthplace of
Moses Mendelssohn. There the aging Kapellmeister, Friedrich Schneider,
led his pupils in an open-air performance of a threnody he had composed
to this affecting text: "Angel voices sang thus, 'Lov'd one come and join
our choir. Thy exalted songs have soar'd above to God's high throne!' Then
the singer gently bow'd his head when they had sung. He, the unsurpassed
source of holy music, gently bow'd his dear head, and died."[188] Schneider's
composition (**ex. 16.21**), scored for male choir, alluded to Felix's part-songs,
and thus his place in the popular musical culture of the time.

At 6:00 A.M. the casket was transferred in Berlin to a hearse drawn by
six horses covered in black. Thousands followed the procession, accompanied by an arrangement of the funeral march from Beethoven's Piano
Sonata Op. 26, to the cemetery of the Trinity Church before the Halle

Ex. 16.21: Friedrich Schneider, "Engelstimmen klangen" (1847)

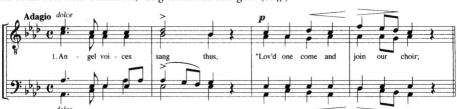

Gate. A hastily convened committee, consisting of Taubert, the violinist Hubert Ries, and the music publisher Bock, organized the choral music for the service, at which the Pastor Berduscheck officiated. The Domchor, for which Felix had composed sacred music, again sang the chorale *Jesus, meine Zuversicht*, and Rungenhagen, Felix's old nemesis at the Singakademie, directed part of that organization in a motet composed by Grell. Felix was then laid to rest next to Fanny in the family plot he himself had visited only weeks before.

In December 1846, when Felix had last seen Fanny in Berlin, she gently upbraided him for not having celebrated her birthday with her in several years. When he parted from her, he is reported to have said, "Depend upon it, the next I shall spend with you."[189] In this promise, he kept his word.

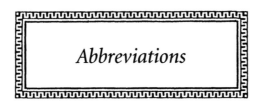

Abbreviations

AfMw	*Archiv für Musikwissenschaft*
AmZ	*Allgemeine musikalische Zeitung*
BadV	*Briefe an deutsche Verleger* (Felix Mendelssohn Bartholdy: 1968)
BamZ	*Berliner allgemeine musikalische Zeitung*
BJ	Biblioteka Jagiellońska, Kraków
BL	British Library, London
BLB	*Bulletin of the Leo Baeck Institute*
BN	Bibliothèque Nationale, Paris
DM	*Die Musik*
DR	*Deutsche Rundschau*
GB	Green Books, Bodleian Library, Oxford, M. Deneke Mendelssohn Collection
GM	*Goethe and Mendelssohn* (Karl Mendelssohn-Bartholdy: 1874)
HHI	Heinrich-Heine Institut, Düsseldorf
JAMS	*Journal of the American Musicological Society*
LA	*Briefe aus Leipziger Archiven* (Felix Mendelssohn-Bartholdy: 1972)
LAWFMB	*Leipziger Ausgabe der Werke Felix Mendelssohn Bartholdy*, Leipzig
LBI	*Leo Baeck Institute Year Book*
LC	Library of Congress, Washington, D.C.
MA	*Mendelssohn Archiv*, Staatsbibliothek zu Berlin—Preussischer Kulturbesitz

MahW	*Mendelssohn and his World* (Todd: 1991)
MDM	Margaret Deneke Mendelssohn Collection, Bodleian Library, Oxford
MF	*The Mendelssohn Family (1729–1847) from Letters and Journals* (Sebastian Hensel: 1882)
Mf	*Die Musikforschung*
ML	*Music & Letters*
MLL	*Felix Mendelssohn: A Life in Letters* (Elvers: 1986)
MMR	*Monthly Musical Record*
MN	*Mendelssohn Nachlass* (Staatsbibliothek zu Berlin and Biblioteka Jagiellońska, Kraków)
MQ	*The Musical Quarterly*
MS	*Mendelssohn Studien*
MT	*The Musical Times*
NYPL	New York Public Library, New York, Mendelssohn Family Correspondence
NZfM	*Neue Zeitschrift für Musik*
19CM	*19th Century Music*
PML	The Pierpont Morgan Library, New York
SBB	Staatsbibliothek zu Berlin—Preussischer Kulturbesitz
VfM	*Vierteljahrsschrift für Musikwissenschaft*

Notes

Preface

1. See Anne Elliott, *The Music Makers: A Brief History of the Birmingham Triennial Musical Festivals 1784–1912*, Birmingham, 2000.
2. Nietzsche, *Beyond Good and Evil* (1886), no. 245.
3. See Marek, 320–21, and, for a photograph of the statue, 324. In 1947 a bust of the composer was placed on the site of the former statue, and on March 10, 1993, a new statue was unveiled in a ceremony before the Neues Gewandhaus in Leipzig. Concurrently the conductor Kurt Masur spearheaded an initiative to restore the composer's final Leipzig residence. See Treue, Schinköth, and the literature cited therein.
4. See Treue, Schinköth, and the literature cited therein.
5. See "Mendelssohn in Germany," *New York Times*, December 2, 1934, where Herbert Peyser reported: "In the face of threats from higher up that the pressure of boycott might be applied to his works, Strauss went so far as to intimate that he could not surpass Mendelssohn and might, perhaps, not even be able to equal him."
6. Luzi Korngold, *Erich Wolfgang Korngold: Ein Lebensbild*, Vienna, 1967, 64.
7. Gerald Abraham, *A Hundred Years of Music*, Chicago, 1964, 59, 60–61.
8. Radcliffe: 1954, 117, 127, 133, 137, and 140.
9. Werner: 1963, 293, 358.
10. Botstein: 1991, 7.
11. See Michael Musgrave, *The Musical Life of the Crystal Palace*, Cambridge, 1995.
12. Elizabeth Sheppard, *Charles Auchester*, Chicago, 1900, II, 167.
13. E. D. Mackerness, "Music and Moral Purity in the Early Victorian Era," *Canadian Music Journal* 4/2 (1960), 20.
14. *NZfM* 33 (1850), September 3 and 6, 1850.
15. "Robert Schumann mit Rücksicht auf Mendelssohn-Bartholdy und die Entwicklung der modernen Tonkunst überhaupt," *NZfM* 22 (1845), *passim*; parts are translated by Jürgen Thym in Todd: 1994, 317–37. See also Thym: 1984.
16. On Wagner's essay, see in particular Botstein: 1991, 9ff.; Mintz: 1992; and Ringer.
17. On the connection between Mendelssohn's incidental music and fairy illustrations, see the forthcoming study by Marian Wilson Kimber, "Victorian Fairies and Felix Mendelssohn's *A Midsummer Night's Dream* in England"; on the genre of the fairy paintings, see Jane Martineau, ed., *Victorian Fairy Painting*, London, 1997.
18. *A Dictionary of Music and Musicians*, London, 1890 (reissue of the first edition of 1879–1889), II, 305.
19. *The Star* (London), February 23, 1889.
20. On the shifting images of Mendelssohn's masculinity, see especially Marian Wilson Kimber: 2002.
21. Michael Mason, *The Making of Victorian Sexuality*, Oxford, 1995, 18.

22. *Encyclopaedia Britannica*, 11th ed., Cambridge, 1911, XVIII, 124; see further Mintz: 1992, 127ff.
23. Botstein: 1991, 16.
24. Ibid., 17.
25. Matthew Sweet, *Inventing the Victorians*, Oxford, 2001, ix.
26. Sposato: 1998; see also the rejoinders by Michael Steinberg and Leon Botstein, and response by Sposato in *MQ* 83 (1999).
27. Botstein: 1991, 23.
28. See further Marian Wilson Kimber: 2003.
29. Reich: 1991b.
30. See Wehner: 2002b.
31. Robert to Clara Schumann, September 18, 1854, in F. G. Jansen, ed., *Robert Schumanns Briefe: Neue Folge*, Leipzig, 1904, 398.
32. Friedrich Niecks, "On Mendelssohn and Some of His Contemporary Critics," *MMR* 5 (1875), 164.

Prologue

1. Peter Gay, *The Rise of Modern Paganism*, N.Y., 1966, 334.
2. Sorkin: 1996, 8–9.
3. *MF*, I, 27. A fuller account is in Joseph Mendelssohn's *Lebensgeschichte* of his father, published in the first vol. of Moses Mendelssohn: 1843, 3–56, and partially trans. in Brown: 2003, 85–88.
4. Altmann: 1973, 66.
5. Letter of March 29, 1840, Cécile Mendelssohn Bartholdy to Elise Jeanrenaud, MDM d. 24.
6. *MF*, I, 22–23.
7. Ibid., I, 1–2; Lewald: 1861, I, 205f.
8. Lewald: 1992, 257.
9. See Porstmann, 344.
10. July 8, 1829, Abraham to Felix, in E. Werner: 1963, 37.
11. *La Palingénésie philosophique ou idées sur l'état passé et sur l'état futur des êtres vivants*. On the Lavater affair, see Altmann: 1973, 194–263.
12. Cited in ibid., 209.
13. See Sorkin: 1996, 95–107.
14. Moses Mendelssohn: 1983, 37.
15. Ibid., 38.
16. Altmann: 1973, 521.
17. Sorkin: 1987, 70.
18. Ibid., 99.
19. Altmann: 1973, 583.
20. Moses prepared the lectures during morning sessions with the fifteen-year-old Joseph, who acted as a secretary; Altmann: 1973, 643.
21. Altmann: 1975, 19.
22. Altmann: 1973, 684.
23. Sorkin: 1996, 151.
24. Ibid.
25. See Elvers and Klein, 126, 128.
26. According to Lowenstein: 1991, 186, the *Meierei* (dairy) was purchased in 1771; according to Jacob Jacobson: 1960, 255, in 1779.
27. Spiel, 1991, 20–21; and Lowenstein: 1991, 185–87.
28. *MF*, I, 63.
29. See Gilbert: 1975, xix.
30. Hertz: 1991, 214.
31. Hertz: 1988, 6–7.
32. See Wilhelmy, 719ff.
33. Lewald: 1992, 247.
34. A. van Hoboken, *Joseph Haydn: Thematisch-bibliographisches Werkverzeichnis*, Mainz, 1971, II, 94.
35. Martin Falck, *Wilhelm Friedemann Bach: Sein Leben und seine Werke*, Lindau, 1913, 51.
36. See E. R. Jacobi.

37. Wollny, 658.
38. September 5, 1789, Johanna Maria Bach to Sarah Levy, in C. P. E. Bach: 1994, 1309–16.
39. On the activities of the Singakademie see Schünemann: 1928; concerning Sarah Levy, cf. Uldall, 11f; E. Werner's article in *Die Musik in Geschichte und Gegenwart* 8 (1960), 684; and Hertz: 1988, 102–3.
40. Lewald: 1992, 248.
41. Cécile Mendelssohn Bartholdy to Elisabeth Jeanrenaud, October 22, 1849, MDM d. 24; a trans. of the letters is in preparation by Joan Benson.
42. See further Neumann, 136–42.
43. "Der edle Mensch sei hülfreich und gut" (*WoO* 151).
44. Quoted in Spiel, 111–12; for a facs., see the entry for Daniel Itzig in *Encyclopaedia Judaica*, Jerusalem, 1971, IX, 1150. According to Felix Gilbert, at the time no other Jewish family received a similar patent of citizenship (Gilbert: 1975, xvii–xviii).
45. Spiel, 112–13.
46. Ibid., 161.
47. Ibid.
48. See Hertz: 1988, 228ff. A more detailed study of the issue of conversion is in Lowenstein: 1994, 120–33. Lowenstein discerns three waves of conversions: (1) 1770–1805, distinguished by a striking number of women and illegitimate infants, (2) 1800–1820, affecting elite families and including conversions of entire families, and (3) 1822–1830, characterized by an increased number of men.
49. Schleiermacher, 238, 241. Henriette did not convert until 1817, after the death of her mother, while Rahel converted in 1814 to marry the writer-diplomat Karl August Varnhagen von Ense.
50. For the particulars, see Cohn.
51. Lowenstein: 1991, 195.
52. See Spiel, 159–60; and Gilbert: 1975, xxviii.
53. See Jacobson: 1960, 254.
54. Letter of August 26, 1799 (*MF*, I, 67).
55. For particular examples, see Lowenstein: 1991, 197 fn. 43.
56. In the early eighteenth century the Prussian Baron Friedrich Christian von Bartholdy had owned the dairy.
57. *Reisebilder* II, cited in *MF*, I, 100.
58. Regarding the frescoes, see William Vaughan, *German Romantic Painting*, New Haven, 1980, 178–80.
59. Curiously enough, in 1812, the year of the Prussian Edict of Emancipation, Bella Salomon herself adopted the name Bartholdy, though she did not convert. See Jacobson: 1960, 256.
60. *MF*, I, 75; no date for the letter is given.
61. It appeared in a list of the Berlin Jewish congregation; see Jacobson: 1960, 257; and Gilbert: 1975, 315.
62. For the text of the decree, see Schoeps, 81ff.
63. A *Vorvertrag* signed by the parties in Berlin on December 8, 1821 established the new organization. Klein: 1995b, 100–102.
64. See, e.g., his letter of December 9, 1823 to Zelter, in F. Mendelssohn Bartholdy: 1984, 29–30. A facs. of the original, in HHI, is in E. Werner: 1975, 22–23. An earlier letter to Zelter, written on August 22, 1822, i.e., *before* his parents' conversion, is signed Felix Mendelssohn (Mendelssohn Bartholdy: 1984, 26–28). At least two letters of Lea, from December 25, 1822, to Wilhelm Hensel and July 29, 1823, to Moritz [Maurice] Schlesinger, are signed Lea Mendelssohn Bartholdy. See Gilbert: 1975, 51; and Elvers: 1974, 48. Finally, a drawing by Wilhelm Hensel, probably executed for the birthday of Felix's sister Fanny on November 14, 1822, is titled "Fanny Mendelssohn Bartholdy als Schutzheilige der Musik Cäcilie." See plate 6.
65. Dubnov, IV, 650–51. See also p. 430, below.
66. The two conjoined as one quotation in *MF*, I, 32. For the original sources, see Altmann: 1973, 728.
67. Henriette (Hinni) Meyer (1776–1862), daughter of the Mecklenburg-Strelitz "court Jew" Nathan Meyer. Several of her letters are published in Gilbert: 1975.
68. April 16–22, 1815, Zelter to Goethe; Hecker I, 424.
69. *MF*, I, 33. Joseph's firm was situated at Spandauer Str. 68, which had been the residence of his father. See Elvers and Klein, 126, 128.
70. Benjamin served in the War of Liberation against Napoleon of 1813 and embraced the Protestant faith in 1816, when he changed his name to Georg Benjamin Mendelssohn. Recent studies include: Gilbert: 1975b, 183–201; Stolzenberg: 1979; Klein: 1990; and Stolzenberg: 1990.

71. Klein: 1995b, 89, 91.
72. *Moses Mendelssohns gesammelte Schriften*, ed. G. B. Mendelssohn, 7 vols., Leipzig, 1843–1845. See Altmann: 1968, 80; and Reissner: 1969, 212f.
73. A reference to Adalbert von Chamisso's popular story *Peter Schlemihl* (1813), in which the title character exchanges his shadow to the devil for everlasting wealth. Abraham made these comments during a visit in St. Petersburg with Maximilian Heine, brother of the poet. See M. Heine, 245. In *MF*, I, 61, Sebastian Hensel transmits an abridged version. Despite the self-denying assertion, Hensel claims that Abraham was a "harmonious, independent, vigorous character, and had nothing of the epigone in him."
74. See Klein: 2000 and Barbier, 45.
75. On his way Abraham had met Goethe in Frankfurt in August; on September 1, Abraham reported about the visit: "'Are you a son of Mendelssohn?' he asked me, and that was the first time that I heard my father mentioned without an epithet, as I always wished." Kippenberg, 73.
76. September 7, 1803, Zelter to Goethe, Hecker I, 56.
77. A. B. Marx: 1865, I, 110; see also Marx: 1991, 209.
78. "The response was an unprecedented, truly fearsome one, the crowd inflamed to the point of madness. Mendelssohn went backstage to see the composer even before the performance was over, and found him stalking up and down in feverish excitement: 'Ah, ç'a frappé, ç'a frappé! [That has struck home, that has struck home!].'" Ibid. The opera left its mark on Beethoven's "rescue opera" *Fidelio* and was admired by Felix Mendelssohn Bartholdy, who would perform the opera in Düsseldorf and the Overture and finales of the first two acts in Leipzig.
79. *MF*, I, 72.
80. April 11, 1800, Brendel Veit to Karl Friedrich Zelter; in the same letter she also describes Abraham as "half-French" (*halbfranzosen*). Körner, 27, 28.
81. *MF*, I, 62.
82. Marx: 1991, 209.
83. Between 1805 and 1808 Pölchau sold many of the Emanuel Bach materials to Abraham Mendelssohn, who gave them to Sara Levy; she, in turn, donated them to the Singakademie and Ripienschule. See Schünemann, 1941, 71; and, more recently, Kulukundis, 159–76.
84. *MF*, I, 72.
85. The business was located on the Mühlendamm in the mansion formerly occupied by Veitel Heine Ephraim, one of Daniel Itzig's partners during the reign of Frederick the Great. See Elvers and Klein, 136–37. Abraham returned to Berlin by the end of May; an entry in a *Judenbürgerbuch* dated May 31, 1804 lists him as a *Berliner Stadtjude*. See Kliem, 130.
86. *MF*, I, 102. Upon his marriage to Lea, Abraham was granted citizenship. Jacobson: 1962, 54.
87. See Klein: 1995b, 91–98. The brother of the banker Simon Veit, former husband of Brendel Mendelssohn (Dorothea Schlegel), Philipp Joseph Veit is not to be confused with Dorothea's son, the painter Philipp Veit, born in 1793.
88. *MF*, I, 43.
89. See her letter of March 2, 1818, in Gilbert: 1975, 38.
90. See Lowenthal-Hensel: 1982, 141–46; and Rabien: 1990, 153–70.
91. See Rabien: 1990b, 295–328; and Sammons, 282–83.
92. Zelter to Goethe, November 16, 1831; Hecker, III, 513.
93. Constant was a member of the *Tribunat* from 1799 until his dismissal in 1802. The following year he accompanied Madame de Staël to Germany and in 1806 began work on the novel *Adolphe*, partly based on their relationship. After authoring an anti-Napoleonic tract in 1814, he sought political asylum in the American embassy in Paris; during the Restoration he was elected to the *Chambre des députés*.
94. *MF*, I, 46.
95. Sebastiani (1772–1851) participated in Napoleon's Italian campaign of 1796–1797 and in the coup d'état of 1799 that ended the Directory. In 1802 he was the ambassador to Constantinople, which he defended against the English; in 1803, he was dispatched on a mission to Syria and Egypt. He later served in the July Monarchy of 1830 and became a field marshal during the reign of Louis-Philippe.
96. *MF*, I, 46.
97. Ibid., 57.
98. Ibid., 55.
99. Several of her letters are printed in Gilbert: 1975; and in Lambour: 1986, 49–76.
100. Cited in Hertz: 1988, 172. Hertz asserts (106) that Brendel was allowed to "join the morning lessons [Moses] offered at the Mendelssohn home to a select group of young students, a group which included her younger brothers Joseph and Abraham and the two von Humboldt

brothers." But on this point, see Gilbert: 1975, xvii, fn. 4, who argues only for Alexander von Humboldt's inclusion in the group.

101. *MF*, I, 36.
102. Ibid., I, 37.
103. See Stern, 50–77.
104. Körner,18.
105. Dilthey, 492.
106. Behler, 289–90.
107. *MF*, I, 40–41.
108. Published in Eichner, 314–368. An English trans. is available in Schlegel: 1990.
109. See Gilbert: 1975, xxii.
110. Cited in Stern, 187.
111. Ibid., 188.
112. Upon converting Jonas became Johann Veit. In 1819, learning that Simon Veit was seriously ill, Dorothea asked for his forgiveness: "I know all too well, that my rigidity, my obstinacy, my vehemence, passion, impetuous restlessness, discontent and fantasizing, and a certainly reproachable striving for the unknown and strange engulfed me, and I alone am responsible for our separation, and for everything for which God wishes to pardon me, as you have pardoned me!" August 28, 1819, in Gilbert: 1975, 44.
113. So called because they wore their hair to resemble Christ.
114. Gilbert, 1975: xxv, fn. 32; and her letters of May 1, 1822, January 1829, and November 25, 1832, to Henriette and Joseph Mendelssohn, in ibid., 49–50, 74–75, and 87–89.
115. See especially Suhr, 107–19.

Chapter 1

1. Sammons, 24.
2. T. Devrient, 329.
3. Nowack, 247.
4. *Leipziger AmZ* 4 (1869), 207. For an illustration of the residence, see Kleßmann, 96.
5. *MF*, I, 72–73. Undated letter (ca. early 1805?) from Lea to her sister Rebecka Seeligmann (1776–1810).
6. Whaley, 88–110.
7. Nowack, 248. Fromet was in Hamburg by April 1806; see her letter of April 4, 1806, in Gilbert: 1975, 4.
8. See Hoffmann: 1962, 53ff.
9. In private possession; quoted in Elvers: 1997, 17.
10. Elvers and Klein, 131–36.
11. Ibid., 136; in 1983 the sum was estimated the equivalent of 100,000 marks.
12. Benedict: 1850, 6.
13. See Elvers: 1997, 17.
14. Letter of May [2], 1809. Lea's letters to Henriette are in private possession; transcribed extracts are in MDM c. 29, fols. 45–62.
15. October 23, 1821; Hecker, II, 139. When the Goethe-Zelter *Briefwechsel* appeared in 1834, the passage was doctored to read: "The father with great sacrifice allowed his sons to learn something and raised them as is proper." The original text was restored by Hecker in 1913. See Elvers: 1997, 18, and p. 292.
16. Leon Botstein has questioned whether Zelter was "being metaphoric (as with, for example, today's use of 'kosher') or literal." See Botstein: 1991, 39–40 (n. 37).
17. Sposato: 2000, 20–21.
18. *Wiener Zeitschrift für Kunst* 7 (1822); facs. in Klein: 1997, 65.
19. *MF*, I, 34.
20. Ibid., I, 58–59.
21. Elvers, "Schenkungen und Stiftungen der Mendelssohns," in Elvers and Klein, 97–98. The Bach materials had belonged to the *Nachlass* of C. P. E. Bach's daughter Anna Carolina Philippina.
22. The text is given in Klein: 1995b, 98.
23. Ibid., 99–100.
24. Kliem, 123–40; and Lowenthal-Hensel: 1990, 141.

25. Alexander: 1979, 10.
26. Klein, "Joseph Mendelssohn," in Elvers and Klein, 21.
27. Hensel incorrectly gives the year of Paul's birth as 1813 (*MF*, I, 74), instead of 1812, confirmed by the baptismal record of the Jerusalemskirche. See Klein: 1997, 20.
28. Treue, 33, fn. 1a.
29. Klein: 1990, 112.
30. Promoted for his knowledge of French to police chief by Marshal Davout, Friedrich Wagner succumbed to typhoid following the battle.
31. Schroeder: 1979.
32. *MF*, I, 74.
33. Elvers: 1997, 21–22. See also "Felix Mendelssohn Bartholdy," in *MT* 38 (1897), 731; J. Werner: 1947, 304; and Ward Jones: 1997b, 6. Elvers dates the portraits from 1813; the other scholars maintain they were taken in Paris in 1816.
34. Letter of April 29, 1814, quoted in Walter Kaufmann, ed., *Hegel: A Reinterpretation*, N.Y., 1966, 341.
35. William Makepeace Thackeray, *Vanity Fair*, Ch. 28.
36. According to the agreement for 1817–1818, M. A. Rothschild & Söhne received 14/32, or nearly half, of the business; the Mendelssohns' share was 5/32. Elvers and Klein, 160.
37. Klein: 1990, 119.
38. The witnesses were Carl Ludwig Ferdinand Heinsius (*Justiz-Commisarius*) and Carl Philipp Stägemann (*Regierungs-Conducteur*). See Elvers: 1997, 18; Kliem, 136; and Sievers.
39. Letter of December 1, 1823, Wilhelm Hensel to his sister Luise, in Gilbert: 1975, 58.
40. Benedict: 1850, 6.
41. The documents, three "monthly reports" and a certificate, are preserved in MDM c. 29, fols. 98–102.
42. July 20, 1818, Lea to Henriette von Pereira Arnstein (extract); MDM c. 29, fol. 45.
43. Stenzel, 79. I am indebted to Dr. Hans-Günter Klein for bringing this source to my attention. Concerning Stenzel's later career, see Lenz, I, 609.
44. Heyse, 11.
45. Lea to Henriette von Pereira Arnstein; MDM c. 29, fol. 45 (extract).
46. Sheehan, 269.
47. See also Eduard Dürre, *Aufzeichnungen, Tagebücher und Briefe aus einem deutschen Turner- und Lehrleben*, Leipzig, 1881, 746, cited in Elvers: 1997, 20–21.
48. April 4, 1816, Zelter to Goethe; Hecker, I, 465. For the date of Abraham's visit, see Steiger and Reimann, VI, 349.
49. April 14, 1816, Goethe to Zelter, in Hecker, I, 468.
50. May 18, 1816, Amalie Beer to her son, Giacomo Meyerbeer. Meyerbeer, I, 313.
51. Henriette Mendelssohn to Lea, November 10, 1816, Gilbert: 1975, 33. On November 9, the Mendelssohns were in Weimar, where Abraham again visited Goethe. See Steiger and Reimann, VI, 430; and Kippenberg, 81.
52. *AmZ* 39 (1837), 846.
53. J. F. Reichardt, *Vertraute Briefe, geschrieben auf einer Reise nach Wien*, ed. G. Gugitz, Munich, 1915, 14th Letter (December 16, 1808).
54. Forbes, 414.
55. Johnson, 204; Fauquet.
56. November 10, 1816, in Gilbert: 1975, 35.
57. Stern, 305.
58. *AmZ* 39 (1837), 845.
59. Gustav Schilling, *Encyclopädie der gesamten musikalischen Wissenschaften oder Universal Lexicon der Tonkunst*, Stuttgart, 1837, IV, 654.
60. SBB, *MA* Ms. 142; see Klein: 1993, 143–44.
61. Elvers and Klein, 145.
62. Elvers: 1997, 20.
63. *MF*, I, 76.
64. March 2, 1818, Rebecka Meyer to Rosa Herz, in Gilbert: 1975, 39.
65. *MF*, I, 88–89. According to Hensel, Fanny was thirteen when she accomplished the feat, thus placing the performance between November 14 and the end of 1818, possibly on December 11, Abraham's birthday.
66. Gilhofer & Ranschberg (October 29–30, 1906).
67. *AmZ* 20 (1818), 791; see also Elvers: 1963. The Salzburg pianist Wölfl had been Beethoven's chief Viennese rival during the 1790s.

68. *AmZ* 39 (1837), 845–46; *Concert militaire* in B♭ major, Op. 40 (1798). No review appears in the *AmZ* of 1818 or 1819, from which we might surmise the concert was a private event, in contrast to Felix's public appearance with the Gugels.
69. Dorn, "Recollections," 398, and Ludwig Rellstab, obituary for Fanny Hensel in the Berlin *Vossische Zeitung*, May 18, 1847.
70. Letter of April 21, 1822, Berger to Jenny Sieber, in Siebenkäs, 233.
71. Plantinga: 1977, 210.
72. *Gesänge aus einem gesellschaftlichen Liederspiele "Die schöne Müllerin,"* Op. 11, Berlin, 1819.
73. Among the more than one hundred documented guests of the salon were the writers E. T. A. Hoffmann, Heinrich von Kleist, and Achim von Arnim (Wilhelmy, 851–60).
74. Youens, 13.
75. Letter of May 6, 1821, Lea to Henriette von Pereira Arnstein (MDM c. 29, extract).
76. *Posthumous Memoirs of Karoline Bauer*, London, 1884, I, 220.
77. Schottländer: 1930, 131–33.
78. Son of the composer Johann Friedrich Fasch (1688–1758), a contemporary of J. S. Bach.
79. The fourth son of Veitel Ephraim, Benjamin Veitel (1742–1811) as a youth knew Lessing and Moses Mendelssohn. In 1790 Frederick William II sent Veitel to Paris to explore an alliance; later he fell under suspicion of espionage and was arrested by French authorities in 1806.
80. Schottländer: 1930, 155–56.
81. K. F. Zelter, *Karl Friedrich Christian Fasch*, Berlin, 1801.
82. Ibid., 17.
83. Ibid., 60.
84. Active in Rome, Benevoli (1605–1672) left several examples of the monumental baroque polychoral style. One of the most imposing seventeenth-century examples, the *Missa Salisburgensis* in fifty-three parts, was formerly attributed to Benevoli but now is thought to have been the creation of H. I. F. von Biber.
85. C. F. C. Fasch, *Sämmtliche Werke*, 2 vols., Berlin, 1839, issued by the Berlin Singakademie; as early as 1802, Zelter intended to send an exemplar of the Mass to Joseph Haydn. See Elvers: 1968.
86. MDM b. 5, fols. 155–61; I am grateful to Peter Ward Jones for alerting me to this source.
87. Among his other polychoral sacred works are Psalm 114, Op. 51, the *Doppel-Quartet "Denn er hat seinen Engeln befohlen über dir"* from *Elijah*, *Drei Psalmen*, Op. 78, *Sechs Sprüche*, Op. 79, and Psalm 98, Op. 91.
88. Schünemann: 1928, 138–71.
89. Zelter, 29–32.
90. *AmZ* 2 (1799), 587.
91. *Zwölf Lieder am Klavier zu singen*; for a facs., see C. F. Zelter, *Lieder*, ed. Reinhold Kubik and Andreas Meier, Munich, 1995, 3–15.
92. Goethe to Zelter, August 26, 1799, Hecker, I, 4.
93. Zelter to Goethe, September 21, 1799, Hecker, I, 9.
94. Schottländer: 1930, 199.
95. Goethe to Zelter, May 11, 1820, Hecker, II, 59.
96. November 12, 1808, Zelter to Goethe, Hecker, I, 224–25.
97. Schünemann: 1941, 28.
98. May 1, 1819, Lea to Henriette von Pereira Arnstein (copy in MDM c. 29).
99. Applegate, 293.
100. For a study and edition of Felix's early composition studies with Zelter, see Todd: 1983. Fanny's exercises have been examined in Schröder. Two other Zelter students, Emil Fischer and G. W. Teschner, are treated in Ruhnke and Seaton: 1981.
101. Marx: 1865, I, 109–10.
102. E. Devrient, *Erinnerungen*, 36.
103. Letter of April 21, 1822, Berger to Jenny Sieber, in Siebenkäs, 233.
104. E. Devrient, *Erinnerungen*, 36.
105. March 10, 1835, Abraham to Felix; P. Mendelssohn Bartholdy: *Briefe*, 1865, 85.
106. July 20, 1829, Felix to Zelter (Berlin, *MA* Ep. 8); quoted in Großmann-Vendrey: 1969, 381.
107. Letter of May 1, 1819, Lea to Henriette von Pereira Arnstein (copy in MDM c. 29).
108. Klein: 1993, 144.
109. Letter of July 14 [*recte* 19], 1819, Lea to Henriette von Pereira Arnstein; quoted in Filosa, 23.
110. Zelter to Goethe, July 20, 1819; Hecker, II, 25.
111. Forbes, 186, 738–39.
112. Ibid., 832–33.
113. Zelter to Goethe, May 13, 1820; Hecker, II, 62.

114. Fanny to Zelter, August 18, 1819; cited in Klein: 1997, 69.
115. MDM c. 43 (see Todd: 1983).
116. May 1, 1819, Lea to Henriette von Pereira Arnstein (MDM c. 29, extract).
117. Ledebur, 233–34.
118. E. Devrient, *Recollections*, 7.
119. In *Die wahren Grundsätze zum Gebrauch der Harmonie*, Berlin, 1773; rep. Hildesheim, 1970, 53–103.
120. In the *Versuch einer geordneten Theorie der Tonsetzkunst*, Mainz, 1817–1821.
121. Kirnberger, *Die Kunst*, II/1, 55–56.
122. May 25, 1826, Zelter to Goethe, in Hecker, II, 424.
123. Schweitzer, I, 405–6. The passage occurs in bar 11. The autograph is in SBB; a facs. was published in 1947: J. S. Bach, *Brandenburgische Konzerte: Faksimile nach dem im Besitz der Deutschen Staatsbibliothek in Berlin befindlichen Autograph*, ed. Peter Wackernagl, Leipzig, 1947.
124. Elvers: 1982, 419.
125. November 1, 1819, Felix to the young horn player Rudolf Gugel, with whom Felix had performed in public in 1818. See Elvers: 1963, 95–97.
126. MDM c. 21, fol. 107. A facs. of the Lied appeared in E. Wolff: 1906, 13.
127. *MA* Ms. 3; see also Klein: 1995, 74.
128. MDM b. 5, fols. 42–52. See further Ward Jones: 2002; J. Draheim has published an edition of the sonata (Wiesbaden, 1998).
129. "Aus Berliner Briefen Augusts von Goethe (19–26. Mai 1819): ein Brief der Ottilie," in *Goethe Jahrbuch* 28 (1907), 35.
130. Treitschke, 102.
131. *MF*, I, 65–66.
132. Treitschke, 110.
133. Sorkin: 1987, 37.
134. Katz: 1980, 77.
135. For a full account, see Katz: 1994.
136. Varnhagen von Ense, IX, 614–15; trans. in Nichols, 9.
137. E. Werner: 1963, 28; on Werner's embellishment of Varnhagen's account, see Sposato: 1998, 193–94.
138. August 9, 1819, Abraham to Henriette Mendelssohn, in Klein: 1997, 42; see also Klein: 2001, 67.
139. Treitschke, 280.
140. *MF*, I, 79.

Chapter 2

1. *MF*, I, 74.
2. Felix Mendelssohn-Bartholdy, *Werke: Kritisch duchgesehene Ausgabe*, Leipzig, 1874–1877. The earliest composition admitted was the Piano Sonata in G minor (1821), posthumously published in 1868 as Op. 105.
3. *Leipziger Ausgabe der Werke Felix Mendelssohn Bartholdys*, Leipzig, 1960–1977. After a hiatus of twenty years, the new *Gesamtausgabe* resumed publication during the 1997 sesquicentennial.
4. December 10, 1824, Zelter to Goethe; Hecker, II, 310. Fanny's fugues appear not to have survived, though some of her chorales are in an autograph volume in Berlin. See Schröder, 23–32.
5. *MF*, I, 82.
6. Ibid., I, 83.
7. Fanny's setting, dated March 22, 1820, is preserved in *MA* Dep. Lohs I, 3; Felix's undated setting is in his composition workbook, MDM c. 43, fol. 21r.
8. See Schröder (n. 4).
9. "Vorrede" to *Geistliche Oden und Lieder*, C. F. Gellert, *Gesammelte Schriften*, ed. H. John et al., Berlin, 1997, II, 108.
10. Including the Fugue in E minor, Op. 35 No. 1; slow movement of the Cello Sonata in D major, Op. 58; and finale of the Piano Trio in C minor, Op. 66.
11. MDM c. 43; see Todd: 1983.
12. Marpurg, *Kritische Briefe über die Tonkunst*, Berlin, 1760; rep. Hildesheim, 1974, I, 266; trans. in David and Mendel, 363.
13. Unpublished, the quartet fugues are examined in Friedrich, 25–29, 34–38.
14. Similarly, Beethoven, whom the Viennese theorist J. G. Albrechtsberger had mentored in the genre during the 1790s, revived it in 1825, two years before his death, in the mystical *Heiliger Dankgesang* movement of the String Quartet Op. 132.

15. *AmZ* 23 (1821), 349.
16. See Schünemann: 1928, 151. According to Ledebur (359), Felix joined the Singakademie on April 11, 1819; more likely, Felix began to attend rehearsals as a visitor around this time.
17. SBB, *MN* 2; MDM b. 5, fols. 69–72. An edition by Pietro Zappalà of several settings has appeared (Stuttgart, 1998).
18. See R. Werner, 4; Zappalà: 1993, 206; and Wehner: 1996, 48–49.
19. Marpurg: 1754, II, 132.
20. See Wehner: 1996, 48–57; and R. Werner, 8–10.
21. Blumner, 56.
22. As, for example, in Psalm 30 (1794), titled *Mendelssohniana: 6 mehrstimmige Gesänge*, and 119 (1795).
23. Sonata in G minor for two pianos (February [1820]), Oxford, MDM b. 5; Piano Sonata in A minor (May 1820), *MN* 1; untitled Piano Sonata in C minor, *MN* 1; Piano Sonata in E minor (July 1820), *MN* 1; Violin Sonata in F major, *MN* 1; Piano Sonata in F minor, *MN* 1 and 2; Piano Sonata in G minor, Op. 105; and Sonatina in E major (December 13, 1821), *MA* Ms. 142.
24. Sonata in G minor for two pianos, ed. J. Draheim, Kassel, 1998; Violin Sonata in F major, ed. R. Unger, Leipzig, 1977; and Op. 105.
25. See Klein: 1993, 146. For facsimiles of the autograph, see Petitpierre, *Romance*, 106–7.
26. Reinecke, 3.
27. In modern usage, the fourth and fifth fingers.
28. July 18, 1820, *MF*, I, 83.
29. Entry of July 6, 1837, wedding diary of Felix and Cécile; Ward Jones: 1997, 62. On August 24, 1820, Abraham, Fanny, Felix, Rebecka, Carl Heyse, and Abraham's colleague Louis Hart signed a visitors' album of the Brömserburg at Rüdesheim. I am grateful to Peter Ward Jones for alerting me to these sources.
30. Thus the American musician Lowell Mason, who visited Berlin in 1852, maintained August Wilhelm was "of the family of the famous John Sebastian." Lowell Mason, *Musical Letters from Abroad*, N.Y., 1854, 98. For a thorough study of A. W. Bach's career, see Sieling; concerning Bach's method of instruction, see Little: 2002, 292–93.
31. Mason, 97; Freudenberg, 25. I am grateful to Prof. Wm. A. Little for drawing my attention to the latter passage.
32. Ibid. The work was the unpublished Prelude in E minor for organ, BWV 533. The student, C. G. Freudenberg, copied the work, which Felix gratefully received at the Singakademie on December 9, 1822; the manuscript survives in *MN* II, 166–67.
33. May 3, 1821, Felix to A. W. Bach, *MLL*, 4.
34. See Felix Mendelssohn Bartholdy, *Complete Organ Works*, ed. Wm. A. Little, London, 1990, V.
35. Rebecka Mendelssohn Bartholdy to Ferdinand David, January 26, 1832, in Eckardt, 41.
36. See Todd: 1983, 69ff.; and Todd: 1998, 172–73.
37. *MN* 1, 3. The *Recitativo* remains unpublished; the Trio and Quartet are edited, albeit unreliably, in McDonald. See also the new ed. of the Quartet by Wulf Konold, Leipzig, 1997.
38. Benedict, 8. Benedict misidentified the work as the Piano Quartet in C minor, Op. 1, which Felix began in September 1822.
39. See further Ward Jones: 1993, 264; piano quartets of Mozart, Prince Louis Ferdinand, and Dussek were in Felix's library (Elvers and Ward Jones, 94, 98–99).
40. Lea to Henriette von Pereira Arnstein (MDM c. 29, extract); the autographs of the first six *sinfonie* (*MN* 3) yield dates only for Nos. 4 and 6, begun on September 5 and 15, 1821.
41. Marx: 1865, I, 111–12; Dorn, 1872b, III, 49.
42. Parts for these symphonies, including Zelter's supplemental wind parts, were in the Singakademie library. Kulukundis, 166.
43. *Über Johann Sebastian Bachs Leben, Kunst und Kunstwerke*, Leipzig, 1802, 44.
44. *AmZ* 5 (1803), 368; from Zelter's anonymous review of Forkel's biography; see Ottenberg, 208ff.
45. The Lieder include *Ave Maria*, "Raste, Krieger," "Die Nachtigall," and "Der Verlassene," of which only the last is dated (September 24, 1821). The two part-songs, in the tradition of Zelter's male choral songs for the Berlin Liedertafel, are "Einst im Schlaraffenland" and "Lieb und Hoffnung." For the solo Lieder, see Leven: 1926; and Leven: 1958.
46. Leven: 1958, 207–8.
47. *Lady of the Lake*, Canto ii, 235–38.
48. *Harmonicon* 10 (1832), 2nd part, 54–55; see the list of editions of Fanny's music in Maurer, 30.
49. *MN* 1, 7–10.
50. See Warrack: 1987, 264; Schünemann: 1923, 507–9.
51. Viz., the seventh scene of Act I, "Giovinette che fate all'amore," the melody of which Felix takes over nearly literally.

52. Henriette Mendelssohn to Fanny (March 3, 1821), in Lambour: 1986, 60. Marianne, who did not convert to Christianity, later became an active philanthropist. At her funeral in 1880 several Mendelssohns participated in a Jewish ceremony for the first time during their lives. See Gilbert: 1975, xvi.
53. February 26, 1821, Lea to Henriette von Pereira Arnstein. MDM c. 29 (extract).
54. A piano-duet arrangement of the overture, presumably used by Felix and Fanny, has survived (*MN* 2, 12–19); most likely, Felix himself rendered the orchestral score of the other numbers at the piano.
55. February 26, 1821, Lea to Henriette von Pereira Arnstein, MDM c. 29 (extract).
56. See Schünemann: 1923, 509–15; Köhler: 1960, 86–89; and Warrack: 1987, 267–71.
57. September 10, 1829, from Mendelssohn to Wilhelm Hensel, in *MLL*, 97.
58. Lea to Henriette von Pereira Arnstein, May 6, 1821, MDM c. 29 (extract).
59. March 22, 1821, from Felix to Gustav Adolf Stenzel, in Felix Mendelssohn Bartholdy, *Briefe*, ed. Rudolf Elvers, Band I, Leipzig, 1997, *Vorabdruck*, 6; and E. Devrient, *Erinnerungen*, 11f.
60. May 6, 1821, Lea to Henriette von Pereira Arnstein (MDM c. 29, extract).
61. E. Devrient, *Erinnerungen*, 11f.
62. T. Devrient, 225ff.
63. Letter of May 6, 1821, Lea to Henriette von Pereira Arnstein. MDM c. 29 (extract).
64. Bauer, I, 223.
65. Rollka, 77.
66. E. Devrient, *Erinnerungen*, 12.
67. Warrack: 1987, 273.
68. E. Devrient, *Erinnerungen*, 15.
69. March 22, 1820 [*recte* 1821], PML; Mendelssohn Bartholdy: 1997, 5–6.
70. Several of Felix's undated math and history exercise books survive at the Bodleian Library (MDM d. 67).
71. An edition with several facsimiles appeared in 1961 (Galley).
72. August Wilhelm Schlegel, *Shakespeares dramatische Werke*, Berlin, 1797–1810, 9 vols.
73. Galley, 30.
74. Lea to Henriette von Pereira Arnstein, February 18, 1819, from a copy of the correspondence in the Mendelssohn-Gesellschaft, Berlin; cited in Lowenthal-Hensel: 1990, 141.
75. Kliem, 136.
76. Bauer, I, 207.
77. Letter of July 28, 1821, Lambour: 1986, 84.
78. February 1821, Lea to Henriette von Pereira Arnstein, MDM c. 29 (extract).
79. Entry of January 1821: "J'aurais fait l'essai d'exprimer sur ce papier mon admiration pour vos rares talen[t]s si la chose m'eut paru aussi facile que de faire une Fugue." Klein: 1993, 145.
80. Hexelschneider, 133.
81. October 19, 1821, Lea to Henriette von Pereira Arnstein. MDM c. 29 (extract).
82. November 6, 1821, Fanny to Felix; Mendelssohn, Fanny and Felix, 21.
83. June 1821, Lea to Henriette von Pereira Arnstein. MDM c. 29 (extract).
84. On Begas see Irmgard Wirth, *Die Künstlerfamilie Begas in Berlin*, Berlin, 1968.
85. Letter of September 1821 from Lea to Henriette von Pereira Arnstein. MDM c. 29 (extract).
86. Berlin, MA Depos. Lohs 1, 45–48. The manuscript, which contains primarily Lieder from 1820 and 1821, is briefly described in Klein: 1995, 81.
87. Lambour, 65, n. 5.
88. One is reproduced in color in Schneider: 1947, 17.
89. See Crum: 1972, 11.
90. Lowenthal-Hensel: 1979, 176.
91. *MF*, I, 96.
92. See Cooper: 1995.
93. Lowenthal-Hensel: 1979b, 184, 193–94.
94. Schadow, I, 143.
95. *MF*, I, 95.
96. On Spontini's opera, which drew upon the romances already composed for the *Lallah Rookh* festival, see Dennis Libby, "Gaspare Spontini and His French and German Operas," Ph.D. diss., Princeton Univ., 1969, 355ff.
97. Helmig, 164.
98. Letter ca. July 1820; *MF*, I, 79.
99. Ibid., I, 75.
100. August 11, 1821, Jacob Bartholdy to Fanny. Lambour: 1986, 87.

101. The loss is alluded to in letters to Fanny from Jacob Bartholdy (August 4 and 11, 1821) and Henriette Mendelssohn (August 7, 1821), Lambour: 1986, 63, 85.
102. September 24, 1821, Lea to Henriette von Pereira Arnstein; cited in Crum: 1984, 87–88.

Chapter 3

1. As reported in Hans von Bülow, *Ausgewählte Schriften: 1850–1892*, Leipzig, 1896, 371.
2. Libby, 206–7.
3. Heine, "Zweiter Brief aus Berlin" (March 16, 1822), in *Sämtliche Schriften*, ed. K. Briegleb, Munich, 1959, II, 25f.; Bauer, I, 213.
4. Jules [Julius] Benedict, *Weber*, London, 1881, 62.
5. Ibid., 66.
6. The Mendelssohns had apparently dined with Weber on June 19, the day after the premiere of *Der Freischütz*. See Petitpierre, *Romance*, 100.
7. Benedict, *Weber*, 73.
8. Libby, 282.
9. Fanny to Felix, October 29/30 1821, in Citron: 1987, 2.
10. August 20–September 20, 1821, Hecker, II, 228.
11. Zelter to Goethe, October 22, 1821, Hecker, II, 139.
12. "Memoir of Ernest-Florens-Friederich Chladni," *Harmonicon* 10 (1832), 163.
13. Chladni provided drawings of more than one hundred patterns in *Entdeckungen über die Theorie des Klanges*, Leipzig, 1787; rep. Leipzig, 1980.
14. E. F. F. Chladni, *Beyträge zur praktischen Akustik*, Leipzig, 1821; rep. 1980, 134.
15. Ibid., 165.
16. Felix to Abraham Mendelssohn Bartholdy, October 30, 1821, in Felix Mendelssohn Bartholdy: 1997, 9.
17. Großmann-Vendrey: 1969, 17 (letter of February 4, 1822).
18. November 1, 1821, in Mendelssohn Bartholdy: 1997, 10–11.
19. Ibid.
20. See Todd: 1991c, 163–71.
21. In Felix's letter of November 4, 1821, to Berlin (NYPL No. 4).
22. Boyle, 233; F. R. Karl, *George Eliot: Voice of a Century*, N.Y., 1995, 180.
23. T. J. Reed, *Goethe*, Oxford, 1984, 29.
24. Steiger and Reimann, VII, 66 (July 14, 1821).
25. Warrack: 1968, 304.
26. Ulrike von Pogwisch (1804–1899), sister of Ottilie.
27. November 6, 1821, Felix to Abraham; *MLL*, 8.
28. *MF* I, 90.
29. Berlin, *MA* Depos. Lohs 1, 27–28; Maurer, 96.
30. *MF* I, 92, but see also Friedlaender: 1891, 116–117.
31. Felix to Lea, March 13, 1825, *MLL*, 29.
32. Bode, 83.
33. November 14, 1821, Felix to Berlin (NYPL No. 8); *GM*, 26.
34. Rellstab, II, 140.
35. Steiger and Reimann, VII, 98 (November 5, 1821).
36. See Elvers: 1970; *GM*, 21.
37. Facs. in Kleßmann, 124; and Selden-Goth, 24. The silhouettes are in MDM d. 8, fols. 31, 37–40; see also *GM*, p. 29n.
38. Rellstab, II, 135–48.
39. *GM*, 12 (after Rellstab, II, 141).
40. Rellstab, II, 143.
41. K. 396 (=K. 385f), Goethe und Schiller Archiv, Weimar. The fragment was "completed" by Mozart's friend and fellow Mason, Anton Stadler, and published as a Fantasy for piano solo.
42. *GM*, 14.
43. Ibid., 15.
44. See J. C. Lobe, "Conversations with Mendelssohn," trans. S. Gillespie, in Todd: 1991, 187–205.
45. Lobe: 1867, 6.
46. In a letter of March 11, 1823, to Goethe, Zelter refers to Felix's new Piano Quartet in C minor, Op. 1, and distinguishes it from the quartet performed for the poet in Weimar in 1821. Hecker, II, 201–2.

47. *GM*, 17 (after Lobe).
48. November 26, 1821, Abraham to Goethe, Friedlaender: 1891, 111.
49. *Vorvertrag* of December 8, 1821; Klein: 1995b, 100–102; the closing and reorganization of the firm was announced on December 31. See Elvers and Klein, 161, No. 55, with facs.
50. Henriette to her son Benjamin, January 4, 1822, in Reissner: 1976, 251.
51. March 19, 1822, Felix to Goethe; Friedlaender: 1891, 78.
52. April 21, 1822, Ludwig Berger to Jenny Sieber; Siebenkäs, 233.
53. January 9, 1822, Felix to Casper. HHI, Sig. 50.538.
54. MDM e. 14, 3; *MN* 9.
55. See further Warrack: 1987, 275, 283; and Schünemann: 1923, 525–32.
56. Warrack: 1987, 283.
57. March 17, 1822, Zelter to Goethe; Hecker, II, 161.
58. It was completed by the date of Zelter's letter, and appears in Fanny's list of Felix's compositions from 1822, narrowing its date to ca. January–March 17, 1822. *MF*, I, 117–18.
59. *MN* 2, 169–74; ed. by Pietro Zappalà in Felix Mendelssohn Bartholdy, *13 Psalmmotetten komponiert 1821/22*, Stuttgart, 1998, 60–68.
60. *MN* 45, 109–72; two editions are available in Hatteberg, and Pietro Zappalà (Stuttgart, 1998).
61. *MN* 45.
62. R. Werner, 17.
63. Elvers and Ward Jones, 89.
64. "Introduction" to Wehner's edition of Felix's *Magnificat* in *LAWFMB* VI:5, Wiesbaden, 1997, xvi.
65. Felix to Zelter, August 9, 1822; Schottländer: 1930, 240.
66. March 29, 1822, Lea to Henriette von Pereira Arnstein; MDM c. 29 (extract).
67. *MF* I, 118.
68. For a modern ed., see H. Allan Craw, ed., *The Symphony 1720–1840*, Series B, XI, N.Y., 1983.
69. Dinglinger: 1993.
70. *Harmonicon* 6 (1828), 251.
71. Fanny included it in her 1822 list of Felix's compositions; *MF* I, 118.
72. See the preface to Renate Unger's edition of both versions in *LAWFMB* II: 6, Leipzig, 1973.
73. For examples, see Hoffmann-Erbrecht.
74. Heyse, 3–6, 9–10, 12.
75. Klein: 1993, 146.
76. Crum: 1984, 87ff.
77. Felix used two drawing books concurrently, now in MDM c. 5, e. 3. Only a few drawings have been published, including views of Wattwyl, the Grindelwald Glacier, Vevay, and Chamonix. See Crum: 1972, No. 6; Petitpierre, *Romance*, 25, 29; Koyanagi, 1 and 54; and Lambour: 1990, 176, which reproduces a view of Vevay drawn for the album of Julie Heyse.
78. July 19, 1822, *MLL*, 12.
79. *MF* I, 115.
80. July 19, 1822, Felix to Zelter; *MLL*, 12.
81. July 19, 1822, Felix and Fanny to Zelter; HHI, Sig. 51.4896.
82. August 27, 1822, Felix to Casper; MDM c. 32, fols. 4–6.
83. August 21, 1822, Lea to Henriette Mendelssohn, in Lambour: 1990, 172.
84. Ibid.
85. August 22, 1822, Felix to Zelter; *MLL*, 14.
86. Ibid.
87. August 21, 1822, Lea to Henriette Mendelssohn, Lambour: 1990, 173.
88. August 22, 1822, Felix to Zelter. *MLL*, 16.
89. Undated letter from Fanny to Marianne Mendelssohn, *MF*, I, 110.
90. *Sehnsucht nach Italien*, August 17, 1822; for an ed., transposed from the original A major to G major, see Fanny Hensel, *Ausgewählte Lieder*, Düsseldorf, 1991, 8–9.
91. About forty-five km. August 21–22, 1822, Lea to Henriette Mendelssohn; Lambour: 1990, 176.
92. September 13, 1822, Felix to Zelter, in Selden-Goth, 25.
93. The commentary supplementing the drawing is in MDM c. 49, fols. 1v–2.
94. *MF* I, 112.
95. "Von allen deinen zarten Gaben" and the lullaby "Schlummre sanft und milde" (September 18, 1822), published in Leven: 1926, 179–80. The Piano Quartet was begun two days later. Autographs of all three are in *MN* II.
96. Felix to Zelter, September 13, 1822, Selden-Goth, 27–28.
97. July 19, 1822, Fanny to Zelter. HHI, Sig. 51.4896.
98. Hiller, *Letters*, 4; Schnyder von Wartensee, 369.

99. E. Devrient, *Recollections*, 11–12.
100. See further Bormann.
101. E. Devrient, *Recollections*, 12.
102. Two autographs survive, dated October 25, 1820 [*recte* 1822] (*MN* 45), and November 4, 1822 (Stadt- und Universitätsbibliothek Frankfurt), bearing a dedication to the Cäcilienverein.
103. Jacobson: 1962, 25. The change was recorded in the Berlin *Judenbürgerbuch* on February 13, 1823; see Kliem, 130.
104. Elvers: 1974, 49.
105. C. H. Müller, 3.
106. See Ward Jones: *Mendelssohns on Honeymoon*, 1997, xv.
107. Steiger and Reimann, VII, 190.
108. *GM*, 34.
109. E. Devrient, *Recollections*, 10.
110. *MF* I, 113.
111. MDM, b. 3, fol. 1.
112. See Montgomery, 201.
113. *AmZ* 25 (1823), 55.
114. Elvers and Klein, 171, No. 68.
115. *MF* I, 101.
116. Elvers and Klein, No. 78, 180–82, with facs.
117. December 25, 1822, Lea to Wilhelm Hensel; Gilbert: 1975, 51.
118. In a letter of June 4, 1822 to Zelter, Fanny lamented, "My quartet progresses slowly. I am in the middle movement. If you are not there, the work will not move at all." Klein: 1997, 70.
119. Ed. Renate Eggebrecht-Kupsa, Kassel, 1990.
120. Cadenbach, 85.
121. Heine, "Dritter Brief aus Berlin," *Sämtliche Werke*, ed. K. Briegleb, Munich, 1959, II, 59 (June 7, 1822).
122. *BamZ* 1 (1824), 168–69.
123. Both versions are available in *LAWFMB* I: 2 (1965).
124. See the more detailed analysis in Todd: 1991c, 167ff.

Chapter 4

1. Dorn: 1872, 399.
2. March 11, 1823; Hecker, II, 201–2.
3. See Ward Jones: 1993.
4. February 11, 1824, Henriette Mendelssohn to Lea, cited in ibid., 269–70.
5. *AmZ* 26 (1824), 181–84.
6. *BamZ* 1 (1824), 168–69.
7. All five are available in *LAWFMB*, I:5, Leipzig, 1967.
8. Mendelssohn, *Complete Organ Works*, Wm. A. Little, ed., London, 1990, V, 69–72.
9. See the Preface to H. C. Wolff's edition in *LAWFMB*, I:3.
10. May 27, 1823, Lea to Henriette von Pereira Arnstein; *Vossische Zeitung* No. 78 (July 1, 1823), 8; both cited in Hellmundt (n. 12), xvi.
11. MDM b. 5, fols. 73–79; the version with string orchestra is in Berlin, *MN* Band 4.
12. Clemens Schmalstich, ed., Berlin, 1960; Christoph Hellmundt, ed. in *LAWFMB*, II:8 (1999).
13. Berlin, *MN* 15; letters of December 9, 1823, Felix to Zelter, *MLL*, 18–19; and December 9, Fanny to Zelter, Klein: 1997, 138.
14. See Lindeman: 1999, and his edition of the original version of the first movement (Madison, Wisc., 1999).
15. Lindeman: 1999, 70.
16. Orazio Frugoni, "The Case of the Captive Concertos," *High Fidelity* 4/3 (May 1954), 26ff.
17. *Sonatensatz* in E major (January 29, 1822), ed. L. G. Serbescu and B. Heller, Kassel, 1991.
18. See further Lindeman: 1999b, 82.
19. Berlin, *MN* 15; see the edition of Karl-Heinz Köhler, with facs., in *LAWFMB*, II:4 (1971).
20. See most recently Leon Plantinga, *Beethoven's Concertos*, N.Y., 1999, 290.
21. They include *Faunenklag, Am Seegestad, Durch Fichten*, and *Ich denke dein* (MDM b. 5 and c. 47).
22. See Walter Frisch, "Schubert's *Nähe des Geliebten* (D. 162): Transformation of the Volkston," *Schubert: Critical and Analytical Studies*, ed. Walter Frisch, Lincoln, 1986, 175–99.

23. *MN* 2, 258–70 (February 23, 1823).
24. Ed. R. L. Todd, N.Y., 1980; see also Todd: 1981.
25. Mendelssohn Bartholdy, *Complete Organ Works*, V.
26. Bormann, 99; ed. G. Graulich, Stuttgart, 1980.
27. See further Wehner: 1996, 131.
28. The first page of the autograph (BL Add Ms. 30900) bears the date March 25, 1823; the last page, March [April] 5. The quartet was first published in Berlin in 1879.
29. In 1848, Felix's widow Cécile gave the autograph, now lost, to the violinist Joseph Joachim, who later described the manuscript to Julius Rietz. See Joachim and Moser, II, 266.
30. *BamZ* 2 (1825), 366.
31. Especially in her *Sonata o Capriccio* in F minor for piano (February 1824).
32. April 8, 1823, Lea to Amalia Beer; Meyerbeer, I, 467–69. See also the letter of September 27, 1823, Amalia Beer to Meyerbeer, in ibid., 554.
33. *MF*, I, 118.
34. The *Allegro molto agitato* in D minor of December 3, 1823, in Fanny Hensel-Mendelssohn, *Frühe Klavierstücke (1823/24)*, ed. Barbara Heller, Kassel, 1996, 24–27.
35. *AmZ* 25 (1823), 271.
36. Letter of April 8, 1823 (n. 32).
37. *AmZ* 25 (1823), 337.
38. *MF* I, 117.
39. Wilhelm Müller to Adelheid Müller, July 29, 1823, in P. S. Allen and J. T. Hatfield, ed., *Diary and Letters of Wilhelm Müller*, Chicago, 1903, 112.
40. Maurer, 80.
41. December 1, 1823, Gilbert: 1975, 57–61.
42. Ibid., 59.
43. Author of the play *Preciosa*, set to music by Carl Maria von Weber in 1821.
44. Goethe to Zelter, August 24, 1823; Hecker, II, 218; see also Löwenthal-Hensel: 1981, 43–44.
45. *MF*, I, 103.
46. Löwenthal-Hensel: 1981, 15.
47. Ibid. For a facs. see Klein: 1997, 53.
48. Abraham and Lea to Wilhelm Hensel, January 4, 1826, in Gilbert: 1975, 62–66.
49. Wilhelm to Luise, December 1, 1823, ibid., 60.
50. *MF* I, 102-03.
51. E. Devrient, *Recollections*, 8.
52. *MF* I, 119.
53. Karl Baedeker, *Northern Germany*, Leipzig, 1900, 260.
54. Ulrich Wegener, "Bad Reinerz: Herrliche Melodien um ein idyllisches Land," cited in Rabien: 1990, 163.
55. *MF*, I, 120.
56. Paul Dengler, *Geschichte des Bades Reinerz*, Reinerz, 1903, cited in Rabien: 1990, 166.
57. Ibid.
58. December 6, 1823, Felix to Latzel, in Liepmannsohn, 64. Friedhelm Krummacher has proposed that a fragmentary violin sonata (*MN* 20, 73–79) was the work intended for Latzel. Krummacher: 1978, 84.
59. E. Devrient, *Recollections*, 57.
60. Ibid., 14–15. Rietz's copy is in MDM c. 68. For a brief description, see Crum: 1983, 30.
61. E. Devrient, *Recollections*, 13.
62. Hiller, *Mendelssohn: Letters and Recollections*, 178.
63. Marx: 1865, II, 85ff.
64. Geck, 19.
65. MDM Green Books IV, 204; see Elvers and Ward Jones, 90.
66. In 1999, a significant part of the library, confiscated by the Russian Red Army at the end of World War II, reemerged in the Ukraine. See "International Sleuthing Adds Insight about Bach," *New York Times*, August 16, 1999; and Christoph Wolff, "Recovered in Kiev: Bach *et al.*: A Preliminary Report on the Music Collection of the Berlin Sing-Akademie," *Notes of the Music Library Association* 58 (2001), 259–71.
67. Friedrich Smend, "Bachs Matthäus-Passion," *Bach-Jahrbuch 1928*, 1–95; Schünemann: 1928, 138–71. For a facs. of the Altnikol Ms., now in SBB, see *NBA* II/5a.
68. SBB, Mus. Ms. Bachautogr. P. 25.
69. *Kritischer Bericht* of Dürr's edition of the Passion for the Neue Bach Ausgabe, II: 5, Kassel, 1974, 15–16, 71, and 94–96.

70. Nos. 4–7, and 25–26. Schünemann: 1928, 148.
71. Geiringer, 199; Carl von Winterfeld first applied the simile in the *Evangelischer Kirchengesang*, Leipzig, 1843–1847.
72. Marx: 1865, II 85ff; for Zelter's reworking of a recitative, see Schünemann: 1928, 149–50.
73. MDM d. 14 (Crum: 1983, 92).
74. The autograph, which fills two volumes (*MN* 10 and 11), bears the first title on its cover, the second at the head of the overture.
75. E. Devrient, *Recollections*, 15; T. Devrient, 279.
76. T. Devrient, 280.
77. A pupil of Zelter and Berger, Dorn (1804–1892) produced his own opera, *Rolands Knappen*, in 1826. A few years later, Robert Schumann studied counterpoint with him in Leipzig.
78. T. Devrient, 279.
79. Dorn: 1872, 399.
80. Ibid.
81. *AmZ* 26 (1824), 107.
82. See Dorn: 1872, 399; Schünemann: 1923, 533ff.; and Warrack: 1987, 285–86.
83. Zelter to Goethe, February 8, 1824; *GM*, 37.
84. E. Devrient, *Recollections*, 15.
85. Ibid., 16.
86. July 6–7, 1824; NYPL No. 11.
87. Dorn: 1872, 400.
88. Klingemann.
89. Ibid., 6; Ward Jones: 1989, 74.
90. Several, including the text of Felix's Singspiel *Heimkehr aus der Fremde*, are in Klingemann, 343–57.
91. Ledebur, 463; Dorn: 1872, 400.
92. See Hake.
93. Sammons, 109.
94. See further Andreas Feuchte, "Hermann Franck (1802–1855): Persönlichkeit zwischen Politik und Kunst," in Lars Lambrecht, ed., *Philosophie, Literatur und Politik vor den Revolutionen von 1848*, Bern, 1996, 399–412.
95. *AmZ* 12 (1809), 630, 652.
96. Marx: 1865, II, 50.
97. See further Scott G. Burnham, "Aesthetics, Theory and History in the Works of Adolph Bernhard Marx," Ph.D. diss., Brandeis Univ., 1988, Ch. 1.
98. *BamZ* 1 (1824), 174.
99. Ibid., 152ff. (April 24, 1824).
100. Thus, in 1826 Zelter commented that Marx "may have been baptized with salt-water, for his excrement has a gray-green-yellow color." Zelter to Goethe, May 25, 1826, Geiger, II, 425.
101. E. Devrient, *Recollections*, 35.
102. Siegfried, 38–39.
103. E. Devrient, *Recollections*, 35.
104. Dorn: 1872, 401.
105. E. Devrient, *Recollections*, 98.
106. Therese Marx.
107. Marx, "Memoirs," 207.
108. Ibid., 211–12.
109. *MN* 49.
110. *MN* 4, 167–76.
111. *MN* 4, 107–65.
112. See the Preface to Gerhard Allroggen's ed., Kassel, 1987.
113. *MN* 4, 89–106.
114. See Todd: 1990, 56–59; and Mendelssohn, *Early Works for Piano*, ed. R. L. Todd, Cambridge, 1985, 5–20. The undated Capriccio may be placed by its clefs before September 1824, when Felix altered the style of clefs in his manuscripts (see p. 132).
115. *MN* 4, 71–87; ed., Leipzig, 1966.
116. London, BL Loan 4, Royal Philharmonic Society Ms. 289. Felix drafted the symphony between March 3 and March 31, 1824. See further the Preface to Ralf Wehner's ed. in *LAWFMB* I:4.
117. See Todd: 1997b, 84.
118. Two of his drawings are reproduced in Ward Jones: 1997b, 15; and Koyanagi, 53.
119. See the letters of July 16 and July 30, 1824, in Schmidt-Beste, 37–41.

120. July 21, 1824, Felix to Fanny; *Fanny and Felix Mendelssohn*, 24.
121. Edition (Amsterdam, 1989).
122. Werner: 1963, 40; also in the revised German version, *Mendelssohn: Neuer Sicht*, 63.
123. Sposato: 1998, 194.
124. Berlin, *MA* Ms. 34, 77.
125. Ed. Liana Gavrila Serbescu and Barbara Heller, Kassel, 1991.
126. Mendelssohn, *Early Works for Piano*, ed. R. L. Todd, Cambridge, 1985, 24–30; with a facs. on xi.
127. See Werner: 1955, 132.
128. In the first movement of the *Eroica* Symphony, and Piano Sonatas, Opp. 31 No. 1 and 53.
129. *AmZ* 25 (1823), 186.
130. I. Moscheles: 1873, 59.
131. Ibid., 10.
132. Jerome Roche, "Moscheles," in *The New Grove Dictionary of Music and Musicians*, London, 1980, XII, 599–600. A selection of Moscheles's solo piano music is available in Jeffrey Kallberg, ed., *Piano Music of the Parisian Virtuosos 1810–1860*, V, N.Y., 1993.
133. *AmZ* 26 (1824), 860.
134. Zelter to Goethe, November 27, 1824, Hecker, II, 306.
135. Polko: 1869, 4–6. Polko (née Elise Vogel, 1823–1899) was an amateur singer who sang in the Gewandhaus concerts of 1846 and 1847 before she devoted herself to a writing career.
136. Lampadius, 17.
137. *BamZ* 1 (1824), 405–7 (November 24, 1824).
138. F. Moscheles: 1888, 1–2. As early as 1822 Lea had attempted to engage Moscheles for lessons (communication from Peter Ward Jones).
139. I. Moscheles: 1873, 65.
140. Ibid., 66.
141. *MN* 13, 49.
142. November 19–22, 1824, Speyer to Spohr, in Speyer, 83.

Chapter 5

1. Children of Bella's daughter Rebecka Seeligmann, who had died in 1810.
2. April 24, 1824, Lea to Henriette von Pereira Arnstein, Lowenthal-Hensel: 1990, 142.
3. Peter Ward Jones has suggested (communication of June 28, 2001) that motivating Bella's decision may have been a practical concern, to bequeath her fortune to the least financially secure members of her family; Bella may have viewed Lea and Abraham as comfortable enough from their own assets.
4. Much of the following discussion derives from two studies: Cullen and Lowenthal-Hensel: 1990.
5. Frederick A. Pottle, ed., *Boswell on the Grand Tour: Germany and Switzerland 1764*, N.Y., 1953, 77–78.
6. *MF* I, 123.
7. Hensel: 1911, 9.
8. E. Devrient, *Erinnerungen*, 45; Cullen, 49.
9. MDM e. 3, facs. in Lowenthal-Hensel: 1990, facing 144.
10. *MF* I, 122.
11. Ibid.
12. Giesau, 58–66.
13. Cited in Lowenthal-Hensel: 1990, 145.
14. Letter of March 13, 1825, *MLL*, 27–30.
15. Soret to Caroline von Egloffstein, March 13, 1825, in *Goethes Gespräche*, ed. F. von Biedermann and Wolfgang Herwig, vol. 3/1, Zurich, 1971, 755.
16. July 8, 1829, Abraham to Felix in London; Werner: 1963, 36–38.
17. Though music publishers occasionally hyphenated Felix's two surnames, he consistently signed his correspondence "Felix Mendelssohn Bartholdy."
18. *MF*, I, 85.
19. March 23, 1825; Elvers, *MLL*, 31.
20. Bellasis, 195.
21. April 1, 1825, Felix to Berlin. *Fanny and Felix Mendelssohn*, 35.
22. April 6, 1825, Felix to Berlin. *MLL*, 37.
23. Zelter to Goethe, May 28, 1825; Hecker, II, 322–23.

24. *AmZ* 39 (1837), 847.
25. March 27, 1825, Henriette to Fanny; Lambour: 1986, 75–76.
26. A piano-vocal score of the work ed. by Ralph Leavis appeared in 1964; a full score ed. by R. L. Todd, in Stuttgart in 1986.
27. See *BamZ* 2 (1825), 211–12.
28. See *GM*, 42n.
29. Onslow's father, a member of Parliament, had been involved in a homosexual affair in 1781, and was compelled to leave England for France.
30. April 1, 1825; Fanny and Felix Mendelssohn, 33–34.
31. Stendhal, *Life of Rossini*, trans. Richard N. Coe, Seattle, 1970, 404.
32. March 25 and April 6, 1825, in *MLL*, 32, 34–35.
33. Unpublished letter of April 18, 1825 (NYPL No. 25).
34. Stendhal (n. 31), 379.
35. April 6, 1825. *MLL*, 36.
36. *MF* I, 126.
37. Warrack: 1968, 227.
38. April 6, 1825; *MLL*, 39.
39. April 20, 1825; *MF* I, 127.
40. May 9, 1825. Ibid., I, 128.
41. Hiller, *Letters*, 4.
42. Lea to Goethe, April 9, 1825; Friedlaender: 1891, 114.
43. Steiger and Reimann, VII, 507; *GM*, 50; Friedlaender: 1891, 126.
44. Hiller, *Letters*, 58.
45. Schubring, "Reminiscences of Felix Mendelssohn-Bartholdy," in *MahW*, 222.
46. Zelter to Goethe, June 7, 1825 (Hecker, II, 340).
47. Dale A. Jorgenson, *The Life and Legacy of Franz Xaver Hauser*, Carbondale, Ill., 1996, 21.
48. Bill, 348. The autograph of the song is in MDM b. 5, fols. 5–6a.
49. The autograph is in PML.
50. In 1826 Weber stayed at Smart's London residence but died after the premiere of *Oberon*; Smart had the misfortune of discovering the composer's body.
51. Cox, 191.
52. See Clive Brown, "The Chamber Music of Spohr and Weber," in Stephen Hefling, ed., *Nineteenth-Century Chamber Music*, N.Y., 1998, 161.
53. Louis Spohr, *Lebenserinnerungen*, ed. Folker Göthel, Tutzing, 1968, II, 134.
54. *MF*, I, 131.
55. Dorn: 1872, 400.
56. The 1825 autograph is in the Whittall Foundation Collection of LC. A facsimile, ed. by Jon Newsom, was published in 1976.
57. Copies of letters from Lea to Henriette von Pereira Arnstein, 1826, in MDM c. 29.
58. *Das Mädchen von Andros, eine Komödie des Terentius, in den Versmassen des Originals, übersetzt von F****, mit Einleitung und Anmerkungen herausgegeben von K. W. L. Heyse*, Berlin, 1826.
59. From the trans. by John Sargeaunt, Cambridge, Mass., 1918, 23.
60. Felix to Goethe, September 30, 1826; *MLL*, 42.
61. *Über die Dichtkunst/Epistel an die Pisonen*, SBB MA Ms. 134.
62. See the review by A. B. Marx in *BamZ* 2 (1825), 364–65 (November 9, 1825), and the unsigned review in *AmZ* 27 (1825), 825.
63. Beethoven [Klingemann] to Fanny, November 8, 1825, in Elvers: 1997b.
64. Schubring: 1991, 229.
65. "Felix Mendelssohns Konfirmations-Bekenntnis," in Klingemann, 358–62. An English trans. is in Brown: 2003, 93–102.
66. Lea to Hensel, January 4, 1826, in Gilbert: 1975, 65.
67. *MF* I, –104 (Lea to Hensel, March 6, 1826).
68. Gilbert: 1975, 66.
69. "Schreibt der Komponist ernst," in a letter of 1826 from Lea to Henriette von Pereira Arnstein (MDM c. 29); published in Galley, 7.
70. *MLL*, 43–4; much of their correspondence was published in Dahlgren.
71. C. H. Bitter, ed., *Carl Loewes Selbstbiographie*, Berlin, 1870; rep. Hildesheim, 1976, 106.
72. I. Moscheles, 89–90; E. Devrient, *Recollections*, 31–32.
73. BL Music Loan 95/2, 92–95 (November 24, 1826).
74. *Vossische Zeitung* (November 13, 1826).
75. *BamZ* 3 (1826), 189–90; see Dorn: 1872, 401.

76. Felix to Fanny, July 7, 1826; Fanny and Felix Mendelssohn: 1997, 48.
77. Berlin, DSB 13, 119–23 (January 5, 1826; unpublished).
78. See further Todd: 1990b. For an edition of the Vivace and Fugue in E♭ see Mendelssohn, *Early Works for Piano*, ed. R. L. Todd, Cambridge, 1985.
79. Blumner, 71; an edition with critical notes by Barbara Mohn is available (Stuttgart, 1997).
80. The manuscript of the fugue shows signs of haste, including, uncharacteristic of Felix, some parallelisms in the voice leading. See R. Werner, 35.
81. They were announced in the *Vossische Zeitung* in February 1827.
82. Dinglinger: 1997.
83. *AmZ* 30 (1828), 63.
84. Robert Schumann: 1888, I, 237.
85. *BamZ* 4 (1827), 288.
86. Schumann: 1946, 210.
87. The autograph is in PML; see further Todd: 1979, 293–328.
88. Ibid., 309–13; see also Todd: 1998, 184–85.
89. The dated autograph is in BN, Conservatoire Ms. 206; according to E. Devrient, the work was heard on a concert of the violinist Louis Maurer, on which Felix also performed the piano part in Beethoven's Choral Fantasia. That concert occurred on November 2, 1825, but the work performed then was the Symphony in C minor, Op. 11 (see n. 62, *supra*).
90. July 7, 1826, Felix to Fanny, in Fanny and Felix Mendelssohn, 48–49.
91. Marx: 1865, II, 229.
92. See Todd: 1993, 41–42.
93. From Weber's 1816 review of the Overture to Spohr's opera *Faust*, also performed on the concert of July 17, 1826. Carl Maria von Weber, *Writings on Music*, ed. John Warrack, Cambridge, 1981, 193.
94. Lea to Henriette von Pereira Arnstein, August 1826 (MDM c. 29, fol. 59, extract).
95. A. W. Schlegel, *Sämtliche Werke*, Leipzig, 1846–1847, VIII, 29; trans. in Wellek, II, 65.
96. In the autograph score Felix specified an English bass horn for Bottom. When he published the overture in 1835, he replaced the instrument with an ophicleide, a member of the keyed bugle family; today, a tuba ordinarily performs the part.
97. Bellasis, *Cherubini*, 203.
98. *MF* I, 130.
99. E. Devrient, *Recollections*, 21.
100. Schubring, "Reminiscences," in *MahW*, 225 (mm. 264ff. of the overture, where the cellos execute a *pianissimo* descending scale).
101. *MF*, I, 130.
102. SBB, MA Ms. 63, 1.
103. See Klein: 1997, 54.
104. "Gab die liebende Natur, / Gab der Geist euch Flügel, / Folget meiner leichten Spur, / Auf, zum Rosenhügel!" The quatrain is from the *Walpurgisnachtstraum* scene of Goethe's *Faust*, Part I.
105. "Gab die liebende Natur / Euch der Kraft Behagen: / Schaffet frei und fröhlich! Nur / Jugend darf es wagen!"
106. E. Devrient, *Recollections*, 31.

Chapter 6

1. *MF* I, 156.
2. Zelter to Goethe, July 1, 1825; Hecker, II, 352.
3. Schünemann: 1941, 40.
4. *AmZ* 29 (1827), 113.
5. E. Devrient, *Recollections*, 32.
6. Zelter to Felix, September 18, 1826; in Schmidt-Beste, 44–45; see also T. Schmidt, 44–46.
7. E. Devrient, *Recollections*, 32–33.
8. *AmZ* 29 (1827), 156.
9. *BamZ* 4 (1827), 84 (March 14, 1827).
10. Felix to A. M. Schlesinger, March 5, 1827; *BadV*, 278.
11. Valeria Gigliucci, *Clara Novello's Reminiscences*, London, 1910, 70.
12. E. Devrient, *Recollections*, 24. Curiously, the English translation of Devrient's memoirs mistranslates the German text ("französischen Kirche") as "Jewish church." Spontini's resi-

dence on Markgrafenstrasse was noted by W. T. Freemantle, in papers for his unfinished Mendelssohn biography (Freemantle Papers in the Whittall Collection, LC).

13. April 6, 1827, Felix to Adele Schopenhauer; *LA*, 215.
14. The revised version was performed in Oxford in February 1987; a recording appeared in 1990.
15. Elvers: 1976.
16. Wellek, II, 28.
17. January 16, 1824; Elvers: 1976.
18. E. Devrient, *Recollections*, 25.
19. *Harmonicon* 8 (1830), 99.
20. E. Devrient, *Recollections*, 27.
21. Klein: 1997, 96.
22. *BamZ* 4 (1827), 141–42 (May 2, 1827).
23. *AmZ* 29 (1827), 410–11.
24. *Revue musicale* (1827), 386–87 (May 1827).
25. *Berliner Schnellpost* 2 (1827), No. 70, 280, quoted in Krettenauer, 26.
26. E. Devrient, *Recollections*, 30.
27. Felix to William Bartholomew, July 17, 1843, Polko: 1987, 186.
28. Zelter to Goethe, April 24, 1827; Hecker, II, 519.
29. E. Devrient, *Recollections*, 40–43. Heinrich Marschner set the libretto in 1833.
30. Waidelich, 160ff.
31. On January 16, 1828, the *AmZ* reported that the opera would be "aroused from its lethargy," but nothing ever came of the idea. *AmZ* 30 (1828), 42.
32. *AmZ* 31 (1829), 356 (June 3, 1829).
33. Werner Obermann, *Der junge Johann Gustav Droysen*, diss., Rheinische Friedrich-Wilhelms-Universität zu Bonn, 1977, 98.
34. Fanny to Klingemann, December 27, 1828; *MF* I, 164.
35. Schubring, "Reminiscences," 224; Droysen: 1902, 109.
36. Lea to Henriette von Pereira Arnstein, ca. September 1827; MDM c. 29, fol. 60 (extract). The matriculation records survive in the *Universitätsarchiv* of Humboldt-Universität zu Berlin. I am indebted to Prof. S. J. Lindeman and Dr. W. Schultze for bringing the archives to my attention.
37. Gans's "Neueste Geschichte" (SBB *MA* Ms. 114); and Ritter's "Geographie von Europa" (MDM d. 67).
38. Hiller, *Letters*, 11.
39. E. Devrient, *Recollections*, 33.
40. W. L. Gage, *The Life of Carl Ritter*, N.Y., 1867, 208.
41. The original Ms. of the fugue for Op. 35 No. 1 was sold in London at an auction on May 10, 1977; the second fugue was originally in *MN* 42, according to a catalogue of the collection prepared by Konrad Schleinitz in 1848 (MDM c. 28).
42. Schubring, "Reminiscences," 227; see also Todd: 1992c, 192ff.
43. Lea to Henriette von Pereira Arnstein, August 1826; MDM c. 23 (extract).
44. Charles Rosen, *The Romantic Generation*, Cambridge, Mass., 1995, 590, 594.
45. T. Devrient, 232–34.
46. *BamZ* 4 (1827), 179 (June 6, 1827).
47. E. Devrient, *Recollections*, 26.
48. SBB, *MA* Ms. 34, 22–24 (November 11, 1823).
49. Schubring, "Reminiscences," 223–24; see the piano part of m. 14.
50. *Die Ruinen des Campo vaccino in Rom*; see Büttner, 87–118.
51. Felix to Lea, July 19, 1842; Selden-Goth, 308.
52. *Rheinblüthen. 4. Jahrgang*, Karlsruhe, 1825.
53. *Harmonicon* 8 (1830), 99.
54. *MF*, I, 133; Droysen: 1902, 195. Not to be confused with the poet Johann Heinrich Voss (1751–1826).
55. Berlin, *MN* 25.
56. See Nancy B. Reich: 1991, 259–71.
57. According to *MF* I, 133n, it was the young physicist Gustav Magnus.
58. Felix to Zelter, February 15, 1832, in P. Mendelssohn Bartholdy: 1869, 338.
59. Felix to Fanny, September 14, 1827; NYPL, part in *MF* I, 136–38.
60. H. G. Reissner, *Eduard Gans: Ein Leben im Vormärz*, Tübingen, 1965, 49.
61. Thibaut, *Purity in Music*, trans. J. Broadhouse, London, 1882, 11.
62. Felix to Berlin, September 20, 1827; *MF* I, 139.

63. Felix to Abraham, September 29, 1827, *MLL*, 49–50; Felix to Lindblad, October 23, 1827, Dahlgren, 16.

64. Reich: 1991, 260.

65. *MN* 25; *Fuga a tempo ordinario*, November 1, 1827 (*MN* 18, 13–18).

66. Felix received a copy of Beethoven's Op. 127 from Ferdinand David as a birthday present on February 3, 1827. See Ward Jones: 1989, 12–13. Curiously, Op. 132 had appeared from Schlesinger in Berlin in September 1827, though the first movement of Felix's Op. 13, which betrays Beethoven's influence, was finished in late July. In a communication to the author (July 28, 2001) Peter Ward Jones has proposed that Felix had access to a prepublication copy of Op. 132.

67. Felix to Lindblad, mid-February 1828, in Dahlgren, 19–20.

68. Ibid., 20.

69. *MA* Ms. 63, 2; for some congratulatory verses on Fanny's birthday, see Klein: 1997, 54–55.

70. See Fanny to Klingemann, December 23, 1827 (*MF* I, 152); and Lea to Klingemann, December 28, 1827 (Klingemann, 43).

71. *AmZ* 30 (1828), 45.

72. *AmZ* 30 (1828), 42, 46. The anonymous reviewer judged Schubert's ballade inferior to settings by Zelter and Reichardt, and "overly rich" (*überreich*) in "modulations and bizarreness."

73. E. Devrient, *Recollections*, 38.

74. *MF* I, 131; dated autograph in the Newberry Library, Chicago, of which a facs., ed. by Oswald Jonas, appeared in 1966.

75. Reich: 1991, 261. The Pistor Collection was eventually sold in 1916 to the publisher C. F. Peters, and is now preserved in the Musikbibliothek of Leipzig. See *Handschriften der Werke J. S. Bachs in der Musikbibliothek der Stadt Leipzig*, Leipzig, 1964, 43–53. The autograph of BWV 133 formerly owned by Felix was donated by Ernst von Mendelssohn Bartholdy in 1908 to the Staatsbibliothek zu Berlin.

76. Reich: 1991, 262.

77. Cairns, 294.

78. Felix to Klingemann, February 5, 1828, Klingemann, 46–49.

79. See further James Garratt, *Palestrina and the German Romantic Imagination*, Cambridge, 2002, 80.

80. *MF*, I, 131.

81. *BamZ* 5 (1828), 9–10.

82. Droysen: 1902, 111.

83. Fanny to Klingemann, December 8, 1828, *MF* I, 163.

84. See Blumner, 71; Schünemann: 1941, 54; *BamZ* 6 (1829), 376, and 7 (1830), 23; and *AmZ* 31 (1829), 829.

85. *Corpus Antiphonalium Officii*, ed. René-Jean Hesbert, Rome, 1968, III, 184 and 260.

86. *BamZ* 7 (1830), 20–23 (January 16, 1830).

87. Reissner: 1959, 95.

88. Schubring, "Reminiscences," 222. In 1963 Eric Werner presented part of an "unpublished" letter from Hegel to Felix dated June 30, 1829 (Werner: 1963, 80) that appeared to discuss the relation of music to logic. But Werner gave no source for the letter, and thus far scholars have been unable to verify its authenticity.

89. Felix's lecture notes, privately owned in 1974, have so far not surfaced; see T. Schmidt: 1996, 53 fn. 108. For a modern edition of the philosopher's lectures, see T. M. Knox, ed. and trans., *Hegel's Lectures on Fine Art*, Oxford, 1975, 2 vols.

90. See J. N. Findlay, *Hegel: A Re-examination*, N.Y., 1958, 340–41; and T. Schmidt: 1996, 53ff., drawn from the fuller discussion in Adolf Nowak, *Hegels Musikästhetik*, Regensburg, 1971.

91. Zelter to Goethe (March 22, 1829), Hecker III, 153; but see also Geck, 60.

92. Felix to Wilhelm Taubert (August 27, 1831), cited in T. Schmidt: 1996, 59.

93. Cited in Hoffheimer, 6.

94. See Reissner: 1959.

95. Fanny to Klingemann, December 27, 1828; *MF* I, 164.

96. Fanny to Klingemann, March 22, 1829; ibid., 173–74.

97. Dated autograph of the Etude (January 4, 1828) in PML.

98. Felix to Klingemann, February 5, 1828, Klingemann, 49.

99. *AmZ* 30 (1828), 282–83.

100. *BamZ* 1 (1824), 391–96.

101. Marx, *Ueber Malerei in der Tonkunst*, Berlin, 1828, 60; see also Silber Ballan, 155ff.

102. Lea to Henriette von Pereira Arnstein, June 1828; MDM c. 29, fol. 60v (extract).

103. *AmZ* 31 (1829), 456.

104. Fanny to Klingemann, September 12, 1828 (*MF* I, 162).
105. Ibid., I, 156.
106. Part of Tölken's address is given in H. Lüdecke and S. Heiland, *Dürer und die Nachwelt*, Berlin, 1955, 209; Levezow's poem is given in German and English in Hatteberg, 182–214.
107. For Schinkel's sketch of the decorations, see Lüdecke and S. Heiland, Pl. 26. For accounts of the festival by Fanny and Levezow, see *MF*, I, 157, and Levezow, *Albrecht Dürer: Lyrische Dichtung zur Gedächtniß-Feier des Künstlers in Berlin, den 18. April 1828* (Berlin, 1828), in Hatteberg, 145–46.
108. See Werner Bollert, "Die Händelpflege der Berliner Sing-Akademie unter Zelter und Rungenhagen," in Bollert, 69–79. Felix's unpublished arrangement of *Acis and Galatea*, modernized in a scoring for flute, oboe, clarinet, bassoon, horn, trumpet, timpani, and strings, was finished in Berlin on January 3, 1829, and survives in MDM c. 74.
109. E. Devrient, *Recollections*, 42.
110. Fanny to Klingemann, December 23, 1827, *MF* I, 151.
111. Douglas Botting, *Humboldt and the Cosmos*, N.Y., 1973, 232.
112. Letter of September 28, 1828, from Chopin to his family in Warsaw. F. Chopin, *Selected Correspondence*, ed. R. E. Sydow, trans. A. Hedley, London, 1962, 17.
113. Fanny to Klingemann, September 12, 1828, *MF* I, 162.
114. Schönewolf, 24–27.
115. Botting (see n. 111), 253 (n. 113).
116. See Todd: 1993, 44–47.
117. Fanny to Klingemann, June 18, 1828, *MF* I, 161.
118. Lea to Henriette Pereira Arnstein, September 1828 (MDM c. 29, fol. 61v, extract).
119. Droysen: 1902: 116.
120. Felix to Leopold Ganz, October 19, 1828; *GM*, 186–88.
121. Entry of January 4, 1829, in Fanny's diary, Berlin, *MA* Depos. 500, 22.
122. Letter of ca. October 24, 1828, from Felix to Berlin (NYPL No. 51).
123. Klein: 1993, 155; a facs. of the autograph faces 151; Fanny to Klingemann, December 8, 1828, *MF* I, 163.
124. See Fanny's letter of September 7, 1838, to Felix; Citron: 1987, 261.
125. Tillard: 1996, 130.
126. Charles Gounod, *Autobiographical Reminiscences*, trans. W. Hely Hutchinson, London, 1896, rep. N.Y., 1970, 91. Gounod confused the *Lieder ohne Worte* with Felix's texted *Lieder*, which, of course, do contain several of Fanny's Lieder, in Opp. 8 and 9.
127. *AmZ* 31 (1828), 18–20.
128. Steiger and Reimann, VIII, 148. A facs. of Felix's autograph, *Festlied zu Zelters siebzigsten Geburtstag MDCCCXXVIII, gedichtet von Goethe, vertont von Mendelssohn*, appeared in Leipzig in 1928.
129. December 27, 1828, Fanny to Klingemann, *MF* I, 164.
130. Regarding Dirichlet's life and career, see further Hans Lausch, "'Der Mathematiker schwimmt in Wollust.' Mathematik bei Moses Mendelssohns—Mathematiker im Familienstammbaum," *MS* 7 (1990), 97–101.
131. *MF* I, 166.
132. Benjamin, 181. Hensel also gave Felix a small diary that he used during his visit to England and Scotland in 1829 (MDM g. 1), and Rebecka a star-shaped diary.
133. Schadow, 238.
134. Poem of January 23, 1829, in Klein: 1997, 155–56.
135. Fanny's diary, Berlin, *MA* Depos. 500, 22, entry of February 4, 1829.
136. *MF* I, 167.
137. Ibid.
138. Helmig and Maurer, 139–61.
139. All conveniently examined in Geck.
140. Schubring, "Reminiscences," 227.
141. See Geck, 23ff.
142. E. Devrient, *Recollections*, 38; T. Devrient, 303.
143. E. Devrient, *Recollections*, 39.
144. E. Devrient, *Erinnerungen*, 62.
145. Schünemann: 1928, 159.
146. Fanny to Klingemann, December 27, 1828 (*MF* I, 165; translation modified).
147. Felix to Zelter, January 8, 1829, *MLL*, 52.
148. Benjamin, 185; the passage is an early version of bars 47–51 of the finale.

149. MDM c. 8, fols. 21–25.
150. LC, Whittall Foundation Collection.
151. Fanny to Felix, April 15, 1829, *MF* I, 177.
152. Fanny's diary (*MA*, 500, 22) entry of February 4, 1829; Hensel's gift, which included a double portrait of Fanny and Rebecka as a frontispiece, is in MDM e. 11.
153. See Geck, 34, based on Schünemann: 1941, 54.
154. E. Devrient, *Recollections*, 60.
155. T. Devrient, 307–8; Marx, report of the performance, Geck, 40.
156. Fanny to Klingemann, March 22, 1829; *MF* I, 171.
157. *MA* Depos. 500, 22, entry of March 9, 1829.
158. See Klein: 1993, 155–56. After Felix left for England in April, Paganini was again invited to the Mendelssohn residence, where he recorded eight measures of a violin Capriccio in Fanny's album.
159. Geck, 36–37.
160. Marissen.
161. Sposato: 2000, 131.
162. Geck, 38.
163. Felix to Schubring, November 18, 1830, in Schubring: 1892, 15.
164. *Vossische Zeitung*, March 13, 1829, in Geck, 52.
165. See Geck, 30; Schünemann: 1928; and Smend.

Chapter 7

1. I. Moscheles, 90.
2. Felix to Moscheles, January 10, 1829, in Moscheles: 1888, 6.
3. I. Moscheles, 149.
4. Zelter to Goethe, March 9, 1829, Hecker, III, 129.
5. Fanny's diary (*MA* 500, 22), entry for April 1, 1829.
6. Ibid., entries for April 1 and 8, 1829.
7. Fanny to Klingemann, March 22, 1829, *MF* I, 173.
8. Now lost, the painting was finished for Lea's birthday. A photograph survives in the Courtauld Institute, London. See further Lowenthal-Hensel: 1997, 15–16 and Illustration 2.
9. Felix to Klingemann, March 26, 1829, Klingemann, 51.
10. Letter of April 13–14, 1829, in *MLL*, 56.
11. Notes for a projected Mendelssohn biography, W. T. Freemantle Collection, LC.
12. Letter of April 21, 1829, *MLL*, 61.
13. Felix to Berlin, April 21, 1829 (*MF* I, 177).
14. Felix to Berlin, April 25, 1829, ibid., I, 180.
15. F. G. Edwards: 1895, 43.
16. Unpublished passages from Felix's letter of April 25, 1829 (NYPL No. 55).
17. I. Moscheles, 150.
18. Rosemary Ashton, *Little Germany: Exile and Asylum in Victorian England*, Oxford, 1986, 82.
19. See Levy: 1985.
20. Letter of July 21, 1829, *MLL*, 79.
21. *Revue musicale* 3 (1829), June; trans. in *The Atlas* and reprinted in the *Harmonicon* 7 (1829), 241–43.
22. *BamZ* 6 (1829), 278ff.
23. Letter of July 8, 1829, in Selden-Goth, 54–55; *Harmonicon* 7 (1829), 193; see also the full account in Jourdan: 1998, 147ff.
24. Robert Elkin, *Royal Philharmonic* (London, 1946), 25.
25. Daniel Pool, *What Jane Austen Ate and Charles Dickens Knew*, N.Y., 1993, 52.
26. See Joel Sachs, "London: The Professionalization of Music," in Alexander Ringer, ed., *The Early Romantic Era: Between Revolutions: 1789 and 1848*, N.Y., 1990, 212. The concert programs are given in Foster.
27. See Jourdan: 1998, 88–95.
28. Unpublished passage of a letter from Felix to Berlin, April 25, 1829, NYPL No. 55.
29. Felix to Berlin, May 26, 1829, *MF* I, 184.
30. Schubring, "Reminiscences," in *MahW*, 228.
31. Cox, 271.

32. Exactly when Felix made the arrangement remains a mystery. Peter Ward Jones has suggested that it predates the English sojourn, though in a letter of May 29, 1829 (NYPL No. 64), Felix mentions the arrangement to Fanny as if it were a novelty. See Ward Jones: 1997c, 65–66; and the detailed discussion in the *Vorwort* to Ralf Wehner's new ed. of Op. 11 in *LAWFMB*, I: 4, Wiesbaden, 2000. The arrangement was published in London in 1911 and recorded by Toscanini in 1945 but it is still rarely played today.

33. *Athenaeum* (June 10, 1829).

34. Felix to the Secretary of the Philharmonic Society, May 26, 1829, Selden-Goth, 49–50. The French version was prepared by Adolphe d'Eichthal (MDM, GB XXVII, 113–14).

35. The *Times*, June 1, 1829, 2 (Argyll-Rooms).

36. Felix to Berlin, June 25, 1829, in Fanny and Felix Mendelssohn, 73–76.

37. Ibid.

38. I. Moscheles, 151.

39. Moscheles's part to the cadenza may survive in MDM c. 86 (for a facs., see Stephan D. Lindeman's edition of the first movement of the Concerto (Madison, Wisc., 1999), xix.

40. *Harmonicon* 7 (1829), 204.

41. See Felix's letters of June 19 to E. Devrient (Devrient, *Recollections*, 81); July 3 to Berlin (NYPL No. 70); and July 17, 1829, to Berlin (NYPL No. 72).

42. See Alexander: 1975, 72–74.

43. MDM c. 34, f. 9–10; in ibid., 74. The anthem was reviewed in *The Musical World* 3 (1836), 189; I am grateful to Peter Ward Jones for this reference.

44. Abraham to Felix, July 8, 1829, in Schneider: 1962, 20. See also p. 139.

45. Fanny to Felix, July 8, 1829 (Citron: 1987, 66).

46. Werner: 1955b, 556; and idem: 1963, 38.

47. See Schneider: 1962, 20–24; and Sposato: 2000, 45ff.

48. See the letters of May 15 and 19, 1829, in *MF* I, 183; and E. Devrient, *Recollections*, 73.

49. July 20, 1829, parts of which are published in Großmann-Vendrey: 1969, 38–39. For Zelter's reply, dated August 9, see Schmidt-Beste, 51–52.

50. June 25, 1829, in Fanny and Felix Mendelssohn, 74.

51. SBB *MA* BA 161; facs. in Kleßmann, 171.

52. June 19, 1829, in *MLL* 69.

53. June 25, 1829, *MF* I, 189–90.

54. Letter of May 1, 1829, in *MLL*, 62.

55. Felix's pocket diary, MDM g. 1, fol. 10; concerning the tunnel, see C. B. Noble, *The Brunels: Father and* Son, London, 1938.

56. I. Moscheles, 140–41.

57. Felix to Abraham, May 1, 1829, in *MLL*, 62–63.

58. Klingemann to Fanny, April 24, 1829, in Klingemann, 52.

59. Maggs Brothers Auction Catalogue 510, London, 1928, No. 1956; see also the edition by Thomas Christian Schmidt, Stuttgart, 1996.

60. Fanny to Felix, February 17, 1835, in Citron: 1987, 173.

61. Letter of March 16, 1834, cited in Großmann-Vendrey: 1969, 211. See further Zappalà: 1991, 106ff.

62. Dated June 12, 1829 (Berlin, *MA* N Mus. Ms. 23), the piece was written not quite two weeks before the performance of Op. 21 on June 24. Later that year Marx published it in the *BamZ*.

63. March 22, 1829, *MF* I, 170.

64. Fanny to Felix, April 18, 1829, in Citron: 1987, 25.

65. Fanny to Felix, May 27 and June 10, 1829, in ibid., 41, 50; Klingemann to Fanny, July 7, 1829, in Klingemann, 57.

66. Fiske, 141.

67. MDM c. 22.

68. See Citron: 1987, 51, n. 19.

69. Fanny to Felix, August 15, 1829, in Tillard: 1996, 161–62; and facs. 11.

70. Fanny to Felix, May 27, 1829, in Citron: 1987, 40.

71. Letter of June 5, 1829, NYPL No. 65; Smart's canon is in Felix's album, MDM d. 8, fol. 70v.

72. Drawing of July 24, 1829, in MDM d. 2, fols. 8 and 10. In January 1847 Felix copied the Scottish drawings as a gift for Klingemann; for a facs., see Klingemann, 55.

73. Felix to Berlin, July 28, 1829; *MLL*, 80.

74. Hadden, 96–97, 103–4.

75. SBB *MA* N Mus. Ms. 111; see also Seaton: 1977.

76. Letter of July 30, 1829; *MT* 39 (1898), 596.

77. Fiske, 127–28.
78. *MF* I, 202.
79. K. F. Schinkel, *"The English Journey": A Journal of a Visit to France and Britain in 1826*, ed. D. Bindman, G. Riemann, New Haven, 1993, 163.
80. *MF* I, 207.
81. Fanny to Felix, August 21, 1829; Fanny and Felix Mendelssohn, 90.
82. *MF* I, 204.
83. Klingemann, August 10, 1829, *MF* I, 205.
84. Ibid., I, 206.
85. Letter of August 15, 1829 (NYPL), in Klein: 1997, 99; the letter is partially printed in *MF* I, 209–10.
86. See Fiske, 141; Tillard: 1996, 154; and Hellwig-Unruh: 2000, 211–12.
87. See Tillard: 1996, 154.
88. Letter of August 25, 1829, *MF* I, 216.
89. Austin, 426; *MF* I, 225–29; and Tudur.
90. The sketch is in Felix's pocket diary, MDM g. 1, fols. 34–35, and transcribed in Wm. A. Little's edition of the organ works, London, 1987, II, x.
91. PML, Heinemann Collection.
92. Paris, BN, Conservatoire Ms. 191.
93. Letter of April 14, 1830, to Ferdinand David. Dated April 13 in *LA*, 126–31; for the corrected text, see Nancy Reich, "The Rudorff Collection," *Notes of the Music Library Association* 31 (1974), 253.
94. See Nancy Reich: 1991, 268–69.
95. Felix and Klingemann to Berlin, September 25, 1829; *MF* I, 232.
96. Berlin, *MA* Dep. Lohs 4, 59–63.
97. The text of the *Ehevertrag* is in Klein: 1997, 156–59.
98. Berlin, *MA* Dep. Lohs 4, 65–66.
99. Letter of October 3, 1829, from Fanny to Felix, Citron, 90–92.
100. Letter of October 27, 1829 (NYPL No. 92).
101. Letter of October 16, 1829 (NYPL No. 90). The copy, finished on November 6, is in Vienna, Österreichische Nationalbibliothek, Musiksammlung Ms. 16536.
102. See Edwards: 1895, 4–7.
103. Sotheby's, November 21, 1990; No. 161.
104. Edwards: 1895, 7.
105. LC, Whittall Collection; the Cramer arrangement substitutes the scherzo of the Octet for the minuet.
106. LC, W. T. Freemantle Collection.
107. Letter of December 17, 1829, from Felix to Mantius, LC; letter of December 28, 1829, Klingemann, 68.
108. PML, New York.
109. For an edition, see Vana.
110. T. Devrient, 315.
111. Klein: 1997, 162.
112. Lea to Klingemann, December 30, 1829, in Klingemann, 70.
113. See Elvers: 1990.
114. Felix to Lindblad, April 11, 1830, in Dahlgren, 34.
115. According to F. G. Edwards, Felix wrote the words (*Musical Haunts*, 39).
116. *Caprice caractéristique*, Op. 76; see Krettenauer, 319–26.
117. Ibid., 260.
118. E. Devrient, *Recollections*, 93.
119. Krettenauer, 274–76.

Chapter 8

1. *GM*, 56.
2. February 10, 1830, to Klingemann, Klingemann, 74.
3. E. Devrient, *Recollections*, 98.
4. For a thorough treatment see Silber: 1987, 14ff.
5. Friedlaender: 1889, 483–89.

6. Silber: 1987, 100–106.
7. Recently, Wolfgang Dinglinger has related it to a Corpus Christi procession Felix witnessed in Munich in June 1830 (Dinglinger: 2002, 117); however, Felix completed the score of the symphony in mid-May.
8. Jourdan: 2000, 118.
9. For the rejected recitative, see Silber: 1987, 129–33.
10. E. Devrient, *Recollections*, 97.
11. Berlin, *MN* 56. See Cooper: 2002, 300–317; and Seaton: 2002, 214–17.
12. Schubring, "Reminiscences," 229. Rust's father was the Dessau violinist F. W. Rust (1739–1796), whose sonatas attracted attention late in the nineteenth century when his grandson, Wilhelm Rust, heralded them as anticipating romanticism. But Wilhelm Rust had rewritten and doctored several of the compositions, which were exposed in the twentieth century as a hoax.
13. May 18, 1830, *MLL*, 118.
14. From *Faust* II, Act I. MDM d. 8, fols. 16–17; for a facs. see Wolff: 1906, 81.
15. May 25, 1830, P. Mendelssohn Bartholdy: 1865, *Letters*, 8. The drawing, by Johann Joseph Schmeller, is in the Stiftung Weimarer Klassik, Weimar. For a facs., see Kleßmann, 181.
16. Letter of May 25, 1830, in Sutermeister, 21.
17. *Albumblatt*, ed. J. Draheim, Wiesbaden, 1984.
18. Ottilie von Goethe, ed., *Chaos*, modern rep. ed. by Reinhard Fink, Bern, 1968.
19. *Chaos*, first series (1830), Nos. 36 and 43, 142–43 and 170–71.
20. Kretschman, 306.
21. June 22, 1830, Felix to Zelter, P. Mendelssohn Bartholdy, *Reisebriefe*, 18.
22. H. A. Köstlin, "Josephine Lang," *Sammlung musikalischer Vorträge*, ed. P. Waldersee, Leipzig, 1881, 59.
23. Letter of July 23, 1830 (NYPL No. 110).
24. MDM g. 2. For an edition of the diary, see Zappalà: 2002.
25. Felix to Rebecka, June 15, 1830, in Silber: 1987, 225; Lea to Felix, June 22, 1830, MDM, GB II, 38.
26. The autograph, BN Ms. 198, is dated June 13, 1830.
27. A. B. Marx to Fanny Hensel, July 21, 1830, *MF* I, 261.
28. MDM d. 8, fol. 66v–67.
29. Berlin, *MA* Depos. 500, 22 (entry for August 6, 1830).
30. Felix to Fanny, June 14, 1830, Sutermeister, 29.
31. S. Hensel: 1911, 13.
32. Felix to Fanny, June 26, 1830; *MF* I, 266–70.
33. Felix to Rebecka, August 22, 1830; *MLL*, 132.
34. Ibid., 134.
35. Felix to Devrient, September 5, 1830, in E. Devrient, *Recollections*, 109–10.
36. February 18, 1836, Felix to Lea, P. Mendelssohn Bartholdy: *Letters*, 1868, 99.
37. See Herfrid Kier, *Raphael Georg Kiesewetter (1773–1850): Wegbereiter des musikalischen Historismus*, Regensburg, 1968.
38. See Hanslick, trans. in *MahW*, 275–309.
39. On the provenance of the sketchbook see Douglas Johnson, Alan Tyson, and Robert Winter, *The Beethoven Sketchbooks*, Berkeley, 1985, 253–59.
40. Rollett, 35–36. Rollett, who attended the event, misdated it to the year 1829.
41. Felix to Paul, September 27, 1830, in Selden-Goth, 84.
42. Unpublished letters to Lea and Abraham of September 10 and 11, 1830 (NYPL Nos. 118 and 119).
43. See R. L. Todd: 1983b. The painting is now known to be by Antonio del Castillo y Saavedra.
44. Felix to Fanny, August 22, 1830, *MLL*, 136. See also the Preface to my edition of the cantata (Madison, Wisc., 1981), viii–ix.
45. Letter of September 26, 1841, Schumann to Krüger, in Jansen, 207.
46. Felix to Abraham, October 6, 1830 (NYPL No. 121).
47. October 18, 1830 (NYPL No. 122).
48. October 10 and 16, 1830, in Sutermeister, 42; Selden-Goth, 89.
49. Felix to Zelter, October 16, 1830, in Selden-Goth, 90.
50. Abraham to Felix, March 10, 1835, P. Mendelssohn Bartholdy, *Letters*: 1868, 68.
51. December 28, 1830, and February 15, 1831, in Sutermeister, 100, and *MLL*, 155.
52. Felix to Paul, October 30, 1830, *MLL*, 130.
53. Letter of November 8, 1830, Sutermeister, 65.
54. Zelter to Goethe, November 2, 1830, Hecker, III, 327.
55. November 8, 1830, Sutermeister, 63.
56. *Memorie storico-critiche della vita e delle opere di Giovanni Pierluigi da Palestrina*, Rome, 1828.

57. Santini to Zelter, ca. 30 December 1830, Hecker, III, 358.
58. SBB *MA* Ep. 380; for a facs. see Klein: 2002, 49.
59. November 23, 1830, P. Mendelssohn Bartholdy: *Letters*, 1865, 68.
60. November 30, 1830, ibid., 70.
61. February 15, 1831, in *MLL*, 159.
62. Gert Schiff, "An Epoch of Longing: An Introduction to German Painting of the Nineteenth Century," in *German Masters of the Nineteenth Century*, N.Y., 1981, 16.
63. Felix to Abraham, December 11, 1830, Sutermeister, 87.
64. February 1, 1831, P. Mendelssohn Bartholdy: *Letters*, 1865, 107.
65. December 10 and 20, 1830, and March 1, 1831, Sutermeister, 83, 96, 115.
66. Armand Dayot, *Les Vernet*, Paris, 1898, 126.
67. See "A Long-Lost Portrait of Mendelssohn," *MT* 46 (1905), 165–66; unpublished letter of September 16, 1831 (NYPL No. 136).
68. January 17, 1831; P. Mendelssohn Bartholdy: 1865, *Letters*, 104.
69. August 27, 1830, *MF*, I, 257.
70. Cairns, 193.
71. May 6, 1831, Berlioz to Gounet *et alia*; Hector Berlioz, *Correspondance Générale I: 1803-1832*, ed. Pierre Citron, Paris, 1972, 441.
72. Cairns, 293.
73. Ibid., 168n.
74. Ibid., 293.
75. March 15, 1831, Sutermeister, 120.
76. March 29, 1831, P. Mendelssohn Bartholdy: *Letters*, 1865, 126.
77. December 11, 1830, ibid., 87.
78. Goethe, *Italian Journey*, trans. W. H. Auden and E. Mayer, N.Y., 1962, 450.
79. Felix to Abraham, February 15, 1831, in *MLL*, 157–58.
80. June 16, 1831, to Zelter, P. Mendelssohn Bartholdy: 1865, *Letters*, 184–85.
81. Ibid.
82. April 4, 1831, ibid., 134; see also June 16, 1831.
83. November 22, 1830, *MLL*, 144.
84. *NZfM* 12 (1840), 144.
85. Zappalà: 1991, 126.
86. December 20, 1830, P. Mendelssohn Bartholdy: *Letters*, 1865, 90.
87. The unpublished autograph is in Berlin, *MN* 49.
88. October 18, 1830; NYPL (No. 122).
89. No autograph survives of the first version; a manuscript copy bearing the title is in MDM d. 58.
90. See Todd: 1993, 81.
91. A facs. of the autograph, now in PML, was published by Hugo von Mendelssohn Bartholdy in 1947.
92. See E. Walker and Abraham.
93. February 25, 1831; MDM d. 13; see Todd: 1993, 33–34.
94. June 6, 1831, P. Mendelssohn Bartholdy: *Letters*, 1865, 164.
95. May 17, 1831, ibid., 151.
96. April 27, 1831, ibid., 149.
97. June 6, 1831, ibid., 166.
98. J. Cottrau, *Lettres d'un Mélomane*, Naples, 1885, cited in Hanslick: 1991, 278.
99. April 27, 1831, P. Mendelssohn Bartholdy: *Letters*, 1865, 147.
100. May 28, 1831, ibid., 156.
101. Ibid.
102. Unpublished letter of June 11, 1831, LC (Music 1055).
103. Pocket diary, MDM g. 3, fol. 17.
104. May 28, 1831 P. Mendelssohn Bartholdy: *Letters*, 1865, 159, and June 11, 1831, to Attwood, unpublished letter in LC (Music 1055).
105. Fanny's diary, entry of March 4, 1831 (Berlin, *MA* Depos. 500, 22).
106. December 28, 1831, P. Mendelssohn Bartholdy: *Letters*, 1865, 319.
107. June 25, 1831, ibid., 193; Butler, *The Way of All Flesh*, ch. 4.
108. MDM g. 3 (July 15, 1831).
109. July 14, 1831, P. Mendelssohn Bartholdy: *Letters*, 1865, 207–8.
110. E. Devrient, *Recollections*, 120.
111. July 7, 1831 (NYPL No. 133).
112. July 24, 1831, P. Mendelssohn Bartholdy: *Letters*, 1865, 216.

113. August 18 [*recte* 4], 1831, in *MLL*, 166.
114. August 10, 1831, P. Mendelssohn Bartholdy: *Letters*, 1865, 243; Felix's autograph of the two Lieder is in PML.
115. August 24 ,1831, P. Mendelssohn Bartholdy: *Letters*, 1865, 269.
116. September 5, 1831, ibid., 291.
117. October 6, 1831, ibid., 295.
118. Ibid., 296; Roberta Werner, "The Songs of Josephine Caroline Lang: The Expression of a Life," Ph.D. diss., Univ. of Minnesota, 1992, I, 110.
119. BN, Conservatoire Ms. 195.
120. Collection of Lilian Kallir, New York; the Ms. is examined in Marian Wilson: 1993, 153ff.
121. Letter of October 6, 1831, from a passage not published in P. Mendelssohn Bartholdy: *Letters*, 1865; the original is in MDM d. 13, fol. 91.
122. Hector Berlioz, *Evenings with the Orchestra*, ed. Jacques Barzun, Chicago, 1973, 218–19.
123. November 13, 1831, published in E. Werner: 1963, 528.
124. Unpublished passage in Felix's letter of November 27, 1831 (NYPL No. 140).
125. Letter of November 29, 1831, in K. L. Immermann, *Briefe*, ed. Peter Hasubek, Munich, 1978, I, 1004–5. See also Immermann, *Zwischen Poesie und Wirklichkeit*, 61.
126. January 11, 1832, P. Mendelssohn Bartholdy: *Letters*, 1865, 323.
127. January 28, 1832, NYPL No. 144.
128. December 20, 1831, to Klingemann, Klingemann, 89.
129. Hiller, *Letters*, 24–25.
130. December 11, 1831, NYPL No. 142.
131. January 11 and 14, 1832, P. Mendelssohn Bartholdy: *Letters*, 1865, 326, 328.
132. See Locke.
133. January 22, 1832, P. Mendelssohn Bartholdy: *Letters*, 334, corrected in Locke, 114.
134. Hiller, *Letters*, 28.
135. Ibid., 26–27.
136. April 11, 1832, Felix to Rebecka, NYPL No. 152.
137. See J.-J. Eigeldinger, "Les premiers concerts de Chopin à Paris (1832–1838)," in P. Bloom, ed., *Music in Paris in the Eighteen-Thirties*, Stuyvesant, N.Y., 1987, 257f.
138. April 16, 1832. Facs. in Leopold Binental, *Chopin: Dokumente und Erinnerungen aus seiner Heimatstadt*, Leipzig, 1932, Abb. 39.
139. Entries in Clara's diaries by her father, February 16 and 26, and March 14 and 23, 1832 (Zwickau, Robert-Schumann Haus 4871, 1-4-A3). An edition by Gerd Nauhaus and Nancy Reich is in preparation.
140. "Nouvelles de Paris," *Revue musicale* 6/8 (1832), 59 (March 24, 1832).
141. See Todd: 1993, 17–18.
142. March 31, 1832, P. Mendelssohn Bartholdy: *Letters*, 1865, 349.
143. Felix to Fanny, January 21, 1832, ibid., 332.
144. Fanny to Felix, February 17, 1835, in Citron: 1987, 173.
145. Ed. C. Misch, Kassel, 1992.
146. See Elvers: 1972, 171.
147. See Hinrichsen, 114–29; and Huber: 1997, 227–45.
148. Fanny's diary entry for January 1, 1832 (Berlin, *MA*, Depos. 500, 22).
149. December 24, 1831–January 21, 1832. Ed. E. M. Blankenburg, Kassel, 1995.
150. For discussion, see Eberle.
151. Ed. E. M. Blankenburg, Kassel, 1994.
152. Fanny to Felix, ca. June 11, 1834, in Citron: 1987, 144. According to Renate Hellwig-Unruh, Fanny completed the overture in April or May 1832. Hellwig-Unruh: 2000, 244.
153. Felix to Berlin, February 28, 1832 (NYPL No. 146); *Harmonicon* 10 (1832), 235.
154. See C. J. Kudlick, *Cholera in Post-Revolutionary Paris: A Cultural History*, Berkeley, 1996.
155. Felix to Heinrich Baermann, April 16, 1832; Nohl: 1873, 310–11.
156. Felix to Berlin, May 11, 1832, P. Mendelssohn Bartholdy: *Letters*, 1865, 351.
157. I. Moscheles, 179, 181; Lampadius, 194.
158. In 1830 fire had destroyed the Argyll Rooms.
159. See *MT* 38 (1897), 732; and Todd: 1991, 195–96.
160. Minutes of the Directors of the Philharmonic for June 17, 1832; London, BL Loan 48.2/2; Berlin *MA* BA 275 (see Klein: 1997, 164).
161. Jourdan, 177ff.
162. Rockstro, 48. See also Little: 2002, 294–96.
163. See Jourdan, 184. When the Reform Bill was finally passed in June, it abolished fifty-six "rotten boroughs" and effectively doubled the size of the electorate.

164. I. Moscheles, 175; *Athenaeum*, May 19, 1832, 326.
165. *Harmonicon* 10 (1832), 142.
166. See most recently, Ward Jones: 1997c, 67–68. In May 2002, the final autograph of the overture, dated June 20, 1832, and known as the "Odling" manuscript, was acquired by the Bodleian Library, Oxford (MDM d. 71), after being held privately for more than fifty years.
167. Edward Lockspeiser, *Music and Painting*, London, 1973, 10–12.
168. Edward Dannreuther, "Wagner," *Grove's Dictionary of Music and Musicians*, London, 1893, IV, 369.
169. See Todd: 1984 and 1993, 79–82.
170. Grey: 2000, 70.
171. No. 4, September 14, 1829 (PML); No. 2, December 11, 1830 (Arturo Toscanini Collection, New York Public Library); No. 6, October 16, 1830 (*MN* 18); and No. 1 (ca. August–September 1831, see Hiller, *Letters*, 17).
172. Schumann: 1946, 210.
173. The autograph from which Moscheles worked survives in the Huntington Library in San Marino, California. For details of the first English edition, see Ward Jones: 1992, 243–44.
174. SBB *MA BA* 157. Felix's addition is dated February 20, 1833. For a facs., see Kleßmann, 203.
175. June 21, 1832, Felix to Dr. Haley Holm, MDM c. 42, fol. 10–11.
176. MDM g. 4, fol. 3 (entry for May 22, 1832).

Chapter 9

1. Felix to Rebecka, P. Mendelssohn Bartholdy: *Letters*, 1868, 10.
2. May 18, 1832, P. Mendelssohn Bartholdy: *Letters*, 1865, 352.
3. See the thorough account in Little: 1992, 72.
4. E. Devrient, *Recollections*, 150.
5. September 4, 1832, Felix to E. Devrient. LC, in Turner, 218.
6. February 4, 1833, Klingemann, 110.
7. E. Devrient, *Recollections*, 155–56.
8. July 4, 1832, Klingemann, 95.
9. August 4, 1832, and January 16, 1833, *GM*, 99, 102.
10. March 17, 1832, F. Moscheles: 1888, 61; unpublished letter to Attwood of February 10, 1833, LC (Music 1055).
11. *Lord, have mercy upon us*, March 24, 1833 (Berlin, MN 28, 1–3), later published in the *Album für Gesang* for 1842.
12. September 26, 1832, F. Moscheles: 1888, 44.
13. July 27, 1832, Felix to Immermann, HHI; E. Devrient, *Recollections*, 143. See also A. B. Marx: 1865, I, 168–70.
14. The *Pagenlied*, published as a supplement to *NZfM* in 1838, and *Weihnachtslied*, Christmas presents for Rebecka (MDM g. 11); and the Fugue in B minor, later released as Op. 35 No. 3. The *Weihnachtslied* is published in Hans Gerber, *Albert Baur*, Freiburg im Breisgau, 1971, 161–62.
15. LC (December 30, 1832; Music 1055). *Die Schlacht bei Prag. Ein grosses Duett für Dampfnudel oder Rahmstrudel, Clarinett u. Bassethorn.*
16. BN Conservatoire Ms. 209; January 6, 1833.
17. Marx: 1991, 213.
18. Berlin, *MA* Ms. 76, examined in Kellenberger and Sposato: 2000, which includes transcriptions of drafts for the libretto preserved in the Bodleian Library.
19. February 4, 1833, Felix to Klingemann; Klingemann, 109–10.
20. Marx: 1865, II, 173.
21. Sposato: 2000, 203, 205.
22. Ibid., ch. 4 for a thorough review of the chronology; in the appendix, Sposato provides complete transcriptions of the libretto drafts for *Paulus*.
23. Marx: 1991, 213.
24. MDM d. 53, No. 88.
25. I. Moscheles, 182.
26. For a facsimile of Felix's dedicatory note, see F. Moscheles: 1888, 49.
27. October 24, 1832, January 26 and February 7, 1833; see *AmZ* 34 (1832), 802–3, 35 (1833), 126; and Klingemann, 110.

28. August 7, 1832, to Immermann, HHI; copy in Weimar, Stiftung Weimarer Klassik.
29. January 17, 1833, to Charlotte Moscheles; F. Moscheles: 1888, 52.
30. See the unpublished letter ca. November 15, 1832 (J. & J. Lubrano, auction catalogue, Autumn 1994, No. 60, 23–24).
31. February 4, 1833, Klingemann, 110.
32. February 13, 1833, Klingemann, 111.
33. *Iris im Gebiete der Tonkunst* 3/47 (November 23, 1832). See further Judith Silber: 1987, 49–50.
34. *Vossische Zeitung* (January 12, 1833), 6–7; *AmZ* 35 (1833), 125.
35. On the early version see especially Hellmundt: 1997.
36. Goethe to Felix, September 9, 1831, as cited in ibid., 105.
37. E. Werner: 1963, 203; Kramer, 78; and Metzger, 94–95. See also Julie D. Prandi, "Kindred Spirits: Mendelssohn and Goethe, *Die erste Walpurgisnacht*," in Cooper and Prandi, 135–46.
38. Foster, 111.
39. Berlin, *MN* Band 27; for a facsimile, see Cooper and Klein: 1997.
40. Felix to Immermann, March 18, 1833, copy in Weimar, Stiftung Weimarer Klassik; the autograph score is in Berlin, MN 56.
41. Benno von Wiese, *Karl Immermann: Sein Werk und sein Leben*, Bad Homburg, 1969, 274.
42. Höffner, 63.
43. Felix to Abraham, February 21, 1832, P. Mendelssohn Bartholdy: *Letters*, 1865, 343; MDM GB II No. 82.
44. Abraham to Lea, May 22, 1833, *MF*, I, 281.
45. Immermann, 119.
46. April 23, 1833, Felix to Robert Reinick, Berlin Mus. Ep. FMB 12; for an edition of the partsong, see *Die Musik* 8 (1908–09), Heft 9, appendix, and the brief comments in Kopfermann, 180. The festival included a prologue by Immermann, transparencies of Dürer's paintings, tableaux vivants, the *Musikantenprügelei*, and scenes from Shakespeare's *Midsummer Night's Dream*. Reinick to Franz Kugler, April 16, 1833, in Höffner, 64–65.
47. Felix to Schubring, September 16, 1835, Schubring: 1892, 92–93. The unpublished orchestral version, titled *Fantasie und Variationen über Preziosa*, was handed down from Ignaz Moscheles's estate to the Russian pianist Anton Rubinstein, and has recently come to light in St. Petersburg. See Wehner: 2002a, 14–15.
48. F. Moscheles: 1888, 64.
49. I. Moscheles, 195.
50. Felix to Abraham, May 7, 1833, NYPL No. 160.
51. See Jourdan, 177; G. I. C. de Courcy, *Nicolò Paganini: Chronology of His Life*, Wiesbaden, 1961, 59–60.
52. Felix added the date of revision, April 10, 1833, at the end of his autograph (BN Cons. Ms. 206).
53. Felix to Watts, April 27, 1833, in Foster, 118.
54. Ward Jones: 1997c, 72–73.
55. Felix to Fanny, April 7, 1834, P. Mendelssohn Bartholdy: *Letters*, 1868, 31–32.
56. *Atlas*, May 19, 1833, 325; see Jourdan, 188–89.
57. For the program, see Foster, 122; also appearing with Felix were the singers Rubini and Cinti-Damoreau, and the violinist Charles De Beriot.
58. *Morning Post* (May 16, 1833); Jourdan: 1998, 188.
59. Berlin, *MN* 28 (July 1834).
60. The history of the work is treated in Cooper: 1994 and 2003, and the prefatory studies in Cooper and Klein.
61. See further Spies, 103–4.
62. Werner: 1963, 267; Konold: 1987, 28–29.
63. As reported by Tovey, in *Essays in Musical Analysis*, London, 1935–39, rep. 1981, 393–94.
64. See Michael C. Tusa, "In Defense of Weber," in R. L. Todd, ed., *Nineteenth-Century Piano Music*, N.Y., 1990, 166–68; and Cooper: 2003, 188–90.
65. The passage (mm. 195ff.) seems to have inspired a similar response by Tchaikovsky in the finale of the *Capriccio Italien* (1880); see mm. 500ff.
66. Pocket diary, MDM g. 4, 13v.
67. For the complete text, see Fischer, 14–15.
68. Abraham to Lea, May 31, 1833; *MF* I, 292; text corrected in Klein: 1999, 49–75.
69. Abraham to Lea, May 26, 1833; *MF* I, 283.
70. Ibid., 283, 285.
71. Ferdinand von Woringen, "Felix Mendelssohn-Bartholdy in Düsseldorf in den Jahren 1833–35," *Neue Berliner Musikzeitung* 1/48, November 16, 1847, trans. in Brown: 2003, 127.

72. See Großmann-Vendrey: 1969, 71–72.
73. See Klein: 1999, 74–75.
74. A. F. Schindler, *Beethoven as I Knew Him*, ed. D. W. MacArdle, N.Y., 1966, 436–37.
75. *Düsseldorfer Zeitung* (June 5, 1833), cited in Esser, 6.
76. Abraham to Lea, ca. June 1833 (*MF* I, 292).
77. Felix to Moscheles, August 10, 1832, F. Moscheles: 1888, 29. See also 65.
78. *Fuga pro organo pleno* and *Andante con moto*, in the fifth volume of Wm. A. Little's edition of the organ works (1990), 60–66. On Novello's album, see Pamela Weston, "Vincent Novello's Autograph Album: Inventory and Commentary," *ML* 75 (1994), 372.
79. For a facsimile see F. Moscheles: 1888, 62.
80. MDM g. 4, fol. 17r; Abraham to Lea, July 6, 1833, *MF* I, 299.
81. *MF* I, 298.
82. Abraham to Lea, July 13, 1833, Klein: 2001, 105.
83. According to Abraham (*MF* I, 301), the soirée occurred on July 6, but other evidence suggests July 9. See Weston (n. 78), 376.
84. M. C. Clarke, *The Life and Labours of Vincent Novello*, London, 1864, 36–37.
85. *Times*, July 17, 1833, 2.
86. Felix to Berlin, July 23, 1833, NYPL No. 165.
87. See Sposato: 2000, ch. 1, for a thorough review of the episode.
88. E. Devrient, *Recollections*, 57.
89. Abraham to Lea, July 23, 1833, in Klein: 2001, 109–10.
90. Two autographs, of which the Horsleys owned one, bear the date August 3, 1833 (Berlin N. Mus. Ms. 79 and Oxford, Bodleian Library, Ms. Horsley b. 1).
91. Fanny Horsley to Lucy Calcott, August 28, 1833, in Gotch, 70.
92. *BadV*, 29–30; Gotch, 70.
93. Letter of ca. July 25, 1833, in Gotch, 46.
94. See Alexander: 1975, 75ff.
95. Mary Alexander to Felix, August 23, 1833, in ibid., 78.
96. *MF* I, 307.
97. Felix to Rosen, September 27, 1833; Klingemann, 118.
98. Meyerbeer to Minna Meyerbeer, May 3, 1833, in Giacomo Meyerbeer, II, 311. The patent, dated May 2, 1833, is in MDM a.1 (Roll), No. 1.
99. Felix to Abraham, December 28, 1833, P. Mendelssohn Bartholdy: *Letters*, 1868, 14.
100. See Schneider: 1958, 47.
101. Felix to Schubring, September 6, 1833, in P. Mendelssohn Bartholdy: *Letters*, 1868, 6.
102. Felix to Rebecka Dirichlet, October 26, 1833, ibid., 8. The march remains unidentified; a possible candidate is a copy of a procession march in E♭ attributed to Felix in MDM c. 50/2, fol. 72.
103. See further Federhofer-Königs.
104. Großmann-Vendrey: 1969, 218–19.
105. October 26, 1833, P. Mendelssohn Bartholdy: *Letters*, 1868, 10.
106. See ibid.; Höffner, 73–80; and Cooper: 1995, 9–26.
107. October 26, 1833, P. Mendelssohn Bartholdy: *Letters*, 1868, 12.
108. Letter of April 3, 1834, to William Horlsey, *GM*, 110.
109. Letter of October 26, 1833, P. Mendelssohn Bartholdy: *Letters*, 1868, 13; MDM GB XXVII, No. 55.
110. *Zum Fest der heiligen Cäcilia*, ed. Willi Gundlach, Kassel, 1998; see Fanny's letter of November 23, 1833, to Felix, in Citron: 1987, 117.
111. Immermann, 133.
112. Felix to Moscheles, February 7, 1834, F. Moscheles: 1888, 88.
113. Esser, 19.
114. Felix to Moscheles, February 7, 1834, F. Moscheles: 1888, 87.
115. Felix to Abraham, December 28, 1833, P. Mendelssohn Bartholdy: *Letters*, 1868, 17.
116. Felix to Breitkopf & Härtel, November 29, 1833, *BadV*, 31.
117. See Mintz: 1957.
118. R. Schumann: 1888, I, 144 (*NZfM* 4 [1836], 7); see further Plantinga: 1984, 14.
119. R. Schumann: 1888, I, 142; also, Felix to Fanny, January 30, 1836, P. Mendelssohn Bartholdy: *Letters*, 1868, 96.
120. Fanny Horsley to Lucy Calcott, October 20, 1833; Gotch, 78.
121. April 7, 1834, Felix to Fanny, Fanny and Felix Mendelssohn, 159.
122. April 1834, Felix to Charlotte Moscheles, F. Moscheles: 1888, 99.
123. See Fanny's letters to Felix of April 27 and June 18, 1834, in Citron: 1987, 137–38, 147–48.

124. January 16, 1834, P. Mendelssohn Bartholdy: *Letters*, 1868, 22.
125. January 22, 1834, Berlin *MN* 28.
126. Berlin *MN* 20.
127. Klingemann, 127–66.
128. Alexander: 1975, 87. Suzanne Summerville has edited the songs in *Three Poems by Heinrich Heine in the Translations of Mary Alexander by Fanny Hensel*, Fairbanks, Alas., 1995.
129. Letter of November 9, 1833; Gilbert: 1975, 93–94.
130. Fanny to Felix, December 1, 1833, Citron: 1987, 118.
131. December 1, 1833, Citron: 1987, 118–19.
132. December 28, 1833, P. Mendelssohn Bartholdy: *Letters*, 1868, 17; and February 19, 1834 (NYPL No. 182).
133. F. W. Riemer, *Mittheilungen über Goethe*, Berlin, 1841, I, 430.
134. See his letter of January 13, 1834, to Mary Alexander, in Alexander: 1979, 15–16.
135. Felix to Berlin, March 28, 1834, NYPL No. 187.
136. Felix to Berlin, July 17, 1834, NYPL No. 205.
137. Hiller, *Letters and Recollections*, 39.
138. Polko: 1987, 37.
139. The two arrangements are in the Brotherton Collection, University of Leeds, and BN, Conservatoire Ms. 94. See Wehner: 2002, 156–61.
140. See further Todd: 1993, 22.
141. February 7, 1834, to I. Moscheles, F. Moscheles: 1888, 85.
142. He did so at a Gewandhaus concert of April 4, 1839. See *NZfM* 10 (1839), 128.
143. February 19, 1834, Felix to Lea (NYPL No. 182); the autograph of *Infelice* is in *MN* 28.
144. Claves Recording, 1999. See also J. M. Cooper, "Mendelssohn's Two *Infelice* Arias: Problems of Sources and Musical Identity," in Cooper and Prandi, 43–97.
145. The *Lieder ohne Worte* Op. 30 No. 5 (December 12, 1833), 30 No. 4 (January 30), and 85 No. 2 (June 9); Capriccio in A minor, Op. 33 No. 1 (April 9); Etude in F major, Op. 104b No. 2 (April 21); and the organ Fugue in C minor, Op. 37 No. 1 (July 30, 1834).
146. October 5, 1833, Schubring to Felix, in Schubring: 1892, 48–63.
147. See Felix's letter to Lea of November 4, 1834 (P. Mendelssohn Bartholdy: 1868, 49), where, however, he confuses the scriptural citation, and associates Paul with Jupiter.
148. January 12 and 13 in Elberfeld and Barmen; February 27 and March 9 in Cologne and Elberfeld.
149. Fétis, "Mendelssohn-Bartholdy," in *Biographie universelle des musiciens*, Paris, 1864, VI, 79.
150. Felix to Lea, May 23, 1834. P. Mendelssohn Bartholdy: *Letters*, 1868, 34.
151. November 19, 1834, Felix to Mde. Voigt, and March 14, 1835, Felix to Hiller; "More Letters by Mendelssohn," *Dwight's Journal of Music* 31 (1871), 58, and Hiller, *Letters*, 47.
152. MDM c. 49, fol. 16v.
153. See Esser, 13–15.
154. May 6, 1834, to Lea, NYPL No. 192.
155. Concerning Burgmüller see Heinrich Eckert, *Norbert Burgmüller*, Augsburg, 1932.
156. Felix to Bauer, January 12, 1835, P. Mendelssohn Bartholdy: *Letters*, 1868, 63.
157. Schumann: 1980, 102.
158. Ferdinand von Woringen: 1847, cited in Brown: 2002, 130.
159. See Großmann-Vendrey: 1969, 61.
160. Probably one of the three marches in MDM c. 50/2.
161. October 12, 1834, *MLL*, 200.
162. Webern, 71–72.
163. March 28, 1834, Felix to Abraham, P. Mendelssohn Bartholdy: *Letters*, 1868, 26.
164. *MF* I, 100.
165. *MN* 20, 51–52, finished on December 9, 1833, and performed on April 26, 1834.
166. Felix to Abraham, March 28, 1834, P. Mendelssohn Bartholdy: *Letters*, 1868, 28.
167. March 10, April 24, and June 7, 1834; LC (Music 1055); only the first has been published (*MLL*, 194–96).
168. Felix to E. Devrient, November 26, 1834, E. Devrient, *Recollections*, 185.
169. September 27, 1834, Felix to H. Baermann, Nohl: 1873, 323.
170. F. Hensel: 2002, 61 (entries of September 29 and November 20, 1834).
171. Felix to Abraham, October 14, 1834 (NYPL No. 210).
172. Diary of Clara Wieck, October 2, 1834, cited in N. Reich: 1985, 218.
173. The librettist, Friedrich Rochlitz, had earlier offered the subject to Felix, already underway with *Paulus*. See Ernst Rychnowsky, "Ludwig Spohr und Friedrich Rochlitz," *Sammelbände der Internationalen Musikgesellschaft* 5 (1903–4), 284.

174. Among Felix's papers is his refutation of claims made by Immermann concerning Felix's duties (MDM c. 49, fols. 9–14).

175. Recently rediscovered at the Brotherton Collection in the University of Leeds. For a full account, see Wehner: 2002.

176. November 4, 1834, Felix to Lea, P. Mendelssohn Bartholdy: *Letters*, 1868, 48.

177. November 26, 1834, Felix to E. Devrient, E. Devrient, *Recollections*, 185.

178. Undated letter (1835?), Abraham to Felix, cited in P. Mendelssohn Bartholdy: *Briefe*, 1865, 68n.

179. November 23, 1834, Felix to Rebecka, P. Mendelssohn Bartholdy: *Letters*, 1868, 55.

180. Immermann, 420–23.

181. January 26, 1835, Felix to Lea (NYPL No. 222).

182. Immermann, 427, 428–38, 441–50. See also Fellner, 302–9.

183. February 26, 1835, Felix to Abraham (NYPL No. 224).

184. Cited in Benno von Wiese, *Karl Immermann: Sein Werk und sein Leben*, Bad Homburg, 1969, 158.

185. Chrysander: 1870.

186. Reproduced in color in Petitpierre, *Romance*, 120.

187. February 11, 1835, Felix to Fanny, Berlin, MA Depos. Berlin 3, 7 (Klein: 1997, 172).

188. February 26, 1835, Felix to Hiller, Hiller, *Letters*, 45.

189. December 25, 1834, and February 7, 1835, Felix to Ignaz and Charlotte Moscheles (F. Moscheles: 1888, 119 and 129), February 26, 1835, Felix to Hiller, Hiller, *Letters*, 44.

190. Ed. Günter Marx, Wiesbaden, 1988. Recent research has shown that two of the movements of the quartet are based on an unfinished piano sonata from 1829. See Hellwig-Unruh: 2000, 222, 254, and the literature cited therein.

191. January 30, 1835, Felix to Fanny, Berlin MA Depos. MG 28 (Klein: 1997, 188).

192. February 17, 1835, Fanny to Felix, Citron: 1987, 173. See also 255.

193. July 17, 1833, Felix to Charlotte Moscheles (F. Moscheles: 1888, 74); November 23, 1834, Felix to Rebecka, P. Mendelssohn Bartholdy: *Letters*, 1868, 57.

194. Berlin *MN* 28, 143–44.

195. Isaac Nathan, *A Selection of Hebrew Melodies, Ancient and Modern*, ed. Frederick Burwick and Paul Douglass, Tuscaloosa, Alabama, 1988, 29; see also Hennemann, 143.

196. BN Bibliothèque du Conservatoire Ms. 200/201 (May 22, 1835).

197. Felix to Attwood, January 11, 1835, LC (Music 1055); Todd: 1992c, "Six Preludes and Fugues Op. 35," 173.

198. June 18, 1834, Fanny to Felix, Citron: 1987, 147.

199. Berlin, *MN* 28, 287–90, 295–97, 299.

200. Berlin, *MN* 29, 120 (July 30, 1834); MA Ms. 6 (January 11, 1835). For an ed. see Mendelssohn Bartholdy, *Complete Organ Works*, I, 8–11, 20–25.

201. Berlin, *MN* 28, 153 (December 12, 1833) and 151–52 (January 30, 1834); and Fanny to Felix, December 27, 1834, which cites Op. 38 No. 2 (Citron: 1987, 167).

202. HHI, and MDM c. 1, fols. 95–102.

203. *BadV*, 191.

204. Felix to Henriette Voigt, March 15, 1835, *Acht Briefe und ein Facsimile von Felix Mendelssohn Bartholdy*, Leipzig, 1871, 17; *Dwight's Journal of Music* 31 (1871), 58.

205. See further Rudolf Elvers's ed. of the *Lieder ohne Worte*, Munich, 1981.

206. Felix to Rochlitz, January 3, 1835, *MLL*, 204. Felix mentions the professorship in his letter to Berlin of the same day (NYPL No. 220).

207. Felix to Abraham, January 15, 1835, *MLL*, 206–7.

208. January 26, 1835, Felix to Schleinitz, ibid., 208; February 6, 1835, Felix to Raymund Härtel, *BadV*, 43.

209. March 15, 1835, Felix to Henriette Voigt, *Dwight's Journal of Music* 31 (1871), 58.

210. May 1, 1835, Felix to *Oberbürgermeister* von Fuchsius, Esser, 41.

211. June 13, 1835, Felix to *Regierungsrath* Heinrich Dörrien, *LA*, 48–49.

212. May 11, 1834, Felix to Moscheles, F. Moscheles: 1888, 104.

213. See the detailed study in Niemöller.

214. Benedict, 25–26.

215. Oxford, Bodleian Library, Deneke 1–32. Six of the volumes have annotations in Felix's hand.

216. Fanny to Felix, April 8, 1835, Citron: 1987, 495; Rebecka to Klingemann, July 6, 1835, Klingemann, 180.

217. Meyerbeer: 1970, II, 468.

218. Brockhaus, I, 291.

219. Facs. in Reinhold Sietz, "Das Stammbuch von Julius Rietz," *Beiträge zur rheinischen Musikgeschichte* 52 (1962), 222–23.

Chapter 10

1. Felix to Friedrich Wilhelm von Schadow and Klingemann, August 9 and 14–16, 1835 (Polko: 1987, 161–63; Klingemann, 188–89).
2. Lea to Rebecka, 1835, *MF* I, 317.
3. Schumann: 1980, 107.
4. See Wolfgang Boetticher, "Neue Materialien zur Begegnung Robert Schumanns mit Henriette Voigt," *Florilegium musicologicum: Hellmut Federhofer zum 75. Geburtstag*, ed. C.-H. Mahling, Tutzing, 1988, 49.
5. Entry for September 13, 1835, in Clara Wieck's diary (Zwickau, Robert-Schumann Haus). See also Clara to Emilie List, September 14, 1835, in Wendler, 58–59.
6. Dörffel, 253.
7. Ibid., 22.
8. On February 21, 1833, February 13, 1834, and April 20, 1834.
9. Dörffel, 78.
10. See Felix's letter of June 13, 1835, to Heinrich Dörrien, *LA*, 49.
11. Schumann: 1946, 219 (*NZfM* 3 [1835], 127).
12. F. Hensel, 71.
13. Felix to Berlin, October 6, 1835, P. Mendelssohn Bartholdy: *Letters*, 1868, 81.
14. I. Moscheles, 216.
15. *NZfM* 3 (1835), 127; Schumann: 1946, 218.
16. Entry for October 4, 1835, from the edition and translation of Clara Wieck's diaries in preparation by Gerd Nauhaus and Nancy Reich.
17. SBB *MA* BA 136; for a facs., see Klein: 1997, 167.
18. *NZfM* 3 (1835), 131; also, I. Moscheles, 215.
19. Ibid., 224.
20. *MF* I, 335; Binder, 269. For another account of the visit, see F. Hensel, 72–73.
21. Felix to Rebecka, November 13, 1835 (NYPL No. 244).
22. Dörffel, 88.
23. BN, Conservatoire Ms. 199, October 29, 1835.
24. Abraham to Varnhagen, November 16, 1835; *MF* I, 326. See also Binder, 288.
25. Fanny's diary, cited in *MF* I, 337. Fanny's account of Abraham's final days is available in F. Hensel, 75–78.
26. Felix to Schubring, December 6, 1835, Schubring: 1892, 99.
27. Luise Hensel to Clemens Brentano, December 9, 1835; Binder, 288.
28. Dörffel, 86.
29. Lea to Charlotte Moscheles, October 6, 1836, in I. Moscheles, 233.
30. December 30, 1835, Dresden, Sächsische Landesbibliothek.
31. Fanny to Felix, December 31, 1835, Fanny and Felix Mendelssohn, 209.
32. Felix to Pastor Bauer, December 9, 1835, P. Mendelssohn Bartholdy: *Letters*, 1868, 87.
33. Fanny to Felix, February 4, 1836, Citron: 1987, 199–200.
34. Felix to Lea, January 29, 1836, NYPL No. 288.
35. Felix to Simrock, January 30, February 27, March 12, and April 2, 1836, *BadV*, 199, 200, 202; Felix to Woringen, March 12, 1836, in Großmann-Vendrey: 1969, 81.
36. Kraków, BJ, *MN* 53 and 54. As he worked on the full score, Felix had a copy made, which he sent to Woringen in April. Felix to Ferdinand von Woringen, March 30, 1836, Fischer, 26.
37. October 12, 1840, Ignaz Moscheles to Charlotte Moscheles; I. Moscheles, 271.
38. By Leon Botstein and the Royal Scottish National Orchestra and Chorus (Arabesque Z6705), from an edition prepared by J. Michael Cooper. The rejected numbers were briefly examined in Grove: 1909, and Kurzhals-Reuter, 103ff.
39. Abraham to Felix, March 19, 1835, P. Mendelssohn Bartholdy: *Letters*, 1868, 68.
40. Here and later in this chapter the numbering of movements from *St. Paul* follows that of the first edition, and of my edition for Carus Verlag (Stuttgart, 1997).
41. Felix to Moscheles, December 25, 1834, F. Moscheles: 1888, 121.
42. F. Hensel, 82 (entry of July 8, 1839).
43. According to Ferdinand von Woringen, Felix sent several movements from Part 2 from Leipzig to Düsseldorf as soon as they were finished, and composed the tenor cavatina "Sei getreu bis in den Tod" (No. 40) only days before the première in May 1836. Woringen: 1847, trans. in Brown: 2003, 135.
44. On a "morning" concert of Joseph Merk, February 21, and benefit concert for Grabau, March 24, 1836.

45. January 29, 1836, Felix to Fanny, P. Mendelssohn Bartholdy: *Letters*, 1868, 94.
46. *AmZ* 38 (1836), col. 105.
47. Felix to Lea, February 18, 1836, P. Mendelssohn Bartholdy: *Letters*, 1868, 98.
48. Fanny to Klingemann, February 12, 1836, *MF* II, 4.
49. February 18, 1836, Felix to Lea, P. Mendelssohn Bartholdy: *Letters*, 1868, 98–99.
50. January 21, 1836, Felix to H. W. Verkenius, Wolff: 1909, 121.
51. January 23 and 29, 1836, Felix to Lea, NYPL Nos. 287 and 288.
52. March 22, 1836, Felix to Klingemann, Klingemann, 199.
53. *AmZ* 38 (1836), 433-36; *NZfM* 4 (1836), 182.
54. MDM GB V, 68; in Richard Wagner, *Sämtliche Werke*, ed. Egon Voss, XVIII/1, xv.
55. Cosima Wagner, II, 247.
56. E. Newman, I, 96n.
57. Schindler to Otto von Woringen, April 13, 1836, in Großmann-Vendrey: 1969, 83.
58. MDM f. 4.
59. April 30, 1837, Felix to Klingemann, Klingemann, 215.
60. Elise Polko: 1868, 60–61.
61. For a facs. see Ward Jones, ed., *The Mendelssohns on Honeymoon*, 126; see also the pencil drawing by Philipp Veit, SBB *MA* BA 132 (facs. in Klein: 1997, 181).
62. *AmZ* 38 (1836), 410.
63. See Cecilia Hopkins Porter, "The New Public and the Reordering of the Musical Establishment: The Lower Rhine Music Festivals, 1818–67" *19CM* 3 (1980), 217f.
64. Davison, 25.
65. April 21, 1836, Felix to Lea, NYPL No. 267.
66. April 25, 1836, Felix to Ferdinand von Woringen, in Fischer, 31–32.
67. Edwards: 1891, 137.
68. New York Public Library, Drexel 4779.
69. Edwards: 1891, 137.
70. Fischer, 33.
71. Charles Klingemann, "Account of the Musical Festival at Düsseldorf," *The Musical World* 2 (1836), 1–6 (June 17, 1836).
72. Fanny to Wilhelm Hensel, May 1836, *MF* II, 8.
73. Schindler, 437.
74. Bischoff to Schindler, June 18, 1836, in Fischer, 38–39.
75. Ferdinand Hiller, *Letters*, 52.
76. May 28, 1836, Felix to Thomas Attwood, in J. R. Sterndale Bennett, 41–42.
77. August 1, 1837, Comité für das Niederrh. Musikfest to Felix, Fischer, 37; see also August 24, 1837, Cécile to Lea, in Ward Jones, *The Mendelssohns on Honeymoon*, 186.
78. Felix to Lea, June 1, 1836, P. Mendelssohn Bartholdy: *Letters*, 1868, 100.
79. See further Stanley Weintraub, *Charlotte and Lionel: A Rothschild Love Story*, N.Y., 2003, 27ff.
80. "Jolly, weird and wonderful animal"; Felix to Klingemann, June 20, 1836, Klingemann, 201.
81. Hiller, 58; see also Felix to Schleinitz, June 30, 1836, *MLL*, 225, and *MF* II, 19.
82. E. Devrient, *Recollections*, 195.
83. Hiller, *Letters*, 60–61.
84. July 13 to Lea and Fanny, and July 24, 1836, to Rebecka, NYPL Nos. 269 and 271.
85. MDM c. 21, fols. 108–9.
86. *MF* II, 22.
87. E. Devrient, *Recollections*, 197.
88. Max Müller, *Auld Lang Syne*, N.Y., 1898, in *MAhW*, 256.
89. *MF* II, 22.
90. E. Devrient, *Recollections*, 193.
91. See further Guenther Roth, "Weber the Would-Be Englishman: Anglophilia and Family History," in H. Lehmann and G. Roth, *Weber's Protestant Ethic: Origins, Evidence, Contexts*, Cambridge, 1993, 97–121.
92. Marianne Weber, *Max Weber*, trans. H. Zohn, New Brunswick, N.J., 1988, 164.
93. MDM b. 5, fols. 18–20.
94. Petitpierre, *Romance*, 47.
95. Ibid., 70.
96. Rebecka to Felix, July 28, 1836, MDM GB V, 110; Fanny to Felix, July 30, 1836, in Citron: 1987, 208.
97. Felix to Hiller, August 7, 1836, Hiller, 64; Felix to Elisabeth Jeanrenaud, August 13, 1836, MDM d. 18.
98. MDM d. 11, f. 5. (August 21, 1836; facs. in Koyanagi, 23).

99. August 20, 1836, Felix to Elisabeth Jeanrenaud, MDM d. 18, fol. 9.
100. Felix to Elizabeth Jeanrenaud, August 13, 1836, MDM d. 18, fols. 6–7.
101. August 20, 1836, Felix to Lea, NYPL No. 275.
102. Felix to Hiller, August 7 and 18, 1836, Hiller, *Letters*, 62–71.
103. August 1836, Felix to Lübeck, in Hartog, 248–49.
104. Felix to Lea, August 20, 1836, NYPL No. 275.
105. Felix to Klingemann, August 12, 1836, in Klingemann, 204–5.
106. An undated autograph, nearly identical to the published version but bearing the title *Des Abends* (*Of Evening*) survives with a note in a second hand explaining the duet was composed in Horchheim around 1836, which might date it from late August 1836 (Opochinsky Collection of Music Manuscripts, Yale University, New Haven, Conn.).
107. F. Hensel, 83 (entry of July 8, 1839).
108. September 13, 1836, Felix to Rebecka, NYPL No. 278.
109. September 20, 1836, Dorothea Schlegel to Lea, in Klein: 1997, 175.
110. Schumann, *Tagebücher* I, 27.
111. Rebecka to Klingemann, October 7, 1836, Klingemann, 205.
112. Schumann, *Tagebücher* I, 29.
113. Edwards: 1909, 95.
114. On the publication history, see further Ward Jones: 1992, 245–46.
115. Eduard to August Franck, November 6, 1836, Feuchte, 69.
116. Entry of November 7, 1836, in Clara Wieck's diary (Zwickau, Robert-Schumann Haus).
117. Fanny to Felix, October 28, 1836, in Citron: 1987, 214.
118. *AmZ* 38 (1836), 767.
119. J. R. Sterndale Bennett, 50.
120. Cited in Großmann-Vendrey: 1969, 142.
121. Felix to Lea, November 26, 1836, NYPL No. 301.
122. Dörffel, 90.
123. See Camilla Cai's ed., Fanny Hensel, *Songs for Pianoforte, 1836–1837*, Madison, Wisc., 1994.
124. Fanny to Felix, November 22, 1836, Citron: 1987, 222.
125. Felix to Fanny, November 14, 1836, in Fanny and Felix Mendelssohn, 234.
126. Müller, *Auld Lang Syne*, in *MahW*, 256.
127. Felix to Klingemann, January 19, 1837, Klingemann, 210; and Fanny to Cécile, December 23, 1836, *MF* II, 27.
128. MDM c. 21; for an inventory, see Crum: 1983, 78–85.
129. One of the Goethe [*recte* Marianne von Willemer] Suleika settings, "Ach, um deine feuchten Schwingen," and Goethe's *Suleika und Hatem*, published as Felix's Op. 8 No. 12. For a facs. of the former, see Maurer, 156. The songs were later transferred to another album (MDM b. 4).
130. December 31, 1836, Felix to Lea, NYPL No. 304.
131. *AmZ* 39 (1837), 317.
132. Seaton: 1997, 174.
133. January 11, 1835, Felix to Attwood, Washington, LC (Music 1055).
134. See Todd: 1992c, 174–79.
135. Schumann, *Tagebücher* I, 31.
136. *Die Schule des Fugenspiels*; see Todd: 1992c, 180–85.
137. G. W. Fink in *AmZ* 39 (1837), 597–99; Robert Schumann in *NZfM* 7 (1837), 73–75.
138. Hensel, *Songs for Pianoforte*, 3–10 (see n. 123).
139. Ed. by Annegret Huber in Fanny Hensel-Mendelssohn, *Lyrische Klavierstücke (1836–1839)*, Kassel, 1996; see also Hellwig-Unruh: 2000, 278.
140. June 24, 1837, Felix to Fanny, in Ward Jones, *The Mendelssohns on Honeymoon*, 168–69.
141. Robert Schumann, in *NZfM* 7 (1837), 47; trans. in Leon Plantinga, *Schumann as Critic*, New Haven, 1967, 213.
142. See Todd: 1992c, 186–88; and Isabelle Bélance-Zank, "The Three-Hand Texture: Origins and Use," *Journal of the American Liszt Society*, No. 38 (1995), 99–121.
143. Brockhaus, I, 335.
144. A facs. of the program is in Klein: 1997, 198–99.
145. In the *Album: Neue Original-Compositionen für Gesang und Piano*, Berlin, A. M. Schlesinger, 1836.
146. March 7, 1837, Felix to Fanny, *MF* II, 30.
147. See Klein: 1997, 195–96, with a facsimile of the cover of the album.
148. March 4, 1837, Felix to Lea, NYPL No. 315.
149. R. Schumann, *Tagebücher* I, 31–32.

150. April 26, 1837, Cécile to Elisabeth Jeanrenaud, in Ward Jones, *The Mendelssohns on Honeymoon*, 143.
151. Lampadius, 233.
152. *AmZ* 39 (1837), 209–10.
153. *NZfM* 7 (1837), 73–75 (September 5, 1837).
154. Robert Schumann: 1946, 194–95.
155. Ibid., 198.
156. Ibid., 198–99.
157. See the excellent discussion of the nineteenth-century German oratorio in Smither, vol. 4; and Martin Geck, *Deutsche Oratorien 1800 bis 1840: Verzeichnis der Quellen und Aufführungen*, Wilhelmshaven, 1971.
158. *AmZ* 39 (1837), 522.
159. Abraham to Felix, March 10, 1835, in P. Mendelssohn Bartholdy: *Letters*, 1868, 70.
160. Sposato: 2000, ch. 4.
161. In the following discussion, the numbering of the oratorio's movements begins with the overture, and includes, for Part 1, Nos. 1–22; for Part 2, Nos. 23–45.
162. December 20, 1831; Klingemann, 90.
163. Lampadius, 246.
164. Sposato: 2000, 487.
165. Klingemann, "Account of the Musical Festival at Düsseldorf," *Musical World*, June 17, 1836, 1.
166. Smither, IV, 154.
167. Julius Schubring, "Erinnerungen," trans. in Todd, *MahW*, 231.
168. Jahn: 1866, 34n.
169. Julius Schubring, "Erinnerungen," *MahW*, 231.
170. Lampadius, 225.
171. See Carl Dahlhaus: 1974b, 58; and Feder, 97–117.
172. March 10, 1835, Abraham to Felix, P. Mendelssohn Bartholdy: *Letters*, 1868, 67.

Chapter 11

1. Felix to Moscheles, November 30, 1839, in F. Moscheles: 1888, 194.
2. March 7, 1837, Felix to Carl Jeanrenaud, HHI, Sig. 52.234; March 24, 1837, Felix to Lea, NYPL No. 316.
3. Petitpierre, *Romance*, 145–46.
4. MDM c. 29, fols. 73–74.
5. Paul to Cécile, November 11, 1836, cited in Ward Jones, *The Mendelssohns on Honeymoon*, xxii.
6. Felix and Cécile to Elisabeth Jeanrenaud, April 15, 1837, ibid., 141.
7. Entry of March 29, 1837, ibid., 1.
8. Entry of April 5, 1837, ibid., 5.
9. No. 1 (1834) was based on a subject upon which Felix had improvised at St. Paul's in London in 1833; No. 2 was finished on December 1, 1836 (Berlin, *MN* 29, 121–23); and No. 3, composed in March 1833, was written for Vincent Novello.
10. April 11, 1837, Felix to Rebecka, in Ward Jones, *The Mendelssohns on Honeymoon*, 136.
11. April 27, 1837, Felix to Elisabeth, ibid., 145.
12. First edited by Leopold Hirschberg for *Jede Woche Musik* (October 29, 1927), 165–66. For a modern edition see Ward Jones, *The Mendelssohns on Honeymoon*, 200–202.
13. Some of his handwritten exercises for her are in MDM c. 29, fols. 1–4.
14. April 25, 1837, Felix to Simrock, in *BadV*, 210.
15. Berlin, *MN* 29, 135–36.
16. April 17, 1837, Felix to Breitkopf & Härtel, in *BadV*, 60-61.
17. Review of Op. 38 in *NZfM* 7 (1837), 58; from the trans. in Schumann: 1946, 212.
18. November 29 and December 12, 1837, Schubring to Felix and Felix to Schubring, in Schubring: 1888, 113 and 116.
19. See further Jost: 1988, 133–37.
20. *AmZ* 39 (1837), 25. Felix's copy of Op. 23 is in the Bodleian Library, Deneke 57 (10).
21. Ward Jones, *The Mendelssohns on Honeymoon*, 49 (June 2, 1837).
22. Ibid., 57 (June 25, 1837).
23. June 24, 1837, Felix to Klingemann, in Klingemann, 216.
24. Ward Jones, *The Mendelssohns on Honeymoon*, 52 (June 7, 1837).

25. June 7, 1837, Lea to Felix; MDM GBVI, 44, cited in Citron: 1987, xli, n. 30.
26. June 24, 1837, Felix to Lea, in Ward Jones, *The Mendelssohns on Honeymoon*, 167.
27. *MF* II, 33.
28. Now incorporated in SBB, *MA* Sammelband Ms. 44. See Fanny Hensel, *Songs for Pianoforte*, vii–xvii, Ch. 10, n. 123.
29. June 2, 1837, Fanny to Felix; Citron: 1987, 233.
30. Ward Jones, *The Mendelssohns on Honeymoon*, 61.
31. See ibid., 65, fn. 1.
32. For a facs. see Max F. Schneider: 1960, and Ward Jones, *The Mendelssohns on Honeymoon*, 66.
33. SBB *MN* 29, 145–49.
34. E. Devrient, *Recollections*, 94; see also Todd: 1997, 117.
35. Felix to Klingemann, February 18, 1837; Klingemann, 212.
36. July 14, 1837, Felix to Schubring, in P. Mendelssohn Bartholdy: 1868, 117.
37. Ward Jones, *The Mendelssohns on Honeymoon*, 73, fn. 9.
38. Polko: 1868, 67–68; Ward Jones, *The Mendelssohns on Honeymoon*, 82 (August 21, 1837).
39. Entry of August 26–27, 1837, ibid., 86.
40. The draft survives in MDM c. 27, 42–44, and is transcribed in Sposato: 2000, II, 235ff. See also the diary entries of August 30 and 31 in Ward Jones, *The Mendelssohns on Honeymoon*, 90–91.
41. Entry for September 3–4, 1837; ibid., 94.
42. From an eyewitness account of H. J. Gauntlett in *Musical World* 6 (1838), 8–10 (September 15, 1837), rep. in Brown: 2003, 213.
43. Ibid.
44. The fugue is in BL Ms. Add. 35007, fol. 99b; for the canon (September 7, 1837) see Ludwig Altmann, ed., *Samuel Wesley and Dr. Mendelssohn: Three Organ Fugues*, London, 1962.
45. Ward Jones, *The Mendelssohns on Honeymoon*, 103 (September 11, 1837), and Philip Olleson, "Samuel Wesley," in *The New Grove Dictionary of Music and Musicians*, 2d ed., London, 2001, XXVII, 307.
46. September 12, 1837; Michael Broyles, ed., *A Yankee Musician in Europe: The 1837 Journals of Lowell Mason*, Ann Arbor, 1990, 125.
47. Ward Jones, *The Mendelssohns on Honeymoon*, 103–5 (entry for September 11, 1837).
48. Felix to Cécile, n.d., cited in Cécile to Lea, September 21, 1837 (NYPL No. 337), in ibid., 192.
49. Entry for September 18, 1837, ibid., 109.
50. See Großmann-Vendrey: 1969, 131.
51. Communication of Peter Ward Jones.
52. See Ward Jones: 1992, 246–47.
53. Felix to Klingemann, November 17, 1837, Klingemann, 224.
54. Schumann: 1946, 208.
55. Fanny to Cécile, October 5, 1837, *MF* II, 36.
56. Ibid., II, 37.
57. F. Hensel, 86 (entry of July 8, 1839).
58. From Clara's journal, cited in Averil Mackenzie-Grieve, *Clara Novello: 1818–1908*, London, 1955, 50.
59. Felix to J. Alfred Novello, November 18, 1837, ibid., 52. To Felix's dismay, Novello distributed lithographed facsimiles of the letter to his friends (Ward Jones: 1992, 247).
60. Mackenzie-Grieve, 54; Felix to Lea, November 13, 1837, NYPL No. 343.
61. *AmZ* 39 (1837), 770.
62. Felix to Fanny, January 13, 1838, Fanny and Felix Mendelssohn, 273; Felix to Hiller, January 20, 1838, Hiller, *Letters*, 111–12.
63. Felix to Lea, July 22, 1837, Ward Jones, *The Mendelssohns on Honeymoon*, 177.
64. Felix to the *Gesellschaft der Musikfreunde*, October 12, 1837, MLL, 236–37.
65. For a facs. see F. Moscheles: 1888, 161.
66. Dated autographs for Opp. 59 No. 1, 41 No. 5, 120 Nos. 3 and 1, and 41 No. 1 between November 23, 1837, and January 1838 survive (SBB *MN* 31, 97; BN Ms. Cons. 197 and 200/201; SBB *MN* 29, 143–44; and MDM c. 16).
67. Felix to Lea, November 13, 1837, NYPL No. 343.
68. Schumann: 1946, 206.
69. Radcliffe: 1954, 152.
70. Werner: 1963, 347.
71. Hiller, *Letters*, 93.
72. Lampadius, 244.
73. Felix to Klingemann, January 9, 1838, Klingemann, 228; Edwards: 1896, 7–8.

74. *Das Waldschloss* and *Pagenlied*, January 26, 1838.
75. April 14, 1838, Felix to Hiller, Hiller, *Letters*, 115; February 8, 1838, Felix to Lea, NYPL 356. See also E. Werner: 1980, 355; and Gantzel-Kress.
76. Felix to Lea, February 11, 1838, NYPL No. 357; Fanny to Klingemann, February 27, 1838, *MF* II, 37; Klein: 1997, 194–95.
77. *The Athenaeum* (1838), cited in Sirota, 91–92.
78. GB IV, 208. See Großmann-Vendrey: 1969, 159–60.
79. Felix to Rebecka, February 24, 1838, NYPL No. 362.
80. Felix to Droysen, March 5, 1838, in Wehmer, 59.
81. J. R. Planché, I, 279–316.
82. Felix to Lea, April 2, 1838, P. Mendelssohn Bartholdy: *Letters*, 1868, 135 (NYPL No. 373).
83. See Hellmundt: 1999, 77–102; an edition is now available (Wiesbaden, 1997).
84. *MF* II, 43.
85. July 15, 1838, Felix to Hiller, Hiller, *Letters*, 124.
86. See Lowenthal-Hensel: 1975, 205, n. 13.
87. See Eric Werner: 1975, 21; Seaton: 1977, 110ff.
88. Felix to David, July 30, 1838, in *LA*, 143.
89. Schumann: 1946, 216.
90. Werner: 1963, 304.
91. Felix to Ferdinand David, July 30, 1838, *LA*, 144.
92. Fanny to Klingemann, November 30, 1838, *MF* II, 48. See also F. Hensel, 90–91.
93. A modern reprint prepared by Rudolf Elvers has been published (Leipzig, 1977).
94. Fanny to Felix, September 7, 1838, Citron: 1987, 261.
95. Dörffel, 92.
96. See Clive Brown: 1984, 216ff.
97. Felix to Rebecka, April 10, 1839, NYPL No. 400.
98. See Deutsch: 1952; the important corrective in Krause; and "Briefe Felix Mendelssohn Bartholdy's an Herrn Professor Ferdinand Schubert in Wien," *Wiener allgemeine Musik-Zeitung* 8/4 (1848), 13–14.
99. Ferdinand Schubert to Felix, April 10, 1839, cited in Krause, 246.
100. See Todd, "The Unfinished Mendelssohn," in *MahW*, 163–84.
101. See the Foreword to Pietro Zappalà's edition, Felix Mendelssohn Bartholdy, *Neun Psalmen und Cantique*, Stuttgart, 1997.
102. *AmZ* 41 (1839), 176.
103. "Denn Sein ist das Meer," Berlin DSB *MN* 31, 51–66, April 11, 1839, published in an English edition by Sir George Grove (London, 1876).
104. Felix to Friedrich Kistner, July 14, 1839, *BadV*, 309.
105. Felix to Lea, March 18, 1839, P. Mendelssohn Bartholdy: 1868, 151.
106. D. F. Tovey, *Essays in Musical Analysis: Symphonies and Other Orchestral Works*, N.Y., 1981, 404.
107. Grey: 2001, 488.
108. April 23, 1839, Felix to Breitkopf & Härtel, *BadV*, 93.
109. Oswald Lorenz, rev. of Op. 47 in *NZfM* 12 (1840), 126; trans. in Seaton: 2001, 699.
110. June 2, 1839, Felix to Lea, NYPL No. 405.
111. See Ulrich Tank, *Die Geschwister Schloss*, Cologne, 1978, 2.
112. Averil Mackenzie-Grieve, *Clara Novello: 1818–1908*, London, 1955, 100–101.
113. Großmann-Vendrey: 1969, 105–6.
114. Felix to Lea, June 2, 1839, NYPL No. 405.
115. Felix to Lea, July 3, 1839, NYPL No. 408.
116. P. Mendelssohn Bartholdy: *Letters*, 1868, 159–60; and Heinrich Hoffmann, *Lebens-Erinnerungen*, Frankfurt, 1985, 170.
117. *Abendmusik an der Oberschweinsteige bei Frankfurt*, Berlin, SBB, Mendelssohn, 24.
118. Felix to Klingemann, August 1, 1839, P. Mendelssohn Bartholdy: *Letters*, 1868, 157.
119. Berlin, *MN* 31, 121–26 (July 13, 14, and 18, 1839); for an edition see Mendelssohn, *Complete Organ Works*, ed. Wm. A. Little, London, 1989, I, 65–87.
120. See Parkins and Todd: 1983.
121. Felix to Fanny, June 18, 1839, P. Mendelssohn Bartholdy: *Letters*, 1868, 152–53. Felix was offered an autograph as a gift and chose the chorale preludes (four preludes from the *Orgel-Büchlein*), which were inserted in one of Cécile's albums; recent research, however, has shown them not to be autograph. I am grateful to Peter Ward Jones for this information.
122. Felix to Ferdinand David, July 24, 1839, *LA*, 148.
123. Schumann, review of Op. 49 in *NZfM* 13 (1840), 198, trans. in Schumann: 1946, 217.

124. Hiller, *Letters*, 154–55.
125. Berlin, *MN* 31, 129–68.
126. Felix to Lea, August 5, 1839, NYPL No. 410.
127. Felix to Lea, August 16, 1839, NYPL No. 411.
128. The dated autograph is in Berlin, *MN* 31.
129. Grove: 1890, II, 304.
130. Dinglinger: 1993b, 117.
131. Sposato: 2000, 485.
132. See further the analysis in Dinglinger: 1993b, 146.
133. *AmZ* 42 (1840), 27–28.
134. *NZfM* 12 (1840), 144.
135. F. Hensel, 94 (entry of August 27, 1839).
136. Henry F. Chorley, *Modern German Music*, London, 1854, I, 9.
137. Ibid., 7–54; *AmZ* 41 (1839), 791–97; and Felix to Lea, September 11, 1839, NYPL No. 412.
138. See David B. Levy, "Wolfgang Robert Griepenkerl and Beethoven's Ninth Symphony," in *Essays on Music for Charles Warren Fox*, ed. J. C. Graue *et al.*, Rochester, 1979, 103–13.
139. Chorley, *Modern German Music*, I, 51.
140. For a full account of the affair, see Werner: 1963, 327–31.
141. F. Moscheles: 1888, 198.
142. MDM c. 49, fols. 24–26. Felix to Klingemann, January 2, 1840, Klingemann, 242.
143. Hiller, *Letters*, 160–61.
144. *Beilage* for June 5, 1839, *AmZ* 41 (1839), after col. 452.
145. Chorley, *Modern German Music*, II, 33.
146. November 14 and 22, 1839; DSB *MN* 31 (Berlin) and 34 (Kraków).
147. The exception is the *Lerchengesang*, Op. 48 No. 4, designed as a round-like canon.
148. Hiller, *Letters*, 152.
149. Radcliffe: 1954, 133; Werner: 1963, 355.
150. See also Douglass Seaton, "Mendelssohn's Cycles of Songs," in Cooper and Prandi, 204–6.

Chapter 12

1. Klingemann, 264.
2. *AmZ* 42 (1840), 53.
3. Ibid., 117.
4. See Todd: 1991c, 196–203.
5. *AmZ* 42 (1840), 227. According to Heinrich Brockhaus, the public was so "electrified" that it succumbed to a *Mendelssohnmanie* and demanded the encore of the Bach. Brockhaus, I, 385.
6. Ibid., 164–65.
7. Cooper: 1997, 157–79.
8. Georg Feder cites forty arrangements in "Geschichte der Bearbeitungen von Bachs Chaconne," *Bach-Interpretationen*, ed. M. Geck, Göttingen, 1969, 168–89.
9. See especially Peter Ward Jones: 1992, 248–50.
10. J. Alfred Novello to Felix, February 18, 1840, MDM, GB XI, 63.
11. H. Probst to Breitkopf & Härtel, February 22, 1840, in H. Lenneberg, ed. and trans., *Breitkopf und Härtel in Paris: The Letters of Their Agent Heinrich Probst between 1833 and 1840*, Stuyvesant, N.Y., 1990, 73.
12. Felix to Edward Buxton, February 25, 1840, LC (Music 1055).
13. John Thomson to Felix, March 13, 1840, MDM, GB XI, 125.
14. February 14, 1840, Felix to Klingemann, Klingemann, 243.
15. Felix to Joseph Mendelssohn, February 20, 1840, in Gilbert: 1975, 128–30. See also Brockhaus I, 388 (March 28, 1840).
16. Hiller, *Letters*, 169–70. One of Felix's Boccaccio translations appeared in Reissmann, 319–20.
17. Sederholm to Felix, November 11, 1838, MDM GB 8, 115. See also Sposato: 2000, 452–53.
18. Gollmick, II, 106.
19. Chorley to Felix, November 3, 1839, MDM GB X, 120.
20. February 28, 1840, Felix to Chorley, in H. F. Chorley: 1873, I, 309–10.
21. Schubring to Felix, February 19–21, 1840, in Schubring: 1892, 156–57.
22. See Bonds, 81.
23. See the detailed accounts in Wm. A. Little: 1992; and Alan Walker, 345–51.

24. *NZfM* 12 (1840), 103.
25. Hiller, *Letters*, 164–65.
26. Ibid., 165.
27. Litzmann, I, 414.
28. D'Agoult, I, 414.
29. Felix to Paul, March 20, 1840, NYPL No. 576.
30. Litzmann, I, 416.
31. F. Max Müller, *Auld Lang Syne*, N.Y., 1898, in *MahW*, 253.
32. Felix's invitation to the orchestra is in MDM GB XI, 97.
33. Details in Felix's letter to Rebecka, March 30, 1840 (NYPL No. 436), cited in Little: 1992, 115–16.
34. *AmZ* 42 (1840), 297; *NZfM* 12 (1840), 118.
35. Felix to Moscheles, March 21, 1840, in Moscheles, 204.
36. Ibid., 203.
37. Hiller, *Letters*, 167.
38. *NZfM* 39 (1853), 6.
39. Therese Marx, 22–24.
40. See Smither, IV, 69ff.; and Zywietz.
41. April 18, 1840, Cécile to Madame Jeanrenaud, MDM d. 40, fols. 18–19.
42. Entries of April 21, 26, 27, May 5, 9, 17 and 18, 1840, in Clara Wieck's diary (Zwickau, Robert-Schumann Haus).
43. May 10, 1840, Felix to Adam, in Tiersot, II, 333. Adam recorded the beginning of a *Christe eleison* in Cécile's album (MDM c. 21, fol. 172); Felix reciprocated by inserting his Lied "O könnt ich zu dir fliegen" in the album of Adam's traveling companion, Mlle. Chérie Couraud.
44. May 24, 1840, Felix to Lea, NYPL No. 434; *AmZ* 42 (1840), 769–70.
45. Felix to Falkenstein, April 8, 1840, P. Mendelssohn Bartholdy: *Letters*, 1868, 183–88.
46. The guidelines appeared in the *Festschrift zum 75-jährigen Bestehen des Königl. Konservatoriums der Musik zu Leipzig*, Leipzig, 1918, 76–77.
47. See the thorough discussion of the festival in Bonds, 80ff., and the account in Brockhaus I, 396–401.
48. Felix to Lea, June 22, 1840, NYPL No. 438.
49. Entry of June 24, 1840, in Clara Wieck's diary (Zwickau, Robert-Schumann Haus).
50. *AmZ* 43 (1841), 822.
51. Felix to Buxton, April 30, 1843, Yale University, New Haven, Conn., Koch Collection.
52. *MT* 38 (1897), 810.
53. See the excellent discussion of the reception history in Bonds, 74–80.
54. A. B. Marx, "Ueber die Form der Symponie-Cantate. Auf Anlass von Beethoven's neunter Symphonie," *AmZ* 49 (1847), 489–98, 505–11.
55. Fétis, *Biographie universelle*, Paris, 1864, VI, 81.
56. *NZfM* 13 (1840), 13.
57. Hauptmann to Hauser, December 10, 1841, in A. Schöne, ed., *The Letters of a Leipzig Cantor, Being the Letters of Moritz Hauptmann to Franz Hauser, Ludwig Spohr, and Other Musicians*, trans. A. D. Coleridge, London, 1892; N.Y., 1972, I, 233; and Hans von Bülow, *Briefe und Schriften*, ed. M. von Bülow, Leipzig, 1896, III, 371. Felix's *Fremdenliste* includes an entry for "v. Bülow (Dresden)" on April 3, 1840.
58. Felix to Klingemann, February 16 and November 18, 1840, in Klingemann, 243 and 251.
59. The autograph Ms. in Kraków, BJ, *MN* 34, is dated November 27, 1840.
60. Bonds, 108.
61. Ibid., 87–96.
62. Felix to Chorley, July 21, 1840, in Chorley: 1873, 314–20.
63. Felix to Lea, August 10, 1840, P. Mendelssohn Bartholdy: *Letters*, 188.
64. See Pape.
65. *NZfM* 13 (1840), 56 (August 15, 1840).
66. See Todd: 1995.
67. *NZfM* 13 (1840), 56.
68. September 7, 1840, Felix to Klingemann, Klingemann, 247.
69. F. Hensel, 196 (entry of September 15, 1840).
70. Fanny to Felix, September 23, 1839, in Fanny and Felix Mendelssohn, 317.
71. *MF* II, 97–98.
72. "Votre frère," Ingres referred to him, "qui joue si bien de la basse." Fanny to Lea Mendelssohn Bartholdy, December 8, 1839, in Fanny Hensel: 2002b, 27.
73. *MF* II, 108.

74. Kupferstich-Kabinett SMPK, Berlin; see Lowenthal-Hensel: 1997, 18.
75. Felix to Lea, September 18, 1840, NYPL No. 444.
76. Dickens, *Hard Times*, ch. 5.
77. I. Moscheles, 268.
78. See F. G. Edwards, "Elizabeth Mounsey," *MT* 46 (1905), 718–21.
79. I. Moscheles, 270.
80. Ibid, 271.
81. *AmZ* 42 (1840), 970.
82. Ibid., 1007–10.
83. See Lockwood; and Todd: 1997, 187ff.
84. K. Olsen and H. Topsøe-Jensen, ed., *H. C. Andersens Dagbøger: 1825–1875*, Copenhagen, 1977, II, 51–52.
85. *MN* 34 (Kraków, BJ).
86. Felix to Lea, December 27, 1840, (NYPL), published with the incorrect date of October 27 in P. Mendelssohn Bartholdy: *Letters*, 1868, 192–93.
87. *MF* II, 250.
88. Barclay, 68ff.
89. Felix to Paul, March 3 [*recte* 4], 1841, NYPL No. 589, published in part in P. Mendelssohn Bartholdy: 1868, 225. Jakoby's pamphlet was banned, and he was prosecuted, though ultimately acquitted, for *lèse majesté*.
90. See C. H. Porter, *The Rhine as Musical Metaphor*, Boston, 1996, 39ff.
91. Felix to Paul, November 20, 1840, P. Mendelssohn Bartholdy: 1868, 202; in February 1840 Felix had set Carl Simrock's poem *Warnung vor dem Rhein*, published posthumously in 1849, but its text deals with the Lorelei legend, not the threat of French aggression.
92. *Josias Freiherr von Bunsen, aus seinen Briefen geschildert von seiner Witwe*, Leipzig, 1869, II, 142; see also Dinglinger: 1997b, 23–25.
93. MDM GB XII, 141.
94. Felix to Paul, December 20, 1840, P. Mendelssohn Bartholdy: *Letters*, 1868, 205–7.
95. Fanny to Felix, December 5, 1840, in Fanny and Felix Mendelssohn, 347.
96. Kraków, BJ, *MN* 34. A fair copy was finished two days later (BL Add. 31801). See Brodbeck: 1991, 43–64.
97. Unpublished portion of Felix to Paul, January 9, 1841, NYPL No. 587.
98. Felix to Klingemann, March 10, 1841, Klingemann, 257–79.
99. P. Mendelssohn Bartholdy: *Letters*, 1868, 233–35; for a facs., see Wolff: 1909, facing p. 148.
100. E. Devrient, *Recollections*, 221.
101. Felix to Paul, June 5, 1841, NYPL No. 596; Felix to Moscheles, June 15, F. Moscheles, 223–24. See also F. Hensel, 201 (entry of January 20, 1841).
102. Felix to Klingemann, July 15, 1841, Klingemann, 264; Felix to Paul, June 15, 1841, *MLL*, 252–54.
103. Reissmann, 230.
104. SBB MA Ep. 376; facs. in Klein: 1997, 233.
105. Heinrich Brockhaus, *Tagebücher*, I, 429.
106. Felix to Spohr, January 8, 1841, MDM c. 42, fols. 25–26.
107. *NZfM* 14 (1841), 88.
108. Felix to Fanny, February 14, 1841, P. Mendelssohn Bartholdy: *Letters*, 1868, 221.
109. Ibid., 222.
110. Kraków, BJ, *MN* 35.
111. See Daverio: 1997, 229ff.
112. Schumann, *Tagebücher* II, 122–23.
113. See Todd, "Zu Mendelssohns 'Allegro brillant' op. 92: Ein Duo für Clara Schumann," forthcoming in the *Kongreß-Bericht* of the *Leipziger Mendelssohn Festtage 1997*.
114. In an edition by E.-G. Heinemann (Munich, 1994).
115. Felix to Paul, January 2, 1841, P. Mendelssohn Bartholdy: *Letters*, 1868, 209.
116. See further the program notes to accompany Christoph Spering's recording of the 1841 version (Paris, Opus 111, 1992).
117. Felix to Eduard Bendemann, April 15, 1841, *LA*, 35. The March was evidently performed in Dresden on April 19, after Felix had returned to Leipzig. The author is grateful to Ralf Wehner for this information.
118. *AmZ* 43 (1841), 613.
119. No. 2 (February 24, 1835, MDM c. 1); No. 1 (February 28, 1839, MDM Horsley b. 1, fols. 17–18); and No. 3 (March 14, 1839, Berlin *MN* 31, 115–18).
120. Horsley, in *MahW*, 241.

121. Dresden, Sächsische Landesbibliothek, Mus. 5543 (May 1, 1841).
122. See *LA*, 233 n. 26. In 1842 Simrock brought out six of the *Lieder ohne Worte* with Christern's texts. See Cooper: 1998.
123. BJ MN 35, p. 36.
124. For a facsimile of the title page and thorough discussion of this source, see Jost: 1992.
125. MDM d. 68; reproduced in Marek, 260.
126. Dibdin to Felix, May 25 and June 19, 1841, in GB XIII, 147 and 258.
127. The prelude appeared, along with a facsimile of the autograph, in *Exeter Hall* 1 (1868), 54–57; for a modern ed., see Mendelssohn, *Complete Organ Works*, I, 91–93, and also *MQ* 5 (1919), 496–97.
128. Felix to Rebecka, July 30, 1841, NYPL No. 508.
129. Felix to Kistner, August 7, 1841, in *BadV*, 311.
130. *AmZ* 44 (1842), 2.
131. MDM GB XIV, 47.

Chapter 13

1. P. Mendelssohn Bartholdy: *Letters*, 1868, 289–90.
2. August 9, 1841, to David, August 14 and 23 to Verkenius, September 6 to Klingemann, and August 28 to Rebecka; *LA*, 156, P. Mendelssohn Bartholdy: *Letters*, 1868, 241–46, Klingemann, 266, and NYPL No. 515.
3. *NZfM* 15 (1841), 94–95.
4. E. Devrient, *Recollections*, 224.
5. From the trans. of Paul Roche, *The Oedipus Plays of Sophocles* (N.Y., 1958), 210; following quotations from the play are also from Roche's translation.
6. Paulin, 337.
7. For a recent study of the composing manuscript, see Boetius.
8. Meyerbeer, III, 375.
9. Becker, 88.
10. Felix to Droysen, December 2, 1841, in Wehmer, 71.
11. Steinberg, 137–57.
12. E. Devrient, *Recollections*, 235.
13. For an illustration, see Jacob, facing 256.
14. Felix to Fanny, March 25, 1845, *MF* II, 317.
15. See Flashar: 1979, 359–60, idem: 1989, 66–81; and Andraschke.
16. E. Devrient, *Recollections*, 225–26.
17. On the variety of scorings, see Seaton: 2001b, 197.
18. Felix to George Macfarren, December 8, 1844, *GM*, 166.
19. Böckh, "Ueber die Darstellung der Antigone," *AmZ* 43 (1841), 965.
20. Felix to Droysen, December 2, 1841, Wehmer, 72.
21. *NZfM* 22 (1845), 147; trans. in *MahW*, 347.
22. Berlin, *MA* Ep. 376.
23. Felix to Klingemann, September 6, 1841, Klingemann, 206.
24. Felix to the *Directeur* and Scribe, January 14, 1841, and January 14, 1842, in Tiersot, 333–34.
25. Felix to B. Schott, December 28, 1841, *BadV*, 336.
26. Bartholomew to Felix, September 21, 1841, MDM GB XIV, 87.
27. Klingemann to Bartholomew, September 18, 1841, in Klingemann, 267.
28. Felix to Bartholomew, October 4, 1841, Polko: 1987, 179.
29. Bartholomew to Felix, October 25, 1841, MDM GB XIV, 132.
30. Ibid., November 23, 1841, MDM GB XIV, 185.
31. Felix to Bartholomew, July 1842, Polko: 1987, 181.
32. Felix to Boettger, December 10, 1841, in *GM*, 195.
33. Schumann, *Tagebücher*, II, 192.
34. Ed. by Liana Gavrila Serbescu and Barbara Heller, 2 vols., Kassel, 1989.
35. For a facs. see Fanny Hensel, *Das Jahr, zwölf Charakterstücke (1841) für das Fortepiano, illustrierte Reinschrift mit Zeichnungen von Wilhelm Hensel*, ed. B. Borchard, Kassel, 2000; see also Thorau.
36. See also Toews.
37. For example, Nubbemeyer: 1997.

38. See Rothenberg, 704.
39. A. Walker, 372.
40. Ludwig Rellstab, *Franz Liszt: Beurtheilungen, Berichte, Lebensskizze*, Berlin, 1842, 2–5; trans. in Adrian Williams, *Portrait of* Liszt, Oxford, 1990, 177–78.
41. Felix to Ferdinand David, February 5, 1842, *LA*, 174.
42. Felix to Liszt, February 1, 1842, in La Mara, I, 38.
43. E. Devrient, *Recollections*, 233.
44. MDM, GB XV, 20.
45. *AmZ* 44 (1842), 234; E. Devrient, *Recollections*, 234.
46. MDM a.1 (Roll), no. 6.
47. Meyerbeer, III, 393.
48. Kraków, *MN* 36.
49. Sterndale Bennett, 123.
50. Felix to David, February 16, 1842, *LA*, 175.
51. *AmZ* 44 (1842), 254.
52. Dörffel, 99.
53. See Seaton: 1977, 212ff. Seaton has located some rejected pages in score for the symphony (DSB MN 19) that also contain sketches for *Antigone*, and partly from this evidence dated the principal work on the symphony to fall 1841.
54. *AmZ* 44 (1842), 258.
55. *NZfM* 18 (1843), 155.
56. Todd: 1984. John Daverio has argued for a similar case for Robert Schumann in "Schumann's Ossianic Manner," *19CM* 21 (1998), 247–73.
57. Felix to J. P. E. Hartmann, December 30, 1840, Copenhagen, Royal Library, Musikforeningens Arkiv. The correspondence with Hartmann is given in Harwell, 239–40.
58. Oxford, Bodleian Library, Deneke 206 (2), arrangement for piano duet.
59. *Ossians Digte*, Copenhagen, 1807–09. See Harwell, 205f., for a transcription of the program, recorded in Gade's composition diary, and 128ff. for a discussion.
60. Grey: 1997, 55ff.
61. Felix to David, March 12, 1842, *LA*, 178.
62. Mercer-Taylor: 1995. To bolster his case, the author seeks to establish similarities between the A-major coda and the Lied from Felix's *Festgesang* for the 1840 Gutenberg festival (specifically, the melody later recast as "Hark! The Herald Angels Sing"). These similarities seem more coincidental than conclusive; still, Felix's reference to a *Männerchor* suggests he had in mind here a German part-song, probably a *Volkslied* and not an English glee.
63. Ludwig Finscher, "'Zwischen absoluter und Programmusik': Zur Interpretation der deutschen romantischen Symphonie," in C.-H. Mahling, ed., *Über Symphonien: Beiträge zu einer musikalischen Gattung*, Tutzing, 1979, 115.
64. Felix to K. H. Hergel, August 1, 1840, BN *Lettres autographes* Mend. 9.
65. Felix to Buxton, March 5, 1842, LC (Music 1055).
66. E. Devrient, *Recollections*, 235–36.
67. Wagner to Eduard Avenarius, May 3, 1842, in Richard Wagner, *Sämtliche Briefe*, ed. G. Strobel and W. Wolf, Leipzig, 1970, II, 76.
68. See Wagner's letter to G. E. Anders, May 13, 1842, in ibid., II, 92.
69. F. Hensel, 209 (entry of June 1, 1842).
70. Esser, 61.
71. Schorn, I, 149.
72. Ibid., I, 150.
73. Letters to Lea and Paul, May 13 and 29, 1842, NYPL Nos. 521 and 604.
74. Cécile to Elizabeth Jeanrenaud, May 29, 1842, MDM d 19.
75. F. Hensel, 209 (entry of June 1, 1842).
76. Felix to Klingemann, September 13, 1842, Klingemann, 271.
77. "Mendelssohn in England: A Centenary Tribute," *MT* 50 (1909), 88. The autographs are in Berlin, *MN* 20, 1–3.
78. A facs. of the Ms. is in *MT* 50 (1909), following 88.
79. MDM d. 56/1–2; on the history of the pieces see *MT* 32 (1891), 592 and 42 (1901), 807. A twentieth-century edition of Op. 72 (ed. H. C. Hieckel, Munich, 1969) includes as a seventh piece an Andante in E♭; the other piece, a Sostenuto in F, remains unpublished.
80. The Austrian national anthem, originally composed for the emperor's birthday and incorporated into Haydn's String Quartet Op. 76 No. 3.
81. "Elizabeth Mounsey," *MT* 46 (1905), 719.

82. Rockstro, 81–82.
83. Felix to Paul, June 17, 1842, NYPL No. 526; Felix to Lea, June 21-22, 1842, P. Mendelssohn Bartholdy: 1868, 255; and *MT* 50 (1909), 88.
84. *The Musical World*, June 16, 1842; Foster, 173n.
85. J. R. Sterndale Bennett, 143.
86. W. Watts to Felix, June 27, 1842, MDM GB XV, 298.
87. Felix to Paul, June 17, 1842, NYPL No. 526.
88. Phillips: 1864, II, 237ff.
89. Rockstro, 83–84. The Ms. was the so-called London autograph of the second volume, formerly owned by Muzio Clementi and purchased at auction by Emett in 1832. It came to the British Museum in 1896 (Add. Ms. 35021). For a facs. see J. S. Bach, *Das wohltemperirte Clavier II*, ed. Don Franklin and Stephen Daw (London, 1980).
90. Felix to Lea, July 19, 1842, *MF* II, 169.
91. Felix to an unidentified court official, June 4, 1842, in English; Kunstsammlungen der Veste Coburg.
92. Felix to Paul, in a postscript to Cécile's letter to Lea dated June 14, 1842, NYPL No. 536.
93. Felix to Lea, June 21, 1842, P. Mendelssohn Bartholdy: 1868, 254, silently blended into which is a relevant passage from Felix to Paul, June 17, 1842, NYPL No. 526.
94. Marek, 293.
95. Felix to Lea, July 19, 1842, *MF* II, 168–71.
96. MDM GB VIII, 160.
97. Arnold Niggli, *Die Schweizerische Musikgesellschaft*, Zurich, 1886, cited in Felix Mendelssohn Bartholdy: 1954, 31–32.
98. See Wanner, 14.
99. Now in Berlin, *MA* Ms. 21; for a facs. of the entire album, see F. Mendelssohn Bartholdy: 1954; the second album, with entries from August 2 to August 30, is in MDM e. 1; of the third, only one drawing has survived (see n. 105).
100. Felix to Klingemann, September 13, 1842, Klingemann, 272.
101. Genast, III, 217–18.
102. Felix to Lea, August 18, 1842, in *MLL*, 257.
103. For a facs. see F. Mendelssohn Bartholdy: 1954.
104. See Grumbacher and Rosenthal, 123–29.
105. Now lost. One page, formerly belonging to Hugo von Mendelssohn of Basel, is reproduced in W. Reich: 1947, 9. It contains an incomplete sketch of Wolfenschiessen.
106. Felix to Lea, September 3, 1842, in Wanner, 6.
107. Felix to Simrock, September 21, 1842, *BadV*, 234–36.
108. Hiller, *Letters*, 183; the sketch, dated September 15, 1842, is reproduced as a frontispiece to the volume.
109. C. E. and M. Hallé, eds., *Life and Letters of Sir Charles Hallé*, London, 1896, 74.
110. *AmZ* 44 (1842), 829.
111. Schumann, *Tagebücher* II, 249.
112. Felix to Hiller, October 8, 1842, Hiller, *Letters*, 194.
113. Felix to von Küstner, October 15, 1842, LC (Music 1055).
114. M. A. Souchay to Felix, October 12, 1842, Bodleian, GB XVI, 69, trans. in Oliver Strunk, ed., *Source Readings in Music History*, rev. ed. by Ruth A. Solie, N.Y., 1998, VI, 158.
115. Felix to M. A. Souchay, Jr., October 15, 1842, in P. Mendelssohn Bartholdy: 1868, 269–71.
116. Op. 57 No. 5, Berlin *MN* 20, 5–6; Op. 63 No. 5, *MN*, 20, 6–7.
117. Felix to Schleinitz, October 17, 1842, *MLL*, 259–60.
118. Felix to von Massow, October 23, 1842, P. Mendelssohn Bartholdy: *Letters*, 1868, 271.
119. Felix to Frederick William IV, October 28, 1842, ibid., 273–75. See also the account in F. Hensel, 213 (entry of November 2, 1842).
120. Felix to Stawinsky (*Regisseur* of the Royal Theater), November 4, 1842, LC (Music 1055).
121. Felix to Lea, December 11, 1842, P. Mendelssohn Bartholdy: *Letters*, 1868, 285.
122. E. Newman, I, 347.
123. Cosima Wagner, II, 138.
124. Felix to Fanny, November 16, 1842, *MF* II, 176.
125. Decree of Frederick William IV, November 22, 1842, in MDM GB XVI, 126/27; see also Dinglinger: 1997b, 27.
126. Felix to Paul, December 5, 1842, P. Mendelssohn Bartholdy: *Letters*, 1868, 283; Felix to Frederick William IV, December 4, 1842, *MLL*, 260.
127. Felix to Lea, December 11, 1842, P. Mendelssohn Bartholdy: *Letters*, 1868, 285.

128. For an account, see F. Hensel, 217–19 (entry of January 2, 1843).
129. *MF* II, 179.
130. Felix to Klingemann, January 17, 1843, Klingemann, 278.
131. Felix to Paul, December 22, 1842, P. Mendelssohn Bartholdy: *Letters*, 1868, 291.

Chapter 14

1. Felix to Hiller, January 19, 1843, Hiller *Letters*, 199.
2. Felix to Paul, January 5, 1843, NYPL No. 612; Felix to Hiller, January 19, 1843, Hiller, *Letters*, 199.
3. See Eppstein.
4. See Jost: 1988, 173ff.
5. Lowenthal-Hensel: 1990, 148. See also F. Hensel, 219–20 (entry of January 20, 1843).
6. E. B. Oliver to Felix, January 24, 1842 [*recte* 1843], MDM GB XVII, 44; and Felix to E. B. Oliver, January 26, 1843, Boston Public Library.
7. Joseph to Felix, MDM GB XVII, 51 (January 27, 1843); trans. in Brown: 2003, 85.
8. Felix to Spohr, January 26, 1843, MDM c. 42, fols. 27–28; Gade to Felix, January 28, 1843, in Gade, 25.
9. Felix to Berlioz, January 25, 1843, Berlioz, III, 60–61.
10. Cairns, 295.
11. See Holoman, 295–96.
12. Cairns, 295.
13. *MF* II, 185.
14. Cairns, 294.
15. Ibid., 297.
16. *AmZ* 45 (1843), 217–21.
17. F. Hensel, 221 (entry of March 13, 1843).
18. Cairns, 297–98.
19. For the complete program, see *NZfM* 18 (1843), 95–98.
20. Felix to Hiller, March 25, 1843, Hiller, *Letters*, 207.
21. Von Massow to Felix, March 27, 1843, MDM GB XVII, 161.
22. For the early history of the *Domchor*, see Scheumann: 1907/08; *idem*: 1908/09; Brodbeck: 1992, 3ff.; and Dinglinger: 1997b, 23ff.
23. *Signale* 1 (1843), 55; the date is sometimes given as April 2, which fell on a Sunday.
24. For a complete roster of students from 1843 to 1881, see Karl Whistling, *Statistik des Königlichen Conservatoriums der Musik zu Leipzig: 1843–1883*, n.p., 1883, reproduced in L. M. Phillips, 247–324.
25. Felix wrote a testimonial for Nottebohm that survives in the LC (March 15, 1843; Music 1055).
26. *NZfM* 18 (1843), 126.
27. *Kämmerer* Minckwitz to Felix, April 13, 1843, MDM GB XVII, 198, cited in Häfner, 246.
28. Richard Wagner, "Das Oratorium 'Paulus' von Felix Mendelssohn-Bartholdy," in Wagner, *Sämtliche Schriften und Dichtungen*, Leipzig, 1912, XII, 149–50.
29. From the diploma awarding the honorary citizenship, cited in *LA*, 106n.
30. See Felix's letter to Paul of April 18, 1843, in NYPL No. 621, the brief report in the *NZfM* 18 (1843), 144, and von Wasielewski: 1897, 36n.
31. See Pape, 29.
32. For their correspondence see especially *LA*, 19–44, and Feder and Hübner, 157–97.
33. Felix to Lea, December 11, 1842, P. Mendelssohn Bartholdy: *Letters*, 1868, 286; trans. modified from the autograph in NYPL No. 530.
34. See further, Pape, 37–40.
35. Felix to Fanny, May 2, 1843, in Fanny and Felix Mendelssohn, 364–65.
36. *AmZ* 45 (1843), 415.
37. J.-G. Prod'homme and A. Dandelot, *Gounod (1818–1893): sa vie et ses oeuvres*, Paris, 1911, 93.
38. Felix to von Massow, May 21, 1843, cited in Scheumann: 1908/09, 260.
39. Sebastian and Fanny Hensel to Felix, postmarked June 17, 1843, MDM GB XVII, 360.
40. Kraków, *MN* 38, 185–95; a modern ed. is in Richard Wagner, *Sämtliche Werke: Band 16, Chorwerke*, ed. R. Kapp, Mainz, 1993, 219–23; see also "Occasional Notes," in *MT* 47 (1906), 385–86.
41. Wagner to Felix, June 3, 1843, in Wagner, *Chorwerke*, 177 (No. 501).
42. Wagner to Avenarius, July 13, 1843, in Spencer and Millington, 110; see also the documents assembled by Kapp (n. 40), 177–79.

43. Felix to Hiller, March 3, 1843, Hiller, *Letters*, 203.
44. MDM g. 6, fol. 27.
45. See Ward Jones: 1992, 251.
46. Including Opp. 59 No. 2-6, 88 Nos. 2 and 4, and 100 No. 2, all in Kraków, *MN* 38/2.
47. Max Thomas, *Heinrich August Neithardt*, diss., Freie Universität, Berlin, 1959, 80.
48. Felix to Paul, July 21 and 26, 1843, P. Mendelssohn Bartholdy: *Letters*, 1868, 303, 307–8.
49. Massow to Felix, July 12, 1843, MDM GB XVIII, 293. See also Brodbeck: 1992, 10–14; and Dinglinger: 1997b, 30–31.
50. Von Massow to Felix, July 14, 1843, MDM GB XVIII, 20.
51. The dated autograph is in Kraków, *MN* 38/2; a modern edition by Roe-Min Kok (Stuttgart, 1996) is available.
52. Fanny Hensel to Franz Hauser, August 10, 1843, in Hellwig-Unruh: 1997, 221; R. Werner, 111.
53. Felix to Paul, July 21, 1843, P. Mendelssohn Bartholdy: *Letters*, 1868, 304.
54. Felix to Rebecka, August 10, 1843, *MF* II, 197.
55. BN Conservatoire Ms. 190.
56. *NZfM* 19 (1843), 68.
57. Andreas Moser, *Joseph Joachim: Ein Lebensbild*, Berlin, 1908, I, 45, 54.
58. Dorn, "Recollections," 404. The melodrama was *Der Zauberer und das Ungetüm* (*The Sorcerer and the Monster*), performed in Berlin on April 20, 1827.
59. Von Küstner to Felix, September 10, 1843, MDM GB XVIII, 16.
60. *AmZ* 45 (1843), 741–42.
61. Felix to the *Rat der Stadt Leipzig*, October 1, 1843, in *LA*, 108–12.
62. Moser, *Joachim*, I, 56.
63. Gade, 42.
64. Fanny to Rebecka, October 18, 1843, *MF* II, 215–19; Hiller, *Letters*, 212–14, and E. Devrient, *Recollections*, 246–50.
65. Ibid., 246–47.
66. Hiller, *Letters*, 214.
67. Fanny to Rebecka, October 18, 1843, *MF* II, 217.
68. On Felix's differing treatments of the motto chords in the overture, see Todd: 1993, 87.
69. *NZfM* 20 (1844), 6–7.
70. E. Devrient, 247.
71. *MA* Ms. 86; an edition by Suzanne Summerville (Fairbanks, Alas., 1994) is available.
72. *MA* Ms. 48; an edition by L. G. Serbescu and B. Heller is available (Kassel, 1991); see also Nubbemeyer: 1999, 108–20.
73. Reinecke, 3.
74. *AmZ* 46 (1844), 76.
75. Felix to Rebecka, December 23, 1843, *MF* II, 238.
76. Felix to Klingemann, November 20, 1843, Klingemann, 283.
77. *Tagebücher von K. A. Varnhagen von Ense*, Leipzig, 1861, rep. Bern, 1972, II, 238.
78. Dr. F. E. Ehrenberg to Felix, October 17, 1843, MDM GB XVIII, 146.
79. They have been edited by Pietro Zappalà (Stuttgart, 1997).
80. See the thorough discussion in Brodbeck: 1992.
81. For the original version of Psalm 2, finished on December 15, 1843, see the new edition of Op. 78 by David Brodbeck (Stuttgart, 1998), 36–58.
82. Kraków, *MN* 38/2, 235–36.
83. Fanny to Rebecka, December 26, 1843, *MF* II, 244.
84. *AmZ* 46 (1844), 79; see also *Allgemeine Wiener Musikzeitung* 4 (1844), No. 1, 4.
85. Felix to David, December 19, 1843, *LA*, 189.
86. Fanny to Rebecka, January 9, 1844, *MF* II, 249.
87. Felix to Paul, February 8, 1844, NYPL No. 655; Fanny to Rebecka, December 26, 1843, *MF* II, 243. The whole issue is carefully reviewed in Dinglinger: 1982, 99–111.
88. Krummacher: 1992, 100ff.
89. Wilfrid Mellers, *Romanticism and the Twentieth Century*, London, 1957, 31.
90. Kraków, *MN* 39, 43–45.
91. Werner: 1963, 415–16, and Werner: 1984, 54–57.
92. MDM GB XVIII, 185; XIX 15, 48, 192, and 223.
93. Kraków, *MN* 39, 43–45.
94. Felix to von Redern, Scheumann: 1908/09, 261.
95. Felix to Droysen, January 19, 1844, Wehner, 86.
96. Richard Wagner, *On Conducting*, 22. When, in 1855, Wagner directed the London Philharmonic, he encountered the Mendelssohnian "style" of performance: "The music gushed forth

like water from a fountain; there was no arresting it, and every Allegro ended as an undeniable Presto." Some corroborating evidence may be found in the memoirs of Robert Schumann, who described the tempo Felix took in the first movement of Beethoven's Ninth as inconceivably fast (*unbegreiflich rasch*; Schumann: 1980, 108). Nevertheless, as Clive Brown has argued, the issue probably had to do with Wagner's growing preference for flexible tempi vs. Felix's tendency to keep strict time. Brown: 1999, 391–94.

97. Wagner to Minna Wagner and Felix, January 8 and 10, 1844, in Spencer and Millington, 116–17.
98. Richard Wagner, *My Life*, trans. A. Gray, Cambridge, 1983, 265.
99. Schumann, *Tagebücher*, II, 316.
100. Felix to Breitkopf & Härtel, January 18, 1844, *BadV*, 138.
101. Felix to Buxton, January 27, 1844, in Selden-Goth, 331, and Schumann, *Tagebücher*, II, 316.
102. A presentation autograph of Nos. 3 and 2 is in the Rudolf Kallir collection in New York.
103. See Todd: 2002.
104. SBB N. Mus. Ms. 241; a facs. of the title page is in Klein: 1997, 220.
105. Lewald, *Meine Lebensgeschichte*, Berlin, 1861, 147; 1989: III, 106.
106. *MF* II, 261.
107. Hiller, *Letters*, 216. See also F. Hensel, 234–35 (entry of April 16, 1844).
108. *AmZ* 46 (1844), 310.
109. Fanny to Rebecka, March 18, 1844, *MF* II, 260.
110. Felix to Rebecka, May 18, 1844, ibid., II, 278.
111. Felix to Paul, May 21, 1844, NYPL No. 661.
112. Bunsen to Felix, April 28, 1844, P. Mendelssohn Bartholdy: 1868, 319.
113. Cited in *MT* 1 (1844), 2 (June 1, 1844).
114. See *The Musical Examiner*, August 10, 1844, 721–22, 725–27, rep. in Nichols, 146–53.
115. Felix to the Secretary of the Philharmonic Society, W. Watts, April 23, 1839, cited in "Schubert's Music in England," *MT* 38 (1897), 83.
116. Ibid., 82.
117. Moser, *Joachim*, I, 62.
118. Felix did attend at least one evening party of Babbage, who gave him a pamphlet with an "account of his calculating machine" for Felix to deliver to Gustav Dirichlet (Felix to Rebecka, July 22, 1844, *MF* II, 293).
119. Rockstro, 96–97. According to a review in *The Spectator* 17 (1844), 618–19 (rep. in Brown: 2003, 219), the cadenza to the first movement combined Bach and Beethoven, while the second, "in which the phrases to be worked were not obvious, fixed attention by its extraordinary ingenuity and science."
120. Felix to Paul, June 11, 1844, NYPL No. 664.
121. Felix to Paul, P. Mendelssohn Bartholdy: *Letters*, 1868, 329.
122. Ella, *Musical Sketches Abroad and at Home*, London, 1878, 251–52.
123. Horlsey, "Reminiscences of Mendelssohn by His English Pupil," in *MahW*, 243–44.
124. F. G. Edwards: 1895, 18–19. See also the review in *The Spectator* 17 (1844), 547, rep. in Brown: 2003, 227–28.
125. Moser, I, 115.
126. Ibid., I, 66 (June 14, 1844).
127. MDM GB XIX, 321; Henry Davison, 56–57.
128. J. R. Sterndale Bennett, 162.
129. MDM g. 9, fol. 14.
130. Grove, *Dictionary of Music*, rep. of 3rd ed., London, 1927, III: 418.
131. Ed. by Robin Langley (London, 1982).
132. Mrs. Grote to Felix, June 22, 1844, MDM GB XIX, 317.
133. On their relationship see Alexander: 1975, 95ff.
134. David B. Levy: 1985.
135. Flowers to Felix, May 11, 1844, and Felix to Flowers, May 16, 1844, MDM GB XIX, 252 and 256.
136. Boyman to Felix, June 17, 1844, ibid., 311.
137. Graves to Felix, June 8, 1844, and Felix to Graves, June 27, 1844, MDM GB XIX, 292 and 325; Felix to Paul, July 19, 1844, P. Mendelssohn Bartholdy: *Letters*, 1868, 330.
138. Macfarren to Felix, April 5, 1844, MDM GB XIX, 211.
139. Felix to Moscheles, March 7, 1845, F. Moscheles: 1888, 252. The letters to the Handel Society are in *GM*, 169–85.
140. *Israel in Egypt, an Oratorio, Composed in the Year 1738; by George Frederic Handel*, London, 1845–1846, Preface, vi. Despite Felix's insistence on the indispensability of the organ part, he laid out the chord progressions in the recitatives to accommodate an alternative performance

in four-part harmony by two cellos, a practice he had observed in his performance of the St. Matthew Passion in Leipzig in 1841.

141. H. C. Wolff: 1959, 182.
142. Chrysander: 1867, 249–67.
143. SBB *MN* 18, 5; see Jost: 1988, 127ff.
144. Kraków, BJ *MN* 39, 6; see Todd: 1992b, 362ff.
145. By July 1844 the *Herbstlied* had replaced the duet *Sonntagsmorgen* (Uhland), which eventually appeared as the posthumous Op. 77 No. 1. See Felix's letter to Kistner, July 18, 1844, in *BadV*, 328.
146. Fanny to Felix, September 7, 1838, Citron: 1987, 261.
147. Felix to Klingemann, July 17, 1844, Klingemann, 295.
148. Felix to Paul, July 21, 1844, NYPL No. 667.
149. Felix to Breitkopf & Härtel, December 17, 1844, *BadV*, 147.
150. See Großmann-Vendrey: 1969, 195, 205–06, and Crum: 1983, 32–33.
151. Felix to Coventry, August 29, 1844, MDM d. 55.
152. On the publication history, see Elvers: 1960, 147–49.
153. All available in Wm. A. Little's edition of the *Complete Organ Works*, London, 1987, II, 2–26.
154. Felix to David, September 2, 1844, *LA* 198; Fanny to Felix, June 22, 1846, Fanny and Felix Mendelssohn, 389.
155. A facs. of the autograph, and of Felix's dedicatory letter to the king, of August 15, 1844, has been published with a postscript by Thomas Schmidt-Beste (Stuttgart, 1997).
156. Mendelssohn, *Complete Organ Works*, II, 27–50.
157. Charles Coventry to Felix, September 19, 1844, MDM GB XX, 90.
158. Felix to David, July 30, 1838, and July 24, 1839, *LA*, 143 and 149.
159. Felix to Breitkopf & Härtel, March 5, 1844, *BadV*, 140.
160. MDM b. 5, fols. 88–100; see Todd: 1982, 80–101.
161. See Worbs: 1959; Gerlach: 1971 and 1974; and Todd: 1979, 384–93.
162. Kraków, BJ *MN*, no number; for a facs., see L. A. Bianchi and F. Sciannameo, eds., *Mendelssohn's Concerto for Violin and Orchestra in E minor, Op. 64*, N. Y., 1991.
163. Kraków, *MN* 39, 99–232; see Greive.
164. Donald Francis Tovey, *Essays in Musical Analysis*, London, 1981, II, 157.
165. MDM d. 11, f. 13.
166. MDM f. 7.
167. Fanny to Cécile, November 19, 1844, *MF* II, 301; Felix to E. Devrient, October 25, 1844, E. Devrient, *Recollections*, 255; Felix to Klingemann, November 5, 1844, Klingemann, 299.
168. SBB, Musikabteilung, 55 MS 42, November 14, 1844; see Klein: 2001b. Felix completed four, three of which reappear as movements in the Organ Sonatas Op. 65.
169. Now lost. A copy possibly made by Ferdinand Schimm in 1844 and a later copy made by Hensel in 1847 survive in the Musik Bibliothek, Leipzig, and Stadtgeschichtliches Museum, Düsseldorf. See Lowenthal-Hensel: 1997, 19–20 and Illustration 3. Of the portrait, Sir George Grove commented, "This, though clever as a picture, can hardly convey the man. The hand is perhaps the most remarkable thing in it, and must be a portrait." Grove: 1890, II, 295.
170. Holland and Rockstro, 119–20.
171. Felix to Griepenkerl, November 18, 1844, *GM*, 197.
172. Ward Jones: 1985; see also Elvers and Ward Jones, 85.
173. The two were published in 1849 as Op. 75 Nos. 1 and 4.
174. For a facsimile of the Ms., dated October 18, 1844, see Fanny Hensel, *"Traum,"* ed. H.-G. Klein, Wiesbaden, 1997.

Chapter 15

1. Jenny Lind to H. M. Munthe, January 12, 1846, Holland and Rockstro, 177.
2. E. Devrient, *Recollections*, 256.
3. C. G. Carus, *Lebenserinnerungen und Denkwürdigkeiten*, Leipzig, 1866, 192–93.
4. Von Minckwitz to Felix, February 1, 1845, GB XXI, 51.
5. Felix to Paul, December 18, 1844, NYPL No. 672.
6. MDM b. 2.
7. Felix to Rebecka and Fanny, January 29, 1844, *MF* II, 312.
8. U. C. Hill to Felix, November 22, 1844, MDM GB XX, No. 288.

9. Felix to U. C. Hill, January 30, 1845, in Wulfhorst, 9; Felix to Paul, January 1, 1845, NYPL No. 675.
10. Kraków, BJ, *MN* 40, 15–16.
11. See Edwards: 1906, 95–100.
12. The complete list is reproduced in "Church and Organ Music," *MT* 47 (1906), 106–07.
13. Felix to Coventry, May 1, 1845, MDM c. 18.
14. Felix to Breitkopf & Härtel, April 10, 1845, *BadV*, 156–59.
15. Ed. by Wm. A. Little, Leipzig, 1977.
16. First identified in Hathaway, 38.
17. Robert C. Mann, 645.
18. See further Großmann-Vendrey: 1974, 191.
19. Kraków, BJ *MN* 40, 49; Berlin, SBB, N. Mus. Ms. 1 (December 18, 1846); for an edition, see Rudolf Elvers's edition of the *Lieder ohne Worte*, Munich, 1981, 150–51.
20. Schlemmer's copy is in MDM c. 47; Klingemann's, in SBB, N Mus. Ms. 38. See also Felix's letters of December 19, 1844, to Lessing, LC (Music 1055), and December 29, 1844, to Hübner, in Feder and Hübner, 189–90.
21. Felix to Klingemann, April 21, 1845, in Klingemann, 308.
22. Kraków, BJ, *MN* 40.
23. Felix to Simrock, May 21, 1845, *BadV*, 244.
24. Felix to Paul, June 10, 1845, NYPL No. 682; see also Felix to Paul, February 12, 1845, NYPL No. 679, and Felix to Simrock, February 12, 1845, in *BadV*, 243–44.
25. Edward Sartoris to Felix, January 28, 1845, MDM, GB XXI, 41.
26. Felix to A. F. Anacker, August 15, 1844, in *Musik und Gesellschaft* 22 (1972), 658.
27. Rev. John Webb to Felix, April 10, 1845, MDM, GB XXI, 131; Felix to Joseph Moore, July 24, 1845, in Edwards: 1896, 31.
28. Eichhorn to Felix, March 2, 1845, Felix to Eichhorn, March 6, 1845, Müller to Felix, March 5, 1845, and Felix to Müller, March 12, 1845, in P. Mendelssohn Bartholdy: *Letters*, 1868, 340–47.
29. MDM b. 5, fols. 102–114; see Todd: 1980.
30. Felix to Ferdinand Schubert, March 22, 1845, "Briefe Felix Mendelssohn-Bartholdy's an Herrn Professor Ferdinand Schubert in Wien," *Wiener allgemeine Musik-Zeitung* 8/4 (1848), 13–14.
31. MDM GB XXI and XXII.
32. Magis to Felix, April 22, 1845, GB XXI, No. 153.
33. Wagner to Felix, April 17 and May 15, 1845, in Wagner: 1970, II, 425–28.
34. Rockstro, 100.
35. Taylor: 1848, I, 108.
36. For an English edition of W. A. Lampadius's German biography, *Felix Mendelssohn-Bartholdy: Ein Denkmal für seine Freunde* (Leipzig, 1848), published in 1865. Cited here are passages from the 1877 ed., 212–13.
37. Grove: 1890, 294.
38. Felix to Paul, April 10, 1845, *MLL*, 270; and Felix to Rebecka, April 11, 1845, *MF* II, 320.
39. SBB N. Mus. Ms. 537; a facs. of the first page is in Klein: 1997, 225.
40. Felix to Fanny, April 20, 1845, *MF* II, 321.
41. I. Moscheles, 329.
42. Krummacher: 1984, 76–80.
43. See the critical ed. of Wm. A. Little, Stuttgart, 1998.
44. Felix to Paul, July 2, 1845, NYPL; Felix to Klingemann, September 29, 1845, Klingemann, 311.
45. Von Falkenstein to Felix, June 30, 1845, GB XXI, 240. The negotiations are examined in detail in Häfner, 251ff.; and Weiss, 77–88.
46. E. Devrient to Felix, September 12, 1845, in E. Devrient, *Recollections*, 265–66.
47. See Musch, 206–11.
48. For a facs. of one, dated July 12, 1845, see E. Wolff: 1909, 169.
49. Felix to Paul, September 5, 1845, NYPL No. 688. The restored residence now houses a museum at Goldschmidtstrasse 12, opened by the Internationale Mendelssohn-Stiftung in 1997.
50. Felix to Klingemann, September 29, 1845, Klingemann, 311; the date is sometimes given as September 15, which, according to Felix's diary (MDM g. 7), would have been the very day he returned from Berlin to Leipzig.
51. Rockstro, 103.
52. *AmZ* 47 (1845), 732.
53. MDM c. 49, fols. 33–56, and c. 33, fols. 83–84 (for a facs. of the latter, see Jacobi: 1915, 26).
54. Edwards: 1896, 35.
55. Grove: 1890, II, 294. In a list of Felix's Berlin engagements (GB XXII, 308), several entries for Magnus appear on November 5, 6, 11, 15, 16, 19, 20, 25, and December 2; presumably the

sittings for the portrait occurred on these dates. According to Grove, Jenny Lind commissioned the portrait. A copy of the original version, a half-length with crossed arms, is in SBB (*MA* BA 191). Other copies showing the composer's hands survive, including one, formerly belonging to his daughter Marie that is now in the Bodleian Library. See also Gläser, 135.

56. Kraków, *BJ* 40, 73 (October 30, 1845). A second version, from January 1846, has been reproduced in facs. See Köhler: 1959.
57. Felix to his parents, August 23, 1831, P. Mendelssohn Bartholdy: *Letters*, 1865, 261ff.
58. *AmZ* 48 (1846), 178–79.
59. Minna to Giacomo Meyerbeer, November 11, 1845, in Meyerbeer, III, 638–39.
60. Though he did inscribe a copy of the score requested by Prince Albert. See Felix to Bartholomew, March 21, 1846, in Polko: 1987, 300–301.
61. V: 8, as translated by C. H. Sisson, Oxford, 1987, 209.
62. Wilhelm Dilthey, *Das Erlebnis und die Dichtung: Lessing, Goethe, Novalis, Hölderlin*, Berlin, 1957, 103.
63. *MF* I, 94.
64. See the "Vorwort" to the ed. by H. Gottwaldt, in *Das Erbe deutscher Musik*, Mainz, 1977, vol. 71, 7–8.
65. British Library, King's Music Library R. M. 21. g. 5.
66. Lampadius, 392.
67. Kraków, *MN* 39, 23–25 ("Qu'on adore ce Dieu").
68. *Berlinische Zeitung*, December 2, 1845, quoted in Holland and Rockstro, 171.
69. MDM GB XXII, 308.
70. According to Clive Brown, papers deposited in the London Mendelssohn Society in 1896 by Jenny's husband, Otto Goldschmidt, but not yet made public, are rumored to corroborate the idea of an affair. Brown: 2003, 33.
71. See most recently, Wullschlager, 219–41.
72. H. C. Andersen, *Das Märchen meines Lebens*, cited in Holland and Rockstro, 163.
73. Felix to Geibel, December 9, 1845, in Schnoor, 114.
74. Polko: 1987, 110.
75. *AmZ* 47 (1845), 895.
76. Holland and Rockstro, 180.
77. Rockstro, 116.
78. Holland and Rockstro, 183n.
79. Felix to Jenny, December 10, 1845, MDM c. 25, fols. 16–17.
80. MDM GB XXVII, No. 94, sent on December 16; see Felix to Schubring, December 16, 1845, in Schubring: 1892, 204–6, and Sposato: 2000, II, 303–16.
81. *AmZ* 47 (1845), 933. The program also included Helen Dolby singing Elvira's entrance cavatina from Act I of Verdi's *Ernani*, the first performance of Verdi in the Gewandhaus.
82. Felix to Jenny, December 23, 1845, published with a facs. in Maude, 53–58.
83. Ibid., 58.
84. Felix to Bernus, October 10, 1845, P. Mendelssohn Bartholdy: *Letters*, 1868, 355.
85. Rockstro, 118.
86. Grove: 1890, II, 299.
87. *NZfM* 24 (1846), 32.
88. Felix to Clara Schumann, January 4, 1846, in N. Reich: 1994, 222.
89. E. Devrient, *Recollections*, 273.
90. *AmZ* 48 (1846), 122.
91. Grove: 1890, II, 299.
92. Letters of October 22 and late November 1845 from Robert to Felix, in Jansen: 1904, 252 and 254, cited in Daverio: 1997, 333.
93. *AmZ* 48 (1846), 123; see also Franz Brendel's review in *NZfM* 24 (1846), 72.
94. "Das musikalische Leipzig in seinem Verhalten zu Richard Wagner," in Hans von Bülow, *Ausgewählte Schriften 1850–1892*, Leipzig, 1896, 21.
95. K. Olsen and H. Topsøe-Jensen, III, 61–63.
96. Wullschlager, 281.
97. F. Hensel, 263. MDM g. 7; letter of February 14, 1846, from Felix to Paul, NYPL No. 699; and Hensel: 1911, 50–51.
98. Von Minckwitz to Felix, March 19, 1846, MDM GB XXIII, No. 163.
99. Schumann: 1980, 104; Schumann, *Tagebücher*, II, 399.
100. Newman, I, 438.
101. See Felix's letter to Hofrat Keil, February 22, 1846, in *LA*, 84–87.

102. Rockstro, 107.
103. Wasielewski: 1894, 333.
104. Rockstro, 109.
105. Felix to Jenny Lind, March 18, 1846, Holland and Rockstro, 192–95.
106. *AmZ* 48 (1846), 277.
107. Felix to Jenny, May 7, 1846, Holland and Rockstro, 210.
108. Felix to E. Devrient, May 9, 1846, in E. Devrient, *Recollections*, 281.
109. Several of the letters appear in W. Reich: 1959, 366–70.
110. Holland and Rockstro, 212.
111. Felix to Devrient, May 9, 1846, E. Devrient, *Recollections*, 277–82.
112. Felix to H.-G.-M.J.-P. Magis, February 23, 1846, in van der Linden, 51. The autograph score (Kraków, BJ *MN* 41, 1–72) is dated at the end February 6, 1846.
113. Kraków, BJ *MN* 41, 73–92.
114. Stanford University Memorial Music Library, Ms. No. 721, dated April 4, 1846.
115. E. Devrient, *Recollections*, 274.
116. Felix to Edward Buxton, March 21, 1846, LC (Music 1055); Robert Schumann, *Tagebücher*, II, 399.
117. Felix to Jenny Lind, May 15, 1846, Holland and Rockstro, 212.
118. Felix to Moscheles, May 23, 1846, F. Moscheles: 1888, 273–74.
119. Bartholomew to Felix, June 23, 1846, in Edwards: 1896, 51.
120. Ibid., 50.
121. Felix to Bartholomew, July 3, 1846, ibid., 53.
122. Naumann, 37–38.
123. Felix to Fanny, June 27, 1846, *MF* II, 331.
124. Esser, 63.
125. Holland and Rockstro, 221.
126. Felix to the *Comité* of the Aachen Musical Festival, April 3, 1846, in Großmann-Vendrey: 1969, 116.
127. The controversy resurfaced in 1977, when the German scholar Peter Gülke published a new edition of Beethoven's symphony that reinstated the repeats of the scherzo and trio. For a full review of the issue, see the Critical Commentary to Jonathan Del Mar's edition of the Fifth Symphony (Kassel, 1999), 55ff.
128. *AmZ* 48 (1846), 461, July 1, 1846 (letter of August 21, 1810).
129. Schindler, 483–86.
130. Onslow's review was carried as well by the *AmZ* (48 [1846], 405ff.).
131. Felix to Hauser, June 8, 1846, Holland and Rockstro, 223.
132. Felix to Fanny, June 27, 1846, *MF* II, 331.
133. Chorley: 1854, II, 323–24.
134. Ibid., II, 326.
135. F. R. Hullah, *Life of John Hullah, L.L.D.*, London, 1886, 44.
136. Chorley: 1854, II, 327.
137. An accretion to the liturgy of the Mass, sung immediately after the Alleluia.
138. Schumann: 1980, 102.
139. Van der Linden: 1954, 53–64. The fugue is included in my edition of the work (Stuttgart, 1996).
140. Felix to Magis, March 13, 1846, in Van der Linden: 1954, 52.
141. Chorley, *Modern German Music*, II, 328.
142. Ibid., II, 331; see also the brief account in Lampadius, 302.
143. *BadV*, 134 (letter of November 20, 1843).
144. Chorley, *Modern German Music*, II, 347–48. Work on the cathedral, having ceased in the sixteenth century, had finally begun again in 1842, and continued until its completion in 1880.
145. Schöne, II, 34.
146. *AmZ* 48 (1846), 457.
147. Moser, 70.
148. See Brown: 1984, 294–95.
149. Spohr: 1861, II, 306–7.
150. *AmZ* 48 (1846), 503.
151. Schubring to Felix, June 15, 1846, Edwards: 1896, 26.
152. Felix to Schubring, May 23, 1846, and Schubring to Felix, June 15, 1846, Edwards: 1896, 24–26.
153. Felix to Jenny Lind, July 23, 1846, Holland and Rockstro, 227.
154. Kraków, BJ *MN* Band 51, dated at the end.

155. Felix to Bartholomew, July 3, 1846, Edwards: 1896, 62.
156. Bartholomew to Felix, July 20, 1846, ibid., 68.
157. It was published in a piano reduction in Bennett: 1883, 182–83.
158. Felix to Bartholomew, August 9, 1846, Edwards: 1896, 72–73.
159. Keudell authored a volume of memoirs of the German chancellor (*Fürst und Fürstin Bismarck*, Berlin, 1901).
160. *MF* II, 325 (translation slightly modified).
161. Fanny to Felix, July 9, 1846, Citron: 1987, 349–51.
162. Felix to Fanny, August 12, 1846, *MF* II, 326 (trans. slightly revised).
163. Diary entry of August 14, 1846, ibid. F. Hensel, 266.

Chapter 16

1. *The Musical World* (August 1846).
2. Edwards: 1896, 76.
3. Henry Phillips, II, 237ff. According to Phillips, Felix gave him the manuscript on September 22, which must be an error for August 22; by September 22, Felix had returned to Leipzig. See also Todd: 1984, 153–60. Felix's autograph is lost; the work has survived in a few manuscript copies.
4. Foster, 199.
5. *The Musical World* (Saturday, August 22, 1846).
6. The *Times* (Monday, August 24, 1846), 9.
7. Quoted in Edwards: 1896, 81.
8. The *Times* (Wednesday, August 26, 1846), 8.
9. Ibid. (Thursday, August 27, 1846), 6.
10. Felix to Moscheles, June 26, 1846, in F. Moscheles: 1888, 274–75.
11. Edwards: 1896, 84; The *Times* (August 27, 1846), 6.
12. Several are in Edwards: 1896, 85–92.
13. The *Times* (August 27, 1846), 6.
14. Felix to Paul, August 26 [*recte* 27], 1846, in P. Mendelssohn Bartholdy: *Letters*, 1868, 363.
15. For the original duet version, see the edition by Jack Werner, Oxford, 1958, and idem: 1965, 81.
16. The *Times* (August 28, 1846), 6.
17. Ibid. (August 29, 1846), 5.
18. Ibid. For the recitative, see Edwards: 1896, 94–95.
19. I. Moscheles, 326.
20. *The Musical World* (September 1846), quoted in J. Werner: 1965, 18.
21. Appia to Felix, May 26, 1846, MDM GB XXIII, 295.
22. Kraków, BJ *MN* 41, 112–13, where it appears beneath the *Spruch* for Ascension Day, Op. 79 No. 3, dated October 9, 1846.
23. Ed. with critical commentary by Barbara Mohn in Felix Mendelssohn Bartholdy, *Neun Psalmen und Cantique*, Stuttgart, 1997.
24. Redern to Felix, May 5, 1846, MDM GB XXIII, 252.
25. Felix to Bote & Bock, October 17, 1846, *BadV*, 342.
26. See the ed. by Günter Graulich, Stuttgart, 1982.
27. Felix to von Redern, November 6, 1846, in Scheumann: 1908/09, 264.
28. By Bote & Bock in the series *Musica sacra*, Berlin, 1853–1855, V and VII.
29. See the ed. with thorough commentary by Judith Silber Ballan (Stuttgart, 1998).
30. I. Moscheles, 327.
31. Dörffel, 114–15.
32. *Leipziger Tageblatt und Anzeiger* 39 (1846), 3541, 3552 (November 7, 1846) and 3560 (November 8). I am grateful to Ralf Wehner for identifying the passage. See also E. Werner: 1963, 479–80.
33. Litzmann, II, 80–81n; Felix to Klingemann, December 6, 1846, Klingemann, 316.
34. Schumann: 1980, 104.
35. Felix to Klingemann, December 6, 1846, ibid., 316. Felix's score is in MDM c. 66–67.
36. E. Devrient, *Recollections*, 287.
37. Ibid.
38. Copied by Felix in his letter to Paul of November 27, 1846 (NYPL No. 712).
39. Felix to Klingemann, December 6, 1846, Klingemann, 316.
40. F. Hensel, 270 (entry of December 30, 1846).

41. By Christmas 1846 Fanny had already received advance copies (F. Hensel, 272).
42. On the publication dates, see H.-G. Klein: 1997, 220.
43. Fanny to Felix, February 1, 1847, Citron: 1987, 363.
44. I. Moscheles, 332.
45. Fanny to Felix, after August 26, 1846, Citron: 1987, 353.
46. MDM c. 21, fols. 133v–4v.
47. See G. A. Müller, 45–46.
48. *AmZ* 49 (1847), 382.
49. See Todd: 2002, 248ff.
50. Fanny to Felix, ca. August 1846, Citron, 353. On the *Gartenlieder*, see the two useful studies of W. Gundlach and S. M. H. Wallace.
51. *NZfM* 26 (1847), 169.
52. P.-A. Koch, 9.
53. On the publication history, see Wallace, 94ff.
54. Franck to Felix, July 26, 1845 and June 2, 1846, MDM GB XXIII, 368 and 301; Felix to Franck, December 22, 1846, Tiersot, *Lettres*, 339; see also van der Elst, 82–84.
55. Buxton to Felix, November 10, 1846, MDM GB XXIV, 130: "I know there are several [music sellers] . . . who have expressed their determination to print the songs if they could get hold of them."
56. T. Brewer, Secretary of the Sacred Harmonic Society, to Felix, September 24, 1846, MDM GB XXIV, 50, and Felix to Brewer, October 7, 1846, Edwards: 1896, 101–2.
57. Felix to Buxton, December 30, 1846, MDM c. 42, fol. 81; on the principal changes, see Edwards: 1896, 99–100; and Joseph Bennett: 1882–1883.
58. I. Moscheles, 329.
59. Felix to Paul, February 14, 1847, NYPL No. 722.
60. Felix to Buxton, February 17, 1847, LC (Music 1055).
61. MDM c. 37. The score was published in London in 1880; a modern edition is available (Stuttgart, 1986).
62. LC, Moldenhauer Archives. See Todd: 2000, 313–20.
63. See Edwards: 1896, 100.
64. Felix to Bartholomew, March 10, and Bartholomew to Felix, March 19, 1847, ibid., 120–22.
65. Felix to Buxton, March 18, 1847, LC (Music 1055); a facs. of the metronome markings is in Edwards: 1896, 125–26.
66. Felix to Carl Grenser, flutist and "Inspector" of the Conservatory, January 10, 1847, in Evans, Todd, and Olson, 137–38.
67. F. Moscheles: 1888, 284.
68. See Häfner, 262–64; E. Devrient, *Recollections*, 290.
69. Felix to Robert Naumann, February 12, 1847, in *LA*, 232; and Kraków, *MN* 42.
70. *NZfM* 26 (1847), 147–48; *AmZ* 49 (1847), 195–96. See also Großmann-Vendrey: 1969, 169.
71. Lampadius: 1877, 155–56.
72. Felix to Lind, October 31, 1846, Holland and Rockstro, 242.
73. Felix to Dirichlet, January 4, 1847, P. Mendelssohn Bartholdy: 1863, 277.
74. Felix to Droysen, April 5, 1847, Wehmer, 104–5.
75. Felix to Klingemann, January 31, 1847; Klingemann, 319. The drawings are now preserved at Yale University, Beinecke Rare Book Library, New Haven, Conn.
76. F. Moscheles: 1888, 286.
77. See ibid., 284–85; I. Moscheles, 333; and F. Moscheles: 1899, 103–5.
78. Felix to Jenny Lind, October 12, 1846, Holland and Rockstro, 233.
79. Lumley, 163.
80. Felix to Paul, February 4, 1847, NYPL No. 718.
81. Chorley, *Modern German Music* II, 389.
82. Lumley, 168.
83. Felix to Geibel, January 30, 1847, in Schnoor, 118.
84. Felix to Klingemann, Lumley, and Gruneison, February 18, 1847, March 10, and March 10, 1847, in Klingemann, 321, 326–27.
85. Schnoor, 120–28; Todd: 1997, 124.
86. Felix to Lattner, March 11, 1847, in *MLL*, 277.
87. Kraków, BJ *MN* 44, 1–10.
88. Buxton to Felix, January 8, 1847, GB XXV, 20; see also Brodbeck: 1994, 198ff.
89. Frederick William IV to his brother Carl, March 19, 1847, cited in Barclay, 126n.

90. *MF* II, 334.
91. Somewhat complicating the issue of borrowing is the existence of a short piano piece by Fanny, based on the theme of her Lied, that appeared posthumously as the second of the *Zwei Bagatellen für die Schüler des Schindelmeisser'schen Musik-Instituts*, Berlin, 1848. No dated autograph survives, leaving open the possibility that the Bagatelle was composed first, then recalled by Felix in the aria from *Elijah*, and finally reused by Fanny in her Piano Trio. On the *Zwei Bagatellen*, see Hellwig-Unruh: 2000, 275–76.
92. Clara Schumann to E. Pacher von Theinberg, June 15, 1847, in Wendler, 148.
93. Rockstro, 126.
94. H. Phillips, II, 243.
95. The *Times*, April 19, 1847, 6, and April 24, 1847, 5. Ironically enough, George Perry had composed his own oratorio on Elijah in 1819.
96. While in Manchester, Felix played the organ at St. Luke's Church, Cheetham Hill, before a large audience. "Mendelssohn in Manchester, 1847," W. T. Freemantle Papers, LC. I am grateful to Peter Ward Jones for this reference.
97. Journal of Edgar Alfred Bowring, April 23, 1847, William R. Perkins Library, Duke University, Durham, N.C.
98. April 24, 1847; trans. in Edwards: 1896, 127. The original, bound in blue silk with gold lettering, is in MDM d. 23.
99. Mary Ann Evans to Mary Sibree, May 10, 1847, in Haight, 42.
100. The *Times*, April 28, 1847, 6.
101. Beatty-Kingston, 35–36. The author reports that he had already heard the composer conduct at a Philharmonic concert, which presumably would have been Felix's last appearance there, on April 26, 1847.
102. A. J. C. Hare, *The Life and Letters of Frances Baroness Bunsen*, N.Y., 1880, II, 98; Alexander: 1972, 86.
103. Entry of May 1, 1847, cited in Marek, 306.
104. I. Moscheles, 340.
105. Morton Latham, *Alfredo Piatti: A Sketch*, London, 1901, 47, 76.
106. E. S. J. Van der Straeten, *History of the Violoncello*, London, 1914, 583.
107. The *Times*, May 5, 1847, 5.
108. Anna Joanna Alexander to Felix, May 6, 1847, GB XXV, 264.
109. The *Times*, May 6, 1847, 5.
110. Royal Library, Windsor. Notwithstanding the account of Jules Benedict (Benedict, 55–56), accepted by Groves and others, Felix did not visit Queen Victoria and Prince Albert at Buckingham Palace on May 8 (communication from Peter Ward Jones).
111. Benedict, 55–56.
112. *The Athenaeum*, after April 16, 1847, cited in J. Werner: 1965, 28; Shaw, 68.
113. Felix to Bartholomew, December 30, 1846, in Edwards: 1896, 106.
114. See Jahn: 1848.
115. On the use of recurring motives, see Smither, IV, 181–82.
116. Friedhelm Krummacher has shown, too, how the fugal subject contains traces of the fugue from the Overture, thus linking the endpoints of the oratorio. See Krummacher: 2001, 333–34.
117. "The Mendelssohnian Cadence," *MT* (1956), 17–19; rep. in *Mendelssohn's 'Elijah'*, 84–92.
118. Hiller, 171; Werner: 1963, 471. The Hebrew melody is cited in Werner: 1980, 498.
119. Sposato: 2000, 355.
120. Werner: 1963, 459–60.
121. Jahn: 1848, in *MahW*, 366.
122. Sposato: 2000, ch. V, upon which the following discussion draws.
123. Ibid., 357.
124. Schubring to Felix, June 15, 1846, Schubring: 1892, 222–23.
125. Felix to Bartholomew, December 30, 1846, Edwards: 1896, 106.
126. See Jack Werner: 1965, 54–56.
127. Staehelin, in *MahW*, 121–36.
128. Krummacher, *Elias der Thisbiter*, Elberfeld, 1828–1833, cited in Staehelin, 129.
129. Jahn: 1848, in *MahW*, 366.
130. See the "Vorwort" to my edition of *Christus* (Stuttgart, 1994), and Sposato: 2000, ch. 6.
131. In a different interpretation communicated to the author, Peter Ward Jones has suggested that Felix's choice was determined by musical considerations or by his desire to avoid replicating Bach's text.

132. Botstein: 1998, 213.
133. Botstein: 1999, 47.
134. Ibid., 48.
135. See Rabien: 1990b, 304–9.
136. The accounts drawn from Felix to Klingemann, June 3, 1847, Klingemann, 329; and Hinni Mendelssohn to Benjamin and Rosamunde Mendelssohn, May 21, 1847, Gilbert: 1975, 143–45.
137. *MF* II, 335.
138. Meyerbeer, IV, 243.
139. *Vossische Zeitung*, May 18, 1847, facs. in Helmig and Maurer, "Briefe aus den Verlobungszeit," 162–63.
140. Felix to Wilhelm Hensel, May 19, 1847, *MF* II, 337 (SBB *MA* Ep. 187).
141. Kraków, BJ, *MN* 44.
142. SBB; for facs., see F. Mendelssohn, *Aquarellenalbum*, ed. M. F. Schneider and C. Hensel, Basel, 1968.
143. Felix to Rebecka, July 7, 1847, P. Mendelssohn Bartholdy: 1868, 385.
144. *MF* II, 338.
145. Felix to Fanny Horsley, July 9, 1847, Oxford Ms. Horsley, c. 1, fols. 43–44.
146. MDM g. 10, fol. 52.
147. Felix to Buxton, July 7, 1847, LC (Music 1055).
148. Washington, D.C., LC, Moldenhauer Archives.
149. See Brodbeck: 1994, 200ff.
150. Felix to Rebecka, July 24, 1847, NYPL No. 731.
151. Felix to Helmina von Chézy, July 11, 1847, in Waidelich, 173.
152. Felix to Ignaz Seydlitz, September 19, 1847 (LC, Music 1055), in which Felix ponders writing a psalm, Mass, or *Te Deum*.
153. Liverpool Philharmonic Society to Felix, September 1847, MDM GB XXVI, 49.
154. Heinrich Hoffmann, 157.
155. Felix to Paul, August 24, 1847, in *MLL*, 282.
156. Chorley, *Modern German Music*, II, 383–400.
157. Felix to Geibel, August 27, 1847, LC (Music 1055).
158. Concerning these unpublished portions, see Todd: 1997.
159. Chorley, *Modern German Music* II, 389n.
160. E. Devrient, *Recollections*, 294.
161. Werner: 1963, 499.
162. Warrack: 1987, 297.
163. I.e., the dominant of a key, say B in the key of E, moving to its submediant (C♯) instead of its tonic.
164. Georg Knepler, *Musikgeschichte des 19. Jahrhunderts*, Berlin, 1961, II, 770.
165. Krummacher: 1984, 80–84. See also Klein: 1982, for an examination of the changes in the autograph score.
166. Felix to Sebastian Hensel, February 22, 1847, *MLL*, 381.
167. Rollett, 36.
168. Felix to Geibel, September 30, 1847, LC (Music 1055); *MF* II, 338.
169. Rockstro, 130.
170. Dörffel, 116, 254.
171. I. Moscheles, 338–44.
172. Moscheles to Josef Fischhof, November 7, 1847, in Rychnovsky, 143.
173. MDM b. 5, fol. 40.
174. I. Moscheles, 341.
175. Ward Jones: 2001, 212–13.
176. Felix to Frederick William IV, October 17, 1847, *MLL*, 284.
177. Rebecka to Felix, October 21, [1847], in Elvers: 1989; Felix to Paul, October 22, 1847, NYPL No. 739.
178. *New-York Tribune*, December 13, 1847.
179. I. Moscheles, 341–44; Rychnovsky; R. Sterndale Bennett; and Benedict; for two short accounts by Charlotte Moscheles, see Alexander: 1972, 102–5.
180. Ward Jones, 2001.
181. Several accounts survive: Lampadius, 314ff.; E. Devrient, *Recollections*, 294–301; Dörffel, 116–19; Gade, 107–9; Rychnowsky; I. Moscheles, 338ff.; Rockstro, 132ff; Reissmann, 298ff., and Brockhaus I, 145–48.

182. *AmZ* 49 (1847), 791.
183. MDM b. 1; a second version was published in Jacob, facing 257.
184. Three copies survive at the Leipzig Hochschule für Musik und Theater; Oxford, Bodleian, Cons. Res. Objects 1; and *MA* BA 21.
185. E. Devrient, *Recollections*, 297.
186. Ibid., 299.
187. Issued between 1855 and 1859, and translated into English in 1882. See the Introduction to Otto Jahn, *Life of Mozart*, trans. Pauline D. Townsend, London, 1882, i.
188. *MT* (May 1, 1848).
189. E. Devrient, *Recollections*, 301.

Bibliography

Abraham, Gerald. "The Scores of Mendelssohn's 'Hebrides.'" *MMR* 78 (1948): 172–76.

Agoult, Marie d'. *Correspondance de Liszt et de la Comtesse d'Agoult.* Edited by D. Ollivier. Paris, 1933, I.

Alexander, Boyd. "Felix Mendelssohn and the Alexanders." *MS* 1 (1972): 81–106.

———. "Felix Mendelssohn Bartholdy and Young Women." *MS* 2 (1975): 71–102.

———. "Some Unpublished Letters of Abraham Mendelssohn and Fanny Hensel." *MS* 3 (1979): 9–50.

Allgemeine musikalische Zeitung 1–50 (1798–1848).

Altmann, Alexander. "Moses Mendelssohns gesammelte Schriften: Neuerschlossene Briefe zur Geschichte ihrer Herausgabe." *BLB* 11/42 (1968): 73–115.

———. *Moses Mendelssohn: A Biographical Study.* University of Alabama, 1973.

———. "Moses Mendelssohn's Proofs for the Existence of God." *MS* 2 (1975): 9–29.

Andraschke, Peter. "Felix Mendelssohns *Antigone.*" In C. M. Schmidt: 1997, 141–66.

Applegate, Celia. "How German Is It? Nationalism and the Idea of Serious Music in the Early Nineteenth Century." *19CM* 21 (1998): 274–96.

Austin, Mrs.[Sarah]. "Recollections of Felix Mendelssohn." *Fraser's Magazine for Town and Country* 37 (April 1848): 426–28.

Bach, C. P. E. *Briefe und Dokumente: Kritische Gesamtausgabe Band II.* Edited by E. Suchalla. Göttingen, 1994.

Barbier, Frédéric. *Finance et politique: La dynastie des Fould, xviiie-xxe siècle.* Paris, 1991.

Barclay, David E. *Frederick William IV and the Prussian Monarchy 1840–1861.* Oxford, 1995.

Bauer, Karoline. *Posthumous Memoirs of Karoline Bauer.* London, 1884–1885.

Beatty-Kingston, William. *Men, Cities, and Events.* London, 1899.

Becker, Heinz, and Gudrun Becker. *Giacomo Meyerbeer: A Life in Letters.* Trans. M. Violette. Portland, Oregon, 1989.

Behler, Ernst. *German Romantic Literary Theory.* Cambridge, 1993.

Bellasis, E. *Cherubini: Memorials Illustrative of his Life and Work.* London, 1912, repr. 1971.

Benedict, Jules, *Sketch of the Life and Works of the Late Felix Mendelssohn Bartholdy.* London, 1850.

Benjamin, Phyllis. "A Diary-Album for Fanny Mendelssohn Bartholdy." *MS* 7 (1990): 179–217.

Bennett, Joseph. "'Elijah': A Comparison of the Original and Revised Scores." *MT* 23 (1882): 525–28, 588–91, 653–56; *MT* 24 (1883), 6–10, 67–72, 123–25, 182–85.

Bennett, J. R. Sterndale. *The Life of William Sterndale Bennett.* Cambridge, 1907.

Bennett, R. Sterndale. "The Death of Mendelssohn." *ML* 36 (1955): 374–76.

Berliner allgemeine musikalische Zeitung 1–7 (1824–1830).

Berlioz, Hector. *Correspondance générale.* Edited by Pierre Citron. Paris, 1978, III.

Bill, Oswald. "Unbekannte Mendelssohn-Handschriften in der Hessischen Landes- und Hochschulbibliothek Darmstadt." *Mf* 26 (1973): 345–49.

Binder, Franz. *Luise Hensel: Ein Lebensbild.* Freiburg im Breisgau, 1904.

Blumner, Martin. *Geschichte der Sing-Akademie zu Berlin.* Berlin, 1891.

Bode, Wilhelm, ed. *Goethes Schauspieler und Musiker: Erinnerungen von Eberwein und Lobe.* Berlin, 1912.

Boetius, Susanne. "'. . . da componirte ich aus Herzenslust drauf los . . .': Felix Mendelssohn Bartholdys kompositorische Urschrift der Schauspielmusik zur 'Antigone' des Sophokles, op. 55." *Mf* 55 (2002): 162–83.

Bollert, Werner. *Sing-Akademie zu Berlin: Festschrift zum 175jährigen Bestehen.* Berlin, 1966.

Bonds, Mark Evan. *After Beethoven: Imperatives of Originality in the Symphony.* Cambridge, Mass., 1996.

Borchard, Beatrix, and Monika Schwarz-Danuser. *Fanny Hensel geb. Mendelssohn Bartholdy: Komponieren zwischen Geselligkeitsideal und romantischer Musikästhetik.* Kassel, 1999.

Bormann, Oskar. "Johann Nepomuk Schelble 1789–1837." Ph.D. diss., Universität Frankfurt, 1926.

Botstein, Leon. "The Aesthetics of Assimilation and Affirmation: Reconstructing the Career of Felix Mendelssohn." In *MahW*, 5–42, 1991.

———. "Mendelssohn and the Jews." *MQ* 82 (1998): 210–19.

———. "Mendelssohn, Werner, and the Jews: A Final Word." *MQ* 83 (1999): 45–50.

Boyle, Nicholas. *Goethe: The Poet and the Age.* Vol. 1. Oxford, 1991.

Brockhaus, Heinrich. *Aus den Tagebüchern.* 2 vols. Leipzig, 1884.

Brodbeck, David. "Some Notes on an Anthem by Mendelssohn." In *MahW*, 43–64, 1991.

———. "A Winter of Discontent: Mendelssohn and the *Berliner Domchor*." In Todd, ed. *Mendelssohn Studies*, 1–32, 1992.

———. "*Eine kleine Kirchenmusik*: A New Canon, a Revised Cadence, and an Obscure 'Coda' by Mendelssohn." *Journal of Musicology* 12 (1994): 179–205.

Brown, Clive. *Louis Spohr: A Critical Biography.* Cambridge, 1984.

———. *Classical and Romantic Performing Practice 1750–1900.* Oxford, 1999.

———. *A Portrait of Mendelssohn.* New Haven, 2003.

Büttner, Fred. "'Zwischen Gaeta und Kapua': Grillparzers Gedicht als Liedkomposition." *Neues musikwissenschaftliches Jahrbuch* 1 (1992): 87–118.

Cadenbach, Rainer. "Vom Gang des Herankommens—Fanny und Felix wetteifern in Klavierquartetten." In Helmig, 81–92, 1997.

Cairns, David., trans. and ed. *The Memoirs of Hector Berlioz.* New York, 1969.

Chorley, Henry Fothergill. *Modern German Music.* London, 1854. Repr. 1973.

———. *Autobiography, Memoir, and Letters.* London, 1873.

Chrysander, Friedrich. "Mendelssohn's Orgelbegleitung zu Israel in Aegypten." *Jahrbücher für musikalische Wissenschaft* 2 (1867): 249–67.

———. "Mendelssohn's Wirksamkeit als Musikdirector an Immermann's Theater in Düsseldorf, 1833–1834." *Leipziger Allgemeine musikalische Zeitung* 5 (1870): 221–22, 228–30, 251–52, 258–60.

Citron, Marcia, ed. *The Letters of Fanny Hensel to Felix Mendelssohn.* Stuyvesant, N.Y., 1987.

Cohn, Warren I. "The Moses Isaac Family Trust: Its History and Significance." *LBI* 18 (1973): 267–80.

Cooper, John Michael. "Felix Mendelssohn and the Italian Symphony: Historical, Musical and Extramusical Perspectives." Ph.D. diss., Duke University, 1994.

———. "'And the Effect of the Whole Was Indescribably Beautiful': Music and *Tableaux Vivants* in Early Nineteenth Century Germany." *Literary and Musical Notes: A Festschrift for Wm. A. Little.* Ed. G. C. Orth. Bern, 1995, 9–26.

———. "Felix Mendelssohn Bartholdy, Ferdinand David und Johann Sebastian Bach: Mendelssohns Bach-Auffassung im Spiegel der Wiederentdeckung der 'Chaconne.'" *MS* 10 (1997): 157–79.

———. "Words without Songs? Of Texts, Titles, and Mendelssohn's *Lieder ohne Worte.*" In *Musik als Text: Bericht über den Internationalen Kongreß der Gesellschaft für Musikforschung.* Ed. H. Danuser and T. Plebuch. Kassel, 1998, II, 341–46.

———. "Mendelssohn's Works: Prolegomenon to a Comprehensive Inventory." In Seaton, *The Mendelssohn Companion*, 701–85, 2001.

———. *Felix Mendelssohn Bartholdy: A Guide to Research.* New York, 2001b.

———. "Of Red Roofs and Hunting Horns: Mendelssohn's Song Aesthetic, with an Unpublished Cycle (1830)." *Journal of Musicological Research* 21 (2002): 277–317.

———. *Mendelssohn's "Italian" Symphony.* Oxford, 2003.

Cooper, John Michael, and H.-G. Klein, ed. *Felix Mendelssohn Bartholdy: Sinfonie A-dur op. 90, "Italienische": Alle eigenhändigen Niederschriften im Faksimile.* Wiesbaden, 1997.

Cooper, John Michael, and Julie D. Prandi, ed. *The Mendelssohns: Their Music in History.* Oxford, 2003.

Cox, H. B., and C. L. E. Cox, ed. *Leaves from the Journals of Sir George Smart.* London, 1907, repr. 1971.

Crum, Margaret. *Felix Mendelssohn Bartholdy.* Oxford, 1972.

———. *Catalogue of the Mendelssohn Papers in the Bodleian Library, Oxford, Vol. I: Correspondence of Felix Mendelssohn Bartholdy and Others.* Tutzing, 1980.

———. *Catalogue of the Mendelssohn Papers in the Bodleian Library, Oxford, Vol. II: Music and Papers.* Tutzing, 1983.

———. "Mendelssohn's Drawing and the Doubled Life of Memory." In *Festschrift Albi Rosenthal.* Ed. Rudolf Elvers. Tutzing, 1984, 87–103.

Cullen, Michael. "Leipziger Straße Drei: Eine Baubiographie." *MS* 5 (1982): 9–77.

Dahlgren, L., ed. *Bref till Adolf Fredrik Lindblad från Mendelssohn, . . . och andra.* Stockholm, 1913.

Dahlhaus, Carl, ed. *Das Problem Mendelssohn.* Regensburg, 1974.

———. "Mendelssohn und die musikalischen Gattungstraditionen." In Dahlhaus, *Das Problem Mendelssohn*, 55–60, 1974b.

———. "'Hoch symbolisch intentioniert': Zu Mendelssohns 'Erster Walpurgisnacht.'" *Österreichische Musikzeitschrift* 36 (1981): 290–97.

———. "Studien zur romantischen Musikästhetik." *AfMw* 42 (1985): 157–65.

Daverio, John. *Robert Schumann: Herald of a "New Poetic Age."* Oxford, 1997.

David, Hans T., and Arthur Mendel, eds. *The New Bach Reader: A Life of Johann Sebastian Bach in Letters and Documents.* Rev. by Christoph Wolff. New York, 1998.

Davison, Henry, ed. *From Mendelssohn to Wagner, Being the Memoirs of J. W. Davison.* London, 1912.

Deutsch, Otto Erich. "The Discovery of Schubert's Great C-major Symphony: A Story in Fifteen Letters." *MQ* 38 (1952): 528–32.

Devrient, Eduard. *Meine Erinnerungen an Felix Mendelssohn-Bartholdy und seine Briefe an mich.* Leipzig, 1869; Eng. trans., Natalia Macfarren, *My Recollections of Felix Mendelssohn Bartholdy and His Letters to Me.* London, 1869; repr. New York, 1972.

Devrient, Therese. *Jugenderinnerungen.* Stuttgart, 1905.

Dilthey, Wilhelm. *Leben Schleiermachers.* Berlin, 1870.

Dinglinger, Wolfgang. "Ein neues Lied: Der preußische Generalmusikdirektor und eine königliche Auftragskomposition." *MS* 5 (1982): 99–111.

———. "Felix Mendelssohn Bartholdy: Der 96. Psalm op. 46—'. . . von dem nur ein Stück mir ans Herz gewachsen war. . . .'" *MS* 7 (1990): 269–86.

———. "Felix Mendelssohn Bartholdys Klavierkonzert a-moll: Umgang mit einer Modellkomposition." *MS* 8 (1993): 105–29.

———. *Studien zu den Psalmen mit Orchester von Felix Mendelssohn Bartholdy.* Berlin, 1993b.

———. "Sieben Charakterstücke op. 7 von Felix Mendelssohn Bartholdy." *MS* 10 (1997): 101–30.

———. "Mendelssohn—General-Musik-Direktor für kirchliche und geistliche Musik." In C. M. Schmidt, 23–36, 1997b.

———. "'Er war immer mit hinein verflochten': Die Freunde Eduard Rietz und Felix Mendelssohn Bartholdy und ihre Briefe." *MS* 12 (2001): 129–48.

———. "The Programme of Mendelssohn's 'Reformation' Symphony, Op. 107." In Cooper and Prandi, 115–33, 2002.

Dörffel, Alfred. *Geschichte der Gewandhausconcerte.* Leipzig, 1884, repr. 1972.

Dorn, Heinrich. "Recollections of Felix Mendelssohn and His Friends." *Temple Bar*, February 1872: 397–405.

———. *Aus meinem Leben.* Berlin, 1872, III, 43–81, 1872b.

Droysen, G. "Johann Gustav Droysen und Felix Mendelssohn-Bartholdy." *DR* 111 (1902): 107–26, 193–215, 386–408.

Dubnov, Simon. *History of the Jews*, trans. Moshe Spiegel. New York, 1973.

Eberle, Gottfried. "Eroberung des Dramatischen: Fanny Hensels *Hero und Leander*." In Helmig, 131–38, 1997.

Eckardt, J. W. A. von. *Ferdinand David und die Familie Mendelssohn-Bartholdy.* Leipzig, 1888.

Edwards, Frederick George. "First Performances. I.—Mendelssohn's 'St. Paul.'" *MT* 32 (1891): 137–38.

———. *Musical Haunts in London.* London, 1895.

———. *The History of Mendelssohn's Oratorio "Elijah."* London, 1896.

———. "Mendelssohn's Organ Sonatas: A Comparison of the Original Autograph with the Published Version." *MT* 47 (1906): 95–100.

Eichner, Hans. "'Camilla': Eine unbekannte Fortsetzung von Dorothea Schlegels Florentin." In *Jahrbuch des Freien Deutschen Hochstifts 1965.* Tübingen, 1965, 314–68.

Elst, Nancy van der. "Felix Mendelssohn en Cesar Franck." *Mens en Melodie* 8 (1953): 82–84.

Elvers, Rudolf. "Verzeichnis der von Felix Mendelssohn Bartholdy herausgegebenen Werke Johann Sebastian Bachs." In *Gestalt und Glaube: Festschrift für Vizepräsident Professor D. Dr. Oskar Söhngen zum 60. Geburtstag.* Witten, 1960, 145–49.

————. "Ein Jugendbrief von Felix Mendelssohn." In *Festschrift Friedrich Smend zum 70. Geburtstag*. Berlin, 1963, 95–97.

————. "Ein nicht abgesandter Brief Zelters an Haydn." *Musik und Verlag, Karl Vötterle zum 65. Geburtstag*. Ed. R. Baum and W. Rehm. Kassel, 1968, 243–45.

————. *Endreim-Spiele mit Felix Mendelssohn, Weimar, November 1821*. Berlin, 1970.

————. "Verzeichnis der Musik-Autographen von Fanny Hensel im Mendelssohn-Archiv zu Berlin." *MS* 1 (1972): 169–74.

————. "Acht Briefe von Lea Mendelssohn an den Verlag Schlesinger in Berlin." In Dahlhaus, 1974, 47–54.

————. "Weitere Quellen zu den Werken von Fanny Hensel." *MS* 2 (1975): 215–20.

————. "*Nichts ist so schwer gut zu componiren als Strophen": Zur Entstehungsgeschichte des Librettos von Felix Mendelssohns Oper "Die Hochzeit des Camacho."* Berlin, 1976.

————. "Verlorengegangene Selbstverständlichkeiten: Zum Mendelssohn-Artikel in *The New Grove*." *Festschrift Heinz Becker zum 60. Geburtstag*. Ed. J. Schläder and R. Quandt. Laaber, 1982, 417–21.

————, ed. *Felix Mendelssohn: A Life in Letters*. Trans. Craig Tomlinson. New York, 1986; German edition as *Briefe*. Frankfurt, 1984.

————. "Der letzte Familienbrief: Rebecka Dirichlet an Felix Mendelssohn Bartholdy." *Festschrift Wolfgang Rehm zum 60. Geburtstag*. Ed. D. Berke and H. Hackmann. Kassel, 1989, 193–96.

————. "Ein Schwede besucht die Mendelssohns: Aus den Reisebriefen des Hendrik Munktell 1829/30." *Neue Musik und Tradition: Festschrift Rudolf Stephan zum 65. Geburtstag*. Ed. J. Kuckertz *et al*. Laaber, 1990, 233–37.

————. "Frühe Quellen zur Biographie Felix Mendelssohn Bartholdys." In C. M. Schmidt, 17–22, 1997.

————. "Der fingierte Brief Ludwig van Beethovens an Fanny Mendelssohn Bartholdy." *MS* 10 (1997), 97–100, 1997b.

Elvers, Rudolf, and Hans-Günter Klein, ed. *Die Mendelssohns in Berlin: Eine Familie und ihre Stadt*. Berlin, 1983.

Elvers, Rudolf, and Peter Ward Jones. "Das Musikalienverzeichnis von Fanny und Felix Mendelssohn Bartholdy." *MS* 8 (1993): 85–104.

Eppstein, Hans. "Zur Entstehungsgeschichte von Mendelssohns Lied ohne Worte, op. 62,3." *Mf* 26 (1973): 486–90.

Esser, Joseph. "Felix Mendelssohn-Bartholdy und die Rheinlande." Diss., Rheinische Friedrich-Wilhelm-Universität zu Bonn, 1923.

Evans, David R. A., R. Larry Todd, and Judith E. Olson. "A Welsh Collection of Mendelssohniana: Letters at Aberystwyth." *Current Musicology* 65 (2001): 116–40.

Fauquet, Joël-Marie. "La musique de chambre à Paris dans les années 1830." *Music in Paris in the Eighteen-Thirties*. Ed. P. Bloom. Stuyvesant, N.Y., 1987, 299–326.

Feder, Georg. "Zwischen Kirche und Konzertsaal: Zu Felix Mendelssohn Bartholdys geistlicher Musik." In *Religiöse Musik in nicht-liturgischen Werken von Beethoven bis Reger*. Ed. W. Wiora. Regensburg, 1978, 97–117.

Feder, Georg, and Peter Hübner. "Felix Mendelssohns Briefe an Pauline und Julius Hübner." In *Festschrift Rudolf Elvers zum 60. Geburtstag*. Ed. E. Herttrich and H. Schneider. Tutzing, 1985, 157–97.

Federhofer-Königs, Renate. "Der unveröffentlichte Briefwechsel Alfred Julius Becher (1803–1848) Felix Mendelssohn Bartholdy (1809–1847)." *Studien zur Musikwissenschaft* 41 (1992): 7–94.

Fellner, Richard. *Geschichte einer Deutschen Musterbühne: Karl Immermanns Leitung des Stadttheaters zu Düsseldorf*. Stuttgart, 1888.

Feuchte, Andreas. "Felix Mendelssohn Bartholdy als Freund von Eduard Franck." *MS* 10 (1997): 57–76.

Filosa, A. J. "The Early Symphonies and Chamber Music of Felix Mendelssohn Bartholdy." Ph.D. diss., Yale University, 1973.

Finson, Jon W., and R. Larry Todd. *Mendelssohn and Schumann: Essays on Their Music and Its Context*. Durham, N.C., 1984.

Fischer, W. H. *Niederrheinisches Musikfest Düsseldorf 1926: Festschrift*. Düsseldorf, 1926.

Fiske, Roger. *Scotland in Music: A European Enthusiasm*. Cambridge, 1983.

Flashar, Hellmut. "F. Mendelssohn-Bartholdys Vertonung antiker Dramen." In W. Arenhövel and C. Schreiber, ed. *Berlin und die Antike*. Berlin, 1979, 351–61.

————. "August Böckh und Felix Mendelssohn Bartholdy." In W. Schmidt-Biggemann, ed. *Disiecta Membra: Studien Karlfried Gründer zum 60. Geburtstag*. Basel, 1989, 66–81.

Forbes, Elliot, ed. *Thayer's Life of Beethoven.* Princeton, 1970.

Forkel, J. N. *Über Johann Sebastian Bachs Leben, Kunst und Kunstwerke.* Leipzig, 1802; repr. 1970.

Foster, M. B. *History of the Philharmonic Society of London: 1813–1912.* London, 1912.

Freudenberg, C. G. *Aus dem Leben eines alten Organisten.* Edited by W. Viol. Leipzig, 1872.

Friedlaender, Max. "Ein Brief Felix Mendelssohns." *VfM* 5 (1889): 483–89.

———. "Briefe an Goethe von Felix Mendelssohn-Bartholdy." *Goethe Jahrbuch* 12 (1891): 77–98, 110–124.

Friedrich, Gerda. "Die Fugenkomposition in Mendelssohns Instrumentalwerk." Diss., Rheinische Friedrich-Wilhelms-Universität zu Bonn, 1969.

Gade, Niels W. *Aufzeichnungen und Briefe.* Edited by D. Gade. Leipzig, 1894.

Galley, Ursula, ed. *Paphlëis: Ein Spott-Heldengedicht von Felix Mendelssohn.* Basel, 1961.

Gantzel-Kress, Gisela. "Karl Mendelssohm Bartholdy 1838–1897." *MS* 8 (1993): 197–225.

Geck, Martin. *Die Wiederentdeckung der Matthäuspassion im 19. Jahrhundert.* Regensburg, 1967.

Genast, Eduard. *Aus dem Tagebuche eines alten Schauspielers.* Leipzig, 1865, III.

Gerber, Hans. *Albert Baur: Ein Lebensbild.* Freiburg im Breisgau, 1971.

Gerlach, Reinhard. "Mendelssohns Kompositionsweise: Vergleich zwischen Skizzen und Letztfassung des Violinkonzerts opus 64." *AfMw* 28 (1971): 119–33.

———. "Mendelssohns Kompositionsweise (II): Weitere Vergleiche zwischen den Skizzen und der Letztfassung des Violinkonzerts, opus 64." In Dahlhaus. *Das Problem Mendelssohn.* 149–67, 1974.

Giesau, Peter. "Das Palais Mendelssohn Bartholdy in Berlin und die Entwürfe Carl Theodor Ottmers zum Umbau aus dem Jahr 1825." *MS* 12 (2001): 55–66.

Gilbert, Felix, ed. *Bankiers, Künstler und Gelehrte: Unveröffentlichte Briefe der Familie Mendelssohn aus dem 19. Jahrhundert.* Tübingen, 1975.

———. "Georg Benjamin Mendelssohn und Karl Mendelssohn Bartholdy—Zwei Professoren aus dem 19. Jahrhundert." *MS* 2 (1975): 183–201, 1975b.

Gläser, Ludwig. *Eduard Magnus: Ein Beitrag zur Berliner Bildnismalerei des 19. Jahrhunderts.* Berlin, 1963.

Gollmick, Carl. *Auto-Biographie nebst einigen Momenten aus der Geschichte des Frankfurter Theaters.* Frankfurt, 1866, II.

Gotch, Rosamund Brumel, ed. *Mendelssohn and his Friends in Kensington: Letters from Fanny and Sophy Horsley Written 1833–36.* London, 1938.

Greive, Tyrone. "The Mendelssohn Violin Concerto in E minor: A Second Manuscript Score." *The Violexchange* 5/2 (1990): 97–108.

Grey, Thomas S. "*Tableaux vivants:* Landscape, History, Painting, and the Visual Imagination in Mendelssohn's Orchestral Music." *19CM* 21 (1997): 38–76.

———. "*Fingal's Cave* and Ossian's Dream: Music, Image, and Phantasmagoric Audition," M. L. Morton and P. L. Schmunk, ed. *The Arts Entwined: Music and Painting in the Nineteenth Century.* New York, 2000, 63–99.

———. "Orchestral Music." In Seaton, *The Mendelssohn Companion,* 395–533, 2001.

Großmann-Vendrey, Susanna. *Felix Mendelssohn Bartholdy und die Musik der Vergangenheit.* Regensburg, 1969.

———. "Stilprobleme in Mendelssohns Orgelsonaten op. 65." In Dahlhaus, *Das Problem Mendelssohn,* 185–94, 1974.

Grove, Sir George. "Mendelssohn." In Sir George Grove, ed., *A Dictionary of Music and Musicians.* London, 1890 (reissue of first edition, 1879–1889), II, 253–310.

———. "Mendelssohn's Oratorio 'St. Paul.'" *MT* 50 (1909): 92–94.

Grumbacher, Rudolf, and Albi Rosenthal. "'Dieses einzige Stückchen Welt...': Über ein Albumblatt von Felix Mendelssohn Bartholdy." *MS* 5 (1982): 123–29.

Gundlach, Willi. "Die Chorlieder von Fanny Hensel—eine späte Liebe?" *MS* 11 (1999): 105–30.

Hadden, J. Cuthbert. "Mendelssohn, Moscheles, and Chopin in Scotland." *Scottish Review* 33 (1899): 94–100.

Häfner, Klaus. "Felix Mendelssohn Bartholdy in seinen Beziehungen zu König Friedrich August II. von Sachsen." *MS* 7 (1990): 219–68.

Haight, Gordon Sherman, ed. *Selections from George Eliot's Letters.* New Haven, 1985.

Hake, Bruno. "Mendelssohn als Lehrer, mit bisher ungedruckten Briefen Mendelssohns an Wilhelm v. Boguslawski." *DR* 140 (1909): 453–70, trans. S. Gillespie. In Todd, *MahW,* 310–37.

Hanslick, Eduard. "Briefe von Felix Mendelssohn-Bartholdy an Aloys Fuchs." *DR* 57 (1888): 65–85, trans. Susan Gillespie. In Todd, *MahW,* 275–309, 1991.

Harmonicon, 11 vols., 1823–1833.

Hartog, Jacques. *Felix Mendelssohn Bartholdy en zijne werken.* Leiden, 1908.

Harwell Celenza, Anna. *The Early Works of Niels W. Gade.* Aldershot, 2001.

Hathaway, Joseph W. G. *An Analysis of Mendelssohn's Organ Works.* London, 1898.

Hatteberg, K. E. "*Gloria* (1822) and *Große Festmusik zum Dürerfest* (1828): Urtext Editions of Two Unpublished Choral-Orchestral Works by Felix Mendelssohn with Background and Commentary." D.M.A. diss., University of Iowa, 1995.

Hecker, Max F., ed. *Der Briefwechsel zwischen Goethe und Zelter.* 3 vols. Leipzig, 1913–1918.

Heine, Maximilian. *Erinnerungen an Heinrich Heine und seine Familie.* Berlin, 1868.

Hellmundt, Christoph. "Mendelssohns Arbeit an seiner Kantate *Die erste Walpurgisnacht*: Zu einer bisher wenig beachteten Quelle." In C. M. Schmidt, 76–112, 1997.

———. "Anton Christanell und seine Beziehungen zu Felix Mendelssohn Bartholdy." *MS* 11 (1999): 77–102.

———. "'Indessen wollte ich mich Ihnen gern gefällig beweisen': On Some Occasional Works, with an Unknown Composition by Mendelssohn." In J. M. Cooper and J. D. Prandi, 169–80. 2002.

Hellwig-Unruh, Renate. "'Ein Dilettant ist schon ein schreckliches Geschöpf, ein weiblicher Autor ein noch schrecklicheres. . .': Sechs Briefe von Fanny Hensel an Franz Hauser (1794–1870)." *MS* 10 (1997): 215–26.

———. *Fanny Hensel geb. Mendelssohn Bartholdy: Thematisches Verzeichnis der Kompositionen.* Adliswil, 2000.

Helmig, Martina, ed. *Fanny Hensel, geb. Mendelssohn Bartholdy: Das Werk.* Munich, 1997.

Helmig, Martina, and Annette Mauer. "Fanny Mendelssohn Bartholdy und Wilhelm Hensel: Briefe aus der Verlobungszeit." In Helmig, 139–61, 1997b.

Hennemann, Monika. "Mendelssohn and Byron: Two Songs Almost without Words." *MS* 10 (1997): 131–56.

Hensel, Fanny. *Tagebücher.* Edited by Hans-Günter Klein and Rudolf Elvers. Wiesbaden, 2002.

———. *Briefe aus Rom an ihre Familie in Berlin 1839/40.* Edited by Hans-Günter Klein. Wiesbaden, 2002. 2002b.

Hensel, Sebastian. *Die Familie Mendelssohn (1729–1847) nach Briefen und Tagebüchern.* Berlin, 1879; 15th Auf., Berlin, 1911; *The Mendelssohn Family (1729–1847) from Letters and Journals.* Trans. Carl Klingemann, [Jr.] London, 1882, 2 vols.

———. *Ein Lebensbild aus Deutschlands Lehrjahren.* Berlin, 1911.

Hertz, Deborah. *Jewish High Society in Old Regime Berlin.* New Haven, 1988.

———. "Work, Love and Jewishness in the Life of Fanny Lewald." *From East and West: Jews in a Changing Europe.* Edited by F. Malino and D. Sorkin. Oxford, 1991, 202–22.

Hexelschneider, Erhard. "Wilhelm Küchelbecker—ein frühes ausländisches Urteil über Felix Mendelssohn Bartholdy." *MS* 8 (1993): 131–40.

Heyder, Bernd, and Christoph Spering, eds. *Blickpunkt Felix Mendelssohn Bartholdy: Programmbuch Drei Tage für Felix vom 30.10 bis 1.11.1994.* Cologne, 1994.

Heyse, Paul. *Jugenderinnerungen und Bekenntnisse.* Berlin, 1900.

Hiller, Ferdinand. *Felix Mendelssohn Bartholdy: Briefe und Erinnerungen.* Cologne, 1874; trans. M. E. von Glehn, *Mendelssohn: Letters and Recollections.* London, 1874; repr. New York, 1972.

Hinrichsen, H.-J. "Kantatenkomposition in der 'Haupstadt von Sebastian Bach': Fanny Hensels geistliche Chorwerke und die Berliner Bach-Tradition." In Helmig, 115–29, 1997.

Höffner, Johannes, ed. *Aus Biedermeiertagen: Briefe Robert Reinicks und seiner Freunden.* Bielefeld, 1910.

Hoffheimer, Michael H. *Eduard Gans and the Hegelian Philosophy of Law.* Boston, 1995.

Hoffmann, Heinrich. *Lebens-Erinnerungen.* Frankfurt, 1985.

Hoffmann, Paul Th. *Die Elbchaussee: Ihre Landsitze, Menschen und Schicksale.* Hamburg, 1962.

Hoffmann-Erbrecht, Lothar. "Klavierkonzert und Affektgestaltung: Bemerkungen zu einigen d-Moll-Klavierkonzerten des 18. Jahrhunderts." *Deutsches Jahrbuch der Musikwissenchaft* 16 (1971): 86–110.

Holland, H. S., and W. S. Rockstro. *Jenny Lind the Artist: 1820–1851.* London, 1893.

Holoman, D. Kern. *Berlioz.* Cambridge, Mass., 1989.

Horsley, C. E. "Reminiscences of Mendelssohn by his English Pupil." *Dwight's Journal of Music* 32 (1872): 345–47, 353–55, 361–63. In *MahW*, 237–51.

Huber, Annegret. "In welcher Form soll man Fanny Hensels 'Choleramusik' aufführen?" *MS* 10 (1997): 227–45.

Immermann, Karl. *Zwischen Poesie und Wirklichkeit: Tagebücher 1831–1840.* Edited by Peter Hasubek. Munich, 1984.

Jacob, H. E. *Felix Mendelssohn and His Times*. Trans. R. and C. Winston, London, 1963.
Jacobi, E. R. "Das Autograph von C. Ph. E. Bachs Doppelkonzert in Es-dur für Cembalo, Fortepiano und Orchester (Wq. 47, Hamburg 1788)." *Mf* 12 (1959): 488–89.
Jacobi, Martin. *Felix Mendelssohn Bartholdy*. Bielefeld, 1915.
Jacobson, Jacob. "Von Mendelssohn zu Mendelssohn-Bartholdy." *LBI* 5 (1960): 251–61.
———. *Die Judenbürgerbücher der Stadt Berlin: 1809–1851, mit Ergänzungen für die Jahre 1791–1809*. Berlin, 1962.
Jahn, Otto. "Ueber F. Mendelssohn Bartholdy's Oratorium Paulus." Kiel, 1842, repr. in Otto Jahn, *Gesammelte Aufsätze über Musik*. Leipzig, 1866, 13–37.
———. "Ueber F. Mendelssohn Bartholdy's Oratorium *Elias*." *AmZ* 50 (1848): 113–22, 137–43. Trans. in *MahW*, 364–81.
Jansen, F. Gustav, ed. *Robert Schumanns Briefe: Neue Folge*. Leipzig, 1904.
Joachim, Johannes, and A. Moser, ed. *Briefe von und an Joseph Joachim*. Berlin, 1911–13.
Johnson, James H. *Listening in Paris: A Cultural History*. Berkeley, 1995.
Jonas, Oswald. "An Unknown Mendelssohn Work." *American Choral Review* 9 (1967): 16–22.
Jost, Christa. *Mendelssohns Lieder ohne Worte*. Tutzing, 1988.
———. "In Mutual Reflection: Historical, Biographical, and Structural Aspects of Mendelssohn's *Variations sérieuses*." In Todd, *Mendelssohn Studies*, 36–63, 1992.
Jourdan, Paul. "Mendelssohn in England 1829–37." Ph.D. diss., Cambridge University, 1998.
———. "The Hidden Pathways of Assimilation: Mendelssohn's First Visit to London." In Christina Bashford and Leanne Langley, ed. *Music and British Culture, 1785–1914: Essays in Honour of Cyril Ehrlich*. Oxford, 2000, 99–119.
Katz, Jacob. *From Prejudice to Destruction: Anti-Semitism, 1700–1933*. Cambridge, Mass., 1980.
———. *Die Hep-Hep-Verfolgungen des Jahres 1819*. Berlin, 1994.
Kellenberger, Edgar. "Felix Mendelssohn als Librettist eines Moses-Oratoriums." *Musik und Kirche* 63 (1993): 126–39.
Kimber, Marian Wilson. "Zur frühen Wirkungsgeschichte Fanny Hensels." In Borchard and Schwarz-Danuser, 248–62, 1999.
———. "The Composer as Other: Gender and Race in the Biography of Felix Mendelssohn." In Cooper and Prandi, 335–51, 2002.
———. "The 'Suppression' of Fanny Mendelssohn: Rethinking Feminist Biography." *19CM* 26 (2003): 113–29.
Kinsky, Georg. "Was Mendelssohn Indebted to Weber?" *MQ* 19 (1933): 178–86.
———, ed. *Musikhistorisches Museum von Wilhelm Heyer in Cöln*. Vol. 4. Cologne, 1916.
Kippenberg, Anton. "Ein Brief Abraham Mendelssohns an Zelter über Goethe." *Jahrbuch der Sammlung Kippenberg* 4 (1924): 72–91.
Kirnberger, Johann Philipp. *Die Kunst des reinen Satzes in der Musik*. Berlin, 1776–1779; repr. Hildesheim, 1968.
———. *Die wahren Grundsätze zum Gebrauch der Harmonie*. Berlin, 1773; repr. Hildesheim, 1970.
Klein, Hans-Günter. "Korrekturen im Autograph von Mendelssohns Streichquartett Op. 80." *MS* 5 (1982): 113–122.
———. "Aus dem Briefwechsel Benjamin Mendelssohns mit seinen Eltern 1811–1818." *MS* 7 (1990): 107–22.
———. "'. . . dieses allerliebste Buch': Fanny Hensels Noten-Album." *MS* 8 (1993): 141–57.
———. *Die Kompositionen Fanny Hensels in Autographen und Abschriften aus dem Besitz der Staatsbibliothek zu Berlin—Preußischer Kulturbesitz*. Tutzing, 1995.
———. "Die 'Societäts-Contracte' der Mendelssohn-Bank 1806–1876." *MS* 9 (1995): 89–118, 1995b.
———, ed. *Das verborgene Band: Felix Mendelssohn Bartholdy und seine Schwester Fanny Hensel*. Wiesbaden, 1997.
———. "Verzeichnis des im Autograph überlieferten Werke Felix Mendelssohn Bartholdys im Besitz der Staatsbibliothek zu Berlin." *MS* 10 (1997): 181–213, 1997b.
———. "'Wir erleben einige Freude an diesem jungen Mann': Die Briefe von Abraham Mendelssohn Bartholdy vom Niederrheinischen Musikfest 1833 nach Berlin." *MS* 11 (1999): 49–75.
———. "'. . . die glücklichsten Momente meines Lebens': Der 22jährige Abraham Mendelssohn schreibt an Karl Friedrich Zelter." *Bunte Blätter: Klaus Mecklenburg zum 23. Februar 2000*. Edited by R. Elvers and A. Moirandat. Basel, 2000, 124–37.
———. "Abraham Mendelssohn Bartholdy in England: Die Briefe aus London im Sommer 1833 nach Berlin." *MS* 12 (2001): 67–128.
———. "Eine (fast) unendliche Geschichte: Felix Mendelssohn Bartholdys Hochzeitsmusik für seine Schwester." *MS* 12 (2001): 179–86, 2001b.

————, ed. *Die Mendelssohns in Italien: Ausstellung des Mendelssohn-Archivs der Staatsbibliothek zu Berlin-Preußischer Kulturbesitz*. Wiesbaden, 2002.

Kleßmann, Eckart. *Die Mendelssohns: Bilder aus einer deutschen Familie*. Zurich, 1990.

Kliem, Manfred. "Die Berlin Mendelssohn-Adresse Neue Promenade 7." *MS* 7 (1990): 123–40.

Klingemann, Karl, Jr., ed. *Felix Mendelssohn-Bartholdys Briefwechsel mit Legationsrat Karl Klingemann in London*. Essen, 1909.

Koch, Paul-August. *Fanny Hensel geb. Mendelssohn (1805–1847), Kompositionen: Eine Zusammenstellung der Werke, Literatur und Schallplatten*. Frankfurt, 1993.

Köhler, Karl-Heinz. "Zwei rekonstruierbare Singspiele von Felix Mendelssohn Bartholdy." *Beiträge zur Musikwissenschaft* 2 (1960): 86–93.

————. *Felix Mendelssohn-Bartholdy*. Leipzig, 1966.

————. "Mendelssohn," *The New Grove Dictionary of Music and Musicians*, ed. Stanley Sadie, London, 1980, xii, 134–59.

————, ed. *Mendelssohn: Die Frauen und die Sänger nach dem Gedicht "Die vier Weltalter" von Friedrich Schiller*. Basel, 1959.

Körner, Josef, ed. *Briefe von und an Friedrich und Dorothea Schlegel*. Berlin, 1926.

Konold, Wulf. *Felix Mendelssohn Bartholdy: Symphonie A Dur, Op. 90*. Munich, 1987.

————. "Mendelssohns Jugendsymphonien: Eine analytische Studie." *AfMw* 46 (1989): 1–41, 155–83.

————. *Die Symphonien Felix Mendelssohn Bartholdys: Untersuchungen zu Werkgestalt und Formstruktur*. Laaber, 1992.

Kopfermann, Albert. "Zwei musikalische Scherze Felix Mendelssohns." *DM* 8 (1908–09): Heft 9, 179–80.

Koyanagi, Reiko, ed. *F. Mendelssohn Bartholdy*. Tokyo, 1992.

Kramer, Lawrence. "*Felix culpa*: Goethe and the Image of Mendelssohn." In Todd, ed., *Mendelssohn Studies*, 64–79, 1992.

Krause, Peter. "Unbekannte Dokumente zur Uraufführung von Franz Schuberts großer C-Dur-Sinfonie durch Felix Mendelssohn Bartholdy." *Beiträge zur Musikwissenschaft* 29 (1987): 240–50.

Kretschman, Lily v. "Felix Mendelssohn-Bartholdy in Weimar." *DR* 69 (1891): 304–08.

Krettenauer, Thomas. *Felix Mendelssohn Bartholdys "Heimkehr aus der Fremde."* Augsburg, 1994.

Krummacher, Friedhelm. "'fein und geistreich genug.' Versuch über Mendelssohns Musik zum Sommernachtstraum." In Dahlhaus, *Das Problem Mendelssohn*, 89–118, 1974.

————. *Mendelssohn—der Komponist: Studien zur Kammermusik für Streicher*. Munich, 1978.

————. "Mendelssohn's Late Chamber Music: Some Autograph Sources Recovered." In Finson and Todd, *Mendelssohn and Schumann*, 71–86, 1984.

————. "Composition as Accommodation? On Mendelssohn's Music in Relation to England." In Todd, *Mendelssohn Studies*, 80–105, 1992.

————. "Art—History—Religion: On Mendelssohn's Oratorios *St. Paul* and *Elijah*." In Seaton, *The Mendelssohn Companion*, 299–382, 2001.

————. "On Mendelssohn's Compositional Style: Propositions Based on the Example of the String Quartets." In Seaton, *The Mendelssohn Companion*, 551–68, 2001b.

Kulukundis, E. N. "C. P. E. Bach in the Library of the Singakademie zu Berlin." *C. P. E. Bach Studies*. Edited by S. Clark. Oxford, 1988, 159–76.

Kurzhals-Reuter, Arntrud. *Die Oratorien Felix Mendelssohn Bartholdys*. Tutzing, 1978.

La Mara, Marie Lipsius. *Briefe hervorragender Zeitgenossen an Franz Liszt*. 3 vols. Leipzig, 1895–1904.

Lambour, Christian. "Quellen zur Biographie von Fanny Hensel, geb. Mendelssohn Bartholdy." *MS* 6 (1986): 49–105.

————. "Ein Schweizer Reisebrief aus dem Jahr 1822 von Lea und Fanny Mendelssohn Bartholdy an Henriette (Hinni) Mendelssohn, geb. Meyer." *MS* 7 (1990): 171–78.

Lampadius, W. A. *The Life of Felix Mendelssohn-Bartholdy*. Trans. W. L. Gage. London, 1877.

Ledebur, Carl von. *Tonkünstler-Lexicon Berlins*. Berlin, 1861; repr. 1965.

Lenz, Max. *Geschichte der Königlichen Friedrich-Wilhelms Universität zu Berlin*. Halle, 1920.

Leven, Luise. "Mendelssohn als Lyriker, unter besonderer Berücksichtigung seiner Beziehungen zu Ludwig Berger, Bernhard Klein und Adolph Bernhard Marx." Diss., Universität Frankfurt am Main, 1926.

————. "Mendelssohn's Unpublished Songs." *MMR* 88 (1958): 206–11.

Levy, David B. "Thomas Massa Alsager, Esq.: A Beethoven Advocate in London." *19CM* 9 (1985): 119–27.

Lewald, Fanny. *Meine Lebensgeschichte*. Berlin, 1861; ed. Ulrike Helmer. Frankfurt am Main, 1989.

————. *The Education of Fanny Lewald: An Autobiography*. Trans. and ed. H. B. Lewis. Albany, N.Y., 1992.

Libby, Dennis A. "Gaspare Spontini and his French and German Operas." Ph.D. diss., Princeton University, 1969.

Liepmannssohn, Leo. *Versteigerung von Musiker Autographen aus dem Nachlass des Herrn Kommerzienrates Wilhelm Heyer in Köln*. Berlin, December 1926–February 1928.

Lindeman, Stephan D. "Mendelssohn and Moscheles: Two Composers, Two Pianos, Two Scores, One Concerto." *MQ* 83 (1999): 51–74.

——. *Structural Novelty and Tradition in the Early Romantic Piano Concerto*. Stuyvesant, N.Y., 1999b.

Little, Wm. A. "Mendelssohn and the Berlin Singakademie: The Composer at the Crossroads." In *MahW*, 65–85, 1991.

——. "Mendelssohn and Liszt." In Todd, ed., *Mendelssohn Studies*, 106–25, 1992.

——. "Felix Mendelssohn and his Place in the Organ World of his Time." In Cooper and Prandi, 291–302, 2002.

Litzmann, Berthold. *Clara Schumann: Ein Künstlerleben nach Tagebüchern und Briefen*. Leipzig, 1902–08.

Lobe, J. C. "Gespräche mit Mendelssohn." *Fliegende Blätter für die Musik* 1/5 (1855), 280–96; repr. in *Goethes Schauspieler und Musiker: Erinnerungen von Eberwein und Lobe*. Edited by W. Bode. Berlin, 1912, 192–99; Eng. trans. by Susan Gillespie as "Conversations with Felix Mendelssohn" in *MahW*, 187–205.

——. "Ein Quartett bei Goethe." *Die Gartenlaube* 1 (1867): 4–8.

Locke, Ralph. "Mendelssohn's Collision with the Saint-Simonians." In Finson and Todd, 109–22.

Lockwood, Lewis. "Mendelssohn's Mozart: A New Acquisition." *Princeton University Library Chronicle* 34/1 (1972): 62–68.

Lowenstein, Steven M. "Jewish Upper Crust and Berlin Jewish Enlightenment: The Family of Daniel Itzig." In *From East and West: Jews in a Changing Europe*. Edited by F. Malino and D. Sorkin. Oxford, 1991, 182–201.

——. *The Berlin Jewish Community: Enlightenment, Family and Crisis, 1770–1830*. New York, 1994.

Lowenthal-Hensel, Cécile. "Wilhelm Hensel in England." *MS* 2 (1975): 203–14.

——. "Wilhelm Hensels 'Lebenslauf' von 1829." *MS* 3 (1979): 175–79.

——. "Theodor Fontane über Wilhelm Hensel." *MS* 3 (1979): 181–99, 1979b.

——. *Preußische Bildnisse des 19. Jahrhunderts: Zeichnungen von Wilhelm Hensel*. Berlin, 1981.

——. "'Diese Schreibart erkläre ich hiermit für unrichtig': Dreimal Mendelsohn, [sic] im Militärkirchenbuch von Neisse." *MS* 5 (1982): 141–46.

——. "Neues zur Leipziger Straße Drei." *MS* 7 (1990): 141–51.

——. "Wilhelm Hensel: Fanny und Felix im Porträt." *MS* 10 (1997): 9–24.

Lumley, Benjamin. *Reminiscences of the Opera*. London, 1864, repr. 1976.

McDonald, J. A. "The Chamber Music of Felix Mendelssohn-Bartholdy." Ph.D. diss., Northwestern University, 1970.

Mann, Alfred. *The Study of Fugue*. New York, 1965.

Mann, Robert C. "The Organ Music." In Seaton, *The Mendelssohn Companion*, 625–56, 2001.

Marek, George R. *Gentle Genius: The Story of Felix Mendelssohn*. New York, 1972.

Marissen, Michael. "Religious Aims in Mendelssohn's 1829 Berlin-Singakademie Performances of Bach's St. Matthew Passion." *MQ* 77 (1993): 718–26.

Marpurg, F. W. *Die Abhandlung von der Fuge*. Berlin, 1753–1754; repr. Hildesheim, 1970.

——. *Kritische Briefe über die Tonkunst*. Berlin, 1760; repr. Hildesheim, 1974.

Marx, Adolf Bernhard. *Die Kunst des Gesangs, theoretisch-praktisch*. Berlin, 1826.

——. *Ueber Malerei in der Tonkunst*. Berlin, 1828.

——. *Erinnerungen aus meinem Leben*. Berlin, 1865.

——. "From the Memoirs of Adolf Bernhard Marx." Trans. S. Gillespie, in *MahW*, 206–20, 1991.

Marx, Therese. *Adolf Bernhard Marx' Verhältniß zu Felix Mendelssohn-Bartholdy in Bezug auf Eduard Devrient's Darstellung*. Leipzig, 1869.

Mason, Lowell. *Musical Letters from Abroad*. New York, 1854; repr. 1967.

Maude, J. M. C. *The Life of Jenny Lind*. London, 1926, repr. 1977.

Maurer, Annette. *Thematisches Verzeichnis der klavierbegleiteten Sololieder Fanny Hensels*. Kassel, 1997.

Mendelssohn, Fanny and Felix. *Die Musik will gar nicht rutschen ohne Dich: Briefwechsel 1821 bis 1846*. Edited by Eva Weissweiler. Berlin, 1997.

Mendelssohn, Moses. *Moses Mendelssohns gesammelte Schriften*. Edited by G. B. Mendelssohn. 7 vols. Leipzig, 1843–1845.

————. *Jerusalem, or On Religious Power and Judaism.* Trans. Allan Arkush. Hanover, N.H., 1983.

Mendelssohn Bartholdy, Felix, trans. *Das Mädchen von Andros, eine Komödie des Terentius.* Edited by K. W. L. Heyse. Berlin, 1826.

————. *Werke: kritisch durchgesehene Ausgabe.* Edited by Julius Rietz. Leipzig, 1874–1877.

————. *Reisebilder aus der Schweiz 1842.* Edited by Max. F. Schneider. Basel, 1954.

————. *Leipziger Ausgabe der Werke Felix Mendelssohn Bartholdys.* Leipzig, 1960–1977; edited by Christian Martin Schmidt, 1997–.

————. *Briefe an deutsche Verleger.* Edited by Rudolf Elvers. Berlin, 1968.

————. *Briefe aus Leipziger Archiven.* Edited by H.-J. Rothe and R. Szeskus. Leipzig, 1972.

————. *Briefe.* Edited by Rudolf Elvers. Frankfurt, 1984. Trans. C. Tomlinson, *Felix Mendelssohn: A Life in Letters.* New York, 1986.

————. *Complete Organ Works.* Edited by Wm. A. Little. 5 vols. London, 1987–1990.

————. *Briefe: Band I, 1817 bis 1829.* Edited by Rudolf Elvers, Serie XI of *LAWFMB.* Vorabdruck. Wiesbaden, 1997.

Mendelssohn-Bartholdy, Karl, ed. *Goethe and Mendelssohn (1821–1831).* Trans. M. E. von Glehn. London, 1874, repr. 1970.

Mendelssohn Bartholdy, Paul, ed. *Reisebriefe aus den Jahren 1830 bis 1832.* Leipzig, 1869, 8th Aufl. Trans. Lady Wallace, *Letters from Italy and Switzerland,* 3rd ed. London, 1865.

————. *Briefe aus den Jahren 1833 bis 1847.* Leipzig, 1865, 5th Aufl. Trans. Lady Wallace, *Letters of Felix Mendelssohn Bartholdy from 1833 to 1847.* London, 1868.

Mercer-Taylor, Peter. "Mendelssohn's 'Scottish' Symphony and the Music of German Memory." *19CM* 19 (1995): 68–82.

————. "Rethinking Mendelssohn's Historicism: A Lesson from *St. Paul.*" *Journal of Musicology* 15 (1997): 208–29.

Metzger, Heinz-Klaus. "Noch einmal: *Die erste Walpurgisnacht.*" In Metzger and Riehn, 93–96, 1980.

Metzger, H.-K., and Rainer Riehn, ed. *Felix Mendelssohn Bartholdy.* Munich, 1980.

Meyerbeer, Giacomo. *Briefwechsel und Tagebücher.* Edited by Heinz and Gudrun Becker. Vols. 1–4. Berlin, 1959–1985.

Mintz, Donald. "*Melusine:* A Mendelssohn Draft." *MQ* 43 (1957): 480–99.

————. "The Sketches and Drafts of Three of Mendelssohn's Major Works." Ph.D. diss., Cornell University, 1961.

————. "1848, anti-Semitism, and the Mendelssohn Reception." In Todd, ed., *Mendelssohn Studies,* 126–48, 1992.

Montgomery, David L. "From Biedermeier Berlin: The Parthey Diaries." *MQ* 74 (1990): 197–216.

Moscheles, Felix. *Fragments of an Autobiography.* London, 1899.

————, ed. and trans. *Letters of Felix Mendelssohn to Ignaz and Charlotte Moscheles.* London, 1888.

Moscheles, Ignatz. *Recent Music and Musicians.* Edited by C. Moscheles. New York, 1873, repr. 1970.

Moser, Andreas. *Joseph Joachim: Ein Lebensbild.* Berlin, 1908–1910.

Müller, C. H. *Felix Mendelssohn, Frankfurt am Main und der Cäcilien-Verein.* Darmstadt, 1925.

Müller, G. A. "'Leichen-' oder 'Blüthenduft'? Heine-Vertonungen Fanny Hensels und Felix Mendelssohn Bartholdys im Vergleich." In Helmig, 42–50, 1997.

Musch, Hans. "Felix Mendelssohn Bartholdy in Freiburg und im Schwarzwald." *Musik am Oberrhein.* Edited by H. Musch. Kassel, 1993, 181–213.

Mussulman, Joseph A. "Mendelssohnism in America." *MQ* 53 (1967): 335–46.

Naumann, Emil. *Nachklänge.* Berlin, 1872.

Neue Zeitschrift für Musik 1–27 (1834–1847).

Neumann, Werner. "Welche Handschriften J. S. Bachscher Werke besaß die Berliner Singakademie?" *Hans Albrecht in Memoriam.* Edited by W. Brennecke and H. Hasse. Kassel, 1962, 136–42.

Newman, Ernest. *The Life of Richard Wagner.* Vol. 1. London, 1933, repr. Cambridge, 1976.

Nichols, Roger, ed. *Mendelssohn Remembered.* London, 1997.

Niemöller, K. W. "Felix Mendelssohn-Bartholdy und das Niederrheinische Musikfest 1835 in Köln." *Studien zur Musikgeschichte des Rheinlandes III.* Edited by U. Eckard-Bäcker. Cologne, 1965, 46–64.

Nohl, Ludwig, ed. *Musiker-Briefe.* Leipzig, 1873, 2nd ed. Trans. Lady Wallace, *Letters of Distinguished Musicians.* London, 1867.

Nowack, Natalie. "'Martens Mühle soll leben.'" *MS* 10 (1997): 247–49.

Nubbemeyer, Annette. "Italienerinnerungen im Klavieroeuvre Fanny Hensels: Das verschwiegene Programm im Klavierzyklus *Das Jahr.*" In Helmig, 68–80, 1997.

————. "Die Klaviersonaten Fanny Hensels: Analytische Betrachtungen." In Borchard and Schwarz-Danuser, 90–120, 1999.

Olsen, K., and H. Topsøe-Jensen. *H. C. Andersens Dagbøger 1825–1875*. Copenhagen, 1977, III.

Ottenberg, H.-G. "C. P. E. Bach and Carl Friedrich Zelter." In Stephen L. Clark, ed., *C. P. E. Bach Studies*. Oxford, 1988, 185–216.

Pape, Matthias. *Mendelssohns Leipziger Orgelkonzert 1840*. Wiesbaden, 1988.

Parkins, Robert C., and R. Larry Todd. "Mendelssohn's Fugue in F minor: A Discarded Movement of the First Organ Sonata." *Organ Yearbook* 14 (1983): 61–77.

Paulin, Roger. *Ludwig Tieck: A Literary Biography*. Oxford, 1985.

Petitpierre, Jacques. *Le mariage de Mendelssohn 1837–1937: un centenaire*. Lausanne, 1937. Trans. G. Micholet-Coté, *The Romance of the Mendelssohns*. London, 1947.

Phillips, Henry. *Musical and Personal Recollections during Half a Century*. London, 1864, 2 vols.

Phillips, L. M., Jr. "The Leipzig Conservatory: 1843–1881." Ph.D. diss., Indiana University, 1979.

Planché, J. R. *Recollections and Reflections*. London, 1872.

Plantinga, Leon. *Clementi: His Life and Music*. Oxford, 1977.

———. "Schumann's Critical Reaction to Mendelssohn." In Finson and Todd, 11–19, 1984.

Polko, Elise. *Erinnerungen an Felix Mendelssohn-Bartholdy: Ein Künstler- und Menschenleben*. Leipzig, 1868. Trans. by Lady Wallace as *Reminiscences of Felix Mendelssohn-Bartholdy: A Social and Artistic Biography*. London, 1869; repr. 1987.

Porstmann, Gisbert. "Zum Judenporzellan." *Moses Mendelssohn: Porträts und Bilddokumente, Mendelssohn Jubiläumsausgabe 24*. Stuttgart, 1997, 343–45.

Rabien, Ilse. "Die Mendelssohns in Bad Reinerz: Zur Familie Nathan Mendelssohns." *MS* 7 (1990): 153–70.

———. "Arnold und Wilhelm Mendelssohn: Zur Biographie zweier bemerkenswerter Brüder." *MS* 7 (1990): 295–328, 1990b.

Radcliffe, Philip. *Mendelssohn*. London, 1954. 3rd. ed. rev. by Peter Ward Jones, 1990.

Reich, Nancy B. *Clara Schumann: The Artist and the Woman*. Ithaca, 1985.

———, ed. and trans. "From the Memoirs of Ernst Rudorff." In *MahW*, 259–71, 1991.

———. "The Power of Class: Fanny Hensel." In *MahW*, 86–99, 1991b.

———, ed. and trans. "The Correspondence between Clara Wieck Schumann and Felix and Paul Mendelssohn." In Todd, *Schumann and his World*, 205–32, 1994.

Reich, Willi. *Felix Mendelssohn Bartholdy: Denkmal in Wort und Bild*. Basel, 1947.

———. "Mendelssohn sucht einen Operntext." *Musica* 13 (1959): 366–70.

Reichwald, Siegwart. *The Musical Genesis of Felix Mendelssohn's Paulus*. Lanham, Md., 2001.

Reinecke, Carl. "Mendelssohn und Schumann als Lehrer." *NZfM* 78 (1911): 2–4.

Reininghaus, Frieder. "Zwei Emanzipationswege aus Berlin: Anmerkungen zum Verhältnis Meyerbeers und Mendelssohns." In S. Döhring and J. Schläder, ed. *Giacomo Meyerbeer—Musik als Welterfahrung: Heinz Becker zum 70. Geburtstag*. Munich, 1995, 223–35.

Reissmann, August. *Felix Mendelssohn-Bartholdy: Sein Leben und seine Werke*. Berlin, 1872.

Reissner, H. G. "Felix Mendelssohn-Bartholdy und Eduard Gans." *LBI* 4 (1959): 92–110.

———. "Henriette Mendelssohn: Unresolved Conflicts of Integration." *LBI* 21 (1976): 247–58.

Reissner, H. G., and G. Ballin. "Mendelssohn-Miszellen." *BLB* 12/46–47 (1969): 212–14.

Rellstab, Ludwig. *Aus meinem Leben*. Berlin, 1861, vol. 2.

Ringer, Alexander R. "Felix Mendelssohn oder das Judentum in der Musik." In Leo Karl Gerhartz, ed. *Felix Mendelssohn Bartholdy—Repräsentant und/oder Außenseiter?* Kassel, 1993, 67–91.

Rockstro, W. S. *Mendelssohn*. London, 1884.

Rollett, Hermann. *Begegnungen: Erinnerungsblätter (1819–1899)*. Vienna, 1903.

Rollka, Bodo. "Tageslektüre in Berlin (1740–1780)." *MS* 4 (1979): 47–80.

Rothenberg, Sarah. "'Thus Far, but No Farther': Fanny Mendelssohn-Hensel's Unfinished Journey." *MQ* 77 (1993): 689–708.

Ruhnke, Martin. "Der Zelter-Schüler Emil Fischer." In *Festschrift Arno Forchert zum 60. Geburtstag*. Edited by G. Allroggen and D. Altenburg. Kassel, 1986, 208–15.

Rychnovsky, Ernst. "Aus Felix Mendelssohn Bartholdys letzten Lebenstagen." *DM* 8 (1908–09): 141–46.

Sammons, Jeffrey L. *Heinrich Heine: A Modern Biography*. Princeton, 1979.

Schadow, J. G. *Kunstwerke und Kunstansichten: Ein Quellenwerk zur Berliner Kunst- und Kulturgeschichte zwischen 1780 und 1845*. Berlin 1849; Neuausgabe, ed. Götz Eckardt, Berlin, 1987.

Scheumann, A. R. "Major Einbeck: Der Organisator der Militär-Kirchenchöre unter Friedrich Wilhelm III. und des Königlichen Hof- und Domchores zu Berlin." *DM* 7 (1907/08): 323–34.

———. "Briefe berühmter Komponisten aus dem Archiv des Königlichen Hof- und Domchores zu Berlin." *DM* 8/11 (1908/09), 259–70.

Schilling, Gustav. *Encyclopädie der gesammten musikalischen Wissenschaften, oder Universal-Lexicon der Tonkunst*. Stuttgart, 1837. Vol. 4, 654–56.

Schindler, Anton Felix. *Beethoven as I Knew Him*. Edited by D. W. MacArdle, trans. C. S. Jolly. New York, 1966.

Schinköth, Thomas. "'Es soll hier keine Diskussion über den Wert der Kompositionen angeschnitten werden': Felix Mendelssohn Bartholdy im NS-Staat." *MS* 11 (1999): 177–205.

Schlegel, August Wilhelm. *Shakespeares dramatische Werke*. Berlin, 1797–1810. 9 vols.

Schlegel, Dorothea Mendelssohn Veit. *Florentin: A Novel*. Edited and trans. Edwina Lawler and Ruth Richardson. Lewiston, N.Y., 1988.

———. *Camilla: A Novella*. Edited by Hans Eichner, trans. Edwina Lawler. Lewiston, N.Y., 1990.

Schleiermacher, Friedrich. *On Religion: Speeches to Its Cultured Despisers*. Trans. John Oman. New York, 1958.

Schmidt, Christian Martin, ed. *Felix Mendelssohn Bartholdy: Kongreß-Bericht Berlin 1994*. Wiesbaden, 1997.

Schmidt, Thomas C. *Die ästhetischen Grundlagen der Instrumentalmusik Felix Mendelssohn Bartholdys*. Stuttgart, 1996.

Schmidt-Beste, Thomas. "'Alles von ihm gelernt?' Die Briefe von Carl Friedrich Zelter an Felix Mendelssohn Bartholdy." *MS* 10 (1997): 25–56.

Schneider, Max F., ed. *Felix Mendelssohn Bartholdy: Denkmal in Wort und Bild*. Basel, 1947.

———. *Ein unbekanntes Mendelssohn-Bildnis von Johann Peter Lyser*. Basel, 1958.

———, ed. *Zarter Blumen leicht Gewinde: Ein bisher ungedrucktes Goethe-Lied von Mendelssohn*. Düsseldorf, 1960.

———. *Mendelssohn oder Bartholdy? Zur Geschichte eines Familiennamens*. Basel, 1962.

Schnoor, Arndt. "Briefe von Felix Mendelssohn Bartholdy in der Stadtbibliothek Lübeck." *Der Wagen* 1997/98: 111–37.

Schnyder von Wartensee, Xaver. *Lebens-Erinnerungen*. Zurich, 1887.

Schöne, Alfred, and Ferdinand Hiller, ed. *The Letters of a Leipzig Cantor, Being the Letters of Moritz Hauptmann to Franz Hauser, Ludwig Spohr, and Other Musicians*. Trans A. D. Coleridge. London, 1892, repr. 1972.

Schönewolf, Karl. "Mendelssohns Humboldt-Kantate." *Musik und Gesellschaft* 9 (1959): 24–27.

Schoeps, J. H. "1786–1871: Ringen um Reform und Emanzipation." In *Juden in Berlin, 1671–1945: Ein Lesebuch*. Berlin, 1988, 64–125.

Schorn, Karl. *Lebenserinnerungen: Ein Beitrag zur Geschichte des Rheinlands im neunzehnten Jahrhundert*. Bonn, 1898, I.

Schottländer, J. W. "Zelter und die Komponisten seiner Zeit." *Jahrbuch der Sammlung Kippenberg*. Leipzig, 1930, VIII, 134–248.

———, ed. *Carl Friedrich Zelters Darstellung seines Lebens*. Weimar, 1931.

Schröder, Gesine. "Fannys Studien." In *Helmig*, 22–32, 1997.

Schroeder, Johann Karl v. "Um das eiserne Kreuz von 1813: Wilhelm Hensel in den Freiheitskriegen." *MS* 3 (1979): 163–73.

Schubring, Julius. "Reminiscences of Felix Mendelssohn-Bartholdy." *Musical World* 31 (May 12 and 19, 1866), repr. in *MahW*, 221–36, 1991.

———, ed. *Briefwechsel zwischen Felix Mendelssohn Bartholdy und Julius Schubring, zugleich ein Beitrag zur Geschichte und Theorie des Oratoriums*. Leipzig, 1892, repr. 1973.

Schumann, Robert. *Gesammelte Schriften über Musik und Musiker*. Edited by Heinrich Simon. Leipzig, 1888.

———. *On Music and Musicians*. Edited by Konrad Wolf, trans. Paul Rosenfeld. New York, 1946.

———. *Erinnerungen an Felix Mendelssohn Bartholdy*. Edited by Georg Eismann. Zwickau, 1947.

———. "Aufzeichnungen über Mendelssohn." Edited by Heinz-Klaus Metzger and Rainer Riehn. In Metzger and Riehn, *Felix Mendelssohn Bartholdy*, 97–122, 1980.

———. *Tagebücher, I (1827–1838)*. Edited by Georg Eismann. Leipzig, 1971.

———. *Tagebücher, II (1836–1854)*. Edited by Gerd Nauhaus. Leipzig, 1987.

———. *Haushaltbücher (1837–1856)*. Edited by Gerd Nauhaus. Leipzig, 1982.

Schünemann, Georg. "Mendelssohns Jugendopern." *Zeitschrift für Musikwissenschaft* 5 (1923): 506–45.

———. "Die Bachpflege der Berliner Singakademie." *Bach-Jahrbuch 1928*: 138–71.

———. *Die Singakademie zu Berlin: 1791–1941*. Regensburg, 1941.

Schweitzer, Albert. *J. S. Bach*. Trans. Ernest Newman. London, 1923, repr. New York, 1966.

Seaton, Douglass. "A Draft for the Exposition of the First Movement of Mendelssohn's 'Scotch' Symphony." *JAMS* 30 (1977): 129–35.

———. "A Study of a Collection of Mendelssohn's Sketches and Other Autograph Material, Deutsche Staatsbibliothek Berlin *Mus. Ms. Autogr. Mendelssohn 19*." Ph.D. diss., Columbia University, 1977, 1977b.

———. "A Composition Course with Karl Friedrich Zelter." *College Music Symposium* 21 (1981): 126–38.

———. "The Problem of the Lyric Persona in Mendelssohn's Songs." In Schmidt, C. M., 167–86, 1997.

———, ed. *The Mendelssohn Companion*. Westport, Conn., 2001.

———. "Mendelssohn's Dramatic Music." In Seaton, *The Mendelssohn Companion*, 143–243, 2001b.

———. "With Words: Mendelssohn's Vocal Songs." In Seaton, *The Mendelssohn Companion*, 661–98, 2001c.

———. "Mendelssohn's Cycles of Songs." In Cooper and Prandi, 203–9, 2002.

Selden-Goth, G., ed. *Felix Mendelssohn: Letters*. New York, 1945; repr. 1972.

Shaw, George Bernard. *London Music in 1888–1889 as Heard by Corno di Bassetto (Later Known as Bernard Shaw) with Some Further Autobiographical Particulars*. London, 1937. 3rd ed., 1950.

Sheehan, James J. *German History 1770–1866*. Oxford, 1989.

Siebenkäs, Dieter. *Ludwig Berger: Sein Leben und seine Werke unter besonderer Berücksichtigung seines Liedschaffens*. Berlin, 1963.

Siegfried, Christina. "'Der interessanteste und problematischste seiner Freunde'—Adolph Bernhard Marx (1795–1866)." In Heyder and Spering, 35–44, 1994.

Sieling, Andreas. *August Wilhelm Bach (1796–1869)*. Cologne, 1995.

Sietz, Reinhold. "Die musikalische Gestaltung der Loreleysage bei Max Bruch, Felix Mendelssohn und Ferdinand Hiller." *Max Bruch-Studien, zum 50. Todestag des Komponisten*. Edited by D. Kämper. Cologne, 1970, 14–45.

Sievers, Hans-Jürgen. "Die Familie Mendelssohn-Bartholdy in den Kirchenbüchern der Evangelisch-reformierten Kirche zu Leipzig." *In der Mitte der Stadt: Die evangelisch-reformierte Kirche zu Leipzig von der Einwanderung der Hugenotten bis zur Friedlichen Revolution*. Ed. by H.-J. Sievers. Leipzig, 2000, 100–03.

Silber, Judith K. "Mendelssohn and the *Reformation* Symphony: A Critical and Historical Study." Ph.D. diss., Yale University, 1987.

Silber-Ballan, Judith. "Marxian Programmatic Music." In Todd, *Mendelssohn Studies*, 149–61, 1992.

Sirota, Victoria R. "The Life and Works of Fanny Mendelssohn Hensel." D.M.A. diss., Boston University, 1981.

Smend, Friedrich. "Zelter oder Mendelssohn?" *Monatsschrift für Gottesdienst und kirchliche Kunst* 34 (1929): 207–9.

Smither, Howard E. *A History of the Oratorio*. Chapel Hill, 2000. Vol. 4.

Sorkin, David. *The Transformation of German Jewry, 1780–1840*. New York, 1987.

———. *Moses Mendelssohn and the Religious Enlightenment*. Berkeley, 1996.

Spencer, Stewart, and Barry Millington, eds. *Selected Letters of Richard Wagner*. London, 1987.

Speyer, Edward. *Wilhelm Speyer der Liederkomponist 1790–1878*. Munich, 1925.

Spiel, Hilde. *Fanny von Arnstein: A Daughter of the Enlightenment 1758–1818*. Trans. C. Shuttleworth. New York, 1991.

Spies, Claudio. "Samplings." In *MahW*, 100–20, 1991.

Spohr, Louis. *Selbstbiographie*. Kassel, 1861. 2 vols., Eng. trans., London, 1865; reissued as *Lebenserinnerungen*. Edited by Folker Göthel. Tutzing, 1968.

Sposato, Jeffrey S. "Creative Writing: The [Self-] Identification of Mendelssohn as Jew." *MQ* 82 (1998): 190–209.

———. "Mendelssohn, *Paulus*, and the Jews: A Response to Leon Botstein and Michael Steinberg." *MQ* 83 (1999): 280–91.

———. "The Price of Assimilation: The Oratorios of Felix Mendelssohn and the Nineteenth-Century Anti-Semitic Tradition." Ph.D. diss., Brandeis University, 2000.

Staehelin, Martin. "*Elijah*, Johann Sebastian Bach, and the New Covenant: On the Aria 'Es ist genug' in Felix Mendelssohn-Bartholdy's Oratorio *Elijah*." Trans. Susan Gillespie. In *MahW*, 121–36.

Steiger, Robert, and Angelika Reimann. *Goethes Leben von Tag zu Tag*. Zurich, 1982–1996. 8 vols.

Steinberg, Michael. "The Incidental Politics to Mendelssohn's *Antigone*." In *MahW*, 137–57.

Stenzel, K. G. W. *Gustav Adolf Harald Stenzels Leben*. Gotha, 1897.

Stern, Carola. "*Ich möchte mir Flügel wünschen*": Das Leben der Dorothea Schlegel*. Hamburg, 1990.

Stolzenberg, Ingeborg. "Georg Benjamin Mendelssohn im Spiegel seiner Korrespondenz." *MS* 3 (1979): 81–161.

———. "Georg Benjamin Mendelssohn an August Twesten." *MS* 7 (1990): 287–93.

Suhr, Norbert. "Felix Mendelssohn Bartholdy und Philipp Veit: Unveröffentlichte Briefe." *MS* 6 (1986): 107–19.

Sutermeister, Peter, ed. *Felix Mendelssohn Bartholdy: Eine Reise durch Deutschland, Italien und die Schweiz.* Tübingen, 1979 (reissue of *Felix Mendelssohn Bartholdy: Briefe einer Reise durch Deutschland, Italien und die Schweiz, und Lebensbild.* Zurich, 1958).

Taylor, J. Bayard. *Views A-Foot, or Europe Seen with Knapsack and Staff.* New York, 1848.

Thorau, Christian. "'Das spielende Bild des Jahres': Fanny Hensels Klavierzyklus Das Jahr." In Borchard and Schwarz-Danuser, 73–89, 1999.

Thym, Jurgen. "Schumann in Brendel's *Neue Zeitschrift für Musik* from 1845 to 1856." In Finson and Todd, 21–36, 1984.

Tiersot, Julien, ed. *Lettres de musiciens écrites en français du xve au xxe siècle.* Paris, 1936. 2 vols.

Tillard, Françoise. *Fanny Mendelssohn.* Paris, 1992; Eng. trans. Camille Naish. Portland, 1996.

Todd, R. Larry. "The Instrumental Music of Felix Mendelssohn-Bartholdy: Selected Studies Based on Primary Sources." Ph.D. diss., Yale University, 1979.

———. "Of Seas Gulls and Counterpoint: The Early Versions of Mendelssohn's *Hebrides* Overture." *19CM* 2 (1979): 197–213, 1979b.

———. "An Unfinished Symphony by Mendelssohn." *ML* 61 (1980): 293–309.

———. "A Sonata by Mendelssohn." *Piano Quarterly* 29 (1980–81): 30–41.

———. "An Unfinished Piano Concerto by Mendelssohn." *MQ* 68 (1982): 80–101.

———. *Mendelssohn's Musical Education: A Study and Edition of his Exercises in Composition.* Cambridge, 1983.

———. "A Passion Cantata by Mendelssohn." *American Choral Review* 25 (1983): 3–17, 1983b.

———. "Mendelssohn's Ossianic Manner, with a New Source—On Lena's Gloomy Heath." In Finson and Todd, 137–60, 1984.

———. "A Mendelssohn Miscellany." *ML* 71 (1990): 52–64.

———. "From the Composer's Workshop: Two Little-Known Fugues by Mendelssohn." *MT* 131 (1990): 183–87, 1990b.

———, ed. *Mendelssohn and his World.* Princeton, 1991.

———. "The Unfinished Mendelssohn." In *MahW*, 158–84, 1991b.

———. "Mozart according to Mendelssohn: A Contribution to *Rezeptionsgeschichte.*" In *Perspectives on Mozart Performance.* Edited by R. L. Todd and Peter Williams. Cambridge, 1991, 158–203, 1991c.

———, ed. *Mendelssohn Studies.* Cambridge, 1992.

———. "'Gerade das Lied wie es dasteht': On Text and Meaning in Mendelssohn's *Lieder ohne Worte.*" In *Musical Humanism and Its Legacy: Studies in the History of Music Theory.* Edited by Nancy K. Baker and Barbara Hanning. Stuyvesant, N.Y., 1992, 355–79, 1992b.

———. "*Me voilà perruqué*: Mendelssohn's Six Preludes and Fugues Op. 35 Reconsidered." In Todd, *Mendelssohn Studies*, 162–99, 1992c.

———. *Mendelssohn: "The Hebrides" and Other Overtures.* Cambridge, 1993.

———, ed. *Schumann and his World.* Princeton, 1994.

———. "New Light on Mendelssohn's *Freie Phantasie* (1840)." In G. C. Orth, ed. *Literary and Musical Notes: A Festschrift for Wm. A. Little.* Bern, 1995, 205–18.

———. "On Mendelssohn's Operatic Destiny: *Die Lorelei* Reconsidered." in C. M. Schmidt, 113–40, 1997.

———. "Mendelssohn." in D. Kern Holoman, ed. *The Nineteenth-Century Symphony.* New York, 1997, 78–107, 1997b.

———. "The Chamber Music of Mendelssohn." In Stephen E. Hefling, ed. *Nineteenth-Century Chamber Music.* New York, 1998, 170–207.

———. "Felix Mendelssohn-Bartholdy, Overture to *Elijah*, Arrangement for Piano Duet (1847)." In Jon Newsom and Alfred Mann, ed. *Music History from Primary Sources: A Guide to the Moldenhauer Archives.* Washington, D.C., 2000, 313–20.

———. "Felix Mendelssohn (-Bartholdy)." *The New Grove Dictionary of Music and Musicians, Second Edition.* Edited by S. Sadie. London, 2001, XVI, 389–424.

———. "Piano Music Reformed: The Case of Felix Mendelssohn Bartholdy." In Seaton, *The Mendelssohn Companion*, 579–620, 2001b.

———. "On Stylistic Affinities between the Works of Fanny Hensel and Felix Mendelssohn Bartholdy." In J. Michael Cooper and Julie D. Prandi, 245–61, 2002.

———. "'Ein wenig still und scheu'—Clara Wieck/Schumann as Colleague of Felix Mendelssohn Bartholdy." In Bernhard R. Appel, Ute Bär, and Matthias Wendt, eds. *Schumanniana Nova: Festschrift Gerd Nauhaus zum 60. Geburtstag.* Sinzig, 2002, 767–84, 2002b.

Toews, John E. "Memory and Gender in the Remaking of Fanny Mendelssohn's Musical Identity: The Chorale in 'Das Jahr.'" *MQ* 77 (1993): 727–48.

Treitschke, Heinrich von. *History of Germany in the Nineteenth Century*. Edited by Gordon A. Craig, trans. E. and C. Paul. Chicago, 1975.

Treue, Wilhelm. "Das Bankhaus Mendelssohn als Beispiel einer Privatbank im 19. und 20. Jahrhundert." *MS* 1 (1972): 29–80.

Tudur, Alwyn. "Mendelssohn's Visit to Wales." *Welsh Music* 4/4 (1973): 43–49.

Turner, J. Rigbie. "Mendelssohn's Letters to Eduard Devrient: Filling in Some Gaps." In R. L. Todd, ed. *Mendelssohn Studies*, 200–239, 1992.

Uldall, Hans. *Das Klavierkonzert der Berliner Schule*. Leipzig, 1928, repr. 1976.

Vana, Marilee A. "Fanny Mendelssohn Hensel's *Festspiel, MA Ms. 37*: A Modern Edition and Conductor's Analysis for Performance." D.M.A. diss., University of North Carolina at Greensboro, 1995.

Van der Linden, Albert. "Un fragment inédit du 'Lauda Sion' de F. Mendelssohn." *Acta musicologica* 26 (1954): 48–64.

Varnhagen von Ense, K. A. *Denkwürdigkeiten und vermischte Schriften*. Leipzig, 1843–1859.

Vitercik, Greg. *The Early Works of Felix Mendelssohn*. Philadelphia, 1992.

Wagner, Cosima. *Diaries*. Edited by Martin Gregor-Dellin and Dietrich Mack, trans. Geoffrey Skelton. New York, 1976–1978. 2 vols.

Wagner, Richard. *Sämtliche Briefe*. Edited by Gertrud Strobel and Werner Wolf. Leipzig, 1970, II.

———. *On Conducting*. In *Three Wagner Essays*. Trans. Robert L. Jacobs. London, 1979.

Waidelich, Till Gerrit. "'Wer zog gleich aus der Manteltasche ein Opernsujet?' Helmina von Chézys gescheiterte Libretto-Projekte für Felix Mendelssohn Bartholdy." *MS* 12 (2001): 149–78.

Walker, Alan. *Franz Liszt: The Virtuoso Years 1811–1847*. New York, 1983.

Walker, Ernest. "Mendelssohn's 'Die einsame Insel.'" *ML* 26 (1945): 148–50.

Wallace, S. M. H. "The *Gartenlieder*, Op. 3, by Fanny Mendelssohn Hensel (1805–1847)." D.M.A. diss., Michigan State University, 2000.

Wanner, G. A. *Felix Mendelssohn Bartholdy und Basel*. Basel, 1974.

Ward Jones, Peter. "The Library of Felix Mendelssohn Bartholdy." *Festschrift Rudolf Elvers zum 60. Geburtstag*. Edited by E. Herttrich and H. Schneider. Tutzing, 1985, 289–328.

———. *Catalogue of the Mendelssohn Papers in the Bodleian Library, Oxford, Vol. III*. Tutzing, 1989.

———. "Mendelssohn and his English Publishers." In Todd, *Mendelssohn Studies*, 240–55, 1992.

———. "Mendelssohn's Opus 1: Bibliographical Problems of the C minor Piano Quartet." In *Sundry Sorts of Music Books: Essays Presented to O. W. Neighbour on his 70th Birthday*. Edited by C. Banks, A. Searle, and M. Turner. London, 1993, 264–73.

———, ed. *The Mendelssohns on Honeymoon. The 1837 Diary of Felix and Cécile Mendelssohn Bartholdy*. Oxford, 1997; German ed. *Felix und Cécile Mendelssohn Bartholdy: Das Tagebuch der Hochzeitsreise*. Zurich, 1997.

———. *Mendelssohn: An Exhibition to Celebrate the Life of Felix Mendelssohn Bartholdy (1809–1847)*. Oxford, 1997, 1997b.

———. "Mendelssohn Scores in the Library of the Royal Philharmonic Society." In C. M. Schmidt, 64–75, 1997c.

———. "Felix Mendelssohn Bartholdys Tod: Der Bericht seiner Frau." *MS* 12 (2001): 205–26.

———. "Mendelssohn's First Composition." In J. M. Cooper and J. D. Prandi, 101–13, 2002.

Warrack, John. *Carl Maria von Weber*. London, 1968.

———. "Mendelssohn's Operas." *Music and Theatre: Essays in Honor of Winton Dean*. Edited by N. Fortune. Cambridge, 1987, 263–97.

Wasielewski, W. J. von. "Felix Mendelssohn-Bartholdy und Robert Schumann." *DR* 19 (1894): 329–41.

———. *Aus siebzig Jahren: Lebenserinnerungen*. Stuttgart, 1897.

Webern, Emil von. "Felix Mendelssohn Bartholdy aus den Erinnerungen des Generalleutnants Karl Emil von Webern." *DM* 12/4 (1913): 67–94.

Wehmer, Carl, ed. *Ein tief gegründet Herz: Der Briefwechsel Felix Mendelssohn-Bartholdys mit Johann Gustav Droysen*. Heidelberg, 1959.

Wehner, Ralf. *Studien zum geistlichen Chorschaffen des jungen Felix Mendelssohn Bartholdy*. Sinzig, 1996.

———. "'. . . ich zeigte Mendelssohns Albumblatt vor und Alles war gut': Zur Bedeutung der Stammbucheintragungen und Albumblätter von Felix Mendelssohn Bartholdy." In C. M. Schmidt, 37–63, 1997.

———. "Bibliographie des Schrifttums zu Felix Mendelssohn Bartholdy von 1972 bis 1994." In C. M. Schmidt, 297–351, 1997a.

———. "'. . . das sei nun alles für das Düsseldorfer Theater und dessen Heil . . .': Mendelssohns Musik zu Immermanns Vorspiel 'Kurfürst Johann Wilhelm im Theater' (1834)." *Mf* 55 (2002): 145–61.

————. "'It Seems to Have Been Lost': On Missing and Recovered Mendelssohn Sources." In Cooper and Prandi, 3–25, 2002b.

Weiss, Hermann F. "Neue Zeugnisse zu Felix Mendelssohn Bartholdy und Johann Paul von Falkenstein." *MS* 9 (1995): 53–88.

Wellek, René. *A History of Modern Criticism 1750–1950.* Cambridge, 1981. Vol. 2.

Wendler, Eugen "*Das Band der ewigen Liebe': Clara Schumanns Briefwechsel mit Emilie und Elise List.* Stuttgart, 1996.

Werner, Eric. "Two Unpublished Mendelssohn Concertos." *ML* 36 (1955): 126–38.

————. "New Light on the Family of Felix Mendelssohn." *Hebrew Union College Annual* 26 (1955): 543–65, 1955b.

————. "Mendelssohn." *Die Musik in Geschichte und Gegenwart* 9 (1961): 59–98.

————. *Mendelssohn: A New Image of the Composer and His Age.* New York, 1963; rev. German ed., *Mendelssohn: Leben und Werk in neuer Sicht.* Zurich, 1980.

————. "Mendelssohniana dem Andenken Wilhelm Fischer." *Mf* 28 (1975): 19–33.

————. "Felix Mendelssohn's Commissioned Composition for the Hamburg Temple: The 100th Psalm (1844)." *Musica Judaica* 7/1 (1984–1985): 54–57.

Werner, Jack. "Felix and Fanny Mendelssohn." *ML* 28 (1947): 303–37.

————. "The Mendelssohnian Cadence." *MT* 97 (1956): 17–19.

————. *Mendelssohn's "Elijah."* London, 1965.

Werner, Rudolf. "Felix Mendelssohn Bartholdy als Kirchenmusiker." Diss., Universität Frankfurt am Main, 1930.

Whaley, Joachim. *Religious Toleration and Social Change in Hamburg: 1529–1819.* Cambridge, 1985.

Wilhelmy, Petra. *Der Berliner Salon im 19. Jahrhundert (1780–1914).* Berlin, 1989.

Wilson, Marian. "Felix Mendelssohn's Works for Solo Piano and Orchestra: Sources and Composition." Ph.D. diss., Florida State University, 1993.

Wirth, Irmgard. *Die Künstlerfamilie Begas in Berlin.* Berlin, 1968.

Wolff, Ernst. *Felix Mendelssohn Bartholdy.* Berlin, 1906.

————. "Briefe von Felix Mendelssohn-Bartholdy an seine rheinischen Freunde." *Rheinische Musik- und Theater-Zeitung* 10 (1909): 86–88, 104–6, 121–22, 136–37, 149–51, 163–65, 182–83.

Wolff, Hellmuth Christian. "Mendelssohn and Handel." *MQ* 45 (1959): 175–90.

Wollny, Peter. "Sara Levy and the Making of Musical Taste in Berlin." *MQ* 77 (1993): 651–88.

Worbs, H. C. "Die Entwürfe zu Mendelssohns Violinkonzert e-moll." *Mf* 12 (1959): 79–82.

Woringen, Ferdinand von. "Felix Mendelssohn-Bartholdy in Düsseldorf in den Jahren 1833–35." *Neue Berliner Musikzeitung* 1/48 (November 16, 1847). Trans. in Brown, 2003, 124–37.

Wulfhorst, Martin. "Hill, Spohr, Mendelssohn and Beethoven's Ninth Symphony: A Mid-Nineteenth-Century Music Festival in New York." *Newsletter of the Institute for Studies in American Music* 15/2 (1986): 8–11.

Wullschlager, Jackie. *Hans Christian Andersen: The Life of a Storyteller.* New York, 2001.

Youens, Susan. "Behind the Scenes: *Die schöne Müllerin* before Schubert." *19CM* 15 (1991): 3–22.

Zappalà, Pietro. *Le "Choralkantaten" di Felix Mendelssohn-Bartholdy.* Venice, 1991.

————. "Di alcuni mottetti giovanili di Felix Mendelssohn Bartholdy." In F. Izzo and J. Streicher, eds. *Ottocento e oltre: Scritti in onore di Raoul Meloncelli.* Rome, 1993, 203–33.

————. "Autographe von Felix Mendelssohn Bartholdy in Italien." *MS* 10 (1997): 77–95.

————. "Dalla Spree al Tevere: il diario del viaggio di Felix Mendelssohn Bartholdy verso l'Italia (1830–1831). Edizione e commento." In Giacomo Fornari, ed. *Album Amicorum Albert Dunning.* Brepols, 2002, 713–88.

Zelter, Karl Friedrich. *Karl Friedrich Christian Fasch.* Berlin, 1801, repr. 1983.

Zywietz, Michael. *Adolf Bernhard Marx und das Oratorium in Berlin.* Eisenach, 1996.

Bold numbers refer to pages with musical examples.

General Index

Unless otherwise indicated, family relationships are to Felix Mendelssohn Bartholdy [FMB]. **Bold** numbers refer to pages with musical examples. Readers may wish to refer to the comprehensive index available on the Internet (www.oup.com/us/sc/0195110439).